A COMMENTARY ON HEBREWS 11

PILGRIM CLASSIC COMMENTARIES

BOARD OF CONSULTANTS

Gerald T. Sheppard, Series Editor
Marvin W. Anderson
John H. Augustine
Nicholas W. S. Cranfield

VOLUMES IN THE SERIES

The Geneva Bible
A Commentary on Galatians
William Perkins

A COMMENTARY ON HEBREWS 11 (1609 Edition)

William Perkins

INTRODUCTORY ESSAYS BY

John H. Augustine

Donald K. McKim

Gerald T. Sheppard

Richard A. Muller

EDITED BY

JOHN H. AUGUSTINE

THE PILGRIM PRESS

NEW YORK

Library of Congress Cataloging-in-Publication Data

Perkins, William, 1558–1602.
[Cloud of faithful witnesses]
A commentary on Hebrews 11 / William Perkins ; introductory essays
by John H. Augustine . . . [et al.] ; edited by John H. Augustine.
p.   cm.
Reproduced from the 1607 ed. of A cloud of faithful witnesses
which is in the possession of St. Mark's Library of the General
Theological Seminary.
Includes bibliographical references.
ISBN 0-8298-0856-6 : $35.00 — ISBN 0-8298-0857-4 (pbk.) : $19.95
1. Bible. N.T. Hebrews XI-XII, 1—Commentaries.   I. Augustine,
John H.   II. Title.   III. Title: Commentary on Hebrews eleven.
BS2775.3.P34   1991
227'.8706—dc20   90-22542
CIP

The Pilgrim Press, 475 Riverside Dr., New York, NY 10115

1   3   5   7   9   10   8   6   4   2

This book is printed on acid-free paper.

Printed in the United States of America.

Contents

A COMMENTARY ON HEBREWS 11
(1609 Edition)

William Perkins

Editor's Introduction

William Perkins' exposition of Hebrews 11:1—12:1, entitled *A Cloud of Faithful Witnesses*, began as sermons originally preached at Cambridge in the 1590s and retained a distinctive pastoral note of personal application despite editorial alteration and expansion for posthumous publication.[1] Since William Perkins died before he could edit the *Commentary* himself, William Crashaw and Thomas Pierson took up the task of editing the volume. The volume's contemporary editors acknowledge in their Dedicatory Epistle that the "notable light in this learned Commentarie" is "much obscured, for lacke of the refining hand of the godly author himselfe."[2] Nevertheless, they invite readers to "use this our Lampe," since it is fed with oil "received in the Lords Sanctuarie," as a practical guide for living as a Christian.

Best known to students of Renaissance literature as the author of the first comprehensive English Protestant manual of casuistry, William Perkins wrote *The Whole Treatise of the Cases of Conscience, Distinguished into Three Bookes* (1606), which was published after his death; it provided a practical application of Christian moral ideals to the daily life of laypersons by appealing to principles derived from Scripture. Perkins is also remembered for his *A Golden Chaine, or the Description of Theologie, containing the Order of the Causes of Salvation and Damnation, according to Gods Woord* (1590; tr. 1591 by Robert Hill), another work that places Reformed theology, and the concept of a step-by-step order of salvation, in the context of contemporary English culture. Offering practical and realistic counsel, the *Golden Chain* is grounded on Scripture, and the work is documented throughout with specific scriptural passages. Although Perkins regards the Reformers highly, he relies more on original sources, especially the Bible, as well as on the writings of St. Augustine and other church Fathers such as Jerome, Polycarp, and Cyprian.

Since respect for Scripture stood at the center of Perkins' works, and because he was a prolific spokesperson for Reformed Protestantism in England, biblical commentary has an important place in his *oeuvre*. He wrote expositions of the Lord's Prayer (1592), *A Digest or Harmonie of the Bookes of the Old and New Testament* (1613), and discussions of specific biblical texts: Philippians 3:7 (1601), Galatians (1604), Revelations 1—3 (1604), Zephaniah 2:1—2 (1606), the Temptation of Christ (1606), Jude (1606), Hebrews 11:1—12:1 (1607), the Sermon on the Mount (1608). His last work was the *Commentary or Exposition upon the Five First Chapters of the Epistles to the Galatians* (1604). A mark of his importance as a biblical expositor was that his followers edited his sermons and published them as biblical commentary. These works include his commentary on Hebrews 11, *A Cloud of Faithful*

Witnesses (1607), a work considered with his well known *Treatise on Vocations, or Callings of Men* (1603) as particularly influential in extolling and developing the virtues of diligence and thrift in colonial America.[3]

Perkins' life spanned nearly the entire reign of Queen Elizabeth in England.[4] Educated in the Reformed tradition at Christ's College, Cambridge, as were Richard Rogers, Laurence Chaderton, and, later, John Milton, Perkins graduated with a Bachelor of Arts degree in 1580 or 1581. Like his tutor Laurence Chaderton (d. 1640), one of the translators of the King James Bible, the moderate Perkins worked to purify the established church from within rather than join the radical Puritans who advocated separation from the established church. However, Perkins' primary concerns did not include church polity; instead, he concentrated his efforts on addressing pastoral inadequacies and deficiencies in the church. At the age of twenty-four he joined Christ's College as a Fellow, and in 1584 he received his Masters Degree. After his ordination, Perkins was appointed lecturer at Great St. Andrews Church, Cambridge. Having become an extremely popular preacher, he served as the public catechist at Corpus Christi College, where he lectured weekly; he was Dean of Christ's College from 1590–1591. Upon his marriage in 1595, Perkins left his Cambridge post; he continued to lecture, to preach, and to write until his death in 1602 at the age of 44.

If the innumerable editions of Perkins' works are any indication, his writings were held in high regard. R. T. Kendall notes that "by the end of the sixteenth century Perkins had replaced the combined names of Calvin and Beza as one of the most popular authors of religious works in England," witnessing the publication of "seventy-six editions (including repeated issues) during his lifetime, seventy-one of which came after 1590."[5] According to H. C. Porter, more than fifty of the 210 books printed in Cambridge between 1585 and 1618 were written by Perkins.[6] A one-volume edition of Perkins' works was published in 1600; this edition was followed by an expanded, three-volume edition which contained nearly forty separate titles, including a number of his biblical commentaries.

The essays gathered in this volume introduce Perkins' *A Cloud of Faithful Witnesses* from various perspectives and with differing emphases. To begin, John H. Augustine's essay on the role of exemplary figures in Perkins' *Commentary* shows that the Reformed doctrine of vocation undergirds Perkins' review of the heroes of faith in Hebrews 11. Arguing that the literary example could assist Perkins' audience to follow their divine calling, " 'Notable Precedents': The Vocational Rhetoric of Exemplary Figures" focuses on Perkins' use of the idea of "calling" to persuade his hearers that they too are called to imitate these exemplary figures of faith.

In "William Perkins' Use of Ramism as an Exegetical Tool," Donald K. McKim demonstrates how Ramism was appropriated as an exegetical tool by English Puritans. Peter Ramus (1515–1572) attempted to reform the arts curriculum by making logic more useful. He developed the idea that rhetoric consisted entirely of style and delivery, and he considered the other three traditional parts of rhetoric—invention, disposition, and logic—as part of logic. McKim then discusses how Perkins applied Ramist tools of logic to link the understanding of doctrine with its practical use; theology thus informed ethics.

Gerald T. Sheppard's essay first raises problems of method inherent in any modern assessment of the history of interpretation before offering his own examination of Perkins' vision of the biblical text. His essay, "Christian Interpretation of the Old Testament between Reformation and Modernity," explores how Perkins sought to find the same testimony to saving faith in both testaments, and to offer a positive role for Old Testament law and example. By making good works and obedience to the law the effect rather than the cause of justification, Perkins found himself obliged to develop rules to govern the relevance of biblical law and example for Christian conduct. Finally, Sheppard suggests some contemporary implications for our own late modern interpretation of Scripture.

In "William Perkins and the Protestant Exegetical Tradition: Interpretation, Style and Method," Richard A. Muller surveys the tradition of Protestant biblical interpretation that influenced Perkins' *Commentary*, paying close attention to the close relationship between sermon and commentary characteristic of sixteenth- and seventeenth-century English Protestantism. In addition, Muller discusses the text of the *Epistle to the Hebrews* used by Perkins in his *Commentary*. By comparing Perkins' text with the 1560 Geneva Bible, the Bishop's Bible of 1566, and the 1576 Laurence Tomson revision of the Geneva Bible, he concludes that Perkins follows the Tomson edition of the Geneva New Testament in nearly every aspect.

This Pilgrim Press edition of *A Cloud of Faithful Witnesses*, the first complete one since a Dutch edition in 1662, is reproduced by kind permission of St. Mark's Library of The General Theological Seminary in New York from their copy, No. STC 19653b. volume 3. Perkins' *A Cloud of Faithful Witnesses* is the second entry in this copy of volume three (1631) of *The Workes of That Famous and Worthie Minister of Christ in the Universitie of Cambridge, M. W. Perkins*, 3 volumes (London, 1609–31). Perkins' editors bound together extant imprints of his earlier works in three separate volumes, retaining the original title page of each imprint with its printing information. The first item in volume three is *An Exposition of Christ's Sermon on the Mount* (1608), separately paginated, pages 1–264. The remaining items, beginning with Perkins' *A Cloud of Faithful Witnesses*, are paginated 1 to 700. However, the signatures are consecutive throughout the volume. I wish to acknowledge the generous advice and assistance of the librarian, Dr. David Green, in preparing this edition. In addition, Janice A. Rossen, Lynn Fauth, Richard Hays, and Michael Piret provided expert advice and their usual encouragement in the development of this edition.

The General Theological Seminary volume reproduced here is in exceptionally fine condition. In a few places the type is shadowed slightly by the type on the other side of the page, but not so as to make the text unreadable (see, for example, p. 204). This Pilgrim Press edition is a thirteen percent reduction of the original trim size of the volume. The collation is: Aa2, Bb1–Ss6, Tt1 = 105 folios, or 210 pages. Folios 1 and 2 have no page numbers; the following folios are paged consecutively from 1 to 206.

This book is dedicated to the memory of Harold H. Augustine (1905–1990), whose life was an exemplary figure of faith.

JOHN H. AUGUSTINE
Yale University

ix

NOTES

1. There is disagreement over the date of Perkins' original sermons on Hebrews. Ian Breward gives the date as 1591 ("The Life and Theology of William Perkins 1558–1602" [diss., University of Manchester, 1963], 30). Alternatively, Donald K. McKim suggests that the Hebrews exposition should perhaps be dated around 1596. He writes that "Perkins referred to having already expounded the Apostles' Creed which would have been in his *Exposition of the Symbole, or Creed of the Apostles* (I, 117–322) which was published in 1595" (*Ramism in William Perkins' Theology*, American University Studies 7, Theology and Religion 15 [New York: Peter Lang, 1987], 193).

2. William Perkins, *A Cloud of Faithfull Witnesses, leading to the heavenly Canaan: Or, A Commentarie upon the 11. Chapter to the Hebrewes, preached in Cambridge by that godly and judicious Divine, M. William Perkins. Long Expected and desired; and therefore published at the request of his Executors, by Wil. Crashaw and Th. Pierson, Preachers of Gods Word: who heard him preach it, and wrote it from his mouth* (1609), 36, vol. 3 of *The Works of that Famous and Worthy Minister of Christ in the Universitie of Cambridge, M. William Perkins* (London, 1631). Subsequent references to this work are cited parenthetically in the text. I have silently regularized i/j, u/v, w/u, and i/y. For a discussion of William Crashaw and Thomas Pierson's editorial work, see H. C. Porter, *Reformation and Reaction in Tudor Cambridge* (1958; reprint, Hamden, Conn.: Archon Books, 1972), 264–67.

3. See Louis B. Wright, *Middle-Class Culture in Elizabethan England*, Huntington Library Publications (Chapel Hill: University of North Carolina Press, 1935), 170–71, 282; idem, *The Cultural Life of the American Colonies: 1607–1763* (New York: Harper & Brothers, 1957), 34. Perkins' writings were widely available in New England; they can be found on most lists of books in New England and were included in the libraries of colonial leaders such as William Brewster: Massachusetts Historical Society, *Proceedings of the Massachusetts Historical Society, 1880–1881* (Boston: Historical Society, 1881), 8.423, 427; Perry Miller, *The New England Mind: The Seventeenth Century* (Boston: Beacon Press, 1961), 520; Samuel Morison, *The Intellectual Life of Colonial New England* (Ithaca, N.Y.: Cornell University Press, 1956), 134.

4. For a discussion of the life of Perkins, see Thomas Fuller, *The Holy and Profane State* (London: William Tegg, 1841), 80–83; and idem, *Abel Redevivus or the Dead Yet Speaking* (London: William Tegg, 1867), 145–154; D. Neal, *The History of the Puritans* (New York: Harper, 1844), 1.536; Frederick Colville, *The Worthies of Warwickshire Between 1500–1800* (London: Henry Cooke, 1870), 573–76; G. Smith, *Dictionary of National Biography* (London: Breams, 1882), 1.275–76; J. Peile, *Biographical Register of Christ's College* (Cambridge: Cambridge University Press, 1910), 2.129–136; Ian Breward, *The Works of William Perkins*, The Courtenay Library of Reformation Classics 3 (Appleford, Eng.: The Sutton Courtenay Press, 1970), 3–13.

5. R. T.. Kendall, *Calvin and English Calvinism to 1649*, Oxford Theological Monographs (Oxford: Oxford University Press, 1982), 52–53.

6. H. C. Porter, *Reformation and Reaction in Tudor Cambridge*, 264.

A COMMENTARY ON HEBREWS 11

"Notable Precedents":
The Vocational Rhetoric
of Exemplary Figures

JOHN H. AUGUSTINE

William Perkins opens his exposition of Hebrews 11:1—12:1, *A Cloud of Faithful Witnesses* (1609), with an extended definition of faith, singling out the maxim in v. six—"without faith it is impossible to please God"—as one of the "most excellent principles of all *Practical Divinitie*."[1] Taking the lead from the Genevan text of this encomium on faith, Perkins locates the Christian doctrine of vocation, or "calling," at the center of his examination of faith. He specifies that "saving faith" dwells only "in the heart of those effectually called" (1) and frequently admonishes his readers to "framc [their] lives in light of God's calling" (63). Like Luther before him, Perkins expresses strong concern about the dangers of becoming too involved with the secular world.[2] He warns his readers that they are called out of the "sea of temptations" (5) that surround them. And like Calvin as well, he encourages them to persevere in their faith amidst the afflictions of this life.[3]

Perkins emphasizes the idea of "calling" in his discussion of the exemplary figures of faith depicted in Hebrews 11 in order to persuade his audience that they, in turn, are called to imitate these exemplary figures rather than to follow those captive to more temporal concerns. In Perkins' words, readers are called to imitate "the religious presidents of your Honourable Parents" (Aa6v) and thus substantiate "their shadows" and perform "their promises" (37–38). Relying on the force of these exemplary figures, Perkins invites readers to reorient their own frame of life into the biblical one and, in a sense, to enter into a biblical "estate" (186, 154), or "pattern of life" (200–201), by "participating" (199) with these "worthy examples" (200–201) on a journey led by a "cloud of faithful witnesses." As a means to explain these concepts, the use of the literary example could assist his audience in perceiving and in following its divine calling.

CALLED TO FAITH

An exacting and meticulous expositor, Perkins divides his *Commentary* into two parts. His outline of the chapter exhibits the centrality of the example:

John H. Augustine is an associate fellow of Pierson College, Yale University.

1. A generall *description* of *Faith,* from the 1. v. to the 4.
2. An *illustration* or declaration of that description, by a large rehearsall of manifold *examples* of auncient and worthie men in the old Testament, from the 4. v. to the ende. (1)

The "generall *description of Faith*" consists of "*three actions or effects* of faith." This description paraphrases vv. 1–3 in a highly ordered manner:

The first effect in the 1. vers. *Faith* makes things *which are not* (but onely are hoped for) after a sort to *subsist and to be present with the beleever.*
The second is in the 2. v. *Faith makes a beleever approved of God.*
The third in the 3. v. *Faith makes a man understand and beleeve things incredible to sense and reason.* (1)

Moving from general statements to particular analyses, Perkins explains further that "Faith in the word of God, is specially of three sorts: Historicall, Miraculous, Justifying or saving faith" (1). However, the "general scope" of the chapter, according to Perkins, concerns "saving faith" (2). His discussion of the author of Hebrews' general description of faith and his specific illustrations of that faith through exemplary figures pays close attention to the notion of vocation:

Saving (commonly called *Justifying*) *faith* . . . is, A special perswasion wrought by the holy Ghost in the heart of those that are effectually called, concerning their reconciliation and salvation by Christ. (2)

The careful expositor searches for the "true meaning of the words" and "what instruction they doe naturally yield unto us" (1); he concludes that "it becomes us therefore to learn carefully the instructions that concerne the practise of this faith, for it is no lesse then a saving faith" (2). At the center of Perkins' understanding of "justifying faith" is the importance of the spiritual development of those called to faith along the familiar lines of Reformed doctrine: justification, sanctification, resurrection, glorification and life everlasting.[4] The basis for this progression comes from Rom. 8:29–30: "For those which he [God] knew before, he also predestinate[d] to be made like to the image of his sonne, that hee might be the first borne among many brethren. Moreover whom hee predestinated, them also he called, and whom he called, them also he justified, and whom he justified, them he also glorified":[5]

1. *Justification,* standing in the remission of sinnes.
2. *Sanctification* in this life.
3. The perfection and accomplishment of our *sanctification* after this life.
4. The *Resurrection* of *the bodie,* and reuniting it with the soule.
5. *Glorification* of bodie and soule.
6. *Life everlasting,* and glorie with God in heaven. (2)

Perkins solidly anchors his series of lengthy sermons on Hebrews 11 in the central Reformed doctrines of *sola fide* and *sola Scriptura,* which he defined in very practical terms. His response to "But how doth God worke this faith?" one of many rhetorical questions throughout the text, captures the Reformed emphasis on justification by faith as revealed in Scripture:

> But how doth God worke this faith? By his word: for as God is the author and worker of faith, so God hath appointed a meanes whereby he workes it, and that is his *Word;* which word of God is the onely ordinarie outward meanes to worke faith. (39)

In a discussion of Abel's faith (11:4), Perkins singles out "humiliation for sinne" and "desire of reconciliation" as the "summe of religion." The anaphoric repetition of the first person singular pronoun drives home an important assumption of Reformed doctrine: humanity stands apart from God due to what Perkins calls "originall corruption" (205):

> Reason not with thy selfe, I worke hard and follow my calling, I hurt no man: thus could *Cain* reason, and yet but cursed *Cain.* Thou must then beside these, get that that *Cain* did not; Learne in thy conscience to see and feele thy sinne, to be grieved for it, so as thou maist say: My sicknesse, my povertie, my crosses grieve me: but nothing so much as my owne sinnes, these trouble me above all, and this griefe swalloweth up all the rest. And there is another thing which I seek above all: not gold, silver, or promotion; but reconciliation with my God, his saviour in Jesus Christ: If thou hast these two, then thou goest beyond *Cain,* then shalt thou stand before God with *Abel,* and be accepted. Remember these two: humiliation for sinne, and desire of reconciliation: these two is the summe of religion. (15)

Juxtaposed to the disorder that sin introduced into the world is an ordered prelapsarian world depicted with a liberal use of third person singular pronouns to emphasize the gap between the two worlds and to create an atmosphere of abundance:

> So God created man rich in all blessings, put him into the Palace of the world: garnished this house of the world with exceeding beauty: his meate, his apparell, his recreation, his house were all excellent and glorious: hee made all other creatures, amongst which there was nothing but concord, love, agreement, uniformity, comelinesse, and good order. (12)

Later, Perkins commends his audience to make an explicit accounting of their sins in order to determine their standing before God. In an encouraging, pastoral style Perkins includes himself in a graphic exhortation: "Let us teach us all to looke to our *lives,* and make conscience of all *sinnes;* especially great & capitall, and *crying sinnes:* for the sinnes of a people are *wormes and Cankers,* eating out the life and strength of a common-wealth" (60).

Due to the extent of human sinfulness, any reconciliation with God depends on faith alone in Christ. Yet Perkins also carefully balances the proper fear of God and an accompanying need for humility with a pastoral emphasis on "the loving care that God hath over them, who have a care to feare and serve him" (39). He reveals his own understanding of the basic structure of faith, while making a number of characteristically lengthy generalizations derived from his discussion of Noah's faith. Perkins commends Noah for heeding God's warning that the world would be destroyed by a flood; he built an ark "in reverence to this message from God" (37). According to Perkins, "Out of which his practise, we may learne two things" (38). In Ciceronian prose that relies heavily on complication of the subject clause, he claims, first, that "*faith is* a supernaturall worke of God in those mens hearts that have it. That it is a *worke of god,* it appeareth in that it alwaies acknowledgeth and beleeveth gods word: that it is *supernaturall,* it appeareth in that it apprehendeth and beleeveth whatsoever Gods word delivereth" (38–39). His second point establishes that justification by faith [alone] in Christ, or what he calls "the promise of salvation by *Christ,*" is the "*principall* object of true faith" (39). Adopting a humble and gently persuasive stance characterized by his use of the phrase "here we learne," Perkins says,

> The whole *Object of faith,* or what is all that that faith beleeveth; namely, nothing but Gods word, and all and every word of God. So that faith hath two objects, differing not in nature, but in degree, principal, and inferiour. The *principall* object of true faith, is the promise of salvation by *Christ.* The *inferious* object thereof, are all other particular promises, of safety, deliverance, providence; helpe, assistance, comfort, or what other benefit soever is made either to the whol Church, and so inclusively to any particular man; or which are personally made unto him. For, saving faith beleeveth not only the graund promise of salvation, but all other promises either of spirituall or corporall blessings, which are subordinate to the great Promise, and doe depend of it, and are therefore apprehended by the same faith.[6] (39)

Perkins' "saving faith," a phrase he repeats frequently in his sermons on Hebrews 11, refers in shorthand fashion to the Reformed doctrine of justification by faith. In commenting on the phrase "*By the which hee obtained witnesse that he was righteous*" from the discussion of Abel's faith in v. 4, Perkins suggests,

> By *faith* hee meanes saving faith, which makes a man just before God, and no other. For whereas hee had said afore, that by faith our *Elders had obtained a good report:* Hee prooves that generall, by this example of *Abell;* therefore that saving faith which was meant there, is also meant here. (18)

His "use" or application deriving from this central doctrine is to warn readers of the dangers of what he calls "a maine pillar of romish religion" (19): justification by works. In contrast to the conclusion of the doctrine section which begins with Perkins' familiar pastoral observation that "here we learn a worthy lesson of Christianity," Perkins' comments in the application section, perhaps best suited for oral delivery, reiterate his warning with a heavy concentration of stern, exclusive terms such as "none" and "never," combined with a large number of negative clauses. In this particularly weighty paragraph, he ponders the significance of *sola fide.* The cumulative effect of these terms is to concentrate one's attention on the singular importance of Perkins' exhortation on "saving faith":

> There is none of us so vile, none so profane, but wee desire salvation. If we doe, then we must tread the beaten way to it. For, we are not borne heires

of it; neither can wee come thither by chaunce: but there is a way that must bee taken, and that way is but one: all other are misleading by-waies. Againe, that way must be taken in this life; else, it is too late. Now, this way is to be a just & righteous man. With this, never man failed: and without this, never man attained to salvation; for, *No uncleane thing can come into the kingdome of heaven.* Never was man justified there, which was not just before: & that must here be begun, which in heaven is to be perfected. In this life therefore wee must seeke to be just. Now, our good work will not serve to make us just: for they are all unable to indure the triall of Gods justice. And if we stand to them, and they proove not able to satisfie Gods justice; then, instead of saving us, they will condemne us. Therefore with *Abell,* let us goe out of our selves, denie our selves, and cleave onely to Christs righteousnesse, in life and death: this is the way that never will deceive us. (18–19)

Perkins distinguishes between "generall faith" and "saving faith" in an extremely detailed exposition of v. six, *"But without faith it is impossible to please God"* (26–36), a verse he extols as containing "a generall Maxime or Canon of *Divinitie*" and "one of the wayghtiest principles in religion" (26). At its center is Perkins' idea of "true saving faith." Although careful to rule out a place for works in attaining salvation, he does indicate that a conscious awareness of what he calls a purified heart—which in turn leads to good works—is the distinguishing mark between "general" and "saving" faith:

Now if any man would know, whether his faith be sound and saving, or not; it is knowne by this: If it purifie the heart: for so saith S. *Peter, That god by faith did purifie the heart of the profane and filthie Gentiles.* If then thy faith doe not *purifie thy heart,* and cleanse thy life, and cause thee to abound in good workes, it is no sound nor saving faith, it is but a generall faith, it is but an historical knowledge, & cannot save the soule: he therefore that upon examination of his heart and life, findeth his *faith* to bee such, let him not content himself, but turne his generall *faith* into a saving *faith,* which in this world will *purifie his heart,* and at the last will *save his soule.*[7] (27)

Before advancing to his discussion of the important practical dimensions of "saving" faith, Perkins links his definition of faith to the Reformed doctrine of *sola Scriptura.* He considers the two inseparable. In his discussion of Abraham's faith (v. 19), Perkins reiterates that "our reasoning in matters of faith, must bee grounded on the word":

Here we learn, that it is a necessarie thing for a man that beleeves, to have good knowledge in Gods word: that when a temptation comes against his faith, by knowledge & reasoning out of Gods word, he may be able to put backe the same: for, all our reasoning in matters of faith, must bee grounded on the word: so doth *Abraham* in this place, against this strong temptation, reason out of Gods word to stay himselfe: so that knowledge in the word of God, is necessarie to him that beleeves. (119)

In comments on Enoch's example of faith in v. 5, Perkins uses chiasmus to convey this linkage between the Word of God and faith:

If therefore mens actions must proceede from faith, then consequently must they have their ground and warrant from *the word:* for *faith* and the *word* are relatives, and the one dependes upon the other; No *faith*, no *word* to binde: no *worde*, no *faith* to beleeve. But all actions that *please God*, must be done in *faith;* therefore all actions that please God, have some ground and direction in the *word of God*, without which word of God there can be no faith. (28)

The Scripture teaches by either rule or example, and, in either case, contains particular teachings that apply to each person's individual calling. For instance, Perkins says,

> *Particular* rules for particular callings are many: *for Kings*, they must *read Gods booke, and not have many wives,* nor *gather too much silver and gold:* They must be *wise and learned:* and *kisse the sonne of God Christ Jesus,* and many other: for *Minister*, they must be *apt to teach, watching, sober,* not *young Schollers* & many other: & so consequently the most of the callings that are in the common wealth, have their particular direction in plaine rules. (28)

However, it is the specific scriptural example, whether it be of God's or man's actions, that primarily concerns Perkins in these sermons, for "in all the actions of our lives and callings" (29) these examples provide a unique "warrant and direction." Thus Perkins grounds his case for the importance of the scriptural example in a discussion of the Reformed doctrine of the Word of God.

Like the flames of a fire, which need to be fed regularly to remain vibrant, so also believers are called to apply themselves to the study of Scripture:

> The nature of faith is like unto *fire,* which will not goe out so long as wood, or other fewell is put unto it, but will take hold thereof, and growe unto a greater flame; and so will faith growe up to a full perswasion in all those that conscionably applie themselves to the Worde and Prayer. (98)

But, as Perkins frequently points out, knowledge of Scripture must be followed by obedience to Scripture. In fact, Perkins considers obedience to Christian doctrine to stem from true faith. Using vivid imagery, he interprets the often debated phrase "the obedience of faith" from Rom. 1:5 in the context of Abraham's faithful obedience to a divine calling:

> Learne here the true nature of true faith: it brings forth true obedience where ever it is: and therefore Christian obedience is called *the obedience of faith,* Rom. 1.5. And these two cannot be seperated, no more then light from the *sunne,* or heate from *fire.* For as the *sunne* naturally; and necessarily gives *light,* and the *fire heate*; no lesse doth true *faith* yeeld true *obedience* to Gods commaundements. Which being so, it teacheth us, for the use. (64)

Later, he explains that "so long as we remaine ignorant; or else having knowledge doe not joyne practise therewith, in obedience from a good conscience: undoubtedly we have no sparke of true faith in us" (196).

Nevertheless, Perkins is careful to recognize that, in contrast to what he claims to be the Roman Catholic position, the obedience of faith he describes does not involve human merit in the process of justification. He suggests that Roman Catholic doctrine expands the doctrine of justification to include aspects of the practice of faith that more properly fall under the doctrine of sanctification. Linking "doctrine" to what he calls "use" or "application," Perkins observes,

> Where is more knowledge, there should be more obedience: therefore it concerneth all those that professe themselves to be Christians, and submit themselves to heare and learne the word of God taught unto them; not to content themselves with bare *knowledge,* though it be never so much: But withall, to bring forth the fruits of *obedience* in their lives and conversations. (98)

In reference to Noah's faithful construction of the ark, he repeats a similar maxim: "[W]here true *faith* is, there followeth true *obedience* to every commaundement of God" (44). Perkins suggests that the way to increase one's faith is to follow the examples of the Patriarchs depicted in Hebrews 11. Inviting his audience to join him in this endeavor, the pastor comments that "we must learne to follow this notable practise of these godly Patriarchs, and looke what meanes they used for the increase of their faith; the same also must we use, and that diligently: so shall wee growe, and increase, and waxe stronge in faith, as they did" (99).

In addition to emphasizing the practical dimensions of the Reformed doctrine of faith, Perkins explains the call to faith in Reformed terms which involves a comparison between faith before and after Christ's incarnation. Such a comparison sharpens his definition of faith and establishes a general framework for the catalog of examples of called individuals that constitute the heart of the *Commentary.* While Perkins' audience shares the "same general promise" of a "justifying faith" in Christ with the patriarchs, they do not share a "like particular promise" with the patriarchs because, as Perkins explains, "we which now live in the Church, are much more bound in conscience to beleeve, then they that lived in the olde Testament. For, we have received the promise of Christs incarnation: They received it not, and yet beleeved" (196). Old Testament figures "hoped for" rather than saw "1. The incarnation of Christ. 2. The publishing of the Gospel." Nevertheless, "their faith gave these two things a beeing in their hearts and soules, though they came not to passe many hundreth yeares after" (2). Perkins observes that although the patriarchs' faith exceeds our own, fuller knowledge of Christ brings an even greater obligation to live an obedient life of faith:

> For though *Abraham, Isaac, and Jacob,* in regard of faith did goe far before us: yet seeing we have more knowledge then they had in the Messias, we must labour to become like unto them in the *obedience* of our lives: their faith was stronger then ours; but our obedience should be greater then theirs, because we have more cause to beleeve then they. (98)

Thus, in order to help his readers to identify with "the Fathers of the old testament," he points out that "there are other things which we hope for as well as they, which are to come, & not seene in respect of us both," including justification, sanctification, the resurrection of the body, the glorification of the body and soul, as well as life everlasting (2). In other words, we share the same calling to salvation as the exemplary figures of faith.

"MANY ARE CALLED"

As Perkins moves from his discussion of the general description of faith in Heb. 11:1–3 to his "rehearsall of the most excellent patterns & ensamples of *faith*, which flourished in the Church of the old Testament" in vv. 4–32, he carefully distinguishes between "naturall *Israelistes*" and those "*strangers from the Church of God*" that were "called extraordinarily" (14). Regardless of their origin, Perkins takes a particular interest in the vocation, both spiritual and temporal, of the examples of faith in Hebrews 11, whether it be Abraham's call to a strange place as "father of the faithfull" (60), Gideon's struggles with his calling to be a judge to his people (173), or Hezekiah's "weighty calling" to serve as king over his people (180). His concern with the Reformed doctrine of vocation in *A Cloud of Faithful Witnesses* can be understood more clearly in the context of his essay, "A Treatise of the Vocations, Or Callings of Men" (1603).[8]

In his *Institutes of Christian Religion*, Calvin explains the double meaning which vocation had for Perkins—a call to salvation and to an earthly occupation—and defines the relationship between the two aspects of vocation.[9] According to Calvin, this call to salvation is of two sorts, general and special:

> This is the general call, by which God invites all equally to himself through the outward preaching of the word—even those to whom he holds it out as a savor of death (cf. II Cor. 2:16), and as the occasion for severer condemnation. The other kind of call is special, which he designs for the most part to give to the believers alone, while by the inward illumination of his Spirit he causes the preached Word to dwell in their hearts. (3.24.8)

The special call, or, as Perkins identifies it, the "effectual calling," forms the basis of Christian faith. Perkins explains the nature of this "effectual calling" in contrast to the idea of a "universal calling" in his discussion of Rahab's faith:

> The consideration of this limited estate of the Church of God for so long time, serves to discover unto us the errour of those, that maintaine and hold *universall calling* of all and every man to the estate of grace and salvation: but if that were so, then in former ages the Gentiles would have beleeved; whereas we see, that before the ascension of Christ, the Church of God was but a small remnant, among the people of the Jewes onely: and not one of tenne thousand beleeved among the Gentiles. Now, if all men had beene effectually called, then all would have received the promise of the Gospel: but many nations in former ages never heard of Christ: and therefore there was never in all ages a generall effectuall calling of all men. (165–66)

The term "call," or "vocation," also referred to an individual's role in society. The central text here is 1 Cor. 7:20: "Let every man abide in the same vocation wherein he was called" (83). According to Perkins, "A vocation or calling is a certain kind of life, ordained and imposed on man by God for the common good."[10] In addition, he writes that it "is the execution of some particular office, arising of that distinction which God makes betweene man and man in every societie."[11] In "Treatise of the Vocations," Perkins delineates five ethical imperatives that follow from the Reformed understanding of the "particular," or "personal" calling. In turn, he includes these imperatives in his *Commentary on Hebrews 11*.[12]

First, everyone ought to have a particular occupation, according to Perkins' "Treatise of the Vocations."[13] Likewise, Perkins warns explicitly in his *Commentary* of the folly of those who "live *in no calling*, but spend their time in eating, drinking, sleeping, and sporting, because they have livings of their owne, and lands left by their parents" (63–64). Second, "every man must judge that particular calling in which God hath placed him, to be the best calling for him." In addition, Perkins urged Christians to be diligent in their callings.[14] Throughout the *Commentary on Hebrews 11*, Perkins exhorts his audience to join him in walking "diligently in our callings, as *Moses* did; and though crosses meete us, so that *Pharaoh* fall out with us, if Kings become our enemies; yet we must not lay aside the duties of our callings; But after *Moses* example, goe on therein with courage" (149). Third, individuals must link the pursuit of their personal callings with their more fundamental ones as Christians. At this point Perkins' *Commentary* echoes directly his broad imperative from the "Treatise of the Vocations" about the need for one's vocation to serve the "common good":

> *Every man within the compasse of his calling, must not onely intend and labour for his owne good; but for the common good, in that Church & common wealth wherein he liveth.* The blinde would out of their carnall mindes, have learned this for a rule, *Every man for himselfe, and God for us all*: and this is many a mans practise, he wil labour diligently in his calling: but, all is for himselfe. But, he that propoundeth onely this end in his calling, to benefit himselfe alone, dealeth unjustly, both towards the Church and common wealth, in which he liveth; who ought to have a part of his care with himselfe. (177)

Fourth, those with public callings must first reform themselves if they wish to be considered worthy of imitation—an activity which occurs in private, though it has public consequences. While discussing the faith of Israel in crossing the Red Sea in his *Commentary on Hebrews 11*, Perkins emphasizes the need to "have care that all our sinnes, whether they bee of heart or life, little or great, new or olde, may be mortified or abolished" if we wish to "walke worthy of the calling of Christianitie" in the community (162). Fifth, a "particular calling must give place to the generall calling of a Christian, when they cannot both stand together."[15] Thus one is called first of all to serve God, and only within that primary focus is one called to a particular, temporal occupation. Robert S. Michaelsen, in his discussion of this passage, writes: "The general calling is more basic than the particular, although the two cannot be separated."[16]

It is the idea of a particular vocation or calling that primarily concerns Perkins in his discussion of Hebrews 11. He expands the Reformed idea of calling in his explication of the phrase from the Geneva Bible (v. 8), "By faith Abraham when he was called." In fact, he says that he "enlarged" the idea of calling "because it is of speciall use in the Christian life" (63). He explains "the *meanes* how he calleth, and the severall *states* whereto he calleth men" (61). According to Perkins, there are two means of being called by God: "immediately"—directly by God—or by human mediation. Abraham, like "the extraordinarie *Prophets* in the old Testament, and the *Apostles* in the new" (61), was called "*immediately*" by God.[17] Others, explains Perkins, were called "mediatly [*sic*] by men directed by himselfe, and furnished, or inabled for that dutie: and so were called the ordinarie Prophets and Priests of the old: and the Evangelists, Pastors, and Doctors of the new Testament" (61).

Perkins then establishes three callings for the "estates of life": general, particular, and personal. First, God's "*Generall* calling is, whereby he calleth all men to repentance by the Gospel, and so to life eternall" (61). Second, a "*particular calling* is, when he calleth and assigneth men to some particular estate and dutie, in Family, Church, or Commonwealth: as, when a man is called to be a Magistrate, Minister, master of a family, lawyer, physitian, &c" (61). Perkins' third category of a personal calling discussed in his *Commentary* is not explicitly identified in his "Treatise of the Vocations." However, it is actually a special case of the particular calling whereby someone such as Abraham is called by God "to some private *personall* dutie, which he designeth not to others, but to be done by them alone" (61). Specifically, Abraham's personal calling was to "*leave his countrey,* his kindred, his lands, his possessions, and to goe seeke another: and to be the *father of the faithfull,* and to receive the covenant: and this dutie belongs to none, but who shall personally, and by name be *called* unto it" (61).

As in his five rules concerning the personal calling in his "Treatise of the Vocation," Perkins' discussion of calling in Hebrews 11, and Abraham's call in particular, subordinates the particular to the general calling, while maintaining the importance of diligence in one's particular vocation. He instructs his audience: the primary "calling of a Christian, is to professe the Gospel of Christ" (62). Emphasizing his point with *parison*, Perkins warns of the cost involved in following God's general calling:

> As the Magistrates is to *defend* it, the Ministers to *teach* it, so all mens to *professe* it: now it is as impossible to *build* without *cost*, or to *fight* without *power* of men, as to *professe* Christ in any *calling*, either generall or particular, without *crosses*. Wee must therefore consider first what our calling and profession will *cost us*: it is sure to cost us a dangering of our credits and estimation in the world; it may be our goods, our liberties, it may bee our *lives* themselves. (62)

Frequently Perkins relies on images involving direction when he discusses the idea of the personal calling; he talks of "framing our lives according to Gods calling" (63, 149), of learning to follow the Judges' and David's faith "within the compasse of our calling" (177), of seeking "the square for all our actions" as called individuals in the Word of God (177), and of the difficulty of walking worthy of "the calling of Christianitie" and finding "the way to heaven" (162). By emphasizing one's need for God's direction in charting one's personal life, in accordance to one's calling, Perkins acknowledges that vocational success depends to a large degree on

God's action, not on human merit or diligence alone. Thus he succeeds in depicting faith as essential to one's particular calling, for the emphasis on one's calling as an area of response to divine grace rests ultimately on the Reformed doctrine of justification by faith.

In addition, a reliance on justification by faith rather than on human merit allows one to place diligence in one's personal vocation within the proper perspective. Perkins chastises those whose "hearts are [so] wholly taken up with the world, for matters of profit and delight; that they can spare no time, to seeke for this pretious gift of faith" (69). William Crashaw and Thomas Pierson, the *Commentary's* editors, simply commend readers "to increase in grace, and trust the Lord with your outward greatnesse" (Aa6v). Faith places the burdens of one's calling upon God. Throughout *A Cloud of Faithful Witnesses* Perkins holds up for imitation "notable precedents" (149, 173) who lived life in accordance with this emphasis on the place of the particular occupational call within the more general call to faith.

CALLED TO
IMITATE EXEMPLARY FIGURES

In going beyond the text of Hebrews 11 itself in emphasizing the role of God's call in the lives of various heroes of faith, Perkins not only reflects the importance of the Reformed doctrine of vocation but elevates the stature of the individuals discussed as models for imitation. In addition to commending believers to follow these "notable precedents," Perkins warns them to avoid becoming too attached to temporal, secular pursuits and to walk, like Abraham, as "pilgrims in a strange land" (73). Moreover, he claims that the "great force" (131) and "power" (77) of these examples will assist believers in the actual "practise of faith" (Aa6v). Using visual imagery, he invites his audience to "see" the world with the "eye of faith" (97, 150) as exemplified by the "faithful Witnesses" (Aa6v) in Hebrews 11 and thus to "conform" their lives to the framework of scriptural patterns and examples.

The two short biblical maxims placed prominently on the cover of *A Cloud of Faithful Witnesses* provide an early indication that the imitation of exemplary figures is central to this exposition:

> *Looke on them that so walke, as yee have us for an example.* Philippians 3.17.

> *Whose faith follow, considering what hath beene the ende of their conversation.* Heb 13.8.

Alluding to Phil. 3:17 in the context of a discussion of Joseph's imitation of the "godly examples of his father Jacob" (v. 22), Perkins concludes that the primary lesson from this passage is that "wee must learne of these godly Patriarches, both to give and to followe good examples" (132). Moreover, Perkins places this call to imitate exemplary figures in close relation to his earlier stress on the importance of the doctrine of justification by faith. In his discussion of the faith of Abraham, Isaac, and Jacob (v. 13), Perkins links a believer's call to "saving faith" with the imitation of the "notable example of *Abraham* and the Patriarchs":

> But if we looke to be saved by *faith*, as these men were, we must learne by their example, not to be ashamed of the profession of Christianity, whereto we are called; but must follow this notable example of *Abraham* and the Patriarchs, who were not ashamed, nor afraid to testifie their profession among the heathen, whensoever any occasion was offred [*sic*]: for *whosoever is ashamed of Christ in this world, Christ will be ashamed of him at the Last Judgement; before his Father in the world to come,* Luke 9.26. (101)

Salvation itself rests upon our ability to follow these examples. Earlier, he implores his audience to learn from "the example of these men" that "our calling is to professe the Gospel and religion of Christ," and that "being called hereunto, [we] must never be ashamed of it; much less denie or forsake the same" (101). Not only does Perkins stress the divine call that directed the lives of heroic figures of faith, in order to establish their important precedent; here he goes a step further by suggesting that our own call to "saving faith" depends on our ability to learn from the patriarchs' example.

Yet faith plays a still more primary role than does imitation. The phrase "by faith" is used again and again—eighteen times in 11:3–31—to underscore the role of faith in motivating the exemplary actions of notable men and women in Scripture.[18] After recounting with brief allusive phrases the faithful acts of numerous people of faith throughout history, the author of Hebrews comments in v. 39 that these Old Testament figures, though they "received not the promise" of Christ's incarnation in their lifetime, still "all through faith obtained good report" (196). Perkins explains that God communicated the nature of saving faith to these individuals "partly by his word, and partly by his spirit in their consciences, and partly by his Church" (196). Although Perkins commends the examples of faith in this particular exposition, the thrust of his comments go beyond commendation to calls for imitation.

In responding to questions about whether Abraham's "hope in God" and assurance of salvation offers a "generall warrant to us" or only a "rare example," Perkins answers that Abraham's faith is not only for our commendation but for our imitation. He suggests that

> [Abraham's] faith is a patterne for all Christians to follow: for else, why doth the Apostle so farre extoll, and set forth that faith of his, above 1300. yeares after his death; shall it be onely for his commendation, and not for our imitation also? Therefore every man that will walke in the steps of holy *Abraham,* may come with him to that measure of *faith*, that he may waite for heaven, with assurance to enjoy it. (79)

Like his comments on Abraham, Perkins' discussion of the other heroes of faith naturally lead to exhortations to follow their examples. For instance, his comments on v. 13–17 about Abraham, Sarah, Isaac, and Jacob's "endurance and constancie" (95) of faith and desire for "an heavenly countrey" reflect this linking of commendation and call for imitation:

> Now whereas the Patriarchs, beeing our fore-fathers in faith, and patternes whome wee must followe, *did desire heaven*: by their example everyone of

us is taught the same duty, to aime at another and a better *Country*, then that in which we live, even at the kingdome of heaven: and not to thinke that this world is the Country wee are borne for. (107)

Again, his commendation of Sarah is coupled with a call to imitate her faith:

> Yet withall we may observe, howe few the holy Ghost here recordeth; namely, but one or two women, amongst many men. For so it hath beene in all ages, those that have beene good, were excellent; but they were few in comparison of men: which, as it is the more commendation to them that are good, so it must stirre up all women professing religion, to labour in the imitation of the faith of their grandmother *Sarah*; that so they may bee some of those fewe.[19]

Perkins characterizes the "faithfull Witnesses" themselves as "excellent and most worthy examples" (14, 201), "a patterne" (48, 79, 107, 201), "our rule" (140), as well as "notable precedents" (149, 173). As Crashaw and Pierson ask in the Dedicatory Epistle, "And what estate of life can possibly befall us, wherein we have not a lively patterne and forerunner leading us the way to Heaven, within the compasse of this Cloud?" (Aa6v). Perkins even goes so far in his admiration of scriptural examples as to claim that "there is no action that can fall out in the life of a Christian man, for which he hath not out of the Scripture either a *rule generall* or *particular*, or else some *example* to follow, which is as good as a rule unto him" (29).

In perhaps his clearest articulation of the relation between the exemplar and its imitation, Perkins discusses the phrase "by which faith he also beeing dead yet speaketh" (v. 4), which refers to Abel. He says that Abel's faith

> yet speaketh, because it admonisheth all men every where, who either heare or read this storie, to become such as *Abel* was, namely, true worshippers of the true God: for, in *Abels* example, it provokes all men to be like him because it assureth them of the same regard and reward with God that *Abell* had: and so *Abels* faith is a never dying Preacher to all ages of the Church. Here we learne, that the holy Examples of Gods children are reall teaching, and loude preaching to other men. For there is a double teaching, namely in word, or deede. (22)

Perkins then applies the notion of "preaching" by word and deed to the minister, claiming that if the minister's "*reall Sermons*," that is, his deeds, are characterized by virtue, then his virtues, too, will "speak for him to all posterities when he is dead":

> It sufficeth not for him to teach by *vocall Sermons*, that is, by good doctrine; but withall by *reall Sermons*, that is, by good life: His faith, his zeale, his patience, his mercy, and all other his vertues must speake, and cry, and call to other men to be like unto him: which if he practise carefully in his life as *Abel* did, then shall his vertues speake for him to all posterities when he is dead. (22)

Throughout the *Cloud of Witnesses* Perkins offers case after case of the exemplary actions of men and women for commendation and imitation. He observes simply and directly that "as the examples of wicked men are every way to be eschewed, so *good mens* are to be followed" (28). In addition, Perkins endorses Paul's admonitions to imitate himself in Phil. 3:17 (131–32) and in 1 Cor. 11:1 (201). However, Perkins is quite careful when commenting on 1 Cor. 11:1 and limits the imitation of Paul to only those things that he does in imitation of Christ: "So *Paul* bids the Corinthians, *bee followers of him*; yet not absolutely in every thing; but *as he followes Christ*: and so must we follow the Fathers, as they went on in faith in Christ" (201). Elsewhere, he holds up Christ's suffering as an example, asking "Why should any bee dismayed with that estate, which Christ Jesus and his deerest servants have undergone for his example" (192). Perkins even refers directly to God's behavior as an example for our imitation in discussing God's promise to Abraham that he would father a nation (v. 12):

> God spake plainely and deceived not *Abraham*: and after at the time performed it; So must we deale plainly and simply in our words and bargaines, and thinke that to deceive and over-reach by craftie words, and double meanings, and equivocal phrases are not beseeming Christianity. (94)

But it is in his exposition of Enoch's faith (v. 5) that Perkins defines his views of the *imitatio Christi* most fully. Unlike a number of Reformed Protestants, whose view of human depravity excluded the possibility of any human imitation of Christ incarnate, Perkins encourages the idea. By distinguishing between the divine nature and mission of Christ as redeemer of humanity from his exemplary actions as a man, Perkins protects the primacy of the Reformed doctrine of justification by faith while still retaining the Christ-as-exemplar theme. He says that Christ's actions are for "our instruction and imitation" (28) and that they can be followed with divine assistance. At the same time, he restricts the *imitatio Christi* to only those actions of Christ

> as *a man*, or as a Jew borne, they are both our instruction and imitation, and they are good directions for our actions: as, his *obedience*, his *zeale*, his *patience*, his *humilitie*, and all other *vertues*. Concerning all which he saith himselfe to us, *Learne of me, for I am humble and lowely*. And againe, when he had washed his Apostles feete, he bad them *learne of him to love one another*: For (saith he) *I have given you example that you should do even as I have done to you*. These his examples are rules of direction to all men in the like case. (28)

Thus the moderate Perkins stands between the relatively optimistic views of human nature that caused some Protestants to encourage the emulation of Christ and the assumption of human depravity that caused other Protestants to discount the imitation of Christ as an unrealistic standard.[20]

Unlike the actual text of Hebrews 11, which primarily employs third-person descriptions, Perkins uses the first person when he exhorts his listeners to follow the examples of faith. He may take his direction from the surrounding texts of Hebrews which often summon the reader by using the first-person. Similarly, Perkins addresses his audience through the use of first-person plural subjunctives, as though by counting himself as a fellow striver he can encourage them more effectively: "*Let us*," he frequently implores, "therefore stirre up our selves, and looke about us; and seeing all the world on a fire about us, namely flaming in contention, hatred, and all disorder; *let us* for our parts seeke to quench it: which because we cannot, therefore lament and bewaile it: but much more lament and be humbled for our sinne, which kindled this fire of disorder in the world" (13, emphasis added). Later, attempting to motivate his hearers to share his commitment to the Word of God, he says that "we must remember *Abraham the father of our faith*; and when we heare Gods word, we must with him captivate our reason, and subdue our affections to it" (69).

Perkins interprets the purpose of Hebrews 11 as a straightforward call: to persuade believers to persevere in faith. After stating this point directly, he elaborates on the idea from various angles, repeating his own purpose in explication in an immediate, personal style that employs frequent stops, starts, and parallelisms intended to convey immediacy and sincerity. Speaking of the authority of Hebrews, he says:

> Now, in this chapter he continues the same exhortation: and the whole chapter (as I take it) is nothing else in substance, but one reason to urge the former exhortation to perseverance in faith; and the reason is drawne from the *excellencie of faith*: for this chapter doth divers waies set downe what an excellent gift of God faith is: his whole scope therefore is manifest to be nothing else, but to urge them to persevere & continue in that faith, prooved at large to be so excellent a thing: and indeede he could not bring a better argument to moove them to love and hold fast in their faith, then by perswading them of the excellencie of it. (1)

In order to "moove them to love and hold fast their faith," the writer of Hebrews had presented an extended series of examples of faith in action. Perkins seeks to do the same for his audience. His exposition of these figures stresses "the power of a great mans example, how forcible it is" (77) in persuading his listeners of the "excellencie of faith." In discussing Jacob's influence on his son Joseph (v. 22), for instance, he claims that

> the good examples of *Superiours* (whether they be civill or Ecclesiasticall) are of great force to bring other men on, and to make them forward in the duties of religion: their zeale (as *Paul* saith to the Corinthians in the case of almes) provoketh many . . . therefore *Superiours* must looke to all their sayings and doings carefully, that they may be worthy examples to their *inferiours*, to drawe them on in religion, and in the feare of God. (131)

It is an effective strategy. Crashaw and Pierson note the persuasive abilities of these examples: "The religious presidents of your Honourable Parents (Right Noble and hopefull Gentlemen) must perswade you much to be found, and constant in the faith" (Aa6v).

While calling his hearers to follow the examples set by praiseworthy individuals, Perkins also warns that "the examples of wicked men are every way to be eschewed" (28). These "bad examples" (2), according to Perkins, often follow "the common course of the world to get a good name" for themselves by laboring for various things of this world such as "riches, preferments, honour, wisdome, and learning" in order "to encrease their credit and name with men." In the meantime "saving faith is never remembered, which must procure them a good name with God" (8). Nevertheless, he counts these things of the world as "blessings" (8), for they originate as "good gifts of God" (142) and only become the "*pleasure of sinne*" (142) when they are misused. Faith remains, throughout, of primary importance. Responding to a series of his own rhetorical questions, in which he asks his listeners to consider their own ability in comparison to the superior gifts of the heroes of the faith, Perkins suggests that even these remarkable achievements, though "not to be contemned," cannot "purchase the favour and acceptation of God" (6).

> Has thou strength? so had *Golias* as well as *Sampson*: has thou beautie? so had *Absalom* as well or more then *David*: hast thou wisedom? so had *Achitophel* (though not like *Salomon*, yet) above ordinarie men: hast thou riches? *Esau* was richer then *Jacob*: has thou lived long? so did *Caine*, and *Ismael* as well as *Isaac*: has thou many children? so had *Ahab* as well as *Gedion*: hast thou learning (the glorie of nature?) so had the *Egyptians* as well as *Moses*: for there *Moses* learned it. All these thou maist have, and yet be a *vile person* in the sight of God: so farre from beeing approved of God, as that he will not vouchsafe (unlesse it be in his anger) once to regard or looke at thee: hast thou therefore any of those outward gifts? it is not to be contemned, it hath his use; thanke God for it, and use it well: and use it so as by it thou maist be approved amongst men: but stand not to it before God: for though it be wisdome, or learning, or never so excellent a gift; it cannot purchase the favour and acceptation of God: but *true faith* is able to please God both in this life, and especially at the day of Judgement. (6)

Perkins' solution to the dilemma of self-doubt for believers is to maintain a loose connection to the world, recognizing that "while we live in this world, our bodies are tents and tabernacles wherein our soules doe dwell, for a time: and besides, this time is uncertaine; for there is no man that can say certainely, he shall live to the next houre" (107).

Thus the idea that believers are called out of the world to follow in the steps of their elders as "strangers" and "pilgrims" in the world is an important aspect of the literary example in *A Cloud of Faithful Witnesses*. In a two step process, Perkins advises his hearers first to follow in the steps of exemplary figures of the past: "See where he hath cast off, and left behind him this and that sinne: see where he hath taken up, and caried with him these and those vertues and graces of God: marke, here is a print of his faith, here is a print of his hope, here are prints of his love" (6). Second, he advises his initiates to "be as carefull to leave behind us our steps; namly, token and prints of our faith, our hope, and love: which if we doe, then mark the excellent use of those steps" (6). As a "stranger" in the world, or "one that is a going throrough a forraine Country to his owne home" (101), Perkins reminds his listeners that they should follow in the steps of Abraham, Isaac, and Jacob, because these figures "were alwaies readie to goe whithersoever God would call them: and in all places wheresoever they were, still they waited on God, and sought to him for the kingdome of heaven" (101).[21]

At the same time, Perkins recognizes that the journey of faith to which he refers so frequently is not without its obstacles (19, 71, 149, 162, 205): "We must not be discouraged because of these crosses and afflictions: but labour with patience to beare that part of affliction, what-ever it be, that shall light upon us in our journey" (206). He exhorts his listeners to "walke diligently" in their "callings as Moses did" so not to let "crosses," or afflictions hinder "the duties" of their "callings" (149).[22]

Further, Perkins acknowledges the gravity of such a commitment. While discussing the persecution and affliction described in Heb. 10:32–34 and 12:3–4, Perkins follows Calvin; he encourages hearers to persevere with patience "through the whole course of their lives" (147). Calvin had suggested that "faith" in Hebrews 11 does not refer to the nature of faith as a whole but to "that part which fits his purpose, namely that it is always joined to patience" (157). Both men see this admonition as necessary because of the many obstacles to "effectual faith" in the temporal world. Perkins frequently employs images of the dangerous "sea of this world" (202) in order to warn his hearers to stand firm in their Christian commitment (5, 114, 138). He reminds them that even Noah's grand ark "would have beene broken in pieces: and so it had, but that God himselfe was the Master and Pilot in that voyage" (42). He describes the rushing flood water in cascades of phrases linked by repeated words, in a compound sentence that lacks the heavy subordination that characterizes so much of the *Commentary*. At the end of this description Perkins simply concludes, "and so in the *midst* of danger they were out of danger":

> For as it proved folly in them that trusted to their high houses, or carchthold on the hils, if they were *out of the Arke*: so will it proove much greater folly to them that shall trust to any means of salvation, if they be *out of Christ*. And contrariwise, as they that were *in the Arke* were sure to be saved, doe the water, windes and weathers, stormes and tempests all they could; and so that still, the more the waters rose, the *Arke* rose also, and was ever higher then they; and the higher it was caried by the violence of the waters, the safer it was from the danger of hills & rockes: and so in the *midst* of danger they were out of danger, & were saved in the midst of the water. (50)

As for those who have sheltered themselves in the safety of the ark, "He that is once truly in Christ, is sure of salvation, nothing can hinder it" (50).[23]

THE "EYE OF FAITH" AND THE
LITERARY EXAMPLE

The significance of the literary example as a rhetorical strategy has long been accepted by rhetoricians and poets alike. Since Aristotle it has been considered to be one of the primary means of persuasion, and Thomas Wilson in his popular *Arte of Rhetorique* (1560) restated a frequently expressed view among Renaissance rhetoricians: "He that mindeth to perswade must needes be well stored with examples."[24] As John D. Lyons claims in his recent study of the example in the Renaissance, "Example, rather than syllogistic or purely assertive discourse, took on a dominance that merits for the period from the fifteenth through the early seventeenth centuries the appelation 'the age of exemplarity.' "[25] An examination of the role that the literary example played in Renaissance poetics in light of Perkins' use of the example in his discussion of vocation is designed to demonstrate some of the important connections between biblical exposition and poetics as well as to illuminate Perkins' understanding of the literary example.

In English Renaissance thought, the example was not only designed to serve as a mere decoration for a particular sentence; it often constituted the actual terms of discussion. Certain logicians considered it to be one of the four kinds of argument. For instance, Thomas Wilson writes in *The Rule of Reason, conteinyng the Arte of Logique* (1550) that "there be foure kyndes of argumentes, Syllogismus, Enthymema, Inductio, Exemplum."[26] In addition, the Ramists treated example as an important element in their efforts to persuade readers by moving from the general to the particular case, or in their various classifications, categories, and divisions of an argument.

A number of different types of illustrative stories were considered to be examples. For instance, Francis Bacon's third category of poetry, "allusive, or parabolical," includes both illustrative stories providing "variety of examples" used "to express some special purpose," and fictional stories concealing wisdom allegorically.[27]

The key point here is that the ability of the literary example to persuade depends on its ability to depict behavior that will be imitated by its readers. Exemplary characters do not stand for a virtue or a vice. Instead, they are themselves individuals exercising the virtue or vice. In the case of exemplary scriptural figures, the actions of certain historical figures depicted in Scripture are held up to exemplify a laudable moral characteristic.

Like the exemplary scriptural figures depicted in Hebrews 11 and amplified for imitation by Perkins, an important quality of exemplary fiction is that its characters are either to be imitated or avoided as examples. They provide exemplary conduct for living or, as Sidney says in *The Defense of Poesy* (1595), they feign "notable images of virtues, vices" intended to be imitated or avoided by readers in their own lives.

> But it is that feigning notable images of virtues, vices, or what else, with that delightful teaching, which must be the right describing note to know a poet by, although indeed the senate of poets hath chosen verse as their fittest raiment, meaning, as in matter they passed all in all, so in manner to go beyond them: not speaking (table talk fashion or like men in a dream) words as they chanceably fall from the mouth, but peizing each syllable of each word by just proportion according to the dignity of the subject.[28]

Exemplary fiction, as described by Sidney, was linked with the rhetorical conception of poetry that attempted to persuade the reader to imitate its examples. According to this conception, Cicero's threefold definition of the orator's aims—*docere, delectare, et permovere*—were applied to the poet.[29] Poetry did not teach merely by setting examples but also by displaying them rhetorically in such a way that the reader would be moved to emulate or to disdain them.

Besides the term "example," various other terms were used to explain the idea of exemplary fiction.[30] For instance, poetry was thought to teach by "notable images of virtues, vices," by "patterns of virtues," or by "types"—all representations of particular behavior which prompted the reader either to follow or to reject it.[31] For Perkins, the term "type" in *A Cloud of Faithful Witnesses* usually refers to the traditional system of biblical typology whereby Old Testament characters, events, and objects prefigured Christ or some aspect of Christian doctrine. For instance, he refers to the land of Canaan as a type of heaven and Jerusalem as a type of the heavenly city (66, 78); he refers to Isaac as a type of Christ (122). He also refers to the manner in which Christ was "shewed and signified" in the Old Testament

> in ceremonies, rites and types; which were in number many, and in signification some of them darke and obscure; but now these types and ceremonies are abolished; the shadow is gone, and the substance come: and in steade of dark signes and figures, we have two most plaine and sensible Sacraments. More plainely, the covenant of grace in the olde Testament, was sealed by the blood of Lambs, as signes of the blood of Christ: but now to his Church in the new Testament, Christ himselfe hath sealed his Testament by his owne blood. (198)

Perkins generally uses the word "type" to refer to an analogy such as that between a seafaring ship and a Christian. In this particular case, loaded with precious cargo, the ship is carefully balanced with various weights to allow it to maintain its balance amidst the waves of the sea. This picture represents God's use of temptations in the lives of his grace-filled servants in order to humble them (like the weights of a ship) lest they become too proud of their own accomplishments:

> We may see a type hereof in worldly affaires: The best ship that floateth on the Sea, when it carieth in it most precious Jewel, is ballaced with gravell or sand, to make it sinke into the water, and so sayle more surely, least floating too high, it should be unstable: even so dealeth the Lord with his servants, when he hath given them a good measure of his graces, then doth he also lay temptations upon them, to humble them least they should be puffed up in themselves. (114)

While this is seen as a "type," when Perkins applies particular lessons from the lives of Old Testament figures to individual Christians he usually employs the term "example."

Sidney made a particularly important contribution to this notion of the literary example. A consistent phrase in Sidney's poetics is "notable images of virtues, vices," which draws attention to the exemplary function of certain images designed to present either virtues to be followed or vices to be avoided. This phrase, with its alternates "notable examples" (107) and "perfect patterns" (110), is regularly used in the *Defense* and it elevates the use of the literary example as precedent.[32] Most of Sidney's examples are taken from history or from exemplary fiction. For instance, he invites his readers,

> See whether wisdom and temperance in Ulysses and Diomedes, valour in Achilles, friendship in Nisus and Euryalus, even to an ignorant man carry not an apparent shining; and, contrarily, the remorse of conscience in Oedipus, the soon repenting pride of Agamemnon, the self-devouring cruelty in his father Atreus, the violence of ambition in the two Theban brothers, the sour-sweetness of revenge in Medea.[33]

In addition, poetic examples are not "captived to the truth of a foolish world."[34] Consequently, poetry is able to develop examples more impressive than those of history. As Sidney writes when he compares history to poetry, "Her world is brazen, the poets only deliver a golden."[35]

Thus a poet is free to examine and to promote certain laudatory qualities by depicting an exemplary character that excludes everything which might detract from the aim of a particular example. Sidney refers to this method in the *Defense* as being "poetical of a perfect pattern" (110). Due to this freedom, particular characteristics—whether virtuous or evil—are depicted in a way that, though simplified, displays their essential qualities more clearly: "If the poet do his part aright, he will show you in Tantalus, Atreus, and such like, nothing that is not to be shunned; in Cyrus, Aeneas, Ulysses, each thing to be followed."[36] Consequently, exemplary characters are clearly depicted in such a way that they can readily attract or discourage. On the other hand, the historian is required to depict "doings, some to be liked, some to be misliked. And then how will you discern what to follow, but by your own discretion which you had without reading Quintus Curtius?"[37]

According to Reformed Protestants such as Sidney, this type of influence is essential in order to make literary persuasion effective, since "our erected wit maketh us know what perfection is, and yet our infected will keepeth us from reaching unto it."[38] As Sidney puts it later in the *Defense*, "Poetry ever setteth virtue so out in her best colours."[39]

In Sidney's conception of poetry, the example is primarily designed to produce a change in behavior. Thus it requires a reader to identify with it.[40] Sidney likens a reader who is "entice[d]" to "enter into" the poet's fictional world to a traveler encouraged not only to undertake but to continue on a journey by the offer of "a cluster of grapes":

> For he doth not only show the way, but giveth so sweet a prospect into the way, as will entice any man to enter into it. Nay, he doth, as if your journey should lie through a fair vineyard, at the first give you a cluster of grapes, that full of that taste, you may long to pass further. He beginneth not with obscure definitions, which must blur the margent with interpretations, and load the memory with doubtfulness; but he cometh to you with words set in delightful proportion, either accompanied with, or prepared for, the well enchanting skill of music; and with a tale forsooth he cometh unto you, with a tale which holdeth children from play, and old men from the chimney corner. And, pretending no more, doth intend the winning of the mind from wickedness to virtue.[41]

The evocative and specific imagery of this journey through a "fair vineyard" is set in contrast to the abstract and obscure scholastic arguments of other forms of persuasion. Sidney tries to make the point that this type of influence can only be exerted by the example.

The acknowledgment of a poetics that relies on the literary example has profound implications for the kind of ideas present in much Elizabethan and Jacobean literature. By identifying explicitly this mode of interpretation, readers of Renaissance poetry and prose are prepared to understand the dynamic of literary examples. Renaissance methods of scriptural interpretation such as those exhibited by Perkins provided a model for the interpretation of secular texts which gave added significance to the use of the "example," "type," or even simply "hero" in Elizabethan and Jacobean poetics.

Using Scripture to support his case for poetry as fiction or as exemplary imitation, Sidney claims that by virtue of feigning notable images of virtues and vices, poetry above all other arts furnishes mankind with the noblest ideals and the most perfect models, even vying with or transcending nature. By means of the vivid, concrete pictures conjured into being by their creative imaginations, poets are able to present examples of ideal truth that may "strike, pierce" and "possess the sight of the soul."[42] While Sidney and Puttenham commended the imaginative example as superior to that found in reality, Perkins sought to find an approximation of the ideal in the scriptural record that he considered to be actuality itself; scriptural biography provided examples of how faith motivated the life of notable individuals of the past.

Another important aspect of the exemplary method of biblical interpretation involved the application of parallels from the Old Testament to New Testament and to contemporary events. Biblical expositors attempted to correlate the events of biblical history with episodes in their own lives. Barbara K. Lewalski calls these applications "correlative types."[43] These scriptural parallels and examples were widely used in sermons, biblical expositions, and general treatises, as well as in poetry. As with exemplary methods of biblical interpretation, writers attempted through these examples to influence the reader's emotions.

Literary examples, like those contained in Hebrews 11, were intended to encourage the reader to develop the character qualities depicted by the example. Throughout this *Commentary*, Perkins invites readers to enter into a new estate of life as a Christian, or, as the Dedicatory Epistle puts it, to "live under the Gospel" (Aa6r) in the world of scriptural examples and thus be moved by their exemplary force. In his discussion of Heb. 12:1, he challenges readers to follow the notable example of Old Testament figures heralded in Hebrews 11 for their constancy in the faith:

> In these words, the holy ghost propoundeth a worthy exhortation to the Christians of the newe Testament; that they should labour to be constant in the profession of the faith; that is, in holding, embracing, and beeleeving, true christian religion. And his reason is framed thus; *The Saints of God in the olde Testament, were constant in the faith; and therefore, you must likewise be constant in the faith, that live in the new Testament.* The first part of the reason is laid downe in all the examples of the former chapter. The conclusion or sequel is contained in this 1 verse. (573)

In analyzing this phenomenon several centuries later, Barbara Lewalski emphasizes that the individual Christian's entry into this new world plays a significant role for those like Perkins who understood the doctrine of the Word of God in this manner. She writes, "Along with this legitimation of typological symbolism, the shift in emphasis in reformation theology from *quid agas* to God's activity in us made it possible to assimilate our lives to the typological design, recognizing the biblical stories and events, salvation history, not merely as exemplary to us but as actually recapitulated in our lives."[44]

Reformed Protestants were indeed particularly adept at seeing metaphors of the human condition in the Bible and reading their own life and times in terms of it. And yet this kind of typological interpretation sometimes deteriorated in Protestant biblical interpretation into strict moral examples, resulting in a rather pedestrian interpretation of Scripture among some extreme Puritans. At times even Perkins could write in a limiting way. For instance, a number of his treatments of certain heroes of the faith in his exposition of Hebrews 11 merely record and repeat certain laudatory truisms about these figures rather than show how they could function as exemplary figures for particular listeners. Even so, when astutely applied, Protestant correlative typology could rise above this tendency toward moralistic read-ings. In his discussion of Heb. 11:1, for example, Perkins gives an imaginative explanation of how "*faith* makes things absent, present" which states the case quite aptly:

> The *faith* of the receiver knoweth best; and yet reason can say something in this case: for suppose a man looke earnestly upon a starre, there are many thousand of miles betwixt his eye & the stars yet the starre and his eye are so united together, as that the starre is after a sort present to his eye. So if we regard locall distance, we are as farre from Christ as earth is from heauen; but if we regard the nature of *Faith*, which is to reach it selfe to Christ, wherever he be, in that regard Christ is present: and why should not this be so: for if the bodily eye, so feeble and weake, can reach so farre as to a starre, and joyne it to it selfe, and so make it present; why should not much more the piercing eye of the soule reach up to Christ, and make him present to the comfortable feeling of it selfe? (3)

Similarly, Perkins later extends this use of visual imagery in connection with the nature of faith to his discussion of individual examples of faith in Hebrews 11. He uses metaphors of vision to convey the notion of entering into the world of biblical values.[45] Sin is thus depicted as capable of blinding one's eyes (162), while faith is pictured as enabling one's eyes to see spiritual values. It is only "saving faith," Perkins' allusion to the Reformed doctrine of *sola fide*, that is able to make the invisible become visible to the "eye of the minde" with "infallible arguments grounded upon the promise of God":

> It is an evidence: that is, whereas life everlasting and all other things hoped for are invisible, and were never seene of any beleever since the world beganne: this saving faith hath this power and propertie, to take that thing in it selfe invisible, and never yet seene, and so lively to represent it to the heart of the beleever, and to the eye of his minde, as that after a sort he presently seeth and enjoyeth that invisible thing, and rejoyceth in that sight, and enjoying of it: and so the judgement is not onely convinced, that such

a thing shall come to passe, though it be yet to come: but the minde (as farre as Gods word hath revealed, and as it is able,) conceives of that thing, as being really present to the view of it. (2)

In addition, faith opens the "eye of the soule" so that one's soul "seemeth to apprehend and enjoy this life everlasting" (2). Perkins' exposition of v. 1— *"Now faith is the ground of things which are hoped for: and the evidence of things not seene"*—explains how "saving faith" allows one to gain a new, spiritual perspective on life. Working by contrasting phrases, he says,

> *Faith* makes that present which is *absent*: and makes that manifest and visible, which in it selfe is invisible: invisible to the eyes of the bodie, it makes visible to the eye of the soule; the sight of which eye is both given, and continued, and daily sharpned by *saving faith*. (3)

Thus faith allows a believer to see biblical promises anew so that spiritual values "shall have a beeing to his soule: in that both his judgement knoweth assuredly they shal come to passe; and his soule in most lively and joyfull representation, seemeth to enjoy them" (3).

Throughout *A Cloud of Faithful Witnesses* Perkins uses the term "eye of faith" to convey this notion of spiritual insight and perspective, whether it be that shown by Enoch, who *"walked with God*, because he saw him by the eye of faith in al his affaires," or by Joseph, who resisted the temptations of Potiphar's wife because of "the feare of God, whom he saw by faith," or by Moses, who endured his battles with the Egyptian Pharaoh because "the seeing of God by faith, takes away fear and gives spirituall boldnesse" (150). In discussing the phrase "But sawe them afarre off" from v. 13, Perkins notes that Old Testament figures such as Abraham, Sarah, Isaac, and Jacob could not have seen Christ, "but afarre off, by the eye of faith, in the promises of the Messias" (97). He then suggests that the phrase "afarre off" is borrowed from "Mariners: who beeing farre on the sea, cannot descrie townes, and coasts afarre off, but onely by helpe of some tower or high place, which their eye will sooner disceren, though it be afarre off" (97). The "eye of faith" transforms a person's perspective and makes him or her alert to the spiritual realities that exist within the fabric of daily life. Like a pair of spectacles, faith allows one to bring into focus *"spirituall* and eternal" values that are "promised and shadowed under the *temporal*":

> Men use for their use, spectacles in reading: but they take no pleasure in looking upon them, but at other things by and through them: So should Christians, through all temporall blessings looke *at spirituall* and eternall, which are promised and shadowed under the *temporall*. (78)

Finally, Perkins also employs visual imagery to challenge us to look within ourselves "to see what manner of persons wee ought to bee" (121). After considering Abraham's "unmatchable example" (110) of obedience and faith, when he showed himself willing to sacrifice his son Isaac, Perkins turns the mirror toward his audience, telling them, "This practise of *Abraham*, must be a looking glasse for us, wherein to see, what manner of persons wee ought to bee. Looke what God commands us to doe, that we must doe: and what he forbids us, that we must not doe" (121).

23

CONCLUSION

On one level, tracing these connections merely demonstrates that William Perkins read the Bible in accordance with what literary critics today would consider to be its own rhetorical form. But on another level, the interaction between biblical exposition and poetics is more complex than that usually allowed, for correlative typology appeared frequently in secular literature as well. The examples of faith in Hebrews 11 influenced Perkins in the way in which poetry's "images of virtues [and] vices" influence Sidney. Both men invite audiences to participate in their narratives and respond to it by imitating a particular exemplary action. Like Rembrandt's interpretation of biblical subjects in terms of his viewers' contemporary experience, as in paintings such as "The Holy Family" (1645), Reformed Protestant writers often interpreted their own life in terms of the Bible.

Given its importance in contemporary culture, a study of the use of literary terms such as "example" and "type" in the context of Perkins' exposition of Hebrews 11 can thus increase our understanding of their use in imaginative literature as well as in scriptural exposition. For instance, Raphael's account of the fall of the angels in book 6 of Milton's *Paradise Lost* refers to the lessons that can be gained from the "terrible example" of the fallen angels:

> . . . let it profit thee to have heard
> By terrible Example the reward
> Of disobedience; firm they might have stood
> Yet fell; remember, and fear to transgress.[46]

Likewise, Perkins believed that the literary example of scriptural figures could assist its readers to achieve the full measure of their divine calling. In this he followed the example of the writer of Hebrews, whose stirring conclusion in Heb. 12:1 encourages readers to persevere in their calling by means of a metaphor:

> Wherefore, let us also, seeing we are compassed with so great a cloud of witnesses, cast away every thing that presseth downe, and that sinne that hangeth so fast on: let us runne with patience the race that is set before us. (199)

As Perkins interprets these words, "The exhortation is inferred upon the former examples; which are all here applied as presidents and directions unto us, for constancy and perseverance in the faith" (199). Using sight imagery to convey the way in which the literary example assists hearers in fitting their own frame of life into the biblical, Perkins explains that "in the same manner must we set before our eyes, for a patterne of life, the worthy examples of beleevers in the old Testament" (200–201). These "worthie beleevers" are compared to "*a cloud compassing us*," says Perkins, "because they give us direction in the course of Christianitie, as the cloud did the Israelites in the wildernesse" (200). Such guidance is also what Perkins wished to provide by emphasizing the idea of vocation in his exposition of the exemplary figures in Heb. 11:1—12:1.

NOTES

1. William Perkins, *A Cloud of Faithful Witnesses, leading to the heavenly Canaan: Or, A Commentarie upon the 11. Chapter to the Hebrewes, preached in Cambridge by that godly and judicious Divine, M. William Perkins. Long Expected and desired; and therefore published at the request of his Executors, by Wil. Crashaw and Th. Pierson, Preachers of Gods Word: who heard him preach it, and wrote it from his mouth* (1609), 36, vol. 3 of *The Works of that Famous and Worthy Minister of Christ in the Universitie of Cambridge, M. William Perkins* (London, 1631). Subsequent references to this work are cited parenthetically in the text. I have silently regularized i/j, u/v, w/u, and i/y.

2. *Luther's Works: Lectures on Titus, Philemon, and Hebrews,* vol. 29, ed. Jaroslav Pelikan, (St. Louis: Concordia Pub. House, 1968), 231. Luther's *Lectures on Hebrews,* given 1517–18, survived as two sets of student lecture notes and were first published in 1929.

3. *Calvin's Commentaries: The Epistle of Paul the Apostle to the Hebrews,* trans. William B. Johnston, ed. David W. Torrance and Thomas F. Torrance (Edinburgh: Oliver & Boyd, 1963), 187–89.

4. William Haller points out that this process was "more than an abstract formula. It became the pattern of the most profound experience of men through many generations" (*The Rise of Puritanism* [New York: Columbia University Press, 1938], 93).

5. 8:29–30. *The New Testament of our Lord Jesus Christ,* trans. Theodore Beza (1607; New York: Pilgrim Press, 1989), 76. All quotations from the New Testament are from this edition.

6. In a discussion of the faith of Abraham and Sarah, Perkins draws a similar distinction between what he calls "saving faith" and other aspects of faith: "Where we learne, that saving faith apprehendeth not onely the great promise of *redemption* by Christ, but all other inferiour promises that depend upon it. For, here we see *Abraham* and *Sarah* take hold of the promise of a temporall blessing, by the same faith, whereby formerly they had laide holde on the promise of eternall salvation by the *Messias:* so that the object of true faith is,

    1. *Principall:* the promise of salvation by Christ.

    2. *Secondarie:* all inferiour promises annexed thereunto" (86).

7. R. T. Kendall argues that Perkins' doctrine of faith—including one's calling, election, and assurance of salvation—places Perkins closer to the views of Beza than to Calvin's. Kendall claims that Perkins encouraged an "experimental predestinarian tradition" characterized by an emphasis on personal introspection leading, ultimately, to various forms of legalism (*Calvin and English Calvinism to 1649* [Oxford: Oxford University Press, 1979], 51–76). Alternatively, Paul Helm disputes Kendall's argument in "Calvin, English Calvinism and the Logic of Doctrinal Development" *Scottish Journal of Theology* 34 (1981): 179–85. See also C. M. Dent, *Protestant Reformers in Elizabethan Oxford* (Oxford: Oxford University Press, 1983), 98–102, 221–24, 238–44.

8. Perkins, *Workes* (Cambridge, 1608) 1.727–56. References are to volume and page number.

9. 3.10.6, 3.24.6. John Calvin, *Institutes of Christian Religion,* Library of Christian Classics, Ford Lewis Battles, ed. John T. McNeil, (Philadelphia: Westminster Press, 1960). Citations are to book, chapter, and section.

10. Perkins, *Workes,* 1.727.

11. Ibid., 1.731.

12. For a discussion of the "general" and "particular" calling among English

Protestants in the Elizabethan and Jacobean period, see Charles H. George and Katherine George, *The Protestant Mind of the English Reformation 1570–1640* (Princeton: Princeton University Press, 1961), 126–43.

13. Perkins, *Workes,* 1.735.

14. Ibid., 1.735.

15. Ibid., 1.734.

16. Robert S. Michaelson, "Changes in the Puritan Concept of Calling or Vocation," *New England Quarterly* 26 (1953): 324, argues that there is a distinct movement from a religious doctrine of vocation in early Puritanism toward the beginnings of a secular doctrine of vocation among the later Puritans. He places his discussion of the Puritan concept of calling within the framework of the Reformed doctrine of justification by faith: "Although the Protestant doctrine of vocation underwent change in the hands of the early Puritans, a central theme appears to have remained. This is the emphasis on the calling as an area of response and obedience to God's grace and love in Jesus Christ. This, then, rested on the basic Protestant doctrine of justification by faith. That doctrine had the practical effect of levelling all men before God. Common work received new value, not necessarily through this levelling process, but as a primary area of man's response to God" (325).

17. Among others, Perkins says that Moses also "had a calling immediatly [*sic*] from God to do as he did" (148) in leading Israel from Egypt.

18. See Michael R. Cosby, *The Rhetorical Composition and Function of Hebrews 11: In Light of Example Lists in Antiquity,* (Macon, Ga.: Mercer University Press, 1988), for a study of the rhetorical techniques of Hebrews 11 compared with techniques employed in other ancient example lists. Cosby suggests that the anaphoric use of "by faith" in Heb. 11:3–31 is used to reinforce "the connection between the introductory statements in 11:1–2 and the specific examples of faith in the lives of famous men and women of the past. This connection is hammered into the mind of the listener by the tremendous emphasis that each notable action recorded in the list was accomplished 'by faith' " (41). In addition, Leland Ryken provides a helpful discussion of Heb. 11:1—12:2 in the context of the conventional formulae used in an encomium. In fact, he refers to "the important motif that these past examples of faith are living models for later generations" (*The Literature of the Bible* [Grand Rapids: Zondervan, 1974], 211).

19. Perkins' unique pedagogical strategy here betrays a low view of women's abilities. He even considers it necessary to note that "saving faith, and consequently salvation it selfe, is not proper to one sexe, but to both; man and woman." To Perkins' credit, he expresses his disgust at what he calls "the monstrous and unnaturall madnesse of some men, who have called into question the possibility of their [women's] salvation; yea, some, whether they have soules, or no." He counters by proclaiming that God "hath made their soules partakers with them [men], of the same hope of immortal life." Nevertheless, Perkins considers it significant and especially blameworthy that, according to the biblical record (Tim. 2:14), "The woman indeed was the first that brought in sinne; and being deceived her selfe by the devill, she deceived man" (84). Earlier in the same discussion of Sarah's faith, Perkins grounds his view of women on the idea of male headship, basing his comments largely on the fact that Abraham is placed before Sarah in Heb. 11:8–11: "He placeth *Abraham* first, to shew the dignitie and preheminence of the man, whome for her sinne, God hath set over her; not onely for her head, but for her guide and governour: and to teach the man, that he, and his example should be first, and should be a light unto her; to shame them who come behinde their wives in faith and holinesse. Hee placeth *Abraham* both afore and after her, and her in the midst; to teach her, that her glorie and honour, every way, is in the vertue and worthinesse of her husband; her head under God: who is to goe before her, to give

her good example: and to come after, to oversee her courses; and on all sides, to be a shelter and defence unto her" (84).

20. J. Sears McGee argues that differing assumptions about human moral capacity led to contrasting responses to the *imitatio Christi* theme among so-called Anglicans and Puritans. Citing important studies by Norman Pettit, Gerald R. Cragg, and M. M. Knappen, McGee observes that "Anglican divines frequently recommended that Christians use Christ as an exemplar for human behavior, and laymen took the doctrine quite seriously. Puritans, on the other hand, spoke a great deal of the importance of 'possessing' Christ or having an 'interest' or 'portion' in him, but they rarely suggested the use of Christ's actions as a model" (*The Godly Man in Stuart England: Anglican, Puritans, and the Two Tables, 1620–1670* [New Haven: Yale University Press, 1976], 107); See Norman Pettit, *The Heart Prepared: Grace and Conversion in Puritan Spiritual Life,* Yale Publications in American Studies 11 (New Haven: Yale University Press, 1966), 29–30; Gerald R. Cragg, *From Puritanism to the Age of Reason: A Study of Changes in Religious Thought within the Church of England, 1660–1770* (Cambridge: Cambridge University Press, 1966), 30; M. M. Knappen, *Tudor Puritanism: A Chapter in the History of Idealism* (Chicago: University of Chicago Press, 1965), 376. More recently, John Morgan, *Godly Learning: Puritan Attitudes toward Reason, Learning, and Education, 1560–1649* (Cambridge: Cambridge University Press, 1986), explains that for Puritans, "The imitation of Christ incarnate was an unrealistic standard for those who still bore the sin of Adam. Rather, puritans settled on the figure of Paul as their role model—Paul the epitome of assured conversion; Paul the chief proselytizer of the true religion in hostile circumstances; Paul who had a covenant with the Lord; Paul who demonstrated the strength of the individual mediator between God and those who sought proof of their election. . . . Paul, through his remarkable combination of faith and good works, provided an example above suspicion of the godly individual in an imperfect world" (p. 38). Elizabeth K. Hudson writes that "conservative Protestants were more likely to recommend Jesus as the model for human behavior than were their puritan contemporaries" (541). She offers two explanations: (1) Puritan doubts about human ability to emulate so perfect a model, and (2) the close identification of the *imitatio Christi* theme with traditional Catholic piety ("English Protestants and the *imitatio Christi*, 1580–1620" *Sixteenth-Century Journal* 19 [1988]: 541–58).

21. Charles H. George and Katherine George discuss the Reformed Protestant concept of vocation in *The Protestant Mind of the English Reformation 1570–1640*. They demonstrate that English Protestant divines "emphasize the iniquity of using the calling to the end of securing material reward, they nonetheless assure the Christian that in connection with, if not as a consequence of, the diligent and God-fearing performance of one's proper work in the world, material reward may be confidently expected" (p. 137). Louis B. Wright claims that *A Cloud of Faithful Witnesses* was "a favorite book with the merchant class" in Elizabethan England because it showed by scriptural examples how faith in the Lord led to worldly success. Wright traces the movement of one copy of Perkins' *Commentary* owned by a prosperous merchant as it accompanied him from England to New England in 1636, and, eventually, to Boston in 1725 (*Middle Class Culture in Elizabethan England* [Chapel Hill: University of North Carolina Press, 1935], 282). However, Wright's claim is not substantiated by the *Commentary* itself. Even recognizing the Georges' point about the confident expectation of material gain despite cautions from Protestant divines about directly using one's calling for material gain, Wright's assertion ought to be read in light of consistent warnings in the *Commentary* itself about the dangers of becoming too attached to the things of this world as well as Perkins' call for Christians to be "strangers" and "pilgrims" in the temporal world. See also Wright's discussion of

Perkins' *A Treatise of the Vocations* in *The Cultural Life of the American Colonies: 1607–1763* (New York: Harper & Brothers, 1957), 140.

22. "Crosse" is a general term used in Renaissance England for any suffering experienced by the body or mind. Perkins makes frequent references to the term in his *Commentary* (15, 61–65, 78, 135, 141–43, 186–87, 193). Perkins explains that its "use" is "to teach us to make true use of our afflictions, and of those many hard crosses that must fall upon us in our course of serving God; namely, to know that they are sent from God, not as a hard-hearted, or cruell *Judge;* but as a wise and mercifull *Father,* who wisheth our good, and who will so blesse unto us the hardest and heaviest crosses, that befall us in our lives (if we receive them in patience and faith) that we shall say with David, Psal. 119.71. *It is good for us that we have beene in trouble, for thereby wee have learned to know God, and our selves better"* (65).

23. See also pp. 19, 29, 57–58, 118–19, 148–49, 156, and 186 for other references to the doctrine of assurance in *A Cloud of Faithful Witnesses*. For a discussion of the doctrine of assurance in Perkins, see Donald K. McKim, "William Perkins and the Christian Life: The Place of the Moral law and Sanctification in Perkins' Theology," *Evangelical Quarterly* 59 (1987): 125–37; Paul Helm, "Calvin, English Calvinism and the Logic of Doctrinal Development," *Scottish Journal of Theology* 34 (1981): 179–85; R. T. Kendall, *Calvin and English Calvinism to 1649* (Oxford: Oxford University Press, 1979), 51–76.

24. Thomas Wilson, *Arte of Rhetorique,* ed. G. H. Mair (reprint, Oxford: Clarendon Press, 1909), 190.

25. John D. Lyons, *Exemplum: The Rhetoric of Example in Early Modern France and Italy* (Princeton: Princeton University Press, 1989), 12. Lyons traces the development of the example in the Renaissance, paying close attention to non-narrative and noninjunctive examples by such writers as Machiavelli and Montaigne. According to Lyons, "To claim a limit for example by arguing that it functions merely to alter the behavior of readers is to neglect its role of organizing a type of knowledge. Particularly in the major prose authors of the sixteenth and seventeenth centuries, example serves as an instrument for relating the individual to sources of authoritative knowledge" (p. 237). E.g., Lyons suggests that latent in the term "imitation" itself, is this broader conception of exemplary rhetoric: "Imitation signifies, on the one hand, the representation of being in text (sometimes called *mimesis*) and, on the other, the representation of a text in our own being, in our ethical conduct (as in such expressions as *imitatio Christi* or *imitatio sanctorum*). In the former case (*mimesis*), the text becomes the model *of* reality; in the latter (imitation), the text becomes a model *for* reality" (p. 236).

26. Facsimile ed., The English Experience 261 (New York: Da Capo Press, 1970), F7v.

27. Francis Bacon, *The Advancement of Learning and New Atlantis*, ed. Arthur Johnston (Oxford: Clarendon Press, 1974), 2, chap. 4, sect. 3.

28. Philip Sidney, *The Defense of Poesy,* ed. Geoffrey Sheppard (reprint, London: Thomas Nelson & Sons, 1965), 103.

29. Cicero, *De Oratore,* trans. E. W. Sutton, introd. H. Racham, 2 vols., Loeb Classical Library (Cambridge: Harvard University Press, 1942), 3.14.

30. I employ the term "example" in a broad sense. I apply it not only to exemplary actions, but also to individual persons, whether fictional or historical, whose character and actions exemplify particular virtues and vices. Just as the story of the gospel is recalled in Paul's letter to the Galatians through allusive phrases such as "Jesus Christ crucified" (3:1), so also the poet can allude to certain names in order to evoke specific characteristics. The poet can evoke Job, for instance, as an example of patience severely tested, Aeneas as an example of fortitude and dedication to a cause, or Hercules and Samson as exemplars of strength. See John M. Steadman,

The Lamb and the Elephant: Ideal Imitation and the Context of Renaissance Allegory (San Marino, Calif.: Huntington Library, 1974), 71–105; and Richard B. Hays, *The Faith of Jesus Christ: An Investigation of the Narrative Substructure of Galatians 3:1–4:11*, Society of Biblical Literature Dissertation Series 56 (Chico, Calif.: Scholars Press, 1983), 7.

31. The standard, comprehensive study of medieval typology is Henri de Lubac's *Exégèse Mediévale*, 4 vols. in 2 (Paris: Aubier, 1959–64). Auerbach substitutes the term *figura* for typology. He distinguishes two medieval concepts, *allegoria* and *figura*, and bases his explanation of them on differing practices of various scriptural exegetes. He explains that in a figural relation both terms, the figures and the figured, are to be thought of as concrete realities, though the figured is likely to be felt as more "real." Consequently, *figura*, unlike *allegoria*, is tied closely to specific events in time: "The difference between Tertullian's more historical and realistic interpretation and Origen's ethical, allegorical approach reflects a current conflict, known to us from other early Christian sources: one party strove to transform the events of the New and still more of the Old Testament into purely spiritual happenings, to "spirit away" their historical character—the other wished to preserve the full historicity of the scriptures along with a deeper meaning" (p. 36). (Eric Auerbach, "*Figura*" trans. Ralph Manheim, *Scenes From the Drama of European Literature* [New York: Meridan, 1969], 11–76, *Neue Dantestudien*, [Istanbul, 1944], 11–71). See Beryl Smalley, *The Study of the Bible in the Middle Ages*, 2d ed. (Oxford: Oxford University Press, 1952); and Jean Danielou, *From Shadow to Reality*, trans. Wulstan Hibberd (London: Burnes & Oates, 1960). There is no comprehensive study of typology in the Reformation. Preus pinpoints some of the differences between medieval and Lutheran typology but covers only Luther's early commentaries on the Psalms.

32. Sidney, *Defense of Poesy*, 103, 107, 110.

33. Ibid., 108.

34. Ibid., 111.

35. Ibid., 100.

36. Ibid., 110.

37. Ibid., 110.

38. Ibid., 101.

39. Ibid., 111.

40. Ibid., 113.

41. Ibid., 113.

42. Ibid., 107.

43. Barbara K. Lewalski, *Protestant Poetics and the Seventeenth-Century Religious Lyric* (Princeton: Princeton University Press, 1973), 111–44. A number of recent studies have examined the idea of correlative typology from diverse perspectives and disciplines. In a section titled "Exemplary Scriptural Characters in *Paradise Lost*," Mary Ann Radzinowicz reminds us that the "roll call of the faithful" in Hebrews 11 "was the sanction for much typological interpretation in Milton's time and earlier." She demonstrates that "Michael's selection of case histories from the Old Testament to be dealt with in Book XII again owes something, but by no means everything, to the selection in Hebrews which greatly influenced typological understanding of the Bible" (*Toward "Samson Agonistes": The Growth of Milton's Mind* [Princeton: Princeton University Press, 1978], 287, 289).

Georgia B. Christopher's important study of Milton and Reformation biblical hermeneutics establishes that "traditional typology was still in use, but it no longer enjoyed the status of norm or underpinning of natural theology." She contends that it is "Luther's attention to the narrative texture that set the style for Protestant commentary. In a way that anticipates Auerbach, he noted that Old Testament stories were mere lattices, and urged the exegete to weave himself into the sense by filling in the interstices with details of situation and psyche from his own experience." Thus, Christopher concludes, "In a very important sense, faith became a 'poetic' activity—a passionate reading of a divine text (in which the figures were identified and read aright) followed by a reading of experience through this text. With the Reformation, religious experience, to an overwhelming degree, became 'literary' experience" (*Milton and the Science of the Saints* [Princeton: Princeton University Press, 1982], 13, 68, 7).

Hans Frei's influential study of "realistic narrative" in biblical hermeneutics posits a "precritical realistic reading" that "envisioned the real world as formed by the sequence told by the biblical stories." He looks primarily to Calvin for this understanding: "More schematically inclined than Luther, Calvin saw a correlation even broader than that of the progression from law to gospel with that from Old to New Testament and from promise of salvation to its fulfillment. History, doctrine, description of shape of life, all converged for him and were held together by their common ingredient in the storied text of the scriptural word, and by the Holy Spirit's internal testimony to that text through his awakening of the reader's and hearer's faithful beholding" (*The Eclipse of Biblical Narrative: A Study in Eighteenth- and Nineteenth-Century Hermeneutics* [New Haven: Yale University Press, 1974], 2, 1, 21).

Linda H. Peterson's study of Victorian spiritual autobiography from the perspective of biblical typology examines seventeenth-century notions of correlative typology and shows how Victorian writers appropriated typology in the development of the genre of spiritual autobiography. Commenting on John Ruskin's autobiography *Praeterita,* she claims that "typology supplied the episodic structure, narrative patterns and interpretive framework of the genre as Ruskin and the Victorians knew it." Earlier, she states her thesis using the terms of correlative typology: "From Bunyan's era to Ruskin's, the spiritual autobiography demanded an intense introspection and retrospection of the writer's life and a rigorous interpretation of his experience in terms of biblical texts or patterns of biblical history" (*Victorian Autobiography: The Tradition of Self-Interpretation* [New Haven: Yale University Press, 1986], 68, 1).

Chana Bloch claims in her study of George Herbert's poetry that beliefs about correlative typology influenced Herbert's "poems in which a seventeenth-century Christian uses his knowledge of typology as a way of coming to terms with his own life. That Herbert regards himself as both correlative type and antitype accounts for their complexity" (*Spelling the Word: George Herbert and the Bible* [Berkeley: University of California Press, 1985], 131).

Richard Hays explores the idea of correlative typology to explain in part Paul's use of Old Testament texts, claiming that Paul's "typological reading strategy extends a typological trajectory begun already in the texts themselves." However, he later contends that even such typological categories "offer insufficient power of discrimination to probe the distinctive properties of Paul's interpretations." Instead, he concludes that "Paul's fundamental reading strategies are profoundly *dialectical*. The word of Scripture is not played off as a foil for the gospel, not patronized as a primitive stage of religious development, not regarded merely as a shadow of the good things to come. Paul's urgent hermeneutical project, rather, is to bring Scripture and gospel into a mutually interpretive relation, in which the righteousness of God is truly disclosed." Though not directly related either to Perkins or to Renaissance notions of correlative typology, Hays' study suggests an extension of correlative typology to consider in light of Perkins' lively and heavily intertextual treatment of Hebrews 11 (*Echoes of Scripture in the Letters of Paul* [New Haven: Yale University Press, 1989], 164, 173, 176).

Most English Renaissance studies on the subject of correlative typology, including those listed above, owe a great deal to William Whitaker's 1588 *A Disputation on Holy Scripture* (trans. William Fitzgerald, Parker Society Publications 46 [Cambridge: Cambridge University Press, 1849]); William Tyndale's works (1525–1536) contained in *Doctrinal Treatises And Introductions to Different Portions of The Holy Scriptures* (ed. Henry Walter, Parker Society Publications 43 [Cambridge: Cambridge University Press, 1848]); and the biblical commentaries of Luther and Calvin.

44. Barbara K. Lewalski, "Typological Symbolism," 82.

45. Calvin also uses the metaphor of vision to describe Scripture's function as "guide and teacher" in enabling its readers to see God at work in creation: "Just as old or bleary-eyed men and those with weak vision, if you thrust before them a most beautiful volume, even if they recognize it to be some sort of writing, yet can scarcely construe two words, but with the aid of spectacles will begin to read distinctly; so Scripture, gathering up the otherwise confused knowledge of God in our minds, having dispersed our dullness, clearly shows us the true God" (*Institutes*, 1.6.1). See also Edward A. Dowey, *The Knowledge of God in Calvin's Theology* (New York: Columbia University Press, 1952), 90–147, for a discussion of Calvin's use of visual metaphors in describing divine revelation.

46. John Milton, *Complete Poems and Major Prose*, ed. Merritt Y. Hughes (Indianapolis: Odyssey Press, 1957), 909–12. Later, Adam responds to Michael's extended prophetic revelation of the course of history. Adam at last has his "fill of knowledge," taught "by his example whom I now / Acknowledge my Redeemer ever blest" (12.572–573).

William Perkins' Use
of Ramism as an
Exegetical Tool

DONALD K. McKIM

The influence of the French philosopher–logician Pierre de la Ramee (Peter Ramus; 1515–72) was extensive throughout the sixteenth and seventeenth centuries.[1] While a university professor in Paris, Ramus and his colleague, Amdomarus Talaeus (Omer Talon; ca. 1510–62), wrote prolifically[2] concerning educational reforms, specifically the reorganization of dialectic and rhetoric. Ramus is known chiefly for his "Ramist logic," which in the tradition of Renaissance humanism sought a simplified logic to the reigning scholastic logic built on the works of Aristotle. To succeed in his goal of subjecting all the liberal arts to the rules of logic, Ramus needed a system of logic that could be taught quickly and grasped easily by young students. The system he developed, Ramism, was applied by his followers throughout the catalogue of the liberal arts. Ramus' conversion to Protestantism gave special impetus to the application of his system to theology and was useful for many English Puritans, in particular, who found it an ideal method for carrying out their theological aims.[3]

The Puritans used Ramism as a framework for doing biblical exegesis. Ramist Puritans such as Laurence Chaderton (1536?–1640), William Perkins (1558–1602), George Downame (1565?–1634), Paul Baynes (d. 1617), Arthur Hildersham (1563–1632), and William Ames (1576–1633) used the Ramist philosophy and logic not only for presenting their systematic theological writings but also as a method of approaching and exegeting Scripture. Ramism proved a powerful exegetical tool. It provided a theoretical background and sanction for Puritan practices in exegeting scripture and also helped to shape those practices through the insights it provided as to how a text (or a subject) should be "logically analyzed," "resolved," or "unfolded" (frequent Ramist terms).

To understand better how Ramism was appropriated as an exegetical method by English Puritans, we will first look at its formation. Next, I discuss the highly influential English Puritan, William Perkins, who advocated the Ramist principles and practiced them in his approach to exegesis.

Donald K. McKim is the author of *Ramism in William Perkins' Theology* (1987) as well as numerous articles on English Reformed Theology and William Perkins.

From this, I draw certain conclusions about how Ramism functioned as an exegetical tool for English Puritanism.

RAMISM

Ramus stood in the stream of the Renaissance humanist logical reforms of Lorenzo Valla (1407–57) and Rudolph Agricola (1444–85).[4] He sought relief from the vast complexities of the scholastic logic as taught in the *Summulae Logicales* of Peter of Spain (1210/1220–1277), who was at his death Pope John XXI.[5] To simplify logic, the humanists and Ramus taught that the major divisions of dialectic were "invention" (*inventio*) and "judgment" (*judicium*). These served to "discover" and "dispose" arguments, which they did by drawing on the "topical" or "commonplace" tradition developed by the ancient rhetoricians. Rhetoric itself was to serve only as a means for ornamentation and delivery of what logic had produced. Thus logic was not to be divided into a logic of science and a logic of opinion; for Ramus there should be only one logic for both. "Method" was to be the key for organizing all that logic discovered. Thus the logician and the rhetorician were equipped to give full expression to human thought.

According to Ramus, with the art of dialectic divided into invention and judgment, invention had the function of arranging the individual concepts or arguments by which discourse was constructed. Judgment served to join these arguments. Judgment proceeded by three steps. The first step was related to the syllogism; the second was concerned with the linking together of arguments (from this step came Ramist "method"); and the third was related to religion.[6]

Ramist Method

Ramus' development of "method" from his second step in the judgment process became his most important and influential contribution to communication theory and to the application of his logic to written texts.[7]

For Ramus, the joining together of arguments to form an intelligible discourse occurred principally by definition and division. To him, a sentence emerged from the sentence before it, by either defining or dividing something which was there. He wrote that "the principles of the arts are definitions and divisions; outside of these, nothing."[8] While syllogisms were helpful, they did not function as they did in scholastic logic, namely, to summarize the truth,[9] but rather functioned to solve doubts when questions arose in matters of definition and division. The syllogism was not so much an argument in itself as a way of arranging an argument.

"Method" for Ramus meant basically the proper arrangement of propositions or axioms. True method was to move from "universals" to "singulars," from the general to the specific.[10] This procedure of organization moved forward by definitions and divisions. By applying this method, any discourse could be either constructed or analyzed. The prime illustration of method for Ramus was the arts. He wrote:

The chief examples of method are in the arts. Here, although all the rules are general and universal, nevertheless there are grades among them, insofar as the more general a rule is, the more it precedes. Those things which are most general in position and first in order which are first in luminosity and knowledge; the subalterns follow, because they are next clearest; and thus those things are put down first which are by nature better known (*natura notiora*), the less known are put below, and finally the most special are set up. Thus the most general definition will be first, distribution next, and if this latter is manifold, division into integral parts comes first, then division into species. The parts and species are then treated respectively in this same order in which they are divided. If this means that a long explanation intervenes, then when taking up the next part or species, the whole structure is to be knit back together by means of some transition. This will refresh the auditors and amuse them. However, in order to present things more informally, some familiar example should be used.[11]

Thus Ramus moved from a reliance on the syllogism, which had been the hallmark of scholastic logic, to a dependence on the right ordering of self-evidencing axioms or propositions, which were the components of discourse.[12] The ultimate goal of all dialectic for Ramus was discourse. The task of combining propositions (whether self-evidencing axioms or conclusions derived from syllogisms) was given to method. The proper method of discourse was also the best method of teaching. He wrote, "Method is the intelligible order (*dianoia*) of various homogeneous axioms ranged one before the other according to the clarity of their nature, whereby the agreement of all with one another is judged and the whole committed to memory."[13]

The procedure by which method moved, namely, by definition and division, makes it possible to lay out a Ramist treatise in the form of a bracketed chart. A Ramist "analysis," that is, an "unweaving" or disentangling of the various strands or threads of argument that ran throughout a discourse, reduced discourse to its simplest components. To Ramus this reduction showed the true meaning of the discourse. Divisions or lineaments on which the discourse was built were what stood, and these could easily be diagramed and their form exposed. The result was a bracketed outline that spread in a geometrical pattern of bifurcation since most often Ramus found that divisions of an axiom could be made into dichotomies. One division could be subdivided, divided again, and thoroughly "analyzed" down to its smallest unit or most particular member. The chart spread horizontally across a page as opposed to the vertical or downward-like thrust of the syllogism in scholastic logic. The task of the logician became classification. The logician's job was to arrange everything under proper headings or rubrics and thus ultimately to lay bare the basic propositions or self-evident axioms of which true discourse was composed.[14]

It was this "logical analysis" that was the trademark of the Ramist handling of a text. A text was reduced to its simplest divisions. Then the process could be reversed. By "genesis" the parts could be reassembled to produce the discourse. The spatial diagrams or charts that the Ramist method produces became the most obvious sign that a writer was a Ramist. If a discourse could be outlined in the bracketed fashion, it was certain that the Ramist method of composition had been employed. Indeed, in the sixteenth and early seventeenth centuries, the term "logical analysis" was a term "so unmistakably partisan that no one but a professing Ramist or one intellectually descended from a professing Ramist would use it."[15]

WILLIAM PERKINS' USE OF RAMISM IN BIBLICAL INTERPRETATION

William Perkins, Fellow of Christ's College, Cambridge, and preacher at the Great Saint Andrews Church from 1584 until his death in 1602, was one of the most respected and influential Puritan leaders during the reign of Elizabeth I. His *Works* were widely read and in the three-volume edition published between 1616 and 1618 total 2736 pages.[16] Many of these pieces originated as sermons. Collectively they include polemical, theological, and exegetical works as well as "cases of conscience," Christian ethical teachings centered on specific pastoral issues.

Perkins imbibed his Ramism at Cambridge, most probably from his tutor Laurence Chaderton, an important leader of the Elizabethan Puritan movement.[17] Recent study has shown that Ramism was pervasive in nearly everything Perkins wrote and in every category of his writings. This is so much the case that nearly all of his works can be diagramed as Ramist charts.[18] Perkins' work, thus, is most appropriate to examine in order to discern the use and importance of Ramism as an exegetical tool for English Puritans.

Ramist Biblical Exegesis

Perkins' biblical commentaries followed the Ramist pattern, or method. Earlier commentators had most often exegeted texts in a straightforward fashion, proceeding verse by verse,[19] digressing into a discussion of doctrine.[20] Some continental commentators, such as Johannes Piscator (1546–1625), had begun to apply "logical analysis" in the tradition of Ramus to the books of the Bible.[21] Others such as Francis Junius (1545–1602) and Lambert Daneau (1530–95) did the same.[22] In addition, they frequently used their knowledge of rhetoric when they commented on Scripture. Often they very carefully analyzed various figures of speech in what can be called "rhetorical exegesis."[23] This approach was complemented by their studies of individual words and terms. This was frequently called "grammatical exegesis."[24]

In England, Dudley Fenner (1558?–87) published a small Ramist commentary on Philemon.[25] In 1591, Richard Turnbull of Oxford used the Ramist logic to set forth *An Exposition of the Book of James*. This was complete with "the Tables, Analysis, and resolution both of the whole Epistle, and everie Chapter thereof: with the particular resolution of everie singular place." Turnbull claimed this was the most ample exposition available and "also more orderly than by any heretofore." He further asserted that he was the first to use the logical method on Scripture "in such a methode, as (to my knowledge) none hath laboured, either in this, or other like places of the

Holy Scripture."[26] But despite these precedents, none of the English predecessors of William Perkins used the Ramist logical method to the same extent he did for biblical exposition.

Perkins' biblical commentaries show that he approached the scriptural books with the tools of the Ramist philosophy firmly in hand. Some of his biblical expositions begin with Ramist charts so the entire scriptural book is already "methodized" or "analyzed" or "resolved" according to Ramist method.[27] Others were clearly drawn according to the method.

In his commentary on the first three chapters of the book of Revelation, Perkins wrote clearly of justifying his approach to Scripture through the use of "the art of Logicke" (which for him was apparently synonymous with Ramist logic).

> Hence observe, the lawfulnesse of the art of Logicke: for divisions are lawfull, (else the holy Ghost would not here have used them) and so by proportion are other arguments of reasoning: and therefore that art which giveth rules of direction for the right use of these arguments, is lawfull and good. Those men then are farre deceived, who account the arts of Logicke and Rhetoricke to be frivolous and unlawfull, and in so saying, they condemne the practise of the holy Ghost in this place.[28]

Perkins not only believed the exegete needed to use the arts of logic and rhetoric, but also that the Bible itself contained the natural divisions which it was the exegete's job to uncover using the tools of logic and rhetoric. In this sense, Perkins perceived the tasks of the logician and the scriptural exegete to be exactly as Ramus had said: to discover and dispose of matter.[29] The logician's job was to define, divide, and classify so that the thought of the discourse might become clear. To Perkins the task of the biblical exegete was precisely the same.

Perkins' Use of Ramism for Exegesis

William Perkins produced a wide range of exegetical works. He wrote commentaries on complete books, such as Galatians and Jude, and on parts of books, such as the first three chapters of Revelation and Hebrews 11, as well as expositions of individual texts of Scripture. Often these textual treatments served as springboards for his further treatment of a particular theological issue, such as witchcraft (Exod. 22:18), idolatry (1 John 5:21), or Christian equity (Phil. 4:5).[30]

A full survey of Perkins' use of Ramism in his biblical exegesis cannot be undertaken here. But Perkins' exposition of Hebrews 11 in his commentary on the eleventh chapter of the Book of Hebrews entitled *A Cloud of Faithful Witnesses Leading to the heavenly Canaan* is instructive in showing both how Perkins worked with Scripture as one committed to the Ramist method and how that method functioned for him as a biblical exegete, theologian, and preacher. This work was originally preached as a series of Cambridge sermons, evidently around the year 1595. It began with the Ramist style division: "Concerning Faith, two points are necessarie to be knowne of every Christian; the *doctrine*, and the *practise* of it." Perkins said the whole doctrine of faith ("beeing grounded and gathered out of the word of God") is found in the Apostles' Creed, "which beeing alreadie by us expounded."[31] It "followeth in order (next after the doctrine) to lay downe also the practise of faith: for which purpose we have chosen this 11 chap. to the Hebrewes, as beeing a portion of Scripture, wherein the said practise of faith is most excellently and at large set downe."[32] Perkins used the "doctrine/practice" pattern as he most often did. This time, he said, it was the pattern to be followed not only with each text or passage from the Bible but in the whole enterprise of Christian faith itself. Perkins would expound both the Apostles' Creed and Hebrews 11 to give the full balance of faith. "Faith" and "works" must both be represented; according to Perkins, they both are "necessarie to be knowne by every Christian."[33]

Perkins' commentary on Hebrews 11 differed from his commentary on the book of Revelation in that it was not prefaced by a chart of "general analysis." But though the Ramist map was absent, the commentary can be outlined in the Ramist fashion. Perkins dichotomized this chapter:

> The partes of this whole chapter are two;
> 1. A generall *description of Faith*, 1.v. to the 4.
> 2. An *illustration* or declaration of that description, by a large rehearsall of manifold *examples* of auncient and worthy men in the olde Testament, from the 4.v. to the end.[34]

Then Perkins proceeded to divide the "description of faith" into three "actions or effects" (in the first three verses of the chapter). The first two of these were dichotomized into "meanings/instructions," and "meaning/uses," thus maintaining again the "doctrine/practice" paradigm. These were further divided, as was the third, "action or effect."

Perkins also divided his second major part in two.[35] The divisions were of examples of faith in the Old Testament, and were categorized as those (1) "such as are set downe severally one by one" (11:4–31), and (2) "such as are set downe joyntly many together" (11:32–40). The first group, those listed "severally," was further divided into "natural Israelites" and these either "living near or after the flood" or "after the flood"; and he categorized them as "strangers from the church of God."

The first person Perkins dealt with was Abel (11:4). The three sections of the verse describing Abel formed the basis for Perkins' discussion of him: his sacrifice was greater than Cain's; he obtained testimony with God; and, though Abel is dead, he "yet speaketh." Each of these divisions was dichotomized by Perkins and then further divided several times. A few of these, when dichotomized, fell further into the "doctrine/use" rubric. Perkins introduced this pattern by saying "here we learne a worthy lesson of Christianitie." In the next paragraph he moved in a natural way to say, "for the use of this doctrine." The "word/deed" pattern was graphically made clear when Perkins wrote of Abel being dead and yet "still speaking." There a bracket was drawn in the text to show the two ways in which the example of Abel's faith was a "never-dying Preacher to all ages of the Church": "in word or deede."[36] The order for Perkins was invariably the same. First would be the doctrine, or lesson or "theory"; then the use, or instruction or "practice." Transferred to the realm of logic, Perkins, like Ramus, marshaled the "arguments" (invention) which to both men were self-evidencing axioms, or "propositions." Then they were arranged for "disposition" (judgment) or "exercise" (use) according to the laws of method.[37]

The divisions that make up the headings for a chart of Perkins' work were not arbitrarily selected. Perkins' main divisions and the different sections of the chart are set off by paragraphs in his works. That is, when he partitioned a subject, he named his divisions and the parts of them in such a way that each point almost always had a paragraph devoted to it. Perkins would begin with a topic sentence which served in a chart to name or define a division. The heading of a division when it was not a single word could usually be captured in a short phrase which came right from the text of Perkins itself. It is true that someone writing without Ramist method in mind could do this as well. A scholastic logician or theologian could also list points in a one, two, three fashion with a topic sentence to identify them. But there are important differences between the scholastics and Ramists at this juncture. The scholastic would move toward a conclusion by deriving points from the proposition and from the point derived immediately prior to it. The Ramist would not do this. Each of the points Perkins listed for either "doctrine" or "use" are points he apparently perceived to spring directly and immediately from his major proposition itself. He did not deduce them through a number of intervening propositions, also deduced. He did not use syllogisms to prove one point before moving on to the next. He did not construct a logical platform from which to display a final conclusion. Perkins did not so much seek to prove the points he made as simply to "unfold" them, to draw them out directly from his text.

On occasion, when he was expounding the Bible, Perkins did use the reasoning process to secure his points. He found examples of the Holy Spirit's use of reasoning, which to Perkins was perfectly valid. For example, on Heb. 11:5 about Enoch that read in part "neither was he found, for God took him away," speaking of the Holy Spirit, Perkins wrote:

> And for his proofe, he first laieth downe *his ground*: then hee thereupon frameth *his argument*, consisting of divers degrees of demonstration . . . the holy Ghost frames his *argument*, to proove that *Henoch* was taken away by faith: and it consisteth of many degrees of evidence. *For before he was taken away, he was reported of that he had pleased God.*
>   *But without faith, it is impossible to please God.*
>   The degrees of the argument are these:
>   1. *God himselfe tooke* Henoch *away.*
>   2. *Before he was taken away, he pleased God.*
>   3. *But without faith no man can please God.*
>   *Therefore* Henoch *by faith was taken away.*[38]

Perkins then expounded on each of the elements of this "argument," missing no opportunity to apply a practical exhortation for each point.

Perkins was concerned throughout his *Commentary* that his audience learn "not in judgment and knowledge onely, to be able to talke of it (which is soone learned:) but in conscience and practise."[39] Yet even though he used a syllogistic form and spoke of the "proof" of the argument, he was still only seeking to "unfold" how the Holy Spirit showed that Enoch was "by faith taken away." The three points from which Perkins deduced his opinion were taken directly from the biblical text itself; they were not Perkins' own propositions. He set them forth as he did to show how he perceived the Holy Spirit had "framed" the Spirit's argument to prove that Enoch was taken by faith. These propositions of Scripture themselves did not need to be proved. They were self-evident, "axiomatic." But by using the syllogistic form, Perkins could portray the interior "logic" of Scripture and make it plain how, in this case, Enoch was taken away "by faith." The first part of the verse Perkins was expounding clearly said, "by faith, Henoch was translated." What came immediately following was the Holy Spirit's "proof" that "Henoch beeing taken into heaven, must needes to be taken away by faith."[40] Perkins "unfolded" the logic of the Spirit's statement.

Here too Perkins displayed a Ramistic understanding of the place and function of syllogistic reasoning. The syllogism served only to clear doubtful propositions by deriving them from self-evident axioms. Perkins generally treated the statements of Scripture as axioms or true propositions. By expounding the Scriptures as he did, using Ramist method, he displayed graphically (whether the charts were prefixed to the work or could be drawn from them) how these axioms fit together in a pattern. If any part of the scriptural record needed further elucidation, the tools of logic were at hand. Perkins shared Ramus' conception of logic. He saw the Holy Spirit as using the logical forms in Scripture to demonstrate how logic as an "art" was to be done. The Spirit demonstrated this by "arguing" through the proper forms, so the syllogism for both Ramus and Perkins was not an argument in itself. It was merely a way for the logician (and the biblical exegete) to arrange an argument. This was all Perkins was doing when he used the syllogism to display the scriptural argument concerning Enoch.

In his exposition of Hebrews 11, Perkins devoted considerable space to explaining what lessons were to be learned and practiced from the examples of the "faithful" mentioned in the chapter. His exegesis proceeded phrase by phrase. Yet one is conscious that Perkins saw all these phrases as fitting together as parts of a larger whole, the "general analysis" of the chapter itself. This meant that at many points Perkins took the words of the scriptural text, the phrases, and grouped them or "translated" them into other words or phrases that served as the main heads for his divisions. For example, Heb. 11:13 read: "All these died in faith, and received not the promises, but sawe them afarre off, and beleeved them: and received them thankefully, and confessed that they were strangers and pilgrimes on the earth." Perkins' treatment of this verse was phrase by phrase. But before he embarked on this exegesis, he grouped the phrases under headings, writing:

> Hitherto the Holy Ghost hath particularly commended the faith of divers holy beleevers. Now from this verse to the 17. he doth generally commend the faith of Abraham, Sarah, Isaac, and Jakob together; yet not so much their faith, as the durance and constancie of their faith. Particularly the points are two.
>   1. Is laid downe their constancie and continuance; *All these died in faith*.

2. That constancie is set forth by foure effects.
    1. *They received not the promises, but sawe them afarre off.*
    2. *They beleeved them.*
    3. *Received them thankefully.*
    4. *Professed themselves strangers and pilgrimes on the earth.*[41]

Thus the phrases of this verse could be charted Ramistically as "constancy of faith" and "effects" of this constancy. In this sense Perkins systematized or categorized the biblical texts in his expositions. He gave attention to the biblical phrases themselves and always drew "uses" from the "doctrines" they taught.

The "order" that Perkins brought to the handling of the texts by grouping them and providing headings for them must have been done to facilitate "method." A chart constructed from Perkins' handling of Hebrews 11, would show not merely a grouping of the biblical phrases alone; it would show that Perkins had filtered the text and set the phrases as parts of larger groupings. From Perkins' perspective, the reader is actually observing the logical method used by God through the Holy Spirit in framing this discourse of Scripture. In this sense, the implications of the apparently innocuous Ramist philosophy become startling. The system was more than just classificatory logic when applied to biblical interpretation. It was an attempt to perceive the logical plan in the mind of God that expressed itself through the flow of the scriptural material. If this plan were to be uncovered, it could therefore also reveal the true hermeneutics for scriptural interpretation. The exact meaning of a text could be ascertained if the procedure used was able to uncover the mind of God behind the text. All other methods of interpreting that text would be false.

The Bible was the Word of God for William Perkins.[42] The Holy Spirit stood behind the writing of Scripture as well as with the interpreter who exegeted Scripture.[43] The Ramist logic applied to Scripture by proponents such as Perkins identified the very thought processes of the divine mind that caused the Scriptures to be written.[44] So, when Scripture was "methodized" and "analyzed" after the Ramist fashion, the reader of the Ramist chart had instant access to God's thought as it expressed itself in a portion of Scripture. Thus, when applied to biblical exegesis, the Ramist philosophy had metaphysical implications.

The connection in Perkins' mind between his interpretation of the biblical texts and the work of the Holy Spirit in framing them is apparent in such remarks in his *Commentary on Hebrews 11* as, "The holy Ghost divideth this reason into two parts, and handleth the same severally"; "here the holy Ghost prooveth the second part of the former argument"; and "but our Translation in this place is true and right, according to the words of the Text, and the meaning of the holy Ghost."[45] It is true that Perkins at times mentioned rules for proper hermeneutics.[46] But at the most basic level, he apparently did not doubt that he was able to peer into the Holy Spirit's mind because he was "properly dividing" the scriptural texts that the Spirit caused to be written. While Perkins gave a proper place to the use of logic and to human reasoning rightly applied,[47] the goal of such work was to see clearly how the Spirit had constructed this pericope of scripture. By laying out his "analysis" in biblical exposition (after the Ramist method), Perkins was making plain how the specific parts of Scripture (parts of verses, verses, chapters) were related to a broader whole. By giving each of these small pieces a heading, or "keyword," Perkins could diagram the section or book, thereby laying out clearly what the Holy Spirit actually had in mind as the Spirit caused the Scripture to be written.

RAMISM AS AN EXEGETICAL TOOL FOR ENGLISH PURITANISM

For this survey of Ramus and William Perkins' use of Ramism in biblical interpretation, the relationship between Ramist philosophy and the English Puritans' appropriation of Ramism as an exegetical tool becomes plain. Ramism provided Puritanism with tools of logic to be applied in the grammatical, rhetorical, and logical analysis of Scripture. These tools of "analysis" helped Puritans to a "resolution" of a passage of Scripture. A text was placed in its context, the words of the text were defined, and then the process of dividing or "distributing" the text was begun.

The Puritan exegete and the Ramist logician both sought to discover and dispose of matter. Ramist method taught that proper procedure included defining, dividing, and classifying from general to specific. The result was a Ramist chart. The "branches" or divisions of this chart served as the exegete's "arguments" in the Ramist sense of being the "topics" or "commonplaces." When arranged according to proper method, these provided one-word summaries of textual divisions that enabled one to see the basic outline or subject of a division at a glance. When preached, these commonplace heads were the key words that triggered the preacher's memory.

The Ramist-Puritan approach differed markedly from the practices of Protestant scholastic theologians. Perkins and his colleagues did not use the Aristotelian categories and language of the scholastics. Their goal in scriptural interpretation was to discover the "arguments" already present in the text. The exegete "uncovered" and classified these as Ramus taught. The scholastic method (and the view of logic that Ramus opposed) was based on deductions that could be made "logically" from the texts. For the scholastics, the ultimate means for arriving at truth was the syllogism. Proper inference based on the process of deduction yielded truth in the scholastic view. Ramist-Puritans in the humanist tradition did not rely on the syllogism as the master instrument for making truth compelling. Ramus taught that the first step in judgment was either syllogism *or* method; method was used more often. Ramists believed texts could be "unfolded" (as some of their charts literally had to be folded to fit into their books) by the proper method. When this method was completed, the interior logic or thought pattern of the author could be plainly shown. All inner relationships of a discourse became immediately visible. William Perkins never attempted to justify or prove the division he made. To him these divisions had yielded self-evident axioms, the validity of which was beyond question. It was only when dealing with "crypticall" places where the "plain meaning" of Scripture was not readily apparent that Perkins resorted to the use of syllogisms.

Thus Ramism was an attractive and powerful tool for English Puritans looking for a key to the right understanding of Holy Scripture. Besides providing tools of logic, right method, and a way of directly perceiving the mind of the Holy Spirit behind the texts of Scripture, Ramism as an exegetical tool helped keep theology itself and the exegesis of Scripture from becoming a purely theoretical discipline. Ramus had stressed the practicality and "use" of each art. When Ramist logic applied to theology and to biblical interpretation, the theologian and exegete asked both what is the *doctrine* taught here and what is its *use*. This had the effect of tying together theology and ethics. As such it was attractive to Puritans, who were bent on the reform of the English church yet who insisted that this reform be theologically grounded. Ramism provided a method of doing theology and approaching Scripture that maintained the unity of theology and ethics while also providing a theoretical framework whereby the application of scriptural principles to the lives of people could be part of every sermon. This was most valuable for those who wished for the spiritual reformation of the English church. Scriptural interpretation and theological reflection were not ends in themselves for Ramist Puritans. Instead, biblical exegesis and theological thought served a more vital and practical purpose. They were to function as ways for William Perkins' definition of the purpose of theology to be realized: "to live blessedly for ever."[48]

NOTES

1. The major work on Ramus is Walter J. Ong, *Ramus, Method, and the Decay of Dialogue* (1958; reprint, New York: Octagon Books, 1974).

2. Ibid., 5. See Walter J. Ong, *Ramus and Talon Inventory* (Cambridge: Harvard University Press, 1958), for a catalogue of these editions.

3. The connection between Ramus and the Puritans was pointed out and elaborated upon by Perry Miller in *The New England Mind: The Seventeenth Century* (1939; reprint, Boston: Beacon Press, 1954). Cf. Donald K. McKim, "The Functions of Ramism in William Perkins' Theology," *Sixteenth Century Journal* (Winter 1985): 503–17; and idem, "Ramism in William Perkins" (Ph.D. diss., University of Pittsburgh, 1980; University Microfilms #8112622).

4. See Lisa Jardine, "Lorenzo Valla and the Intellectual Origins of Humanist Dialectic," *Journal of the History of Philosophy* 15, no. 2 (April 1977): 143–64; and Wilbur Samuel Howell, *Logic and Rhetoric in England 1500–1700* (1956; reprint, New York: Russell & Russell, 1961); and Ong, *Ramus*, chap. 5.

5. See Joseph P. Mullally, ed. and trans., *The "Summulae Logicales" of Peter of Spain* (Notre Dame, Ind. n.p., 1945); and Ong, *Ramus*, chap. 4.

6. A full discussion of the Ramist philosophy is given in Ong, *Ramus*; and McKim, "Ramism in Perkins," chap. 2.

7. See Howell, *Logic and Rhetoric in England*, 160.

8. Ramus, *Aristotelicae animadversiones* (Paris, 1543; reprint, Stuttgart-Bad Cannstatt: Friedrich Frommann, 1964), fol. 58. See Ong, *Ramus*, 188.

9. See Ernest A. Moody, *Truth and Consequence in Medieval Logic* (Amsterdam: North-Holland Pub. Co., 1953); and J. Maritain, *Formal Logic*, trans. Imelda Choquette (New York: Sheed & Ward, 1946).

10. See Ramus, *Dialectici commentarii tres authore Audomaro Talaeo editi* (Lutetiae, 1546), 83, cited in Ong, *Ramus*, 245.

11. Ramus, *Dialectica* (Basel, 1569), bk 2, pp. 542–43, as in Ong, *Ramus*, 249.

12. Miller wrote that for Ramus "the stuff of judgment is not the syllogism but the axiom; the aim of an orator or preacher is a succession of sentences, not a display of deductions. When he has laid out the arguments and combined them into several axioms, he then ought to perceive from the axioms themselves what are their interconnections and what is their order; he should use the syllogism only when in doubt about formulating a particular proposition, or when incapable of recognizing the order of precedence among several statements" (*New England Mind*, 134). Alexander Richardson, a follower of Ramus, wrote that "syllogisms serve but for the clearing of the truth of axioms" (*The Logicians School-Master: or, A Comment upon Ramus Logick* [London, 1657], 335).

13. Ramus, *Dialecticae libri duo* (Lutetiae, 1574; same text as 1572), bk 2, pp. 72–73, as trans. in Ong, *Ramus*, 251. Cf. Ong, *Ramus*, chap. 11.

14. Ong reproduces some charts from Ramus' works in *Ramus* (181, 200–202), as does Miller (*New England Mind*, 126). McKim ("Ramism in Perkins," 443–502) produces over 50 Ramist charts from Ramus or his followers.

15. Walter J. Ong, "Johannes Piscator: One Man or a Ramist Dichotomy?" *Harvard Library Bulletin* 8 (1954): 153.

16. All citations from Perkins are from *The Workes of that Famous and Worthy Minister of Christ in the Universitie of Cambridge, Mr. William Perkins*, 3 vols. (Cambridge: John Legatt, 1616–18). Hereafter cited as *Works*.

17. On Chaderton, see Patrick Collinson, *The Elizabethan Puritan Movement* (1967; reprint, London: Jonathan Cape, 1971); and Peter Lake, *Moderate Puritans and the Elizabethan Church* (Cambridge: Cambridge University Press, 1982). On Chaderton's Ramism, see McKim, "Ramism in Perkins," 118–21. A sermon attributed to Chaderton on Rom. 12:3–8 has a Ramist chart at its beginning. It is reproduced in McKim, "Ramism in Perkins," fig. 5.

18. See McKim, "Ramism in Perkins." Cf. Donald K. McKim, *Ramism in William Perkins' Theology* (New York: Peter Lang, 1987).

19. Luther's and Calvin's commentaries were set up in this way, as were Nicholas Ridley's. See Ian Breward, "The Life and Theology of William Perkins" (Ph.D. diss., University of Manchester, 1963), 70.

20. Breward points to Peter Martyr's *Commentaries*, esp. pp. 41a–44b, where Martyr discusses the Mass. Breward writes, "This was the Protestant counterpart of the medieval scholion, and occurs frequently in Luther's commentaries" (p. 70).

21. On Piscator, see Ong, "Johannes Piscator"; and idem, *Ramus*, passim. Ramist-style charts appear in Piscator's *Analysis logica Epistolarum Pauli* (1591).

22. Francis Junius (DuJoy) was professor of divinity at Leiden. For his "logical analysis," see his *The Apocalyps* (Cambridge, 1596), 26; and the table in the Eng. trans. of his *Apocalypsis* entitled *A Briefe and Learned Commentarie Upon the Revelation of Saint John . . .* (London, 1592). This is reproduced in McKim, "Ramism in Perkins, fig. 21.

Lambert Daneau was an associate of Theodore Beza in Geneva and became a well-known Calvinist theologian. Some of Daneau's Ramistically styled charts are reproduced in Olivier Fatio, *Methode et Theologie Lambert Daneau et les debuts de la scolastique reformee* (Geneva: Droz, 1976). Cf. Daneau's *Twelve Small Prophets*, trans. J. Stockwood (Cambridge, 1594), 228–41; and John Platt, *Reformed Thought and Scholasticism: The Arguments for the Existence of God in Dutch Theology, 1575–1650*, Studies in the History of Christian Thought, ed. Heiko A. Oberman (Leiden: E. J. Brill, 1982), 119–22.

23. See Daneau, *Twelve Small Prophets*, 270.

24. Breward, "Life and Theology of William Perkins," 70.

25. Fenner became pastor of the Reformed Church in Middelburg, The Netherlands, after a stormy English pastorate. He translated Ramus' and Talon's works into English in 1584 as *The Artes of Logike and Rethorike*, and in 1585 published *The Sacred Doctrine of Divinitie Gathered out of the Word of God*, a Ramist systematic theology. See McKim, "Ramism in Perkins," 128–31. Ramist charts for his *Oeconomie* (*The Order of Householde . . .*); *Epistle to Philemon*; and *The Sacred Doctrine of Divinitie* are found in McKim, "Ramism in Perkins," figs. 8, 9, 10.

26. See Richard Turnbull, *An Exposition Upon the Canonicall Epistle of Saint James (London, 1591), "To the Reader."* Turnbull's chart is reproduced in McKim, "Ramism in Perkins," fig. 22.

27. See the charts at the beginning of Perkins' *Exposition upon the whole Epistle of Jude* (*Works* 3:479); and *Commentarie upon the Three First Chapters of the Revelation* (*Works* 3:207).

28. *Works* 3:259. See also 2:650, and 3:95, where Perkins approves the study of logic so that "false collections" of doctrines would be avoided.

29. See above, n. 8.

30. See Perkins, *An Exposition upon the five first chapters of the Epistle to the Galatians* (*Works* 2: 153–343); *An Exposition of the three first Chapters of the Revelation of S. John* (*Works* 3:207–370); *A Commentarie upon the 11. Chap. to the Hebrewes, containing the Cloud of faithfull Witnesses* (*Works* 3: 1–206); *A Discourse of the Damned Art of Witchcraft, grounded on Exod. 22.18* (*Works* 3: 607–52); *A Warning Against the Idolatry of the Last Times* (*Works* 1:669–716); *Epiekeia, or A Treatise of Christian Equity and Moderation* (*Works* 2:434–52).

31. *Works* 3:1.

32. Ibid.

33. Ibid.

34. Ibid.

35. Ibid., 14.

36. Ibid., 22.

37. See Ong, *Ramus*, 283–84.

38. *Works* 3:24.

39. Ibid., 26.

40. Ibid., 26.

41. Ibid., 95.

42. Perkins said often: "The Scripture is the word of God written in a language fit for the Church by men immediately called to be Clerkes, or Secretaries of the holy Ghost" (*Works* 2:647); ". . . the holy Scripture is no device of man, but the very word of the everliving God" (*Works* 2:474).

43. See *Works* 1:122; 2:649. Perkins wrote: "When any particular man comes to understand the Scripture this is by the working of Christ, hee opens his eyes. He gave the Disciples understanding as they went to Emmaus, to understand the Scriptures" (*Works* 3:220). Perkins was confident that even when there are diverse understandings of a Scripture text, "we must still have recourse to Christ." Using the "tools" that God has given for understanding, Perkins claimed that "a man shall be able to find out the true sense: for Christ in Scripture expoundeth himself."

44. This was the "inspiration" of Scripture: "And these are not onely the pure word of God, but also the scripture of God: because not onely the matter of them; but the whole disposition thereof, with the style and the phrase was set downe by the immediate inspiration of the holy Ghost" (*Works* 1:122).

45. *Works* 3:103, 105, 129. In his more formal theological definitions, Perkins stressed the role of the Holy Spirit as the prime agent in the writing of Scripture. As he worked with the Scripture through exegesis and interpretation, he did, however, pay attention to the human writers of Scripture and urged proper exegesis

to ponder every sentence of Scripture "and every circumstance of time, place, [and] person" (*Works* 2:244). Perkins believed "the sense of Scripture is rather to be judged the word of God, then the words and letters thereof" (*Works* 3:104). As Breward comments, it is this emphasis which "kept the christological reference of the earlier reformers and did not fall with the conclusion of Illricus that if the text was inspired, its inspiration must even extend to the Hebrew vowel points." See *The Work of William Perkins*, ed. Ian Breward, Courtenay Library of Reformation Classics (Appleford, Eng.: Sutton Courtney Press, 1970), 48. Cf. Jack B. Rogers and Donald K. McKim, *The Authority and Interpretation of the Bible: An Historical Approach* (San Francisco: Harper & Row, 1979), chaps. 2–4, for historical perspectives on the inspiration of Scripture.

46. See Perkins' manual on hermeneutics, *The Arte of Prophecying* (*Works* 2:643–73; 1:583.

47. See *Works* 3:95, 259; 2:650.

48. *Works* 1:11. Ramus said theology was "the art of living well" (*bene vivendi*). See Peter Ramus, *Commentariorum de religione Christiana, libri quatuor* (Frankfurt, 1576; reprint, Frankfurt: Minerva, 1969), 6: "Theologia est doctrina bene vivendi."

Interpretation of
the Old Testament between
Reformation and Modernity

GERALD T. SHEPPARD

William Perkins' exposition is one of the greatest achievements in literary-theological sophistication among Protestants just prior to the dawn of the modern era. No other English Protestant of the late sixteenth century more strongly influenced the course of biblical exposition in both England and in the New World, especially during the time of the thirteen colonies. His biblical exposition is a high moment in the history of interpretation, though one, like all others, with its own cultural and temporal liabilities. At times, Perkins' commentary is so logically fastidious and doctrinally exhaustive that it can easily be criticized as "scholastic," especially when compared with the blunt, discursive style of Martin Luther or the aesthetic restraints of John Calvin. At other times, Perkins seems so naive in matters basic to later modern historical criticism that, compared with modern "exegetes," he might be labeled a "biblicist." He addresses us historically from between the periods of the Reformation and modernity, an era often dismissed by modern historians of biblical interpretation as one of inert sophistry. At the same time, the British divines considered themselves exceptional in this regard. Citing the works of William Perkins and twenty or so other preachers and theologians, Joseph Hall could declare with confidence in 1624, "Stupor mundi clerus Britannicus" (The wonder of the world is the British clergy).[1]

Precisely because of the chaotic and formative nature of this period, Perkins' lucid exposition deserves a fresh assessment. He is especially significant now when we have begun to reevaluate elements within the consensus of a "modern historical consciousness" and their influence on textual interpretation.[2] At a minimum, we find in Perkins' work the specific premodern possibilities that existed prior to the elegant simplification of early modernity, with its own novel and confident conception of "exegesis."

While I will seek here to illustrate these issues, my concern is with Perkins' interpretation of the Old Testament. Exposition on the book of Hebrews, especially chapter 11, has always provided scholars with an ideal place to look for answers to questions of the sort I raise.[3] In practical terms,

Gerald T. Sheppard is professor of Old Testament Literature and Exegesis at Emmanuel College at the University of Toronto.

I will offer a critical but empathetic discussion of Perkins' interpretation of the Old Testament within his exposition of Hebrews 11. In conclusion, I will suggest implications for contemporary interpretation of the Bible.

OBSERVATIONS ON METHOD

Before discussing Perkins' work, I want to challenge an assumption common in the modern interpretation of the history of interpretation. This assumption is so pervasive that it deserves to be called "the standard modern hermeneutical fallacy." By this phrase I refer to assessments of premodern interpretation that presume that the "real" semantic content, "the literal sense," of a biblical text, must, as a matter of fact, coincide with our modern historical estimate of "the (historical) author's intent," "the original sense," or "what the text originally meant" (as distinguished from "what it means" as a register of its contemporary significance). In the parlance of the biblical theology movement of the 1930s to the early 1960s, modern scholars have regularly asserted that, using historical criticism objectively, we can now isolate "what a text meant" as a first step before the second, which is the evaluation of what a later interpreter correctly or incorrectly thought it meant or what it "means" (its current significance). The assumption is often made, as, for example, in *The Cambridge History of the Bible,* that modern scholars know what a biblical passage "meant" and can thus judge premodern interpreters in terms of how well each one anticipated such knowledge or, at least, did not violate it in the course of theological explication.[4] Before stating my own descriptive ideal, it is necessary to demonstrate why this pervasive modern model is so misleading and why a modern reexamination of the history of interpretation is so desperately needed.

In *Historians' Fallacies: Toward a Logic of Historical Thought*, David Hackett Fischer examines a variety of fallacies which well-known historians have accepted as truth. Most entail some subtle form of anachronism. What I called "the standard modern hermeneutical fallacy" is a cumulative error in judgment that usually combines at least three of Fischer's simpler fallacies: (1) the fallacy of misplaced literalism, (2) the fallacy of essences, and (3) the moralistic fallacy.[5] In order to show how foundational the standard modern hermeneutical fallacy has become, my illustrations come from Frederick W. Farrar's famous Bampton Lectures of 1885, which have gone through several printings under the title *History of Interpretation* (London, 1886). These lectures are a modern classic in the field, dominating it up to the 1960s. Even more recent assessments in the history of interpretation often perpetuate Farrar's model of evaluation, which I now criticize according to Fischer's fallacies.[6]

The Fallacy of Misplaced Literalism

Farrar can easily cite various figures in the history of interpretation who state that Christian doctrine should be derived only from the "literal sense" rather than from other senses of Scripture and, more importantly for our

NB

~ martin

purposes, that "the literal sense" corresponds to "the author's intent." For example, Farrar quotes Calvin's advice, "It is the first business of an interpreter to let the author say what he does say, instead of attributing to him what we think he ought to say."[7] Farrar thinks he states the same thing when he argues, "The one aim of the interpreter should be to ascertain the specific meaning of the inspired teacher, and to clothe it in the forms which will best convey that meaning to the minds of his contemporaries."[8] Thus for Farrar, Luther and Calvin express and refine a correct consensus in the history of interpretation, despite his admission that they both fail in practice to follow consistently this principle. Farrar dismisses as insignificant, for instance, the Reformers' appeal to the "analogy of faith," despite acknowledging that it is "a watchword which occurs hundreds of times," because according to Farrar it is merely "a misapplication of a scriptural phrase." However, in a footnote he concedes that the phrase expressed for them an understanding that Scripture interprets Scripture, an "obscure rule" for Farrar "which exegetically considered has no meaning."[9] By so underestimating the significance of such key hermeneutical features, Farrar can claim to find precedents in the history of interpretation for exactly the same aims as embraced by what he accepts as the modern "science of biblical criticism."[10]

In this use of historical precedents, Farrar employs the fallacious logic of misplaced literalism because he takes a premodern expression, "the author's intent," to signify the same implied ostensive reference to an "original" author as those same words convey in the vocabulary of modern historical criticism. As seen in the hermeneutical rules of Flacius, upon whom Perkins partially relies, the "literal sense" is thought to be disclosed by "the scope, purpose, or intention of the whole book."[11] At a minimum, the Reformers think that the intent of authors will complement the pattern, design, context, or scope of the scriptural text rather than shatter it into fragments assigned to various known and anonymous "authors." The same assumption explains why the Reformers appeal to the analogy of faith in order to hold text and subject matter together within the context of Scripture as a whole.[12]

Modern criticism discovered a new problem and new set of possibilities unanticipated by these premodern formulations about the literal sense, namely, an awareness of the radical difference that often exists between the *biblical* presentation of "authors" (for example, David of the psalms, Solomon of the Solomonic books, Paul of the Pauline epistles) and what we can detect about the originating *historical* authors and editors of these same works. Therefore, peculiar to the modern period is the awareness that the "intent" of a purported biblical author in association with the canonical context of a biblical book cannot be uncritically equated with the "original intents" of various historical authors/editors in the history of the formation of a biblical book.

Moreover, we should recognize that most of the historical authors of traditions now retained in the Bible never "originally" intended to write "Scripture" at all. In most cases, a decisive semantic transformation has taken place between the diverse moments when ancient prebiblical traditions originated and later moments when the traditions came to belong to a canonical context within the specific form and function of Jewish or Christian Scripture. Just as the quest for the historical Jesus must not uncritically be equated with an effort to comprehend the presentation of the Christ of faith in the Gospels, so historical authors must be carefully distinguished from the contextual presentation of biblical "authors." In his study of modern Roman Catholic conceptions of the literal sense of Scripture, Robert Robinson has shown explicitly how the older premodern formulation relating the literal sense to an author's intent is entirely misunderstood when it is reduced to a nearly scientific principle and inverted to read: the (modern reconstruction of the "original" historical) author's intent is the same as the literal sense.[13]

In my view, any description of premodern interpretation should initially endeavor to understand the terms peculiar to the older form of discourse without assuming that hermeneutical expressions from one era will carry the same semantic import in another. Certainly, a modern consciousness of the difference between historical authors/editors and the presentation of biblical authors forces us to make hermeneutical decisions heretofore unnecessary and points to further differences in what might be signified by the term "author" as well as the historical and referential character of any appeal to "intention."

In the late nineteenth century, particularly in the United States, so-called liberals and some conservative evangelicals (especially later "fundamentalists" in the 1920s) each claimed precedent in premodern interpretation for their positions. The "conservatives" often tried to use modern historical knowledge to prove the historical accuracy of biblical authorship in order to validate the canonical context or the scope of biblical books. Conversely, the "liberals" stressed the "author's intent," even when the context of Scripture had to be replaced in that pursuit by a set of reconstructed texts together with original or "genuine" authors (J, E, D, P, or Second Isaiah).

My point here is that the modern era faces historical possibilities regarding the nature of the "author's intent" which are alien to the premodern period. Both conservative and liberal modern views are similarly tempted to find precedence in the past formulations by means of misplaced literalism.[14] Instead, it is important to recognize that when expressed as though they were modern terms some elements of the older formulation—for example, the correspondence of "authors" to the "scope" of whole biblical books—can no longer be expressed precisely in the way they once were. From the perspective of liberal historical criticism, one must either (1) ignore the premodern emphasis on scope and the analogy of faith, as has Farrar, to press forward rigidly in terms of a modern idea of the historical author's intent or (2) reassess what is signified by a modern appeal to the "author's intent" in a way that will again sustain the context and scope of biblical books. I believe the latter option holds more promise because it can share more closely aims of premodern biblical interpretation without compromising modern historical consciousness.

A far better correlation than Farrar's would be, first, to consider all forms of modern historical criticism pertinent at least to what premodern interpreters called the "grammatical sense" of a text, which was an effort to understand the language, grammar, and other aspects in the historical etymology of the text preliminary to a recognition of its literal sense. Second, we can seek to clarify in what specific ways historical criticism is also essential to demarcate ambiguity, heighten realism, and clarify vagueness within the "literal sense" of Scripture. This literal sense is identified by its canonical context, its intertext, and its subject matter which corresponds to the scope and analogy of faith in older hermeneutical terms. To this degree, what literary critics such as Northrop Frye have called the "shape" of a biblical book and what Brevard Childs has further identified as "the canonical context" approximates far more closely the premodern conception of the "scope" of the "literal sense"—as well as the premodern appeal to an implicit "author's intent"—than do any of our modern references to the original intent of reconstructed "genuine" or "historical" authors.[15] Regardless, a modern effort can claim to continue a tradition of premodern biblical interpretation only by venturing a bold transformation of the premodern technical language of hermeneutics for use in modern interpretive discourse in order to avoid the fallacy of misplaced literalism.

The Fallacy of Essences

Farrar also limits the historical value of his survey from the outset by skewing his descriptions, relying on his own point of view regarding the essential nature of Scripture. As Fischer observes, no historian *qua* historian can tell us "the essence"—the inner reality—of historical events, ideas, or written documents without help from either a meta-historical, philosophical certitude or the eye of God. An essentialist method better serves apologetic interest than it sheds light on basic historical problems and possibilities in the estimate of past events.

What Farrar opposes is perhaps best illustrated by his claim, "Whoever was the first dogmatist to make the terms 'the Bible' and 'the Word of God' synonymous rendered to the cause of truth and of religion an immense disservice."[16] Behind this caveat is his own view that the Bible "contains" the Word of God and that "it is avowedly the record of a progressive revelation."[17] Only by recovering the historical authors' intentions can the biblical text play its true role as a human record of divine revelation and can this entirely human effort be weighed according to reason and our own discernment of the Holy Spirit. Farrar seeks to reassert for Scripture a "divine authority" that can best be ensured by "the removal of the false methods" of biblical interpretation in earlier eras.[18] While such a goal may be noble, its *historical* liability is that it assumes anachronistically a particular definition of the essential nature of Scripture, one that is freighted with peculiarly modern ideas about the role of texts as essentially referential "records" of past events. It should come as no great surprise that past efforts at interpretation, presupposing a different role for Scripture, fail to measure up.

My objection then is not with Farrar's opinion about Scripture so much as with the way this opinion becomes a "fact" that can be assumed pertinent to a perforcely historical inquiry. Even if such a fact is true, it is not a "fact" in a historical study of the past in that it is not a true description of how earlier interpreters envisioned Scripture. It therefore obscures rather than discloses their own perceptions of unity and difference in the biblical text. Furthermore, it impedes the possibility that we might be able to recognize in their own perception of continuities and discontinuities within the biblical text correspondences between their view of "the literal sense" and other modern literary-critical conceptions besides only one modern model of historical reconstruction.

Specifically on the issues of how Christians have interpreted the Old Testament in relation to the New, Farrar's essentialist definition of Scripture allows him to devalue, at the outset, many significant efforts at biblical interpretation. By accepting a particular, essentialist notion of "progressive revelation" within Scripture, Farrar can immediately condemn those who "deal with the Old Testament as if it stood on the same level of revelation as the New" and warns about those who "give the title 'Word of God' as indiscriminately to the books of Chronicles or Ecclesiastes, or to books in which as in Esther or Canticles, the name of God does not so much as once occur, as we do to the Gospel of St. John." So, he reasons, any effort to find in "the crudest and least spiritual narrative of Genesis and Judges the same theological value and supernatural infallibility as to the words of Christ is a deathblow to all sane, all manly, all honest interpretation."[19] Of course, if past efforts at interpretation can be dismissed categorically as attempting what is essentially impossible, then we are not likely to seek to understand further why interpreters agonized over texts in the way that they did.

The Moralistic Fallacy

Finally, a more insidious error illustrated by Farrar reflects what Fischer calls the "moralistic fallacy." While we have every right to voice our own moral, theological, and metaphysical points of view about the failures of the past, it is important that we exercise care when making *historical* judgments about past practices lest we play into cruder forms of moralizing prejudice. Farrar assures his readers that "the party theologians" have through proof-texts "gone astray" but that hope of true interpretation survived among "the simple," who intuitively and piously relied on the Holy Spirit to reveal to them "the few great moral principles" of the Bible.[20] The same "intuition" aided by the Holy Spirit is how the historical authors of the Bible "learnt by experience the lessons which they recognized to be eternal and divine."[21] By employing a Hegelian scheme, Farrar opines, "We shall see that past methods of interpretation are erroneous because the course of history has stripped off the accidents which pertained to the enunciation of truth, and given us a near insight into the truth itself."[22] The rise of modern historical method and a proper method of exegesis is heralded as the time when "the stone is rolled away from the door of the sepulchre." As just one among many examples of the rewards of modernity, Farrar notes that after seventeen hundred years of confusion we have at last "discovered the continuous design and central conception of the First Epistle of St. John."[23] It is ironic that Joachim Oporim is now nearly forgotten, along with his theory of the design and center of 1 John.

Behind the failure of preceding generations, Farrar sees everywhere the specter of Jewish misinterpretation, so that he can rationalize the mistakes of premodern "Christian expositors," as saying, "There is hardly an error in their pages that cannot be traced back to the Rabbis or to Philo."[24] Instead of helping us understand the logic of midrashic interpretation, Farrar dismisses the Talmud because "for every one text on which it throws the slightest glimmer of light, there are hundreds which it inexcusably perverts and misapplies."[25] Farrar blames the rabbis both for the view of Scripture as verbally inspired and for theories of interpretation that misled the earliest Christians. He summarizes, "The age of the rabbis lost itself in worthless trivialities, and suffocated the warmth and light of Scripture under the white ashes of ceremonial discussion, yet in preserving the text of the Old Testament it rendered services of inestimable value."[26] In other words, what I have called the standard modern hermeneutical fallacy leads to easy charges of "perverting" the truth with overtones of immoral or selfish manipulation. The same tone lies behind Farrar's overture to the modern era:

> It would have been shameful if we had remained content with the exegesis of the Rabbis, who were children of an imperfect and abrogated dispensation, or the Fathers who "lived among the falling and fallen leaves of the old world," or the Schoolmen in the ages of an all but universal ignorance.[27]

Regarding what a historian describes as "shameful" is inevitably subject to our own cultural prejudice. Historian David Fischer wisely cautions us, "Moral judgments consist in judging people by their own standards; moralizing is judging them by other people's standards."[28]

I will try in this essay to describe what I perceive to be Perkins' own implicit vision of the biblical text. I am aware that deconstructionists such as Jacques Derrida have radically challenged our understanding of texts by pointing to the circularity inherent in any modern appeal to a particular centered structure. Derrida in particular, while attacking the assumption of "objectivity" in literary arguments for structure, has not doubted the necessity of opting for some structure, no matter how provisional and capricious it might be, in order for there to be a particular interpretation.[29] Once a structure is chosen, its proportions and center become discrete and interpretation itself becomes subjected to its own aesthetic rules of a profound interplay between text and interpreter. Within this delimited assessment of a text, there is a relative "objectivity" that corresponds to the activity of interpretation once the rules of the game are established. Naturally a game to one interpreter may be a matter of life and death to another.

William Perkins supposes, as we shall see, that there is a natural structure or "scope" to Scripture which will help one find the "plaine sense." It is this "plaine sense" rather than any later modern notion of "original sense" that is the locus of the testimony of the Holy Spirit to God's revelation of the Gospel. A consideration of how Perkins treats the Old Testament proves especially rewarding because he confronts there the greatest possible tension between his vision of the Old Testament text and his own Christian doctrinal preunderstanding. After this examination, we will consider what are some implications for our own peculiar late modern situation.

BASIC ELEMENTS IN
PERKINS' PRACTICE OF EXPOSITION

Perkins' approach to Scripture sought to advance and refine what he regarded as the real achievements of the continental "restorers of the Gospel." When Perkins was born in 1558, Luther had been dead for over a decade; both Calvin and Melancthon died by Perkins' seventh year. His contemporary on the continent was Theodore Beza (1519–1605). Beza's Latin annotations to the Old and New Testament were selectively translated into English by the Marian exiles in Geneva so that they became an integral feature of the Geneva Bible of 1560 and its subsequent editions. As had Beza, Perkins read extensively in the works of Calvin, Luther, Melancthon, and Flacius. His goal was to preserve the Protestant position principally against the threat of its own internal corruption. At the same time, Perkins maintained a strong polemic with the Roman Catholic Counter-Reformation, symbolized by the decisions of the Council of Trent.[30]

For all of these reasons, much of Perkins' technical language about biblical exposition was already familiar to Protestants, though he employs it with his own nuance. By what seemed to be modest innovations, Perkins tried to strengthen the Protestant defense regarding the sufficiency of the plain sense of Scripture for establishing Christian doctrine. As Donald McKim illustrates in this volume, Perkins' argument against the use of either human reason or church tradition as an authority comparable to Scripture was accompanied by his own sophisticated reliance on logic and Ramus' rhetoric system. These strategies of deduction helped Perkins to demonstrate not only the sufficiency of Scripture but its richness as a source of Christian doctrine. In order to understand further Perkins' use of the Old Testament, I begin with the more elementary aspects in his vision of the biblical text preliminary to his application of logical or rhetorical strategies.

In standard Protestant fashion Perkins emphasizes that the "object" of both faith and Scripture is "the Word of God"—"nothing but God's word, and all and every word of God" (39).[31] This term "object" translates the Latin *res*, which has often been cited as the "subject matter" of Scripture by later theologians. Perkins readily affirmed that the Scripture "is the word of God" (16), though the very necessity of a proper "exposition" in order properly to render that divine word implies that the relation between "the text" of Scripture and its "object" or subject matter can be misconstrued. Therefore, Perkins' concern is to show us how to read the Bible as Scripture so that "the text" is held together with its "object." This assumption underlies his assertion, in contrast to the Roman Catholic position, that "the word of God registered in the holy Scriptures, doth containe in it sufficient direction for all action and duties of a man's life" (27–28). Precisely how the Word of God is "registered in the holy Scriptures" constitutes a major concern for Perkins. Three general aspects of Perkins' hermeneutical perspective deserve more detailed treatment.

First, Perkins wants to speak of Scripture in "two waies": (1) "as written and penned by holy men" sometime after the church was formed and (2) "as it is the word of God" which existed long before the church or any Christian

Bible. Using the term Scripture in these two ways, Perkins concludes, "So then the Scripture was afore the church; but penned after" (16). The term "Scripture" can refer, therefore, to either the revealed Word of God itself or the Word of God as "registered" in the form of a written Old and New Testament. For that reason, Perkins recognizes that Cain and Abel "had no [written] scripture, it was penned many yeares after; namely, by Moses first of all." Yet, they were "taught the same religion and, delivered the same doctrine to his children . . . neither by [written] Scripture, nor revelation, nor their owne invention, but by the instruction of their Parents" (15, my bracketed addition).

At a minimum, the Word of God is "registered in" Scripture, but it was also communicated prior to written Scripture in other ways and through other means. The goal of interpreting Scripture presupposes for Perkins that the expositor must discern in the words of "the text" its true "object," namely, the saving Word of God which existed and was known to some people in an essential manner millenia before Scripture itself was written. In modern times, we might say that he resists a rigid objectification of the text by acknowledging Scripture's temporal and pragmatic capacity to serve as a vehicle of its true object, the eternal Word of God.

Second, this orientation of Perkins to Scripture causes his practice of exposition to be text-oriented, on the one hand, but also more concerned with what the Holy Spirit says than with what a human author intends, on the other. Rather than referring to a human author and that author's argument or feelings, Perkins tends to spell out the content of the text itself ("the Text is plaine" [72]) or to anthropomorphize it ("the Text addeth" [107]; "the Text saith" [119]; "For so saith the Story" [51]). A key feature in his control of the content of a passage is to identify its "scope," a term that signified the relation between the perceived form and function of a text. Perkins uses the term in a manner analogous to how someone might survey a geographical territory or, in the vernacular of his own day, a "scope" of land. Perkins therefore speaks not about the scope of an author but the scope of a text, passage, place, story, chapter, or book ("the scope of this place" [14]; "the scope of the first commandment" [29]; "the scope of all of these verses is to prove" [103]). The ocular domain of scope is maintained in the way Perkins resolves possible contradictions in stories by "seeing" through "reading," and "finding" solutions in the wider context ("in the historie at large" [162]; or, "if we would see the history at large, we must read . . ." [134]). From this perspective, Perkins presents himself as a seasoned explorer who roams through the very human territory of the text in an effort to find, to see, and to hear the Word of God.

Alongside this humanistic and anthropomorphic description of "the text," Perkins repeatedly identifies the principal voice that speaks through the text as "the holy Ghost." His most common expression is "the Holy Spirit saith," which he uses before either specifying a textual feature or summarizing the content of a passage. Perkins' assumption of a full noetic complement accompanying this voice is shown by his appeals to an inner logic that orchestrates what and how the holy Spirit speaks in a text—for example, "Thus reasoneth the holy Ghost here" (78); "the holy Ghost proceedeth to amplifie and enlarge the commendation" (103); "Here then the holy Ghost setteth down two notable reasons" (141). Perkins assumes that the Holy Spirit has a special relation to the formation and function of Scripture. For example Perkins relies on spiritual discernment and confirmation to attest to the genuineness of Scripture (38). Again, Perkins shows no interest here in the precise role of the human author, the nature of his or her "inspiration" or possible "accommodation" to the limits of human discourse and temporal knowledge of the world. Nor by linking the voice of the text to the Holy Spirit does Perkins advocate a spiritual or mystical interpretation. He argues in true Protestant fashion for giving priority to the "plaine sense" as an authority above all others. By focusing on the voice of the Holy Spirit expressed within the voice of the human author, Perkins minimizes the need to reconstruct the human author's consciousness with its unique psycho-social historicality.

In sum, Perkins' vision of the biblical text is governed both by literary and theological judgments regarding both the "scope" of Scripture and its relation to the Word of God which is the true "object" of Scripture. The text is interpreted according to its capacity to bear witness to its subject matter rather than according to a theory that construes the semantic import of a text primarily in terms of its reference to the historical intentionality of its human author. Certainly, as seen in Perkins' commentary on Galatians, he observes both the "scope" and the "occasion" of a text. The occasion values the temporal conditions out of which singular human voices, as depicted and presented in Scripture, can be heard. Whenever Perkins affirms the "inerrancy" of Scripture in these terms his conception is quite different from that of certain modern fundamentalists who seek to secure inerrancy by locating it in terms of the inspired but historically accommodated author's intent. While modern fundamentalists presuppose that the essential semantic function of a biblical text is *to refer* outside of itself to a historically particular intentionality of an inspired human author, Perkins finds his semantic clues in the "scope" of individual passages, chapters, or whole books. In this respect, Perkins' approach is far more immediately text-oriented than is a fundamentalist orientation which moves, first, from the text to a modern reconstruction of an author's intentionality and then to some type of theological adjudication of that intentionality, rather than to an assessment of the text itself.

Third, we should observe the evidence of how Perkins pragmatically handles passages in Scripture which exhibit difference, contradiction, and resistance to his mode of understanding Scripture. Hebrews 11:2 states that the Israelites passed through the Red Sea "by faith," but Perkins admits that in the Exodus story, "when the people came to the redde sea, they were wonderfully afraid, and murmured against Moses . . ." (157). Perkins concludes they murmured "at first," but that after Moses spoke comforting words to them they followed "by faith." So, too, Heb. 11:24–26 says Moses "refused to be called a son of Pharaoh." Perkins assures us that Moses was not "rude" in so doing. At stake might be his disobedience of the commandment to obey one's parents. Perkins observes that commandments in the Second Tablet "doe binde us no further then our obedience unto the Commandments of the first tablet." Furthermore, "if we read the whole Historie of Moses, we shall not find" that he never openly rejected the designation of "son," so that his refusal must have been "not in word but in deede" (138).

Again as an example, Perkins is impressed with the seemingly minor contradiction that Heb. 11:21 describes Jacob as worshiping "on top of his staff," while Gen. 47:31 tells us that "he worshiped towards the ende or top of his bed." Perkins remarks, "there is a great difference between these two," and asks, "How therefore can they stand together?" (126). His answer is that just before Jacob died, he raised himself toward the head of the bed and, being weak and feeble, steadied himself on his staff. With this answer, Perkins offers the general rule that the same thing may be spoken by the Holy Spirit in a "diversity of words" which may "enlarge" the meaning rather than "corrupt or deprave the same" (129).

Finally, Perkins can appeal to the reason of the human author to account for differences. Hebrews 11:14–16 observes that the Hebrew slaves in the wilderness not only looked toward the Promised Land, but sought "a heavenly country." Perkins, first, notes that "the holy Ghost" divides the reason into two parts: (1) they sought a country and (2) it was heaven itself (103). Second, Perkins remarks that "the Author of this Epistle had diligently read the History of Abraham, Sarah, Isaac, and Jacob" (104) and had observed "in reading" that they often spoke of themselves as "pilgrimes and strangers." The author "gathered from their confession" the truth that they were not in their own country. Perkins, then, proceeds to encourage ministers through "reading, meditation, and observation" to "gather from Scripture" similar insights. Furthermore, Perkins argues that the author of this epistle has learned from Scripture some truths "by just consequence," for "though not literally, yet in sense and meaning they are contained in the Scripture." Similarly, the doctrines of "the proceeding of the holy Ghost from the sonne; and the baptizing of children . . . are not expressed in Scripture," but these "are true doctrines, no less to be beleeved, then that which is plainly expressed" (105).

This last example illustrates well what I described before about the relation between Perkins' appeal to what the Holy Spirit says and the ideas of the human author. Though these instances include some blatant efforts at harmonizing, they also demonstrate Perkins' determination both to sustain the biblical text and to admit that the text presents differences that are not easily reconciled within his larger vision of it. In other words, if we are unimpressed by the ease with which he speculates in order to reconcile some contradictions, we should admire his willingness to acknowledge the presence of differences that threaten his assumptions about the unity of the text. The text itself exercises pressure on him as an interpreter and Perkins feels compelled to find an explanation. There is a degree of objectivity within this hermeneutical circle such that a minor feature of no doctrinal importance—whether Jacob rested on his staff or bed post—constitutes "a great difference." Even the crudest effort to harmonize inadvertently pays homage to the differences that evoked its clumsy response, sustaining, however artificially, the hope of a unified reading in the light of a singular conception of reality and truth.

In these examples we see clearly that the intertext of Scripture inspires the discovery of truths that may not be literally expressed but can be "gathered out of Scripture" (see, for example, pp. 104, 118, 123). This way of describing how an expositor extracts hidden truth from Scripture by inference recalls Michael Fishbane's recent summary of the goal of Jewish interpretation as suggested by Ps. 119:18: "unveil my eyes that I may behold wonderful things *from out of* your Torah."[32] What Perkins thinks can be "soundly gathered out of Scripture" though not plainly expressed is similar to much that is found in Jewish "midrash." Perkins' "gathering out of Scripture" aims not at a mystical or spiritual sense but at an implicit truth of the literal sense indicated by a troubling silence, unnecessary difference, or provocative ambiguity (105). Sometimes this aspect of the text provokes Perkins to attempt historical or psychological explanations similar to modern historical reconstructions. For instance, in the story of Abraham's testing in Genesis 22, Perkins is perplexed by the readiness of the patriarch to sacrifice his own son. On the basis of the evidence elsewhere in Scripture that God will always honor God's promises. Perkins speculates here—"not as certane but as most probable" (112)—that Abraham must have had faith that God would somehow provide a substitute for his son.

In a different way, some biblical texts present a problem not because of internal contradiction but because the plain sense of the text seems to violate the subject matter of Scripture. So, alongside the possibility that every action by key figures in the Old Testament is potentially a positive example, Perkins asserts the rule that actions that are "contrary to the word" ("Noah's drunkenness, Lot's incest, David's adulterie, and many other infirmities and such like") "are, therefore, to be avoided" (28–29). In the case of Jepthah (Heb. 11:32), Perkins sees the danger in the Old Testament story in which Jepthah makes a vow and kills his own daughter (Judges 11). Because, Perkins reasons, Jepthah "had knowledge in God's will and words," he surely knew that "God would never accept of such a vowe." The words of the oath seem plain—"It shall be the Lord's, (And) I will offer it"—but Perkins appeals to another possible translation based on "the words in the originall": "It shall be the Lord's, (*or*) I will offer it" (174). Here, Perkins finds the idea that if an animal appears it will be sacrificed, but if a human appears, that person will "be the Lord's" in the sense of becoming a Nazarite. Jepthah weeps over his daughter not because she is dead but because of the severe restrictions that she as a Nazarite must observe. Perkins concludes this self-consciously precarious speculation by repeating what is most certain to him: "Believing and godly Jepthah . . . undoubtedly . . . could not think that God would be pleased" by the sacrifice of his daughter (174–75). Consequently, we see that in his determination to hold the text and its presumed subject matter together, Perkins employed different strategies of response to the various possibilities within the literal sense of the biblical text. In this respect, his approach, if not always satisfying, always endeavors to take seriously the literal sense of the text itself.

THE ROLE OF REASON

Another dimension to Perkins' interpretation of Scripture is his appeal to reason. He does not hesitate to attack Roman Catholics for reliance on esoteric scholastic or philosophical terminology (51). Perkins often comments on how the Scripture compels us to accept by faith ideas and occurrences that are "impossible to reason," "against reason," or "beyond reason" (44, 71, 56). We are advised that it is necessary for us to "capitulate our reason" and that "the obedience of reason" stands in opposition to "the obedience of faith" (69). Even though faith "doeth farre surpasse all worldly wisedome," Perkins still fully values what "worldly wisdom" positively "teaches us" (163, 107). What becomes obvious is that faith may summon us to assent to things the world will regard as unreasonable, but "worldly reason" can still pertain to the truth of God and will always be of service to us when it finds support in the Word of God. So, in Perkins' assessment of Heb. 11:19, he observes that "the text saith" that Abraham "reasoneth with himselfe, that God was able to raise up his sonne againe." This statement from Scripture confirms for Perkins that "all our reasoning in matters of faith must bee grounded on the word; so does Abraham in this place, against this strong temptation, reason out of God's word to stay himselfe: so that knowledge in the word of God, is necessarie to him that beleeves" (119).

Perkins himself drew heavily on logical and rhetorical theory to aide his expositions of Scripture, despite his awareness that much of biblical interpretation and the language of faith will inevitably seem irrational to the world. He admitted the value of "worldly wisdom" and presumed that Scripture itself leaves room for its value. The qualification in the above quotation concerning "our reasoning in matters of faith" allows for a greater role for reason shared with the rest of the world outside of concerns with faith and doctrine. Nevertheless, he considered the Word of God a precious asset to reason, providing it with a ground it could not otherwise have. The Word of God is the superior foundation that lies, as it were, above and below all other appeals to wisdom. For Perkins, reason, logic, and rhetoric are not negated or devalued but are given their true basis and sense of direction through Scripture.

THE PRESENTATION OF FAITH IN
THE OLD TESTAMENT AND
THE NEW TESTAMENT

Perkins especially tried to refine the understanding of faith and its relation to both conscience and obedience of the law. His treatment of Hebrews 11 provides perhaps the best illustration of how he interpreted Scripture along these lines. At the outset, he distinguishes "three sorts" of faith in Scripture: "historical," "miraculous," and "saving (commonly called Justifying) faith." The first two entail belief in, respectively, God and God's power to perform miracles; they are forms of faith exhibited even by "the devill themselves" and Judas, as well as the rest of the disciples. Elsewhere, the first two sorts of faith are each called "generall faith," distinct from "saving faith." Though Perkins finds in Hebrews 11 some statements pertinent to general faith, he argues, "The general scope in this chapter is principally of that faith that saves a man" (2).

Perkins praises Old Testament figures for "their faith" which is expressly more than merely "an action of a sanctified minde and a good grace of God," such as are humility, love, and the fear of God. Instead, their faith provides examples of "saving faith," which derives for them, as for us, only from the imputed justification by the righteousness of Christ. In this way, Perkins affirms the basic conviction of the Reformation on the matter of justification by faith alone. General faith may masquerade as saving faith, but it will fail to "purify thy heart, and cleanse thee and cause thee to abound in good works." The absence of good works is a sign that saving faith is not present (26). Though we should not judge others who are in the church, God will confirm in our conscience that we have received the gift of saving faith (58, 119). So Perkins assures us that for Old Testament figures "God testified it to their owne consciences . . . that he did accept them in the Messias to come" (5–6). Consequently, he heightens the family resemblance between us and them by asserting further, "If they have the same faith, they have the same conscience" (77). Here we see Perkins' rationale for why, even for later Christians, persons in the Old Testament can be models of "saving faith."

Elsewhere Perkins explores more explicitly the relation between saving faith and works when he discusses "the means . . . set downe by God's word" by which we can "live in true faith." First, we gain knowledge from Scripture and look for help from the teachers of the church: "for without learning the Catechisme, it is impossible to learne religion." Second, we must learn the promises of God and hide them in our hearts. Finally, "we must conforme ourselves throughout (heart and life) unto the holy laws of God" (96). These characteristics of faith lie at the heart of Perkins' exposition of Hebrews 11 as it is concerned with the Old Testament figures in Hebrews 11.

Perkins is careful not to confuse legal obedience with works worthy of justification. He repeatedly calls good works and obedience to the law the "effects" or the "fruits" of saving faith (97). He epitomizes this position elegantly: "Faith is a hand to take hold on Christ and his benefits, love is a hand to give out tokens of faith both to God and to man" (59). Of course, this delicate compromise, which lets good deeds and virtue serve as confirming signs to the conscience regarding the presence of saving faith, enhances his commemoration of the obedience and virtue of Old Testament figures. Since they were no more saved by legal observance than are we, the law, with the obvious exception of ceremonial legislation, was for them and remains for us a guide to the obedient life that constitutes the "fruits" of saving faith.

Perkins' positive assessment of the Old Testament and its presentation of faith and the law stands in contrast to the more pejorative estimates of the Old Testament found in Erasmus and common in the left wing of the Reformation. Perhaps one of his best summaries on this topic is:

> We in the newe Testament, have greater measure of knowledge, more lively discerning of the Messias, and a clearer light of understanding, in the mystery of our salvation by Christ, then the Church had, under the olde Testament; howsoever they excelled in faith yet in the knowledge, and discerning of Christ, they were inferior to us. (97)

Because, Perkins reasons, "more knowledge" ought to conjoin "more obedience," then "their faith was stronger then ours; but our obedience should
be greater then theirs, because we have more cause to beleeve then they"
(98).

Likewise, Perkins recognizes that the figures depicted in the New Testament did not yet have a written New Testament to guide their faith. For
instance, Peter's refusal to accept Jesus' words about his impending death on
the cross (Matt. 16:21–23; Mark 8:31–33) shows "the Apostles were ignorant
of some maine points of the Gospel." Perkins elaborates further the variety
of things the disciples "did not know": "how Christ should be a Saviour"
and "his resurrection." Even at the ascension, Perkins reasons, "they knew
not the nature of Christ's Kingdom" because they had to ask him if he
would now restore the kingdom (see Acts 1:6). The fact that the disciples
still "had true faith" despite this lack of knowledge basic to the Gospel
remains for us "a most comfortable truth," since we are assured that if we
hold to Christ our faith will be sufficient and we can proceed from their
testimony "to learn the doctrine of the Gospel" (167). Unlike those in the
Old and the New Testament periods, we have "the Scriptures perfect and
complete" (37). Perkins' view that the human response to faith prior to the
existence of a written Scripture would necessarily be "stronger" or "greater
than ours" means that the Old Testament stories on their own can provide
excellent, if not superior, examples of Christian faith (97).

Perkins not only allowed for significant limitations about what Old and
New Testament figures could know about the doctrine of saving faith prior
to the formation of Christian Scripture; he also sought to describe ways in
which God's activity in relation to ordinary human life had been indelibly
altered due to the appearance of Christian Scripture. I will note two of his
distinctions. First, in the prebiblical period, God usually called prophets,
disciples, and apostles "immediately," but today "men" are called to the
ministry "by means," especially through the recognition of their calling by
other ministers (61). Second, in the Old Testament far more than "now
under the Gospel," we find instances of God's direct revelation to individuals.
Any similar revelations today are likely to be given only to ordained
ministers, are "more ordinary" (concerned with "personal and private"
matters, "not directly touching salvation"), and, in general, "are ordinarily
nothing else, but these; the true meaning of Scripture, and a discerning of
true Scripture from forged, of true Sacraments from supposed, of true
doctrine from false, of true Pastors, from false prophets" (37–38). Elsewhere,
Perkins states similarly, "In former times men had visions and dreames and
Angels from God himselfe to reveal his will unto them: yet this Ministrie of
Gods world in the new Testament is as sufficient a meanes of the beginning
and increasing of true faith, as that was then" (132).

Even more than many modern exponents of a "biblical theology,"
Perkins is highly attentive to the historical differences between the nature of
faith in the prebiblical period and what informs a postbiblical faith so typical
of later Christianity. In this perspective, the presence of a Scripture has
indeed altered what we might expect of a believer's faith. Scripture betrays
the advantage we have over earlier periods of hindsight through the lens of
God's full revelation. So, earlier beliefs and religious traditions that once

were "scriptural" only in the sense that they truly mediated the Word of God have, secondarily and in a distinctive fashion, become "scriptural" in the sense that they now belong to the intertext of a written Bible and that Scripture alone, not the prebiblical faith or traditions, conveys to us the full doctrine of the Gospel. This orientation to the Bible and to its pre-history asserts a much sharper distinction than is typical in, for example, most modern "biblical theologies," between the import of Scripture and what the biblical authors actually thought or believed. Perkins' approach is obviously a "text-oriented" strategy of only one sort, based in this case on additional assumptions about the true form and function (scope) of Scripture and its relation to its object, the Word of God.

From our modern vantage point, we may observe that Perkins allowed for the potential of a rich conversation between Christians and Jews. He described more positively than had earlier Reformers the historical differences between a Christian understanding of saving faith and the same saving faith as understood by ancient Isarel and by the disciples of Jesus. At a minimum, this assessment grants to the Old Testament religious significance independent of the New Testament as a guide to saving faith.

Furthermore, the faith of the Old Testament is presumed to stand on the same promises, however dimly perceived, as those that later attained specific Christian definition in the teaching of the resurrected Lord. Of course, in the second century rabbinic Judaism, with the codification of the Mishnah (oral torah), also changed how it offered a precise account of the Torah revealed in Scripture. The legacy of Christian anti-semitism in the period of the Reformation casts a shadow over some of its most profoundly humane achievements. Unfortunately, Perkins' positive view of the faith of Old Testament figures did not lead him to an equal appreciation of the faith of "Jews and Turks" in his own day. Still, he avoided some of the worst Christian portrayals of ancient Israel and of later Judaism as narrowly "legalistic" in matters of faith. This corrective is made possible by Perkins' ability to see ancient Israelite and Jewish obedience to the law as the effect rather than the cause of saving faith or a way of earning it.

As an alternative to the highly philosophical Roman Catholic moral theology, Perkins also sought to be aggressively concerned with cases of conscience yet still base his arguments solely on Scripture. On the subject of Old Testament law, Perkins takes Rom. 10:3—"Christ is the ende of the Law to all that beleeve"—to signify that Christ is "not the taker away, or abrogater of the law, but the fulfiller of it . . . the abrogater of the Ceremoniall, so the fulfiller of the Morall law" (56). Perkins might be accused by some modern scholars of reading the Old Testament text anachronistically in confirmation of Protestant assumptions about justification by faith and of introducing a positive function for the law that exceeds the explicit teaching of the Gospel. However, he views Scripture as more than a chronological record of persons, places, and events. For Perkins, Scripture is, first and foremost, a witness through past humans and events to the reality of the Word of God that remains true for all times and places. What does seem remarkable is the room he has made for Christian conformity to the example of Old Testament lives and to the nonceremonial parts of the Old Testament law. Excessive and inflexible conformity came to be a hallmark of "Puritans" in the minds of their detractors, though nothing in Perkins' own work would, as we shall see, require it.

THE ETHICAL IMPORT OF
OLD TESTAMENT EXAMPLES GOOD AND BAD

Perkins is careful to distinguish between an assessment of biblical figures as either "ensamples" or "types." As "types" they foreshadow truths of the Gospel in a nonliteral fashion, but as examples in Scripture they exhibit the revealed human drama of people who obey or disobey the law and the wisdom of God. This capacity of biblical presentation of figures is partly defended on purely logical grounds when Perkins asks, "Can a man walke in this way, and not leave marks and steps behind him. . . ?" (5). The narratives, therefore, by their cumulative depiction constitute a revelation of a universal reality in which readers can locate themselves as a figure. So, Perkins explains, 'The practise of Abraham must be a looking glass for us, wherein to see, what manner of persons we ought to bee" (121).

Hans Frei has brilliantly described the nature and prevalence of the realistic mode of interpreting biblical narrative in Calvin, Luther, and among selected theologians in the eighteenth and nineteenth centuries.[33] By over-looking the seventeenth century, Frei missed some of the most provocative efforts to maintain this approach shortly after the Reformation and just before the full effects of modernity became commonplace in biblical studies. Clearly, premodern realistic mimetic assessments of the literal sense of Scripture had implications for theological anthropology, but Perkins' contribution was to find in this reading a normative resource for a systematic, even casuistic, understanding of Protestant ethics.

In his search for a Protestant ethic based solely on Scripture, Perkins attacks the Roman Catholic position of moral theology. He argues logically that, "If therefore men's actions must proceede from faith, then consequently must they have their ground and warrant from the word." In a polemical challenge to Roman Catholics, he then seeks to prove the sufficiency of Scripture in this regard (28). First, he appeals to "the evident testimonies of the holy Ghost" by citing 2 Tim. 3:16–17 and 1 Tim. 4:4–5. Second, he considers the objection that since Scripture was written long ago and the Commandments are only ten in number, it is dubious that Scripture alone can offer us today "sufficient directions." This objection touches on a key issue generally for Perkins, namely, how we derive "instruction" from Scripture (see, for example, pages 76, 106, 115). Perkins' answer is that the plain or literal sense of Scripture offers ample guidance of this sort, "either by rules, or by Examples" (28).

Through his treatment of examples, Perkins makes clear that the patterns of their obedience provide figural correspondence and direction to our attempts to "conform" our lives to them. Here he assumes that lives depicted in Scripture correspond realistically to our lives; the lives in the Bible and our lives pertain to the same vision of reality as revealed by God through Scripture. Hence, by figural correspondence the pattern of realistic depictions of a life in Scripture parallel a pattern of action and circumstance in our contemporary experience so that each may illuminate the other. On the one hand, the scriptural example by its explicit depiction may shed light on a similar action contemplated by a contemporary reader, indicating whether it would, in fact, be commendable or unworthy. On the other hand, the reader may illuminate and heighten the realism of the biblical text by certain modest appeals to experience or even human psychology.

Perkins speculates, for instance, that Abraham probably told Isaac at the altar that God had asked him by "a special commandment" to offer his son as a sacrifice since, otherwise, youthful Isaac would have most likely over-powered his father rather than submit to such a strange situation (112). Also, God used many words in calling Abraham from Ur in order to make sure that he was "furnished with strength and resolution" to follow through after accepting (62). Similarly, Perkins can also appeal to the context of a whole story or to the larger intertext of Scripture, including related information found elsewhere in Scripture. In these ways the realism implicit in both the canonical context of a text and the contemporary experience of the reader is critically considered so that the perception of correspondence is measured and limited rather than entirely subjective.

Each of these categories—rules and examples—can be further subdi-vided, according to Perkins, into instances that are of a "general" or a "particular" nature. The general rules include the Ten Commandments "for all men in all ages" and a few rules in the New Testament (Matt. 7:12; 1 Cor. 10:31; 16:14; 10:24). For rules to be practical, they must be particular, and Perkins thinks that the particular rules one should obey will "fall within the compasses of some of these [general] rules" (brackets added). Perkins expresses confidence that we can frame rules that are both "pleasing to God" and "comfortable" to us by observing "the tenour of some of these" general rules in Scripture. With examples, we can distinguish between God's "ex-traordinary examples" and those of "good men" which offer evidence of "ordinary workes of God's wisedom in his creatures." Though Perkins is not explicit, the general use of examples appears to be for our understanding from them of God's "justice towards sinners, of his mercie towards his children, of his care and providence towardes all" (28). Perkins is convinced that no action will lack either some guidance of a general or particular rule or an example and, therefore, "the Scripture affoords directions for all our actions" (29).

Besides this traditional use of examples, we should consider briefly how Perkins treats a number of hermeneutical problems confronting such an approach to Scripture: (1) the occurrence of immoral or exceptional cases intermingled with exemplary conduct; (2) the special case of Jesus' exemplary life; and (3) differences between the Old Testament and the New Testament.

Immoral or Exceptional Cases

In the history of exemplary interpretation, Jews and Christians have always acknowledged that there are some actions that seem exceptional or immoral intermingled with commonplace exemplary depictions. Perkins continues that tradition but develops it into a casuistry. For example, the command that Abraham offer his son obviously violates one of the commandments. However, God's request is a "special commandment." Perkins, then, argues that some commandments are more binding than others. The first Table, for example, is more binding than the second in the Ten Commandments. He concludes, "this rule may be set down; that when two Commandments crosse each other, then a man must preferre the greater" (110).

Likewise, we find in Scripture some special events which we should not expect to repeat. While we possess the same "general promise" as did the Hebrew slaves at the Red Sea, we should not presume to share in their "particular promise" that God will divide the waters of that river for their escape. We should not expect to have a similar experience since such rare and extraordinary events reflect "God's special warrant" (159). Finally, Perkins is fully aware that there are many "examples or actions" that are "contrary to the word," and he recalls the general principle of interpretation that a proper hearing of Scripture must hold the text together with its true object, so examples or actions are commendable only if they are "directly agreeable with the word of God" (28–29). In this last "rule" of interpretation, the word of God itself is a criterion for assessing what provides positive "instruction" of the Holy Spirit and what belongs to the realistic account of obedience or disobedience according to Scripture.

Jesus as an Example

Jesus is a special case since he is "God and man." Perkins distinguishes three sorts of actions performed by Jesus. First are actions that confirmed "his Godhead," such as his ability to walk on water. Second are many actions indicative of his role as "mediator," such as "his fasting fourtie dayes, his passion and his merits." These two types of actions by Jesus offer "no direction for our actions." What remains for "our instruction and imitation" is a third group of actions which are "done by him as a man, or as a Jew borne." In support of the need for us to conform our lives to such actions, Perkins can cite Jesus' invitation to "learn of me" and his statement, "I have given you an example" in Matt. 11:29 and John 13:14–15 (28). Once again, Perkins must carefully adjudicate between different types of actions, some of which are special or serve a nonexemplary purpose—for example, establishing the Godhead or mediatorial office of Christ—others which provide paradigmatic patterns integral to the concerns of Christian ethics.

Differences between the
Old Testament and the New Testament

Perkins is clear that obedience to the law is not a way for Christians to "please God" as Adam once did because "now that is past, that power is lost" (24). Still, we have already seen that he does think that obedience to Old Testament law becomes a "fruit" or "effect" of justification by faith alone and an assuring sign of the same to the believer's conscience. This tension in the use of the law and the import of the Gospel becomes even more explicit when Perkins considers the question of how Rahab in Heb. 11:31 could be saved by faith if she is a harlot (compare 1 Cor. 6:9). He answers that her condemnation is "true according to the Law, but the Gospel gives this exception, unlesse they repent" (166). Moreover, even the ceremonial law which is "ended with Christ" can be a source of instruction. In the case of Cain's offering a proper sacrifice, "this law binds us not." Nonetheless, it teaches us the wisdom that we are to give the best we have to God (17). In other words, Perkins sapientializes it in order to ascertain the wisdom of God implicit in this obedience to law which is in itself now out of style.

Here we see that wisdom, law, prophecy, and Gospel serve as different idioms of revelation and that one idiom might be appropriate at one place and not at another. Perkins can also go beyond the literal sense to explain the relation of the ceremonial law to later Christian practices. When Perkins considers the Passover, he avers, "I consider it one of the Sacraments of the old Testament." He treats circumcision similarly. Though Christians share "the same faith" as the Old Testament figures, they now view the earlier "sacraments" of the Passover and circumcision as types foreshadowing the Lord's Supper and baptism respectively (151–52). In these ways, Perkins is able to assert a continuity in the examples of saving faith in both the Old and New Testaments while rationalizing some of the different actions as conforming to different economies of divine revelation.

CONCLUDING OBSERVATIONS

My analysis of Perkins' handling of specific features of the Old Testament leads me to two general observations about "the literal sense" and "saving faith" then and now. These concern (1) the role of the author's intent; and (2) the idioms of a literal-sense interpretation.

The Role of the Author's Intent

Perkins consistently treats the words of Scripture as human words "written and penned by holy men." Yet, more often than not, he identifies the voice behind the literal sense as that of "the holy Ghost." This perspective should be distinguished from that of Aquinas who argued that the literal sense is the human author's intent when it coincides with God's intent and that the presence of divine intention explains why the literal sense contains within it multiple spiritual or mystical senses. Perkins would agree with Whitaker, his contemporary, who argued that there is only one true literal sense and that other so-called "senses" can be deemed at best to be only "uses" and "applications" of the literal.[34] While, as we have seen, Perkins does not hesitate to describe the argument of "the holy Spirit" in a given text, he clearly assumes it can be inferred only through the human witness of the text itself.

If we ask what criteria Perkins uses to guide his recognition of an author's intent and purpose, we find emphasis again on the human character, of the biblical text rather than its divine origin. Not anticipating the modern predisposition to find an "original" historical author and, as such, an "original" or "genuine" sense, Perkins assumes that the literal sense coheres within the syntactical wedding of the presentation of a single human *persona* as the "author" to the dimensions of a whole book. For that reason, he explicitly speaks of "the author of this Epistle" and segments the parts of the book according to the "argument" of that author. In modern terms, we might say this canonical context of Scripture, rather than its strictly historical context, offers the primary guide for Perkins to organize the parts of the text under one or many "scopes." He describes how Hebrews 11 "is dependent on the former" chapter and summarizes: "For this chapter . . . his whole scope, therefore, is manifest to be nothing else, but to urge them to persevere and continue in that faith . . ." (1). In this effort Perkins shows interest in the human author only insofar as that author is a witness to the subject matter of Scripture. Consequently, he pays no attention to any historical biography of the author, nor does he speculate about whether the writer of Hebrews is the apostle Paul; and Perkins never views the religious content of the text as valuable primarily for its insight into a "theology" embraced by the historical person responsible for the biblical text.

From a modern perspective we find in Perkins' work a proper warning against reducing the meaning of a text to the biography of an author, especially if the text is Scripture. After all, our modern consciousness of history makes us aware that virtually none of the "original" writers of earliest traditions which later became scriptural intended to write Scripture. Therefore, "Scripture" as a special type of religious literature is usually a secondary adaptation of the "original" authors' intentions, in service to a later canonical context and semantic capacity which, then, alters the angle by which their intentions are relevant to the form and function of Scripture.

In Perkins' appeals to the "argument" and "scope" of the biblical text itself, he relies more on what we in the modern period might call the contours of the canonical context than on speculation about the reconstructed world of the ancient writers or the depicted figures. However, Perkins often did presume a continuity between textual depiction and the possibility of accurate contemporary knowledge about ancient historical events that would prove untenable in the modern period. A defense of the "scope" of biblical books, in Perkins' sense, cannot be upheld by such referential appeals to historical authorship but could find support in a different, equally modern, literary-critical assessment of the relation between a specific text or book and the realistic presentation of an authorial *persona* within it.

Certainly within the modern period, an awareness of the complex historical authorship of most biblical books need not negate an appreciation for the theological significance of the effect achieved by the realistic depiction of a single "author," for example, Moses, Isaiah, or Paul, in association with a certain book (for example, Isaiah) or a collection of books (for example, the pentateuchal Torah or the Pauline Epistles). Such an ordering of ancient tradition provokes us as readers to find a coherent reading of the diverse prebiblical traditions within the arena established by the context of Scripture itself. The presentation of biblical "authors" in such books serves a significant function within Scripture by anchoring the words of the text in a specific "historical" and realistic human voice. This aspect is enhanced further by a recognition of how the canonical context has orchestrated the diverse underlying historical intentions so that the reader is compelled to find within a given book a coherency of argument that conjoins here and there with the distinctive personality and idiomatic expressions of the biblical author.[35] While Perkins' approach to the relation between biblical authors and the scope of biblical books will not offer a satisfying response to the range of historical issues raised in the modern period, his approach does recall a basic orientation toward the biblical text, when it is read as a Scripture, that cannot be entirely forfeited without loss of the Protestant tradition itself.

The Idioms of a Literal
Sense Interpretation

Heiko Obermann has highlighted some of the problems confronting any literal-sense interpretation of the Old Testament during the period prior to and including the Reformation.[36] A major debate arose around a possible distinction within the literal sense between its historical and its prophetic import. Nicholas of Lyra went so far as to speak of a double literal sense, one primarily concerned with matters of history, therefore, a semantic level of the literal sense shared with Jews, and one that included prophecy with a distinctly Christian view of the fulfillment of the Old Testament in the New. In general, the Reformers rejected this proposal, but the debate over the historical and prophetic nature of biblical texts became an increasing point of controversy in the modern period.

Here I note only that Perkins' understanding of Scripture suggests the importance of other matters than idioms alongside of prophecy and history in the explication of the literal sense of Scripture. When Perkins claims that Abraham had "saving faith" and "saw me [Christ]," he does not defend these statements by appeal to prophecy or any form of psychic foreknowledge or prediction. He argues that "in faith" aspects of reality that are yet unknown are made present. In this case, Abraham and other Old Testament figures exhibit faith in Christ "because their faith gave them right and title in Christ, and in their hearts they felt the efficacie of his death and resurrection." In support of this view, Perkins makes appeal to "reason" by stating that when we observe a star it may be present to our eyes even though it is actually very far away (3).

My point is that in much, if not most, of Perkins' exposition of Hebrews 11 we find no primary reliance on either strictly historical interpretation or a prophetical reading of the Old Testament text as promise that finds fulfillment in the New. Instead, he offers what we might call a sapiential or wisdomic interpretation of the depictive realism of the text, which is amplified, given depth, or illuminated by appeal to the revealed reality of the law, prophecy, and gospel. By "wisdom" I refer to the biblical idiom epitomized in the Solomonic books, distinct from Torah and prophecy in the context of the Old Testament. In wisdom we find stress on "reason" which comprehends God's revelation of reality in terms of the typical, recurring patterns of human experience, including the activities of the wise and foolish, the righteous and the wicked. Exemplary interpretation of biblical figures immediately belongs to this biblical genre.[37] Concurrently, Perkins explores the relation, predisposed by the intertext of Scripture itself, between this wisdom idiom and other idioms of revelation in Scripture whether of the law, prophecy, or the Gospel. In other words, much modern interpretation of the Bible has been preoccupied with such important matters as "(salvation) history" or, more recently, "narrative." However, an examination of Perkins ought to remind us that in the premodern period non-narrative idioms, especially wisdom, were often just as significant in the history of interpretation and warrant renewed consideration in our own models of modern exegesis.

NOTES

1. See Patrick Collinson, *The Religion of the Protestants: The Church in English Society 1559–1625* (Oxford: Oxford University Press, 1982), 92–93. For a survey of various pejorative assessments of the seventeenth century, see Frederick W. Farrar, *History of Interpretation* (Grand Rapids: Baker Book House, 1961; reprint of the 1886 edition published by E. P. Dutton), 357–78, esp. 360 n 1. Regarding this period Farrar avers, "In this day men repeat the vague and extravagant assertions of seventeenth-century divines, which furnish no assistance and solve no difficulty, and which can only be maintained in detail by an accumulation of special pleas" (p. 27). Though he does not comment specifically on Perkins, he does grant that "English Christians were happily insulated from the incessant bickerings of the Lutheran and Reformed churches" (p. 376). For a more positive recent hermeneutical assessment, see Henning Graf Reventlow, *The Authority of the Bible and the Rise of the Modern World,* trans. John Bowden (Philadelphia: Fortress Press, 1985), p. 91–184.

2. Cf. Ernst Troeltsch, *Protestantism and Progress: The Significance of the Rise of the Modern World.* Fortress Texts in Modern Theology (reprint Philadelphia: Fortress Press, 1986); and David Tracy, *Blessed Rage for Order* (New York: Seabury, 1975), 10ff.

3. E.g., Helmut Feld, *Martin Luthers und Wendelin Steinbachs Vorlesungen über den Hebräerbrief: Eine Studie zur Geschichte der Neutestamentlichen Exegese und Theologie* (Wiesbaden: Franz Steiner, 1971); Kenneth Hagen, *A Theology of Testament in the Young Luther: The Lecture on Hebrews* (Leiden: E. J. Brill, 1974); and idem, *Hebrews Commenting from Erasmus to Béze 1516–1598* (Tübingen: J.C.B. Mohr, 1981).

4. See *The Cambridge History of the Bible: From the Beginnings to Jerome,* vol. 1, ed. P. R. Ackroyd and C. F. Evans (Cambridge: Cambridge University Press, 1970). In his historical descriptions, R.P.C. Hanson judges that the pervasive assumption that the psalms and other Old Testament books were to be read as "prophecies" reflects, "to be honest, the limitations which the Father imposed on themselves." He then observes "the distorting effect which these ideas had upon their understanding of the Bible" (p. 422). In his treatment of Origen, Hanson volunteers what an interpreter can properly do—"present the intention of the text as it is seen through the medium of a particular mind and as it can be expressed in terms of a particular living culture"—and concludes, accordingly, that Origen is a "wayward genius" who "as an interpreter . . . fails" (pp. 488–89). Insofar as these evaluations presume one particular modern standard for "the literal sense" of Scripture (the historical author's

original intent; see p. 420) and one alien to premodern interpretation generally, they constitute *as historical descriptions* an anachronistic assessment well beyond the bounds of a strictly historical investigation.

5. David Hackett Fischer, *Historians' Fallacies: Toward a Logic of Historical Thought* (New York: Harper & Row, 1970), 58–61, 68–70, 78–82.

6. E.g., E. Earle Ellis, *Paul's Use of the Old Testament* (Grand Rapids: Baker Book House, 1957), is so confident that the literal sense is a "grammatical-historical" recovery of the historical author's intent that he must rationalize the apostle Paul's apparently nonliteral use of the Old Testament on the basis that for the apostle "the grammatical and historical meaning are assumed" (p. 147).

7. Farrar, *History of Interpretation*, 347.

8. Ibid., 4; see also his rules 2 and 3.

9. Ibid., 322 n. 1.

10. Ibid., 337.

11. My translation from the 1719 print of the *Clavis* of Matthias Flacius Illyricus in *De Ratione Cognoscendi Sacras Literas: Über den Erkenntnisgrund der Heiligen Schrift*, ed. Lutz Geldsetzer (Dusseldorf: Stern-Verlag Janssen & Co., 1968), 91. On scope, see my essay, "Between Reformation and Modern Commentary: The Perception of the Scope of Biblical Books," in *William Perkins' Commentary on Galations*, Pilgrim Classic Commentaries, ed. Gerald T. Sheppard (New York: Pilgrim Press, 1989), xlviii–lxxvii.

12. On the "analogy of faith," see William Whitaker, *Disputation on Holy Scripture* (reprint; New York: Johnson 1968; orig in Latin, 1588), 472—73. So, too, Martin Chemnitz, *Examination of the Council of Trent*, pt. 1, trans. Fred Kramer (St. Louis: Concordia Pub. House, 1971; orig. 1565–1573), defends the freedom of interpretation to warrant a departure from a consensus of church tradition if it is consonant with "the words of Scripture, the circumstances of the text, and the analogy of faith" (p. 213). Regarding the related role of the rule of faith, see Rowan Greer and James Kugel, *Early Biblical Interpretation*, ed. Wayne Meeks (Philadelphia: Westminster Press, 1986), 171ff.

13. Robert Bruce Robinson, *Roman Catholic Exegesis Since Divino Afflante Spiritu: Hermeneutical Implications*, SBL Dissertation Series #111 (Atlanta: Scholars Press, 1988), 23–24.

14. For a more detailed argument, see my chapter, "How Do Neo-Orthodox and Post Neo-Orthodox Theologians Approach 'Doing Theology' Today," in *Doing Theology in Today's World*, ed. John Woodbridge (Grand Rapids: Zondervan Pub. House, forthcoming).

15. See Northrop Frye, *The Great Code: The Bible and Literature* (New York: Harcourt Brace Jovanovich, 1982), xii–xiii; and Brevard S. Childs, *Introduction to the Old Testament as Scripture* (Philadelphia: Fortress Press, 1979), 69–83.

16. Farrar, *History of Interpretation*, 369.

17. Ibid., 8, 4.

18. Ibid., 18.

19. Ibid., 28.

20. Ibid., 133, 131, 134–37.

21. Ibid., 7.

22. Ibid., 9.

23. Ibid., 31.

24. Ibid., 11; cf. 9–10, 429.

25. Ibid., 10.

26. Ibid., 15.

27. Ibid., 79.

28. Fischer, *Historians' Fallacies*, 79.

29. *The Structuralist Controversy: The Languages of Criticism and the Human Sciences,* ed. Richard Macksey and Eugenio Donato (Baltimore: Johns Hopkins University Press, 1972), 271. Cf. Frank Lentriccha, *After the New Criticism* (Chicago: University of Chicago Press, 1980), 174–77.

30. See Perkins' reference to "the Councell of Trent," 38.

31. All page citations from the Hebrews 11 reprint will appear in parentheses within the text as here.

32. Michael Fishbane, *Biblical Interpretation in Ancient Israel* (Oxford: Clarendon Press, 1985), 539.

33. Hans W. Frei, *The Eclipse of Biblical Narrative: A Study in Eighteenth- and Nineteenth-Century Hermeneutics* (New Haven: Yale University Press, 1974).

34. Whitaker, *Disputation on Holy Scripture,* 405–10.

35. Cf. David G. Meade, *Pseudonymity and Canon: An Investigation into the Relationship of Authorship and Authority in Jewish and Earliest Christian Tradition* (Grand Rapids: Wm. B. Eerdmans, 1986).

36. Heiko Obermann, "Biblical Exegesis: The Literal and the Spiritual Sense of Scripture," in his *Forerunners of the Reformation: The Shape of Late Medieval Thought Illustrated with Key Documents* (Philadelphia: Fortress Press, 1981), 281–96.

37. On the wisdom character of such lists of examples or exemplary interpretation, see Otto Michel, *Der Brief an die Hebräer* (Göttingen: Vandenhoeck & Ruprecht, 1966), 370–71; and Thomas R. Lee, *Studies in the Form of Sirach 44–50,* SBL Dissertation Series 75 (Atlanta: Scholars Press, 1986), 29–48. For details about a contemporary and highly significant Dutch debate questioning from a salvation historical perspective the validity of exemplary interpretation, see Sidney Greidanus, *Sola Scriptura: Problems and Principles in Preaching Historical Texts* (Toronto: Wedge Publishing Foundation, 1970).

William Perkins and the Protestant Exegetical Tradition: Interpretation, Style, and Method

RICHARD A. MULLER

William Perkins, remembered today primarily as the author of *A Golden Chaine*, a highly schematized treatise on the order of the causes of salvation and damnation, and *A Case of Conscience*, one of the foundational treatises for the Puritan program of self-examination, was respected in his own time not only as a dogmatic theologian but also as a preacher and an expositor of Scripture.[1] Among his works,[2] we find extended expositions of the Lord's Prayer,[3] Galatians,[4] the Sermon on the Mount,[5] the eleventh and twelfth chapters of Hebrews,[6] the first three chapters of Revelation,[7] a commentary on the temptation of Christ,[8] a meditation on Zephaniah 2:1–2,[9] Jude,[10] *A Digest or Harmonie of the Bookes of the Old and New Testament*,[11] and the highly influential *The Art of Prophecying*, also known by its subtitle, *A Treatise Concerning the Sacred and Onely True Manner and Methode of Preaching*.[12] The extent of these writings makes clear that Perkins devoted by far the greatest portion of his literary exertions to the exposition of Scripture.

Thomas Fuller, writing in the middle of the next century, commented of Perkins' preaching that "the Scholar could hear no learneder, the Townsmen plainer Sermons." Perkins combined, in other words, great skill in theological argumentation with unsurpassed clarity and piety. "What was said of Socrates," Fuller continued, "that he first humbled the towring speculations of Philosophers into practice and morality; so our Perkins brought the schools into the Pulpit, and unshelling their controversies out of their hard school-termes, made thereof plain and wholesome meat for his people."[13] Of the sermons collected and published as Perkins' *A Commentarie on . . . Galatians*, their editor, Ralph Cudworth, the elder, commented (perhaps with some hyperbole) that the exposition surpassed all previous commentaries.[14] These characteristics of Perkins' preaching, together with his ability to codify and digest a vast array of medieval and Reformation teaching, account for the influence of Perkins for years to come: his works

Richard A. Muller is professor of historical theology, Fuller Theological Seminary.

were widely distributed, with printings at Cambridge, Geneva (in Latin), and Amsterdam (in Dutch).

Perkins came to the forefront of the theological world at a time when English theologians were hardly viewed as eminent. Before his time, no major English system had appeared since the days of Scotus, Ockham, and Bradwardine. In the sixteenth century the most published author in England was John Calvin, and the second after him, Theodore Beza. Major systems published in England also included those of Musculus, Vermigli, Ursinus, and Hemmingius. These were supplemented by a spate of treatises from the pens of continental authors such as Zanchi and Olevian. Perkins stands, on the merit of his *A Golden Chaine*, *An Exposition of the Symbole or Creed*, and *A Treatise on the Manner and Order of Predestination*, as the first theologian either British or continental to be more widely published in England than Calvin or Beza[15] and as the first native English Protestant theologian to have a major impact not only in the British Isles but also on the continent.[16]

The theology of these works has been aptly described as "high Calvinist" and "scholastic." But Perkins, because of the practical, evangelical thrust underlying his thought, also deserves the title "the father of pietism" given him by Heinrich Heppe.[17] On the one hand, Perkins' theology evidences an abiding sense of the divine sovereignty in full, double predestination, in the saving work of grace in the elect, in the satisfaction made by Christ, and in the empowering of the elect by the Spirit; but, on the other hand, he never allows the divine sovereignty, as primary cause, to overwhelm the secondary causality.[18] He evidences a strong theological interest in the role of the individual believer in the work of salvation as hearer of the word, follower of Christ, and inward warrior of the conscience. For all his emphasis on election and on the power of God in Christ, his theology, like that of the Puritan and Presbyterian writers of seventeenth century England, never diminishes the importance of the individual life of piety.[19] Like the Puritans, he certainly hoped to purify the church of abuses, but he never opposed episcopacy. His chief interests were in the reform of souls and the teaching of sound doctrine, emphases which are apparent throughout his writings, though perhaps most prominent in the commentaries.

THE PROTESTANT EXEGETICAL TRADITION: STYLES AND METHODS[20]

Perkins' commentaries or expositions of Scripture belong to a tradition of interpretation reaching back into the Middle Ages[21] but influenced strongly, in its late sixteenth- and early seventeenth-century expression, by both the humanism of the Renaissance and the exegesis and theology of the Reformers, both English and continental European. From the Middle Ages, Protestant exegesis received and initially followed (as is evident from Luther's work) the medieval pattern of presenting the text, providing it with a running commentary or "gloss," and then, in places where the text made special demands on the reader or offered one of the *loci classici theologiae* or *sedes doctrinae*, developing an extended discussion of issues, the *scholion*.[22] Reference to the medieval sources, such as the great *Glossa ordinaria*, attributed to Walafrid Strabo, or to later medieval commentators such as Nicholas of Lyra, Paul of Burgos, or Dionysius the Carthusian, typically cited in later medieval or Roman Catholic expositions of the text, dropped rapidly from the Protestant commentaries as polemic between Protestant and Roman Catholic became heated. A close examination, however, of the exegetical works of the great Reformers—Luther, Bucer, Calvin, Oecolampadius and others—manifests a continuing use of the theological results of this exegetical tradition, as well as of the frequently cited commentaries of eminent patristic writers such as Augustine, Chrysostom, and Jerome.[23]

From the Middle Ages—at least from one line of development of medieval exegesis—the Protestant commentators also received the assumption that the literal sense was preeminent as the source of meaning of the text. Aquinas had argued pointedly that a "multiplicity of senses" arose not because any word signified more than one thing but because the thing signified by a given word might itself be a type of other things. "Thus," he concluded, "in holy scripture no confusion results, for all the senses are founded on one, the literal."[24] Because of the Thomistic insistence that the literal sense was the primary sense of the text and the other senses (allegorical, tropological, and anagogical) derivative and resting on the typological character of the things signified by the words of the text, late medieval exegetes who accepted Aquinas' approach were pressed to find ways of identifying doctrinal points, once grounded on allegory, as arising from the literal meaning of the text. This pressure can be recognized as one of the sources of various late medieval hermeneutical models such as the double literal sense (*duplex sensus literalis*) of Lyra, the ecclesially determined *sensus literalis* of Jean Gerson, and the highly christologized unitary spiritual/literal model of Lefevre d'Étaples.[25]

A certain continuity of development in hermeneutics explains, at least in part, why the Protestant exegetes of the first half of the sixteenth century—the founders of the Protestant exegetical tradition—were able to maintain a doctrinal orthodoxy in their expositions of most of the key *loci* in Scripture at the same time that they set aside the *quadriga*, or fourfold exegesis, and various late medieval models. Medieval exegetes had already begun to find the dogmas of the church in the "literal sense" of the text, as defined by the significance, the tendency, or the "scope" (*scopus*) and "foundation" (*fundamentum*) of the whole of Scripture. The theological significance of texts, as mediated by a long catholic tradition of exegesis, remained much the same, particularly with reference to the great dogmas of the church such as the Trinity and the person of Christ.

For all this fundamental continuity, Protestant commentaries did develop into two intitial patterns of exposition, both partially different from but partially reminiscent of the medieval model. On the one hand, Melanchthon followed a pattern of brief, running comment on the text, reminiscent of the gloss, while, on the other, Bucer developed a pattern of textual analysis followed by massive theological exposition, reminiscent of the *scholion*. The Melanchthonian model incorporated not only the Renaissance emphasis on linguistic skills already found in Luther's work, but also the Renaissance emphasis on the right *methodus*, or "way through" the text, locating meaning always in the *literalis sensus*.[26] It was Melanchthon's intention not to produce a set of annotations on the text but to identify the topics or *loci* in the text and to move through them in an orderly fashion: he accordingly broke the verses or pericopes of the text into logical components and explained the meaning of each of these parts.[27]

An approach similar in intention but very different in its formal result is found in the commentaries of Martin Bucer. As Parker comments, "Bucer poured all his theology into the commentaries, so that they represent, in all their massive, uncouth, ill-written and badly arranged form, the vigour and profundity of his restless and creative mind."[28] Like Melanchthon, Bucer held that the development of dogmatic *loci* out of the text was an essential part of the work of the commentator—and, in view of the Protestant insistence on the biblical norm, the one sure method for formulating Protestant doctrine. But Bucer also assumed that the text had to be exposited closely, verse by verse—leading to a vast concatenation and intermingling of exegetical remarks and dogmatic conclusions.[29]

In addition, both Melanchthon and Bucer modified the *scholion* to conform to the new place-logic of Rudolf Agricola. Agricola had, in the mid-fifteenth century, brought about a major revolution in the teaching of logic. He argued that Aristotle's categories of predication were too cumbersome and not necessarily grounded in the subject under examination. The first step in logical analysis, therefore, ought to be the elicitation of the topics (*topoi*) or places (*loci*) belonging to the subject, followed by the establishment of a suitable order of discussion. In the theological and exegetical works of the early sixteenth century—notably Melanchthon's *Loci communes* on the Protestant side and Cano's *De locis theologicis* on the Catholic—this method was used both as a way of drawing topics out of Scripture for the sake of extended exposition similar to the medieval *scholia* and for the sake of organizing works of doctrinal theology.

Calvin, who came to the task of exegesis from his training as a humanistic scholar in the classical languages—and not from either the medieval exegetical model or from an interest in the Agricolan place-logic—brought about a further development in the Protestant exposition of Scripture. He objected both to Bucerian prolixity and to the Melanchthonian topical theological comment, preferring a model much more akin to Bullinger's verse by verse exegesis, preceded by a brief statement of the occasion or historical background of the work and, at the beginning of each chapter, a statement of the argument or scope.[30] Perhaps precisely because Melanchthon's topical discussions functioned better when gathered into a theological essay, the *Loci communes*, and Bucer's vast dogmatic essays only prolonged the difficulty of working through his highly influential theological commentaries, Calvin chose to divide the labor. He restricted his exegetical expositions to the commentaries and his *disputationes* on doctrinal points to the *Institutes*, rendering unnecessary any dogmatic expansion of the commentaries.[31] Because of this careful, perhaps we should say, esthetic, distribution of the theological task, Calvin stands as one of the founders of the Protestant textual commentary.

There is also a very close resemblance between the method of textual analysis found in Calvin's commentaries and the expository method followed both in his lectures and in his sermons. Indeed, many of the commentaries began as lectures in the Genevan Academy and were later edited by Calvin for publication—while many of his sermons have the appearance of lectures, or even of commentaries on the text.

In all of these works, Calvin echoed his predecessors in the Protestant exegetical tradition by emphasizing a direct address to the grammar and meaning of the text as the primary work of the exegete: he is frequently quoted as using terms or phrases such as *simplex, literalis,* and *genuina sensus*—the simple or unitary, literal, and genuine sense of the text—as opposed to various forms of allegorical interpretation.[32] Parker judiciously notes that the term *simplex sensus* ought to be understood as an alternative to the late medieval *duplex sensus*.[33] Nonetheless, it remains the case that Calvin understood the text as a living word capable of addressing the contemporary people of God on matters of faith and morals—indeed, on matters of contemporary doctrinal import. His understanding of terms such as "literal sense" included patterns of typology, of doctrinal interpretation drawing on the scope or argument of a chapter or book or of Scripture as a whole, and of multiple referents, not altogether unlike the spirit of the medieval methods whose excesses he strove to avoid.[34] Calvin did not solve, but rather helped to carry forward in a Protestant form, the question of the relationship of the meaning of the text of a holy book to a contemporary significance in the community of faith.

It is not the case that Calvin's method became the sole standard for Protestant commentary. While his close textual/theological approach was adopted by Beza in his famed *Annotationes in Novum Testamentum,* the Bucerian model of combining exposition with extended dogmatic disquisition, saved from some of its verbosity, was followed by such major Reformed exegetes as Wolfgang Musculus, Peter Martyr Vermigli, and Jerome Zanchi. In Perkins' own time, Johannes Piscator followed a threefold method of verse-by-verse textual "analysis," followed by short "*scholia*" and lengthier "*observationes*." In Piscator's exegesis of Hebrews, these latter comments frequently took the form of typological interpretations designed to press a soteriological or christological point.[35] All of these writers exerted a considerable influence on English theology and exegesis. Their commentaries, moreover, manifest a common ground with Reformed preaching. As J. W. Blench has shown, a particular method of exposition, based on the topical or place-logic approach to commentary and on the scholastic *quaestio,* passed over into English preaching from works like Musculus' commentary on Romans.[36] Musculus' commentary not only developed doctrinal disquisitions in the context of exposition, it also divided the disquisitions into "observations," "questions," and "answers" identified by marginal headings.[37] Blench notes the presence of the form in the sermons of John Hooper, whose sermons proceed *secundum ordinem textus*—following the text itself as the basic rule of organization—and, after the text of the passage has been identified, drawing doctrinal lessons from the text and offering discussion of the "use" or application of the doctrine.[38]

This method was carried forward on the Reformed or Calvinistic side of the English Reformation by Thomas Cartwright. Like Hooper's sermons, Cartwright's stand as technical theological disquisitions drawn out of the theological *loci* or *topoi* identified in the text. In the case of Cartwright's *A*

Dilucidation, or Exposition of the Epistle of St. Paul to the Colossians,[39] the sermons function both as homilies and as detailed exegetical works. Throughout, Cartwright's assumption as exegete is that the meaning of the text is lodged in the literal, grammatical construction of the text—but also that the individual verse or phrase in Scripture stood in a larger, scriptural context of meaning, capable of broad, biblical elucidation and capable also of a direct address, often by means of types and figures, to the present situation of the church.[40]

PERKINS' *A CLOUD OF FAITHFUL WITNESSES* AND THE REFORMED THEOLOGICAL TRADITION

From the full title of Perkins' commentary, *A Cloud of Faithful Witnesses, leading to the Heavenly Canaan: Or, A Commentarie upon the 11. Chapter to the Hebrews, preached in Cambridge by that godly and judicious divine M. William Perkins*[41] we understand the close relationship of sermon and commentary. Perkins' model for the sermon, as presented in his *Treatise Concerning the . . . Method of Preaching,* was a highly technical theological model, based more on the tradition of the Reformed commentary as mediated by Musculus and Zanchi than on earlier homiletical models.[42] This is not to imply, in disagreement with Thomas Fuller's glowing commentary on the plainness and popular wholesomeness of Perkins' homiletical style, that the text partakes of a technical and scholastic dryness, but rather that lively elements of homiletical style are wedded to the commentary and render the somewhat strict theological format of each section suitable both for the spoken and the written form. Perkins' success in this approach assured the continued use of the model by generations of Puritan preacher/commentators.[43]

Perkins' *A Cloud* is a highly textual commentary in the sense that it remains, throughout, close to the words of the *Epistle,* studying each phrase minutely, but, unlike purely textual commentaries in the tradition of Calvin, it has no direct recourse to the Greek (although it does offer occasional evidence of Perkins' work as a translator) and its purpose is not primarily the elucidation of the grammatical meaning but, via a union of sermon and commentary, to move toward large scale theological exposition of the chapter. The text of Hebrews runs through the commentary—to paraphrase one modern scholar's characterization of Gregory the Great's *Moralia*—like a fine silver thread, around which Perkins created a theological tapestry of highly intricate texture and weave. The tapestry draws on the theme of the chapter, but to that one crucial thread, it adds strands from the scholastic and orthodox Reformed theology of the day and from the older theological tradition, all joined together in patterns of Ramist logic designed to draw out the theological "parts" of each idea or definition generated by the reading of the *Epistle.*

Granting the closeness of Perkins' examination of the text of the *Epistle* and granting his strongly Protestant assertions throughout his works that Scripture alone must be the authoritative ground for theological formulation, the text chosen by Perkins should be of some importance to our study—and may shed some light on Perkins' theological position. As we have already noted, Perkins evidences little interest in the Greek text of the *Epistle*. And as one might easily conclude from that characteristic of his commentary, the translation is not his own. Perkins had, of course, several translations available to him: he had both the Bishops' Bible of 1566, as revised in 1572 under the superintendence of Giles Lawrence, then professor of Greek at Oxford, particularly in its version of the New Testament; and the Geneva Bible, much improved over the 1560 translation by Laurence Tomson's 1576 retranslation and revision of the New Testament on the basis of Beza's *Annotationes*.[44] As a comparison of Perkins' text with the 1560 Geneva, the Bishops' Bible, and the Tomson revision of the Geneva Bible makes clear, although Perkins' text is not identical with any version, it is drawn virtually entirely, with a few significant alterations, some in the direction of Beza's original, from the Tomson revision. Where, on occasion, phrases in the main citations follow the Bishops' Bible, Perkins' use of the text in the body of the commentary typically returns to Tomson. (Given the posthumous editing and publication of the work, variants in the main citations at the head of each sermon may have arisen from editorial work, whereas it is unlikely that editors are responsible for variants that are integral to Perkins' expositions.)

If the text of the epistle, noting Perkins' usage in the body of the commentary, is compared with Tomson, twenty-three of the forty-one verses cited are verbally identical, disregarding minor alterations in spelling. Ten of these verses evidence variants in punctuation, virtually all of which relate to the logical patterns of Perkins' argument, and none of which appear to reflect differences found in other translations. (Perkins has a tendency to add commas and change commas into semi-colons or, more frequently, colons, in order to indicate the sections of the verse being exposited and to emphasize the almost syllogistic logic of the chapter.) Of the nearly one thousand words of the text, some eighteen are altered, with half of the changes (and, arguably, the only substantive ones) resting on Perkins' exegesis and not on other versions. Only one of the alterations (v. 29) clearly favors the Geneva (1560) or the Bishops' Bible, probably for stylistic considerations. Five words are added or dropped for syntactical reasons; and there are four transpositions of words, none of which bear any relation to either the Geneva 1560 or to the Bishops' Bible. There is also one place in the text (v. 8) where one phrase in the main citation appears to look to the Bishops' Bible, but the citation in the body of the commentary, on which Perkins' argument rests, reverts to Tomson. Perkins, in short, followed the Tomson's English version of Beza's text.

What is remarkable—granting the intellectual proximity of Perkins and Beza on many points, including the strong resemblance between Perkins' *A Golden Chaine* and Beza's somewhat notorious *Tabula praedestinationis*[45]—is that Perkins follows the text of the Beza/Tomson New Testament, but pays scant attention to its marginal notes. Perkins tends not to follow out the suggested cross-references from the Tomson/Beza margins, and he ignores entirely one of the major annotations offered by them. In the margin at v. 6 ("he is a rewarder of them that seeke him") the Tomson New Testament comments, "This reward is not referred to our merits, but to the free promise, as Paul teacheth in Abraham the father of all the faithfull, Rom. 4.4."[46] The text of Hebrews itself has not yet reached the example of Abraham: it has noted Enoch (v.5) and is about to pass on to consider Noah (v.7). Perkins holds to the flow of the text, ignoring both the marginal comment and the reference to Romans.

There may be a reflection of Tomson's marginal note in Perkins' lengthy examination of the faith of Abraham in v. 8–10 ("Abraham is the father of the faithfull, Rom. 4.11"), but Perkins' exegetical and theological interest in this verse lies primarily in the great theme of active, practical faith and not in the marginal comment's concern for a forensic justification apart from merit.[47] For Perkins, the doctrine of justification by grace alone through faith, apart from the works of the law stands as a presupposition to be noted at various points in his exposition rather than as the primary point of this particular verse. In vv. 8–10, the issue for Perkins is the obedience that arises from faith and the character of the life that is framed by faith. Perkins' contemporary, David Paraeus, had similarly indicated that "faith is here generally described, not only as it justifies, but also as it acts toward God and lays hold on his past, present, and future promises, works, and blessings revealed in his word."[48] (Perkins will, of course, return to the theme of justification by faith for substantive discussion, as the text warrants.)[49] Perkins evidences, in other words, a textual reliance on Tomson and Beza, while at the same time showing an exegetical and theological independence in his interpretation.

Perkins' exposition offers a separate chapter or sermon for virtually every verse of the chapter—thus accounting for the size of the commentary (206 pages in folio!)—and uses his own recommended pattern for sermons throughout its length. (In the discussion that follows, therefore, I will trace out only the very representative pattern of argumentation in the sermon on chapter 1, v. 1, but will draw ideas and issues from the entire commentary in order to show in detail the relationship of Perkins' commentary to earlier works in the Reformed tradition.)

Perkins begins his commentary with a citation of v. 1, "Now Faith is the ground of things which are hoped for and the evidence of things [which are] not seen." He then immediately moves to identify and define faith— inasmuch as this is the great theme of the chapter—and to set the chapter into its literary and textual context in the epistle by noting its relation to the preceding chapters.[50] This first sermon thus serves a dual purpose of intro- ducing the entire commentary and offering an exposition of the first verse, in which Perkins understands the great theme of the chapter to be summa- rized.

Perkins' initial statements on faith indicate both his tendency to use Ramist bifurcation and the close relationship that he sees between the work of the commentator, the preacher and the dogmatic theologian. (This use of Ramist bifurcation, granting the roots of the method in the logic of Rudolf Agricola, should be regarded as quite of a piece with the tendency of Perkins' exegetical and homiletical method to draw on Agricolan place-logic and, like Musculus and Zanchi, to develop doctrinal topics or *loci* from the text.) Perkins begins:

Concerning Faith, two points are necessarie to be knowne of euery Christian, the *doctrine*, and the *practise* of it: the whole *doctrine* of faith (beeing grounded and gathered out of the word of God) is comprised in the *Creede*, commonly called the *Apostles Creede*: which beeing alreadie by us expounded it followeth in order (next after the *doctrine*) to lay downe the *practise* of faith: for which purpose we have chosen this II. chap. to the Hebrewes, as beeing a portion of Scripture wherein the saide practise of faith is most excellently and at large set down.[51]

Perkins refers here to his *An Exposition of the symbole or Creede of the Apostles*, which, more than the famous *A Golden Chaine*, should be considered as his theological system,[52] as the first part of his theological task, and the commentary on Hebrews II as the second. The first exposits the faith as doctrine, the second exposits the faith as practice.

This interpretation of the chapter, moreover, is justified by an examination of the text of the epistle: in the tenth chapter, Perkins comments, we read that many Jews "received the faith" and gave their "names to Christ" but subsequently fell away. The chapter is an exhortation to perseverance in faith in response to the temptations leveled against believers to fall away. Chapter II "continues the same exhortation" now through the recounting of examples:

And the whole chapter (as I take it) is nothing else in substance, but one reason to urge the former exhortation to perseverance in faith . . . for this chapter doth in divers waies set down what an excellent gift of God faith is: his whole scope therefore is manifest to be nothing else, but to urge them to persevere and continue in that faith, prooved at large by so excellent a thing."[53]

This approach to the work of exposition, signaled by Perkins' use of the crucial term "scope,"[54] a term that looks back through the exegetical tradition of the sixteenth century to Erasmus,[55] has a kinship with what contemporary exegetes identify as canonical and rhetorical criticism: Perkins' intention is to set the theological stage for the exposition of individual verses and parts of verses. He is adept, in a logical and scholastic sense, at the division and subdivision of a topic and at the detailed analysis of a finely divided text, but he never allows the close analysis of parts to stand in the way of his sense of the meaning of the whole. The initial concentration on "scope," indicating the focus or "target" of the text as a whole,[56] provides Perkins with a point of reference that unifies and gives significance to the various parts of his exposition. Whether *A Cloud* is examined as a commentary or as a set of sermons, the theological unity of Perkins' remarks is drawn directly from his initial exposition of the scope, the focus of argument of the text.

Here Perkins reflects not only the doctrinal *locus*-model of commentary and sermon offered by Musculus and Zanchi but also the textual, grammatical approach of Calvin. For although Calvin did not use the term "scope" as much as other exegetes of the era, he invariably began his commentaries with a statement of the *argumentum* of the book—a chapter by chapter overview of the meaning of the work, akin in intention to Perkins' emphasis on scope.[57] Indeed, Calvin had noted the connection between the chapters, had argued that chapter 11 was an exposition by example of the exhortation to patience in faith offered in chapter 10, and had commented that "whoever made this the beginning of the chapter eleven, improperly disrupted [its] context."[58]

Perkins appears to be satisfied with the division of the chapter, granting that chapter 11 stands as a unity of exhortation, resting on the thetically stated definition of faith in the first verse: the connection with chapter 10 is important as a way of establishing the context of exegesis, but to Perkins' Ramist mind, there could be no problem in accepting the transition between the chapters as a formal division of the subject, with the second part beginning correctly with the definition. And it suits the homiletical purpose of his commentary to isolate the eleventh chapter—except for the inclusion of a homily on 12:1 to close out the commentary.

The method employed by Perkins in the exegesis of individual texts divides the verses up into component parts, argues the meaning of the parts, and then draws out the argument of the text in terms of the grammatical and logical relation of the parts—a model not unlike that noted in Melanchthon's early Reformation adaptation of the *locus* model. This topical structuring of the text appears to be the basis for most of Perkins' changes in punctuation. Thus, Perkins puts a colon in place of a comma in v. 1 ("... things which are hoped for: and the evidence . . .") in order to identify the co-equal propositions in the text and more easily to permit him to argue that v. 1a (explained by 1b), v. 2 and v. 3 present "three *actions* or *effects* of faith."[59] Similarly, in verse 8, Perkins replaces Tomson's sixth comma with a colon, yielding, "By Faith, Abraham, when he was called, obeied God, to goe out into a place, which he should receive for inheritance: and he went out, not knowing whither he went."[60] The text refers, notes Perkins, to the "first example" of Abraham's faith and "concerning this his faith and obedience . . . laieth downe two points: 1. The *cause* or ground thereof; which was Gods calling: he was *called of God*. 2. The first fruit or *effect* of his faith: he *hearkened and obeied*." The portion of the text before the colon, then, contains two basic points concerning the causality of Abraham's faith: efficient cause and the effect. Perkins continues, with reference to the portion of the text following the colon, "And this his obedience is amplified by divers particulars: 1. The *matter* of it; he *went out* of his countrey. 2. The *ende*, to take possession of a countrey, which he should not enjoy of a long time. 3. The *manner; he went out, not knowing whither he should goe.*"[61]

This method of division of the text is followed throughout the epistle, as a means of both identifying the parts of the chapter and indicating the logical flow of the parts themselves. Thus in his exegesis of the first chapter, Perkins notes that the chapter as a whole falls into two parts: "1. A generall *description* of Faith from the 1 v. to the 4" and "2. An *illustration* or declaration of that description by a large rehersall of manifold *examples* of ancient and worthie men in the Old Testament, from the 4 v. to the ende."[62] The text, therefore, is ideal as a basis for a series of interrelated homiletical expositions. Perkins takes the points in order, subdividing as he moves forward:

The description of Faith consists of *three actions or effects* of faith, set downe in three severall verses.

The first effect in the 1. verse. *Faith* makes things *which are not* (but onely are hoped for) after a sort *to subsist and to be present with the beleever.*

The second is in the 2. v. *Faith makes a beleever approoved of God.*

The third in the 3. v. *Faith makes a man understand and beleeve things incredible to sense and reason.*

Of these in order. . . .[63]

Perkins now cites the first verse again in full and turns to his exposition, discussing, first, "the true meaning of the words," that is, their literal or grammatical sense, and, second, "what instructions they doe naturally yield unto us." For the meaning," he continues, "we must examine the words severally."[64] First, the two initial words, "Now Faith"; faith can have any of three distinct meanings—historical, miraculous, or "justifying or saving faith." Perkins defines the three meanings, reflecting the scholastic Protestantism of his day: "Historicall faith, is not onely a knowledge of the word, but an assent of the heart to the truth of it"—such as all people, good and bad, and even devils have. Miraculous faith is a special inward persuasion wrought for a particular purpose by the Spirit, and, again, not saving. The chapter, Perkins notes, narrowing his focus of argument, discusses saving faith as its "primary scope."[65]

Second, "this faith is the ground or substance." The text, Perkins notes, refers to the substantial existence or subsistence of promises in the heart of the believer by faith, "so that the thing which never had, nor yet hath a beeing in the heart of the beleever; this I take to be the true meaning."[66] Perkins' exegesis of the definition of faith manifests an acquaintance with the interpretive questions of his time. He accepts the translation of Tomson, "faith is the ground of things which are hoped for," but immediately elaborates, "ground or substance," commenting that "the word signifieth both."[67] Perkins perhaps knew that Lefevre D'Étaples had rendered *hypostasis* as *fundamentum,* or "ground," but that the earlier consensus from the days of Jerome and Augustine to the time of Calvin and Beza had been to read *hypostasis* as indicating not the foundation but the reality of what was hoped for—thus *essentia* (Augustine), *substantia* Jerome, Calvin, Piscator), or *illud quo subsistunt* (Beza).[68] Perkins' exposition clearly leans toward Calvin, with a hint of Beza's movement from *substantia* toward *subsistentia,* in its argument that "the meaning is: things hoped for, as yet are not, and so have no beeing or substance: "Now faith . . . gives to these things which yet are not (after a sort) a substance or subsistence in the heart of the beleever. . . ."[69] If Perkins' comments on the first half of the definition tend to set aside the translation in favor of the Latin of Calvin and Beza, his comments on the second half do not: "the evidence of things which are not seene," qualified by a description of faith as offering "infallible arguments," looks to Jerome's translation of *elenchos* as *argumentum,* to Augustine's *convictio,* to Erasmus' *indicium* (evidence or testimony), and to Piscator's rendering of the word as *index* rather than to Calvin's and Beza's *demonstratio.*[70]

It follows, Perkins continues, that the text must proceed to identify "of what things this faith is the ground or substance . . . namely, of *things hoped for,* and things *not seene."* Here Perkins is able to establish how the text, in its literal meaning, without allegory, addresses the contemporary audience, for these things "be of two sorts: either in regard of the Fathers of the old testament alone, or of them and us both." Belonging to the first sort are "the incarnation of Christ" and the "publishing of the Gospel . . . in a glorious manner," things that "we have seene" but which for the Old Testament fathers "had a beeing onely in *faith.*"[71] Of the second sort are "things which we hope for as well as they, which are to come, and not seen in respect of us both," such as justification, sanctification, the "resurrection of the bodie," the glorification of body and soul, and life everlasting. The text, therefore, addresses the church of the present day with the "evidence" of these hoped for things, "yea, compelleth it by the force of reasons unanswerable to beleeve the promises of God certenly."[72]

After his highly theological exposition of the meaning of the text, Perkins turns to the second part of his exposition, "the instructions this first effect thus unfolded doth minister to us."[73] His exposition divides into five points, one of which (the fourth) contains a formal "objection" and an "answer" to the objection. In the fourth point, we learn from the text that "the nature" of this faith as evidence "stands not in doubting but in certainty and assurance." By way of objection, some would say that "doubting is a part, or at least a companion of faith, for we doubt as well as beleeve: and who is so faithful as doubteth not?" This objection is connected in Perkins' mind with "Romish doubting of the essence of faith" and "joining faith and doubting," perhaps a reference to the anti-Protestant Pyrrhonism of Charron.[74] The premise, Perkins answers is false: surely we do doubt, but the command of God is not to doubt or to doubt and believe, but simply to believe. Faith is a virtue, a work of grace and of the Spirit in us; doubt is a vice and a work of the flesh. It cannot be joined to faith.[75]

Finally Perkins comes to the "uses" that derive from his exposition of the "instructions" of the "first effect." There are many uses of this faith, Perkins comments, but "especially two": first, when believers are tempted by the devil and try to rely on their own strength they find "that to resist is a harder matter than [they] dreamed of." The verse teaches us to hold fast to faith and in moments of temptation "to call to mind Gods promises, beleeve them, that is applie them to thy selfe."[76] Second, when we are burdened under the weight of our own sins and seek strength to bear the weight, we can look to faith, which, "resting on the word of God, and beleeving the promises, not formally but truly, will put such substantiall spiritual strength into" us.[77] The structure of Perkins' comment, thus, follows the *locus* model of the English commentary and sermon, looking back to the work of Musculus, Hooper, and Cartwright, and, in the case of Perkins' *A Cloud,* following specifically the version of the *locus* model outlined in Perkins' own *Treatise Concerning the . . . Method of Preaching:* the reading or presenting of the text, an exposition of the text in order "to give the sense and understanding of it beeing read, by the Scripture it selfe," a gathering of "profitable points of doctrine out of the naturall sense" of the text coupled with the answering of objections to those points, and finally an application of the doctrine "to the life and manners of men."[78]

Perkins stands very clearly with Beza, Piscator, and, indeed, with the majority of commentators, against Calvin's reading of v. 3b. Calvin had argued the parallel not between this text and Rom. 4:17 but between it and Rom. 1:20, "the invisible things of him from the creation of the world are clearly seen, being understood by the things that are made, even his eternal power and Godhead." In other words, the visible order manifests the invisible things of God. In order to argue this reading of Heb. 11:3b, Calvin assumes that the preposition *ek* can be understood as fused with the participle *phainomenon,* and the text read "so that the things not seen are made visible" rather than "so that the things that are seen were made from things which do not appear." The text does not refer, in other words, to the act of creating out of nothing but to the truth, based on God's creative work (v. 3a), "that we have in this world a visible image of [invisible] God."[79] Perkins, with Beza and Piscator (and, in this case, virtually the entire exegetical tradition),[80] argues that the text "saith, *The things that we see,* that is, all the world, *were made of things never seene:* that is, of a flat nothing, which is here saide not to be seene, or not to appeare; because how can that appeare or be seene, which is not?" The point of the text, for faith, concerns the relationship between God's creative and providential power: if God created the world out of nothing, "then he can preserve us also by nothing, that is, without meanes, or by weake meanes, or contrarie to meanes." By faith "we ought not onely to see Gods providence, when we see no meanes; but even when the meanes are against us."[81] And, "secondly, if he made all things of nothing, then he is able also, in respect to his promises made in Christ, *To call such things that are not, as though they were,* Rom. 4.17."[82]

We gain brief entry into Perkins' approach to translation in his comments on vv. 17 and 21, where he proposes a reading of the text quite different from the standard translations of his time and defends his approach textually. Perkins refers to the Tomson translation (which he has tended to favor) and defends his variant:

> In the ordinary translation, it is read thus, *When he was tried:* But this is not so fit, beeing rather an exposition of the meaning, then a translation of the word. For the very word signifieth, *to be tempted:* and the meaning is, when he was *tried.* I would therefore rather read it thus: *when he was tempted;* or, *being tempted,* as the word signifies.[83]

The point is similar to Calvin's (*tentatus est*) and Beza's (*ut tentaretur*), who both indicate a *tentatio* (trial or temptation) but proceed to argue that the text in no way contradicts James 1:13: God, in the literal sense of the word, tempts no one. Rather God tests or, in Perkins' probable reflection of Calvin, "prooves," the faithful: Calvin comments, "Verbum tentationis nihil quam probationem significat."[84] Perkins' rendering, "when he was tempted," may be a replacement of Tomson's version with a more cognate rendering of Beza's *cum tentaretur,* itself a reflection of the Vulgate.

Similarly, in translating v. 21, where he has again seen fit to differ from the usual and more feliciitous English readings, Perkins makes a particular point of noting the rectitude of "our Translation in this place . . . according to the words of the Text, and the meaning of the Holy Ghost, *that he worshipped upon the ende of his staffe.*" He debates with a Roman Catholic reading, "and adored the top of his Rod," used by Rome as a biblical proof of the veneration of relics. "They leave out," he comments, "a substantiall word of the text, to wit, this word *upon*."[85] At one level, Perkins' translation parallels Beza's *Annotationes,* both in its rendering of the text as "Et adoravit super extremo baculo suo," and in its protest—in Beza's case, against Sebastian Castellio (and, by implication, against the Vulgate)—that the preposition "upon" (*epi*) cannot be omitted without doing violence to the text.[86]

Of more existential importance to Perkins—registered in his angry declamation against possible Roman Catholic use of the misread text and in his somewhat stentorian declaration that his translation was not only "according to the words of the text" but that it also witnessed the "meaning of the Holy Ghost"—was the translation and the explanation offered in the Rheims Bible, translated by exiled English Roman Catholics and filled with anti-Protestant annotations. The "Rhemists" had rendered the text, "By Faith, Iacob dying, blessed every one of the sonnes of Ioseph: and adored the toppe of his rodde." And they had added, in obvious polemic against Protestant translations from the original languages, that their version, based on the fathers' acceptance of "the authentical Latin," reproduced the "sense of the Holy Ghost."[87]

Neither does the fine English of the Geneva and Tomson Bibles' "leaning on the end of his staffe" suit Perkins' taste.[88] The point of the text, according to Perkins, is that Jacob, in his final illness (cf. v. 29), raised himself up reverentially for worship with the aid of his staff. Perkins' rendering indicates either a careful—and literal—recourse to the Greek text or yet another movement from Tomson's translation back to Beza's version. In either case, it conforms to the letter of the Greek text and follows the pattern of interpretation indicated in Perkins' discussion of the translation of v. 17: he preferred to strive for a precise verbal reflection of the original and to offer a subsequent explanation of the text rather than to follow a pattern of dynamic equivalency, embodying an interpretation in the translation itself.

Perkins' reading also stands in general agreement with Calvin's equally literal rendering, "et adoravit ad summitatem virgae eius,"[89] although Perkins, writing at a time when the precise verbal integrity of the text was a far more intense polemical issue than in Calvin's day, ignores Calvin's simple textual explanation. Calvin had noted that the account of Jacob's old age in Genesis spoke of him worshiping at the head or top of his couch (Gen. 47:31)—and that by a simple misunderstanding of the vowels implied by the text, the translators of the Septuagint had read "staff" for "couch." "This," then, Calvin concludes, "is one of the places from which it is possible to conjecture that at that time the [vowel] points were not in use among the Hebrews."[90] Beza also raises this possibility, assuming, however, that the translators misread the pointing and thereby ignoring the problem thus caused by the use of the Septuagint by the writers of the New Testament, while Piscator follows Calvin in assuming that the translation had been made from an unpointed text.[91] Perkins, like other Protestant exegetes of the late sixteenth and early seventeenth centuries, was profoundly sensitive to the Roman Catholic complaint that human errors had crept into the text of Scripture and that the churchly magisterium was necessary to correct interpretation: the late dating of the vowel points was rapidly becoming a theologically dangerous opinion, particularly when it implied significant discrepancies in the text.[92] Perkins also most certainly had in hand the Rheims annotation, which had taken Calvin to task for his comments on the vowel points and had assumed both the late dating of the points and the correctness of the reading in Hebrews 11:21—a textual having one's cake and eating it too:

> the Apostle doth not tie him selfe to the Hebrue in the place of Genesis . . . but foloweth the Septuaginta, though it differ from the Hebrue, as also the other Apostles and Evangelists and our Saviour him selfe did: neither were they curious (as men now a daies) to examine all by the Hebrew only, because they writing and speaking by the Holy Ghost, knew very well that this translation is the sense of the Holy Ghost also. . . . Even so we that be Catholikes, folow with al the Latin fathers the authentical Latin translation, though it be not alwaies agreable to the Hebrue or Greeke that now is. But Calvin is not onely very saucie, but very ignorant, when he saith that the Septuaginta were deceived, and yet that the Apostle without curiosity was content to folow them: because it is evident, that the Hebrue being without pointes, might be translated the one way as wel as the other.[93]

Perkins, therefore, avoiding the Scylla of inauthentic pointing and the Charybdis of apostolic "curiosity," ignores the textual explanation and proceeds to reconcile logically the account in Genesis with the text of Hebrews:

> for when *Jacob* was about to give up the Ghost, and was ready to die, hee raised up himselfe upon his pillowe towards the beds head, and thereon rested his body. Now because his body was weake and feeble, he staide himselfe also upon his staffe: and thus comparing the places together, wee see there is no repugnancie in them.[94]

Something of the fluidity of the early Reformation use of the text is lost, but the context of argument has changed considerably.

In his interpretation of Moses' flight from Egypt, Perkins again reflects the debates within the tradition of interpretation, recognizing that there are two possible readings of the text: it indicates either Moses' earlier flight alone to Midian or his later flight leading the children of Israel out of Egypt. Perkins agrees (not identifying any sources for his opinion other than the text of Scripture) with the conclusions of Calvin that the text refers to Moses' second flight, against patristic opinion (for example, Chrysostom, Theodoret and Theophylact) and against Piscator.[95] He does not, however, reflect the entirety of Calvin's exposition, where the basis of the patristic opinion is taken into consideration: it is only after this flight, in the following verse that the Passover is mentioned, and, in the verse after that, the flight through the Red Sea.[96] Unlike Calvin, Perkins views as utterly conclusive the fact that in the first flight (Exod. 14:15), Moses "fledde for feare," whereas the epistle clearly states that "he departed, not fearing. . . ."[97] Perkins' comments on this verse, therefore, appear to reflect only a rejection of the shorter comment of Piscator or, perhaps, an entirely theological consideration, resting on the problem of faith as Perkins understands it to be addressed by the text.

Verse 29 also marks a point of departure, albeit a minor one, from the Genevan rendering of the text. Tomson gives, "the Egyptians . . . were swallowed up," reflecting not only Beza's but also Calvin's and Piscator's *Egyptii adsorpti sunt*, a literal rendering of *katepothesan*.[98] Perkins, somewhat in contrast with the principles of interpretation he had advocated previously, reflects not the literal meaning of the text but the obvious intention of the biblical author: Perkins extends the meaning of the verb and offers "were drowned," following the lead, most probably, either of the 1560 Geneva Bible or of the Bishops' Bible. There appears to be not doctrinal or polemical point at stake in the choice of translation. Perkins does add, as a matter of exegetical precision that the "redde sea" was typically called by the authors of the Old Testament "the sea of rushes" or "sedges." He explains the change of name on the assumption that the sea was called "red" either because of the color of its sand or because of the color of some of the rushes "which, by reflection, may make the same colour appear on the water." In any case, he concludes, the "Holy Ghost" here uses one of the common names given to that body of water by the people of the region: the text causes no difficulty.[99] Calvin had passed over the problem in silence though the problem of the name had been registered by Protestants since the time of Luther, who had rightly rendered the Hebrew of Exod. 13:18 as *Schilfmeer* (the sea of reeds or rushes).[100]

Perkins' literalism surfaces here also in the contrast between his and Piscator's theological treatment of the drowning of the Egyptians. Perkins emphasizes the historical situation—the Israelites are fleeing, pursued by "a huge great Armie." It is the mistake of the Egyptians, who have no divine protection, to follow the Israelites across the dry seabed. In his theological application, Perkins remains close to the text and to the event in salvation-history:

> Here, by this fact of *Pharaoh* and his men, we learne, that when God forsakes a man, and leaves him to himselfe, he doth nothing else but run headlong to his owne destruction. *God* (as *Moses* saith) *raised up Pharaoh to shew his power upon him*.[101]

Perkins' application to the present, in other words, holds fast to the theological meaning of the text for Israel and finds the point of contact with the present in a generalization from God's dealings with Pharaoh to God's dealings with human beings in general. Piscator, by way of contrast, sees the primary meaning of the drowning of the Egyptians as a typological reference to eternal reprobation.[102]

In his comments on v. 35, Perkins once again follows Tomson in the reading, "others also were racked" and, therefore, Calvin (*distenti fuerunt*) and Beza, in arguing on the model of Erasmus that the Greek *etumpanis-thesan* had a more technical meaning than simply "imprisoned" (*carcera-tos*).[103] Here again, Perkins faces a problem of post-Tridentine polemics that had not yet been registered by Calvin in 1549 when his commentary had appeared in print:[104] if the text indeed indicates a major persecution such as implied by mention of the rack, occurring after the time of the prophets and before the time of Christ, and involving martyrs who died in hope of the resurrection, it must be a reference to the Maccabees, and therefore to an example of faith drawn from a book regarded by Protestants as noncanonical. Perkins explains the procedure of the "Author of this Epistle" and thereby, by extension, justifies the Protestant definition of the canon by noting that the biblical authors frequently refer to extracanonical books, such as the sources noted in Kings and Chronicles, the reference in Jude to the prophesies of Enoch, and Paul's references to Aratus (Acts 17:28), Menander (1 Cor. 15:33), and Epimenides (Tit. 1:12).[105]

SOME CONCLUSIONS

Perkins' commentary on Hebrews 11 stands in the tradition of the sixteenth-century Protestant and, specifically, Reformed commentators in both its basic style and method and its exegetical detail. He evidences a preference for a close, literal/grammatical location of the meaning of the text coupled with, as was true of the work of his predecessors in the Reformed tradition, a strong sense of the direct theological address of the text to the church in the present. Although Perkins cites none of his sources, his address to various textual, theological and polemical issues evidences a broad use of the work of previous commentators and translators, and in some cases, such as his protest against the Rheims translation of 11:21, the assumption that his audience was also fairly well-apprised of the issues at stake in addressing the text. And it must also be said that, despite the number of technical problems noted by Perkins either directly or by implication, the commentary as a whole, in most of its four hundred columns follows out the pattern and the intention of the sermon. As evidenced in the identification of Moses' flight (v. 27) as the exodus rather than the flight to Midian, Perkins stresses the power and the exercise of faith throughout the work, never losing sight of the "scope" of the chapter, as identified by him in his exposition of v. one.

His model throughout the commentary is the homiletical model developed by him in his *Treatise Concerning the Only True Manner and Method of Preaching*. Since this model was derived from the pattern of scriptural exposition used in the commentaries of Melanchthon, Bucer, Musculus, and Zanchius, its presence here in no way negates the character of *A Cloud of Faithful Witnesses* as a biblical commentary. Rather—as demonstrated by Perkins' integration of textual and critical with theological, polemical, and hortatory elements into the text of each section or homily—its presence indicates the intimate relationship between sermon and commentary characteristic of sixteenth- and seventeenth-century Protestantism. Together with Perkins' emphasis on the scope of focus and argument of the text, this stylistic character of his work underlines the continued sense, typical of the highly biblical theology of the Reformers, that right exegesis opens Scripture to the life of the church. Perkins' exposition of Hebrews 11 moves directly from the text and its presentation of the promises to the address and the practical encouragement offered to the contemporary church by those same promises—in its doctrine, in its polemic and, primarily, in its practice of the faith.

NOTES

1. On Perkins' life and thought, see Sidney Lee, "Perkins, William" s.v. *Dictionary of National Biography*; Donald K. McKim, *Ramism in William Perkins' Theology* (New York: Peter Lang, 1987); Ian Breward, "The Life and Theology of William Perkins, 1558–1602" (Ph.D. diss. University of Manchester, 1963; idem, "The Significance of William Perkins," *Journal of Religious History* 4 (1966–67): 113–28; idem, "William Perkins and the Ideal of Ministry in the Elizabethan Church," *The Reformed Theological Review* 24 (1965): 73–84. See also, R. W. Frank, "William Perkins— Puritan Minister," *McCormick Speaking* 2, no. 9 (June, 1949); Perry Miller, *Errand into the Wilderness* (Cambridge: Harvard University Press, 1956), 52, 54, 57–59; and, on the style and impact of Perkins as preacher, William Haller, *The Rise of Puritanism: Or, the Way to the New Jerusalem as Set Forth in Pulpit and Press from Thomas Cartwright to John Lilburne and John Milton, 1570–1643* (New York: Columbia University Press, 1938; repr. New York: Harper & Row, 1957), 87–93 and passim.

2. William Perkins, *The Workes of that Famous Minister of Christ in the University of Cambridge, Mr. William Perkins*, 3 vols. (Cambridge, 1608–1609). Perkins' works appeared in England in six editions following his death: two one-volume, partial editions appeared in 1603 and 1605, followed by augmented editions in three volumes appearing in 1608–09, 1612–13, 1616–18, and 1626–30/31. There was also a printing of vol. 1 in 1635. The dates of these volumes typically represent points at which extant imprints were gathered and bound together in large folio volumes, not necessarily dates of separate printings. New title pages at the beginning of the volumes indicate the date of binding and publication, while the title pages of individual treatises within the volumes sometimes indicate earlier years for the actual printings. Titles of works tend to vary slightly from printing to printing and the works that were gathered together into vols. 2 and 3 are typically paginated separately. In view of these variations between printings, references to individual commentaries in the following notes give the place of publication and date of first editions.

3. William Perkins, *An Exposition of the Lords Prayer* (London, 1592).

4. William Perkins, *A Commentarie or Exposition upon the Five first Chapters of the Epistle to the Galatians: With the Continuation of the Commentary Upon the Sixth Chapter* (Cambridge, 1604).

5. William Perkins, *An Exposition Upon Christs Sermon on the Mount* (Cambridge, 1608).

6. William Perkins, *A Cloud of Faithful Witnesses . . . a Commentarie Upon the Eleventh Chapter to the Hebrews* with *A Commentarie Upon Part of the Twelfth Chapter to the Hebrews* (Cambridge, 1607).

7. William Perkins, *Lectures Upon the Three First Chapters of Revelation* (London, 1604); *A Godly and Learned Exposition or Commentarie Upon the Three First Chapters of the Revelation*, 2d ed., rev. (Cambridge, 1606).

8. William Perkins, *The Combat Betweene Christ and the Devil Displayed, or a Commentarie Upon the Temptations of Christ* (London, 1606).

9. William Perkins, *A Faithfull and Plaine Exposition Upon the Two First Verses of the Second Chapter of Zephaniah . . . Containing a Powerfull Exhortation to Repentance* (London, 1606).

10. William Perkins, *A Godly and Learned Exposition Upon the Whole Epistle of Jude* (London, 1606).

11. William Perkins, *A Digest or Harmonie of the Bookes of the Old and New Testament* (Cambridge, 1613).

12. William Perkins, *The Art of Prophecying* (London, 1607).

13. Thomas Fuller, *Abel Redivivus: or the Dead yet Speaking. The Lives and Deaths of the Moderne Divines* (London, 1651), 434; and idem, *The Holy State and the Profane State* (London, 1642), 89–90.

14. Cf. Perkins, *Galatians*, in *Workes*, 2:157.

15. Cf. Charles D. Cremeans, *The Reception of Calvinistic Thought in England* (Urbana: University of Illinois Press, 1949), 65.

16. Cf. Heinrich Heppe, *Geschichte des Pietismus und der Mystik in der reformierten Kirche namentlich in der Niederlande* (Leiden, 1879), 24–26; August Lang, *Puritanismus und Pietismus* (Neukirchen, 1941), 109–19; F. Ernest Stoeffler, *The Rise of Evangelical Pietism* (Leiden: E. J. Brill, 1965), 55.

17. Heppe, *Geschichte des Pietismus*, 24.

18. Cf. Richard A. Muller, *Christ and the Decree: Christology and Predestination in Reformed Theology from Calvin to Perkins* (Durham, N.C.: Labyrinth Press, 1986; reprint, with corrections and bibliography, Grand Rapids: Baker Book House, 1988), 160–73.

19. Cf. Stoeffler, *Rise of Evangelical Pietism*, 55.

20. This essay has been restricted, for the most part, to consideration of exegetes in the Reformed tradition. On parallel developments in Lutheran exegesis, see e.g., Hansjoerg Sick, *Melanchthon als Ausleger des Alten Testaments* (Tübingen: J.C.B. Mohr, 1959); Arno Schirmer, *Das Paulus-Verständnis Melanchthons, 1518–1522* (Wiesbaden: Steiner, 1967); Timothy Wengert, *Vivum Evangelium*: Philip Melanchthon's *Annotationes in Johannem* in Relation to Its Predecessors and Contemporaries (Ph.D. diss. Duke University, 1984); Rudolf Keller, *Der Schlüssel zur Schrift, Die Lehre vom Wort Gottes bei Matthias Flacius Illyricus* (Hannover: Luther Verlagshaus, 1984); and Robert Kolb, "Teaching the Text: The Commonplace Method in Sixteenth-Century Lutheran Biblical Commentary," *Bibliothèque d'Humanisme et Renaissance* 49 (1987): 571–85.

21. The preeminent study of medieval exegesis remains Henri De Lubac, *Exégèse médiévale: les quatre sens de l'Écriture*, 4 vols. (Paris: Beauchesne, 1959–64). See also, P. C. Spicq, *Esquisse d'une histoire de l'exégèse latine au moyen age* (Paris: Beauchesne, 1944); Beryl Smalley, *The Study of the Bible in the Middle Agaes*, 2nd ed. (Notre Dame: University of Notre Dame Press, 1964); and James S. Preus, *From Shadow to Promise: Old Testament Interpretation from Augustine to the Young Luther* (Cambridge: Harvard University Press, 1969).

22. Cf., e.g., Martin Luther, *Dictata super Psalterium* in *D. Martin Luthers Werke: Kritische Gesamtausgabe* (Weimar: Bohlau, 1883–), vols. 3–4, hereafter cited as *WA*; and idem, *Divi Pauli apostoli ad Hebreos epistola*, in *WA*, vol. 57, pt. 3, 1–238.

23. Note Luther's use of Lombard, Augustine, Nicholas of Lyra, Paul of Burgos, Dionysius the Areopagite, and Bonaventure in his exposition of Hebrews: in *WA*, vol. 57 pt. 3, 98–112. Cf. Scott Hendrix, *Ecclesia in Via, Ecclesiological Developments in the Medieval Psalms Exegesis and the Dictata Super Psalterium of Martin Luther, Studies in Medieval and Reformation Theology*, vol. 8 (Leiden: E.. J. Brill, 1974); David C. Steinmetz, *Luther and Staupitz: An Essay in the Intellectual Origins of the Protestant Reformation*, Duke Monographs in Medieval and Renaissance Studies 4 (Durham, N.C.: Duke University Press, 1980); Susan Schreiner, *Theater of His Glory: Nature and the Natural Order in the Thought of John Calvin* (Durham, N.C.: Labyrinth Press, 1990); and idem, "Double Justice and Exegesis in Calvin's Sermons on Job," *Church History*, 58 (1989): 322–38.

24. Thomas Aquinas, *Summa theologiae*, Ia, q.1, art.10, ad 1. Cf. Beryl Smalley, "The Bible in the Medieval Schools," in *The Cambridge History of the Bible*, vol. 2: *The West from the Fathers to the Reformation*, ed. G.W.H. Lampe (Cambridge: Cambridge University Press, 1969), 215–16.

25. Cf. Preus, *From Shadow to Promise*, 67–71, 79–81, 137–41.

26. Cf. Philip Melanchthon, *Elementorum rhetorices libri II*, in *Opera quae supersunt omnia*, ed. C. G. Bretschneider and H. E. Bindseil, 28 vols., in *Corpus Reformatorum*, vols. 1–28 (hereafter cited as *CR*) (Halle: Schwetschke, 1834–60), 13, col. 469. On *loci communes* see ibid., cols. 451–54.

27. Cf. Philip Melanchthon, *Commentarii in Epistolam Pauli ad Romanos* (1540), *CR*, vol. 15, cols, 545–59, with the analysis of T.H.L. Parker, *Calvin's New Testament Commentaries* (Grand Rapids: Wm. B. Eerdmans, 1971), 33–35.

28. Parker, *Calvin's New Testament Commentaries*, 42.

29. Cf. Martin Bucer, *Metaphrases et enarrationes perpetuae Epistolarum D. Pauli Apostoli. Tomas primus. Continens metaphrasim et enarrationem in Epistolam ad Romanos* (Strasburg, 1536).

30. Cf. Heinrich Bullinger, *In omnes apostolicas epistolas divi videlicet Pauli . . .* (Zurich, 1537), with the analysis of Bullinger's style and method in Joachim Staedke, *Die Theologie des jungen Bullinger* (Zurich: EVZ, 1962), 283–85.

31. Cf. Calvin's comments in the *Institutio christianae religionis*, in the preface to the reader: "si quas posthac scripturae enarrationes edidero, quia non necesse habebo de dogmatibus longas disputationes instituere, et in locos communes evagari, eas compendio semper astringam," in *Opera quae supersunt omnia*, ed. Baum, Cunitz and Reuss (Brunswick: Schwetschke, 1863–1900), vol. 2, p. 4, (hereafter, *CO*), with Parker, *Calvin's New Testament Commentaries*, 49–54.

32. In particular, note Calvin's comments on exegesis in the exposition of Gal. 4:22–24, *CO*, 28, col. 236.

33. Parker, *Calvin's New Testament Commentaries*, 64.

34. Cf. Brevard S. Childs, "The *Sensus Literalis* of Scripture: An Ancient and Modern Problem," in *Beiträge zur Alttestamentlichen Theologie: Festschrift für Walter Zimmerli*, ed., H. Donner, R. Hanhart, and R. Smend (Göttingen: Vandenhoeck & Ruprecht, 1976). I discuss this issue in "The Hermeneutic of Promise and Fulfillment in Calvin's Exegesis of the Old Testament Prophecies of the Kingdom," in *The Bible in the Sixteenth Century*, ed. David C. Steinmetz (Durham, N.C.: Duke University Press, 1990).

35. Cf. Johannes Piscator, *Commentarii in omnes libros Novi Testamenti* (Herborn, 1613; 1658). I follow the 1658 edition in this and subsequent comments. Note that Piscator's comments on Hebrews 11 understand Abel primarily as a type of Christ and Enoch as a type of the eternal life offered to the church (*Commentarii*, p. 716, col. 1) and that he views Moses faith as an indication that "the ancients believed in Christ as much as we [today]" (ibid., p. 717, col. 1). Perkins usually follows a far more literal approach to exegesis and application. Piscator is better known for his (somewhat overenthusiastic) Ramism. Unlike Perkins, who used Ramist bifurcation as a means of organization in his writings, including his commentaries, Piscator assumed that a preliminary step to understanding the text of Scripture was to divide the entire text into Ramist dichotomies. See, e.g., his *Analysis logica in epistolarum Pauli* (London, 1591) and *Analysis logica septem epistolarum apostolicarum* (London, 1593).

36. J. W. Blench, *Preaching in England in the Late Fifteenth and Sixteenth Centuries. A Study of English Sermons 1450–c. 1600* (Oxford: Basil Blackwell, 1964), 94, 101–2.

37. Wolfgang Musculus, *In epistolam apostoli Pauli ad Romanos commentarii . . .* (Basel, 1555).

38. Blench, *Preaching in England*, 94. Cf. John Hooper, *Early Writings of John Hooper, D. D., Lord Bishop of Gloucester and Worcester*, ed. S. Carr (Cambridge: Parker Society, 1843), 443–55.

39. Thomas Cartwright, *A Dilucidation, or Exposition of the Epistle of St. Paul to the Colossians, Deliuered in Sundry Sermons*, ed. A. B. Grosart (Edinburgh, 1864).

40. On Cartwright and the English tradition of preaching and exegesis before Perkins, see Blench, *Preaching in England*; Irvonwy Morgan, *The Godly Preachers of the Elizabethan Church* (London: Epworth, 1965); and Erwin R. Gane, "The Exegetical Methods of Some Sixteenth-Century Anglican Preachers: Latimer, Jewel, Hooker, and Andrews," *Andrews University Seminary Studies* 17 (1979): 23–38, 169–88; and idem, "The Exegetical Methods of Some Sixteenth-Century Puritan Preachers: Hooper, Cartwright, and Perkins," *Andrews University Seminary Studies* 19 (1981): 21–36, 99–114. Note the discussion of Cartwright's relationship to the "Puritan" or Reformed style of preaching in Haller, *The Rise of Puritanism*, 10–25, 82–85.

41. Printed for Leonard Greene (1609), in *Workes*, vol. 3 (unaltered from the 1609 ed., with original title page and separate pagination).

42. On Perkins' style and method, see John H. Augustine, "Authority and Interpretation in Perkins' *Commentary on Galatians*," in William Perkins, *A Commentary on Galatians*, Pilgrim Classic Commentaries, ed. Gerald T. Sheppard (New York: Pilgrim Press, 1989), 15–23.

43. E.g., Thomas Manton, *The Complete Works of Thomas Manton*, 22 vols. (London: J. Nisbet, 1870–75). Cf. esp. the sermons on Hebrews 11 in vol. 13, 317–492; John Owen, *The Works of John Owen*, ed. William H. Goold, 17 vols. (London and Edinburgh: Johnstone & Hunter, 1850–53); John Flavel, *The Fountain of Life: A Display of Christ in His Essential and Mediatorial Glory*, in *The Works of John Flavel* (1820; reprint Edinburgh: Banner of Truth, 1968), vol. 1, 17–561. Also note Owen's detailed, technical *An Exposition of the Epistle to the Hebrews*, ed. William H. Goold, 7 vols. (London and Edinburgh: Johnstone & Hunter, 1855).

44. E.g., for a representative edition near to the time of Perkins' commentary on Hebrews 11, see *The New Testament of our Lord Jesus Christ, translated out of Greeke by Theod. Beza: With briefe summaries and expositions upon the hard places by the said Author, Ioac. Camer. and P. Loseler, Villerius*. Englished by L. Tomson. Together with the Annotations of Fr. Junius upon the Revelation by S. John. Imprinted at London by the Deputies of Christopher Barker, Printer to the Queens most Excellent Majestie, 1599. On the theological impact of the Geneva Bible, see, Irena D. Backus, *The Reformed Roots of the English New Testament* (Pittsburgh: Pickwick Press, 1980); Dan G. Danner, "The Contributions of the Geneva Bible of 1560 to the English Protestant Tradition," *Sixteenth Century Journal* 12 (1981): 5–18; Maurice S. Betteridge, "The Bitter Notes: The Geneva Bible and Its Annotations," *Sixteenth Century Journal* 14 (1983); and *The Geneva Bible: The Annotated New Testament, 1602 Edition*, Pilgrim Classic Commentaries, ed. Gerald T. Sheppard (New York: Pilgrim Press, 1989).

45. Cf. Richard A. Muller, "Perkins' *A Golden Chaine*: Predestinarian System or Schematized *Ordo Salutis*?" *The Sixteenth Century Journal* 9 (April 1978), 69–81.

46. Tomson here reproduces *not* one of the marginal glosses from Beza's text, as was his typical practice, but a sentence from the text of Beza's *Annotationes* on v. 6: see Theodore Beza, *Jesu Christi Domni Nostri Novum Testamentum, sive Novum Foedus, cuius Graeco contextui respondent interpretationes duae: una, vetus; altera, Theodori Bezae. Eiusdem Theod. Bezae Annotationes, in quibus ratione interpretationis vocum reddita . . .* (Cambridge, 1642), p. 684, col. 1, ll. 20–23.

47. Cf. *A Cloud*, 74.

48. David Paraeus, cited in John Calvin, *Commentaries on the Epistle of Paul the*

Apostle to the Hebrews, trans. John Owen (Edinburgh: Calvin Translation Society, 1853; reprint Grand Rapids: Baker Book House, 1979), 261, n.1.

49. Cf. *A Cloud*, 203.

50. Ibid., 1.

51. Ibid., 1.

52. *An Exposition of the Symbole or Creede of the Apostles*, in *Workes*, 1: 123–322. Not only does Perkins state that *An Exposition* is his system or body of doctrine, it is also nearly twice the length of *A Golden Chaine* and offers a more complete presentation of Christian doctrine. See Richard A. Muller, *Christ and the Decree*, 132; and, idem, "Perkins' A Golden Chaine," 80–81.

53. *A Cloud*, 1.

54. See Gerald T. Sheppard, "Between Reformation and Modern Commentary: The Perception of the Scope of the Biblical Books," in Perkins, *A Commentary on Galatians*, 42–71.

55. See Marjorie O'Rourke Boyle, *Erasmus on Language and Method in Theology* (Toronto, 1977), 72–81.

56. Cf. *Oxford English Dictionary*, s.v. "scope," with the *Confessio helvetica prior* (1536), chap. 5, "*Scopus Scripturae*"; and chap. 12, "*Scopus evangelicae doctrinae*"—where, in the German version, *scopus* is translated as *Zweck*, i.e., the target or bull's eye of the gospel: text in Philip Schaff, *The Creeds of Christendom, with A History and Critical Notes*, 6th ed., 3 vols. (New York: Harper & Row, 1931; reprint, Grand Rapids: Baker Book House, 1983), 3: 212, 217.

57. Cf. John Calvin, *Commentarius in Epistolam ad Hebraeos*, CO, 55, cols. 5–8.

58. Calvin, *Ad Hebraeos*, CO, 55, col. 143. Beza, *Annotationes*, p. 686, col. 1–2, makes no mention of this problem, but presses immediately into linguistic issues.

59. *A Cloud*, 1.

60. Cf. Perkins' citation of the text, p. 60, with his citations on pp. 60 and 68. I have followed the version of the text found in the body of Perkins' commentary.

61. *A Cloud*, 60.

62. Ibid., 1.

63. Ibid., 1.

64. Ibid., 1.

65. Ibid., 2.

66. Ibid., 2.

67. Ibid., 2.

68. Calvin, *Ad Hebraeos*, CO, 55, col. 140, offers, "Porro fides est rerum sperandarum substantia, demonstratio eorum quae non videntur"; Beza, *Annotationes*, p. 683, text, gives, "Est autem fides, illud quo subsistunt quae sperantur, and quae demonstrat quae non cernuntur"; the Vulgate gave, "Est autem fides, sperandarum substantia, rerum argumentum non apparentium."

69. *A Cloud*, 2.

70. Ibid., 2. Cf. ibid., 3; Calvin, *Ad Hebraeos*, CO, 55, col. 140; and Beza, *Annotationes*, p. 683, text, as cited above, n 68.

71. *A Cloud*, 2.

72. Ibid., 2.

73. Ibid., 3.

74. Cf. Richard H. Popkin, *The History of Skepticism from Erasmus to Spinoza*, 2d ed. (Berkeley: University of California Press, 1979).

75. *A Cloud*, 4.

76. Ibid., 4.

77. Ibid., 5.

78. *Art of Prophecying* in *Workes*, 2:673. See Blench *Preaching in England*, 101–2.

79. Calvin, *Ad Hebraeos, CO*, 55, col. 145: "Hinc autem natus est error quod praepositionem *ek* separant a participio *phainomenon*. Ita exponunt, Ut fierent visibilia ex non apparentibus. . . . Dicendum enim erat, *ek me phainomenon*. . . . Quare aliter, si quis verbum e verbo transferre velit, non potest hoc membrum exponi quam sic: Ut non apparentium fierent visa, hoc est spectacula: ut praepositio *ek* sit composita cum participio. Continent porro haec verba optimam doctrinam: quod in hoc mundo conspicuam habemus Dei imaginem. Adeoque idem hoc loco docet apostolus noster quod Paulus ad Romanos capite 1, 20."

80. Cf. Beza, *Annotationes*, p. 683, text cited above, n. 66; Piscator, *Ad Hebraeos*, p. 712, col. 1: "Per fidem intelligimus, constructum fuisse mundum verbo Dei, ita ut quae cernimus, non sint ex apparentibus facta."

81. *A Cloud*, 13.

82. Ibid., 14.

83. Ibid., 112. Calvin has *quum tentatus est*, i.e., when he was tested or tried.

84. Calvin, *Ad Hebraeos, CO*, 55, col. 156. Cf. Perkins, *A Cloud*, 112; and Beza, *Annotationes*, p. 684, text, and p. 685, col. 1, ll. 43–44, where Beza clarifies the *cum tentaretur* with the comment, "id est, cum exploraret eum Dominus."

85. *A Cloud*, 129.

86. Beza, *Annotationes*, p. 685, col. 1, l. 49; cf. col. 2, ll. 51ff.: "De quo ut nemo jam posset dubitare, ausus etiam est Castellio nuper hunc locum ita interpretari, *Et Josephi virgae caput veneratus est*. Atqui primum omnium, ut demus Josephum, hoc passurum fuisse . . . quorum hoc ad praedicandam Jacobi fidem. Deinde, quo jure debet excludi praepositio *epi*?" The Vulgate gives, "Et adoravit fastigium virgae eius."

87. Cf. *The New Testament of Jesus Christ*, translated faithfully into English, out of the authentical Latin . . . in the English College of Rhemes . . . (Rheims, 1582), in loc. (annotations following on p. 633).

88. Similarly, Piscator, *Commentarii*, p. 712, col. 2, offers, "Et adoravit, summo baculo suo nixus" (And he worshiped, resting on the top of his staff).

89. Calvin, *Ad Hebraeos, CO*, 55, col. 159; Beza, in. loc., disputes Castellio's and therefore Calvin's *virga* as implying a "scepter" and substitutes *baculum*, a walking stick.

90. Calvin, *Ad Hebraeos, CO*, 55, col. 159: "Hic unus est ex iis locis unde coniecturam facere licet, puncta olim apud Hebraeos non fuisse in usu . . ." N.b., pointed in one way, the Hebrew of Gen. 47:31 reads *mittah*, "bed"; pointed differently, the consonants remaining the same, it can read *matteh*, "staff."

91. Cf. Beza, *Annotationes*, p. 686, col. 1, ll. 8ff., with Piscator, *Commentarii*, p. 715, col. 1.

92. Cf. Richard A. Muller, "The Debate Over the 'Vowel Points' and the Crisis in Orthodox Hermeneutics," *Journal of Medieval and Renaissance Studies* 10 (Spring, 1980): 53–72.

93. *The New Testament* (Rheims), annotation on Heb. 11:21 (p. 633).

94. *A Cloud*, 129.

95. Cf. Calvin, *Ad Hebraeos, CO*, 55, col. 162–63, with Piscator, *Commentarii*, p. 715, col. 1.

96. Calvin, *Ad Hebraeos, CO*, 55, col. 162–63.

97. *A Cloud*, 147. Note that Beza does not comment on the problem: cf. *Annotationes*, p. 686, col. 2, ll. 29ff. John Owen, *An Exposition of the Epistle to the Hebrews*, vol. 7, 160–61, agrees with Perkins.

98. Cf. Calvin, *Ad Hebraeos, CO*, 55, col. 163–64, with Piscator, *Ad Hebraeos*, p. 713, col. 2.

99. *A Cloud*, 159.

100. Cf. Calvin, *Ad Hebraeos, CO*, 55, col. 164.

101. *A Cloud*, 160.

102. Piscator, *Commentarii*, p. 717, col. 2.

103. Calvin, *Ad Hebraeos, CO*, 55, col. 168.

104. The fourth decree of Trent, defining the canon of Scripture as including the Apocrypha was issued on 8 April 1546; the earliest Protestant confessional documents defining the canon without the Apocrypha are the *Gallican Confession* (1559) and the *Belgic Confession* (1561).

105. *A Cloud*, 184.

A
CLOWD OF
FAITHFVLL WITNESSES, LEA-
ding to the heauenly Canaan:

OR,

A Commentarie vpon the 11. *Chapter to the Hebrewes,* preached in Cambridge by that godly and iudicious Diuine,
M. WILLIAM PERKINS.

Long expected and desired; and therefore published at the
request of his Executors, by WIL. CRASHAVV, and TH. PIERSON, *Preachers*
of Gods Word: who heard him preach it, and wrote it
from his mouth.

PHIL. 3. 17.
Looke on them that so walke, as yee haue vs for an example.

HEB. 13. 8.
Whose faith follow, considering what hath beene the ende of their conuersation.

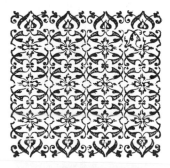

Printed for LEONARD GREENE.
1609.

TO THE NOBLE
AND VERTVOVS GENTLEMEN,
Sir IOHN SHEAFFIELD, Knight; and M. O-

LIVER S. IOHN: Sonnes and Heires to the Right Ho-
nourable EDMVND *Lord Sheaffield, Lord Preſident of the*
North, and OLIVER Lord S. IOHN, Baron of
Bletſho : Grace, and peace.

He gracious promiſes of God (Honourable and moſt worthy
Gentlemen) made to the holy Patriarchs, touching the Land of
Canaan, were ſingular comfort to the beleeuing Iſraelites, in
their bondage of Egypt. And the renewing of the ſame by the
hand of *Moſes* (whoſe words God confirmed by ſo many miracles)
muſt needs augment their ioy aboundantly, although their bonds
at that time encreaſed. But, the pledge of Gods preſence in the
cloudie pillar, whereby he led them in the wilderneſſe both night and day, did ſo far
exceede all his promiſes for matter of conſolation, that euen *Moſes* himſelfe deſired
rather to be detained from the promiſed Land, then depriued of the comfort of that
his preſence in the way: *If thy preſence* (ſaith he) *goe not before vs, bid vs not depart hence.* Exod.33.15.
Now, theſe things beeing *enſamples* vnto ys, and euident types of our eſtate who liue 1.Cor.10.6.
vnder the Goſpel, ſhewe apparantly, that howſoeuer Beleeuers be greatly cheered
in their ſpirituall trauell, by the gracious promiſes which God in Chriſt hath made
vnto them; yet this their ioy is much encreaſed, by the view of thoſe that haue gone
before them in the way of faith; who are vnto them as a *Cloud of witneſſes, or a cloudie
Pillar.* For, howſoeuer the truth of God be the onely ground of ſound conſolation:
yet becauſe we are a kin to *Thomas*, and will not beleeue vnleſſe we ſee, and feele;
therefore it is, that by the example of Beleeuers (wherein is ſome ſenſible euidence of
the comfort of Gods truth) we are farre more cheered, then by the promiſe it ſelfe
alone.

Here then beholde what great cauſe we haue to caſt our eyes vpon this *Cloude of
Witneſſes*; which the holy Ghoſt hath errected as a pledge of his preſence, and a direction to all thoſe that ſhall followe their ſteps in the practiſe of faith, till the worlds
ende. Shall *Moſes* affect that Cloude ſo much, which led them onely the way to a
temporall inheritance: and ſhall not we much more be rauiſhed with delight in *this
Cloud*, which leades vs to the kingdome of heauen ? In all eſtates *the iuſt muſt liue by* Heb.10.38.
faith: For, *We walke by faith, and not by ſight.* And what is the hope and happineſſe of a 2.Cor.5.7.
Chriſtian man, but to receiue at laſt the ſaluation of our ſoules, which is the ende of our 1.Pet.1.9.
faith, and period of this walke. But any faith will not ſupport vs herein: ſome begin
in the *Spirit*, who end in the *Fleſh*, going out with *Saul* for a while; but at length re- Gal.3.5.
turns with *Demas* to the world, neither can they doe otherwiſe: for, *Apoſtaſie is the* 2.Tim.4.10.
Cataſtrophe of Hypocriſie. He that would deceiue in his profeſſion is vſually deceiued
of his ſaluation.

Wherefore this ſhall be our wiſedome, to ſee to our ſoules, that our faith (as the
beloued *Apoſtle* ſaid of loue) *be not in word, and tongue; but indeede and in truth.* And for 1.Ioh.3.18.
our better direction in trying the truth of our faith, we haue here many notable preſidents in this *Cloud of Witneſſes :* conſiſting of moſt worthie Beleeuers in all ages be-

fore

fore CHRISTs incarnation: all which ſhewed the life of faith by their workes;and we in them may ſee how to put our faith in practiſe. Now, the rather muſt we attende hereunto, becauſe in all eſtates we muſt practiſe faith. For, *without faith it is impoſſible to pleaſe God.* And what eſtate of life can poſſibly befall vs, wherein we haue not a liuely patterne and forerunner leading vs the way to Heauen, within the compaſſe of this Cloud? Art thou a *King* or *Magiſtrate?* behold DAVID, HEZEKIAS, and the *Iudges:* art thou a *Courtier?* Looke on MOSES: art thou a *Martiall-man?* Behold SAMSON, DAVID, IOSVAH. Here is ENOCH, NOE, and the Prophets for *Miniſters:* the *Patriarches* for Fathers: SARA and the *Shunamite* for mothers: ISAAC and IOSEPH for children: Here is ABEL for Shepheards, and RAHAB for victuallers: Here are ſome that liued in honour, in peace, and plenty, ſome in want, and ſome in ſickneſſe: but moſt of all in perſecution; becauſe therein is the greateſt *tryall of faith.* So that, which way ſoeuer we turne vs, if we walke by faith, we haue here ſome faithfull witneſſe to goe before vs. And to cleare their ſteps the better to our ſight, that ſo we may *followe hard towards the marke* without wandring, we haue here a notable light in this learned Commentarie; which, we muſt confeſſe, is much obſcured, for lacke of the refining hand of the godly Author himſelfe: but now, ſeeing that ſhining light is quenched, vſe this our Lampe; it is fed with ſuch oyle as we receiued in the Lords Sanctuarie, from that Oliue Tree, whence many a one did fill his veſſell. And beeing importuned to expoſe the ſame for the Common good, we haue preſumed to place it vnder the ſhelter of your Honourable names;beſeeching God it may helpe *to guide your feete in the way of peace.*

The religious preſidents of your Honourable Parents (Right Noble and hopefull Gentlemen) muſt perſwade you much to be ſound, and conſtant in the faith: for declining in religion brings [a] ſtaine of honour, and decay [b] euen of temporall portion. But, labour you to encreaſe in grace, and truſt the Lord with your outward greatneſſe. Honour him, and he will honour you: delight in him, and he will giue you your holy hearts deſire; his faithfulneſſe will be your ſheild, to the griefe of thoſe that enuie your happineſſe. But, beware of bad example, and euill counſell, which are the bane and poyſon of younger yeares. Walke with God like *Enoch:* vſe the world as *Abraham* did, and followe *Moſes* in the matters of delight, forſaking them when they become the pleaſures of ſinne. So ſhall you *obtaine good report,* and your memories ſhalbe bleſſed with your Poſterities,like theſe faithfull Witneſſes. NOVEMBER, 10. 1607.

Yours in the Lord to be commanded,

William Craſhaw,
Thomas Pierſon.

Heb.6.

1.Pet.1.7.

Phil.5.14.

Luk.1.79.

a Ier.22.15. &c.to the ende.
b 1.King.11. 11.
1.Sam.2 30.
Pſal.37.4.

Heb.11.5.

verſ.10.
verſ.24.&c.
Heb.11.39.

A COMMENTA-RIE VPON THE

11. Chapter of the Epiftle to the Hebrewes.

VERSE I.

Now Faith is the ground of things which are hoped for: and the euidence of things not feene.

Oncerning Faith, two points are neceffarie to be knowne of euery Chriftian ; the *doctrine*, and the *practife* of it : the whole *doctrine* of faith (beeing grounded and gathered out of the word of God) is comprifed in the *Creede*, commonly called the *Apoftles Creede*: which beeing alreadie by vs expounded, it followeth in order (next after the *doctrine*) to lay downe alfo the *practife* of faith : for which purpofe we haue chofen this 11.chap. to the Hebrewes, as beeing a portion of Scripture, wherein the faide practife of faith is moft excellently and at large fet downe.

This chapter depends on the former, thus ; We may read in the former chapter, that many Iewes hauing receiued the faith, and giuen their names to Chrift, did afterward fall away ; therfore towards the ende of the chapter, there is added a notable exhortation tending to perfwade the Hebrewes to perfeuere in faith vnto the ende, as alfo to fuffer patiently what euer fhall befall them in the profeffion of it : and to vrge the exhortation, there are diuers reafons, not needefull to be alleadged ; for they concerne not the prefent purpofe.

Now, in this chapter he continues the fame exhortation : and the whole chapter(as I take it)is nothing elfe in fubftance, but one reafon to vrge the former exhortation to perfeuerance in faith ; and the reafon is drawne from the *excellencie of faith :* for this chapter doth diuers waies fet downe what an excellent gift of God faith is : his whole fcope therefore is manifeft to be nothing elfe, but to vrge them to perfeuere & continue in that faith, prooued at large to be fo excellent a thing : and indeede he could not bring a better argument to mooue them to loue and hold faft their faith, then by perfwading them of the excellencie of it. For common reafon bids vs not onely chufe, but

A hold faft that that is excellent.

Out of this coherence we may learne in a word, that perfeuerance in faith is a matter not of ordinarie neceffitie, nor of meane excellencie, to the vrging whereof the author of this Epiftle vfeth fo large and fo forcible an exhortation ; in fo much as, whereas ordinarie exhortations occupie the roome of one or fome *few verfes*, this is continued through *diuers chapters*.

The parts of this whole chapter are two :

1. A generall *defcription* of *Faith*, from the 1.v. to the 4.

2. An *illuftration* or declaration of that defcription, by a large rehearfall of manifold *examples* of auncient and worthie men in the old B Teftament, from the 4. v. to the ende. Of thefe two in order.

The *defcription* of Faith confifts of *three actions or effects* of faith, fet downe in three feuerall verfes.

The firft effect in the 1. verf. *Faith* makes things *which are not* (but onely are hoped for) after a fort *to fubfift and to be prefent with the beleeuer.*

The fecond is in the 2.v. *Faith makes a beleeuer approoued of God.*

The third in the 3.v. *Faith makes a man vnderftand and beleeue things incredible to fenfe and reafon.*

C Of thefe in order.

Now Faith is the ground of things which are hoped for: and the euidence of things which are not feene.

This firft v. containes the firft effect in the defcription of faith, wherein firft let vs fee the true meaning of the words : fecondly, what inftructions they doe naturally yeild vnto vs. For the meaning, we muft examine the words feuerally. *Now faith*

Faith in the word of God, is fpecially of three forts ; Hiftoricall, Miraculous, Iuftifying or fauing faith.

1. *Hifto-*

1. *Hiſtoricall faith*, is not onely a knowledge of the word, but an aſſent of the heart to
the truth of it: and this faith is generall not
onely to all men, good and bad, but euen to
the deuills themſelues: Iam. 2.19. Thou beleeu-
eſt there is one God, thou doeſt well: the deuills alſo beleeue it and tremble. Now he that
will beleeue out of the Scripture there is one
God, he will beleeue hiſtorically any thing in
the Scriptures.

2. *Miraculous*, or the faith of miracles:
which is, An inward perſwaſion of the heart,
wrought by ſome ſpeciall inſtinct of the holy
Ghoſt in ſome man, whereby hee is truely perſwaded, that God will vſe him as his inſtrument
for the working of ſome miracles: this alſo is
generall, both to elect and reprobate, *Iudas* had
it with the reſt of the Apoſtles.

3. *Sauing* (commonly called *Iuſtifying*) faith,
which is, A ſpeciall perſwaſion wrought by the
holy Ghoſt in the heart of thoſe that are effectually called, concerning their reconciliation
and ſaluation by Chriſt.

Of theſe three ſorts of *faith*, the third is
principally meant, in this place. And although
in the deſcription, & ouer all the chapter, there
are ſome things that agree to other faith then
it; yet I ſay the generall ſcope in this chapter, is
principally of that faith that ſaues a man. It becomes vs therefore to learne carefully the inſtructions that concerne the practiſe of this
faith, for it is no leſſe then a ſauing faith.

Secondly, it is ſaid; This faith is the *ground
or ſubſtance*; for the word ſignifieth both. The
meaning is: things hoped for, as yet are not, and
ſo haue no beeing nor ſubſtance: Now faith
that beleeues the promiſes, and applieth them,
that faith giues to theſe things which yet are
not (after a ſort) a ſubſtance or ſubſiſtence in
the heart of the beleeuer: ſo that that thing
which neuer had, nor yet hath a beeing in it
ſelfe, by this faith hath a beeing in the heart of
the beleeuer; this I take to be the true meaning.

Thirdly, it followeth of what things this faith
is the ground or ſubſtance: namely, of *things
hoped for*, and things *not ſeene*. And theſe be of
two ſorts: either in regard of the Fathers of
the old teſtament alone, or of them and vs both.

Of the firſt ſort were theſe two: 1. The incarnation of Chriſt. 2. The publiſhing of the
Goſpel, both to Iew and Gentile in a glorious
manner: both theſe were *hoped for* of them; but
we haue *ſeene them*: to them they had a beeing
onely in *faith*: to vs a beeing in themſelues.

Now vnto the Fathers of the old teſtament,
their faith gaue theſe two things a beeing in
their hearts and ſoules, though they came not
to paſſe many hundreth yeares after.

There are other things which we hope for
as well as they, which are to come, & not ſeene
in reſpect of vs both: and they be ſixe.

1. *Iuſtification*, ſtanding in the remiſſion
of ſinnes.

2. *Sanctification* in this life.

3. The perfection and accompliſhment of
our *ſanctification* after this life.

4. The *Reſurrection* of *the bodie*, and reuniting it with the ſoule.

5. *Glorification* of bodie and ſoule.

6. *Life euerlaſting*, and glorie with God in
heauen.

Theſe they ſaw not with the eye of the bodie, neither doe we; yet they hoped for them,
and ſo doe we: they had no beeing in themſelues to them, neither haue they as yet to vs:
but this true *ſauing faith* gaue to them, giues to
vs, and will giue to euery beleeuer, whilſt the
world laſteth, ſuch a certaine aſſurance of them
that they ſeeme preſent to vs, and we ſeeme
preſently to enioy them: we cannot enioy any
of them fully; but ſauing *Faith* hath this power, to giue them all a preſent beeing in our
hearts, and vs ſuch a reall poſſeſſion of them, as
greatly delighteth a Chriſtian ſoule: inſomuch
as the feeling of the ſweetneſſe of this glorie,
though it be to come, ouerwhelmeth the feeling of a worldly miſerie, though it be preſent.

Fourthly, it is added, *And the euidence*

This word ſignifieth and teacheth vs two
things concerning faith.

1. *Faith is an euidence, &c.* that is, Faith ſo
conuinceth the minde, vnderſtanding, & iudgement, as that it cannot but muſt needes, yea it
cōpelleth it by force of reaſons vnanſwerable,
to beleeue the promiſes of God certenly.

2. It is an euidence: that is, whereas life e-
uerlaſting and all other things hoped for are
inuiſible, and were neuer ſeene of any beleeuer
ſince the world beganne: this ſauing faith hath
this power and propertie, to take that thing in
it ſelfe inuiſible, and neuer yet ſeene, and ſo
liuely to repreſent it to the heart of the beleeuer, and to the eye of his minde, as that after a
ſort he preſently ſeeth and enioyeth that inuiſible thing, and reioyceth in that ſight, and enioying of it: and ſo the iudgement is not onely
conuinced, that ſuch a thing ſhall come to
paſſe, though it be yet to come: but the minde
(as farre as Gods word hath reuealed, and as it
is able,) conceiues of that thing, as being really
preſent to the view of it.

Let one example ſerue for all: Life euerlaſting is a thing hoped for: now *Faith*, not onely
by infallible arguments grounded vpon the
word and promiſe of God, conuinceth a mans
iudgement, that it ſhall come to paſſe, (inſomuch as hee dare ſay; that he knoweth as certainly, there is a life euerlaſting, as that hee
liueth and mooueth,) but this *Faith* alſo (as
much as Gods word hath reuealed, and as
farre forth as the minde of man is able to conceiue of it,) ſo repreſenteth this life euerlaſting to the eye of the ſoule, as that the ſoule
ſeemeth to apprehend and enioy this life euerlaſting; yea, and often in ſuch meaſure, as that
he contemneth the world, & all the preſent fe-
licity of it, in compariſon of that meaſure of the

ioyes

ioyes thereof, which *faith* reprefenteth to his foule: and thus *faith* makes that prefent which is *abfent :* and makes that manifeft and vifible, which in it felfe is inuifible : inuifible to the eyes of the bodie, it makes vifible to the eye of the foule; the fight of which eye is both giuen, and continued, and daily fharpned by *fauing faith.* And thus faith is amoft excellent *euidence* of things not feene. So then the whole fumme of this firft effect, is briefly thus much; whereas things to be beleeued, as perfection of fanctification, refurrection, glorification, &c. are not yet feene, neither can be, in that they are not yet come to paffe; yet if a man haue grace certainely to *beleeue* the promifes of God, thefe things fhall haue a beeing to his foule: in that both his iudgement knoweth affuredly they fhal come to paffe; and his foule, in moft liuely and ioyfull reprefentations, feemeth to enioy them.

Hitherto of the meaning of the firft effect.

Now in the fecond place, let vs fee what inftructions this firft effect thus vnfolded doth minifter vnto vs.

Firft, whereas *faith* giues a fubftance, & being things to that are not, wee learne that the Fathers in the old Teftament that liued before the incarnation of Chrift, were truely partakers of the bodie and blood of Chrift.

If any alleadge that this is ftrange, confidering that Chrift had then no bodie and blood, neither had he any vntill the Incarnation : and how then could they receiue that, which then was not?

I graunt it is true, they then had no beeing, and yet the Fathers receiued them: but how can this be? I anfwer by the wonderfull power of *fauing faith,* which makes things that are not in nature, to haue in fome fort a beeing and fubfiftence : and fo was Chrift (though he was to come) prefent to the beleeuers of the olde time. For, Apoc. 13.8. *Chrift is a Lambe flaine from the beginning of the world:* that is, flaine as well then as now : and that not onely in the counfell and decree of God, whereby he is borne and flaine in all times and places : nor onely in regard of the eternall power, efficacie, and merit of his death, but alfo euen in refpect of the heart of the *beleeuer,* whofe faith makes that, that is locally *abfent,* after a fort truly and really *prefent :* euen fo alfo is Chrift a Lambe flaine from the beginning of the world.

See a plaine demonftration hereof in Ioh. 8. 56. *Abraham faw me* (faith Chrift) *and reioyced :* How could this be, when as Chrift was not borne of a 1000. yeares after. *Anf.* This could not be in reafon, but it was indeede to *Abrahams faith:* whereby he faw Chrift more liuely, and more to his ioy and confolation, fo many. 100. yeares afore he was; then many which liued in Chrifts time, and faw him, and heard him, and conuerfed with him: for they

liuing with him, yet were as good as abfent from him, becaufe they beleeue not in him: And *Abraham,* though Chrift was fo far from him, yet by his faith was prefent with him. Againe, 1. Cor. 10 3. the auncient beleeuing Ifraelites *ate the fame fpirituall bread, and dranke the fame fpirituall rocke, and that rocke was Chrift:* How could they eate and drinke Chrift fo long afore he was? I anfwer, they did it by reafon of that wonderfull power of *faith,* which makes a thing abfent, prefent to the beleeuer : by that faith they receiued Chrift, as liuely, as effectually, as much to their profit and comfort, as we doe fince his comming.

If any man afke how could their faith apprehend that, that then was not; I anfwer by giuing them intereft and title to it: and fo the Fathers are faid by faith to haue receiued Chrift, becaufe their faith gaue them right and title in Chrift, and in their hearts they felt the efficacie of his death and refurrection, whereby they died to finne, and were renewed in holineffe, as well as we are now by the fame efficacie.

Secondly, whereas *faith* makes things abfent, prefent;

Here they are confuted that teach that the Lords fupper is no Sacrament, vnleffe the bodie and blood of Chrift be either truely turned into the bread and wine, or at leaft be in or about the bread; and that fo he is locally prefent, and muft locally and fubftantially be receiued: and this (fay they) is the moft comfortable receiuing of Chrift : for what comfort is it to receiue one abfent? but thefe men know not this notable prerogatiue of true faith, *Faith* giues beeing to things which are not, and makes things prefent which are abfent : they therefore that will haue Chrift locally prefent, they take this noble prerogatiue from faith: for here is nothing abfent, which faith fhould make prefent: we neede not goe in this Sacrament to require a corporall prefence : it is fufficient if wee haue true faith; for that makes him prefent much more comfortably, then it might be his bodily prefence would be vnto vs?

If any man afke how this can be ? I anfwer, The *faith* of the receiuer knoweth beft; and yet reafon can fay fomething in this cafe: for fuppofe a man looke earneftly vpon a ftarre, there are many thoufand miles betwixt his eie & the ftarre, yet the ftarre and his eye are fo vnited together, as that the ftarre is after a fort prefent to his eie. So if wee regard locall diftance, we are as farre from Chrift as earth is from heauen. but if we regard the nature of *Faith,* which is to reach it felfe to Chrift, where euer he be, in that regard Chrift is prefent: & why fhould not this be fo? for if the bodily eie, fo feeble and weake, can reach fo farre as to a ftarre, and ioyne it to it felfe, and fo make it prefent; why fhould not much more the piercing eye of the foule reach vp to Chrift, and make him prefent to the comfortable feeling of it felfe?

Thirdly, here we learne how to behaue our

felues in a ftrange temptation, whereby God vfeth to exercife his children. The Lord after that he hath receiued his children into his fauour, continueth not alwaies to manifeft that fauour vnto them; but often times pulls backe the feeling of it for a time; that afterward, he may fhew it againe in more comfortable manner vnto them, and that they may afterward more fenfibly feele it, and more earneftly loue it, and more carefully labour to keepe it, when they haue it.

Now for the time of this eclipfe of the fauour of God, he not onely darkeneth his loue, but makes them feele alfo fuch a meafure of his wrath, as that they will often thinke themfelues caftawaies from the fauour of God. *Dauid* and *Iob* were often exercifed with this temptation, as appeareth by their moft lamentable and bitter complaints: yea, *Dauid* doubts not, Pfal. 77. 9. to chalenge the Lord, that *he hath forgotten to be gratious, and hath fhut vp his louing kindneffe in difpleafure.* And Iob, chap. 15. 26. complaines to the Lord, that *he writeth bitter things againft him, and makes him to poffeffe the finnes of his youth*; words, as it may feeme, of men forfaken of God: and indeede fo for that time they thought of themfelues. If it pleafe the Lord thus to deale with vs, fo as we feele nothing elfe but his wrath wraftling with our confciences, neither can thinke otherwife by prefent feeling, but that God hath forfaken vs; what fhould we doe in this pitifull cafe? fhould we defpaire, as reafon would bid vs? no, but take this courfe; Call to minde Gods mercifull promifes, and his auncient former loue; and caft thy felfe vpon that loue, though thou canft not feele it: when thou haft moft caufe to defpaire, then labour againft it: when thou haft no reafon to beleeue, then beleeue with all thy power. For, remember the power and prerogatiue of thy *faith:* it beleeues not things *that are,* and manifeftly appeare, fo much as fuch things *that are not,* and haue no beeing. So then, when Gods fauour feemes to be loft, and to haue no beeing to thee, then is Gods fauour a fit obiect for thy faith, which beleeues thofe things that *are not.* Let all the deuills in hell fet themfelues againft thy poore foule, and if thou holdeft faft this faith, they cannot all make thee finke vnder it: for when the deuill faith, Thou haft loft Gods fauour; by faith a man anfwereth, though Gods fauour be loft vnto my feeling, yet to my faith it is not: My faith giues it a beeing, and fo long (fay what thou wilt) I will neuer feare that it is loft. When God pulls backe his fauour, and fights againft thee with his wrath; doe as *Iacob* did, Gen. 32. 27. 29. wreftle with God, though thou haue but one legge: that is, though thou haue but one little fparke of *faith,* fight with that *little faith,* lay hold by it on God, and *let him not goe vntill he hath bleffed thee,* in turning againe vnto thee his fauourable countenance: and fay with Iob, 13. euen in the very

heate of thy temptation, *O Lord, though thou kill this bodie and flefh of mine, yet will I truft in thee for euerlafting life:* yea, and though Gods anger fhould feeme to encreafe, yet for all that take fafter hold, and faint not; for *faith* will neuer faile thee: it will reftore Gods loue when it feemes loft; it will fet it before thine eyes, when it feemes to be hid. For, marke well but this one reafon; if *faith* will giue life euerlafting a beeing, and make it prefent to thy foule, which indeede yet neuer had beeing to thee: how much more can it giue a beeing to Gods fauour, and make it prefent to thy foule, which once had, and indeed hath ftill a beeing, and was neuer loft indeede, but onely to a mans feeling? Thus, true faith is able to anfwer this temptation, whether it come in life, or in the pangs of death.

Fourthly, whereas *faith* is called an *euidence;* hence we learne, that the nature of faith ftands not in doubting, but in certentie and affurance. The Romifh doubting of the effence of *faith,* is as contrarie to true faith, as darkneffe to light: for faith is an *euidence of things hoped for,* that is, it conuinceth the iudgement by vnfallible arguments; knowing as certainly the truth of the promifes, and of the things hoped for, as that God is God. But Rome will needes ioyne *faith and doubting,* which indeede fight like fire and water, and can neuer agree together in euery refpect, but one will in the ende deftroy the other.

Obiection. But it feemeth, doubting is a part, or at leaft a companion of faith, for we doubt as well as beleeue: and who is fo faithfull as doubteth not? *Anf.* We doe fo: but what then? we fhould not; for God commands vs to beleeue, and not to doubt: therefore to beleeue, becaufe it is commanded of God, is a vertue: and if it be a vertue, then to doubt is a vice; faith and doubting are both in a good man, but faith is a worke of grace and of the fpirit; doubting is a worke of the flefh, and a piece of the corruption of the old man.

Fiftly, if *faith* be a fubftance of *things* hoped for, much more is it a fubftance to the *beleeuer;* if it giue thofe things a beeing which are out of him, much more doth it giue a permanent beeing vnto the beleeuer himfelfe, ftrengthening him to ftand and continue in all affaults. So, Heb. 3. 14. *Faith is that, whereby a beleeuer is fuftained and vpholden:* fo that indeede we may fitly fay, Faith is the fpirituall fubftance, and the fpirituall ftrength of a Chriftian man: and according to the meafure of his faith, fuch is the meafure of his fpirituall ftrength.

This confideration hath diuers comfortable vfes, but efpecially two: 1. When any of vs are out of the reach of a temptation, fo long are we confident of our owne ftrength: but when we are affaulted by the Deuill, the world, and our owne flefh, then we fhall finde, that to refift is a harder matter then we dreamed of: for, as poffible as it is for wa-

ter

ter to burne, or fire to put out it felfe : fo poffible is it for vs of our felues to refift finne; in fo
much, as it is a thoufand to one, but that at euery affault our nature yeelds. Now if it be fo
hard to rule ouer one finne, how fhall we doe
againft that fea of temptations, that ouerwhelmeth a Chriftian life? this doctrine teacheth
thee how ; namely, to flicke to thy faith, and it
will doe it for thee : for if it be the fubftance of
the things thou hopeft for , which yet neuer
were ; much more will it yeeld vnto thee fpirituall ftrength and fubftance, to make thee ftand
in all temptations. When thou art tempted,
then call to minde Gods promifes , beleeue
them, that is, applie them to thy felfe, and be
refolued that they were made, and fhall be performed euen to thee : then though thou haue
no more power of thy felfe , then fire hath to
ceafe to burne ; yet whilft thou doeft thus,
thou fhalt feele thy foule fpiritually ftrengthe-
ned againft all temptations: and, feeling the experience of this , denie them thine owne
ftrength , and magnifie the power that God
hath giuen vnto true *faith*.

Againe, though now we are moft of vs quiet *vnder our owne vines and fig getrees :* yet we
know not how foone the hand of the Lord
may be vpon any of vs , in pouertie, fickeneffe,
imprifonment, banifhment loffes, famine, or
how it pleafeth him : how fhall a poore Chriftian ftand and buckle himfelfe to beare thefe?
I anfwer, true *fauing faith* refting on the word
of God, and beleeuing the promifes , not formally, but truly, will put fuch fubftantiall fpirituall ftrength into him , as that at firft, though
he bow vnder it , yet fhall he be able to recouer himfelfe againe, and buckle himfelfe to goe
forward in his profeffion, and fhall follow
Chrift manfully with this his croffe: This wonderfull power hath God giuen to fauing faith,
both to refift temptations , and to vndergoe all
croffes.

And thus much of the firft action or effect
of faith : the fecond followeth.

Verse 2.

For, by it our Elders were well reported of.

THis verfe containeth the *fecond effect of
fauing faith:* which is, *that faith is a means
whereby a beleeuer is approoued of God.* This
verfe hath fpeciall relation to the fift verfe: For
that, that is laide here of all the Elders in géne-
rall, is there affirmed fpecially of *Enoch* : namely, that *he was reported of to haue pleafed God.*

Let vs firft fearch the true meaning of the
words.

Elders] That is, all fuch men as liuing vnder
the old Teftament, beleeued in Chrift: amongft
which (though all be vnderftood) yet fome
were more *excellent in faith* and obedience
then others, and fo more honourable , and of
higher eftimation with God and men: and of

them it is fpecially to be vnderftood.

Now concerning thefe Elders, it is further
faid, that they were well reported of: hereby
are meant three things :

1. That God *approoued*, and allowed of thé.

2. That God did *approoue* of them, *becaufe
of their faith* in the Meffias.

3. That God gaue a teftimonie, and *declared that he approoued* of them.

For the firft , it may be asked , How were
they *approoued* of God?

Anf. Chrift the fonne of God is he, *in whom
the Father is well pleafed.* Now they beleeuing
in Chrift, their finnes were laid on him , and
made his by imputation : and contrariwife
his holineffe, obedience, and fatisfaction, were
imputed to them, and by the fame imputation
made theirs : Now that beeing theirs , God
beeing fo well pleafed with Chrift, could not
but alfo for Chrifts fake approoue of them. If
this feeme hard vnto any , I make it plain by
this comparifon. Looke as *Iacob* a yonger brother , puts on *Efaus* garment , the elder brother, and in it was taken for *Efau*, and obtained
his fathers bleffing and partimonie , which by
himfelfe he could not haue got: euen fo we are
as younger brethren, Chrift is *our elder brother*,
wee haue no right nor title to our fathers bleffing, nor to the kingdome of heauen: wee muft
put on the robe of perfect righteoufneffe,
which is the garment of Chrift, our elder brother: we, ftanding clothed with it, purchafe our
fathers fauour, and with his fauour his bleffing,
and his bleffing is the right and title to euerlafting life. And thus by Chrift *they were approoued.*

Secondly, for what were they *approoued*? The
text faith. *By faith*; not becaufe *faith* is an action of a fanctified minde and a good grace of
God : for fo are humility, loue , feare of God
(all which are graces of the fanctifying fpirit,
as faith is) : but becaufe it is a worthy inftrument in the heart of the beleeuer , which apprehends, and applieth to the foule that righteoufneffe of Chrift, by which he is iuftified; thus,
it being the hand and inftrument of their iuftification, by it (it is faid) they were approoued.

3. The text addeth, that God did not onely
approoue of them, but that *he teftified and made
it manifeft to all the world* that he did fo.

And this teftimonie
God gaue of them } 1. In his word.
2. In their owne confci-
ences.

The truth of the firft is manifeft , in that not
onely in this chapter , but often alfo in the old
teftament , God hath made fuch honourable
mention, and giuen fuch honourable titles vnto many of thefe Elders, calling *Abraham the
friend of God*, 2. Chron. 20. 7. and *Dauid, a
man after Gods owne heart*, 1. Sam. 13. 14. and
them all, his *anointed* and *deare chofen children*,
Pfal. 105. 15. Thus God hath teftified of them
in his word.

2. God teftified it to their owne confciences,

Matth. 3. 17.

in that hee gaue them his spirit, inwardly to assure their consciences that he did accept them in the Messias to come : and thus these Elders *receiued a testimonie* both outward to all the world, and inward to their consciences, that God in Christ *approued* and loued them: so the sense is plaine, the vse hereof manifold.

1. In that it is said these *Elders were approued by faith :* here wee learne what is the olde and ancient way, the right and straight way (that hath no by-wayes) to life euerlasting : namely, this onely, To relie on the mercy of God in Christ for pardon of sinne; this is the way wherein all the ancient Elders walked to heauen : this is the way that God hath opened and made vnto his Court: it is the Kings high way, the beaten way, common to euery one that knowes how to walke in it: aud deceiued none that euer went in it ; and beside which, there is no other. Seeing then, God hath consecrated it, and our *Elders* haue trode this way before vs, let vs follow them; that so we may attaine that kingdom whereto it hath brought them.

If any yet doubt whether this be the way or no: the spirit of God puts it out of doubt, Esay 30. 21 ; First, affirming peremptorily *This is the way:* Secondly, bidding vs therefore *walke in the same: This is the way, walke in it.* Our Elders obayed this commandement of the spirit: and, walking in this way, found the end of it, euerlasting life. If we would attaine the same end of the iourney, we must walke the same way.

But the world will say, this is a needlesse exhortation ; for we walke this way, we deny our selues, and looke to be approued of God onely by Christ : but it is strange to see how men deceiue themselues. Can a man walke in a way, and not leaue marks and steps behind him; euen so he that walks in this way, follow him, and you shall see steps of his continuall dying vnto sinne, and liuing vnto holinesse; insomuch that a man that followeth him, and marketh the course of his life in this way, may euidently say, See where he hath cast off, and left behind him this and that sinne: see where he hath taken vp, and caried with him these and those vertues and graces of God: Marke, here is a print of his faith, here is a print of his hope, here are prints of his loue. And may a child of God be followed and traced all the way to heauen, euen vntill he come to his death, which is the gate of heauen. How mightily then are they deceiued, which thinke they haue walked all their liues in this way, and yet there is not one step to bee seene : for assuredly this way is so beaten and troden, that no man euer trode in it since the world began ; but he left behind him manifest and visible steps, that all men that would looke at him, might see hee had gone that way. As therefore we all desire to come to heauen, and as we professe we walke in the way thither: so let vs be as carefull to leaue behind vs

our steps; namly, tokens and prints of our faith, our hope, and loue: which if we doe, then mark the excellent vse of those steps. 1. They testifie vnto all that see them, that wee walked the right way to heauen: and secondly, they will serue for marks and directions for them that shall walke in the same way after vs. By the 1. wee shall leaue an honorable testimonie of our selues behind vs : by the 2. we shall mooue others to magnifie Gods name, to whome our steps haue beene markes and directions, helps, and furtherances in the way to heauen.

Secondly, for what were these *Elders approoued? for their faith :* for nothing else. Amongst these Elders *Sampson* was wonderfull in strength : *Salomon* in wisdome : *Ioshua* in courage : *Moses* in learning: many of them, in the honour and pompe of the world, in beauty, riches, and other externall gifts, and the most of them all in long life ; yet not for one or all of these are any of them said to be regarded of God: but it is plainely saide, that *for their faith God did approoue them.* Here then learne what is the thing amongst all things that must make vs acceptable vnto God: euen this, To denie our selues, and to rest vpon the mercie of God in Christ; this will doe it and nothing else. Hast thou strength ? so had *Golias* as well as *Sampson:* hast thou beautie? so had *Absalom* as well or more then *Dauid:* hast thou wisedome? so had *Achitophel* (though not like *Salomon,* yet) aboue ordinarie men : hast thou riches? *Esau* was richer then *Iacob:* hast thou liued long? so did *Caine,* and *Ismael* as well as *Isaac:* hast thou many children? so had *Ahab* as well as *Gedion:* hast thou learning (the glorie of nature?) so had the *Egyptians* as well as *Moses:* for there *Moses* learned it. All these thou maist haue, and yet be *a vile person* in the sight of God: so farre from beeing approoued of God, as that he will not vouchsafe (vnlesse it be in his anger) once to regard or looke at thee: hast thou therefore any of those outward gifts? it is not to be contemned, it hath his vse; thanke God for it, and vse it well: and vse it so as by it thou maist be approoued amongst men : but stand not to it before God: for though it be wisdome, or learning, or neuer so excellent a gift; it cannot purchase the fauour and acceptation of God : but *true faith* is able to please God both in this life, and especially at the day of Iudgement.

This doctrine first confuteth the errour of some grosse Papists, who hold and write that many *Philosophers* for their good vse of the light of Nature, for their deepnesse in learning, and for their ciuill liues, are now Saints in heauen : a most manifest and shamefull vntruth, and here as manifestly confuted : for was *Salomon* not accepted, for all his wisedome, and shall *Socrates*? was *Moses* not accepted for all his learning, how then should *Aristotle*? if faith made all of them accepted, and nothing but faith ; how is it possible they should be accep-

ted

ted which neuer heard of faith? nay I lay more: If many a man which liueth in the Church, as deepe (it may be) in humane learning as they, and of great knowledge also in the whole doctrine of Religion(which they neuer knew)and yet could not, nor euer shall be accepted of God, onely for want of this sauing faith; How absurd is it to imagine saluation for them, which neither had sparke of faith nor knowledge of Christ? Let vs then hold, that *as there is no name whereby to be saued, but onely the name of Christ:* so no meanes to be saued by that Christ, but onely faith, euen that *faith, for which these Elders were accepted of God.*

Secondly, this excellencie of faith aboue other gifts, shewes the vanitie of the world; so carefull and earnest in seeking honour, riches credit, wisedome, learning, (all which can but make them esteemed and approoued to the world)and so carelesse and negligent in getting true faith, which will both approoue a man vnto the world, and make him honourable in the eyes of the Lord God.

Thirdly, by this doctrine, the Popish doctrine is iustly condemned, which teacheth that a man is iustified by his works, and that faith is not the most excellent of Gods graces. Here we are taught other diuinitie : for, *that for which a man is accepted, by that he is iustified:* but for their faith only were they accepted:therefore iustification is onely by faith. Againe, that which makes a man accepted of God, that must needs be the most excellent thing of all. For God which is goodnesse it selfe, regardeth that that is the best: but God esteemed them onely for their faith: therefore it is the chiefe of all graces of God, in regard of making a man accepted of God.

Fourthly, here is a paterne and president for Gods children, how to bestowe and measure out their loue and estimation in the world. God loued *Salomon* more for his faith, then for all his glory and wisedome; and esteemed more of *Moses* for his faith, then for all his learning. So deale thou with thy wife, thy child, thy seruant, thy friend, and with all men. Hast thou a wife neuer so beautifull, louing, honest, and thrifty; neuer so toward and obedient a child; a most wise and trusty seruant; a friend for faithfulnesse like thy owne soule? These are indeede much to be esteemed; yet thinke not thy selfe in a paradise, when thou hast such: for there is a greater matter behind, then all these. Looke therefore further: Is thy wife, thy child, thy seruant, thy friend endued with sauing faith? that is worth more then all the rest:that is it that makes them beloued of God. Let that therefore make them best beloued of thee:& that which makes them so honourable before God, let that make them most honourable and most esteemed of thee: So in all men, loue that in a man best which God loueth; and so thou shalt be sure not to loose thy loue. Esteeme of a man, not as the world esteemeth, not according to his strength,

beautie, high place, or outward gifts: but as God esteemeth him, namely, according to the mesure of *sauing faith*, which thou seest in him; for is not that worthy of thy loue, which hath purchased the loue of the Lord God himselfe?

Fiftly, here is comfort for all such seruants of God, as hauing true faith, yet are in base estimation for worldly respects: some are poore, some in base callings, some deformed in body, some of meane gifts, many in great distresse and miserie all there liues ; most of them some way or other contemptible in the world : Yet let not this discomfort any child of God: but let them consider what it is that makes them *approued of God*: not beautie, strength, riches, wisedome, learning (all these may perish in the vsing)but true faith:if then thou hast that, thou hast more then al the rest. If thou hadst al them, they could but make thee esteemed in the world: but hauing true faith, thou art esteemed of God ; and what matter then who esteemes thee, and who not ? This crosseth the corrupt censure of the world, who more esteeme a man for his outward gifts, & glory of riches or learning, then for sauing graces. Let Gods children when they are abased, contemned, mocked, and kept from all place & preferment in the world, let them I say, appeale from their vniust iudgement to the iudgement of God; and be comforted in this, that though they want all things (without them) that should make them esteemed in the world, yet they haue that (within them)for which God will esteeme, approue, and acknowledge them both in this world, and in the world to come. And they haue that that will stand by them, when strength and beautie are vanished, when learning, and riches, and honour are all ended with the world.

Thus much of the second doctrine.

3. In that our *Elders by faith obtained a good report*, Here wee learne the readiest and surest way to get a good name. A good name is a good gift of God; Eccles. 7.3. *It is a pretious ointment:* it is a thing that all men would haue : These Elders had it, and they haue laide vs downe a platforme how to get it, and it is this; 1. Get into fauour with God, please him, that is, confesse thy sinnes, bewaile them, get pardon, set the promises of God in Christ before thee, beleeue them, applie them to thy selfe as thine owne, be perswaded in thy conscience that Christ did all for thee, and that he hath purchased thy acceptation with God.

Thus when thou art assured that God approues of thee, God can easily giue thee a comfortable testimonie in thine owne conscience, and hee can mooue the hearts of all men to thinke well, and open their mouthes to speake well of thee; for hee hath the hearts of all men in his hand. And therefore those that are in his fauour, he can bend the hearts of all men, to approue them ; yet this must be vnderstood with some cautions.

Act.4.12.

1. God will not procure his children a good name amongſt all men: for then they ſhould be curſed: for Luk. 6. 26. *Curſed are yee when all men ſpeake well of you:* But the Lord meaneth, that they ſhall be accepted, and haue a good name with the moſt and with the beſt. For indeed, a good name (as all other graces of God) cannot bee perfect in this life: but they ſhall haue ſuch a good name, as in this world ſhall continue and increaſe, and in the world to come be without all blot: for ſinne is the diſgrace of a man; therefore when ſinne is aboliſhed, good name is perfect.

2. God will not procure all his children a good name, nor alwaies: for, a good name is of the ſame nature with other externall gifts of God: ſometime they are good to a man, ſometime hurtfull: to ſome men good, to others hurtfull. Euery one therefore that hath true faith, may not abſolutely aſſure himſelfe of a good name: but as farre forth as God ſhall ſee it beſt for his owne glorie, and his good.

3. The good name that God will giue his children, ſtands not ſo much in outward commendation, and ſpeaking well of a man: as in the inward approbation of the conſciences of men. They muſt therefore be content ſometime to be abuſed, mocked, ſlandered; and yet notwithſtanding they haue a good name in the chiefe reſpect: for they whoſe mouthes doe abuſe and condemne them, their very conſciences doe approue them.

Out of all theſe the point is manifeſt, that God will procure his children a good name in this world, as farre forth as it is a bleſſing, and not a curſe: & that becauſe they are aproued of him, and by faith iuſtified in his ſight: for ſo to be is the onely way to get a good name. For in reaſon it ſtands thus: that thoſe who are in eſtimation, and good name with the Lord himſelfe; much more will God make them eſteemed, and giue them a good name with men like themſelues. Hence we learne, firſt, that the common courſe of the world to get a good name, is fond, and wicked, and to no purpoſe: They labour for riches, preferments, honour, wiſdome, and learning; by them to get eſtimation in the world: yea, many abuſe theſe bleſſings in vaine oſtentation, to encreaſe their credit and name with men: and in the meane time ſauing faith is neuer remembred, which muſt procure them a good name with God. This is a wrong courſe: firſt, wee muſt labour to bee approoued of God; and then after the good name with God, followeth the good name in the world. Hee therefore that labours for fauour with men, and neglects the fauour of God; hee may get a good name, but it ſhall prooue a rotten name in the end. Prou. 10. 7. *The memoriall of the iuſt ſhall be bleſſed, but the name of the wicked ſhall rot.* The good name of the wicked is rotten: 1. Becauſe it is loathſome and ſtinking in the face of God, though it bee neuer ſo glorious in the world. 2. Becauſe it

A will not laſt the wearing out, but in the end vaniſheth and comes to nothing, vnleſſe (as a rotting thing leaues ſome corruption behind it, ſo) their good name in the end being vaniſhed, leaues infamy behind it. And this is the name which commonly is gotten in the world, becauſe men firſt ſeeke not a good name with God: but that good name which is obtained by faith, will ſtand and continue all a mans life, and at his death leaue behind it a ſweet perfume, and abideth for euer in the world to come.

Secondly, this maintaines the excellencie of our religion againſt Atheiſts, and all enemies of it, which eſteeme and call it a baſe and contemptible religion, and of which can follow no credit nor eſtimation. But ſee, their malice is here controlled: our religion is a moſt glorious and excellent profeſſion, it is the high way to get true credit and eſtimation: it makes a man honorable in the ſight of God and men: for by it our Elders obtained a good report, which continueth freſh to this day.

In the fourth place, *Were they well reported of for their faith?* therefore their *faith* was not hid in their hearts; but manifeſted in their liues: for, the world cannot ſee nor commend them for their faith; but for the practiſe of faith, Here it is plaine, that men muſt not be content to keepe their *faith* cloſe in their hearts, but they muſt exerciſe the fruits of it in the world; and then both theſe together will make a man truely commendable. Thy *faith* approoues thee vnto God; but the practiſe of it is that that honours thee and thy profeſſion in the world.

Laſtly, in that faith was that which approoued our Elders vnto God; here is a ſtorehouſe of comforts, for all true profeſſors of this faith.

Art thou *poore?* thy faith doth make thee *rich* in God.

Art thou *ſimple* and of meane reach? thy faith is true *wiſedome* before God.

Art thou any way *deformed?* faith makes thee *beautifull* vnto God.

Art thou weake, feeble, *or ſicke?* thy faith doth make thee *ſtrong* in God.

Art thou *baſe* in the world, and of no account? thy faith makes thee *honourable* in the ſight of God and his holy Angels. Thus thou art poore, and fooliſh, and deformed, and ſicke, and baſe in the world; but marke how God hath recompenſed thee: he hath giue thee faith, whereby thou art rich, and beautifull, and wiſe, and ſtrong, and honourable in heauen with God: ſay therefore with *Dauid*, the *lot is fallen vnto thee in a faire ground, & thou haſt a goodly heritage,* namely, thy faith which thou wouldeſt not change for all the glorie of the world. Faith is the true riches, the ſound ſtrength, the laſting beautie, the true wiſedome, the true honour of a Chriſtian man: therefore take thy ſelfe 10000. times more beholden vnto God, then if he had giuen thee the vncertaine riches, the

Pſal. 16. 6.

craftie

crafty (and yet foolish) wisedome, the decaying strength, the vanishing beauty, the transitorie honour of this world.

If thou hast true faith, thou art sure to haue enemies: 1. The wicked of the world will neuer brooke thee, but openly or priuily hate & hurt thee. Then the deuill is thy sworne enemie: how canst thou deale with so powerfull an enemie, and all his wicked instruments? Here is found comfort: if thou hast faith, thou hast God thy friend: labour therefore for this true faith, and then care not for the deuil, and all his power. Night and day, sleeping and waking, by land and sea thou art safe and secure, the deuil cannot hurt thee, thy faith makes thee accepted of God, and brings thee within the compasse of his protection. That same little sparke of faith, which is in so narrow a compasse as thy heart, is stronger then all the power and malice of Satan. As for the malice which his instruments, wicked men in this world, shew against thee in mocks and abuses, much lesse care for them: for their nature is to speake euill, and cannot doe otherwise: looke not therefore at them, but looke vp into heauen by the eye of thy soule, where *thy faith makes thee beloued & approoued of God himselfe*, and honourable in the presence of his holy Angels.

And thus much of the second action or effect of faith, the third followeth.

VERSE 3.

Through faith wee vnderstand that the world was ordained by the word of God, so that the things which wee see, are not made of things which did appeare.

IN this verse is contained the third action or effect of *faith*, namely this; Faith makes a man to vnderstand things beyond the reach of mans reason. This third effect is set out in these words, by the instance of a notable example; namely, of the Creation of the world; 1. By the word of God. 2. Of nothing: both which, that wee may the better vnderstand, let vs consider of the words as they lie in order.

Through faith

1. By *faith*, in this place (as I take it) is not meant that sauing-faith, which iustifies a man before God; but a generall *faith*, whereby a man imbraceth Christian religion: or whereby a man beleeueth the word of God in the doctrine of the law and the Gospel, to be true. My reason is, because a man that neuer had iustifying and sauing *faith*, and is no member of the catholike Church, nor child of God, may haue this gift, To beleeue that God by his word made the world of nothing. Therefore, I thinke that this is an action of a generall, and

not of sauing faith.

We vnderstand

That is, whereas there are many things beyond the reach of reason, and therefore by reason cannot be apprehended or vnderstood, yet by vertue of this faith a man is brought to vnderstand them, and to beleeue them to bee true.

Now then whereas generall faith brings vnderstanding of many things which reason cannot reach vnto; here, such as be students in humane learning, and which labour to attaine to the deepenesse and perfection of it, are taught, with their trauell in humane studies, to haue care to ioyne faith and knowledge of religion. For there are many things which our vnderstanding by reason cannot conceiue; and many truthes which Philosophy cannot reach vnto; nay, many also which it denies: but faith is able to perswade and demonstrate them all, and it inlightens the minde, and rectifies the iudgement, when as Philosophy hath left the mind in darknesse, and the iudgement in error. Now, in whom sound knowledge in Philosophy, and this faith in religion doe concurre together, hee is a man of a most rectified iudgement, and of a deepe reach in the greatest matters: but, separate *faith* from humane knowledge, and hee will stumble at many truthes, though hee had the wit of all the Philosophers in his owne head: For example, that God should make the world of nothing: that it should haue beginning and ending: that God should be eternall, and not the world: that mans soule beeing created, is immortall: These and many other truthes, reason cannot see, and therefore Philosophy will not admit: but ioyne faith to it, and then that crooked vnderstanding is rectified and made to beleeue it. It is therefore good counsell, to ioyne both these together. Religion hinders not humane learning, as some fondly thinke; but is a furtherance and helpe, or rather the perfection of humane learning, perswading, and proouing, and conuincing that, which humane learning cannot. And thus we see how faith makes vs to vnderstand.

But, what doth it make vs to vnderstand? the text saith, *That the world was ordained*, &c. Amongst many Expositions we may most safely set downe and approoue this; God by his word or commandement hath *ordained*, that is, made in good order: *the ages*, that is, the world and all in it; and all this he did by his word, and (which is more strange then that) made them all of nothing. This is a wonderfull thing: reason conceiues it not, but disputes against it: Philosophy grants it not, but writes against it: but marke the priuiledge of this faith; it makes a man beleeue it, and shewes him also how it is.

Now for our better perceiuing the excellencie of this power of faith, here are foure points set downe: 1. What was created: *The worlds.*

2. In what manner: *Ordained.* 3. By what meanes: *By Gods word.* 4. Of what matter: *Of nothing.* Of theſe in order.

The firſt point is, What was made? The text anſwereth, *The worlds.* The word ſignifieth, in the originall, *Ages:* and ſo it is alſo taken, Heb. 1.2. God made the worlds or ages by Chriſt: by this word thē he meaneth theſe two things, Firſt, times and ſeaſons, which are ordinarie creatures of God, as well as other: for amongſt other creatures (Gen. 1.) are recorded alſo times and ſeaſons to bee Gods creatures. Secondly, he vnderdſtandeth the world alſo, and all in it: and ſo it is truely tranſlated. For with good reaſon may the word *ages* ſignifie *the world,* becauſe the world and all in it had their beginning in time, haue their continuance in time, and ſhall haue their end in time againe. Time begun them, time continues them, and time ſhall end them: and ſo the *world* is euery way meaſured by the compaſſe of time: and therefore it pleaſeth the holy Ghoſt to tearme the world, and all in it, *Ages,* or times.

Now whereas it is ſaid, *Ages,* that is, times and ſeaſons were *ordained* of God; we learne, that if time bee a creature or an ordinance of God (created for ſo great purpoſes, as to be the meaſure of all things) to take heede of abuſing ſo excellent an ordinance: if thou haſt ſpent it well, ſpēd it ſtil better. Time is ſo good a thing, it cannot be ſpent well enough. But haſt thou miſſpent time (that is, abuſed it) take Saint *Pauls* counſell, Eph. 5. 16. *Redeeme the time:* that is, ſeeing what is paſt cannot be recall'd; then recompence the loſſe of it, by the well beſtowing of time to come. Spend euery houre well: and that thou maieſt doe ſo, be alwaies either doing good to other, or receiuing good from other: doe either, and time is well ſpent. And take heede thou bee not of the number of thoſe that often ſay, they cannot tell how to driue away *time:* and therefore they deuiſe many toyes, and conceits, and vaine pleaſures, yea, many wicked and vnlawfull delights: and all to ſhift off (as they ſay) and deceiue the *time.* It is wonderfull to ſee, that the wicked, whoſe *time* of ioy is onely in this world, ſhould ſeeke to haſten it, and make it ſeeme ſhorter; yet ſo it is, the deuill blinding them: but howeuer it is, ſeeme it ſhorter or longer, that ſame one ſinne of miſſpending their time, ſhall condemne them if they had no more; for if *account muſt be giuen for euery idle word,* a fearefull account remaines to be made for ſo many idle houres. Let vs then be very carefull in the vſe of this good ordinance of God, and neuer deuiſe how to paſſe away *time:* for there is no man that is a profitable member in the place where he is, that can finde one houre ſo idle, that hee knowes not how to imploy it, either in receiuing or doing ſome good.

Were ordained

The ſecond point, in this example, is the manner. Did God make a peſect or an imper-

fect world? The text anſwereth, it *was ordained.* The word ſignifieth thus much; God framed the *Ages,* that is, all creatures, viſible and inuiſible, in a moſt excellent, perfect, and abſolute *order.* As in a campe euery man keeps his ranke and order, and no man goeth out of his ſtanding appointed him: So euery creature hath his due place, and his proper vſe aſſigned him of God: ſo that the workmanſhip of the world in euery creature, and in euery reſpect was abſolute: and thus (*ordained*) is as much as perfectly made. And the whole world was as the perfect body of a man, where euery member, bone, ioynt, veine, and ſinew, is in his proper place, and nothing out of ſquare.

Ob. Was euery thing created in his *order* and due place? Whence then come ſo many *diſorders* in the world? The deuill hath his kingdome, authoritie, lawes, and ſubiects; hee rules in the wicked. Now can there be any order in Satans kingdome? Againe, whence are ſo many alterations and ſubuerſions of Kingdomes; ſo many wars, ſo much effuſion of blood? The Goſpel is tranſported from Country to Country; ciuill diſſenſions in Cities and priuate families; betwixt man and man; betwixt man and ſome creatures: betwixt creature and creatures; yea, hatred often vnto the death: yea, often hatred betwixt creaturs of the ſame kind. All theſe being ſo, where then is that excellent order wherein they were created?

I anſwer: the ſtate of all creatures is changed, from that wherein they were created, by the fall of our firſt parents. God made no diſorder, *He ſaw euery thing that he had made, and lo it was very good:* therefore it was in a moſt perfect order: For, orderly comelineſſe is a part of the *goodneſſe* of a thing: but diſorder is the effect of ſinne: it entred with ſinne; and it is both a companion and a reward of ſinne. Had we continued in our innocence, all creatures had continued in their excellent *order:* but when we had broken the perfect *order* that God had appointed vs; immediately all creatures broke that order wherein they were afore both towards vs, and one amongſt another. Whil'ſt wee obeyed God, all creatures obeyed vs: but when wee ſhooke off the yoke of obedience vnto god, and rebelled againſt him, then they became diſobedient vnto vs. Whil'ſt wee loued God, all creatures loued and reuerenced vs: but when we fell to hate the Lord, then began they to hate vs, and not before. If therefore thou ſeeſt any diſobedience and hatred in the creatures towards thee, any diſorder and vanity amongſt themſelues, thanke thy ſelfe for it, thou broughteſt it into the world with thy ſinne.

This beeing ſo, we are hence taught when wee ſee any diſorder in any creature, not to blame the Lord nor the creature, but to turne backe to our ſelues, to take notice of our owne ſinnes and corruptions, and to acknowlegde this was not ſo at the fiſt, but our ſinne was the

Gen. 1.31.

cause of it; and therefore be humbled and ashamed of our selues, that we should confound that excellent *order* which God made, and all creatures (but for vs) would haue kept till this day: but the common practise is contrary, as I will prooue in particulars.

God made mans bodie pure and holy, and therefore it had no neede to be couered: but with sinne came shame, and thence came it that God gaue vs *apparell* to couer that shame that sinne had brought vpon vs: so oft therefore as a man puts on his apparel, he should be humbled and ashamed by it: and thinke thus with himselfe, This was not so at the first; *Adams* bodie was glorious: whence came this ignominie and shame, which wee must couer with apparell? it came from my sinne; therfore so often as a man puts it on, so oft should he be quite ashamed of himselfe, which hath brought this shame vpon himselfe: so as now he must needes haue a cloake to couer his shame. But doe men make this ende of their apparell? nay, rather they make it a banner to display their pride and vanity; and so farre are many from beeing ashamed of it, as that they are contrariewise proud of it. But this is as abominable, and cursed, and senselesse a pride, as if the prisoner should be proud of his bolts and fetters, which are signes of his misdemenour: for, what is thy apparell (make the best of it) it is but a beautifull cloake of thy filthie shame: then, as bolts and fetters are burdenous, and shamefull, though they be of gold: so is the cloake of thy shame, thy apparell, though it be silke, siluer, or gold: for we should not be ashamed onely of ordinary apparell, or base, but euen of the most gorgeous; knowing that once we had a glorie of our owne, farre aboue all the glorie of apparell: and the ignominie that sinne hath brought vpon vs, is greater then this glory of apparell can take away.

Here I denie not the vse of gorgeous apparell, to those to whom it belongs: But I say to the rich men (who, by their abilitie) to men in authoritie, who (by their place and calling) may weare costly apparell: yea, and to Princes, who may lawfully weare silke, siluer, gold, and the most excellent ornaments of pretious stones, or whatsoeuer: to all them, I say, God hath granted you the vse of these; but withall, bee not proud of them, for you once had a glorie greater then these, but lost it by sinne: and sinne brought a shame, which these cannot hide. For though thy apparell hide it from the world, yet can it not from God: onely *faith* can couer it from God: therefore glorie in nothing but thy faith, be ashamed of thy apparell: yea, of thy robes and costly ornaments. And know further, that whereas thy bodie by sinne is become so vile, a meaner couer and baser apparell were fit for it. And therefore know, that whereas God hath giuen thee vse of costly apparell, and pretious ornaments, he giues them not to honour thy bodie, but the place thou art in: and to a-

dorne that part of his owne Image, which he hath set in thee by thy calling. And know lastly, that if thou hadst keept that order, wherein God at thy creation (as the text saith) *ordained* thee: thy naturall glorie would more haue adorned thee and the place thou bearest, then all this accidentall and artificiall glorie can: and therefore glorie not so much for the one, as be ashamed for the losse of the other; and let thy apparell teach thee this lesson.

Thirdly, many men take much delight in some kinde of *meate*; some in varietie of meats; and some so loue their bellie, as they care not how many creatures, or kind of creatures doe die, for their belly sake: this is to be considered. For I take it a great fault, for men either to bee too lauish and carelesse, how many creatures they cause to die, or (though they eate but one kinde) to doe it without all vse or further consideration. For, marke whence comes this, that man cannot now liue, or not so well; but his life must be the death of other creatures, his nourishment and preseruation, the destruction of other creatures. At the beginning before sinne was, this was not so: no creature did either serue to cloath or feede *Adam*: but this came with sinne; sinne brought this vanitie vpon creatures, to die for the feeding and cloathing of man: and had we stood without sinne, no creature should haue lost his life to bee our meate. I take it therefore the dutie of a man to make great vse of his meate in this regard. And first, for the meate that he loues best, let him be humbled for his sinne: knowing that if hee had not sinned, hee should haue had much more sweetnesse in other meate, which notwithstanding should not haue cost any creature his life. And secondly, for variety be not too lauish, nor too riotous: consider euery dish is the death of a creature of Gods creation: consider againe whence comes this, that creatures must die to feed thee; not from the creation, creatures were not made to that end: Innocencie would haue preserued all creatures to more excellent ends.

Sinne it was, and thy sinne that destroyes so many creatures for the belly of man: it is a vanitie come vpon creatures for mans sinne, that they must die for mans meate. The death therefore of euery creature, should be a corasiue to a mans heart: when he seeth it, it should touch him to the quicke, and make him say, This creature dieth not for it selfe, but for me; not for it owne fault, but for mine. Miserable sinner that I am, if I had right, I should rather die then it. God made it once for a better end, but my sinn hath brought it to this corruption. If this consideration tooke place, men would not eate their ordinarie fare with so little vse: nor at extraordinarie occasions be so carelesse how much they spend, and how many creatures they cause to die.

But you will say, God hath giuen vs libertie in meates: differences of meats are taken away in Chrift, and God hath giuen vs vfe of his creatures, not onely for neceffitie, but more liberall vfe euen for greater delight and comfort. I anfwer; I grant all this and more too, to a man that hath faith. I grant, feafts and bankets are lawfull for fome men on fome occafions. I take not away any mans liberty in meats: God hath granted it, and man ought not to take it away. I onely wifh that when we eate, wee alfo would make this vfe of it: and that wee would not too riotoufly abufe that liberty that God hath giuen vs for diuerfity of meates: faith giues leaue and libertie to eate; yet faith denies not a man to make a holy vfe of his eating, for his owne humiliation, but rather commaunds it.

Fourthly, we fee in the world, that creatures not onely die for mans feeding, but one creature feedes on another, and one creature deftroyeth another to eate him. The Hawke preyeth on diuerfe kindes of birds: the Fox feedeth on tame birds: the Wolfe on the Lambe: greater fifhes deuoure the leffe: Dogs will eate diuerfe kindes of creatures, if they can come by them. Thefe things are manifeft, and fome of them be common fports in the world.

Now whence comes this fearefull diforder in nature, that one creature fhould deuoure another? came it from the creation? was the world ordained in this ftate, that one creature fhould eate vp another? the greater feede vpon the leffe? no: but finne brought this confufion, our finne caufed this pitifull maffacre of all creatures one by another. Let vs therefore at thefe fights be humbled for our finne, which caufed fo fearefull a diforder: when thou feeft thy Hawke flie fo fircely and fo cruelly murder a filly birde: thy Hound, the Hart, Hare, or Connie; then, as God hath giuen thee leaue in good order, meafure, and manner, thus to deale with the creatures, and therefore thou maift take delight in it: fo, withall make this vfe of it; Whence comes this? it was not fo from the beginning: When finne was not in the world, thefe would all haue lodged in one cage and cabbin, and one neuer haue offered to haue eaten another: my finne caufed this iarre, and this diforder betwixt thefe two creatures. This fhould humble a man, becaufe of his finne, and reftraine his life from too much libertie, and his affection from too much delight in thefe kind of paftimes.

Againe, when we fee the crueltie of the Fox, the Wolfe, the Beare, toward the fheepe and other creatures; Blame not too much the crueltie of the beafts: for this was not in them at their creation; but thy finne made them thus cruel one againft another. Turne then into thy felfe, and be afhamed of it: and blame not fo much the crueltie in them, as thine owne finne which caufed it in them.

Againe, fome creatures are vnperfect, fome in parts of their bodie, fome in fome fenfes: and fome are loathfome and vgly to behold: and fome are venomous, and hurtfull to the world. When thou feeft it, confider whence is this. They were not thus created: for God [ordained] that is, made all creatures in perfect *order*: but this comes from thy finne: enter into thy felfe, and acknowledge this, and be humbled for it: and doe not fo much contemne this creature for his imperfection, nor loath him for his deformitie, nor hate him for his venome; as contemne, and loath, and hate thine owne finnes which were the caufe of all thefe.

Laftly, fome take great delight in faire buildings, and make no vfe of them but for delight and pleafure: but if they confider well, they haue no fuch caufe: it was not fo at the creation. *Adam* in his innocencie had a more fumptuous Palace *ordained* for him; namely, the Paradife of heauen and earth: and yet trees were not cut in pieces, nor the earth had her ftones rent out of her bowels, for the building of it. Thy finn it was that deftroied this Palace; and finne hath caufed the neceffitie of thefe buildings: How then canft thou glorie in thy buildings; Wilt thou glorie in thy fhame? Canft thou be proud of thefe, when thy finne bereft thee of a better? As therefore thy houfe is a comfort, ftrength, fecurity, and delight vnto thee: fo adde this one vfe alfo; let it in this confideration be a caufe to humble thee for thy finne.

The diforder that finne hath brought into the world, might be fhewed in more particulars: but thefe may fuffice, beeing thofe of whom we haue moft common vfe, and therefore doe moft commonly abufe.

To conclude this point, I fay vnto all men: Doeft thou fee what diforder is now in the world, in thy apparell, meate, recreations, buildings? Seeft thou the confufion, vanity, corruption of all creatures: the variance, diffenfion, and hatred of creatures amongft themfelues? Canft thou fee all this, and either not regard it at all, or elfe take delight in it? This is a curfed and abhominable delight. If a rich man fhould confume all his wealth, or throw it all on heapes, and then defperately fet his houfe on fire, hath he any caufe of ioy to fee this? If he fit ftill at this, you will fay he is fenfeleffe: but if he laugh at it, he is madde: So God created man rich in all bleffings, put him into the Palace of the world: garnifhed this houfe of the world with exceeding beauty: his meate, his apparell, his recreation, his houfe were all excellent and glorious: hee made all other creatures, amongft which there was nothing but concord, loue, agreement, vniformity, comelineffe, and good order: now man by finne fell; and by his fall, not onely fpent all his riches (that is, defaced the glorie of his owne eftate:) but alfo fet his houfe (that is the world) on fire: that is, defaced the beauty of heauen and earth: brought confufion, corruption, vanity, deformity, imperfection, and monftrous diforder on all creatures; fet all the world together by the

eares,

all creatures; set all the world together by the eares, and one creature at variance and deadly hate with other; so that one creature doth fight teare, wound, destroy, and eate vp another. O cursed and damnable sinne of man, that hath so shamefully *disordered* that heauenly *order*, wherein God created all things at the beginning! and miserable men are we, which can sit still and see this, and not be mooued: but if we reioyce and delight in it; certainly, then a spirituall madnesse hath bewitched our soules. Let vs therefore stirre vp our selues, and looke about vs; and seeing all the world on a fire about vs, namely, flaming in contention, hatred, and all disorder; let vs for our parts seeke to quench it: which because we cannot, therefore lament and bewaile it: but much more lament and be humbled for our sinne, which kindled this fire of disorder in the world.

Hitherto of the manner of the Creation.

By the word of God.

The third point is, by what meanes? The Text answereth; the world was ordained in that excellent order, *by the word of God.* By this word is meant, 1. not any *vocall* word, as if the Lord should speake vnto the creatures: nor secondly, the *substantiall* word of the Father, the second person; although I confesse that by *him were made all things.* Yet I take it, it is not so meant in this place: but rather as *Moses* doth, Gen. 1. when he saith, that in the creation *God said:* It is in both places a comparison taken from a Prince, who bids his seruants doe this, and they doe it presently. The Lord in this place is like a Prince, he hath his word whereby he commanded the world to be made. That word, I take it, is *his will:* for, Gods willing of any thing, is an effectuall commanding of it to be done: yea, it is the doing of it: for his willing of a thing to be, is more then all the commandements of all men in the world. For if he doe but will it, the thing is done what euer it be: whereas all the world may command, and yet it is no neerer. From hence, I take it this is manifest to be the surest sense for this place; God willed the beeing of all creatures, and according as he willed, they presently were: and that his will was his word here mentioned.

Here then first marke a speciall point, that sets out the glorie of the Creator: he vsed no labour, no motion, no paines, no seruants, no meanes as men doe. He onely *spake the word, and they were made; he commanded, and they were created,* Psal. 148. 5. This shewes how glorious a God he is, and his power how omnipotent it is, who at his owne will and word produced such a glorious frame of heauen and earth, so many thousand sorts and kinds of creatures in their order and due place. *Dauid* most seriously considered of this, when he made the 104. Psalme, as appeareth if we read it. We ought also so deeply to meditate of this his glorious power manifested in this miraculous creation, as that we (seeing it) may

Ioh. 1. 3.

acknowledge with the Psalmist, Psal. 115. 3. *Our God sitteth in heauen, and doth whatsoeuer he will.*

2. Did the Lord make all things *by his word?* learne we then for our instruction thus much; Euer when we see what is Gods will concerning our selues in any crosse or affliction whatsoeuer; let vs subiect our selues to it and beare it, because it comes from so mightie a God, as whome there is no resisting. For see, he that commanded all the world to be, and it presently was so, and nothing could disobey; then if he command any crosse to seaze vpon thee, wilt thou resist him? nay, rather take Saint *Peters* holy counsell, 1. Pet. 5. 5. *Humble thy selfe vnder this so mightie hand of God, that he may exalt thee in due time.* If thou then see his crosse comming towards thee, meete it, receiue it with both hands, beare it with both shoulders: if he will humble thee, resist not thou: for when againe he pleaseth to exalt thee, all the deuills in hell are not able to resist him.

It followeth; *So that the things which we see, are not made of things which did appeare.*

The fourth and last point is the *matter,* whereof the world was made: the Text saith, *The things that we see,* that is, all the world, *were made of things neuer seene:* that is, of a flat nothing, which here is saide not to be seene, or not to appeare; because how can that appeare or be seene, which is not? So the meaning is, when there was nothing in the world, then God made the world to be: This is the strangest thing of all in this fourth effect: For it is not so strange that the world should be created in excellent *order;* or that God should make it by his *word;* as that he should make it of *nothing.* Reason denies it, Philosophie disputes against it as absurd, and neuer will yeild vnto it: but here is the power of *faith* manifest, for it makes vs beleeue and know it is so.

Hence we learne, 1. If he created the world of nothing, then he can preserue vs also by nothing, that is, without meanes, or by weake meanes, or contrarie to meanes: he that did the one, can doe the other, for the same reason is of both. This is a speciall point of our religion, Not to tie Gods prouidence vnto meanes. Men vse neuer to acknowledge it but with meanes: but that is no worke of *faith.* But we ought not onely to see Gods prouidence, when we see no meanes; but euen when other meanes are against vs, then to see it, is a point of *faith:* and that is our dutie, though it be hard. Giue men health, wealth, libertie, peace, let them be guarded about with Gods blessings; then they will magnifie the prouidence of God: but take these away, and lay vpon them penurie, sickenesse, or any crosse, then they rage, and rayle, and distrust, yea blaspheme, and say, No prouidence, no God. And thus God is beholding to the meanes, for else men would flatly denie him. But this argues the want of faith. For had we that faith in vs,

where-

whereby we beleeue ftedfaftly, that God made all the world without meanes, that *faith* would alfo perfwade vs that he can preferue vs beeing made, though meanes be wanting, or though they be againft vs. This we may make vfe of, whether we be in neceffitie, and would be re-leeued: or in any perill, and would be fuc-coured: or in what extremitie foeuer, when meanes doe faile vs.

Secondly, if he made all things of nothing, then he is able alfo, in refpect of his promifes made in Chrift, *To call fuch things that are not, as though they were,* Rom. 4. 17. As, a man by nature is the child of wrath, and of the deuill: he is able to make him a feruant of God, and child of grace.

This may teach vs, 1. Not to defpaire of any mans faluation, though he feeme almoft paft all grace: for God can make any thing of nothing, and therefore can put grace into that heart wherein afore was none.

And 2. this is a comfort to all them which through weakneffe of faith, cannot perfwade themfelues of their election. For, fuppofe thou be full of wants and imperfections, and haft a rebellious and froward heart: What then? Re-member God made thee once a creature, of no-thing; he can now againe make thee a new crea-ture, of nothing: hee created thee without meanes; he can faue thee, though neuer fo many meanes doe feeme to be againft thee.

And thus much of thefe three effects of faith; and confequently

Of the firft part of this Chapter, containing a defcription of faith in generall.

Abels faith.

Verse 4.

By Faith, Abel offered vn-to God a greater facrifice then Cain: by which he obtained witneffe that he was righteous; God teftifying of his gifts: by which faith he alfo beeing dead yet fpeaketh.

He fecond part of the Chap-ter, containeth an illuftrati-on and proofe of the former defcription, by a rehearfall of the moft excellent pat-ternes & enfamples of *faith,* which flourifhed in the Church of the old Teftament.

These examples be of two forts: 1. Such as are fet downe *feuerally* one by one, from the 4. v. to the 32. 2. Such as are fet downe *ioyntly* many together, from thence to the ende.

The examples fet downe feuerally are of two forts: 1. Such as were naturall *Ifraelites,* and borne members of the Church vifible. 2. Such as were not naturally members, but *ftran-gers* from the Church of God, till they were called extraordinarily.

Examples of fuch as were members of the vifible Church, are alfo of two forts: 1. Such as liued about the flood: or, 2. after the flood.

Firft, of fuch as liued afore, or about the time of the flood, there be three faithfull men, whofe faith is here recorded: 1. *Abel,* and 2. *Enoch* before. 3. *Noe,* both before and after. All thefe three in order.

Thefe excellent and moft worthie exam-ples, are all grounded on fome place of the old Teftament, and are continued from the begin-ning of the world almoft to Chrifts incarnati-on: for he beginneth with *Abel,* which is fo neere the beginning, that he was the *fecond* good man that liued in the world: yea, and the *firft* of all that had this true *faith,* as the onely meanes of his faluation. For, as for *Adam,* he afore his fall had not this faith, neither fhould it haue faued him: but when the firft meanes failed him, then came this *faith* as the fecond and more effectuall meanes of his faluation: but *Abel* was neuer in poffibilitie to be faued by any thing, but by this *faith.* And therefore *Abels* faith hath the firft place of commendati-on, and that in this verfe.

Abels faith is here commended for three things: 1. In that *he offered by it a greater facrifice then Cain.* 2. By it *he obtained tefti-monie with God.* 3. By it dead *Abel yet fpeaketh.*

The firft effect of *Abels* faith, is thus fet downe by the holy Ghoft, *By faith, Abel offe-red vnto God a greater facrifice then Cain.*

The ordinarie Expofition of thefe words, is this: That *Cain* and *Abel* comming to offer, there was no difference in the matter of their facrifice, but onely in the manner of offering, in that *Abel* offered by faith, and fo did not *Cain.*

This Expofition though it be good, yet it fits not the fcope of this place, nor the fourth of Gen. The right fenfe therefore feemes to bee this; *Abel* hauing *faith;* this faith mooued him to teftifie his thankfull heart to God. This he did by offring vnto God the *beft and coftlieft facrifice* that he could: namely, the *firft fruites and fatteft of his fheepe;* Whereas vnbeleeuing *Cain,* hauing no loue to teftifie vnto God, brought onely of the fruite of his ground: not of the beft as *Abel* did: but whatfoeuer cam firft to hand. This beeing the true meaning of the whole: let vs come to the particular points laid downe in this effect, and they are three.

1. That

1. That *Cain* and *Abel offered*, that is, serued God.

2. That they offered *Sacrifices*.

3. That *Abel* offered a better then *Cain*.

The firſt point containes their ſeruice in generall: the ſecond, their ſeruice in particular: the third, the difference of their ſeruice: wherein eſpecially will appeare the excellencie of *Abels* faith.

Firſt, *Abel* and *Cain*, the two firſt brethren in the world, *offered* ſacrifice to the true *God*. How learned they this? for they had no Scripture, it was penned many yeares after; namely, by *Moſes* firſt of all. I anſwer, when their parents *Adam* and *Eue* had fallen, god gaue them (of his infinite goodneſſe) a couenant of grace, *that the ſeede of the woman ſhould breake the ſerpents head,* Gen. 3. 15. we doubt not but our firſt parents receiued this couenant, and beleeued the promiſe: and this their *faith,* taught them how to worſhip the true God aright.

You will ſay: thus *Adam* and *Eue* learned of God; but how came this to *Cain* and *Abel*: I anſwer, when they had beene thus inſtructed of God, *Adam* as a faithfull ſeruant of God, taught the ſame religion, and deliuered the ſame doctrine to his children: and by it they were taught, what, to whome, and in what manner to offer ſacrifice. And thus they did it neither by Scripture, nor reuelation, nor their owne inuention, but by the inſtruction of their Parents.

Hence let all Parents learne a leſſon of *Adam,* the firſt parent that was in the world; namely, to procure the good of their children: he nourtered his children excellently: 1. He prouided for them till they came to age. 2. Then he left them not, but appointed them their callings: for one was a husbandman, and the other a ſhepheard. 3. Not thus onely, but he taught them to worſhip the true God, both in their callings, and in the practiſe of religion: and therefore he taught them to offer ſacrifice in way of thankfulneſſe vnto God: all this did *Adam.*

So muſt thou doe with the children which God hath giuen thee. 1. Prouide for them carefully till they be of age, take heede they miſcarie not any way for want of things needfull. 2. So bring them vp, as that they may be apt to liue in ſome godly calling whereby to doe good in his Church: and that calling thou muſt appoint them, according to the finenſſe of their gifts. *Adam* appointed thē not both one calling, but diuers callings, according to the diuerſitie of their gifts: and thou muſt ſee it be a lawfull and honeſt calling, for ſo are both theſe. Then 3. (the greateſt matter of all theſe) teach them religion, and the true manner of fearing and worſhipping God; that as by the two firſt, thy child may liue well in this world, ſo by this he may be made an heire of the kingdome of heauen.

Adam was the firſt father, and father of vs all; let all then follow him in this practiſe: and if we follow him in one, follow him in both. Diuers will be as carefull for their bodies and for their callings as *Adam* was, but how few are as carefull to teach them religiou for the preferment of their ſoules to life eternall? but parents muſt haue care of both theſe: els they ſhall anſwer for their child at the day of iudgement: and though he periſh in his owne ſinne, yet his blood will God require at the fathers hands. For God made him a father in his roome, and he diſcharged not the dutie of a father vnto their child.

Secondly, in that *Cain* offered as well as *Abel*; hence we learne diuers inſtructions.

1. It is a common opinion, that if a man walke duly and truly in his calling, doing no man harme, but giuing euery man his owne, and ſo doe all his life long, God will receiue him, and ſaue his ſoule: but the truth is this; If men doe thus, it is good and commendable, and they muſt be exhorted to continue: but if they ſtand vpon this for ſaluation, they caſt away their ſoules. For marke here, *Cain* was a man that walked in an honeſt calling, and more then that, he tooke paines, and laboured in it (which all men doe not which haue honeſt callings:) And more then all theſe, when *Abel offered,* he came and worſhipped God alſo; and he did outwardly in ſuch ſort, as no man could blame him, but onely God that ſaw his heart: And for all this, yet is he a *wicked Cain,* and that is all that the word of God giues him, 1. Ioh. 3. 12. Then it is manifeſt, that to walke in a mans calling iuſtly and vprightly, doing no man harme, will not ſerue the turne. *Cain* did it, and yet was accurſed: we muſt then goe further then *Cain,* els we ſhall goe with *Cain* to the place where he is.

Reaſon not with thyſelfe, I worke hard and follow my calling, I hurt no man: thus could *Cain* reaſon, and yet but curſed *Cain.* Thou muſt then beſide theſe, get that that *Cain* did not; Learne in thy conſcience to ſee and feele thy ſinne, to be grieued for it, ſo as thou maiſt ſay: My ſickneſſe, my pouertie, my croſſes grieue me: but nothing ſo much as my owne ſinnes, theſe trouble me aboue all, and this griefe ſwalloweth vp all the reſt. And there is another thing which I ſeek aboue all: not gold, ſiluer, or promotion; but reconciliation with my God, and his fauour in Ieſus Chriſt: If thou haſt theſe two, then thou goeſt beyond *Cain,* then ſhalt thou ſtand before God with *Abel,* and be accepted. Remember theſe two; humiliation for ſinne, and deſire of reconciliation: theſe two is the ſumme of religion. If thou haſt theſe, thou art bleſſed with *Abel*; if not, curſed with *Cain,* howſoeuer thou liueſt in the world. If thou ſay, *Cain* killed his brother, and ſo would not I doe for all the world, I will doe no man hurt in bodie or goods; This will not ſerue: for it is ſaide that

God had no respect to *Cain* afore he killed his brother, euen when he *offered his sacrifice:* and therefore this dutie is most necessarie, and there is no shifting it off.

2. *Cain* offered as well as *Abel*; yea, *Cain* offered *afore Abel*, as it is manifest in Gen. 4. 3. And yet *Abels* sacrifice was better when it came to the proofe, and was accepted, and not *Cains* which came first. Hence we learne, that a man may be more forward then many other in many outward duties of religion, and yet not be accepted of God: another may be not so forward to the dutie, and yet when he comes, be better accepted. Whence comes this? what? is forwardnesse in good duties a fault? Nothing lesse: but hence it is, he that outwardly is most forward, may come in hypocrisie and without *faith*; the want whereof makes his forwardnesse nothing worth. Many such haue we in our Church: great frequenters of places and exercises of religion; and yet they come but as *Cain* did, or it may be in worse intents. Thy forwardnes is to be commended; but take this with thee also; Care not so much to be first at the Sermon, or to be there oftner then other, as to goe with true faith, repentance, and a heart hungring for grace: if not, boast not in thy forwardnes: *Cain* offered afore *Abel*, and yet not accepted: and so there may come an *Abel* after thee, and bring faith with him, and be accepted, when thou with thy hypocriticall forwardnes shalt be reiected as *Cain* was.

Thirdly, did *Cain* offer as wel as *Abel*? Hence we learne, that the *Church militant* is a mixt and compounded companie of men: not of one sort, but true beleeuers and hypocrites mingled together: as here in the very infancie of the church, there was a *Cain* worshipping in shew, as well as *Abel* that worshipped in truth. So was it in the infancie, so in her perpetuall growth, and so shall it be in the last age of the Church: the good shall neuer be quite separated from the bad, vntill Christ himselfe doe it at the last iudgement. Goates shall alwaies be mingled amongst the sheepe, *till Christ the great shepheard doe separate them himselfe*, Matth. 25. 34. And he that imagineth a perfect separation till then, imagineth a fancie in his braine, and such a Church, as cannot bee found vpon the earth.

This beeing so, let no man therfore be afraid to ioyne himselfe to the visible Church: neither let any that are in it goe out of it, because the bad are mingled with the good; for so it hath beene alwaies, and euer will be: he then that will goe out of a Church, because there be hypocrites in it, must goe out of the world; for such a Church is not found, but triumphant in heauen.

Fourthly, in that *Caine* and *Abel offered*, hence we learne, that the church of God which truly professeth his name, hath beene euer since the beginning of the world. For this Church was in the houshold of *Adam*, when there was

no more but it in the world: for *sacrifice* to God is a signe of the Church: yea, and beside the sacrifice, they had a place appointed where *Adam* and his family came together to worship God. For, so much *Cain* intimateth, Gen. 4. 14. and 16. *Cain went out from the presence of the Lord*, that is, not onely out of his fauour and protection, but from the place of his solemne seruice, and where he wonted to manifest his speciall *presence* to his children seruing him: and therefore *Cain*, as beeing excommunicate, complaines (vers. 14.) because he must leaue it. Thus the Church hath beene from the beginning, and therefore is truly called Catholike.

The Papists abuse this place notoriously: for whereas the *Church* hath beene so auncient, they argue therefore it is aboue the *Scripture*: yea, and that we could not know it to be *Scripture*, but by the auncient testimonie of the Church.

We must know the Scripture is two waies to be considered: first, as it was written and penned by holy men, and so it is later then the Church: for *Moses* was the first penman of Scripture: but secondly, as it is *the word of God*, the substance, sense, and truth thereof is much more auncient then the Church: yea, without the word of God, there can be no Church: For, without faith is no Church (because the Church is a companie of beleeuers) and without the word is no faith: therefore no word, no faith; no faith, no Church. So then the Scripture was afore the Church, but penned after.

Thus we see that *Cain* and *Abel offered*.

Now secondly, what offered they? *sacrifices*. Sacrifices were vsed in the worship of God for two ends. 1. When a sacrifice was offered, especially of beasts, when a man saw the blood of the beasts powred out, it put him in minde of his owne sinnes, and the desert of them, and taught him to say thus: Euen as this creature is here slaine, and his blood distills and drops away; so my sinnes deserue that my blood should be shed, and my soule be drenched in hell for euer. This creature can die but one death, for it sinneth not; but my sinnes deserue both the first and second death.

Secondly, sacrifices serued to put them in minde of the Messias to come; and the slaying of the beasts shewed them how the Messias should shed his blood, and giue his life for the sinnes of the people. These are the two principall endes of sacrifices, and for these two endes did *Cain* and *Abel* offer; *Cain* in hypocrisie and for fashion sake; *Abel* in truth, conscience, and sinceritie.

As it was in the old sacrifices, so is it in our Sacraments of the new Testament: whereof, the sacrifices were all types: 1. In baptisme, sprinkling of the water, serues to shewe vs how filthily wee are defiled with our owne sinnes.

2. It signifies the sprinkling of the blood of

vpon the heart of a finner, for his fanctification from finne.

2. In the fupper, the breaking of the bread fignifies, 1. how we fhould be broken in humiliation for our finne: and the pouring out of the wine, how our blood and life fhould be fhed, and poured out for our finnes, if wee had that that we deferue. And fecondly, they reprefent vnto vs how the bodie of Chrift was broken, and his blood poured out for our finnes: which he was content to fuffer vnder the wrath of his Father, for our fakes: fo that wee fee, both the facrifices and facraments of the old, as alfo of the new Teftament, all aymed at thefe two ends; to fhewe vs our finnes, and our miferie by finne; and to foretell or reprefent our reconciliation by Chrift. Which beeing fo, our leffon is this;

We haue all receiued thofe two Sacraments: the firft once, the fecond often. Now if they haue beene duly receiued of vs, they ought to haue this double vfe vnto vs: 1. To caufe vs to make a fearch of our owne finnes, and of our miferie by finne: and feeing it, to be caft downe and humbled, confidering how corrupt our hearts are, and how wicked our liues. And fecondly, when this is fo, then to make vs feeke for reconciliation with God by faith in Chrift, to make vs defire it, loue it, and pray for it aboue all things in the world. *Abel* not onely offred, but offred fo, as that it put him in minde of his finne, and of his redemption, by the death of the Meffias to come. So wee muft not onely outwardly receiue the Sacraments; but fo receiue, as that wee may fee and be humbled for our finne, and feeke to be reconciled to God in Chrift.

Such vfe alfo ought wee to make of hearing the word, and not to bee content with bare hearing of it, or to get a generall knowledge out of it: but it muft giue vs a fpeciall fight of our owne eftate by finne: and vrge vs forward to feeke the fauour of God in Chrift. Religion ftands not in hearing the word, and receiuing the Sacraments with the congregation, though it bee done neuer fo often, and neuer fo formally: But fo to heare and fo to receiue, as that they may worke in vs thofe two things: and that is the pith and life of religion. And whofoeuer he be that profeffeth religion, & fheweth not the fruit of it in thefe two, that mans profeffion is in vaine, and it will goe for no payment at the day of iudgement.

Thus wee fee they offred, and what they offred. It followeth; *A greater facrifice then Cain.*

The third and laft point, is the difference of thefe facrifices. For although *Cain* offred as well as *Abel:* and offred *facrifice* as well as *Abel:* yet was there a difference in there facrifices: for *Abels* was *better* then *Caines.* This is the chiefe point: for this fets downe what was that excellencie of his *faith*, for which he is here commended. *Abel* is not commended for

offring, by his faith; for fo did *Cain* that had no faith: nor for offering facrifice, by his faith; for fo did *Caine* that had no faith: but becaufe that by his faith he offered *a better facrifice* then *Cain* could.

The holy Ghoft calls *Abels* a *better* or *greater* facrifice, becaufe *Abel* brought the beft & fatteft of his fheepe, and fo beftowed the moft coft he could; as fignifying that hee woud haue beftowed more coft, had he knowne how to haue don it. For he that giues as he hath, would giue more if he had it. And hee that doth the beft he can in any thing, it is certaine he would doe better if he could. *Caine* contrariwife brought not the beft of his fruits, but either the worft, or whatfoeuer came firft to hand; as thinking that whatfoeuer hee brought, was good enough: therefore worthily is *Abel* faid to haue offered a better facrifice then *Cain.*

And further, this holy practife of *Abel*, came to be a law written, euen one of the commandements of the Ceremoniall law; namely, that *the firft borne fhould be offred to God,* Exod 34.19. And the *firft fruites of the corne,* Leuit. 23. 10. &c. And that *nothing that was lame, blind, maymed, or had any blemifh in it, fhould be offred to the Lord.* Deut. 15. 21. *Abel* here did euen that which thefe lawes commanded: and thefe lawes commanded the fame that he did. Thus God vouchfafed to honour his feruant *Abel*, for his obedient and honeft heart; euen to make his practife the ground and beginning of one of his owne lawes: that fo the Ifraelites in all their generations, might in their daily practifes, remember this worthy deede of holy *Abel* to his perpetuall honour.

Now for vs the truth is, this law bindes vs not: for it was a ceremony, & is ended in Chrift. Yet the equitie and vfe of it reacheth euen to vs: namely it teacheth vs when wee will giue any thing vnto God, to giue the beft wee haue. This is the equitie of thofe lawes ceremoniall, which commanded them to giue to the Lord their firft borne, and their firft fruites, and the fatteft of their cattell: and fo much of them doe ftill binde vs. Now from this rule, are taught diuerfe duties.

1. To the *Parent.* Haft thou many children, and wilt giue fome to the Lord? namely, to ferue him in the minifterie? The practife of the world, is to make the eldeft a Gentleman, the next a Lawyer, the next a Merchant: hee that is youngeft, or leaft regarded, or that hath fome infirmity in wit, or deformitie in bodie, fet him to fchoole, let him bee a Minifter. But *Abells* facrifice controlles this profane courfe of the world. Learne therefore by him, whomfoeuer of all thy children thou findeft fitteft in gifts and graces of bodie and minde; whom thou loueft beft, and moft efteemeft, he is fitteft for the Lord, and the Lord is moft worthy of him: confecrate him to the Lord, for his feruice in the minifterie.

2. To the *young man*. Hee beeing in the ſtrength and ripeneſſe of wit, ſenſes, memorie, capacity, and in the beſt of his age: he ſaith, I will take my pleaſure now I am fitteſt for it: I will repent at the end of my dayes, and that is a fitter time. This is a vile policie of the deuill, to diſhonour God, and to caſt away their ſoules. What a griefe is it to giue the deuill his young yeares, the ſtrength of his bodie and wit, and to bring his withered old age vnto God? nay, be ſure, *God* will not accept thy rotten ſacrifice of old age, but rather giue thee vp to the deuill, that he may haue thee altogether, which hath had the beſt: then follow rather *Salomons* counſell, Eccles. 12. 1. who bids thee *remember thy Creator in the dayes of thy youth:* Remember *Abels* ſacrifice, it was of the beſt. So, thou haſt no ſacrifice but thy ſelfe to offer: offer then the beſt: thy young yeares is the beſt time, giue them vnto God.

3. To all *Chriſtians*. *Abell* offred the beſt: it teacheth vs all, if wee will profeſſe and ſerue God, not to doe it by the halfes; or for ſhew and faſhion ſake, or negligently, as not caring how. Thus to doe, is but to offer the ſacrifice of *Cane*, and that makes the moſt profeſſors goe away with their ſeruice vnaccepted as *Cains* was: for God will haue all or none, hee is worthy to haue no partner: he muſt be ſerued with all the heart, with ſoule and bodie, ſo that a man muſt conſecrate himſelfe wholly vnto him. 2. King. 23. 25. It is the ſpeciall commendation of good King *Ioſias*, *that hee turned vnto the Lord with all his heart, and ſoule, and might:* and for that, hee is preferred afore all Kings afore or after him: not that *Ioſias* could fulfill the lawe perfectly, as it required; but it is meant of the endeuour of his heart and life, by which hee ſtraue with all his might to ſerue God as well as he could: his example is ours.

We profeſſe religion, wee muſt looke that our hearts affect it: we profeſſe a turning from ſinne, we muſt take heed it be not formall, and from the lips, but from the heart. So, when we practiſe any dutie of religion, whether we pray or heare the word, or receiue the Sacrament (this is the ſacrifice that we can offer) wee muſt not doe them coldly and careleſly; but with zealous affection & reſolution from the heart. Otherwiſe, if we ſerue God for faſhion ſake, and our hearts are on the world, and our owne luſts, wee offer the *ſacrifice* of curſed *Cain*, and wee with our formall religion ſhall goe to him. But let vs offer the *ſacrifice of Abell:* that is, though it bee neuer ſo little, yet let it bee the beſt wee can, and all wee can, and God will accept vs as hee did *Abell*. And thus the Parent ſhould giue God his *beſt childe:* the young man his *beſt yeares:* euery man his *beſt part*, which is his *heart*. And thus wee follow the ſteps of holy *Abell*, who offered to God *the beſt ſacrifice* hee had. This was the fruite of his faith: euen ſo that Parent, that young man, that profeſſor that hath true faith,

will doe ſo likewiſe.

Hitherto of the firſt effect of *Abells* faith: It followeth; *By the which hee obtained witneſſe that he was righteous*

This is the ſecond effect of *Abells* faith, whereby it is commended. 1. For the meaning. By *faith* hee meanes ſauing faith, which makes a man iuſt before God, and no other. For whereas hee had ſaid afore, that by faith our *Elders had obtained a good report:* Hee prooues that generall, by this example of *Abell*; therefore that ſauing faith which was meant there, is alſo meant here.

Theſe words ſet downe two benefits which *Abel* had by his ſauing faith: Firſt, he was *iuſt* by it. Secondly, God *teſtified* that he was ſo.

For the firſt: *Abels faith* made him *iuſt and righteous*, not becauſe his faith was an excellent quality of that vertue in it ſelfe, as to make him iuſt; but becauſe it was an inſtrument whereby hee apprehended and applied to himſelfe the righteouſneſſe of the Meſſias to come, whereby hee might ſtand iuſt before God. This was his righteouſneſſe, which hee had *by faith:* for hee truſted not to any holineſſe of his own, though (it is out of queſtion) hee knew hee was the ſonne of that man who once was perfectly righteous: but the truſt and confidence of his heart was in the righteouſneſſe of that bleſſed ſeed, which, God had promiſed, *ſhould breake the ſerpents head*. This Promiſe hee knowing, beleeued it, applied it to himſelfe, and this faith made him righteous.

Here we learne a worthy leſſon of Chriſtianity; namely, that the true and the vndoubted way to heauen, is a holy and liuely faith in Ieſus Chriſt: for, this faith makes a man righteous, and that righteouſneſſe opens him the gate of heauen. To this ende (ſaith the Apoſtle) *Beeing iuſtified by faith, wee haue peace with God:* but by whom; *through our Lord Ieſus Chriſt*.   Rom.5.1.

For the vſe of this doctrine, wee muſt renue our former exhortation, which indeede cannot bee too often preſſed to the conſcience. There is none of vs ſo vile, none ſo profane, but wee deſire ſaluation. If we doe, then we muſt tread the beaten way to it. For, we are not borne heires of it; neither can wee come thither by chaunce: but there is a way that muſt bee taken, and that way is but one: all other are miſleading by-waies. Againe, that way muſt be taken in this life; elſe, it is too late. Now, this way is to be a iuſt & righteous man. With this, neuer man failed: and without this, neuer man attained to ſaluation; for, *No vncleane thing can come into the kingdome of heauen.*   Apoc.21.27. Neuer was man iuſtified there, which was not iuſt before: & that muſt here be begũ, which in heauen is to be perfected. In this life therefore wee muſt ſeeke to be iuſt. Now, our good works will not ſerue to make vs iuſt: for they are all vnable to indure the triall of Gods iuſtice. And if we ſtand to them, and they prooue not able to satisfie Gods iustice ; then, in stead of sauing vs, they will condemne vs. Therefore with *Abell*, let vs goe out of our selues, denie our selues, and cleaue onely to Christs righteousnesse, in life and death: this is the way that neuer will deceiue vs.

But some will say, We walke in this way. I answer; He, that walketh in a way, may be traced by his steps: so then, shew your steps of holinesse, of deuotion, of charitie, &c. these must shew your faith: leaue these steps behinde you, and then your faith is good. Thus did holy *Abell*: beleeue thou it, acknowledge it, and follow thou after him: & renounce all by-paths which the Papists, or thy owne braine imagineth. Let this one doctrine sinke into thy heart in stead of many, and let not the deuill strake it out. For, if thou walke in this way, my soule for thine it will bring thee to heauen: if not, at the last day this doctrine will condemne thee, because it shewed thee this way, and thou wouldest not walke in it.

Secondly, obserue: He saith, *Abell* was *approoued* and accepted of God. How prooues he that? Because his works pleased God: as who say, his works cannot please God, vnlesse his person doe : therefore in that his workes doe, thence he concludeth that his person did: it is the reason of the holy Ghost, and therefore infallible.

In the framing of this reason, the holy Ghost teacheth vs a great point of our religion: namely, that first a mans person must please God afore his actions can. And after the person, then the actions. This is plaine in these words: for it is said, he *first obtained witnesse that hee was righteous* himselfe, and then *God testified of his gifts*: So likewise more plainely, Gen. 4. 4. God had respect *first to Abell, and then to his offring*: So that the truth is manifest, No work pleaseth God afore the worker doe. This beeing so, hath excellent vses.

First, it ouerthroweth a maine pillar of Romish religion: *Iustification by works*: For how can a man be iustified by his workes, when hee himselfe must be iust afore the works can be? Vnlesse he be iust, his works be wicked: if they be wicked afore his person be iust, how can they then iustifie him. And if the person be once iust, what needes it then to be againe iustified by workes? Good works make not a man good: but a good man makes a worke good: and shall that worke that a man made good, returne againe and make the man good? 1. That is absurd in reason: And 2. It is needelesse. For, the man is good alreadie: else the worke could not haue beene good. We may therefore say, workes are rather iustified by the person of a man, then his person by the workes : and it is a most vaine thing to looke for Iustification from that which thou thy selfe must first iustifie afore it be iust: if we had no other reasons against iustification by workes but this, this were sufficient.

Secondly, hence wee learne, that till a man bee called, and his person iustified and sanctified, all that euer he doth is sinne. 1. His *common actions*, his eating, drinking, sleeping, walking, talking, are all sinnes. Yea 2. the *workes of his calling*, and his labour in the same, though neuer so iust, equall, and vpright. 3. Further, his *ciuill actions*, namely, the practise of ciuill vertues : his outward grauitie, meekenesse, sobrietie, temperance, quietnesse, vprightnesse, and all outward conformitie, are all sinnes. Yea more then all this, his *best actions*, namely, his practising of the parts of Gods worship, or his deedes of charitie, his praier, his hearing the word, his receiuing of the sacraments, his giuing of almes; they are all sinnes vnto him, if he haue not a beleeuing and penitent heart : yea such sinnes as shall condemne him, if hee had no other. *Obiect.* This should seeme strange diuinitie, that the most holy actions, as praier, &c. should be damnable sinnes. I answer, they are in themselues holy and good, and as farre forth as God hath commanded them; yet in the doer they are sinnes, because he doth them from a foule and vnholy heart : for the same action may bee holy in it selfe, and in regard of God the author of it, and yet a sinne in him that is the doer of it. As cleere water, pure in the fountaine, is corrupted or poisoned by running thorough a filthie and polluted channell; so are euen the best actions, sinnes: as euen the preaching of the word to a minister, whose heart is not cleansed by faith, and his person accepted of God; it is a sinne vnto him, and (if he repent not) shall be his condemnation. *Cain* sinned not onely in hating and murthering his brother, in lying and dissembling with God; but *Caine* sinned also euen in offring sacrifice. And *Abels* sacrifice had bene a damnable sinne, but that his person was iustified before God. And the reason of all this is good; for nothing in the worke is able to make an action acceptable to God, but onely the acceptation of the person by Christ. This beeing so, it stands vs euery one in hand to looke to our selues; and to labour aboue all things for faith and repentáce: that so our persons may be accepted righteous before God, and thereby our actions accepted also. If it be a miserable thing, that all thy actions, euen holy actions should be sinnes, then labour to bee iustified; for that onely can make thy workes accepted: if not, then though thou labour neuer so much to be approoued in the world, and set neuer so glorious a shew vpon thy workes to the eyes of men, they are all abhominable sinnes in the sight of God: and at the day of iudgement they shal goe for no better. Preach, and teach all thy life long; nay, giue thy life to die for religion: giue all thy goods to the poore, depriue thy flesh of all delights : build Churches, Colledges, bridges, highwaies, &c. and there may come a poore shepheard, and for his keeping of his sheepe be accepted, when thou with all this pompe of outward holinesse, maist bee reiected. And why this? only becaufe hee had faith, and thou haft none; his perfon was iuftified before God, and thine is not. Therefore let this be my counfell, from *Abel*: Labour not fo much to worke glorious workes; as that which thou doeft, doe it in faith. Faith makes the meaneft worke accepted; and want of faith makes the moft glorious worke reiected: for fo faith the Text, *Abel muft be accepted, elfe his facrifice is not.* Thus wee fee *Abel* was iuft, and God fo accounted him. The fecond point is, That God gaue teftimonie hee was fo: In thefe words,

God giuing teftimonie.

What *teftimonie* it was that God gaue of *Abel* and his gift, it is not expreffed in the word; and fo it is not certaine: but it is very likely, that when hee and *Cain* offred, God in fpeciall mercy fent *fire from heauen*, and burnt vp *Abels* facrifice, but not *Cains*: for fo it pleafed the Lord often afterward when he would fhewe that he accepted any man, or his worke, he anfwered them by fire from heauen. So hee burnt vp the facrifice that *Aaron* offred, Leuit. *9.24.* So he anfwered *Salomon*, 2.Chron.*7.1*. And fo *Elias.*2. Kings, *18. 28.* And fo it is likely that he gaue this teftimonie that he accepted *Abel* and his offring. This was a great prerogatiue that *Abel* and the Fathers in the old teftament had. We haue not this, but wee haue a greater; for we haue that that is the fubftace, and truth, and bodie of this: For we haue alfo the fire of God, that is, his fpirit comes downe into our hearts euery day, not vifibly, but fpiritually, and burnes, vp in the heart of a beleeuer his finnes and corruptions, and lights the light of true faith, that fhall neuer be put out.

The vfe hereof is this; As no facrifice in the old law pleafed God, but fuch as was burnt by fire from heauen, fent downe either then or afore: fo our facrifices of the new Teftament (that is, our inuocation of Gods name, our facrifice of praife, our duties of religion, our workes of mercie and loue,) neuer pleafe God, vnleffe they proceede from a heart purged by the fire of Gods fpirit, that is, from a beleeuing and repentant heart: both which are kindled and lighted, and daily continued by that fire of Gods fpirit. Therefore it is, that *Paul* faith, 1. Tim. *1.4. that loue muft come out of a pure heart, and good confcience, and faith vnfained.* The duties of religion, and works of loue comming from this purged heart, afcend into the prefence of God, as a fmoake of moft acceptable facrifices, and are as a fweet perfume in the nofethrils of the Lord.

Now, of what did God thus teftifie? *Of his gift.*

It may here be asked at the firft: how can *Abel* giue *a gift* to God: hath the Lord neede of any thing; and are not al things his? I anfwer, God is foueraigne Lord of heauen and earth, and all creatures: yet hath he fo giuen his creatures vnto man to vfe, as that they becom mans

owne, and fo he may efteeme and vfe them: and beeing mans, a man may in token of his thankfulneffe returne them againe to God; efpecially feeing God accepts them beeing fo offred, as moft free gifts.

This fheweth vs, firft, the wonderfull mercie of God, that whereas wee can offer him nothing but his owne, he vouchfafeth to accept a gift offered of his own, euen as though we had of our owne to offer.

2. See here a difference betwixt the facrifices of the old, and Sacraments of the newe Teftament. In their facrifices they gaue fomething to God, and therefore they are called *gifts*: in our Sacraments wee receiue daily grace from God.

3. In that the facrifices of the old Law are called *gifts*, wee muft knowe that it is typicall, and hath excellent fignifications vnto vs.

1. It fignifieth, that the Meffias fhould bee giuen of God freely, for the faluation of his elect: and that Chrift the Meffias fhould willingly giue himfelfe to be a redeemer.

2. It fignifieth, that euery man that lookes for faluation by Chrift, muft giue himfelfe to God, and all that is in him. So *Paul* exhorteth, Rom. *6. 13. Giue your felues vnto God, and your members weapons of righteoufneffe.* When we giue any thing to a man, we make him Lord of it. If we then giue our foules and bodies to the Lord, we muft giue them fo, as that they may obey and ferue him, and be ruled by him, and ferue for his glory, howfoeuer he fhall vfe them. We profeffe religion, and make great fhewes; but to giue our felues in obedience to God, is the life of religion: But contrary is the courfe of the world. For, moft profeffors are giuen vp to finne and Satan: *their bodies* giuen to drinking, gaming, vncleaneffe, iniuftice; *their foules* to enuying, hatred, malice, reuenge, luft, pride, felfe-loue: God hath nothing except it be *a face*: but that will not ferue the turne: hee will haue all, *bodie and foule*; for he made all, and he redeemed all. We goe againft equitie; Chrift gaue his bodie and foule for vs: why fhould we not giue ours againe to him? Againe, this gift is not as other gifts; for here all the profit redounds to the giuer: the glorie indeed is his; but the gaine & profit is our owne. Why then fhould we withhold our felues from God? it argueth, we knowe nor feele not, what Chrift hath giuen vs: for if wee did, if we had 10000. liues, wee would thinke them all too little for him.

And thus much of the firft and fecond effect of *Abels* faith; the third followeth.

By which Abel *beeing dead, yet fpeaketh.*

The 3.*effect*, whereby *Abels faith* is commended, is laide downe in thefe words. Concerning the meaning whereof there is fome difference, which is briefly to be examined. Some thinke the words fhould be thus tranflated, *By which alfo* Abel *beeing dead, is yet fpoke of*; making

the

the meaning to be, that by his faith he obtained a good name to all posterities: but it seemes this cannot stand, for two causes: First, because that is alreadie affirmed of *Abel* and all the rest, in the second verse, that *through faith they had obtained a good report*: which therefore might seeme needeles so soone to be repeated againe. Secondly, for that afterward Christs blood and *Abels* beeing compared together, it is not said that Christs blood is *better spoken of* the *Abels*, but that it *speaketh better things* the *Abels* did. Therefore the words are rightly translated.

Now for the true sense of them, it is likely the holy Ghost here hath relation to the storie whence it is taken; where, vpon *Cains* murther God saith to him, *The voice of thy brothers blood crieth to me from the earth:* and why crieth ir? Namely, for vengance against so monstrous a murder; and crieth to all men to behold it, & to abhor the like: and so after a sort he continueth to speake, to this day. So that the words, in the true and full sense of them, doe import these two points;

   1. That *Abel spake* when he was *dead*.
   2. That in a sort *Abel still speaketh*.

For the first: *Abel spake* and cried *when hee was dead:* but how? not with a vocall speach: but the phrase is figuratiue, and imports thus much, as if the Lord had said to *Caine:* thou hast killed thy brother closely, and it may bee hast hid him in the sand, or buried him, and thinkest no man knoweth of it: but thou must know *Cain*, this thy fact is euident to me, as if *Abel* had told me; I know thou killedst him: and if thou wonder how I knowe, I tell thee his blood told me; for it cried in my eares, and yet it crieth out against thee: for though *Abel* bee dead, his blood yet speaketh. As this is true of *Abels*, so of all mens *blood:* and as of *blood*, so of all other *oppressions*, though done by neuer so great men. Murders, oppressions, and all wrongs done to Gods children, they crie to God against the oppressors, though the poore oppressed men dare scarce name them; they neede not, for their blood doth; yea euen their very *teares* cannot be shed, but *God takes them vp, and puts them in his bottle*, and will knowe who shed them. Thus blood crieth against them that shed it, yea teares crie against them that cause them. This affordeth vs a double instruction. First, here it is apparant that God seeth & knoweth the sinnes of men, though the men be neuer so mighty, or their sinnes neuer so secret. For though men conuay them neuer so closly, and labour to hide them with all the meanes that the wit of man can deuise: yet the very dead creatures crie out, and doe proclaime the sinnes and sinners in the eares of God, as fully as the voices of liuing men, can discouer any thing vnto men. Priuy oppressions, and goods gotten by deepe deceit, lie hidde to the world: But *the stone out of the wall shall crie, and the beame out of the timber shall answer it; Woe be to him that buildeth his house with* blood, and erects a Citie by iniquitie: as though he had saide, God knoweth euery stone and euery piece of timber in their stately houses, which they haue gotten by deceite or oppressing of the poore. Priuy conspiracies, and plots of treason are laid against Princes and Magistrates; and often in so secret manner, as in mans reason is not possible to be discouered. But God hath many wayes to finde them out, and they neuer scape his priuie search: and therefore the holy Ghost aduiseth; *Curse not the King, no not in thy thought, nor the great ones in thy bedchamber: for the fowle of the heauen shall carie thy voyce, and that which hath wings shall declare the matter.* So that whatsoeuer is plotted neuer so priuily, or conspired in the secret closets of vngodly men, God knowes it, and hath meanes enow to disclose it to the world. And in our daily experience God magnifieth himselfe mightily in reuealing murders. For, bring the murtherer before the dead corps, and vsually it *bleedeth*, or giueth some other testimonie, whereby it *speaketh* euen as *Abels* blood did, *This is the murtherer*. Nay more: for, *Abels* blood spake to God, but here euen to men also.

And of this it is hard to giue any reason at all, but the secret and immediate hand of God, thereby shewing himselfe to know all secret sinnes, and to be able to disclose them by strange meanes.

The vse of this doctrine is, to feare all men from sinning, though they thinke it possible to conceale their sinnes from the world: for this is one of the strongest & commonest encouragements that men take, to liue in a sinne, If they thinke it likely to be concealed. But here they see how false a ground that is. For if they can conceale it from men, yet can they not from God: and if God know it, then can he reueale it to the world when it pleaseth him.

Againe, whereas *Abels blood cried when hee was dead;* It teacheth vs, that God had a care of *Abel* both liuing and dead: for it were nothing to say his *blood cried*, if God heard not that cry. But it is apparant he heard it, for he reuenged it, and punished *Cain* when *Abel* was dead, and could not reuenge it himselfe. And this care God had not ouer *Abel* alone, but ouer all his children: and as the Psalmist saith, *Pretious in the sight of the Lord is the death of his Saints:* that which is vile, & of no regard in the world, is pretious with God. Tyrants make hauocke of the Church, and kill them vp by heapes; but God records vp euery one, and will not faile to reuenge it, when they are dead: For if God haue bottles for the teares of his seruants, surely much more hath hee bottles for their blood.

The vse whereof is to teach vs in all extremities of danger or distresse, to learne patience: yea, though we be sure to die, yet (as Christ saith) *To possesse our soules with patience:* For we haue one, will heare the cause, and reuenge our quarrell when we are gone: So that if wee

be

be patient we looſe nothing; but if we be impatient we get nothing. Let vs therefore hold our tongues : for, the *wrong* done to vs *crieth* loud enough to God for reuēge, who wil hēare it as aſſuredly as he did *Abels*. And thus we ſee how *Abel* ſpake then, euen after he was dead.

The ſecond point is, *He ſpeakes alſo yet*: and that three wayes.

Firſt, his faith yet ſpeaketh, becauſe it admoniſheth all men euery where, who either heare or reade this ſtorie, to become ſuch as *Abel* was, namely, true worſhippers of the true God: for, in *Abels* example, it prouokes all men to be like him, becauſe it aſſureth them of the ſame regard and reward with God that *Abell* had : and ſo *Abels* faith is a neuer dying Preacher to all ages of the Church.

Here we learne, that the holy Examples of Gods children are reall teaching, and loude preaching to other men.

For there is a double teaching, namely, in { word, or deede.

It belongs to the *Miniſter* to teach in word; and to *all men* to teach by their deedes, and good exāples. And if the miniſter teach not thus alſo, it is the worſe both for him & his hearers.

It ſufficeth not for him to teach by *vocall Sermons*, that is, by good doctrine; but withall by *reall Sermons*, that is, by good life: His faith, his zeale, his patience, his mercy, and all other his vertues muſt ſpeake, and cry, and call to other men to be like vnto him: which, if he practiſe carefully in his life as *Abel* did, then ſhall his vertues ſpeak for him to all poſterities when he is dead.

Againe, *Abel* though *dead*, may be ſaid *to ſpeake*, becauſe howſoeuer his bodie be dead, yet in ſoule and ſpirit hee liueth with God in heauen. And thus the word *ſpeaketh* may bee vnderſtood, becauſe it is here oppoſed to *death*: by *which he beeing dead, yet ſpeaketh*: that is, being dead in bodie, yet liueth in ſoule: which life with God, was obtained vnto by his true and ſauing faith.

Thirdly, he may be ſaid *to ſpeake yet*, as all other Gods Martyrs are ſaid *to crie* in the Reuelation, *from vnder the altar*, *How long Lord holy and true doeſt thou not auenge our blood on them that dwell on the earth*; As this is true of *all* Martyrs, ſo ſpecially of *Abell* the *firſt Martyr* of all: which words are not ſpoken, neither by him nor them *vocally* with vtterance of voice : but it is ſo ſaid, to ſignifie what feruent deſire the ſeruants of God haue in heauen, of the full manifeſtation of Gods glorie *in their bodies*, and of an vtter aboliſhment of ſinne in *the whole world*. Which their deſire, they doubtleſſe vtter to God in a more excellent manner, then in this world we can vtter any thing with our voice: and thus *Abel ſpeaks yet*, & ſhal ſpeak till the worlds end.

Hitherto of the *firſt* Example, the Example of *Abel*.

Reuel. 6. 10.

The ſecond is of Henoch in theſe words,

By faith Henoch was tranſlated, that he ſhould not ſee death, neither was he found, for God tooke him away: for, before he was tranſlated, hee was reported of that he had pleaſed God, &c.

THe *ſecond example of faith*, is taken alſo out of the old world, before the flood; and it is of *Henoch* the ſeauenth from *Adam*: to whom, ſtrange and miraculous things befell, by reaſon of his faith. Let the meaning of the words be firſt examined.

By faith,

That is, by his confidence in the Meſſias, or his ſauing faith, he was taken away.

Taken away,

That is, from earth to heauen, not by an ordinarie worke, but miraculouſly ; is is euident by the next words.

That he ſhould not ſee death,

That is, that he ſhould not feele death, nor any diſſolution of ſoule and bodie: and therefore his taking away was *miraculous*. For to be taken away by death is an ordinarie worke; but to be taken away, and yet not die, that is miraculous and extraordinary: & ſuch was *Henochs*.

So then the ſubſtance of theſe words is thus much; *Henoch* hauing this grace from God, *to beleeue* ſtedfaſtly in the *Meſſias* to come, was likewiſe honoured with this high prerogatiue, To be taken into heauen, without taſting of death, and to the ende that he might not die. Thus we haue the meaning.

Now concerning this *tranſlation of Henoch*: there are two opinions,

Some thinke he was tranſlated *in ſoule onely*, and not in bodie: and they ſay he died in the tranſlation, ſo as his ſoule onely was taken vp into heauen, and his bodie ſlept in the earth. Though this appeares falſe at the firſt ſight, yet let vs ſee their reaſons, and what they can ſay for themſelues.

Their firſt reaſon is this; No mortall bodie *vnglorified* can enter into heauen ; but there is no mention of his glorification : therefore his bodie could not come in heauen,

Anſwer. It is certaine it was glorified ere it came in heauen. If they reply, it is not mentioned: I anſwer it followeth not, that therefore it was not: for euery circumſtance of euery action is not mentioned. For many circūſtances of actions muſt neceſſarily be ſuppoſed, & ſuch a one was this. Againe, the glorification of his bodie is here plainely enough implied where it is ſaid, he was tranſlated, that he ſhould not ſee

death.

death. Now, if his bodie saw not death, it was made immortall, which is a speciall part of glorification.

Their second reason. Chriſt was the the firſt that euer entred into heauen both in bodie and soule; and for proofe thereof, they bring S.Paul where he saith , *Chriſt is the firſt fruits of them that sleepe.*

1.Cor.15.20.

Answer. True indeede *of them that sleepe,* that is , *of all that die :* for Chriſt entred into heauen both in body and soule firſt of all them: but *Henoch* neuer died; as the Text here auoucheth: therefore that place hinders not, but *Henoch* might be in heauen in his bodie, before Chriſts humane fleſh aſcended thither.

Thirdly, they argue out of Saint Iohn: *No man hath aſcended into heauen, but he that deſcended ; the sonne of man , which is in heauen.* But say they, this son of man is not *Henoch,* but *Chriſt:* therefore none but Chriſt aſcended bodily into heauen.

Answer. That place is not meant of *corporall aſcending ,* but of *vnderſtanding myſticall and heauenly things :* no man aſcendeth to the full knowledge of heauēly miniſteries, but Chriſt alone, who deſcēded frō the boſom of his father.

And thus we see , this opinion hath no ſtrength of Argument to reſt vpon: but we may safely hold (notwithſtanding any thing that can be said againſt it) that *Henoch* was tranſlated both in bodie and soule. And if any man yet doubt , how he could be taken vp in bodie before he was glorified ; Wee are to knowe, though he he died not, yet his bodie was changed, as thoſe men ſhall be, *which ſhall be found aliue at the laſt day.*

1.Cor.15.51.

The second opinion is, that *Henoch* was taken vp in soule and bodie *into Paradiſe*(some say, the heauenly, but the moſt the earthly Paradiſe) and there liues in his mortall and corruptible bodie, and muſt afore the laſt day come againe in his bodie with *Elias,*and fight againſt Antichriſt : and when by their doctrine they haue ouercome him , he ſhall by violence kill them, and so they ſhall die Martyrs : And this is the generall receiued opinion of the moſt Papiſts. But it is a meere conceit, and a dreame, and there is no ground for it: but good argument againſt it.

For firſt, as for the *Earthly Paradiſe,* it was defaced by the flood; nor doe we read that euer man was in it but *Adam.*And some of their owne fables tell vs that *Seth* went to the gates of Paradiſe, when his father o *Adam* was ſicke, to get some Phyſicke out of Paradiſe for his father, but he could not get in:Nor doe we finde any mention of it afterwards So that it is likely in all reaſon, that it was defaced by the vniuerſall flood.

And if they mean, he was tranſlated into the *heauenly Paradiſe;* I anſwer, *thither can no vnclean thing come:*but a mortal bodie is vnclean: and themſelues say , he was taken away in his mortall bodie , and in it ſhall come againe and die. Therefore *Henoch* hauing a mortall and vnglorified bodie, cannot be in the higheſt heauens; into which nothing can enter which is not glorified and made immortall.

If they alleadge Eccleſiaſt. 44. 16. *Enoch pleaſed God,& was tranſlated into Paradiſe,&c.*

I anſwer: we neede not call in queſtion the authoritie of the booke , nor anſwer that it is not in the Canon of faith. For the text is corrupted wilfully by some that ſhewed themſelues in the *latine* too bold with the text, both there and elſewhere:for in the *Greeke* originall, there is no ſuch matter as *Paradiſe ;* but the words are theſe : *Enoch pleaſed God ; and was tranſlated for an example of repentance to the generations.* And thus we see , this opinion is euery way erroneous , and hath no ſhadow of reaſon in it, nor for it.

Seeing therefore both theſe opinions are to be refuſed , let vs in few words ſet downe the true & Orthodoxall iudgement of the Church, out of the Scriptures in the olde and new teſtament. And it is this: That this holy man, by Gods ſpeciall fauour to him, was aſſumed into heauen both bodie and soule; his soule beeing perfectly ſanctified , and his bodie glorified in the inſtant of his tranſlation : and there he remaineth in glorie, expecting the generall reſurrection, and the full glorification of all Gods elect.

Out of this tranſlation of *Henoch ,* we may learne;

Firſt, that there is *a life euerlaſting* prepared of God for his children, wherein they ſhall liue for euer both in soule and bodie ; for hereof hath God giuen vs moſt euident teſtimonies, both here in *Enoch ,* and afterward in *Elias: Elias* a Iew , *Enoch* none : *Enoch* in the firſt world , *Elias* in the second : *Enoch* before the flood, *Elias* after: *Enoch* vncircumciſed , *Elias* circumciſed : *Enoch* married, *Elias* vnmarried, and both were aſſumed into heauen in soule and bodie , and are there to this day, and tarry for vs till the ende of the world; aſſuring vs that our *soules* liue for euer : and that our *bodies,* though they die, ſhall riſe againe to life. Here therefore we haue a notable ground for that laſt (but not the leaſt) article of our faith, where we profeſſe *to beleeue life euerlaſting.*

2. King.

Secondly , in this example we learne, that *God is not tied to the order of Nature.* The order which God eſtabliſhed and ſet downe concerning all men after *Adams* fall is this : *Duſt thou art , and to duſt ſhalt thou returne.* By vertue of this decree, all men are to die, as ſure as they once liued; and when that time appointed by God is come, all the world cannot ſaue one man, but accordingly die he muſt. But here notwithſtanding we see, God that tied man to this order, is not tied himſelfe. *Enoch* and *Elias* are exempted, they die not, their bodies neuer turned to duſt; ſuch is the power of God ouer the order of Nature, in all naturall actions.

Gen.3.19.

Thirdly, whereas the Papiſts holde , that all

the

the Fathers who died before Chriſt, were in *Limbus* (a place out of heauen) and came not in heauen till Chriſt fetcht them thence, & carried them with him at his aſcenſion; Here wee learne it is moſt falſe and forged. For here wee ſee, *Henoch*, and afterwards *Elias* were in heauen both in bodie and ſoule, many hundred yeares before Chriſts Incarnation: whereby (as alſo by many other euidences that might bee brought) it is apparant, that *Limbus Patrum* is nothing but a deuiſe of that heretical Church of Rome.

Hitherto hath the holy Ghoſt *auouched* the tranſlation of *Henoch*. Now he *prooueth* ſubſtantially, that he was taken away.

Neither was he found, for God had taken him away:

And for his proofe, he firſt laieth downe *his ground*: then hee thereupon frameth *his argument*, conſiſting of diuers degrees of demonſtration.

The *ground* is, the plaine and euident teſtimonie of the old Teſtament in Geneſis; where the words are theſe: *Henoch was not found, or not ſeene, for God tooke him away*. Againſt this ground, beeing the very words of the olde Teſtament, no man can take exception. And here in a word, let vs all marke the high and ſoueraigne authoritie of Gods word, which euen the *holy Ghoſt* himſelfe vouchſafeth to alledge for the confirmation of his owne words. It had beene ſufficient that the holy Ghoſt here affirmed *Enoch* to be taken away: but we ſee hee prooues it out of the old Teſtament, ſo alſo did the *Apoſtles*, and *Chriſt* himſelfe all their doctrine.

Let this teach all men to giue due reuerence to the holy ſcriptures: let teachers *alledge* them, let hearers *receiue* them farre aboue all humane teſtimonies, ſeeing the holy Ghoſt himſelfe vouchſafeth to confirme his owne words by the authoritie thereof.

Secondly, hauing laide this *ground*, the holy Ghoſt frames his *argument*, to prooue that *Henoch* was taken away by faith: and it conſiſteth of many degrees of euidence.

- For before he was taken away, he was reported of that he had pleaſed God.

But without faith, it is impoſſible to pleaſe God.

The degrees of the argument are theſe;
1. *God himſelfe tooke* Henoch *away.*
2. *Before he was taken away, he pleaſed God.*
3. *But without faith no man can pleaſe God.*
Therefore Henoch *by faith was taken away.*

The firſt degree, *That* Henoch *was taken away*, and was not found any more in this world, hath beene ſufficiently ſpoken of alreadie.

The ſecond degree is, that *afore he was taken away, hee pleaſed God*: which is not barely affirmed, but it is further added, that *he was reported of*, or he *receiued teſtimonie*, that he pleaſed God.

Now, this report or teſtimonie is taken out of the ſtorie of *Geneſis*, where it is affirmed of *Enoch*, that *he walked with God*: which *walking with God*, is an aſſured teſtimonie that *he pleaſed God*; for (as the Prophet *Amos* ſaith) *Can two walke togetheir vnleſſe they be agreed*: therefore in as much as *Henoch walked with God*, it is proofe ſufficient, that *he pleaſed God*: and becauſe he *pleaſed God*, therefore God *tooke him away*. So that here are two diſtinct points in the ſecond degree; Firſt, that *Henoch* pleaſed God: Secondly, that there is a report or a teſtimonie giuen of him, that he did pleaſe God.

In the firſt let vs obſerue three ſpeciall points of inſtruction.

Firſt, in that *Henoch*, before he was taken away, pleaſed God: let vs learne, that whoſoeuer lookes to haue his ſoule tranſlated into heauen at his death, and both bodie and ſoule at the reſurrection; muſt before hand in this life learne *to pleaſe God*: they muſt ſeeke to pleaſe God, not when the time of tranſlation is come; but *before*, as here it is ſaide *Henoch* did.

If any man demaund, *How ſhall I pleaſe God?* My anſwer is this: *Adam* pleaſed God by keeping *the Law*: but now that is paſt, that power is loſt: we muſt now *pleaſe God* by direction from *the Goſpel*; namely, by faith in Chriſt & true repentãce, together with a holy life (which muſt neceſſarily accompanie true faith and repentance) thus God is pleaſed. And this muſt we not deferre till our death; but doe it in our liues; nor can we looke to be inheritours of the kingdome of glorie as now *Henoch* is, vnleſſe before hand we be in the kingdome of grace, *by pleaſing God as Henoch did*. It is lamentable, to ſee men not care for ſaluation till death, and then they *begin to pleaſe God*: but alas, *God will not be ſo pleaſed*. They begin to learne how to *pleaſe God*, whẽ they haue ſo long *diſpleaſed* him, as there is then feare they can *neuer pleaſe* him: but that man liueth and dieth with comfort, of whom it may be ſaid as here of *Henoch*, *before he was taken away he pleaſed God*.

Againe, whereas he came not in *heauen* till he pleaſed *God*; this diſcouers the madneſſe of ſinnefull men, who will looke for heauen, and yet will leaue no ſinne, but flatter themſelues therein. But, let all impenitent men here take knowledge that they come not in heauen till they pleaſe God: let them therefore ceaſe *pleaſing themſelues* and their corruptions, by liuing in ſinne, and learne to *pleaſe God* by a holy life.

And further: In this point mark how nothing brought *Henoch* to heauen, but his *pleaſing of* God. He was *rich*, for he was one of the greateſt on the earth: he was *royallie deſcended*, for hee was the ſeauenth from *Adam* in the bleſſed line: he was *learned*, for he had the ſixe firſt Patriarkes to teach him, ſixe ſuch *Tutors* as neuer man had: and it is likely he had a comely, ſtrong, and actiue bodie. But ſee, all theſe brought him not to heauen: no, he pleaſed God, and was *therefore taken away*.

Let

Let this teach vs not to reſt in wealth, beauty, ſtrength, honour, humane learning, nor all theſe put together without the feare of God: for ſome of them may pleaſe *thy ſelfe*, and ſome may pleaſe *other men*; but God muſt be pleaſed afore thou come in heauen, if thou wert as good as *Henoch*. Therefore vnto all thy outward bleſſings adde this, To *pleaſe God* by faith and repentance. Then as thy pleaſing of *men* may make thee happy in this world: ſo thy *pleaſing of God*, ſhall tranſlate thee from earth to heauen.

Thus we ſee, *Henoch before he was tranſlated pleaſed God.*

Secondly, as he *pleaſed God*, and elſe could could not haue beene, *tranſlated*; ſo it is added, he *was ſo reported of, or there was ſuch a teſtimonie of him.* That proofe or *teſtimonie* is here concealed; but it is recorded in the ſtorie of Geneſis, where it is ſaid *Henoch walked with God*: which, as we heard before, was an aſſured teſtimonie that God was well pleaſed with him.

But what is this, *he walked with God*: how can a man bee ſaide to walke with God? The meaning is, That *Henoch* liued a godly, righteous, and innocent life in this world: for to liue in holineſſe and righteouſneſſe, is to *walke with God.* And further, his heart was poſſeſſed of two perſwaſions or reſolutions, which were the inducements drawing him to this holy life.

Firſt, that he was alwayes *in Gods preſence*, and that God is alwayes readie to diſpoſe of all things to his good.

Againe, that God did *ſee*, trie, and diſcerne all his *wordes* and *deedes*, yea his cogitations and thoughts, and the whole courſe of his life. Theſe were the holy *reſolutions* of *Henoch*, and theſe made him lead a holy life.

This leſſon is worth learning, and this example worthy to be followed of vs all: our dutie is with *Henoch*, to *walke with God* in this life; if we purpoſe to liue with God in heauen: and *we walke with God* by leading holy and vnblameable liues, in *holineſſe* towards God, and *righteouſneſſe* towards man. But if wee thinke this hard to doe, we muſt labour to be reſolued on theſe grounds: *Firſt*, that God and his prouidence is euer preſent with vs, to diſpoſe of vs alwaies to his glorie, & of all other things to our good.

Secondly, that as we are in Gods preſence; ſo God ſeeth vs, and all our thoughts, words and workes, bargaines and dealings, and will iudge them all.

When theſe two perſwaſions poſſeſſe our hearts, it cannot be, but wee ſhall liue godly, and feare to offend God: for, as a childe is dutifull and obedient in his Fathers preſence; ſo when a man is perſwaded, he is in Gods preſence, it cannot but make him dutifull. When a man is perſwaded that God ſeeth him, he will take heed what he doth; and that God heareth

him, he will temper his tongue; and that God beholdeth all his dealings in the world, he will take heede how he borroweth, lendeth, buieth, or ſelleth, and what he doth in all his actions: and the very cauſe of all careleſneſſe in theſe and all other duties in the world, is, becauſe men are perſwaded *God ſeeth them not.*

To vrge vs therefore to this excellent dutie; we haue, Firſt, *Gods commandement: Walke before me and be vpright* (ſaith God) to *Abraham*, and in him to all the children of his faith.

Againe, we haue *the examples* of Gods children, who are renowned for the obedience of this *Commaundement; Henoch* here, after him *Abraham*, and after him *Dauid*, who teſtifieth of himſelfe, *I will walke before God in the land of the liuing.*

Thirdly, as it is both *commaunded* by precept, and *practiſed* by example: ſo the *proofe* of it is moſt comfortable to all that practiſe it; for it will make them *proſper* in all they goe about. For, as he that is alwaies in the *Kings preſence* and companie, cannot but be in his fauour, and therefore cannot but ſucceede well in all his affaires: ſo he that walkes with God, cannot but proſper in whatſoeuer he ſets his heart and hand vnto. Bleſſed *Abraham* found this moſt true, when he aſſured his ſeruant whom he ſent to prouid *Iſaac* a wife, in a long, and doubtfull, and dangerous iourney; *The Lord, before whom I walke, will ſend his Angell with thee, and proſper thy iourney:* and euen ſo may euery child of God ſay with confidence: *The Lord, before whom I walke, will ſend his Angell with mee, and proſper mee in my proceedings.*

Fourthly, this *walking with god* is a good meanes to make a man *beare the croſſe with patience:* For if he be perſwaded that God ſeeth how wrongfully he is perſecuted or oppreſſed, and that Gods prouidence is alwaies preſent, ſo as no affliction can come vnto him, but by his appointment: and againe, that his prouidence diſpoſeth of all things to his good, how can he but receiue with patience that portion of afflictions which God ſhall lay vpon him? For as he that walks with the King, who dare offer him wrong? ſo he that walks with God, what euill can touch him? This is *Ioſephs* argument to his brethren, when they were diſcomforted, and feared he would puniſh them after their Fathers death: *Feare not* (ſaith he) for *am not I vnder God?* as though he had ſaide, Doe not I walke in Gods preſence? and acknowledge my ſelfe vnder his power? and that God, which you thoght euil againſt me, dipoſed it to good: where the ground of *Ioſephs* reaſon is; that hee *walking with God, his affliction turned to his good.*

Laſtly, this is a meanes to bring a man to *make conſcience of all ſinne*, in thought, word, and deede, and in all his dealings, when he perſwades himſelfe to walk in the preſence of god. When *Ioſeph* was allured to ſin by his miſtreſſe, his anſwer was, *How ſhall I commit this great*

Gen.17.1.

Pſal.116.9.

Gen.25.40.

wickednesse, and so sinne against God? The bridle that restrained him, was the feare of that God in *whose presence he walked*: And because hee *walked with God*, he would not *walke with her* in her wicked way: and because hee kept a holy company *with God*, therefore hee would not keepe *her company*, nor be allured by her temptations.

So then seeing this way of *walking with God*, is euery way so excellent and so profitable, let vs learne it not in iudgement and knowledge onely, to be able to talke of it (which is soone learned): but in conscience and practise (as dutifull children doe before their parents, so) let vs in a heauenly awe and a child-like reuerence walke before God, labouring for a true perswasion of his presence and prouidence, to bee alwayes ouer vs and our whole liues. The want hereof is the cause of all sinne: And if we doe *thus walke with God*, and so please him, as *Henoch* here did, then shall we be sure (though not after the same manner that *Henoch* was, yet) in soule first, and afterwards in soule and bodie both, to be translated into eternall life. But if we will not *walke* this way with *Henoch* in this life, let vs neuer looke to liue in heauen with him; but assure our selues, that as the way of holinesse is the way to glorie, so the way of wickednesse is the way to eternall perdition. And thus much of the second degree.

> *But without faith it is impossible to please God.*

These words containe the third degree, or the third part of the reason. And this degree consists of a generall Maxime or Canon of *Diuinitie*: and the holy Ghost *first* layeth it down; and *then*, because it is one of the wayghtiest principles in religion, he proueth it substantially, in the words following. In the Canon it selfe let vs first examine the meaning, and then vnfold the manifold vse of it.

> *Without faith.*

By *faith*, is meant here the same *faith* as afore; namely, true *sauing faith* in the Messias. And without this sauing faith,

> *It is impossible to please God.*

Impossible how? not in regard of the absolute, infinite, and indeterminable *power* of God, which hath no limits, but his owne *will*: but in regard of that order of the causes and meanes of saluation set downe by God in his word: which is this;

1. Man by sinne hath displeased God.
2. God must be pleased againe, els a man cannot be saued.
3. He that will please God, must please him in Christ the Mediator, els he cannot: therefore he that will please God, and be saued, must needes beleeue *in Christ*. And thus by this order it is impossible. We denie not, but in regard of Gods absolute power, he could saue a man without faith; as he can lighten the world without the Sunne. But as (if he keepe that order of *nature*, which his owne *wisdome* hath ap-

pointed) it is impossible to giue light to the world without the Sunne: so (if he keepe that order for *saluation*, which his owne *Iustice* hath appointed) it is *impossible to please god without faith in Christ*. So then the meaning is laid downe: and now appeares the strength and force of the holy Ghosts argument;

> *He that will be saued and come to heauen, must first please god: But without faith it is impossible to please god: Therefore without faith no man can be saued nor come in heauen: and by consequent, therefore* Henoch *beeing taken into heauen, must needes be taken away by faith.*

Now the vse of this Canon, rightly vnderstood, is manifold and of great profit.

First, here we learne that *faith* is simply and absolutely *necessarie* to saluation, and most necessarie of all other gifts and graces of God whatsoeuer. And though many be required, yet amongst all holy graces this is the principall, and more necessarie in some respects, then any other. For howsoeuer *hope, and loue, and zeale*, and many other graces of God are required, to make the state of a Christian complete; and though they all haue their seuerall commendations in the world: yet, of none of them all is it said in the whole Scripture, as it is here said of faith, that *without it, it is impossible to please god.* And no meruaile, for it is the roote and ground of all other graces, and giues them their life and beeing: for therefore doth a man *feare* God, therefore doth he *loue* God, therefore is he *zealous* for Gods glorie, because he beleeueth that God loueth him in Christ the redeemer.

Now then if *faith* be thus necessarie, then it followeth that those that liue in *ignorance*, and so haue no sound faith, but a foolish *presumption*, are in a miserable case: for how euer they may flatter themselues with conceits of their *deuotions*, and good *meanings*, & good *intents*; it is *faith*, with which they must please God, and nothing can without it. It stands them therefore in hand to lay off ignorance and presumption, and labour for a sound and sauing faith, and that will bring them to the fauour of God.

And againe, as for such as haue receiued *grace to beleeue*, seeing *faith* is of such necessitie, and that they hauing *faith* must needs haue *knowledge*, they therefore must looke and examine by their knowledge, whether their faith be a sound faith or no: for herein many that haue knowledge deceiue themselues, & thinke they haue true faith when they haue not. Now if any man would know, whether his faith be sound, and sauing, or no; it is knowne by this: If it purifie the heart: for so saith S. *Peter, That god by faith did purifie the heart of the profane and filthie Gentiles*. If then thy faith doe not *purifie thy heart*, and cleanse thy life, and cause thee to abound in good workes, it is no sound nor sauing faith, it is but a generall faith, it is but an historicall knowledge, & cannot saue the foule : he therefore that vpon examination of his heart and life, findeth his *faith* to bee such, let him not content himselfe, but turne his generall *faith* into a sauing *faith*, which in this world will *purifie his heart*, and at the last day will *saue his soule*. And this must euery man the rather doe, because what knowledge, or what other gifts of God soeuer any many hath, without *faith* in Christ all are nothing : for it is faith that seasoneth them all, and makes both them and the person himselfe to pleafe God.

Secondly, if it be *impoſſible without faith to pleaſe God*, then here wee see the fond and foolish hypocrifie of the world, who will pleafe God by other meanes : some thinke if they bee glorious in the world, either for their wealth, or their wit, or their honour, or their authority, or their learning, they presently bring themselues into a fooles Paradise ; and because the world makes account of them, and they pleafe themselues, therefore they thinke it certaine, they *muſt needes pleaſe God*. But alas, though all the world admire them, and they be neuer so farre in loue with themselues, *He that ſits in heauen, laugheth them to ſcorne*. For, not all the pompe and glorie, nor all the millions and mountaines of gold in the world, can *pleaſe the Lord* for one of the least of their many thousand sinnes, wherewith they haue prouoked him. Let these men aske *Nabuchadnezzer* if his pompous *pride* : or *Achitophel* if his actiue head, and crafty *wit* : or *Abſalom* if his *golden lockes* : or *Iezabell* if her *painted face* and courtly attire : or *Naball* if his *flockes of ſheepe* : or the *Philoſophers*, if their naturall *learning* : if all of these, or any of these did *euer pleaſe God* : Nay alas, they all haue found and felt, that *without faith it is impoſſible to pleaſe God*.

Thirdly, it is the opinion not of the *Turke* alone in his Alcaron, but of many other as ill, that euery man shall be saued by his owne religion, if he be deuout therein ; be he *Turke, Iewe*, or *Chriſtian*, *Papiſt* or *Proteſtant*. But this is a ground and rule of *Atheiſme*, and appeares here to be moſt false ; for, no saluation without pleasing of God, and *without faith it is impoſſible to pleaſe God :* therefore no religion can saue a man, but that which teacheth a man rightly to *beleeue in Chriſt*, & consequently to *pleaſe god*. But euery religion teacheth not to beleeue in Chriſt, some not at all ; and some not aright ? and therefore it is *impoſſible* for such a religion to saue a man. Againe, be a man what he can be, valeſſe he be within the couenant of grace, he cannot be saued : But he cannot bee within the couenant, but *by faith :* therefore no man can be saued by any meanes, but *by true faith* : nor in any religion, but that which teacheth true faith.

Here therefore not onely *Turkes and Iewes* are excluded : but this alfo sheweth many *Papiſts*, and many *carnall goſpellers* in our Church, how short they come of that religion which must saue their soules. For this is the conceite

Pſal. 2.4.

of the most men, that if they doe some good workes, which carie a faire shew to the world, as *liberalitie* to learning, or *charity* to the poore ; straight they thinke they haue leaue to liue as they lift, and God is bound to forgiue their sinnes, and to giue them heauen : and this they imagine, though they knowe not what it is *to beleeue* in Christ, or *to repent* of their sinnes. One of this religion came to the Prophet *Micha* in his dayes, and asked him this question (vttring that plainely which all such men thinke in their hearts) *Wherewithall ſhall I come before the Lord, and bowe my ſelfe before the high God? ſhall I come before him with thouſands of Rams, and tenne thouſand riuers of oile?* He makes the question, and would faine make answer himselfe : nay, he goeth further, and offers more,) *Shal I giue my firſt borne for my tranſgreſſions, and the fruite of my bodie for the ſinne of my ſoule?* But the Prophet answers him, shewing him his follie, and how little God regards such workes without a contrite heart ; *He hath ſhewed thee O man what is good, and what the Lord requireth of thee : Surely to doe iuſtly, to loue mercie, to humble thy ſelfe, and walke with thy God*. Marke how that answer fits this example of *Henoch*. He *pleaſed God, he walked with God*, and was taken away : So, answereth the Prophet, if thou wouldeſt *pleaſe thy God*, and come to heauen by his fauour ; neuer ſtand vpon *thouſands of Rams, and Riuers of oile*, vpon thy gay and glorious workes : *but humble thy ſelfe, and walke with thy God*. No walking with God (saith *Micha*) no pleasing of God : what is it but all one, as if he had said, *Without faith it is impoſſible to pleaſe God?* Here then is no diſallowance of *good* workes, but of *workes without faith* and true repentance : which though they bee neuer so faire and flouriſhing ; yet it is impoſſible, that without faith they should pleaſe God.

Hereby it is alſo manifeſt, that all the *vertues* of the *heathen*, and the workes of such men as either know not Christ : or, knowing him, acknowledge him not their onely Sauiour : or, acknowledging him, doe not truely *beleeue* in him with such a faith as *puriſieth their hearts* ; are nothing elſe, but as the Fathers called them *ſplendida peccata*, gilded and glittering droſſe, and beautifull deformities. And how-euer this seemes harsh, yet it muſt needes be true ; seeing *without faith it is impoſſible to pleaſe God*.

And here alſo the vanity of some *Papiſh* Writers appeares, who preſumptuously make some *Philoſophers* Saints : whereas they should firſt haue ſhewed that they *beleeued* in Christ ; and then we would beleeue and teach it as willingly as they : but elſe, if they had had all the learning, and all the morall vertues in the world ; this muſt ſtand for a truth, *Without faith it is impoſſible to pleaſe God*.

Laſtly, here wee learne, that the *word of God* regiſtred in the *holy Scriptures*, doth containe in it *ſufficient direction* for all the actions

*Micha.*6.7,8.

and duties of a mans life : for *without faith no man can pleaſe God.* And if no man, then no mans *actions* can pleaſe God which are not *of faith* : for whatſoeuer is not of faith , is ſinne, Rom.14.23.

If therefore mens actions muſt proceede from faith , then conſequently muſt they haue their ground and warrant from *the word:* for *faith* and the *word* are relatiues, and the one dependes vpon the other ; No *faith,* no *word* to binde: no *worde,* no *faith* to beleeue. But all actions that *pleaſe God ,* muſt be done in *faith*; therefore all actions that pleaſe God, haue ſome ground and direction in the *word of God,* without which word of God there can be no faith. And this is true , not onely in *holy actions,* but euen in the *common* actions of mens liues and lawfull *callings.* This is a *principle,* which wee muſt firmely beleeue and receiue. And beſide this *argument* here, it is alſo prooued by the euident teſtimonies of the holy Ghoſt. S.Paul to Timothie; *All Scripture is giuen by inſpiration of God , and is profitable to teach, improoue, correct , and inſtruct in righteouſneſſe, that the man of God may be abſolute, and made perfect vnto all good workes.* How can the ſufficiencie of Scripture be more ſufficiently in words expreſſed? Againe, *Euery creature and ordinance of God , is good,&c. For it is ſanctified by the word of God and praier.* Now if the Scripture make a Chriſtian *perfect in all good works,* how can it be, but it giues him ſufficient *direction for all his workes?* And if euery action be *ſanctified by the word;* how can that be but the word hath warranty and direction for euery action and dutie ; which may fall out in the courſe of a Chriſtian life? And vpon theſe grounds we haue good reaſon to be reſolued of this truth.

But now if any man aske how this can be, for the *Scriptures* were written long agoe, and the ſtories are of *particular men, nations, and times,* and the *Commandements* are knowne to be but tenne; how then can the Scriptures yeild ſufficient directions for euery mans particular actions? I anſwer , the Scripture giues directions for all actions two wayes. Either by *Rules,* or by *Examples:* Rules are of two ſorts, *Generall, or particular. Particular* rules for particular callings are many: *for Kings,*they muſt read *Gods booke , and not haue many wiues,* nor gather *too much ſiluer and gold:* They muſt be *wiſe and learned* ; and *kiſſe the ſonne of God Chriſt Ieſus,* and many other: for *Miniſters,*they muſt be *apt to teach,watchnig,ſober,*not *young ſchollers,*& many other:& ſo conſequently the moſt of the callings that are in the common wealth, haue their particular directions in plaine rules.

Generall rules, are firſt *the tenne Commandements,* which are directions for all ſorts of men in all times , what to be done, what not to be done in all actions towards God and men; and beſides , in the new Teſtament there are ſome fewe rules, which are generall directions for all men all in ages : As,*Whatſoeuer you would that*

men *ſhould doe to you , doe you the ſame vnto them.* Againe , *Whether you eate or drinke, or whatſoeuer you doe , doe all to the glorie of God.* Againe,*Let all things be done to edification,and without offence of thy brother.* Againe , *Let all your workes be done in loue.* Laſtly, *Let no man ſeeke his owne* (alone)*but euery man anothers wealth.* Now there is no action in the world, nor any dutie to be done of a Chriſtian man, be he publike or priuate *perſon,* be it a publike or priuate *action,* be it towards God or man; but if he haue not a particular direction, yet it falls within the compaſſe of ſome of theſe rules: and by the tenour of ſome of theſe, he may frame his worke in ſuch manner , as ſhall be pleaſing to God, and comfortable to himſelfe.

Secondly , beſides rules there are *Examples,* which are ſpeciall directions : and they are either of *God,* or good men. *Extraordinarie examples* of God, namely ſuch as he did in extraordinarie times, or vpon extraordinarie occaſions, they concerne vs not: for theſe he did by the power and prerogatiue of *the Godhead:* as, bidding of *Abraham ſacrifice his ſonne* , bidding *the Iſraelites ſpoile the Egyptians,* and ſuch like. But the ordinarie workes of Gods *wiſedome* in his creatures, of his *iuſtice* towards ſinners , of his *mercie* towards his children , of his care and *prouidence* towardes all , are excellent rules of direction for vs. Hence wee haue theſe rules : *Be ye holy,for I am holy: Be ye mercifull,as your Father in heauen is mercifull* , Luk.6.36.

So for the actions of *Chriſt:* who was *God and man :* the miraculous actions of his power, which argued his *Godhead,* as his *walking vpon the water,* and ſuch like, are no directions for vs.Nor againe, his actions and workes done as he was Mediator, as his *faſting fourtie dayes, his paſſion and his merits,*theſe are no directions for vs to doe the like: But , as the firſt giue vs *inſtruction;* So theſe procure vs *iuſtification.*

But the third ſort of his actions done by him as *a man,* or as a Iew borne, they are both our inſtruction and imitation , and they are good directions for our actions: as, his *obedience,*his *zeale,* his *patience,* his *humilitie* , and all other *vertues.*Concerning all which he ſaith himſelfe to vs, *Learne of me, for I am humble and lowely.* And againe, when he had waſhed his Apoſtles feete, he bad them *learne of him to loue one another :* For (ſaith he) *I haue giuen you example that you ſhould do euen as I haue done to you.* Theſe his examples are rules of direction to all men in the like caſe.

Now as for the *examples* of men, as the examples of wicked men are euery way to be eſchewed , ſo *good mens* are to be followed: for *whatſoeuer is written , is writtten for our learning* , Rom.15.4. And ſo for them we are to know, that their examples or actions, contrary to the word, are therefore to be auoided, becauſe they be contrary: as, *Noahs drunkennes, Lots inceſt,Dauids adulterie,* & many other his

infir-

1.Cor.10.31.

1.Cor.14.26.
1.Cor.10.24.

Gen.22.
Exod.11.2.

Matth.11.29.

Ioh.13.13,
14,15.

2.Tim.3.16,
17.

1.Tim.4.4,5.

Deut.17.17,
18,19.

Pſal.2.

1.Tim.3.2,
&c.

Exod.20.

Math.7.12.

infirmities,and such like. Such as are directly agreeable with the word of God, are to be embraced and receiued as directions for our liues,not for their owne fake, but becaufe they are agreeable to the word. But as for such as are neither commaunded nor forbidden; and beeing done, were neither allowed nor difallowed: thefe beeing done by godly men, and fuch who for their faith were approoued of God, againft which no exception can be taken in the word, they be as rules and directions for vs in the like cafes. Now there is no action that can fall out in the life of a Christian man, for which he hath not out of the Scripture either a *rule generall* or *particular*, or elfe fome *example* to follow,which is as good as a rule vnto him. And thus wee fee how the Scripture affoords directions for all our actions. In the demonftration whereof, wee haue ftoode the longer, becaufe it is a principle of great moment. The vfe hereof is double. Firft, wee muft therefore in all the actions of our liues and callings, take confultation with the *word of God*: and for our direction therein, wee muft fearch for either generall or particular rules, or at leaft for examples of godly men in like cafes. And without the warrant and direction of fome of thefe, wee are by no meanes to enter into any thing, or to doe any worke. If we doe, then wee cannot cleare our felues from finne in fo doing: for we finne,becaufe we *pleafe not God* in doing that action: we pleafe not God, becaufe we haue *no faith* for the doing of it:we haue *no faith*, becaufe we haue *no warrant nor ground in the word* for it. Therefore what-euer a mã prefumeth to do without fome warrant in the word for his directiõ, *he finnes* in fo doing.

Secondly, here *Minifters* muft learne their duty: for if no action can poffibly *pleafe God* that is done *without faith*, nor can be done *in faith* without warrant from *the word*, then muft they be *Gods mouth* vnto the people, to be able to tell them what is lawfull,what is vnlawfull by the word; that fo their people may performe their actions in faith,and confequently pleafe God.

Now hauing laid downe this Rule; becaufe it is a principle of fo great moment, the holy Ghoft in the next words proceedes to the proofe of it.

For he, that commeth to God, muft beleeue that God is, and that he is a rewarder of them that feeke him. Thefe words are a proofe of the former rule,and the reafon ftands thus;

Hee that commeth to God, muft needet beleeue: But *He that pleafeth God, commeth to God.* Therefore *Hee that pleafeth God, muft needes beleeue: and fo, without faith it is impoffible to pleafe God.*

He that commeth to God,
To come to God in the fcriptures,but efpecially in this Example, is to labour to haue fellowfhip with God in Chrift: as is manifeft in three places more. In the fourth Chapter, we are bid *to goe boldly to the throne of grace:* and in the feauenth, *Chrift* is faid *to be able perfectly to faue them that come vnto God by him.* And in the tenth, we are called *to drawe neere with a true heart in affurance of faith.*Out of al which places it appeares,that to come to God, is to haue fellowfhip with God by Chrift.And the reafon why that phrafe is fo often vfed to the Hebrewes;is, for that many of them hauing receiued the profeffion of Chrift,afterward forfooke him againe, and fell from his religion, and by renouncing Chrift,fell away from God. Therefore he exhorteth them to *take heed leaft there be in any of them an euill heart, and vnfaithfull to depart from the liuing God,* Chap. 3. 12. Now,by the contrary,If to renounce Chrift be to fall or goe away from God: then we may gather, that to come to God, is to cleaue to Chrift, and to God by Chrift. So then the meaning is, He that will haue any fellowfhip with God in Chrift, He muft beleeue.

What muft He beleeue? Two things.

1. *That God is.* 2. *That he is a rewarder of them that feeke him.*

He muft firft *beleeue that God is,*

That is, not fo much that *there is a God,* for that we are taught by the very light of Nature: But that this God, whom in Chrift he labours to know, & come nere,*is the true and only God.*

This is a notable point in Chriftian religon to beleeue, *that God is God indeede:* not a fiction, a fhadowe, or imaginarie God,but *God indeede.*For it is the fcope of the *firft commandement,* that God gaue mankind.If any man object, There is no man that knowes God, but confeffeth *God to be God,* no man was fo mad as euer to thinke otherwife:

I anfwer, to beleeue the true God to be God indeede, is a matter of great difficultie. For though a man by nature thinke there is a God, yet doe we not by nature thinke the true God to be God.Nay,by nature euery man is an Atheift, and denieth in his heart *the true God to be God,* and doth impugne the *firft commandement* aboue all other. And this may truely & fafly be affirmed of all men that euer came of *Adam* (Chrift alone excepted)that by nature they are Atheifts, and it may be prooued thus.

By nature, though we know and beleeue *there is a God,* yet the corruption of our nature is fuch, as we frame and faine him to our felues to be fuch a one as we pleafe; for we denie in our hearts his *power,* his *prefence,*and his *iuftice,* But to take away thefe three from him,is to denie the true God *to be God indeede.*

Firft, men by nature denie Gods *prefence:* For men would be afhamed to do many things in the prefence of any man, euen the bafeft in the world; which when they are out of mens fights, and yet in Gods prefence, they commit carelefly and boldly. I fpeake not of naturall actions, which are lawfull;& yet in many whereof there is none fo great fhame, as men naturally refufe to doe them before others: But I meane *sinnefull actions*, which not for any natural vnseemelinesse, but euen for their foulenesse and vglinesse, becaufe they are haynous finnes, men would feare to doe, if any man were prefent. Seeing then men feare not, nor fhame not to doe them, though they be in Gods prefence; it followeth, that therefore they naturally imagine, *that God is not prefent:* for, if they were fo perfwaded, they would not commit them, though they efteemed God no better then a man.

Secondly, men by nature denie *Gods power*, thus; When a man offendes a Magiftrate by breaking any law which may deferue death, or fome great punifhment, he is fore afraid; and all his care is, how he may efcape his punifhing hand. But, let a man offend God neuer fo much, by breaking carelefly all his holy commandements, he neuer feares at all, nor trembles at the punifhment belonging vnto them. How can this be? but that howfoeuer he grants *there is a God*, yet he is not perfwaded that God hath power to reuenge the contempt of his laws, and therefore he neuer feares nor fhrinks at the remembrance of him, nor flieth at all from his reuenging hand, but ploddeth on in finn without feare.

Thirdly, man by nature denieth *Gods iuftice:* for the iuftice of God is to winke at finne in no man, but to condemne and punifh it wherefoeuer he findes it, by inflicting the curfes of the law vpon it. But man denieth this *iuftice:* for though he finne againft Gods law, and his confcience tell him of it; yet he perfwades himfelfe, there is no curfe nor punifhment due for it, at leaft that he fhall efcape it: nay though he fee neuer fo many before him punifhed for the fame finne, yet (our nature is fo blinde and fo corrupt) he thinks for all that, it fhall not light on him. And it is lamentable, yet moft true, that the *God* of the ignorant men is a meere *Idoll*, a God made all of mercie, and which hath no iuftice in him at all, and their finnes they carelefly lay all on Chrift, and fay God is mercifull: and in this conceite they care not how ignorantly, how loofely, how profanely they liue; and their hearts neuer haue a reuerent and awefull thought of the iuftice of God.

Thefe are the pitifull imaginations that all men by Nature haue of God. All thefe may be prooued by euident Scripture: The firft in the Pfalme, where *Dauid* brings in the wicked faying to themfelues, *God hath forgotten, he hides his face, he will not fee, he will not regard.* The fecond, by the blafphemie of *Rabfaketh*, who vttered with his tongue that which all mens hearts thinke by nature, *What God can deliuer you out of my hand?* The third *Efay* prooues apparently, where he tells vs that the wicked fay; *We haue made a couenant with death, and with hell are we at agreement, though a fcourge runne ouer and paffe through, it fhall not come at vs.*

Thus both *Scripture* and plaine *demonftrations* prooue this to be true, That euery man by

Pfal.10.11, 12,13.

Efa 36.18, 19,&c.

Efa.28.15.

nature denieth Gods *prefence, power, and iuftice*; and therefore is by nature a plaine Atheift, not beleeuing *that God is God indeede.* Now furthermore, there are 4. forts of people that put in practife this *Atheifme.*

Firft, fuch as are not afhamed to fay openly, *Is there a God or no?* and dare difpute the queftion, and at laft auouch *there is none*; but that all matters concerning *God* and his *worfhip*, are nothing but deuifes of politique men, to keepe fimple men in awe, and to make fooles faine; but thefe themfelues are fooles of all fooles, and the deuill deuifed that impious conceite, to keepe them in miferable blindneffe. There haue been fuch fooles in all ages, yet in old time *Dauid* faith, *Thefe fooles did but fay in their hearts*; But now the fooles of thefe laft and rottten ages, are ripe in their follie, and they dare *fay with their mouthes: There is no God.* Thefe are Monfters in nature, and *deuils* incarnate, wrofe then the *deuill* himfelfe; for he in iudgement neuer was an *Atheift.* Thefe are to be marked and hated worfe then Toads and Adders: and if fuch a one can be conuicted by any lawfull euidence, if euer Heretike or Traytor deferued death, fuch a one deferues tenne deaths; as beeing a Traytor to God, to mankind, and to Nature her felfe. And though thefe wretches fay there is *no God*, yet make they *a God of themfelues*, facrificing all their affections to their pleafure, and their profit.

Pfal.14.1.

The fecond fort are fuch, as acknowledge & worfhip *a God*, but *a falfe God.* Thefe haue beene in all Countries, and in moft ages, as Hiftories doe fhew: fome worfhipping the Sunne fome the Moone, fome ftarres, fome beafts, birds, fifhes; fome dead Idols, of wood, or ftone, or mettall. And of this fort, and no better, are fome in thefe Churches, where the true God is worfhipped: the Apoftle faith, *Couetoufneffe is idolatrie*; for if a mans heart be fet wholly on riches, then the *wedge of gold is his God.* And to other, whofe affections are all on pleafure, *their belfe is their God.* Let thefe men hold in iudgement as they can, their practife I am fure proclaimes Atheifme.

The third fort are fuch as acknowledge and worfhip the *true God*, but in a *falfe manner:* & of thefe there are 3. principall forts; Firft, *Turks:* Secondly, *Iewes*; who hold the true God, but denie the Trinitie of perfons, and the deity of Chrift. Thirdly, the true *Papift* holds in word one God, & the Trinity of perfons as wee doe; but looke at their doctrine, and (if their words haue any naturall meaning) they denie it: for, if the fecond perfon be *true Chrift*, then hath hee two natures, Godhead and Manhood: but by their fained *Tranfubftantiation*, they quite take away the truth of the Manhood. And againe, *Chrift* hath three offices; he is the True *King, Prieft*, and *Prophet* of his Church: and if he be not fo, he is not Chrift: But the Papifts doctrine in plaine words, and neceffarie confequence denieth them all, as hath beene often prooued vnto their shame, and published to the world: and they neuer yet to this day could or durst answer it: for if they doe, they shall soone either heare vs againe, or else we will recant it. But till then, it appeares, that their God is by their doctrine not the *true God*, but an Idol: for, *he that denieth the Sonne, denieth the Father also*, as saith S. *Iohn*.

The fourth sort of *Atheists*, are such, as acknowledge and worship the true God, and worship him in true manner, for the outward worship; but in their liues and deeds denie him. And these are not to be sought for in *Turkie*, or *Iurie*, or *Italy*: for all Churches are full of such Protestant Atheists. *Italy* may haue more Atheists in iudgement then we: but these hypocrites and Atheists in life, are here also; those tares we haue amongst our corne. Of these speakes the Apostle, that *they professe to know God, but denie him in their works.* Let this seeme no wonder, that such men be called Atheists: for, the Apostle saith plainely; *He that careth not for his family, is worse then an Infidell.* Whereby it appeares, a man may be a professour of the Gospel, or a Christian in profession; and an Infidell or Atheist in his practise: and it is certaine; let any man professe what he will, if his life be nought, his religion is a false religion in him.

Now then, to shut vp this point with the vse thereof: If this be true, that there are so many sorts of Atheists, that almost the world is full, and that we are all so by nature: then, *first* let vs see how hard a matter it is *to beleeue in God* aright, and if no man *come to God*, but he that *beleeueth God* aright, then we see it is no maruell, though so fewe come to God. Let vs therefore goe to God by earnest prayer, to giue vs his spirit to worke true faith in our hearts, and to make vs of a true beliefe. And *secondly*, seeing men may be Christians in profession, and Atheists in practise; let vs all look narrowly to our selues, and ioyne with our profession, *Conscience and obedience:* for else the more we know God, the worse we are. It may please God after to giue vs better mindes; but as yet we are no better then deniers of God: and though we come neere God in profession and in his outward seruice, yet indeed we are farre from him, because wee want that true *faith*, which must professe God, not in iudgement alone, but in practise; and that will bring vs *neere vnto God: for he that commeth to God, must beleeue that God is.* And thus much for the first thing to be beleeued, by him that will come to God and please him.

The second is,

And that He is a rewarder of them that seeke him.

It is a notable sentence, and one of the most comfortable in the booke of God: and containes the second thing to be beleeued. The parts are naturally two:

1. How a man doth *seeke God.*

2. How God *rewards them* that seeke him.

For the first: A man truely *seeketh God*, by doing foure actions.

First, a man must forsake himselfe, goe out of himselfe, and as it were loose himselfe in his owne iudgement, when hee intends to *seeke God.* If any aske how that may be? I answer; Thus: A man must labour to see his sinnes fully and distinctly, and in light thereof be cast down in himselfe, as a man is, when he seeth his debts: then let him looke into himselfe, and see if he can finde in himselfe any ability to pay those debts, or any meanes in the world to satisfie Gods iustice, and purchase pardon. And if vpon due examination he finde none at all, no not the least, nor any thing in himselfe, but an accusing, and raging conscience: Let him then fall out of all loue with himselfe, nay hate and abhorre himselfe and his owne basenesse: and lastly, let him *despaire* of his owne saluation in or from himselfe: and thus doing, he forsakes himselfe, denieth himselfe, and euen looseth himselfe. And thus necessarily must he doe to himselfe, that will set his heart to seeke the Lord. For, God will be found of none that hope to finde helpe at any hand but his: they therefore that seeke God, but will seeke themselues too, do iustly loose both God and themselues.

Secondly, he that will seeke God aright (when hee hath lost himselfe) must hunger in his heart and soule, not after wealth and honours, ease, or pleasures; but after the fauour and mercie of God in Christ, for the forgiuenesse of his sinnes: and one drop of Christs blood, to wash away the guilt and staine of his defiled and sinnfull soule, must be dearer to him then all the pomp and glorie of tenne worlds. Looke how a hungry soule hungers after meat, and a faintie soule thirsteth after drinke; so must his soule *hunger* after Gods mercie, and *thirst* for Christs blood: and these are necessary: For, as a man that vndertakes a long iourney, must be prouided of meate and drinke; so hee that vndertakes the iourney to goe *seeke the Lord*, must haue this prouision for the diet of his poore soule, *Gods mercies, and Christs merits*: and he that seekes, without a soule hungring after these, may seeke long and finde nothing.

Thirdly, if he will truly seeke God, he must not goe in euery path: but take the *true and liuing way*, which Christ hath consecrated *by his blood*: nor take any guide, but trust to Christs spirit alone to be his guide: nor make many mediators or messengers to God, but make Christ alone to God the Father. Wee must therefore goe to him, and yeeld vp our selues to bee taught and guided by him, and leaue our sute to be preferred by him: we must not looke to come to God, by running on pilgrimages to this or that Saints picture, or bones: or to our Lady of *Loreto.* Many haue sought God in these, but who euer found him?

1. Ioh. 2. 23.

Tit. 1. 16.

1. Tim. 5. 8.

Nay, alas thou maift lodge in her forged taber-nacle at *Loreto* all thy life, and lie in hell for all that when thou art dead; and maift kiffe all the Saints pictures, and bones, and haire, and all their reliques in Spaine and Italie, and all can-not get thee one fight of Gods fauourable countenance. Nor againe, muft we looke to come to God by our good works, though we are to doe them: they are good *markes* in the way, and good *euidences* of a right way; but they cannot open heauen, and let thee in. And therefore when thou haft done all thou canft, thou muft forfake them all in matter of iuftifi-cation and comming to God. Onely thou muft goe to God by Chrift, and cleaue to him alone; he is the *doore*, the *way*, the *truth*, the *life*: and certenly neuer man found God, that fought him not in Chrift alone. And when Popifh de-uifes and diftinctions haue done all they can, men will be found liers, and Chrift to fpeake truth, faying, *No man commeth to the Father but by me.*

Laftly, when all thefe are done, then muft thou *beleeue* that God is become thy mercifull Father in *Chrift*, and is reconciled vnto thee in him: for there is no feare, but if thou *feeke God in Chrift*, thou fhalt finde him: and when thou haft done the three former things, thou maieft fafely and affuredly beleeue, that thou haft tru-ly *fought God*. And after all thefe, if thou haue not firme and *liuely faith*, thou doeft not *feeke God*. For, as it is *impoffible without faith to pleafe God*; fo is it *impoffible without faith to finde God*. Thus if a man lofe himfelfe, long af-ter Gods mercie, take Chrift alone for his guide and mediator, and fteadfaftly beleeue his reconciliation with God by Chrift, then he feekes God aright: and to this feeking, belongs a reward and bleffing. Now then *if this be to feeke God*, here is fome light giuen to a great queftion, *Whether the Church of Rome be a true Church*, and their doctrine truly Catholique, or erroneous & failing in fundamentall points? For anfwer; Can that be a true Church, which doth not bring her children to feeke God? or that, Catholique doctrine, which teacheth not her children to feeke God, the right way? but fends them into 1000.by-waies? Surely if this be to feeke God, then fearch all the Popifh do-ctors, and almoft all their writers, and fee whe-ther a man be not taught to feeke God quite in another walke. Which way of theirs, whether it ordinarily bring the feekers to God or no, we leaue to Gods mercifull iudgement. But for our felues, as we fee we haue the true and li-uing way, the fure and infallible way, *by Chrift to God, by the Sonne to the Father*; let vs re-ioyce in the comfort of fo rich a mercie, and be thankefull to the Lord for reuealing himfelfe vnto vs, and opening vnto vs the true way to him, and to his glorie. And thus much for the firft point, How we muft *feeke God*.

The fecond is, *How he is a rewarder of them that feeke him*: I anfwer, God *rewards them that feeke him*,

Firft, by offering himfelfe gracioufly to be found of them that *feeke him*: for he neuer hides himfelfe, nor turnes away from the foule that *feeketh him*; but rather turnes to him, and meetes him that comes to him: he is that good Father, which faw the prodigall fonne a farre off, and met him, and receiued him, Luk. 16. Yea, rather is it true, that *he is found of them that fought him not*, then euer *fought* by any that *found* him not. And hereby God much magnifieth his grace and mercie to mankinde, in beeing fo affuredly found when men feeke him. For in this world it is not fo. *All men feeke the face of the Prince*, faith *Salomon*: true, but all men finde it not. No. Acceffe to great men is not fo eafie: they and their fauour are fo in-clofed, that men may long feeke afore they finde either them or it: but God here is not fo inclofed, as he will not be feene nor fpoke to, he is found of them that feeke him. And as hereby he honoureth himfelfe, fo he highly re-wardeth his feruants: for there is no greater contentment to a fubiect, then to perceiue his feruice pleafeth his Prince; nor greater ioy then to finde his gratious fauour when they feeke it.

Let then this practife of the *great God* of heauen, Firft of all, teach the *great ones* of this world to be willing to be *found* when they are *fought* vnto: thereby fhall they honour them-felues, and cheere vp the hearts of their people, who feeke vnto them. And againe, it may be a rich comfort to the *poore ones* of this earth: who, when they fee they muft long looke, and waite, and pray, and pay, and feeke the face and fauour of great men, and cannot finde; may then remember, yet they haue a God, who will not fhut the doore vpon them, will not turne away, will not keepe fecret, will not feare them away with a rough anfwer, or a fower looke, but hath this honourable and princely grace, *He will be found of them that feeke him*.

Secondly, he *rewardeth them that feeke him*, by beftowing his loue and fauour on them: not onely he, but his fauour fhall be found of all that feeke him. It is Gods fauour that Gods children feeke, and his fauour they fhall be fure *to finde*. This is no fmall reward vnto them: for in this world a man thinks he hath enough if he haue the Princes fauour: and therefore it was the common phrafe in old time, *Let me finde grace or fauour in the eyes of my Lord the King*. So fpeake Gods children vnto the Lord. It is not wealth, nor honours we feeke for at Gods hand; but *let vs finde fauour in the eyes of the Lord our God*: and fo they doe, what euer they finde in this world.

Thirdly, he *rewardeth* them not with his *na-ked fauour*, but with the moft gracious tefti-monies thereof that can be: which are two: *For-giueneffe of their finnes*, and *eternall life and glo-rie with himfelfe*. This is all a Prince can doe to his fubiect, who hath offended him; To forgiue

him

him the fault, and remit the punishment: and to aduance him to honour. This doth the Lord to all that seeke him : he forgiues them the debt they owe him, whereby life, and soule, and all was forfaited to him, and giues them also life e-uerlasting: So plentifull a reward is giuen them from that God, *vnder whose wings they are come to trust.*

Fourthly, he rewardeth them with the be-ginnings of heauen and happinesse euen in this world, *A good conscience. and ioy in the holy Ghost:* the comfort whereof is more, euen in the bitterest affliction, then all the pleasures and contentments in the world.

Lastly, with the *appurtenances of heauen*, and of eternall life : namely, the good blessings of this life, a competent portion whereof God giueth his children in this world, as tokens of his fauour, and as rewards of their seruice, and seeking him.

Now as this place doth ayme at all these re-wards; so principally and directly the holy Ghost meaneth *eternall life:* as though he had said: *Hee that commeth to God,* must stedfastly *beleeue* that God is able, and most willing *to re-ward* all that come to him with a better reward then this world can yeeld, euen with eternall life and glorie for his sonnes sake.

But then will some *obiect;* God rewardeth vs, therefore we merit; therefore good workes deserue.

I answer, this place indeede is grosly abused by the Papists for that purpose: but wee are to know, the truth is farre otherwise; for God *re-wardeth* men for two causes: First, for his *pro-mise* sake, and that is for his owne sake, for it was his owne goodnesse that made him pro-mise, and no former debt hee owed to man. A-gaine, he rewardeth our good workes, not for our merits (for they are nothing, but of death and curses) but for *Christ* and his *merits:* for their worthinesse, are our good workes rewar-ded. So then here are two causes of Gods re-warding, and yet mans merits are neither of both: and so the argument is nought, That *God rewardeth,* therefore *wee merit:* for God doth it for other causes. Thus these spiders ga-ther *poison* out of this flower, but let vs sucke the *honey:* for this notable sentence hath excel-lent vse.

First, if *God be a rewarder of them that seeke him,* then not of them that seeke him not. Who *seeke not God?* wicked and vngodly men, seeke him not, but rather seeke to auoide him, and his seruice: this sentence therefore is heauie a-gainst them. For, when they heare it, their con-science answereth, But we *seeke not God;* There-fore we can look for *no reward* from him. Dost thou seeke the world? then must the world bee thy rewarder : Doest thou seeke to please thy selfe? then must thou reward thy selfe. And if thou will please the deuill by liuing in sinne, then must he be thy paimaster: alas! pitifull and fearefull will these rewards be.

Againe, if God *reward none but them that seeke him:* here appeares the reason why so ma-ny *Papists* die in our religion, and (with vs) cleaue to *Christs merits alone,* when they come to die; because their conscience then tells them, that by their pilgrimages, reliques, will-wor-ships, and many more of their courses (ordina-rie in *Popperie*) they did neuer seeke God, but themselues and their owne honour, gaine, and credit; and full well knowe they that there is no reward due for such seruice: and therefore by their practise they make it a true saying, that *It is good liuing a Papist, but dying a Prote-stant.*

Secondly, if God be a rewarder of them that seeke him, then we see it is most true which the Apostle saith; *It is not in vaine to serue God,* 1. Cor. 15. 58. *for God is a rewarder of them that seeke and serue him.* Therefore the Atheist and profane men of this world (who say: *It is in vain to serue God; and what profit is there that we haue kept his Commandements?*) are here conuinced to be liers against the truth.

Then seeing it is so, let this admonish vs all to seeke and serue God, in all truth and since-ritie, knowing we serue him who *will reward it.* Nothing more encourageth a man to serue his *Lord and King,* then to see that his paines are regarded, and his seruice rewarded; nor more discourageth a man then the contrary. If therfore *God* did euer forget any that serued him, let vs bestowe seruice elsewhere, and thinke him vn-worthie to be *sought to:* but if, contrariwise, he neuer forgot, nor deceiued, nor disappointed any that serued him; then is he most worthie to haue the seruice both of our soules and bodies. *Dauid* indeede once said; *In vain haue I clean-sed my heart, and washed my hands in innocen-cie.* But he was then in a strong *temptation,* as himselfe there confesseth: but afterwards when he *went into the sanctuary of God,* and searched the truth of the matter, he confesseth he was deceiued. And therefore as in the first verse he had acknowledged, that *God was good to Israel:* so in the last he concludeth, that *it is good for him to draw neere vnto God:* and so though the temptation was very vehement, yet as faith appeared in the beginning, so it had victory in the ende, and testified, that *God is good to all that seeke him.* Another time also (for he was a man of many sorrowes and temptations) bee-ing in some great distresse, his corruption so preuailed, that he said *All men are liers:* What-soeuer *Samuel,* or God, or *Nathan,* and other Prophets haue told me of Gods loue, and mer-cie, and of his promises, and prouidence, and fatherly care; I see it is all false, and nothing so. Now surely if *Dauid,* or all the Kings in the world can proue this, then God is not wor-thie to be sought after : but great men thinke they may say any thing, especially when they are mooued, as *Dauid* here was. But when *Dauid* entred into himselfe, and considered the words he had so presumptuously vttred; vpon

better

Malach. 3. 14.

Psal. 73. 13.
&c.

vers. 17.

vers. 1.
vers. 28.

Psal. 116. 11.

verf.11.

verf.12.

Pfal.31.19.

Luk.15.

Pfal.139.2.

better aduife he confeffeth, and writes it vp for all pofterities to Gods glorie and his owne fhame, that it was in paffion, *I faide in my feare all men are liers :* This he faid in his haft, or in his feare: but vpon aduife, in the next verfe, he confeffeth *Gods benefits* were fo many , and fo great to him, as he cannot tell *what to render to the Lord for them:* And in another place he crieth out in admiration; *O how great is thy goodneffe which thou haft laid vp for them that feare thee , and put their truft in thee, euen before the fonnes of men!*

We fee then, that merciful promife of Chrift is euer made good , *Seeke and yee fhall finde,* Matth.7.7. None euer fought God, but found: We may feeke our owne pleafures & liue loofely , and be deceiued, and heare that fearefull queftion , *What profit haue ye of thefe things?* Rom.6.21. What reward but fhame & forrow? but if we feeke God aright, we neuer loofe our labour. Let vs therefore feeke God , let the hand of our hearts *knocke* at Gods mercie gate in Chrift, and we fhall not goe away without *a reward.* The prodigall child fled from his Father, fpent all, and loft his fauour: but he no fooner faid, *I will returne and humble my felfe to my Father;* but he found him, and wan his Fathers fauour againe. So, let vs but offer our felues to God (*God vnderftandeth our thoughts long before*) he will meete vs, and receiue vs, and giue vs a reward.

Thirdly, as God *rewardeth them that feeke him* , fo *all that feeke him:* None miffe him, all finde that feeke. Great ones haue not acceffe, & the poore kept out; but all receiued as they come: no difference; but the more carefully any feeke, the more welcome are they. Here let *Princes & great men* learne their duties at god, by whofe grace and permiffion they are what they are.

Firft , let them thinke it vnbefeeming their *greatneffe* , to let any *ferue* them *without a reward:* and a ftaine to their honour, not to let well deferuing fubiects finde their fauour. Let them not *daunt* their hearts by not regarding them and their paines : but let them *encourage* them to ferue them , by looking at them, by good countenances , and good fpeeches, and by rewarding euery one acording to his worth. All great men fhould efteem this, as one of the pearles of their Crownes , to haue it faid of them , *Such a one is a rewarder of them that ferue him.*

Againe, let them learne to difpenfe their fauour, according to reafon, and not affection onely. *God is* indifferent and *equall to all that feeke him,* fo let Princes be : for that is true honour and iuftice to reward each one as he deferues. And that he may finde the beft , who doth beft, this will make euery one ftriue, who fhould be firft, and forwardeft , in all feruiceable duties.

Further , this muft teach them *not to defpife them* that are vnder them in this world: for,

howfoeuer the ftate of this world requires that difference of perfons, elfe it cannot ftand ; it is nothing fo with God , nor in the world to come. For there the fubiect , the feruant , the poore man, may chalenge his part in Gods fauour as well as the beft: nay, whofoeuer *feeketh* the moft *carefully, fhall finde the beft reward.*

Moreouer , here is a comfort to the poore, and the meaner fort of men , who are appointed by God to be vnderlings in this world: Seeke they fauour here and finde it not? worke they here and doe their duties, and are not rewarded? Let them learne to feek God, who will affuredly both *regard* what they doe, and abundantly *reward it.*

Fourthly , feeing *God is a rewarder of them that feeke him:* here is a comfortable incouragement againft two great impediments, which hinder many a man from feruing God.

Firft, *to feeke God* is but a matter of mockerie to profane men; for, let a man *fet his face to Ierufalem* , there are prefently *Samaritanes,* which for that caufe will hate and mocke him; Let a man fet his heart to feeke God , by hearing the word more carefully, praying to God, inftructing his familie, or keeping the Sabbath more carefully then afore, and forthwith he is the laughing ftocke, and the by-word to profane men: but loe, here is comfort ; The God whom thou feekeft will reward thee , and that fo richly, that thou wilt thinke thy felfe well recompenfed, both for thy feruice, & their mockes. In this world men care not who think or fpeak euill of them, fo the Prince like them: and fhall it not encourage vs to feeke God , though the world mock vs? feeing fo doing we pleafe God, and fo farre doe pleafe him, as he will highly reward vs ? Thofe therefore, that fall from religion for thofe mockers, it appeares *they feeke not to pleafe God, but men.*

Secondly, for a man that is a *Magiftrate* or a *Minifter* , to doe his dutie carefully, is the high way to vndergoe a burthen of contempt and hatred. Infomuch as many good men are afraid to be either *Magiftrates or Minifters:* for firft , *wicked men* muft needes hate them, becaufe the one is to rebuke, and the other to punifh their faults. And againe, euen *good men* are too refpectles of them that are in thefe places, and for the moft part neither yeeld them that reuerence , nor reward, that is due vnto them; but often times a man for all his paines and care taken for Church or common wealth, is recompenced with hatred, enuy, grudges, euill words, and flanderous reports. In this cafe, the comfort is this , that though a man be in the world neither regarded , nor rewarded, as his defert is, yet the Lord feeth what he doth, and is a plentifull rewarder of all *that feeke and ferue him:* and therefore efpecially of them, who not onely themfelues ferue him in his chiefe places of feruice, but alfo doe winne many other to feeke and ferue God.

Fiftly, *if God be a rewarder of them that feeke him,*

A

him, then doubtlesse he is a *reuenger of them that hate him:* for he, that can mightily *reward his* followers, can also mightily be *reuenged* of his enemies. These two are the two parts of a *Kings power,* To be able highly to aduance his friends, and mightily to punish his enemies. therefore principally this belongs to the *King of Kings.* This sentence therefore is a thunder-bolt of a most fearefull threatning against all impenitent sinners; assuring them, that if they persist to profane gods holy name by their care-lesse sinning against him, they shall be sure to finde and feele him a powerfull reuenger of them that hate him. Thus he promiseth him-selfe, Deut. 32. 40. 41. 42. *I lift vp my hand to heauen, and I say, I liue for euer. If I whet my glittering sword, and my hand take hold on iudge-ment, I will execute vengeance on my enemies, & reward them that hate me.* Where also note how the same phrase is vsed: for here the Apo-stle saith, God is *a rewarder of them that seeke him:* So in Deuter. *A rewarder of them that hate him.* If any obiect how these two can stand together; for, a man had as good hate him, as seeke him, if the *same reward* belong to both: I answer; A reward, but not the same belongs vnto them. Theeues and murderers are iustly *rewarded,* when they die for their facts: and the King rewards a good seruant, when he aduan-ceth him to honour. They that seeke God, are rewarded with mercies and fauours aboue their desert: they that hate God, are rewarded with vengeance and torments, according to their de-sert: and this shall all wicked men, and enemies of God, be as sure to finde, as euer any that *sought God,* obtained mercie.

But worldly men will say, we hate not God, we are no *Iewes* nor *Turkes,* we are christened, and come to the Church, according to the law, as good subiects should doe. I answer; neither doe *Turkes* nor *Iewes* hate God, if this be all: for, they denie not the Godhead, but acknow-ledge it, and are circumcised, and liue more strictly in their deuotions then most Christians. Here is therefore more required, or else we shall make them also good friends with God: But a man may hate God, and be neither *Turke* nor *Iew;* he may *acknowledge* Christ and the Trinitie, and yet hate God. For, as Christ saith, *He that is not with me, is against me, and he that gathereth not with me, scattereth:* So is it here; He that seeketh not, serueth not, and loueth not God, hateth God: for there is no man can knowe God, but must needes either for his mercies loue him, or else hate him for his iu-stice against sinne and sinners. Againe, Christ bids vs, *If you loue me keepe my Commandements.* If then to keepe Gods commandements bee a signe of one that loues God, it is a signe that one loues not God, when he hath no care to keepe them. By which two places, it appeares, that whosoeuer makes not conscience of sinne, is Gods enemie, and that God so reputes him: therefore let this feare euery man from liuing

B

C

D

carelesly in his sinne, and driue him to true re-pentance: for else let him assure himselfe, God is not so *plentifull a rewarder* of them that seeke him, but he is as *powerfull a reuenger* vpon those that hate him.

Lastly, *if God bee a rewarder of them that seeke him,* wee learne the great difference be-twext *Gods* seruice and the *deuills.* The deuills seruants are fed with faire words, but get no-thing, the deuill is able to giue them nothing: but Gods seruants (as we see here) are plenti-fully *rewarded.* God is *a rewarder* of them that seeke him: but the deuill is a *deceiuer* of them that serue him. But will some say, There is none so madde to be the deuills seruants. I answer: He that doth any mans worke, is either his ser-uant or his slaue: but euery sinfull wicked man doth the deuills worke: for sinne is the deuills worke; therefore all impenitent sinners are the deuills seruants. It is Christs argument to the Iewes: *You are of your Father the deuill, for the workes of your Father you will doe: murthers and lies are his workes, you liue in these sinnes, and doe these workes; therefore you are his ser-uants.* [Ioh.8.41.44.]

Again, the holy Ghost teacheth vs, that *who-soeuer committeth sinne* (and liueth therein without repentance) *the same is the seruant of sinne.* Now sinne is but the *bawde* or broker to the *deuill:* they that are the seruants of sinne, sinne preferres them to the deuill, and so they become his seruants: therefore whosoeuer is the seruant of *sinne,* is by that meanes the slaue and seruant of the *deuill* also. Which if it bee true, it will fall out vpon the reckoning, that the deuill hath more seruants in the world then God hath: which is so much the more lamenta-ble, in as much as he deludeth all his seruants, & is not able *to reward them,* nor to giue them any good thing. [Rom.6.20.]

But will some say, this is nothing so: for contrariwise, who haue the honours, pleasures, and wealth of this life, who haue hearts ease and the world at will, but such men? I answer: True, it is commonly so; but haue they those from Sathan? No, not the least of them all, but all from God: for euery man is Gods child by creation, and some by grace, to euery one of his children he ordaines and giues *a portion:* but to his children by grace *a double portion;* both here, and in heauen. The wicked men, they will not feare nor serue him; therefore they haue no part nor portion in heauen, but here they haue it: So saith *Dauid;* there are some men, which are *men of this world, and haue their portion in this life: these mens bellies god filleth with his hidden treasures, they and their children haue enough, and leaue the rest for their children after them:* Where it is manifest, that wicked men haue their parts and portions of Gods blessings in this world, and that all their wealth and pleasures are graunted them by and *from god,* as their portion; reseruing the principall part of the portion of his children [Psal.17.14.]

for

for a better life. Therefore all the *good things* of this life, which *Diues receiued,* and all wicked men doe receiue in this life, are not any rewards of *Satan,* but gifts, *of God;* so vnworthie a master is the deuill to serue. Indeede he will promise his poore slaues any thing, but can performe nothing, but will lie vnto them and deceiue them. He told *Christ* confidently; when he let him see the glorie and greatnesse of this world, *All this is mine, and I giue it to whom I will:* but he was a *lier from the beginning,* and so he is here. He lied to the first *Adam,* and no maruell, that he dare auouch so fond and loude a lie in the presence of the *second Adam,* Iesus Christ. He promised the *first Adam,* to make him God, and here the *second Adam* to make him King and Lord of all the world, and the glorie of it: but he performed both alike, he deceiued the first, and so had the second also, if he had trusted him. Nor did euer any trust him, but he deceiued him (I meane euen for the base things of this life); witnesse else all his witches (his most deuoted and professed seruants of all other) if euer he made any one of them wealthie: all ages are not able to shew one. Whereas, on the other side, there was neuer man that serued God, but had a competent measure of comforts for this life (and some, abundance) & yet al that is but the first fruits and beginnings of that *reward,* which is laid vp for them in another world. Which beeing true, is it not a strange and lamentable case, to see men (for all this) debase themselues to this base and slauish seruice of Satan, and to refuse this high and honourable seruice of *almighty God?* A common seruant in this world hath more wit: he, if he can heare of a better seruice, a Master who giues better wages, and who better preferres his seruants, will leaue his old Master, and make meanes to get the other. And shall not we be as wise for both soule and bodie, as they for the bodie alone? Shall they leaue a man for a man, and shall not wee leaue the deuill for God.

Let vs therefore abandon the base seruice of Satan, who neither can, nor will reward them that serue him; put away so ill a Master, who hath not so much as meate and drinke to giue vs (for we haue euen that from God: but of his owne, he hath nothing to giue vs, saue in this world sorrow, and shame, and an *ill conscience;* and in the world to come, the torments of *hell* with himselfe): And let vs all seeke the blessed seruice of God. If we know not how to attaine it, goe to *Christ* by hearty confession of thy sinnes, and earnest prayer, and he will preferre thee to God his Father: for neuer was any denied, that with a good and true heart, offered himselfe to Gods seruice. Then shall we feele and finde what a blessed thing it is to be Gods seruant: of whom, it was euer true, which the holy Ghost here saith, and is and euer shall be, that *He is an honourable rewarder of them that seeke him.*

And thus we haue (in some part) the mea-

ning and vse of this notable sentence: wherein we haue stood the longer, because it is one of the most excellent principles of all *Practicall Diuinitie.*

Now put all together, and we shall see how it prooues *Henoch to be taken away by faith;* which is the first ground, and the maine matter of all this example, and of these two verses.

God is a rewarder of all his children that seeke him by faith: therefore it is *faith by which Gods children please God:* and therefore holy *Henoch* who was *taken vp by God* from earth to heauē, both *pleased God by faith,* and *by faith was taken away.*

And thus much for the commendation of *Henochs faith,* and consequently the examples of such, as liued in the first world *before the flood.*

Now followeth the example of *Noah,* who liued in both worlds, both before and after the flood.

Noahs faith.

VERSE 7.

By Faith, Noah beeing warned of God of the things which were as yet not seene, mooued with reuerence, prepared the Arke to the sauing of his houshold: through the which Arke he condemned the world, and was made heire of the righteousnesse which is by faith.

IN this vers. is contained the *third example,* and the last in order of those who liued afore the flood, in the first and old world; namely, of the renowned Patriarke *Noah,* the tenth from *Adam.*

Of whom and whose faith, great and glorious things are spoken in this verse; and that in a high and excellent stile, full of maiestie, and diuine eloquence.

Concerning *Noahs* faith, two points are laid down; first, the *ground of his faith:* secondly, *the commendation* of it.

The *ground* of his *faith* was a speciall reue-

lation

lation from God, in these words; *Noah beeing warned of God.* The things reuealed, whereof God warned him, are laid downe two wayes: first, generally, to be *things as yet not seene*; then particularly three in number.

1. Gods *Iudgement* vpon the sinfull world, that hee was purposed to destroy it by water.

2. Gods *mercie* on *Noah*, that he would saue him, and his family.

3. That he would saue him by an *Arke*, and therefore he must make one: and these be the things whereof *Noah* was warned of God.

His faith is *commended* by three worthy effects or operations in him. 1. It *mooued in him a reuerence*, or a reuerent regard of the warning sent him from God. 2. It made him *prepare the Arke*: of which Arke there are set downe two ends. 1. It *saued his houshold*. 2. It *condemned the world*. 3. It *made him heire of the righteousnesse, which is by faith.*

This, I take it, is the true resolution of these wordes: and they containe manie excellent things concerning his faith.

By faith Noah *beeing warned of God, of the things which were as yet not seene;*

By faith, that is, by a generall and historicall *Faith*, and also by a true and sauing *faith* in the *Messias* to come, *Noah* beeing warned of God of the iust *Iudgement* hee purposed to bring vpon the world, by an vuiuersall floud; and of his *mercifull prouidence*, to him and his family, that he would saue them by an *Arke* (all which things were then to come, and therefore vnseene) he *beleeued* these forewarnings of God: and therefore, in reuerence to this message from God, hee prepared the Arke, and thereby saued his houshold, and condemned the wicked world. And so his *faith*, by all these appearing to bee a true and liuely *faith*, did make him a iust and *righteous* man in Gods sight. This is the summe and substance of *Noahs* example: let vs speake of the seuerall parts in order.

The first point is, the Ground of his faith, *A warning or an answer from God.* For, he beeing a righteous man in that wicked age, wherein all the world weltred in wickednesse, and walking before God in great holinesse, when no man cared for religion, hee had this speciall fauour from God, that when he purposed to destroy the world for their sinne, hee first of all reuealed to *righteous Noah* that purpose of his. So that these words haue reference to the reuelation which *Noah* had from God, in the 6. of Geuesis. For, this message came not from God by any Prophet (for we know none in those euill dayes, except *Noah* himselfe) but either by the Ministerie of an *Angell*, or else by immediate reuelation from God himselfe: and this fauour he receiued from God, not for any cause in the world, but becuase he was a holy and righteous man.

From hence, we may learne diuers excellent instructions.

First, whereas God maketh choise of *Noah*, to reueale vnto him his counsell, and his iudgements to come; wee learne that this is a prerogatiue which God bestowed on such as feare him, he reuealeth his counsels to them in a speciall manner, whether they be purposes of Iudgements vpon his enemies, or of mercies vnto his Church. Thus dealt he with *Abraham*, Gen. 18. 19. *Shall I* (saith God) *hide from Abraham the thing that I will doe?* which thing was, the destruction of Sodome, and her sisters. And so when the *Sodomites* liued in wanton carelesenesse, and put farre from them the euill day, then *Abraham* knew from God their destruction was at hand. And as in that, so it is generally true in all his great workes: that *the Lord God will doe nothing, but he reueales his secrets to his seruants the Prophets.* Amos 3.7. Now this is not a prerogatiue of Prophets alone, or of such as were extraordinarie men as *Abraham* was: but *the secrets of the Lord are amongst such as feare him*, Psalme 25. 14. All that feare the holy name of God, are Gods friends, and of his Counsaile: and therefore not *Abraham* onely is called *the friend of God*, Iames 2. 23: But of all true beleeuers, saith Christ, Iohn 15. 14. 15; *You are my friends, If you doe what I command you: henceforth I call you not seruants, but friends, for the seruant knoweth not what his Master doth; but all things that I haue heard of my Father, haue I made knowne vnto you:* As if he had said, I will communicate and impart my secrets vnto you, as one friend doth vnto another, as farre as shall be fit for you to know. And the Apostle saith, 1. Cor. 2. 15. *A faithfull and a holy man discerneth into the deepe counsailes of God*; which are reuealed vnto them, as much as concerneth their saluations, and sometimes more; as here, vnto *Noah*, who was fore-warned of God, *of things then not seene.*

This prerogatiue of Gods children, is to be vnderstood with some cautions.

First, that this is more proper to Prophets, and holy Ministers of God, then to ordinarie Christians.

Secondly, that it was more ordinarie in the *old testament*: then now in the dayes of the *Gospell.* If any obiect, Then the state of the Church afore Christ, was better then it is now vnder Christ; I answer: not so; for first, we are recompensed by hauing the Scriptures perfect, and compleate, which they had not: and by hauing the substance of their shadowes, and the performance of their promises: in which respects our state is farre more excellent then theirs. And secondly, for this particular, I answer, they indeed had more ordinarie reuelation of matters *personall and priuate*, and not directly touching saluation: but of such things as are generall, and doe necessarily concerne saluation; we in the time of the new Testament, haue more euident demonstration, and more full reuelation, then they had afore Christ. For example: particular mercies to fome faithfull men, or particular iudgements on Gods enemies, whether particular men or whole kingdomes, were after reuealed to godly men, in thofe daies (as here to Noah:) but faluation by the Meffias, and the manner how the Meffias fhould faue his Church, is more fully and plainly reuealed now, then in thofe daies.

Out of which confideration arifeth the third caution; which is, that reuelations of Gods wil, to be expected now vnder the Gofpel, are ordinarily nothing elfe, but thefe; the true meaning of Scripture, & a difcerning of true Scripture from forged, of true Sacraments from fuppofed, of true doctrine from falfe, of true Paftors from falfe prophets. Thefe and fuch like, as farre forth as they are neceffarie to faluation, ail true and faithfull beleeuers (which out of an humbled heart, by deuout prayer doe feeke it at Gods hand) are fure to haue reuealed vnto them from God. But as for other purpofes of God, of perfonall and particular matters, or what fhall be his bleffings, or what his iudgements to thefe and thefe men, families, cities, or kingdomes; or when, or how he will change States, or tranflate kingdomes; or by what extraordinarie meanes he will haue his Gofpel propagated, or a declining Church or State vpholden; thefe we are not to expect, nor eafily to beleeue any that fhall fay, fuch things are reuealed vnto them. And yet we tie not the Lord in fuch ftrait bonds, but that he may fometime extraordinarily reueale his purpofe therein, to fome his felected feruants: yet prouided, that that reuelation be examined and allowed of the Church. But as for fuch things as concerne immediately the faluation of our foules, gods fpirit doth moft cofortably reueale them vnto vs, in our *praiers*, in his *word*, and in his *Sacraments*: of all which, it is moft true, that *the fecrets of God are amongft them that feare him:*

The vfe of this doctrine is double; for inftruction, and for exhortation. For our inftruction, here we learne how to anfwer the church of Rome: they afke vs, how doe we know true religion from erroneous; or true Scripture, or Sacraments from forged? We anfwer, firft, by it felfe, by fight and fenfe of the excellencie thereof; as we know gold from braffe, or filuer from lead. But what if the braffe or tinne be gilded ouer? I then anfwer fecondly, we can know gold from braffe, and filuer from tinne by the found and fmell, and hardneffe to endure, and by the operation: fo there is a fpirituall found of the Scriptures in the eares of a Chriftian, a fpirituall comfort and tafte in true religion, a fpirituall operation (in holy mens hearts) of the true Sacraments. But what if falfe Prophets come in fheepes cloathing, and by lying wonders, feeme to giue the fame found, tafte, fmell, vertue, and operation vnto their forgeries, or at leaft chalenge it, and fay, that theirs is true? I anfwer laftly; then we know

true Religion, true Scripture, true Sacraments, true Prophets, true Doctrines from falfe, by a holy and fupernaturall reuelation from Gods fpirit; which, by euident and powerfull demonftration, affureth vs what is true and what is falfe, for the fubftance of faluation. And this fpirit is giuen to all, that in true humilitie doe feeke it, in holy praier, and in a holy & frequent vfe of Gods word and Sacraments; and to none els. And furely if the Papifts were as well acquainted with the fpirit of God, as they are with their own forged reuelations, they would neuer denie it. By force of this teftimonie a Chriftian man knoweth, as affuredly as that God is God, that the Pope, as now he is, and as he exercifeth his place and power, cannot be the true *Vicar of Chrift*; and that Poperie, as it is now eftablifhed by the Councell of Trent, and taught by the moft learned of their fide, cannot be the true religion, nor the fafeft way to heauen. And when queftion is, what is the meaning of this place, *there is one God and one Mediatour betwixt God and man, the man Chrift Iefus;* if all the world fhould fay the contrarie, a Chriftian man will know and beleeue there are *no more mediatours to God but Chrift:* or of that place, that *Chrift was offered for our finnes once for all;* that there is no facrifice can purchafe vs pardon, but his; let Papifts colour the matter by vnfound diftinctions as much as they can: and the fame might be fhewed in diuers other points and places. And if any afke how this can be: I anfwer; Noah was *warned of God of things not feene:* So Gods children are warned and affured of God, of fuch things as concerne their faluation, though they be things beyond fenfe and reafon, *Gods fecrets doe belong vnto them.*

The vfe of exhortation is, that if God *warne* his children of his will, and reueale his fecrets to them, this fhould mooue & excite vs to become truly and indeede Gods feruants: for we ferue not a Lord that is ftrange and auftere vnto vs; that will not giue vs a good looke, or a faire word: nay, he is fo farre from that, that he calls vs to his holy *Counfell,* and makes vs know his *fecrets,* and communicates his owne felfe vnto vs by his bleffed Spirit; and by that Spirit reuealeth vnto vs many excellent myfteries of faluation, which the carnall and profane men of the world neuer dreame of.

In the fecond place: let vs obferue, that Noah *beeing thus warned of God* in this particular matter (as he had beene formerly warned and taught of faluation by a Meffias to come) beleeueth not onely the generall promife of faluation, but alfo this particular promife of his preferuation and deliuerance. Out of which his practife, we may learne two things;

Firft, that *faith* is a fupernaturall worke of God in thofe mens hearts that haue it. That it is a *worke of God,* it appeareth in that it alwaies acknowledgeth and beleeueth Gods word: that it is *fupernaturall,* it appeareth in that it apprehendeth and beleeueth whatfoeuer Gods word deliuereth, be it neuer fo incredible to reafon or fenfe. But how doth God worke this faith? By his word: for as God is the author and worker of faith, fo God hath appointed a meanes whereby he workes it, and that is his *Word*; which word of God is the onely ordinarie outward meanes to worke faith. And that word of God is two wayes to be confidered: either as *reuealed* by God himfelfe (as to Noah here); or elfe, beeing *written* by God, is either preached by his Minifters, or read by a mans felfe in want of preaching: and thefe are all one, and are all meanes ordained of God to worke faith; and that not onely to begin it where it is wanting, but to augment it where it is begun.

Which beeing fo, it muft teach vs all, not onely with fpeciall care and reuerence to *heare* the word, by whomfoeuer it is preached; but alfo to heare it read: yea, *to reade* it our felues with all diligence. So doing, it will worke out, and make perfect in vs that holy faith, which will make vs bleffed in our felues, and accepted of God, as it did Noah in this place.

Secondly, here we learne what is the whole *Obiect of faith*, or what is all that that faith beleeueth; namely, nothing but Gods word, and all and euery word of God. So that faith hath two obiects, differing not in nature, but in degree, principal, and inferiour. The *principall* obiect of true faith, is the promife of faluation by *Chrift*. The *inferiour* obiect thereof, are all other particular promifes, of fafety, deliuerance, prouidence; helpe, affiftance, comfort, or what other benefit foeuer is made either to the whol Church, and fo inclufiuely to any particular man; or which are perfonally made vnto him. For, fauing faith beleeueth not only the ground promife of faluation, but all other promifes either of fpirituall or corporall bleffings, which are fubordinate to the great Promife, and doe depend of it, and are therefore apprehended by the fame faith. So, Noah here had alreadie apprehended the maine Promife of faluation by the Meffiah, and had *hid it in his heart:* and afterward when this particular promife of his deliuerance was made, by the fame faith he laid hold on it alfo. And it is good reafon that faith fhould doe fo: for if it apprehend the *greater* promife, then no maruell though it take hold of all other *inferiour* promifes, which are but dependances vpon the principall

By this that hath beene faide, it appeareth, that we are wrongfully charged by them, who fay, we teach that fauing faith beleeueth onely faluation by Chrift, or apprehendeth onely the promife of faluation in Chrift: for, we fay and teach, It apprehendeth alfo other particular promifes, & euen the promifes of outward and temporall bleffings; as appeareth in this example of Noah.

Laftly, in that Noah a faithfull man, is heere warned of God of the dangers enfuing,

that fo he may auoid them; wee may learne the louing care that God hath ouer them, who haue a care to feare and ferue him. Thus dealt hee with his children in all ages, for their comfort and preferuation, to encourage all men to ferue God in truth and vprightneffe, as here Noah did: for, fo doing, they may affure themfelues of Gods care and prouidence ouer them, euen then, when his wrath fmokes againft the finners of the world: and that furthermore in all exigents and extremities, hee will teach them, either from his word, or by the counfell of fome others of his children, or elfe hy his owne fecret infpiration, what they are to doe, and what courfe to take, for their fafetie and deliuerance.

How often fhall a Chriftian man finde in the courfe of his life, that God put into his minde, to anfwer thus or thus, or to forefee this or that; by which his fo doing, he efcaped fome great danger: fo that (though not in the fame manner as Noah was) all faithfull men doe daiely finde, that they are warned by God of fuch things as doe concerne them.

But what were thofe things whereof Noah was warned from God? The text faith: *Of the things which were as yet not feene.*

This hath not relation to the time, when the holy Ghoft wrote thefe words, but when God gaue the warning to Noah; for then *they were not feene*, but were to come: for they were not performed for many yeares after, as fhall appeare in the particulars.

Particularly they were thefe three: Firft, the great and iuft *wrath*, which God had conceiued againft the *finfull world*, for the vniuerfall corruption and generall finfulneffe thereof. Noah was a *Preacher of righteoufneffe* to that wicked age; and as *S. Peter* faith (1. Epiftle 3. 11) The very *fpirit of Chrift preached in him:* but they contemned both him, and the fpirit by which hee fpake, and made a mocke of him, and all his holy admonitions, and folaced themfelues in all their finfull pleafures, without feare or refpect of God or man, pleafing themfelues in their own defiled wayes, and promifing to themfelues, fafety and fecurity. But behold, This Noah, whom they efteemed a bafe and contemptible man, vnworthy of their company; to him is reuealed, how fhort their time is, and that they muft be cut of in the midft of their iollity. Gods children, whome wicked men doe thinke and fpeake of with great contempt, doe know full well the miferable ftate of fuch men, and the fearefull dangers hanging ouer thē; when the wicked mē themfelues are farre frō thinking of any fuch matter.

The fecond thing, which God *reuealed to* Noah, was, that he would *faue him* & his family frō perifhing by the waters, which he would bring vpō the world. His *faith was not in vaine*: God rewarded it with a fingular preferuation. Thus dealt he alwaies with his children; deliuering *Lot* out of Sodome, Gen. 19. *Rahab* out of

Hierico: Ioſhua 6. 22. The *Kenits* from the Amalekits, 1. Sam. 15. and here *Noah* out of that generall deſtruction. And this God aforehand reueales vnto him, for his greater comfort and ſecurity: that when ſignes and ſtrange tokens did foretell and ſhew, that ſtill the deſtruction was neerer and neerer; ſtill *Noah* might comfort himſelfe in the aſſurance of that mercifull promiſe which God had made him of his deliuerance, and of his family alſo for his ſake.

The third thing *reuealed* to him, was the meanes whereby he ſhould be ſaued from the vniuerſall floud; namely, by *an Arke*, which for his more aſſurance he is bid to make himſelfe; that ſo at euery ſtroke he gaue, he might remember this mercifull promiſe of his God vnto him. For as euery ſtroke in the making of the Arke, was a loude ſounding Sermon vnto that ſinfull generation, to call them to repentance: ſo was it alſo an aſſurance vnto *Noah* of his deliuerance. Of which Ark, and of *Noahs* obedience in making it, wee ſhall hereafter ſpeake at large. And thus much concerning the ground of *Noahs* faith, which was a *warning* or reuelation *from God*.

Now followeth a ſecond point: namely, the *commendation* of his faith, or a deſcription of the *excellencie* thereof, by diuers and ſingular effects.

Mooued with reuerence,

The firſt effect of his faith is, It *mooued in him a reuerence*, or a reuerent feare of that *God* that ſpake to him, and of his *iuſtice* towards ſinne & ſinners, and of his *mercie* towards him.

In this effect we are to conſider two points: 1. The *ground* of this reuerence. 2. The *occaſions or motiues* of it.

The *ground* whence this *reuerence* ſprang, was his true & ſauing *faith*: for the holy Ghoſt firſt telles vs of *Noahs* faith, and afterwards of this *reuerent* feare he had of God, and his great workes.

Where we learne, that whoſoeuer is endued with ſauing *faith*, is alſo touched with feare and reuerence at the conſideration of God, and his glorious workes; whether they be works of his *power*, his *wiſedome*, his *mercy*, or his *iuſtice*, or of all together.

For the firſt: *Dauid* could not ſee the works of Gods *power* in the creation, Pſalm. 8. *But when he looked vp and beheld the heauens, the workes of Gods hands, the moone and the ſtarres which he had ordained*; he forthwith fell into a *reuerence* and admiration of Gods mercy to man, for whom & whoſe vſe he made them all.

For the ſecond, the ſame *Dauid* could not enter into conſideration of Gods *wiſedome*, in the admirable frame of mans bodie, Pſal. 139. 13. &c. but he preſently falls into a *reuerence* & admiration thereof in moſt excellent and paſſionate words: *Thou poſſeſſeſt my reines, thou coueredſt me in my mothers wombe: I will praiſe thee, for I am fearefully and wonderfully made.*

Meruailous are thy workes, and that my ſoule knoweth right well: My bones are not hid from thee, though I was made in a ſecret place, yet thy eyes did ſee my ſubſtance when I was without forme, and in thy booke were all my members written, which in continuance were faſhioned, though there were none of them before. How deere therefore are thy counſels to mee, O God! Thus we ſee how this holy King, cannot content himſelfe with any tearmes, to expreſſe his religious & reuerent conceite of Gods maieſtie.

For the third, Gods *mercifull* workes to his Church and children, haue alwayes beene conſidered of by good men with great *reuerence:* And, *What ſhall I giue vnto the Lord*, ſaith Dauid, *for all his benefites poured on mee?* (Pſalm. 116. 12.)

But eſpecially, the *Iudgements* of God haue beene alwaies entertained of Gods children with much *reuerence* and admiration. Bleſſed *Dauid* ſaith, *My fleſh trembleth for feare of thee, and I am afraid of thy Iudgements*, Pſal. 119. 120. How would this noble *King* haue trembled and beene afraid, if he had beene a priuate man? And how glorious is *God*, and his workes of Iudgements, whereat euen *Kings* themſelues doe tremble? And the Prophet *Habbacuk* ſaith, that when hee but heard of Gods iudgements to come, *his belly trembled, his lips ſhooke, rottenneſſe entred into his bones*, Habba. 3. 16. And thus Noah here, hearing of Gods iuſt wrath againſt the ſinfull world, & of his purpoſe to ouerthrowe all liuing fleſh by water, was mooued with great feare and reuerence at this mighty worke of God: and from the view of this his great and iuſt iudgement, his *faith* made him ariſe to a more earneſt conſideration of the Maieſtie of God. By all which, it is more then apparant, that true faith (whereſoeuer it is) worketh a holy feare and reuerent eſtimation of God, and of his workes, and of God in and by his workes: whereby on the contrarie ſide, it followeth, that therefore to thinke baſely or ordinarily of *God*, to thinke ſcornefully of his workes, or to denie his power and his hand, in the great works, either of mercy or iudgement done in the world, is an argumēt of a profane heart, & wāting true faith.

The vſe of this doctrine diſcouers the profaneneſſe, and the great want of *faith* that ordinarily is in the world. And that appeares by two euidences: the firſt, is to mens owne *conſciences*; the other, is to the viewe and ſight of all the *world*.

Firſt, men may ſee in themſelues a profane heart, and voide of *faith*, by this euidence. For, doth a man in his heart thinke baſely of God, his power, his iuſtice, or his mercies? Doth he either doubt of them? or, granting them, doth he thinke of them without feare and amazement? Then aſſuredly his heart is void of true faith, and farre from the life and power of religion. For aſſuredly, where God is *knowne and beleeued*, there that mans heart (though he be

a King)

a King) cannot once thinke of God, without, a reuerence of his Maiestie, and an admiration at *his greatnesse*, and his *owne basenesse* : therefore the want of this, argueth a want of true religion and true *faith* in mens hearts.

Secondly, this profanenesse discouers it selfe to the *world*, by want of reuerence to Gods *workes*. Let the Lord send vnseasonable *weather*, or *famines*, or *plagues*, or any strange signes in heauen or in earth; forthwith they are but fooles that cry out, Behold *the finger of God, the hand of God:* No, this is nature, and is produced by naturall causes. Ill weather comes from the *starres:* famines from ill weather, and mens couetousnesse: Plagues from famines, or from ill aires, or else by apparant infection from another place. But cannot Nature and naturall means haue their place, vnlesse they haue Gods place; God ouerthroweth not them: why should they ouerthrow God? Yet thus it is in the world, and thus God is robbed of his glory: and he is but a simple fellow, which is *mooued with reuerence* at sight of such things, or begins to magnifie Gods power and iustice in thē. This is too apparant to be denied, for, haue wee not now as great causes of feare as can be? *Noah* heard of *water*; and we heare that *fire* is to destroy the world: and yet where is he that is *mooued with reuerence*, as *Noah* was; and yet *Noah* could say, The floud shall not be, these 120. yeares: but who can say and prooue that this world shall not be destroyed by fire within these 120. yeares? And till the floud came, they had doubtlesse many other plagues, which were fore-runners of the generall destruction; all which as they came, *Mooued Noah vnto reuerence:* and so we, in this age, doe see the great workes of Gods Iudgements, vpon men, vpon families, vpon townes, vpon countries, and whole kingdomes, and we feele his heauie hand in many sharpe strokes; but who and where are they whose hearts feare God the more, and doe tremble in the consideration of his Iudgements. Nay, alas, amongst many it is but a matter of mockerie so to doe. This is not the *fault* of our religion, but the *want* of it: for if men truly knew and beleeued in God, they could not thinke nor speake of God, nor looke at his workes, but with feare and reuerence. For as our feare of God is, so is our faith: little feare of God, little faith: and no feare at all, no faith at all. Let therefore all men shewe their religion by their feare of God, and let euery Christian acknowledge God in his workes. England hath beene faulty herein in one point especially. We haue had *great plagues*, which haue taken away many thousands in short time, wherein God hath shewed himselfe mighty against our sinnes: But Gods hand would not be seene nor acknowledged, but onely nature and naturall causes. But let *England* take heed, that God send not a plague so generall and so grieuous, that euen the most profane men, (euen the sorcerers of Egypt if they were

here) doe acknowledge that it it *the finger of God*; and so giue God that *due reuerence*, which in his ordinarie visitation he hath not. Thus we see the ground whence this reuerence in *Noah* sprang; namely, his faith.

Now let vs see the *occasions* or considerations in *Noahs* heart, that made him feare. The *ground* whereupon he feared, was true faith; for else he had not beene capable of any feare or reuerence of God: but the occasions which stirred vp this feare in him, were som things els.

Now if we looke to humane reasons, *Noah* had no cause at all *to feare* as he did. For first, the Iudgement was *farre off*, 120. yeares after: and common reason saith, it is folly to feare any thing so farre off; but it is time enough to feare, when it is neere at hand. Againe, hee was *one single man*, and the world was full of wise and mighty men: they all heard of it, yet none of them feared; therefore their example might preuaile with him, to keepe him from feare, and to make him secure and carelesse with the rest: for examples are strong, especially when they are so generall.

Thirdly, the *strangenesse* of the Iudgement threatned, was such, as might driue any man (in reason) from fearing it at all. For first, who would euer beleeue, that God would drowne *all the world* with water? such a thing neuer had beene, and therefore, how could it be? And againe, If all should bee drowned, who would think that *Noah should escape*, and none but he?

These three considerations, beeing wayed in the ballance of mans reason, would haue kept *Noah* from fearing, or beleeuing this word of God. But, behold the *power of faith:* it goeth beyond all humane reach, fixeth it selfe fast on Gods word: and therefore he not onely beleeueth it, but hath furthermore his heart possessed with a great *reuerence* of Gods Maiestie vpon this message. And there were three *motiues* stirring him vp vnto this *Reuerence*.

First, the consideration of Gods strange Iudgement vpon the sinfull world; to see that his wrath was so prouoked, that hee should bring so vnwonted a plague: so *strange* both for the *nature* of it; a floud of water to drowne men: whereas generally all men can auoide the violence of that element: and for the *measure* of it, so great, as it should drowne al the world, and destroy all men.

Now, that which this *Iudgement* of God wrought in *Noah*, the same effect should Gods Iudgements worke in vs: namely, they should mooue vs with reuerence. For, as Christ saith, *Our dayes are like Noahs: As it was in the dayes of Noah; so shall the dayes be before the comming of Christ* (Matthew 24. 37.) These dayes are as wicked, men are as couetous, as cruell, as malitious, as voluptuous, and yet as secure, as they then were; as full of sinne, and yet as dead in sinne as they were then. Therfore *Noah* looked for a floud 120. years after: & who can tell whether our world shall last so long a time or no? at left we may fafly fay (whatfoeuer the world doth) there is no man liueth, but within far leffe time the 120.years, is affured to be throwen to hell by *a flood* of Gods wrath at his death, vnleffe in the meane time he repent: and yet alas where is hee that is mooued with reuerence at confideration hereof? The wicked man may fcape the *water* of a flood: but he can not fcape the *fire* of hell, he cānot efcape death, he cannot efcape the laft Iudgement. Thefe are to come, yet they are fure: why then doe not men feare as *Noah* did? he feared 120. yeares afore it came. We can indeede tremble a little at a prefent Iudgement: as, when fire breakes out, when waters ouerflowe, when the plague deftroyeth, or when famine confumes: but to tremble at a *Iudgement* threatned, though it be afarre off, this is the worke of *true faith*. This was in *Noah*, and wrought in him a reuerence: and fo would in vs, if it were in vs. When men crie *fire, fire:* we ftirre, we runne, we tremble: but God crieth in his word, the *fire of hell, the fire of his wrath;* and we care not, we ftirre not, we leaue not our finnes, we are not mooued with reuerence, as *Noah* was: therefore it is more then manifeft, that holy faith is wanting in the world, which *Noah* had.

The fecond motiue, ftirring vp this reuerence in him, was the confideration of Gods wonderfull mercie to him and his familie, in fauing them. This mercy feemed fo wonderful to him, both for that he knew it was vndeferued (knowing himfelfe a finnefull man, and therefore not able to merit Gods fauour, and beeing priuie to himfelfe of his owne manifold imperfections) & alfo *vnexpected*, for he neuer thought to haue beene fpared alone in an vniuerfall deftruction: therefore he wondred with reuerence at fo great a mercie. Thus Gods mercies doe not onely winne a mans heart to *loue* God, but euen to *feare* him with much reuerence: this *Dauid* prooueth (Pfalm.130. 4.) *There is mercie with thee, O Lord, that thou maiſt be feared:* as though he had faid; thy great mercies to thy children, O Lord, doe make them conceiue a reuerent eftimation of thee. This made *Dauid* crie out in a holy paffion: *How excellent are thy mercies, O Lord!*

And as Gods children wonder at the excellencies of Gods *mercies* vnto them, fo alfo at their *owne bafeneffe* and vnworthieneffe. Thus doth holy *Dauid*, 2. Sam. 7. 18. (who as hee was a man of much faith, fo was he full of excellent meditations, and reuerent fpeeches of God, which are the true effects of faith) when God had fet him in his kingdom, he faith, *Who am I, O Lord, and what is my houfe, that thou haſt brought me hither?* And 1. Chron. 29. 14. *But who am I, faith he, and what is my people, that we ſhould offer thus vnto the Lord?* And doubtleffe euen fo faid *Noahs* bleffed foule often vnto the Lord, and to it felfe, *Who am I, O Lord, and what is my family,* that we ſhould be chofen out of fo many thoufands, and be faued

when all the world perifheth?

Let vs apply this to our Church and State. If any Nation haue caufe to fay thus, it is *England* God hath deliuered vs out of the thraldome of *ſpirituall Egypt*, and led vs out: not by *a Moſes*, but firft by a childe, then by a woman, and giuen vs his Gofpel, more fully, and freely, and quietly, then any kingdome fo great in the world; and ftill deliuereth vs from the curfed *plots of the Pope*, and tiranous *inuaſions* of the *Spaniard*, who thought to haue marked vs in the foreheads with the brand of infamie, and to haue done to vs as they haue done to other nations whom they haue conquered: but God from heauen fought for vs, & ouerthrew them in their owne deuifes: yea, the Lord *put his hooke in his noſethrils, and his bridle in his lips, and caried him backe againe with ſhame and reproach.* We are vnworthie of fuch a mercie, if our foules doe not often fay vnto God: *O Lord what are we*, and *what is our people*, that thou ſhouldeſt be fo wonderfull in thy mercies vnto vs.

And particularly this muft teach euery Chriftian to be a careful obferuer of the fauours and *mercies* that God vouchfafeth to his foule and bodie, to him or his: and the confideration of them, muft make him daily be *mooued with reuerence*, and reuerent thoughts of Gods Maieftie; and ftill as the Lord is more & more mercifull vnto him, to beare ftill the more *feare and reuerence* vnto him for the fame.

The laft motiue of this *Reuerence* in *Noah*, was the confideration of Gods *power and wiſedome*, both in the *Iudgement*, vpon the world, and in the *mercie* vpon him: for firft, in the *Iudgement* it was wonderfull, that God would chufe fo weake an element as water to deftroy and vanquifh the huge *Giants* of thofe dayes: but therein appeared firft Gods *power*, that by fo weake meanes can caft downe his enemies: And againe, his *wiſedome*; that as an vniuerfall wickedneffe had *polluted* the whole world, fo a flood of *water* fhould *waſh* the whole world. Secondly, the *mercie* was alfo wonderfull, that God fhould chufe to faue *Noah* by fo ftrange a meanes as an *Arke*, which fhould fwimme on the waters. For *Noah* thought, if the Lord will faue me, he will either take me vp into heauen (as he did *Henoch* a little before) or elfe make me build a houfe vpon the top of the higeft mountaine. But, the Lord will faue him by no fuch meanes, but by an *Arke*: wherein appeared, firft Gods power that would faue him by fo weake a meanes, as might feeme rather to deftroy him. For *Noah* muft lie and fwim *in the midſt* of the waters, and yet be faued from the *waters:* and the *Arke* muft faue him; which, in all reafon, if the tempefts had caft it againft the hard rocks and mountaines, or vpon the ftrong Caftles and houfes of the mighty giants, would haue beene broken in pieces: and fo it had, but that God himfelfe was the Mafter and Pilot in that voyage.

And

And secondly, Gods *wisedome* shone cleerely in this meanes ; becaufe God would haue him saued not in such sort, as the world might not see it (as it would haue beene, if he had bin taken vp into heauen, or into the aire): but would haue him saued in an *Arke*; that so all the wicked men, as they were a dying in the water, or expecting death vpon the tops of the hills, might see him liue and be saued, to their more torment, and to their greater shame, who would not beleeue Gods word, as he did. For, as the wicked in hell are more tormented to see the godly in the ioyes of heauen: so doubtlesse were the wicked of *that age*, to see *Noah* saued before their eyes. The view of this power and wisdome of God herein, made *Noah* giue great reuerence to Gods Maieftie.

And no lesse ought it to worke in the hearts of all true hearted English men, and faithfull Christians. For, did not the Lord restore and eftablish the Gospel to our nation, *by a child,* and by a *woman*; and in her time when all other Princes were against her (contrary to the rules of policie)? and did not God in our late deliuerance, ouerthrowe our enemies, not so much by the power of man, as by his owne hand? Did not he fight from heauen? *Did not the starres and the winds in their courses fight againf that Sifera of Spaine?* Let vs therefore with blessed *Noah* stand amazed to see Gods mercies, and with reuerence and feare magnifie his great and glorious name.

And thus we haue the three motiues that mooued in *Noah* this Reuerence of God: the consideration first of his great *Iudgement* on the sinnefull world : 2. Of his great *mercie* in sauing him: 3. Of his admirable *power and wisedome*, shewed both in the Iudgement and in the mercie.

Hitherto of the first effect. It followeth,

Prepared the Arke,

The 2. *effect* of *Noahs faith*, whereby it is commended, is, that he vpon a commandement receiued from God (as we heard before) doth *make and build an Arke*, wherein to saue himfelfe and his familie. Concerning this *Ark*, much might be spoken out of the booke of Gen : but it is not to our purpose: which is no more in this Chapter, but to shew the *obedience and practife of faith*, and therein the excellencie of it. Now the point here to be spoken of, is not the *matter*, nor the *meafure*, nor the *proportion, nor the fashion, nor the ufes* of the Ark; all which in the 6. Chapter of Genesis, are fully described : but the action & *obedience* of *Noah in preparing it*, as God bad him: whereof the holy Ghoft (in Gen. 6. 22.) saith, *Noah did according to all that God had commanded him, euen so did he.*

Now in this action of *Noahs* faith, diuerse points of great moment are to bee considered.

First, why did God bid *Noah make an Arke* 120. yeeres before the flood, when he might

A haue built it in three or foure yeares?

The answer is, God did so for diuers caufes: some respecting the *sinnefull world*, as that they might haue longer time, and more warnings to repent; euery *stroke* of the Arke, during these 120. yeares, beeing a loud *Sermon* of repentance vnto them. Againe, that they might bee without excuse, if they amended not: and lastly, that their iniquities might be full, and their sinnes ripe for vengeance. But of all these, we wil not speake, becaufe they cóceme not *Noah*, of whose faith we are onely to speake: let vs therefore touch onely those caufes which con-

B cerne *Noah*. And in regard of him, the Lord did thus, that he might trie his faith and patience, and exercise other graces of holinesse in him. Thus God dealeth with his seruants alwaies : he exercifeth them many and strange waies in this world. He led the Ifraelits in the deferts of Arabia *fourtie yeares*; whereas a man may trauell from Rameses in Egypt, to any part Canaan, in *fourtie dayes:* and this God did *to humble them, and try them, & to know what was in their heart* (Deut. 8. 2.)

God promised *Abraham* a sonne, *in whom al the nations of the earth should be blessed* (Gen. 12. 3.) But he performed it not of 30. yeares after (Gen. 21. 2.) He gaue *Dauid* the kingdome of Ifrael, and anointed him by *Samuel*, 1. Sam. 16. 13. But he attained it not of many

C yeares after; and in the meane time, was perfecuted and hunted by *Saul, as a flea in a mans bofome: or as a Partridge in the mountaines*, 1. Sam. 24. 15. and 26. 20. And thus God exercifed him, both in that and other his promifes: as he saith, Pfal. 40. 1. In waiting I waited on the Lord : and Pfal. 119. 82. Mine eyes faile for waiting for thy promife! O when wilt thou comfort me? Thus God dealt with them, and thus in fome meafure he deales with all his children, *to humble and to try them, and to know what is in their hearts*; for that, in thefe cafes, men doe alwaies shew themfelues, and their difpofitions. When men enioye all things at their will and wish; who cannot make a faire profeffion? but where men are long deferred, & kept from that is promifed, and they expect, and

D are fo long croffed in their expectations; then they appeare in their owne colours.

And as God dealt with thé, fo wil he one way or other doe with vs : if we be his seruants, he will at fome time of our life or other, lay fome such affliction vpon vs, as may trie vs, and our faith, and our patience, and our humilitie. For if we be hypocrites, and haue no true graces, but onely a shew; this will difcouer it: and if we haue true and found faith, and patience; this will make them shine like orient pearles in their true and perfect beauty.

Secondly, as God bad *Noah build an Arke* fo long time before any neede of it; fo he did, without denying or gainefaying. So faith the ftorie (in Genefis): *He did according to all that God commanded him.* And thus the holy Ghoft faith here, Hee beeing warned of God, by faith *prepared the Arke*: Where wee learne, That where true *faith* is, there followeth true *obedience* to euery commaundement of God: insomuch as a godly beleeuing man no sooner heareth any dutie to be commanded of God, but he thinkes his soule and conscience is tied to obedience: and this is the nature of true faith. And it is as impossible to be otherwise, as it is for fire hauing fewell not to burne. Acts. 15.9. *Faith purifieth the heart*; namely, from carelesse disobedience to Gods word: for if from any corruption at all, then from it especially, because it is most contrarie to the purenesse of true faith.

This being so, sheweth vs, not any fault in our religion (as the Papists slander vs) but the want of our religion, and the want of true faith in the world: for there is almost no obedience to Gods commandement. For first, Turkes and Iewes acknowledge not the Scriptures: and the Papists haue set aside Gods commaundements to set vp their owne. And few Protestants haue the feeling of the power of true religion, and nothing indeed but a bare profession: but it must be a feeling of the power of it, which produceth due obedience. And alas, wee see men obey not Gods commandements, God saith,

Commande-ments 3,4. *Sweare not by my name vainely: keepe my Sabbath.* Where is there a man of many that feareth to breake these; Alas there are more mockers of such as would keepe them, then carefull and conscionable keepers of them. How truly said Christ, *When the sonne of man commeth, shall he finde faith on the earth?* It is likely, therefore, these be the dayes, wherein we may wait for the comming of Christ; for the generall want of obedience, sheweth the generall want of faith.

But this *obedience* of *Noah* is better to bee considered of: for it was very excellent and extraordinarie; there beeing many hinderances that might haue stopped him in the course of his obedience, and haue perswaded him neuer to haue gone about the *making of the Arke.*

As first, the great *quantity* of the Arke, amounting to many thousand Cubits; a worke of huge labour, and great charge.

Againe, the *length* of his labour, to last 120. yeares. It is a tedious thing, and troublesome to mans nature, to be euer in doing, and neuer to haue done.

Thirdly, the building of it was a matter of much *mockery* to the world: for, it signified; 1. the destroying of the whole world; 2. the sauing of him and his. These things were taunted at by the worldly wise men of that sinfull age, and he was loudly laught at by many a man, to thinke all the world should perish; but much more, if all perished, to imagine, that he and his should be deliuered.

Lastly, the building of the Arke was a harsh thing to *nature*, and naturall reason, in many respects; for,

First, that all the world should be destroyed, seemed not *possible* to be, because it neuer had beene.

Secondly, it seemed not *likely* that Gods mercy should be so wholly swallowed vp of his iustice.

Thirdly, they must liue in the Arke, as in a close prison, without comfort of light or fresh aire, and amongst beasts of all sorts, and that for a long time, he knew not how long. Now reason would tell him, he had better die with men, then liue with beasts; and better die a free man and at liberty, then liue a prisoner; and better die with company, then liue alone: And that if God had purposed to saue him, he could haue vsed other meanes, and more easie, more direct, and more safe then this; that therefore his deliuerance was to be doubted of. And lastly, reason would say: I may make my selfe a gazing and mocking stocke to the world for 120. yeares; and it may be then Gods purpose will be altred, and no floud will come; or if it come, I goe into *the Arke*, and it chance to breake against the mountaines, so that I perish with the rest, then am I worst of all, who perish notwithstanding all my labour; therefore I had better let it alone, and take my venture with the rest of the world.

These doubtlesse, and many such naturall considerations came into his minde, and stood vp as so many impediments of his *faith*. But, behold the power of true *faith*, in the heart of a holy man: It ouergoeth all doubts, it breaketh through all difficulties, to obey the will and word of God. Yea, it giues a man *wings*, with which to flie ouer all carnall obiections. Thus wee see it here in *Noah*, and afterward shall as cleerely see it in *Abraham*, and other holy men.

The vse of this doctrine discouereth the weaknesse of many mens faith: for if the doctrine of the *Gospel* go currant with our natural affections, or seeme plausible to our natures, we doe formally obey it: But if it crosse our affections, or goe beyond our reason, or controll our naturall dispositions, then we spurne against it, we call it into question, we are offended at it, and denie our obedience. Here wants the faith of *Noah*, which carried him beyond the compasse of nature, and reach of reason, and made him beleeue and doe that which neither nature could allowe, nor reason like of, and which would be displeasing to his naturall affections. Let vs therefore learne to practise true faith, by beleeuing forthwith what God shall say vnto vs, without asking aduise, or hearing the obiections of flesh and blood. God threatned in times past the ouerthrow of the great *Monarchies* of the *Assyrians, Chaldeans, Persians, Grecians, Romanes*: reason did make doubts how it could be, but *faith* beleeued it, and it is done. God in latter times threatned the fall of *Abbies*, and dispersing of *Monkes*, for their wickednesse. It seemed impossible to reafon: yet faith in fome beleeued it, and it came to paffe.

God now threatneth the ruine of *Babylon*, and the full reuelation of *Antichrift*, and the ouerthrowe of the newe found Hierarchie of the *Iefuites*, which glitter fo in worldly glory, and in outward ftrength: this feemes hard to bring to paffe; but let *faith* beleeue it, for it is Gods word, and fhall be fulfilled in his feafon. God hath faid, that our *bodies* fhall rife againe, euen thefe bodies which are burned to afhes, or eaten of beaftes, or fifhes, or turned to duft in the earth. This is a wonder to nature, an a-mazement to reafon: but faith will beleeue it, and fhall finde it true, for God hath faid it.

God faith, Chrift is in the Sacrament *truly* and *really prefent* to the foule of a Chriftian. Carnall fenfes denie this, and naturall reafon knoweth not how, but aske with the *Caper-naits*, *How can he giue vs his flefh to eate?* But faith beleeueth it, and knoweth how; though to outward fenfe it cannot be expreffed. And it was a holy & diuine fpeech vfed by holy *Mar-tyrs*, who beeing asked how Chrift could bee eaten in the Sacrament, and not with the teeth, anfwered; *My foule knoweth how.* God faith, *Wicked* men though they flourifh neuer fo, are *miferable*; and good men are *bleffed* aboue all other. Reafon and worldly experience fay this is falfe: but *true faith beleeues it*, and findes it true; for neuer did any child of God defire to change his eftate with the mightieft or weal-thieft wicked man in the world. God faith, *He that will follow Chrift, muft denie himfelfe*, and his owne defires, and follow Chrift, in bitter-neffe and affliction. Nature faith, *This is a hard leffon: who can beare it?* But faith beleeues it, yeeldes to it, and endeauours the practife of it, becaufe God hath fo commaunded. Such is the power and excellencie of *true faith*.

Fourthly and laftly, out of this action and obedience of *Noah*, marke a fpeciall leffon. God had reuealed to him, that he would faue him and his family, and affured him hee fhould not perifh. Yet for all this, he *makes an Arke*: whereupon it followeth, that *Noah*, though he knew God would faue him, yet was perfwaded he muft vfe the meanes, or elfe fhould not be faued. He might haue faid to himfelfe, God hath faid, and bound himfelfe by couenant, he will faue me; now if I make not the Arke, yet his word is his word, and he will ftand to it. His will cannot be altred, though I be falfe, he will be true; though I doe not that I fhould doe, yet he will doe what belongs to him: therefore I will fpare my labour and coft of *making the Arke*; efpecially feeing it is a matter of fo much mockery, & fo ridiculous to reafon. But *Noah* is of another minde: he will not fe-uer Gods word from his meanes, he dependeth on Gods *word* for his fafetie, but not on his *bare word* without the *meanes*.

Whence we learne, that though a man bee *certaine* of his faluation, yet he is to vfe the

meanes of faluation: and that not onely though he bee certaine in the *certaintie of faith*, but though he could be affured from God him-felfe by immediate reuelation. For if God fhould fay to a man by his name, thou fhalt be faued; It is no more, then here was faid to *No-ah* for his deliuerance. For to him faid God, *I will deftroy all flefh: but with thee I will make my couenant*, and thou fhalt be deliuered: yet, for all that, *Noah* iudgeth, that if he vfe not the meanes, if he *make not an Arke*, he is to looke for no deliuerance: this was *Noahs* diuinitie;

Contrary both to the diuinitie and practife of fome in this age: who fay, *If I fhall be faued, I may liue as I lift*: and though I liue as I lift, yet if in the ende I can fay, *Lord haue mercie on me*, I am fafe enough. But *Noah* would not truft *his bodie* on fuch conditions, though they be fo prefumptious as to truft their *foules*. Let fuch men be affured, God in his decree hath ti-ed the ende and the meanes together. *Let not therefore man feparate what God hath ioyned together:* he that doth, let him look for no more faluation if he vfe not the meanes, then Noah would haue done for fafetie, if he had made *no Arke*, And thus we fee the fecond effect of his faith. It followeth;

To the fauing of his houfhold.

Now this fecond effect of preparing, is fur-ther enlarged by a particular enumeration of the *Endes* or purpofes, why the *Arke* was made; namely, both of Gods commandement, and his obedience in making it.

1. By it *he faued his houfhold.*
2. Hereby *he condemned the world.*

The firft ende which both God had in com-maunding, and *Noah* in *making the Arke*, was *the fauing of his houfhold:* that is, himfelfe, and all that belonged to him; which were his wife, his three fonnes, and their wiues, Gen.7.7.

But firft of all, it may feeme wonderfull, how this *Arke* fhould *faue him and his houfhold* in this generall deftruction. For it was a great and huge veffell refembling a fhip: yet fo farre vn-like, as it is rather called an *Arke*. It muft flote aboue the water, It muft be *laden* with a hea-uie burthen; and yet without *Anchor* to ftay her, without *maft* to poife her, without *fterne* to guide and mooue her, without *Mafter* to gouerne her. For Noah was partly a husband-man, and partly a Preacher: and though he had much learning, yet the vfe of fayling was not then found out; and therefore in all reafon this Arke would be caried on hills and rockes, by the violence of the Tempefts, and fo flit in pie-ces. Yet, for all this, *it faued him*, euen when heauen and earth feemed to runne together (fo vehement was the raine) euen then it faued him and his. How came this to paffe? Euen becaufe Gods prouidence and his hand was with it: *He was the Mafter*, & the Steres-man. For as God himfelfe *fhut the doore of the Arke vpon him*, when he was in, and made it faft after him, that no water might enter (which was impoffible for Noah himſelfe to haue done.) Gen. 7. 16. So doubtleſſe the ſame God that had vouchſafed to be his *Porter*, was alſo his *keeper and preſeruer*, and the *Maſter* of the Arke during that voyage. And from hence came it to paſſe, that the Arke ſaued him, which otherwiſe in reaſon it could neuer haue done.

Here we learne, firſt, the ſpeciall and extraordinary preſence and prouidence of God ouer his children in great diſtreſſes and extremities. His prouidence is ouer all his workes, for *hee forgets nothing that he hath made*: but the ſpeciall eye of his prouidence watcheth ouer his children; as a Maſter of a family hath an eie ouer his meaneſt ſeruants, yea ouer his very cattell: but his care night and day is for his children. And as God ouerlooketh all his children alwaies: ſo principally his prouidence ſheweth it ſelfe, when they are in the deepeſt dangers, or in the greateſt want of naturall helps. When *Daniel was caſt into the Lyons denne*, God was there with him, and *ſhut their mouthes*, Dan. 6. 22. When the *three children were caſt into the fierie fornace*, God was with them, and tooke away the natural force from the fire: Dan. 3. 27. When the *Iſraelites* were to paſſe through the ſea or elſe die (a hard ſhift) God was with them and made the ſea giue place to his children, *and ſtand like two wals on either ſide them*, Exod. 14. 22. When they were to wander through the the wide wilderneſſe, through ſo many dangers and diſcomforts as Deſerts doe afford, *Chriſt was with them*, and waited vpon them with his continuall comfort and aſſiſtance, 1. Corin. 10. 4. And ſo when Noah was to goe into the *Ark*, and (beeing in) muſt haue the *dore ſhut*, and cloſed vpon him; his caſe was pitifull. For, doe it himſelfe he could not; it both beeing *ſo bigge*, that Elephants and Camels muſt enter in at it: and though he could haue pulled it to: yet beeing within, he could neuer haue ſufficiently *cloſed* it from the water: Nor would any other of that wicked world doe it for him: they did not owe him ſo much loue or ſeruice, but rather mockt him, and laught at him: as *firſt*, for making the Arke; ſo now for entring in, when he knew not how to haue it cloſed. How ſhould he doe? himſelfe *could not*, others would not. *God himſelfe with his owne hand ſhut it for him.* And after, when he was in, and was in danger to be throwen vpon the rocks, and to be ſplit in pieces on the hills, and had no Anchor, no ſterne, no Pilot, no Maſter; God himſelfe was with him, and was *all in all vnto him*. The eye of his loue, and the hand of his power was ouer him, and ſo the Arke *ſaued him & his houſhold*. Such is the prouidence of God ouer his, when they are in the deepeſt diſtreſſes, and moſt deſtitute of all worldy comforts.

The vſe of this doctrine miniſtreth *comfort* vnto Gods children: who as they are ſure of *ſtrange calamities to fall vpon them*; ſo are they ſure alſo of a ſpeciall care of God ouer them, euen in their greateſt extremities. And this may

Gods children (who ſerue him in the true *obediēce of faith*) euer aſſure themſelues of, that the Lord doth neuer forget, nor forſake them in any of their troubles: but will be euer readie with his mercifull hand, to *defend* them from dangers, to *prouide* for them in neceſſities, and to *comfort* them in diſtreſſes, when they know not in the world how to doe. *Eliſha* had an armie of men ſent againſt him, to take him: How ſhould one man eſcape from a whole armie? His man cried, *Alas Maſter, what ſhall we doe?* He anſwered his man, and bad him, *feare not, there were more for him then againſt him*; that is, more *Angels* (though they were vnſeene) for him, then there were men in the Armie againſt him. And ſo when *no man* would ſhut the doore for *Noah*, there were *Angels* enow readie ſent from God to doe it for him: and when all wicked men wiſhed he might periſh with the *Ark* he had made, and aſſured themſelues he would periſh, hauing no ſuch helps as ſhips require; then the holy Angels, or rather God himſelfe, ſupplied all ſuch wants vnto him: and ſo when themſelues periſhed, they ſawe *him and his houſhold ſaued by that Arke*. And no leſſe care hath God ouer his Church and children to this day. And though he worketh not viſible miracles for them, yet they feele and finde that he is oftentimes mighty & wonderfull in *preſeruing* them, in *prouiding* for them, in *aſſiſting* them, and in *comforting* them, when elſe without that prouidence of his, they knowe they had miſcaried.

Againe, whereas *God himſelfe* vouchſafeth in *Noahs* danger to be the *Maſter and Pilot* of this Arke, that ſo it may *ſaue him and his houſhold*; we learne the auntientie and dignitie of the trade of Mariners, Saylers, and Maſters of ſhips. *The auntientie*: For we ſee it is as old as Noah, as old as this ſecond world, euen 4000 yeares olde. The *dignitie* is great; for God himſelfe was both the firſt *author*, and the firſt *practiſer* of it. The *author and firſt deuiſer*: For Noah made not this *Arke* of his owne head, but (as we heard before) he was *warned of God* to doe it. And he was the firſt *practiſer*; for God himſelfe performed all thoſe ſeruices vnto Noah in the Arke: elſe it had neuer ſaued him.

This beeing ſo, It is the more griefe to ſee that worthie calling ſo abuſed, and debaſed as it is; the moſt of them that practiſe it beeing profane, vngodly and diſſolute men. Such men ſhould remember, God made the firſt ſhip, and God was the firſt Maſter, and the firſt *Mariner*, the firſt *Pilot*, the firſt gouernour of a ſhip: and they ſhould labour to be iike him. This is one of thoſe fewe callings, which may ſay, God himſelfe was the firſt deuiſer and practiſer of it. Al callings cannot ſay ſo; why then ſhould they ſo farre forget whom they ſucceede? Indeede vpon the ſeas and in diſtreſſes, they will make ſome profeſſion of religion: but let them come a-ſhore; what *ſwearing*, what *whoring*, what *drunkenneſſe* amongſt them? But let them bee

2. King. 6. 15, 16.

afraid to be so profane, which hold the place, which once God himselfe held: or els let them know they are vn worthy of so good a calling.

And thus we see the reason, and the meanes how the Arke could *saue him and his houshold*; namely, because God did gouerne it.

In the next place, obserue the *end and vse* of the Arke. It was to *saue this holy man and his houshold*. Learne here that Gods seruants in common calamities haue safety: For, God himselfe giueth them security, and prouideth deliuerance. Thus was it euer. When God proceedeth in iudgement against *Hierusalem*, for the sinnes thereof: he *marketh the godly in their foreheads*; namely, such as mourne and cry for the abhominatiõs which are done against God, Ezech. 9. 4.

When *Sodome* must be destroyed, *righteous Lot* and his family, must be drawn out; nay, the *Angell can doe nothing till he be safe*, Gen. 19. 16. 22. When the *destroying Angell* went ouer the land of Egypt, and destroyed the first borne in euery house of the Egyptians (the Israelites dwelling amongst them) he *past ouer* all the *Israelites*, whose doores were sprinkled with the blood of the Paschall Lambe, Exodus, 12. 13: And euen so hee whose heart and soule is sprinkled with the blood of Iesus Christ the lambe of God, no calamity can doe him hurt; nay, when others are smitten he shall be deliuered.

The vse of this doctrine is to *our Church and State*: Wee haue by Gods mercy long enioyed Peace and the Gospell; and both, vnder a gracious gouerment: and with these, manie other blessings. Yet speake truth, and the sinnes of our times call for a *floud*, as in *Noahs* time: and sure a floud of tribulation must come one way or other. For this was alwayes the state of Gods Church; now peace, now persecution. *Peace* abused, causeth *trouble*, and calamities. Therefore as we haue so long had peace and ease; so assuredly looke for a floud: what it will be or when, knoweth no man; onely hee who will send it, the *righteous and almighty God*. How then shall wee doe, when the floud of tribulation is vpon vs; There is no way but one. *Beleeue* in Christ Iesus; settle thy heart in true faith: *repent* of thy sinnes: get Gods *fauour* and forgiuenesse: and then when the floud comes, Gods prouidence shall affoord thee (one way or other) an *Arke of safetie* and deliuerance. Sprinkle thy soule now with *Christs blood* by faith and true repentance: and the destroying Angell of Gods wrath, shall *passe ouer thee and thy houshold*.

Thirdly, obserue the *largenesse* of Gods bounty. Not onely *Noah* shall be saued, but with him *his houshold also*. Why the Lord did so, there bee diuers reasons.

First, for the Propagation and *multiplication of the world* after the floud. If any obiect, *Noah and his wife* might haue serued for that end: I answere, they were olde; for hee was

600. yeares olde, when the flood came: and though he liued 300. yeares after the flood (Gen. 9. 28.); Yet reade we not of any children that he had. If any further obiect; The first world was begun, and multiplied by two alone, *Adam and Eue*, and no more: why then should there be so many for the beginning of the second world? I answere: God did so in the beginning, to shewe that *all mankind came of one blood* (Acts. 17. 26.) and that in regard of bodie or birth, there is no difference originally betwixt man and man: which also was obserued euen in the second beginning. For, though the world was multiplied by three brethren, *Shem, Cham, and Iapheth*: Yet those three were not strangers, but all sonnes to one man *Noah*, so that as at first by *Adam & Eue*; so after from *Noah and his wife* came all men in the world. But in the beginning of the *second world*, there must needes be more lines then one: because now the *blessed seede* was promised, whose line and kindred must needes be kept distinct from all other, vntill his incarnation. Againe, there was more cause now why the world should be speedily replenished then at the beginning. For, first the earth had some glory and beauty left it after the *first curse*; so that it was still a most pleasant and delightfull habitation to *Adam and Eue*. But now by the *second curse* in the flood, all her beauty was gone, she and all her glory was ouerrunne, spoyled, and defaced: so that it had beene a miserable habitation for Noah and his wife, if they had beene without company. Secondly, the earth beeing much defaced, and the vertue of it almost quite perished by the flood, had now more neede to be recouered, by the hands and helps of many mens labours. And to this purpose the Scripture saith, Gen. 9. 19. and 10. 32. that the earth was *deuided amongst the three sonnes of Noah*. And they liued not all together, but *ouerspread the earth* And least the beasts, which then were many, should ouergrowe the world, therefore God would haue the world speedily replenished; and to that ende *Noah* and his *wife* had neuer a seruant in the Arke, but onely such as should haue children: *their 3. sonnes and their wiues*. And thus the multiplication of mankind is the first cause, why God saued *Noahs* children.

The second cause: It is likely that as himselfe was a *righteous man*, so they of his family were more orderly and religious, then others of that wicked Age; for good men make conscience of teaching their families: as *Abraham* Gen. 18. 18. And seeing Noah is commended for a iust and good man, doubtles, he did carefully instruct *his houshold*, and therefore it is to be supposed, that all, or the most of them were holy and righteous persons fearing God.

Thirdly, though al of them were not righteous, yet they were all of the family of *righteous Noah*: and therefore for his sake they were saued;

saued; all beeing his *children*, or his childrens *wiues*. For, the righteous man procureth blessings not on himselfe alone, but on all that belong vnto him, dwel with him, or are in his company. At *Abrahams* requeſt, had there bin but *tenne righteous men in Sodom*, all had beene ſpared *for their ſakes*, (Gen. 18.32.) When *Ioſeph* dwelt in *Egypt*, all *Putiphars houſe*, and all in it (though he were a heathen man) were bleſſed for *Ioſephs* ſake; (Gen. 39. 5.) When *Lot* was deliuered out of *Sodomes* deſtruction, the *Angels* asked him, *Haſt thou any ſonnes in law?* that they might haue beene ſaued for his ſake, (Gen. 19.12.) When *Paul* and 276. *ſoules* with him ſuffered ſhipwracke, and were all in preſent danger of drowning, God ſaued *Paul*, and for his ſake all the reſt : *God gaue him the liues of all that were with him in the ſhip*, Act. 27.24. And ſo here *Noahs* children, and their wiues, are ſpared for *Noahs* ſake.

Let this encourage all men to ſerue God in truth and vprightneſſe; ſeeing thereby they ſhall not make *themſelues* alone bleſſed, but bring downe Gods bleſſing euen on *their houſes*, children, and poſterities: yea, the very *places* where, & the *people* with whom they dwell, ſhall fare the better for them. And thus we ſee the cauſes and reaſons, why not *Noah* alone, but euen his houſhold were alſo ſaued.

In the fourth place, let vs obſerue how the holy Ghoſt ſaith, that *Noah* built the Arke; not for the ſauing of himſelfe, but *of his houſhold:* and it is ſo ſaid for two cauſes.

Firſt, to ſhew that Noah, though he were the *head* and gouernour, yet was *one of the houſhold;* for in the word *houſhold*, himſelfe is comprehended. Maſters and Fathers, though they be gouernours, yet muſt thinke themſelues *members* of the houſhold; ſo will they haue more care thereof, when they eſteeme themſelues members of the bodie, and parts of the whole.

Secondly, to teach vs what care *Noah* had for his family; euen ſo great, as he *prepared the Ark to ſaue them withall.* Here is an example of a worthie Maſter of a houſhold; and yet all this was but for a temporall deliuerance. Now if he was ſo carefull for their *bodily* ſafetie, how much more was he to ſaue them from *hell and damnation*, which he knew to be an eternall deſtruction of both ſoule and body. Therefore doubtles as he was a diligent *Preacher of righteouſneſſe* to that ſinnefull world: ſo principally a diligent *Preacher*, and *Prayer*, and *Chatechiſer* of his owne family; that ſo he might make them Gods ſeruants, and deliuer them from the eternall fire of hell.

Noahs example is to be a patterne to all *Parents* and Fathers of families, to teach them care not onely for the *bodies*, and bodily welfare of their families, but eſpecially for their *ſoules* and ſpirituall welfare. And if they be bound by all bonds of nature and religion, to prouide for the *bodies* of their children; let reaſon iudge,

how much more ſtraightly they are tied to looke to their ſoules. But *S. Paul* ſaith, *He that prouideth not temporall things neceſſary for his family, is worſe then an Infidel*, 1. Tim. 5. 8. Then what is he who prouideth nothing for their ſoules? Surely, his caſe is extremely feareſull. Therefore when thou haſt prouided meat, apparell, a calling, and mariage, houſe and liuing for thy child; thinke not thou haſt done, and ſo maiſt turne them off. The *world* may take them thus: But *God* will not take them ſo at thy hands. No, the greater dutie remaines behind; thou muſt prouide for their ſoules, that they may know God, and feare his name. Thou muſt with *Abraham* (Gen.18. 19.) *Teach thy family, that they may walke in the waies of God: I knowe Abraham*, ſaith God, that he *will doe it*. And ſurely God will knowe all ſuch as do ſo. By doing thus, men ſhall make their houſes *Churches* of God, as here *Noahs* was: and it would be farre better with our Church and State, if men did ſo: *Miniſters* in the Church, and *Iuſtices* in the Country ſhould haue much leſſe to doe, if *Maſters* of families would doe their duties.

But to go further; let vs ſee more *particularly* what this *houſhold* was, that was thus ſaued by the Arke.

Firſt, it was a familie of *foure men* and *foure women*: not men or women alone; but both, and conſiſting of as many *women as men*. Thus God would haue one ſexe to loue another, and one to thinke themſelues beholden to the other: the beginning of the firſt world was by *one man* and *one woman*. Of the ſecond, by *foure men*, and *foure women*; but alwaies equall. And here alſo God would teach men not to contemne the other, though the weaker ſexe: for God ſaued as many of them from the vniuerſall flood, as he did men.

Secondly, how many were they in all? *but eight perſons.* Of the whole world no more were ſaued. A miſerable ſpectacle. See what ſinne can doe. It can bring many *Millions to eight perſons* in a ſhort time. See what it is to offend God. Let vs not then glory in our *multitudes*, but glory in this that we *knowe and ſerue God:* for otherwiſe, if our ſinnes *cry* out to him againſt vs, he can eaſily make vs fewe enow.

Thirdly, what were theſe *eight perſons?* not one *ſeruant* amongſt them all; there were none but *Noah* and his wife, his three ſonnes and their wiues. It is meruailous, that here were none of *Noahs ſeruãts*. Som think he had none, and that the *ſimplicitie* of thoſe dayes required no attendance, but that each one was ſeruant to himſelfe. And they ſeeme to gather it out of Gen. 7. 1. where God biddeth *Noah, Enter thou and all thine houſe into the Ark:* And when they entred, they are recounted in the ſeauenth verſe, to be none but *himſelfe, his wife, and his children*, therefore ſay they, in Noahs houſe, there were no ſeruãts. But why might not *Noah* haue ſeruants, as well as *Abraham and Lot* had?

had? doubtlesse he had. But, behold a wonderfull matter : *Noahs* owne seruants would not beleeue his preaching, but chose rather to liue loosely with the *world*, and perish with it, then to liue *godly* with their *Master*, and be saued with him. This was and will be true in all Ages that in a wicked age, or in a wicked towne, a *Master* shall not be able to gouerne his owne *seruants* ; but the streame of common wickednesse, and ill examples of other men doth draw them from the obedience of their *Masters.* They can readily alleadge for themselues , we will not be vsed more hardly then other mens are , wee will not be tied to our houres, and bound to so many exercises, we will doe as others doe. Thus would *Noahs* seruants doe, and perished with the world. So hard a thing is it for a good man to haue good seruants in such times or places where wickednes raigneth.

And thus we haue seene in some sort, How the *Arke saued* Noah *and his houshold,* and what this *houshold* of his was.

Now besides this *end and vse of the Arke,* we are further to know ; that whereas this *sauing* of them was but a *corporall deliuerance* from a temporall death , this *Arke* hath also a *spirituall* vse, which we may not omit: for as many of *Noahs* family as were *true beleeuers,* it was a means to saue them another way, euen to saue their *soules* : for it taught them many things.

First, it was an assurance of Gods *loue* vnto their *soules* : for if hee was so carefull to saue their *bodies* from the flood, they thereby assured themselues, he would be as good vnto their *soules;* which they knew to be farre more pretious and excellent.

Secondly, it shewed them how to be saued. For, as they saw no safety, nothing but present death out of the *Arke:* So it taught them, that out of *Gods Church,* and out of Gods fauour, no saluation could be expected;& so it taught them to labour to be in Gods fauour, and members of his true *Church.*

Thirdly, they saw they were saued from the flood, by *faith and obedience.* For first , *Noah* beleeued Gods word, that the flood should come ; then he *obayed* Gods commandement, and *made the Arke* , as he was commanded. And thus hee and his, by beleeuing and obaying, were *saued* through the Arke:and without these , the Arke could not haue saued them. This taught them more particularly how to be saued ; namely, by *beleeuing God, and obaying God,* and else no saluation. For, when they saw their bodies could not be saued without them ; it assured them much lesse could their soules be saued without faith and obedience.

Lastly , this *deliuerance by the Arke* was a pawne vnto them from God, assuring them of *saluation,* if they beleeued in the Messias. For, seeing God so fully performed his promise vnto them for their bodily deliuerance vpon their beleeuing: they thereby might assure theselues, he would performe his promise of saluatió vnto

them , vpon their *faith and true obedience.* Moreouer, it strengthned their faith.For, when euer after any promise of God was made vnto them , or any word of God came vnto them, they then remembred Gods mercie and faithfulnesse vnto them in their *deliuerance by the Arke:* and therefore beleeued.

Vnto these and many other *spirituall* vses, did the Arke serue vnto *Noah, and to his houshold,* as many of them as were *beleeuers.*

But what is this to vs? Indeede, the *Arke* serued them for a *temporall* deliuerance, it saued their liues ; therefore they also had reason to make *spirituall* vse of it : But it saued not vs, it serued vs to no vse corporall; therefore how can we make any spirituall vse of it.

I answer; though we had no *corporall* vse of the Arke,yet there ariseth an excellent *spirituall* vse out of the consideration of it.

The *Arke of Noah and our baptisme* , are figures correspondent one to the other : that, that *Noahs Arke* was to them, *Baptisme* is to vs. Thus teacheth S. *Peter,* 1.3. 20. 21. *To the Arke of Noah the figure which now saueth vs, euen Baptisme* agreeth. The same that S. *Paul* here ascribeth to the Arke, S. *Peter* ascribeth to *Baptisme.* The Arke saued them, Baptisme saueth vs. Now the resemblance betwixt these two figures, hath two branches.

First, as it was necessary for them that *should be saued* in the flood, to be in the *Arke;* and out of the *Arke* no possibilitie to escape: So is it for them that will haue their *soules* saued , to be in *Christ,* and of his Church; they must bee *mysticall* members of *Christ* , and visible members of his *Church* : and out of *Christ and his Church,* no possibilitie of saluation. That this is true(for *Christ*) S. *Peter* prooueth apparantly, Acts 4. 12. *Among men there is no name giuen vnder heauen, whereby to be saued,but the name of Iesus Christ; neither is there saluation in any other.*

And that this is true , for the *Church,* hee prooueth , Acts , 2. 47. *The Lord added to the Church daily such as should be saued.* See how such as are to be saued must ioyn themselues to the *Church,* when they see where it is: and all this is signified and taught in *Baptisme.* For the *outward* vse of *Baptisme* makes vs members of the *visible* Church, and the *inward* and powerfull vse of *Baptisme* makes vs members of *Christ himselfe.*

The vse and consideration hereof, should make vs all more carefull to be true members of *Christ,* and of his *Church,* by making not onely a bare profession of religion ; but by seeking to be incorporate into Christ by *faith* and true *repentance* : for this must saue vs when nothing can. As they that were out of *the Arke,* no gold nor siluer could buy out their safetie, no lands nor liuings , no houses nor buildings , no hilles nor mountaines , nothing in the world, nor the whole world it selfe could saue them; but beeing out of the *Arke* they all perished:

shed: So if a man be out of *Chriſt*, and out of his *Church*, no gold nor ſiluer, no honour nor glory, no wit nor policy, no eſtimation nor au-thoritie, no friends nor fauour, no wiſdome nor learning, no hills of happineſſe, nor mountaines of gold can ſaue his ſoule; but he muſt periſh in the *flood* of gods eternal wrath. For as it proued folly in them that truſted to their high houſes, or catcht hold on the hils, if they were *out of the Arke*: ſo will it prooue much greater folly to them that ſhall truſt to any means of ſaluation, if they be *out of Chriſt*. And contrariwiſe, as they that were *in the Arke* were ſure to be ſa-ued, doe the waters, windes and weathers, ſtormes and tempeſts all they could; and ſo that ſtill, the more the waters roſe, the *Arke* roſe alſo, and was euer higher then they; and the higher it was caried by the violence of the wa-ters, the ſafer it was from the danger of hills & rockes: and ſo in the *midſt* of danger they were out of danger, & were ſaued in the midſt of the water: So, he that is once truely in Chriſt, is ſure of ſaluation, nothing can hinder it; *floods* of ca-lamities may aſſault him and humble him, but they hurt not his ſaluation: he is in the *Arke*, he is in *Chriſt*: nay the *gates of hell ſhall not ouer-throwe him*: but through all the waues of the deuills malice, & through all tempeſts of temp-tations, the bleſſed *Arke* of Chriſts loue and merits ſhall carie him vp, and at laſt ſhall con-uay him to ſaluation; this is the bleſſed aſſu-rance of all them that are truely *baptized into Chriſt*. But as for ſuch, as out of their prophan-neſſe, either care not to be in *Chriſt*, or con-temne *Baptiſme*: let them aſſure themſelues, they be out of the *Arke*, and they periſh cer-tainely. This is the 1. part of the reſemblance.

The ſecond is this: *Noahs* bodie going *into the Arke*, he ſeemed therein a *dead* man, going into a graue or tombe to be buried; for he was buried in the *Arke*, and the *Arke* in the waters, and he depriued of the freſh aire and gladſome light; yet by Gods appointment, it was the meanes to ſaue *Noah*, which in all reaſon, ſee-med to be his graue; and if Noah will be ſaued he muſt goe into this graue. So they that will eſcape hell and damnation by *Chriſt*, the true *Arke* of holineſſe, muſt be buried and mortifi-ed in their *fleſh*, and fleſhly luſts; and there is no way to come to life euerlaſting but this. For thy *ſoule* cannot liue, whilſt thy *ſinnes*, the olde man, that is, thy corruptions doe liue; but they muſt die, and be buried, and then thy *ſoule liueth*: and whilſt they liue, thy ſoule is dead, & farre from the *life of grace*, which is in Chriſt Ieſus. All this is affirmed at large, in Rom.6.3. 4. where we may ſee apparantly, that we muſt by baptiſme *die with Chriſt and be buried with him*, elſe we cannot be ſaued by him: our cor-ruptions, our ſinnes, which are the old man muſt die and be buried: that the newe man, that is, the grace and holineſſe of Chriſt, may liue in vs, and our ſoules by it: and he that thus *dieth* not, neuer *liues*; and hee that thus is not

A

buried, neuer *riſeth* to true life. Thus *mor-tification* of ſinne is the way to heauen, and *death* the way of *life* eternall: and he that is not thus *mortified* in his *corruption*, let him neuer looke to be *quickned to grace or glorie*.

If this be ſo, we may then ſee what a miſera-ble world we now liue in, wherein mortificati-on of ſinne is a thing vnknowne: not a man of many that can tell what it is: nay, *grace* is dead, and *holineſſe* is mortified, and I feare *buried* alſo: but the *old man* raignes, *Corruption* liues, and *ſinne* flouriſheth. Mortifying of *Chriſt* by our ſinnes is common: but mortifying of *ſinne* is ſildome ſeene. For, Chriſt is betrayed, crucified, and killed in a ſort by the ſinnes of men. What a fearefull change is this? Chriſt ſhould *liue* in vs, and wee endeuour to *crucifie* him againe: ſinne ſhould be *crucified*, but it liueth in vs. But if we will haue Chriſt to ſaue vs, then muſt we *mortifie* the bodie of our ſinne. *For, he that will liue when he is dead, muſt die while he is aliue.* And he that will be ſaued by his *baptiſme*, muſt looke that baptiſme worke this effect in him, To make him *die*, and be *buried* with Chriſt, that afterwards he may *riſe* and *raigne* with Chriſt. And then ſhall *Baptiſme* ſaue vs, as the *Arke ſaued faithfull Noah, and his houſhold*. And thus much for the firſt end and vſe of the Arke: the ſecond followeth.

By the which he condemned the world.

Here is the ſecond end, why *Noah* prepared the Arke; To the *condemnation of the world* that then was. For, *by it* (not by his *faith*, as ſome would reade it) he condemned that wic-ked generation, both to a *temporall* deſtructi-on of their bodies, and to an *eternall* Iudgement in hell.

In the words, there are two points to bee conſidered. 1. Who are condemned; *The world.* 2. Whereby? *By Noahs Arke.*

For the firſt, it may be asked, what is meant by the *world? S. Peter* anſwereth (2. Ep. 2.5.) *The world of the vngodly*: that is, that genera-tion of ſinfull men, who liued in the dayes of *Noah*, whom alſo in the 1. Epiſt. 3.20. he cal-leth *diſobedient*: and their more particular ſinns are diſcloſed and recorded by *Moſes*, Gen. 6. 4 5. to be, monſtrous abuſe of holy *mariage*, vnnaturall *luſts, cruelties*, and *oppreſſions*: an vtter neglect of Gods *ſeruice*, and *Sabbath*: and an extreame *prophaneneſſe*, and diſſolute-neſſe in euery kinde. And this corruption was not priuate, or perſonall: but vniuerſall, tho-rough all eſtates, ſexes, and ages. This world of the vngodly; this whole race of wicked & diſo-bedient men were condemned: but how was that world condemned by *Noah*? Thus: God vouch-ſafed them 120. yeares to repent in, & appoin-ted *Noah* to preach vnto thē, during that time, to call them to repentance. But they beleeued not God, nor *Noah*, but continued in their *diſo-bedience*, and grew in their *vngodlines*: therfore when that time was expired, God performed his word ſpoken by Noah, brought the flood

B

C

D

vpon them, deſtroied them all, and condemned in hell as many of them as died in impenitencie and vnbeliefe. And thus that wicked world was condemned, according as *Noah* in his Miniſterie had foretold them.

Here we may learne;

Firſt, what the world of this age is to looke for, vnleſſe there be repentance. For, to ſpeake but of our ſelues in this Nation; Haue not wee had the *Goſpell* 30. yeares and more? and with peace, and much proſperity? Haue not we had a gooly time giuen vs to repent? What is our duty, but with reuerence to ſee and acknowledge this goodneſſe of God, to take hold of this mercifull opportunity, this time of grace, and this day of ſaluation? If we doe not, and make no account of the Goſpel, what can we looke for, but to be condemned, as that world was? Looke at the *meanes* and opportunities, which theſe dayes affoord; & they be as *golden dayes*, as euer were ſince *Chriſt*, or as euer can be expected, till his comming againe. But looke at the *profaneneſſe*, and carnality, and ſecurity of this age (euen ouer all *Chriſtendome*) and this is the *Iron age*, theſe be the euill dayes; and ſo euill, as nothing can be expected, but a *riuer* of brimſtone, and a *flood* of fire to purge it.

The dayes of the *comming of the ſonne of Man* (which I take to be theſe dayes) *ſhall bee like* (ſaith Chriſt, Matth.24.37.) *vnto the daies of Noah:* And ſurely in *ſecurity* and profaneneſſe, they are like; and therefore in all reaſon they muſt bee like in puniſhment. Wee muſt therefore take warning by them, and ſhake off this ſecurity, which poſſeſſeth all mens hearts, and waite for the Lord in *watching and prayer*, and thinke euery day may be the *laſt day* of this world; at leaſt, the laſt day *of our liues:* and let vs prepare for it, and liue in the expectation of it. Otherwiſe, if our ſinfulneſſe growe on a little further; nothing can we looke for, but to be condemned in an vniuerſall iudgement, as that world was. Let vs therefore betake our ſelues to a more ſerious ſeruing of God: that the Lord when he commeth, may finde vs ſo doing.

Secondly, in that the whole *world* that then was, was thus deſtroyed and *condemned*, and (as we heard afore) onely *Noah and his houſhold ſaued*; we learne, that it is not good, nor ſafe to follow the multitude. *Noah* was here a man alone, he held and beleeued againſt *all the world*, and yet his iudgement, and his beliefe was true, and all the worlds falſe: and (accordingly) *he ſaued, when they were all condemned.*

It is meruaile therefore the Church of *Rome* ſhould ſo much ſtand vpon *numbers and multitude*, for the gracing of their religion: For, it euer was, and euer will be a weake argument. If multitudes might euer haue beene alledged; then vnto *Noah* eſpecially, to whome it might haue beene ſaid, Who art thou that pretendeſt to be wiſer then all men? & to know more then al the world? Thou that haſt a faith by

thy ſelfe, and haſt no man to beare thee company; thinke not that all *Adams* poſteritie, all the children of holy *Henoch*, and *Methuſalem* are all deceiued, but thy ſelfe alone? Would not theſe and ſuch like obections, haue diſcouraged any man? Yet behold the *force of faith:* Noah had Gods word for it, and therefore beleeueth againſt all the world, and is commended to all ages for this *faith*. It is therefore but a vaine flouriſh of the Papiſts, to preſſe vs ſo much with their *multitudes*, and *vniuerſality*, and *conſent*, and *vnity*, and *ſucceſſion*, and *continuance*. For, all this is worth nothing; as long as they firſt prooue not, that that doctrine or opinion which theſe multitudes hold, hath his ground from Gods word; till then, all the other is vanitie. For, it is better with Noah, to haue Gods plaine word of his ſide, then to beleeue otherwiſe with *all the world*; which was here deceiued and *condemned*, when Noah alone beleeued Gods word, and was *ſaued*.

And thus we ſee who were condemned: the world. To ende this point, one *queſtion* may not vnprofitably be here mooued:

Whether was all the world, that is, *all the men in that world condemned or no?* The words ſeeme to imply that all but Noah, were: and yet it may ſeeme ſtrange, that of ſo many Millions none ſhould repent but he: and if they repented, why were they not ſaued? I anſwer, The world of that wicked age was condemned two wayes.

Firſt, with a corporall deſtruction, and ſo they were all condemned without exception. No high houſes, no hills, no deuiſes of man could ſaue them. For, the *waters roſe* 15. *cubits aboue the tops of the higheſt mountaines vnder heauen*, Gen.7. 20. And ſo, though till then diuerſe of them liued by flying to the *hilles:* yet that beeing their laſt refuge, and beeing thus taken from them, *then all fleſh periſhed that mooued vpon the earth: and euery man, and euery thing that drewe the breath of life*. For ſo ſaith the Story, Gen.7.21.22. And it is but vaine to imagine, that any of them could be ſaued vpon that *Arke:* for, firſt it was ſo made with a ridge in the top (as is moſt probably thought) that no man could ſtand vpon it, much leſſe make any ſtay, in that violent toſſing by tempeſts. Againe, if they could, yet could they not haue liued ſo long for want of foode; the waters beeing (almoſt) a yeere vpon the earth. And thus it is moſt certaine, they all without exception, were deſtroyed with bodily deſtruction.

But ſecondly, they were condemned to an eternall deſtruction in hell: and therefore S. *Peter*, 1.3. 18.ſaith, *Their ſpirits are now in priſon, who were diſobedient in the dayes of Noah*. Now all the *queſtion* is, whether were they all condemned, or no? I anſwer: For ought that we certainely know out of the Scripture, they were all condemned. Yet in the iudgement of *charitie*, we are not ſo to thinke: and the rather, becauſe there are many probable coiectures, that ſome of them repented. For, howſoeuer many of them beleeued not Noah, iudging that he spake of his owne head: yet it is more then likely, that when they faw it begin to raine extraordinarily, at left, when they faw themfelues driuen to the tops of the hilles, & there looked hourely for death; that then diuers of the pofterity of *Henoch, and Methufalem, and Lamech*, were afhamed of their former vnbeliefe, and then turned to God in faith and in repentance. And doubtles, that is the onely or the principall caufe, why God brought the flood *in fourty dayes*, which hee could haue done in foure houres; that fo men might haue time to repent. Gen. 7.

But it will be faide: If any repented, why then were they not faued? I anfwer; becaufe they *repented not in time*, when they were called, by *Noahs* preaching. Repentance is neuer too late, to faue the *foule* from hell: but it may be to late to faue the bodie from a temporall iudgement. And this, I take it, is that that wee may fafely hold: for it feemes too hard to condemne al the pofterity of *Methufalem, Henoch, Lamech*, and other holy Patriarks (who, as the Text faith, *begat fonnes and daughters*) and to thinke, that none of them repented, when they faw the flood come indeed, as *Noah* had faid. It cannot be, but they heard their Fathers preach: and why might not *that* preaching worke vpon their hearts, when the Iudgement came, though afore it did not? But why then did not God record in the Scripture, neither their repentance, nor faluation, but hath left it fo doubtfull?

I anfwer; for the very fame, for which hee would not record *Adams* nor *Salomons*: All for this caufe, that he might teach all men to the worlds ende, what a fearefull thing it is to difobay his commandement, as *Adam* did: or to defer repentance when they are called by Gods word, as *thefe men* did. Therefore to feare vs from the like, though afterwards they repented; it pleafed God not to record it, but to leaue it doubtfull.

This *queftion* being thus difcuffed, yeelds vs two ftrong motiues to *repentance*.

Firft, for if we *repent* not betime, our ftate then is fearefull and *doubtfull*, though not *defperate*; as we fee here the faluation euen of *Methufhelahs children* is doubtfull: for they repented not when they were called, but deferred it, till the iudgement came. So, if we deferre our repentance til our *deaths*, there is great queftion of our faluation: but let vs repent, when we are called by Gods word, and then it is out of queftion, then there is no doubt of our faluation.

Secondly, if wee *repent betime*, we fhall efcape the temporall Iudgement which God fends vpon the world for finne. If not, but deferre repentance till the Iudgement come, wee may then by it faue our *foules*, but our *bodies* fhall perifh in the vniuerfall Iudgement. If the children of *Henoch* and *Methufhelah*, which were neere a-kinne

unto *Noah*, had repented at *Noahs* preaching, they had beene faued with Noah: they did not. But when they flood came indeed, then doubtlefse they beleeued with Noah, and wifhed themfelues in the Arke with him: but it was too late, they faued their foules, but were drowned with the reft. So affuredly, when God threateneth any Iudgement on our Church or Nation, they that beleeue and repent betime, fhall efcape it. But they that will liue in wantonnes with the world, and not repent till God begin to ftrike: If then they doe, when the flood is come (though *faluation* cannot bee denied to *repentance* whenfoeuer) yet let them affure themfelues, they fhall beare their part with the world in the *punifhmēt*, as they did partake with them in their finnes. Let then thefe two confideratiōs mooue vs all to turne to God by timely repentance: then fhall we be fure to efcape both the *eternall* & *temporall* Iudgement; & not be *condemned*, as here this *world of the vngodly* was. And thus we fee who were *condemned*.

The world.

The fecond point is, whereby were they condemned? the Text faith onely, *by which he condemned*, &c. Whereupon fome would vnderftand *faith*, and reade it thus; by which *faith he condemned the world*. Which though it be true (for the *faith* of holy men *condemnes* the vnbeleeuing and misbeleeuing world) yet is it not proper in this place, where the Arke is defcribed by the vfes of it: which are two, whereof this is one; And (befides the Greeke conftruction doth well beare it) the Iudgement of almoft all interpreters referres it to the Arke. And further in all reafon; that that *faued him and his houfhold, condemned the world* alfo: but the Arke is faid to haue *faued them*; therefore *by it he condemned the world*. Neither is this any derogation, but a commēdation of faith: for by faith he made that *Arke*, which *Arke condemned the world*. Now, by the Arke Noah condemned the world two wayes.

1. By his *obedience* in building it.
2. By his *preaching* in building it.

For the firft, God bad Noah build an *Arke*, fo great, and to fuch an vfe, as in all reafon no man would haue don it. Yet Noah by the power of his *faith* beleeued Gods word, and obeyed, and therefore *builded the Arke*. This faith and obedience of Noah to this Commandement of God, condemned the vnbeleeuing & difobedient world, and made them without excufe. So faith Chrift: The *Nineuites*, who beleeued at the preaching of *Ionas*, fhall rife in Iudgement againft the *Iewes*, and condemne them, becaufe they repēted not at *Chrifts* preaching. And the *Queene of Sheba*, who came fo farre to heare *Salomon*, fhall *condemne them*, who then would not heare Chrift, Matth. 12. 42.43.

Euen fo, Noahs obedience fhall condemne thē. For Noah being told of a *miraculous* thing, and beleeuing it, and beeing commanded fo

vnrea-

vnreaſonable a thing, as the making of the Arke, and obaying, ſhall condemne that wicked world, who would not beleeue Gods ordinarie promiſes; nor obey his ordinarie and moſt holy commandements. And as the *Saints* are ſaid to *condemne the world*, 1. Cor.6. 2. by beeing witneſſes againſt them, and approouers of Gods iuſt ſentence: So Noahs fact and faith condemned that world. And thus we ſee it is apparant, that the obedience, and godly examples of good men, doe *condemne the vngodly*.

The vſe whereof, is to encourage vs all to imbrace Chriſtian religion, and not be daunted by the ſcornes, or other euil behauiours of profane men, which cannot abide the Goſpel. For he that walketh in the way of holineſſe, and keepeth good conſcience *in the midſt of a wicked generation*; if his godlineſſe doe not *ouercome their euill*, and conuert them, it ſhall more demonſtrate their wickednes, and *condemne them*. Our Church is full of mockers, and they diſcourage many from Chriſt and religion: but let them know, this will be the ende of it, their obedience whome they contemne and laugh at, will be their condemnation. And thus Noah by his *obedience* in building the Arke, *condemned the world*.

Secondly, ſo did he alſo by his *preaching*, as he builded it. For, the building of the Arke, was a part of his propheticall miniſterie.

The Prophets preached two waies; in word, and in action. For beſide their *verball* preaching, and deliuering of Gods word, they preached in their *liues and actions*; eſpecially in ſuch actions as were extraordinarie. And ſuch was Noahs building of the Arke: it was an *actuall preaching*; yea, euery ſtroke vpon the Arke, was a loud Sermon to the eyes and eares of that wicked world. For, by making it, he ſignified ſome ſhould be ſaued, and the reſt drowned: namely, all that would beleeue and repent, ſhould be ſaued in it; and all that would not, ſhould (out of it) be drowned: and becauſe they beleeued not this, therefore *by it he condemned them*. From this ground we may learne;

Firſt, that a man may be a true and ſincere Miniſter, lawfully called by God & his church, and yet not turne many vnto God, nor by his Miniſterie bring many to repentance. For here Noah a Prophet called immediatly, yet in 120. yeares preaching both in word and action, he cannot turne one to *faith and repentance*. A moſt fearefull thing, if we well conſider it, that both by preaching and making the Arke, he ſhould not turne one of the ſonnes of Lamech, Methuſhelah, or Henoch, to beleeue him: but that they ſhould all rather chuſe to be miſled in the generall vanitie of that wicked world, then to ſerue God with Noah. This was a moſt diſcomfortable thing vnto him as could be, yet this hath beene the caſe and lot of many holy Prophets. Eſai muſt *goe and preach vnto them*, and yet his doctrine muſt *harden their hearts, that they may not be ſaued*, Eſa.6.10. And Eze-

kiel muſt *goe and ſpeake*, and yet is told aforehand, *they will not heare him, nor repent*, Ezek. 3.4.7. And when Saint *Paul* himſelfe preached vnto the Iewes at Rome, *ſome beleeued not*. Act.28.24. There is nothing will more diſcourage a man, and caſt downe his heart, then to ſee that his labours are not onely in vaine, but doe take a contrarie effect; that whereas they were beſtowed to haue ſaued them, they are meanes of their deeper condemnation. Therefore as when their labours bring men to God, they may greatly reioyce, and account thoſe people, as Saint *Paul* did the Theſſalonians, *his crowne, his ioy and glorie*: So when they doe no good (as Noah here) but that men are worſe and worſe; this muſt humble and abaſe them in themſelues, and let them know the power and vertue is not in them, but God. So ſaith S. *Paul* to the vngodly and impenitent amongſt the Corinthians; *I feare*, ſaith he, *when I come, my God abaſe me amongſt you, and I ſhall bewaile many of them which haue ſinned, and not repented*. And ſurely, this or nothing will abaſe a Miniſter, and miniſter matter of great bewailing: yet not ſo, but as ſtill there is matter of true comfort and contentment, vnto all godly and faithfull teachers. For whether thy labour be the *ſauour of life vnto life*, or of *death vnto death*, to thy hearers; it is *to God a ſweete ſauour in Chriſt*.

Againe, we may here learne, that thoſe who are condemned before God, haue their condemnation by the preaching of the word. *The ſecrets of all the world*, ſaith the Apoſtle, *ſhall be iudged by Ieſus Chriſt, according to the Goſpell*: and here the preaching of *Noah*, and his *actuall preaching* by preparing the Arke, *condemnes the world*. Such is the power and might of the Miniſterie of Gods word, vpon all them that reſiſt it.

Which beeing ſo, ſhould teach all men, when they come to heare Gods word, to ſubmit themſelues to the power of it, to obey it, and become penitent: for otherwiſe ſo many Sermons as a man heareth, ſo many *inditements* are preſented to God againſt him. And if at the laſt day there were no Deuills to accuſe; thoſe bills of inditements, would both accuſe *and condemne him*. And this Iudgement is begunne in this life, as their conſciences doe often tell them, and is accompliſht at the laſt day: for there is no dallying with Gods word: if it cannot ſaue, it kills. It is the fire, which if it cannot ſoften, it hardens. Let then all impenitent men, make conſcience to obey gods word: for if now they abuſe it, it will be euen with them, both here and in another world. For, as the very ſame Arke, which ſaued Noah and his houſhold, *condemned* the world; ſo the ſame word of God, which beleeued and obeied by godly men, is their ſaluation; diſobeied, and refuſed by vngodly men, ſhall be their condemnation.

And thus much for the two ends, why *Noah* prepared the Ark: & cóſequently of the ſecond

1.Theſſ.2. 20,21.

2.Cor.12. 21.

2.Cor.2.15, 16.

effect of *Noahs* faith. It followeth:

And was made heire of the righteoufneffe, which is by faith.

Here is the third and laft effect, whereby the excellencie of *Noahs* faith is commended. It made him an heire, and that not of the world: (for fo he was befids) but of that that the world could not yeeld; *of righteoufneffe*, and that of the beft of all, euen of that righteoufnes, which is by faith. Thefe words haue relation to that teftimonie, which God gaue of *Noah* in Genefis, 6. 9. *Noah was a iuft and vpright man, and walked with God.* Now that which is fpoken there more *generally*, is here *particularly* opened and vnfolded; he was iuft or *righteous:* how? hee was righteous by the *righteoufneffe of faith :* fo that thefe words are a commentarie vnto the other.

But becaufe that, that is here affirmed of *Noah*, is a moft glorious thing; his *faith made him an heire*.(that is, made him that was heire of all the earth, a better heire) therefore thefe words are to be well waighed. For their full opening, three points are to be confidered.

    1. What is the *righteoufneffe* here fpoken of.

    2. Why it is called *the righteoufneffe of faith,* or by faith.

    3. How Noah was made *Heire of it by his faith.*

For the firft, That *righteoufneffe* by which Noah and all holy men, are to ftand righteous before God, is not a *righteoufnes* of any nature, but fuch a one as is appointed of *God* for that purpofe. That we may knowe it the more diftinctly, wee muft examine the feuerall kindes thereof.

Righteoufneffe is of two forts: *Created, Vncreated.*

Vncreated; is that which is *in God*, and hath no beginning nor ending, no meanes, nor meafure. Of this fpeaketh the Prophet, Pfalm. 119. 137. *Righteous art thou, O Lord.* This cannot make any man righteous; for two reafons.

Firft; for the Godhead and it are all one, It is in God effentially. A man is one thing, and his righteoufneffe is another. But God and his *righteoufneffe* are all one: And therefore it is as impoffible for any man to haue this *righteoufneffe*, as it is *to be God*.

Secondly, it is *infinite*, and mans foule a *finite* creature, and therefore not capable of any thing that is infinite; and confequently, not of the vnmeafurable righteoufnes which is in the godhead. Therefore this we muft leaue vnto God, as proper to the Deitie.

Created righteoufneffe, is that, which God frameth in the refonable creature, *Men and angels.* Of *Angels* we are not to fpeake, though theirs and mans differed not much in nature at their creations.

Created righteoufneffe of *man*, is of 2. forts, *Legall,* or *Euangelicall.*

Legall righteoufneffe, is that which the Morall *law* prefcribeth.

Euangelicall, that which the *Gofpell* hath reuealed.

Of legall righteoufneffe, I finde there are three forts fpoken of;

    1. One that is a *perfect*
    2. One that is a *ciuill*   *righteoufneffe.*
    3. One that is an *inward*

Perfect righteoufneffe Legall, is the perfect fulfilling of the law in a mans owne felfe. And by this fhall no man liuing be iuftified before God; for, no man, fince the fall of *Adam*, is able perfectly to fulfill the Law. If any can, then fhall hee be righteous by it: but none did, nor euer can; therefore, no man fhall ftand righteous by perfect legall righteoufneffe in himfelfe. Some will obiect: But a *regenerate* man may: for he is reftored by grace; therefore though by *Adams* fall a man is difabled, yet by *regeneration* he is inabled to fulfill the law perfectly.

I anfwer; It were fo, if they were *perfectly* fanctified in their regeneration : but they are fanctified but in part, and it is not perfect vntill death. Obiect. 1. Theff. 5. 23. We are *fanctified throughout, fpirit, foule, and bodie.* If all thofe, what then remaines vnfanctified? therefore our fanctification is *perfect*. I anfwer: It is perfect in *parts*, but not in *meafure* nor degree. As a *childe* is a *perfect man* in all the *parts* of a man, but not in the *quantitie* of any part: So a *childe of God* is perfectly fanctified in all *parts*, but not in the meafure of any part, vntill flefh, and mortality, and corruption haue an end.

Secondly, fome may obiect: The virgin *Mary* finned not. I anfwer: fo teacheth the Church of *Rome*, that fhe neuer finned, that her life was free from finne *actuall*, and her conception from finne *originall*. But fo taught neither the Scripture, nor Gods Church : but contrariwife, it is more then manifeft, fhe was a finner. For firft, fhe confeffeth *her foule reioyced in God her Sauiour :* but if fhe were no finner, fhe ftoode in neede of no Sauiour. Againe, fhe died : but if fhe had not finned, fhe fhould in Iuftice not haue died. For *death entred by finne:* and where no finne is, there death is not due. Thus no man can be righteous by the *perfect* righteoufneffe of the law, in himfelfe.

Secondly, there is a *ciuill* righteoufneffe: and that is, when a man in his *outward actions*, is conformable to the law, efpecially to the Commaundements of the fecond Table. For example; he is free from the outward actions of murther, adulterie, or theeuery, and fuch like : or he can *refraine* his anger, & *ouercome* his paffions, that they fhal not breake out into open violece to the view of the world: and for the firft Table; he comes to the *Church*, and profeffeth religion. All this is a *ciuill righteoufneffe*, and by this can no man be iuftified, nor *made righteous*. For firft, it is not a *perfect*, but a moft imperfect righteoufneffe, and therefore cannot iuftifie. It is fo *imperfect*, that it is as good as none at all in Gods fight : for it is but an outward, and *con-*

ſtrained, and diſſembled obedience, & wants the inward and true obedience of the heart and ſoule.

Secondly, it cannot make a man *righteous*: for wicked men haue it, which are vnrighteous, and cannot be ſaued. *Haman* hated *Mordecay* in his heart: yea, his heart boyled in malice againſt him: yet the Story ſaith; *That neuertheleſſe he reſtrained himſelfe till he came home*, Eſt. 5.10. And therefore Chriſt ſaith, that *except our righteouſneſſe exceede the righteouſneſſe of the Scribes and Phariſes, we cannot enter into the kingdome of heauen*. Matth. 5.20. Now what was theirs but an outward *ciuill* righteouſneſſe, whereby they kept the law, onely in outward actions? as appeareth, in that Chriſt, afterward in the ſame Chapter, expounding the law, doth reduce it to the *inward*, which is to his *full* and proper ſenſe: So then, yet wee haue not found that *righteouſneſſe*, which may make a man *righteous*.

Thirdly, there is a righteouſneſſe, called the *inward righteouſneſſe*, of a Chriſtian man, which is this; A man hauing repented, and his ſinnes beeing forgiuen, he is by the holy Ghoſt *ſanctified inwardly*, in his ſoule, and all the parts and powers of it. This ſanctification is called inward righteouſneſſe. Now the Church of *Rome* ſaith, A man may be *iuſtified by this*. But it is not ſo, as appears by theſe reaſons; Firſt, this righteouſneſſe is in this life imperfect; and that is prooued by the Apoſtle, where he ſaith, *We doe here know but in part*, 1. Corinth. 13.12. Therefore our *vnderſtanding* is but in part regenerate: and as it, ſo conſequently all other parts or powers of our ſoule, are but in part regenerate; and in them all, we are partly *ſpirit*, and partly *fleſh*, Galath. 5.17. Therefore if our ſanctification be imperfect, it cannot iuſtifie vs. Againe, this righteouſneſſe is mingled with ſinne and vnrighteouſneſſe: and from this mixture, comes the combat betwixt the fleſh and the Spirit (ſpoken of, Galath. 5.17). *For theſe two are contrary one to the other*.

If it be mingled with ſinne, then it cannot make vs *righteous*: no, nor the works of grace that come from it, though God in mercie reward them. And though as S. *Iames* ſaith, *They iuſtifie our faith, and make vs iuſt before men*, Iames. 2.21. Yet can they not iuſtifie vs *before Gods iuſtice*; nor at the barre of the laſt Iudgement, will they paſſe for payment. S. *Paul* ſaith 1. Corinth. 4.4. *I knowe nothing by my ſelfe, yet am I not thereby iuſtified, that is, I haue ſo* walked in my calling, ſince I was an *Apoſtle*, and Miniſter of the Goſpel; as I am not priuie, nor guilty to my ſelfe of any negligence therein. If he dare not ſtand to that, to be iuſtified by it, who dare take hold, when he refuſeth. Againe, no man can doe any *perfect good* works, vnleſſe he be *perfectly* iuſt: For, how can perfection come out of imperfection? But no man can be perfectly iuſt in this ſinnefull body: as is prooued in the firſt reaſon; therefore his works

here in this life cannot be ſuch, as may make him righteous.

But it may be obiected: Though our works haue ſome *defects* in them, yet Gods *mercy* accepts them for *righteous* and iuſt; and therefore they may iuſtifie vs. I anſwer: As Gods *mercy* accepts them, ſo muſt his *Iuſtice* be ſatisfied alſo; but they beeing imperfect, cannot ſatisfie his *Iuſtice*, for Gods infinite Iuſtice requires perfect ſatisfaction. But as for our beſt workes, as they are done by vs, weigh them in the balance of Gods Iuſtice, and they are ſo light, as they deſerue damnation: yet *in* Gods *mercy* in *Chriſt*, their defects are couered, and they are reputed good workes, and are rewarded; but we incroach vpon Gods *mercie*, and abuſe his *Iuſtice*, if therefore we imagine they ſhould deſerue Gods mercie, or be able to iuſtifie vs in his ſight. Thus then ſeeing Legall righteouſneſſe faileth vs, let vs come to Euangelicall.

Euangelicall righteouſneſſe, is that that is reueiled in the *Goſpel*, and ſhould neuer haue beene reuealed, if that of the *Law* could haue ſaued vs. But whē it (not by defect in it, but default in *our ſelues*) could not, then God in mercie affordeth vs another in the *Goſpel*.

Euangelicall righteouſneſſe is that, that is in *Chriſt* Ieſus; his it is, that muſt make a man righteous before God: But this *Chriſt* was an extraordinary perſon, conſiſting of two natures, *Godhead and Manhood.*

And accordingly, he hath a double *righteouſneſſe* in his holy perſon.

Firſt, as he is *God*, he hath in his nature the *righteouſneſſe of God*, and that is vncreated, and infinite; and therefore *incommunicable*: and ſo none is, nor can be *righteous* by it.

Secondly, there is in *Chriſt* a *righteouſneſſe* of his *humanitie*: and this, though it be finite and created, yet is it beyond meaſure, in compariſon of the righteouſneſſe of man or Angel: So ſaith S. Ioh. 3.34. *God giueth not him the Spirit by meaſure.*

This *righteouſneſſe* of *Chriſt*, as man or Mediator, conſiſteth in two things;

　1. In the *purity* of his *nature*.
　2. In the *perfection* of his *obedience*.

The firſt branch of our Mediators righteouſneſſe, is the *holineſſe* of his *humanity*; which was perfectly ſanctified in his conception, by the powerfull operation of the *Godhead*: and this was done at the firſt inſtant of his conception in the virgins wombe. From this purity of nature, proceeded his *obedience*, which was as *perfect*, as his nature was *pure*: and ſo pure a nature made a plaine way to *perfect obedience*. And therefore as his conception was free from ſinne originall: ſo was his whole life from the leaſt ſinne actuall.

Now the Mediators obedience was double; *Actiue*, and *Paſſiue*.

And both theſe he performed in his owne perſon.

His *Paſſiue obedience* was his paſſion, or ſuffering of whatsoeuer the Iustice of God had inflicted on man for sinne, whether for soule or bodie.

The *Actiue obedience* of the Mediators person, was his perfect fulfilling of the moall *Law*, in all duties to God or man, in thought, word, or deede; and all this for vs, in our steade and on our behalfe. And here is *true righteousnesse*: for where the *nature* of any person is perfectly pure, and the *obedience* perfect, the *righteousnesse* of that person is perfect. And I say, all this was done by him for vs: he *suffered* all that we should haue suffered, and suffered not: hee *did* that which wee should haue done, and did not. And this is that *righteousnesse*, by which, a sinner is made *righteous* before God. For, seeing *legall* cannot, it is this that must. And now we haue found that *righteousnesse*, by which *Noah* and all holy men were made and counted righteous; namely, that that is resident in the holy person of *Iesus Christ* the Mediator.

And yet this is aboue and beyond all reason, that one should be *iustified* by anothers *righteousnesse*: and the doctrine, though it be of God, and grounded neuer so strongly on Gods word, yet hath it enemies, and is mightily oppugned by the Church of *Rome*. Therefore let vs first *prooue* it: and then *answer* the obiections to the contrarie. Wee prooue it thus;

First, from plaine Scripture, 1. Corinth. 3. 24. *Hee that knew no sinne, was made sinne for vs; that we might be made the righteousnesse of God in him.* What can be said plainer? he was made *sinne* for vs, and we *righteousnesse* by him. Therefore as Christ was no sinner in his owne person, but *our sinnes* were laid vpon him, and so he was made a sinner by *our sinnes*; so though we be not *righteous* in our owne persons, yet hauing *Christs righteousnesse* imputed to vs, wee are made righteous by his righteousnesse.

Againe, the *righteousnesse* that must saue vs, must be the righteousnesse of man and God: as in the aforenamed place it is said, that *we might be made the righteousnesse of God in Christ*. But no mans owne righteousnesse can make him the *righteousnes* of God, nor can Gods righteousnesse be the *righteousnesse of man*: therefore it remaineth, that onely Christ, beeing both God and man, hath in him that righteousnesse, which may make a man the righteousnesse of God.

Thirdly, the Scripture saith, *Christ is the end of the Law to all that beleeue*, Rom. 10. 3. The end of the Law; that is, not the taker away, or *abrogater* of the law, but the *fulfiller* of it: as the abrogater of the *Ceremoniall*, so the fulfiller of the *Morall law*. If he fulfilled the Law, for whom was it? not for himselfe. For as the *Messiah was not slain for himselfe*, Dan. 9. 26. so he obeyed not the Law *for himselfe*. For whom then? for all that beleeue. Therefore Christ doing it for them, they fulfill the Law in Christ: and so Christ *by doing*, and they by

A *beleeuing* in him that doth it, do fulfill the Law. Now if it be not amisse to say, *We doe in Christ fulfill the law*: No more is it to say, *We are made righteous by Christs righteousnesse*: though it be his, and not ours, but onely by faith.

Let vs then see (in the second place) what the Church of Rome obiect against it. They first obiect thus:

As a man cannot be *wise* by another mans wisedome, nor *rich* by a nother mans riches, nor *strong* by another mans strength: So can he not be *righteous* by an other mans righteousnesse.

I answer: The comparison is not a like. For B one man hath no proprietie in *another mans wisedome*, strength, or riches: but we haue a right and proprietie in *Christs righteousnesse*. Againe, the wisedome of one man, cannot be the wisedome of another; because they are two persons, fully and equally distinct: but it is not so betwixt *Christ* and a *sinner*: for euerie beleeuer is spiritually, and yet truly and really conioyned to Christ, and they make one mysticall bodie; Christ beeing the head, and euery true beleeuer beeing a member of that bodie: and therefore, that which is his righteousnesse, may be also truly ours. *His*, because it is in him; and ours, because we are knit to him. For, by reason of this mysticall vnion betwixt him and vs, all blessings of saluation in him, as in *the head*, are diffused into vs, as his *members* or branches; & C yet are as properly still in him, as is the *braine* in the *head* of a man. And thus, though in sense and reason this cannot be, yet by faith & Gods spirit, the righteousnesse of Christ is made ours.

Secondly, they obiect. If this be so, then *God iustifieth wicked men*; but God will not doe so: it is against the nature of his holinesse and Iustice. And againe, he that *iustifies the wicked is abominable to God*, Prou. 17. 15. therefore God will not doe so himselfe.

We answer: The *ground* is good, but the *collection* is vntrue. *God will not iustifie a wicked man*, that is true: but that therefore a man cannot be iustified by *Christs righteousnesse*, is false. For, God doth not iustifie him that lieth rotting in his former sinnes, and weltring in his olde corruptions; but him that beleeueth in Christ, D and repenteth of his sinnes. And that man in his faith is *iustified*, and in his repentance *sanctified*, and so he is made a newe man: yea, as S. *Paul* saith, *He that is in Christ is a newe creature*: 2. Corinth. 5. 17. For, as it is in the first *conuersion*, God turneth nor saueth no man against his will; but first makes him *willing* by his owne worke alone, and then conuerteth and saueth him with his owne free will, working together with Gods grace. So is it in the worke of *Iustification*; God *iustifieth* no wicked man: but makes him first iust and righteous in and by Christ, and then accounts him so. But then (will some say) the sinner hath no righteousnes, but that *of Christs*; and that is *in Christ*, and

not

not in himselfe : therefore he hath none in his owne person: how then can he be any thing, but a wicked man still? I answer: that is not true that is first affirmed. The beleeuing sinner hath more righteousnesse then that that is *in Christ*. That which *iustifieth* him, is in Christs person: But the sinner, when he is iustified, is also *sanctified*, by the mighty worke of Gods grace; and so he is made a holy man, and doth good and holy workes, because he is in Christ, though his sanctification be imperfect. To this end, saith S. *Peter*, Acts, 15. 9. *Faith purifieth a mans heart*; for it is impossible a man should beleeue, and so be *iustified*, but he must also be *sanctified* in his heart and life. Thus a sinner is *iustified* by Christs righteousnesse, *inherent* in Christ himselfe; & *sanctified* by Christs righteousnesse, *diffused* from Christ into the sinner. And therefore his *Iustification* is perfect; because, that that *iustifieth* him, is still in *Christ*: but his *sanctification* imperfect, because that that sanctifieth vs, is in our selues; the one *imputed* to vs, the other *infused* and inherent.

Againe, I answer, that if wee take it in the sense of Scripture, It is true, that *God iustifieth a wicked man*. For S. *Paul* saith, Rom. 4. 5. *To him that worketh not, but beleeueth in him that iustifieth the vngodly, his faith is counted to him for righteousnesse.* See, God iustifieth the vngodly: but how? euen as we heard before; not him that is vngodly *after*, but *afore* he be iustified: him that by nature, and in himselfe is vngodly, God iustifieth by working in him faith and repentance; by which, of an vngodly man, he is made a man iustified and sanctified.

Their last obiection is, If a sinner be *righteous* by Christs righteousnesse, then Christ is a *sinner* by his sinnes: for there is the same reason of both. But Christ is no sinner, but the holy of holiest: and S. *Paul* saith, *He knew no sinne*, 2. Cor. 5. 21. and himselfe for himselfe chalengeth his enemies, *Which of you can reprooue me of sinne?* If then our sinnes cannot make him a sinner, no more can his righteousnesse make vs righteous.

I answer: Here we graunt all, if they speake the words of the Scripture, in the *sense* of the Scripture; for Christ was a true and reputed sinner, in the sight of Gods Iustice: as hee that becomes *surety* for another, is a *debter* in his roome: or as he that vndertakes for a man, body for bodie, must answer for him, his owne bodie for his: so in all reason and iustice, Christ, though hee had no sinnes of his owne, yet beeing our *surety*, and vndertaking for vs, and standing in our steade, our sinnes are iustly accounted his. And as for these places, and many more like, they are all vnderstood of *personall* sinnes: from all which, and the least contagion thereof, hee was perfectly free. And therefore the same place that saith, *He knew no sinnes* (that is, in and for his owne person, knew not what sinne was,) saith also, that for *vs* and in *our stead*, he was made euen *sinne it selfe*, that

wee might bee made the righteousnes of God in him. Thus Christ, in *himselfe* more righteous then all men and Angells; *in our steade* is a reputed sinner: & by the same reason we (most vnrighteous in our selues) are clothed with Christs righteousnes, & thereby are reputed righteous. And as Christ, (though no sinner in himselfe) by beeing *a sinner in our stead*, & hauing our sinnes imputed vnto him, became subiect to the wrath of God, and bare it, euen to *death* it selfe: So we, though not *righteous* of our selues, yet hauing *Christs righteousnesse* imputed vnto vs, are made thereby partakers of Gods loue: and for the worthinesse of *that righteousnesse* of his, so made ours, shall be *glorified* in heauen. And thus, now at last we haue found that true, and that onely righteousnesse, which can make a man as it did *Noah*, righteous in Gods sight. Now it remaines to make vse of it.

First, here we learne how foulely our nature is defiled with sinne, and *stained* with corruption: the *staine* whereof cannot be washed away with all the *water* in the world; no, nor with the blood of all creatures: no, nor couered with the righteousnesse of all men and Angels, but onely with the *righteousnesse of God*. And that sonne of God also, if he will apply that righteousnesse vnto vs, and make it effectuall, must become man, and *liue*, and *die*, and *rise againe* for vs. A meruailous thing is it, and worthie of our often consideration, that all the Angels & men in the world, cannot make *one sinner righteous*; but that Gods sonne must needes doe it: And that our sinnes are so hideous, as nothing can hide the filthinesse thereof, from the eyes of Gods Iustice, but onely the glorious *mercie seate* of Christs righteousnesse. This may therefore teach vs, how to esteeme of our selues, and our owne natures.

Furthermore: See here the great goodnesse of God to man: God put perfect *legall* righteousnesse in *Adams* heart in his creation; he receiued it for himselfe and vs; and lost it for himselfe and vs. God in mercie purposing to restore man, thus by himselfe lost and cast away, giues him another, and a better righteousnesse then before. But because he saw man was so ill a *keeper* of his owne Iewels; he trusts not him with it, but sets that righteousnesse in the person of Christ Iesus, and commits it to him to keepe. Who, as he truly knowes the full *value* and excellencie thereof, and as he deerely loues vs: so he will most safely *keepe it* for vs, and clothe vs with it in his Fathers presence at the last day. A point of vnspeakeable comfort to Gods children, to consider that their saluation is not in their owne *keeping*, where it might againe be *lost*; but in a safe hand, where they shall be sure to finde and haue it, when they haue most neede of it: and to remember that their *righteousnesse* beeing in *Christ*, they cannot loose it. For, though they sinne, and so loose often the comfort of a good conscience for a time; yet they then loose not *their righteousnes*,

which

which is then in Chrift; and to confider, that, when in this world they fuftaine loffes or iniuries, or lofe all they haue vpon the earth; that yet *their righteoufnes* (the riches of their foule) is then in heauen full fafe in Chrifts keeping, and fhall neuer be loft. This fhould make vs learne to know Chrift more and more, and to giue him the loue and affections of our very hearts, that fo we may be able to fay with bleffed *Paul*, 2. Tim. 1. 12. *I know whome I haue beleeued, and I am perfwaded, that he is able to keepe that which I haue committed vnto him againft that day.*

Laftly, if there be fuch a *communion* betwixt Chrift and a beleeuer, that our finnes are made his, and his righteoufnes made ours; this may teach vs *patience*, and minifter vs comfort in all *outward* afflictions, or *inward* temptations; becaufe it is certen all our fufferings are *his*, and he is touched with all the wrongs done to vs. When he was in heauen, he calls to *Saul*, Act. 9.4. *Saul, Saul, why perfecuteft thou me?* and at the laft day, Matth. 25.45. whatfoeuer either good or euill was done to any of his children, he faith, *was done to himfelfe:* and accordingly it fhall be rewarded as done to him.

And thus we haue taught that true *righteoufnes*, which iuftifies a finner, and made *Noah righteous*; and we fee the vfe of that worthie doctrine. And in this firft point we haue the longer infifted, becaufe it is one of the fundamentall points of Chriftian religion.

Hitherto of the firft point; namely, what that righteoufneffe is, which is here fpoken of.

The fecond point to be confidered in thefe words, is, that this righteoufnes is that righteoufneffe, *Which is by Faith.*

It is fo called, becaufe *faith* is the proper inftrument created in the foule of man by the holy Ghoft, to apprehend that righteoufneffe, which is in the perfon of Chrift; nor can it be any waies elfe either apprehended or applied: and therefore it is worthily called *that righteoufnes which is by faith*: that is, which by faith is made a mans own, or whereunto a man hath title *by his faith*. Here therefore two points offer themfelues to our obferuation:

1. That true *faith apprehends* properly this true righteoufnes.
2. That *onely faith* can doe it.

For the firft, it is prooued by apparant euidences of Scripture. S. *Paul* tells the Galatians (3.14.) *They receiued the promife of the Spirit, by faith.* And S. *Iohn* faith, that *as many as receiued Chrift, to them he gaue power to be called the fonnes of God.* And leaft any man fhould thinke, that to receiue Chrift, is not to beleeue in Chrift; he addeth, *Euen to as many as beleeue in his name,* Ioh. 1.12. And therefore faith is fitly compared to a *hand* that takes hold on a garment, and applieth it to the bodie, beeing naked: or to a beggars hand that takes or receiues a Kings almes: fo faith in a mans foule takes hold on Chrifts righteoufnes (which is

the mercifull and liberall almes of the King of heauen) and applieth it to the poore and naked foule of the beleeuer.

If any man aske, how can *faith* applie Chrift to the beleeuer? I anfwer: as a man, beeing in his corrupt nature, hath nothing to doe with Chrift: fo contrariwife, when the holy Ghoft hath wrought *faith* in his heart by a fupernaturall operation; then we are to know, that as faith is the proper inftrument to *apprehend* Chrift; fo is Chrift and his righteoufneffe the proper *obiect* for faith to worke vpon. For though it apprehend and applie all other promifes which God makes to our foules or bodies; yet moft *properly* and *principally*, and in the firft place, it apprehends the promife of faluation, and the righteoufneffe of Chrift. Now for the *particular* manner, how faith doth thus; we are to know, that though it be fpirituall and inuifible, and fo not eafily expreffed to fenfe, yet is it done as *properly* by faith, as a *garment* is by the hand taken and applied to the bodie, or a plaifter to a foare.

If any aske further; But when may a man know, whether his faith haue apprehended and applied Chrifts righteoufneffe to his foule, or no?

I anfwer; when he beleeueth *particularly*, that Chrifts righteoufnes *is his* righteoufnes, and hath reconciled him to God, and fhall *iuftifie* him in Gods prefence, then doth faith worke his true and proper worke: for this cannot be done but by faith: and where faith is, this muft needes be done.

The fecond point is, that *faith alone*, and no other vertue, nor fpirituall power in mans foule, is able to doe this. And this may be prooued by comparing it with all the principall vertues of the foule: for amongft all, there are none that may come into comparifon with faith, but *hope* and *loue:* both which, efpecially loue, haue their feuerall and fpeciall excellencies: yet haue neither of them, nor both of them this vertue to *apprehend and apply Chrifts righteoufneffe*. The propertie of *loue*, is to extend it felfe, and with it felfe to carie many paffions or affections of the heart, and to place them vpon the thing that is *loued*: yet cannot loue be faid properly to apprehend Chrift; for he muft needes be *apprehended*, before he can be *loued*. And the proper action of *Hope*, is to waite and expect for a bleffing to come: fo, hope *waites* for faluation, but properly *apprehends* it not. For faluation muft firft be *beleeued*, and then hoped or expected: fo faith *Ieremie*, Lament. 3. 26. *It is good both to truft and to waite for the faluation of the Lord:* to *truft*, that is, to beleeue affuredly it will come (there is the action of *faith*) and to *waite* till it doe come (that is the action of hope.) Thus we fee the feuerall natures, and actions, of thefe two worthie vertues. But the proper action of faith, is to *apprehend and lay hold* on Chrift, and his righteoufneffe, and to apply them to a mans owne foule:

and

and that beeing done, then come *Loue* and *Hope*, and doe their duties: And so, though *loue* last longer then faith doth, yet *faith* is afore *loue*, and makes the way for it.

To conclude this second point; *Faith* is a hand to take hold on Christ and his benefits. *Loue* is a hand to giue out tokens of faith both to God and man, For (1. Cor. 13.5.) *Loue seeketh not her owne, but others good:* namely, the good of them that are loued. *Hope* is an *eye* looking out, and *wayting* for the good things promised. So that, as *faith* is the *hand* of the soule; so *loue* is the *hand*, and *hope* is the *eye* of faith; *Loue* the *hand* whereby it worketh, and Hope the *eye* whereby it waiteth and looketh for the performance of such things, as *faith* hath apprehended and beleeued. If the Church of Rome thinke this any wrong to this holy vertue of loue, to be the *hand* of faith: let them know it is not ours, it is the doctrine of the Apostle, where he saith, *Faith worketh by loue.* If faith worke by it, then surely loue is the *hand* of faith. Thus faith *worketh* by loue, *waiteth* by hope, but *beleeueth* by it selfe.

And for this cause, the righteousnesse, that makes vs righteous before God, is rather called the righteousnesse of faith, then of any other Christian vertue, or grace of the spirit. And for the same cause is it, that so often in S. *Pauls* Epistles, it is called by the same name; as, Philip. 3. 9.

The third and last point concerning *Noahs* faith; is that, *Noah was made heire* of this righteousnesse.

A speciall commendation of his *faith*, It made him *heire* of true and sauing righteousnesse: that is, it gaue him a true title vnto it, and made him *heire apparant* of that glorie, which it assureth euery one that apprehends it by this true *faith*: and so he was made as certainly, and as truly partaker of it, as the young *Prince* is assured of his Crowne and Kingdome at his time, or the *heire* of his Fathers lands.

Here two most worthy doctrines doe offer themselues to our view.

　1. The excellencie of *faith.*
　2. The excellencie of a *Christian mans estate.*

The excellencie of *faith* appeares thus: It makes a holy man assured and *certaine* of his saluation by Christ Iesus. The Church of Rome saith, it is *presumption* in any man to thinke so, vnlesse he haue an extraordinary *reuelation: but we learne from the Scripture, that* if a man haue true faith; that is able to assure him of saluation. For, *faith* makes him an *heire* of true *righteousnesse*, and of saluation thereby. Now we know, the *heire* is most sure and certaine of his *inheritance:* what euer he gets or loseth, he is sure of that. But this righteousnes and saluation by it, is his *inheritance*; therefore hee may be, and is by faith assured of it. The *Papists* therefore doe wrong vnto this doctrine, and derogate from the dignitie of true

faith: But this is their custome, they will extoll any thing, rather then that which the holy *Scripture* so much extolleth; namely, true *faith.* For, if they knew what it is truly to know *Christ*, and to *beleeue in him by that faith*, which worketh by loue, they would then know, that faith makes a man *heire of happinesse*, and therefore most assured of it.

Secondly, here we may see the *excellencie of a Christian mans estate:* he is not naked, nor destitute of comfort; but *is heire of a glorious inheritance*, by meanes of his faith: and a Christian mans inheritance, is Christs *righteousnesse.* Out of which, we learne,

First, that no man by any good workes done by or in himselfe, can merit true and iustifying *righteousnesse:* the Pharisaicall *Papists* teach so; but their conceite is here ouerthrown, by the doctrine of the holy Ghost. For, sauing righteousnesse is his inheritance: which we know, is always gotten by the Father, and *descendes* from the Father to the Sonne, as a free token of his loue. And it were scornefull and absurd, to see a Sonne offer to buy his inheritance of his Father; it beeing against the nature of an inheritance, to come any other wayes, but by *free gift* from the Father to the Sonne: therefore our righteousnesse that must saue vs, beeing as we see here our inheritance; let vs resolue of it, we cannot buie nor merit it.

Againe, here is sure and solide *comfort* against all the griefes, and crosses, and losses of this world: Gods children must needes haue their *portion* of afflictions in this life. But here is their comfort, they may loose their goods, liuings, possessions, their good names, their healths, their liues; but their *inheritance* standeth sure and firme, and cannot be lost. Let them therefore here learne, not to griue out of measure: for a holy man may say thus to himselfe, and that most truly; My Father may *frown* on me for my faults, and *chastise* me for my sinnes: but I am sure he will not *disinherite* me: for I am *heire, by faith, of Christs righteousnes*; and I may loose many things, but I shall not loose that.

Thirdly and lastly, here must Gods children learne their duties. They are *heires* to a godly and glorious *inheritance:* and Christes righteousnes is *their inheritance;* therefore they must learne to set & settle all their affections on this inheritance. For, there is nothing in the world more worthie to bee affected, then a *faire inheritance.*

We must therefore first labour aboue all worldly things for this inheritance; namely, to be made partakers of this *righteousnesse.* This is that pearle, which we hauing found, must *sell all we haue to buy it.* And when we haue gotten it, we must care to *keepe* it, and therefore must lay it vp in our verie hearts and soules: and keeping it, we must reioyce and delight in it aboue the world, and all the pleasures of it.

This is the glorious *portion* which our God

and

and Father leaueth vs as his children : what should all the care of our hearts be, but to preserue it? *Naboth* had a Vineyard, that came to him from his Father by *inheritance : Ahab* the King would giue him money, or a *better vineyard* for it : but *Naboth* would not : Nay (saith he) *God forbid I should sell my Fathers inheritance*, 1.king.21.3.&c. If he made such account of an earthly *inheritance*, what should we of the heauenly ? if he of a poore *vineyard*, what should we of the glorie of heauen ? If he denied the *King*, to sell it for a better, should not we denie the *Deuill*, to leaue our part in *Chrift* and his *righteousnesse*, for the world, or any thing that he can promise vs? In all such temptations our answer should be ; *God forbid I should sell away my inheritance*, which my God and Father gaue me. Thus did blessed *Paul*, who esteemed *the world*, and all in it *doung and drosse, that he might winne Chrift*, and be made partaker of this *righteousnes*. So must we (if we will be worthie of this *inheritance*) prize and value it aboue this world, and thinke basely of all the pompe and pleasures of this world, in comparison of it : and rather be content to lose the world, then to leaue it.

And lastly, when we haue it, and are thus carefull to preserue it ; where should our content, ioy, and delight be, but in this *our inheritance* ? So doth the heire : nothing so reioyceth him, as to thinke of his *inheritance*. Here therefore the madnesse of carnall men is discouered, who reioyce exceedingly in the honours, profits, and pleasures of this life (as swine in their bellies) and neuer goe further : But alas, this is not their *inheritance*, if they looke to haue their soules saued. Therefore herein they shew themselues voide of grace, and of all hope of a better world. For if they had, they would reioyce in it, and not in the vaine and transitorie delights of this world, *which perish in the vsing*, and are *loft* with more torment and vexation, then they were *kept* with delight. We must learne then *to vse this world, as though we vsed it not*, 1.Cor.7.31. And if the Lord vouchsafe vs any portion of pleasures in this world, we must take it thankefully, as aboue our *inheritance* (and must therefore vse it lawfully and foberly ;) but haue our hearts, and the ioy of them vpon our *inheritance*, which is in heauen, whereof we are made *heires* by faith ; and wherein we are *fellow heires* with this *blessed Noah*, who was *made heire of that righteousnes, which is of faith*.

And thus haue we heard the most glorious commendation of *Noahs faith* : and of *Noah* by his faith, and of all the examples before the flood.

Now follow the second sort of *Examples* ; namely, such as liued in the second world, after the flood.

They are all of two sorts : either such as liued afore the giuing of the *Law*, or after.

Afore the giuing of the Law, here are many:

whereof, as of all the other kinds, some are *men*, some *women*.

The first of those blessed men after the flood, whose *faith* is here renowned, is *Abraham* that great Father : of whome, and whose faith, because he was a Father of so many faithfull, more is spoken then of any one.

Abrahams faith.

Verse 8.

By Faith, Abraham, when he was called, obeied God, to goe out into a place, which he should afterward receiue for inheritance : and he went out, not knowing whether he should goe.

 Oncerning holy *Abraham*, here are more examples then one recorded, and his faith is renowned many waies : more verses are spent of him, then of some fiue others. And the reason is, because his faith was more excellent then any others that followed him. In which regard, he is called the *Father of the faithfull*, oftentimes in the new Teftament, especially in the Epiftles to the *Romanes* and *Galatians*.

The *first* example of his faith (and the *fourth* in order of the whole) is of his leauing his own natiue countrey, and how at Gods commandement he went he knew not whether ; onely he knew God called him, and therefore he would goe : wherein appeared a most worthie faith.

Now concerning this his faith and obedience, the Text laieth downe two points :

1. The *cause* or ground thereof ; which was Gods calling : he was *called of God*.

2. The fruit or effect of his faith ; he *hearkned and obeied*. And this his obedience is amplified by diuers particulars :

1. The *matter* of it ; he *went out* of his countrey.

2. The *ende*, to take poffeffion of a countrey, which he should not enioy of a long time.

3. The *manner* ; he *went out, not knowing whither he should goe*.

The first point, is the cause or ground of *Abrahams* faith in this action, and is laid downe in the first words,

By faith, Abraham *when he was called,*

This ſtorie is taken out of Gen. 12. The cauſe of Abrahams faith, is *Gods calling.* Gods *calling* is an action of God, whereby he appointeth a man to ſome certaine condition, or ſtate of life, in this world, or after this life. And in this regard, God is compared to a *Generall* in the field, which aſſigneth euery *Souldier* his ſtanding and dutie: ſo doth God appoint euery man his place and dutie in the Church.

Concerning theſe *callings,* let vs ſee the *meanes* how he calleth, and the ſeuerall *ſtates* whereto he calleth men. For the meanes or manner; God calleth men two waies : immediately, or by meanes.

Sometime *immediately* by himſelfe and his owne voice : as, the extraordinarie *Prophets* in the old Teſtament, & the *Apoſtles* in the new. So ſaith S. *Paul* of himſelfe, he was *called to be an Apoſtle, not of men, nor by men, but by Ieſus Chriſt, and God the Father,* Gal. 1. 1.

Sometime mediatly by men directed by himſelfe, and furniſhed, or inabled for that dutie : and ſo were called the ordinarie Prophets and Prieſts of the old; and the Euangeliſts, Paſtors, and Doctors of the new Teſtament. The firſt was extraordinarie; this is ordinarie : the firſt is for an vnbeleeuing, or a misbeleeuing people ; the ſecond, is for an ordinarie and eſtabliſhed Church. Now, of theſe two waies, God called *Abraham immediatly* by himſelfe from heauen.

Gen. 12. 1.

Secondly, for the eſtates of life whereunto God calleth men, they are three: *Generall, Particular, Perſonall.*

Gods *Generall* calling is, whereby he calleth all men to repentance by the Goſpel, and ſo to life eternall. Of this ſpeakes the Apoſtle, Rom. 8. 30. *Whom God predeſtinated, them alſo he called:* and Rom. 11. 29. *The calling of God, is without repentance.* Hereby he calls men in this life to the ſtate of grace, and to the ſtate of glorie in heauen ; and this is to all.

His *particular calling* is, when he calleth and aſſigneth men to ſome particular eſtate and dutie, in Family, Church, or Commonwealth : as, when a man is called to be a Magiſtrate, Miniſter, maſter of a family, lawyer, phyſitian, &c.

Thirdly, God calleth ſome men to ſome priuate *perſonall* dutie, which he deſigneth not to others, but to be done by them alone. Such a *calling* had he aſſigned him, that would needes be perfect; *Goe ſell all that thou haſt, &c.*

Matth. 19. 21.

Now the calling of *Abraham* in this place, is to be referred to this third kind. For it was a *priuate* and *perſonall* calling *to leaue his countrey,* his kindred, his lands, his poſſeſſions, and to goe ſeeke another : and to be the *father of the faithfull,* and to receiue the couenant : and this dutie belongs to none, but who ſhall perſonally, and by name be *called* vnto it.

Yet all theſe three callings may concurre in one, as here in him. For he was called to be a Chriſtian (for *the generall*) and a gouernour of a great family (for the *particular* calling:) but

that, that is in this place vnderſtood, is this extraordinarie and *perſonall* calling to leaue his countrey. And in it we are to conſider three circumſtances : 1. Who was called: 2. When: 3. How he was called.

For the firſt: *Abraham* was called, the ſonne of *Terah:* but neither his father *Terah,* nor his brother *Nahor* were called, but *Abrahã* alone.

But it may worthily be demanded, why God ſhould not call his *father and his kinred :* there can be no anſwer but this that the Apoſtle giueth, Rom. 9. 18. *God hath mercie on whome he will, and withholdeth it from whome he will.* He calleth *Iſaak,* and refuſeth *Iſmael :* loueth *Iacob,* and hateth *Eſau :* taketh *Abel,* and leaueth *Cain; euen becauſe he will,* and for no cauſe that we know. But why then calls he *Abraham,* and not his kinred? Is not that partialitie? I anſwer, he is tied to none, he might refuſe all: therefore the meruaile is, that he calls any. But why ſome and not other, why *Abraham* and not his kinred, no reaſon can be giuen : for Gods iudgements are wonderfull. But as that *that is impoſſible with mã, is poſſible with God:* ſo that that is *iniuſtice* or *partiality* with man, is *iuſtice* with God. And it is extreame folly, and intolerable preſumption for vs to weigh Gods actions in the balance of our ſhallow reaſon.

Matth. 19. 26.

For the ſecond : But when was *Abraham* called? for the time, there are two circumſtances worth the obſeruation: Firſt, *Abraham* was called to this dignitie, when he liued in idolatrie with his fathers. So ſaith Ioſhua, 24. 2. *Thus ſaith the Lord, Your fathers dwelt beyond the flood in old time, euen Terah the father of Abraham, and ſerued other gods.* If *Abraham* was called by God, when he was an idolater, then it is apparant he had not purchaſed Gods fauour by his workes. Where we learne, that the whole worke of a mans ſaluation, is to be aſcribed to Gods meere mercie : who (as the Prophet ſaith) *was found of them that ſought him not,* Eſai. 65. 1. *Abraham* neuer dreamed of the true God, nor of any new couenant of grace and ſaluation, when *God called him.* And ſo, when *Paul* was going armed with bloodie furie, and his furie armed with commiſſions and authoritie againſt the Saints, then God from heauen called him ; and of a perſecuter, made him the principall inſtrument of his glorie, Act. 9. 2, &c. Therefore (to applie this to our ſelues) if God haue vouchſafed vs the ſame grace, and taken vs *to be his people,* and made a couenant of ſaluation with vs, which in former times haue been *ſinners of the Gentiles;* we muſt learne here to ſee whence this fauour is, and therefore to aſcribe nothing to our ſelues, but giue all the glorie vnto God.

And *particularly,* for euery one of vs: if God haue been ſo mercifull to any of vs, as when we were *popiſh* or *ſuperſtitious* with our parents, or kindred, to open our eyes, and bring vs home to his holy truth: or, when we weltred in wickedneſſe and ſenſuality with the *profane world,* to touch our hearts: and to call vs to grace and sanctification: let vs often remember, and freely acknowledge this his vndeserued mercie, and say with the holy Prophet: *Vnto thee belongeth mercy, but vnto vs open shame.*

Secondly, for the *time* when *Abraham* was called: It was when he *was 75. yeares of age,* or there-abouts, as is manifest in the Storie, Gen. 12. 4. therefore we see that God for a long time let him lie in his blindnesse, and idolatrie ere he called him. It is more then likely, that *Abraham* in that meane time liued ciuilly, and followed learning and other ciuill courses: and in that time, it is likely he attayned to that measure of knowledge in Astronomie, and other learning, for which, he is renowned in old Writers: But this was the first time that he was called to know and serue the true God in his true seruice.

Here we learne, that though a man perseuere in his sinnes, for a long time, and passe his best yeares in vanitie without repentance, and thereby bee in a grieuous and fearefull estate: yet true beleeuers, and men penitent, must not therefore iudge them *cast-awayes.* For, Gods mercie calls a man in his old age, and toucheth the heart when it pleaseth him. Christ in the Parable *calls some at the* 11. *houre,* Mat. 20. 6. and so God calleth men to grace in their olde age. We must therefore spare these sharpe and vnsauourie censures, which some vnaduisedly cast vpon such men; for *charity thinketh not euill,* 1. Corinth. 13. 5. where it may thinke or suppose any possibility of good: But contrariwise, pray for them, and hope of their conuersions, because we know, that *at what time soeuer a sinner repents of his sinne, God wil forgiue him.*

And yet for all this, men must not presume to liue carelesly in their sinnes, for that is desperately to tempt God: but must follow the holy Counsell of *Salomom,* Ecclef. 12. 1. *To remember their Creator in the dayes of their youth:* and to turne vnto God when they haue meanes, least God take away the *meanes,* and with the meanes, his *fauour* from them. *Abraham* was not *called,* till he was olde; but when he was *called,* he harkened and *obeyed:* So must thou, when God calls thee by afflictions, or by his word, then answer and obey as *Abraham* did; or else *Abrahams calling in his old age,* will be little comfort to thee. Thus much for the time.

Thirdly, for the *manner of his calling,* it is laied down in the Storie of Genesis, to be in an earnest kinde of Counsell. *Goe out,* saith God, *from thy kindred, & from thy Fathers house, vnto the land that I will shew thee:* Where it is to be obserued, hee saith not barely *Goe,* or come forth; but hee amplifieth, and vrgeth it with many wordes and circumstances.

If any aske why God did so, when he might haue giuen the commandement in one word? I answer; the reason is, that *Abraham* might haue cause more seriously to consider of Gods *calling,* and to imprint it more deeply in his

heart; least at the first brunt he should haue obeyed, and afterward haue shrunke backe. For, it is doubtlesse, that this calling was harsh to reason, and that *Abraham* found many hinderances, and therefore it were dangerous hee would haue started backe after some triall of these difficulties he must passe through, if he had had but a bare call, & comandement *to goe.* But when God saith to him, *Goe out of thy natiue Country, let it not stay thee,* that thou wast borne there; nor hinder thee, that *thy kindred* dwels there: but leaue all, and come with me: *forsake all, and trust me,* follow me into the land that *I will shew thee:* I take thee from one, but I will giue thee another: When God, I say, vseth all these, and it may be, many more like words to *Abraham,* its apparant he would haue him furnished with strength and resolution, to goe through with his *calling* after he had once made entrance into it.

Out of which practise of God, we learne this *Instruction;* that God would haue no man enter vpon any calling or dutie, with a fearefull and faint heart, nor with a doubtfull minde; but with a strong and settled *resolution* to goe thorough stitch with it, and not to relent and repent in the midst. And for this end, God would haue all men afore they enter, seriously to consider the *place or duty* they are to vndertake; for the Lord had rather a man should refuse at the first; then hauing entred, to looke back ● againe; and it is great follie for men, hastily and suddainely, or humorously to cast themselues vpon any *calling,* and then vpon triall and experience of the dangers and difficulties thereof, to bee wearie, and wish they had neuer done it. Men in this world are generally *wiser* in matters of the world; If a man bee to *build* a house, hee will not forth-with set vpon building such a house as his humor desireth, but will first of all sit downe and count the *cost,* and then his own *abilitie,* to see if the one will counteruaile the other, else he neuer begins it. So saith Christ (the wisedome of God) *of the wisedome of this world:* and the like also he saith for warre, that no *Prince* wil fight with his enemy on vnequal tearmes, but will knowe himselfe able to sustaine the encounter, Luk. 14. 28. 31.

So the calling of a Christian, is to professe the Gospell of Christ. As the Magistrates is to *defend* it, the Ministers to *teach* it, so all mens to *professe* it: now it is as impossible to *build* without *cost,* or to *fight* without *power* of men, as to *professe* Christ in any *calling,* either generall or particular, without *crosses.* Wee must therefore consider first what our calling and profession will *cost vs:* it is sure to cost vs a dangering of our credits and estimation in the world; it may be our goods, our liberties, it may bee our *liues* themselues. Againe, what enemies we haue to encounter in this spirituall warrefare, the deuill, death, hell, sinne, corruption, and the craftie malice of wicked men: all these we are sure to meete withall.

Ezek. 18 27, 28.

Were it not then folly for a man to vndertake
this profession, and not to confider thus much
aforehand? The want of this is caufe,why fome
put their hands to the plough,and after fhrinke
away,and make themfelues ridiculous to their
enemies corporall and fpirituall.

And for particular callings, the cafe euen
ftandeth fo alfo. Some men thinke the calling
of a *Magiftrate,* a place of *honour:* and therefore ambitioufly plot and defire to raife themfelues into authority; neuer remembring the
burden, and trouble they are fure to finde.
Which when they feele to be too heauie for
their lazie fhoulders to beare with eafe, they
foully fall to plaine carelefneffe, and neglect all
doing good in their places, and wifh they had
neuer bought honour fo deare.

So others thinke the Minifterie nothing, but
a place of *eafe, exemption, and preferment.* And
in thefe conceits rufh prefumptuoufly & rafh-
ly into that holy ftate, neuer thinking aforehad
of that great *charge of foules* they are to take,
nor of that heauie *account* they are to make for
them;nor of the hatred, and contmpt, and extreame difgraces they are fure to finde, if they
doe their duties with confcience. And therefore (when vpon experience they finde it fo to
be) they either fall to carnall courfes with the
world, and *neglect their duties* (that by thefe
two meanes they may pleafe the world) or elfe
they continue in their duties, with much griefe
and vexation, wifhing they had chofen rather
any calling, then the *Minifterie:* and by either
of both, doe expofe themfelues to fhame and
much rebuke. Whereas contrariwife, hee that
aforehand cafts his *account* what it will coft
him to be a *Minifter,* what he muft vndertake,
what he muft lofe, what he is fure to find, is fo
fettled and refolued afore-hand, as he goeth
through all dangers and contempts, with comfort, courage, and contentment. Let vs therefore all learne by this practife of God,when we
thinke to enter vpon any fuch dutie, to reafon
with our felues, as God did with *Abraham,*
what we are *to forfake,* and what wee are to
meete withall. So fhall we not afterward repent
vs, but goe on with much affurance, as *Abraham* did.

This point I haue the more inlarged,becaufe
it is of fpeciall vfe in Chriftian life.

Thus much of the *caufe* of *Abrahams* faith,
Gods calling, and all the circumftances therein.

The fecond point, is the excellencie and
commendation thereof, commended by the
fruite and effect: It made him *yeeld* to this calling of God. And this obedience of his faith, is
fpoken of two wayes:

1. It is laid downe *generally; He obeyed God.*
2. It is further commended by diuers *particulars,*which we fhall fee in their places.

Obeyed God.

Here is the obedience of *Abrahams* faith,
laid down in one generall word: *He obeyed;*that
is when God called him to leaue his Country,

kindred, and friends,he yeelded againft reafon,
becaufe God bad him. When God told him he
would carie him into another land, he *beleeued*
it,and left a certaine for an vncertaine,a poffeffion for an expectation; here was the power &
excellencie of his faith appearing in this obedience. From hence we learne two inftructions.

Firft, feeing *Abraham* is *the Father of the
faithfull,* Rom. 4. 11. and our glorie is to be
children of fathfull Abraham;

Therefore we muft all learne, as *good children to followe our Father,* in framing our liues
according to Gods calling:when G O D *calleth*
vs to any ftate of life, then to obey; and when
not God, but the world or our owne corrupt
humors call vs, then not to obey. For, to obey
the firft, is the *obedience of faith,* but to obey
the fecond, is *the obedience of our corruption.*
Therefore againft this practife of holy *Abraham,* two forts of men doe offend, and thereby
fhew themfelues *children vnlike their Father
Abraham.*

Firft, fuch men as beeing *called by God* to
fome functions or duties, *will not obey:* for examples, wee haue too many. To fome, God
faith, *Leaue thy priuate care,* which is,for none
but thy felfe: *be a Magiftrate,* and vndertake
the *publike care* of the common-wealth: but
they, as though they were born for themfelues,
will not imploy themfelues in publike feruice.

To fome, God faith; *Leaue thy eafe,* and thy
care of worldly credit, and vndertake the teaching of my people, and care not for the contempt of that calling, fo thou maift *faue foules:*
but their carnall credit is more deere vnto them
then *Abrahams kindred is to him;* they will not
forfake them.

Thefe, and all that doe fo, may make what
fhew they will: but they are not *children of A-
braham,* feeing they want his *faith:* and they
want his *faith,* becaufe they faile in his *obedience:* they muft therefore learne to yeeld
when God calleth, and not to ftand vpon fuch
bafe allegations of worldly matters; when A-
braham left Country and kindred to obey God.

Secondly, fuch men as refpect not Gods
calling, but looke what the fwinge of their natures, or the courfe of the wicked *world* carie
them vnto, they prefently yeeld and obey, not
regarding whether it be Gods calling or no.
Three forts of men are moft faulty in this kind.

Firft, fuch as are content to grow in wealth,
either by opreffion, as vfurie or extortion;or by
craft and diffembling, or by any other fuch indirect courfe, whereby their brother is hurt,
looking only at gain,but not regarding whence
it comes.

Secondly, fuch as liue by *dicing, carding,* or
by *playes and Enterludes,* thinking any trade
lawfull that brings in wealth, or that gets money;neuer caring whether God *allow the calling*
or no.

Thirdly,fuch as liue *in no calling,*but fpêd their
time in eating,drinking, fleeping,and fporting,

A

becaufe they haue liuings of their owne, and lands left by their parents.

All thefe and all fuch like, doe obey indeed: but whereunto? not vnto Gods calling: for a-las, he neuer *called them* to thefe courfes, but hath often *recalled* them from it; therefore this is the obedience not of *faith*, but of *corruption*, and of the world, which is a plaine difobedience vnto God. For, as the wifedome of the flefh or the world is foolifhneffe with God, Rom. 8: fo obedience to the flefh or the world, is difobedience & rebellió againft God.

All fuch men, muft know that they are not *the children of Abraham*, becaufe they are not children of *his faith*. Nor can they be heires of his faith, becaufe they practife not his *obedience*: for, Gods *calling*, and no other rule for our liues muft Chriftian men admit. When *hee* calleth they muft obey: and when *he calls not*, or allowes not a courfe of gayning, or a trade of life (though all the world allowed it) wee muft not follow it: this will honour them, and their profeffion, before God. *Abrahams* faith *iuftified* him before God, but his *obedience iuftified his faith: obedience*, faith *Samuel*, 1. Sam. 25. 22. 23. *is better then facrifice: but difobedience is as the finne of witchcraft.* Therefore let all Chriftians approoue their faith by their obedience, hanging on Gods mouth, and attending on Gods calling, for, directions of their whole life: and refolue with *Dauid*, Pfal. 119. 105. *Thy word is a lanterne to my feete, and a light to my pathes.* When *Kings* may not liue, but by this light of Gods calling and Gods word; it is fhamefull prefumption, for ordinary men to frame their liues by lights of their owne making.

In the fecond place out of *Abrahams* obedience, let vs marke, By what meanes *obeyed* he? *by faith.* Learne here the true nature of true faith: it brings forth true obedience where euer it is: and therefore Chriftian obedience is called *the obedience of faith*, Rom. 1. 5. And thefe two cannot be feperated, no more then light from the *funne*, or heate from *fire*. For as the *funne* naturally, and neceffarily giues *light*, and the *fire heate*; no leffe doth true *faith* yeeld true *obedience* to Gods commaundements. Which being fo, it teacheth vs, for the vfe,

Firft, how our *Church and doctrine* are flaundered by the *Papifts*, who pleafe themfelues in faying, We looke to be faued by fole faith, and without workes. For, we teach, that though a man be *iuftified* without refpect to his workes, yet no man was euer *iuftified*, whofe *faith* did not bring forth *good and holy workes*: and we teach, that none is heire of *Abrahams* faith, which is not alfo of his *obedience*. Therefore God will reward their lying tongue.

Secondly, this teacheth vs, that *Abrahams* faith is rare in thefe dayes. Many make profeffion of *Abrahams* religion, but it feemes they are as far deceiued as the Iewes were, Ioh. 8. 39. *The Iewes would be Abrahams children, becaufe*

B

C

D

they were of his flefh: and men now will be fo, becaufe they are of his *profeffion*; but both are farre wide, for we muft be children of *faithfull Abraham*. But if we will be like him in *faith*, we muft be like him in *obedience* alfo: when God calles vs to any dutie, we muft forfake our owne *natures*, and denie our owne *affections*, and croffe our owne *corruptions*, to follow Gods *calling*, and to doe our duties. So fhall we be true children of *Abraham*, when wee are like our Father in his beft vertues. Thus we fee his obedience laied downe generally.

Particularly, In his *Obedience* there are laid downe three points:

1. The *matter* ⎱ all which are laide
2. The *ende* ⎰ down directly in the
3. The *manner* ⎰ Text.

For the matter of his obedience, it followeth in thefe words: *To goe out into a place, &c.*

The particular matter wherein *Abrahams* obedience confifted, was this; At Gods commaundement he went out of his owne country into another: for one which he fhould inherite, he left that which he did inherite.

Here many points of good inftruction may be learned.

Firft, fee here the power and ftrength *of true faith*; It was a wonderfull hard thing for *Abraham* to doe.

For firft, he was well ftriken in yeares, 75. yeares olde. Yong men delight to be ftirring; but men growen into yeares, doe loue to fettle themfelues as birds in their nefts: and it is grieuous vnto them to thinke of remoouing, or taking long iournies.

Secondly, he muft leaue his *owne Countrie*, where he was bred, borne, and brought vp; which all men generally doe loue by nature.

Thirdly, he muft leaue *his goods, and landes: and liuings*, which no doubt were great: for, hauing liued fo long in his natiue Country, and beeing borne as he was, his eftate doubtleffe was very great.

Fourthly, he muft leaue *his acquaintance*, with which he had liued all his life; yea, his *own kindred*, and muft goe liue amongft ftrangers. Thefe foure confiderations were fo many hindrances to his obedience; and ftrong temptations, to make him haue looked backward: but fuch is the power of his faith, he is *commanded of God*, therefore he *obeyeth and goeth out.*

The vfe is, to teach vs what a faith we haue. For, if we meafure all Gods commaundements by our naturall affections, our faith is but a fhadow, and hypocrifie: But if we confult not with flefh & blood, but reft, and rely on Gods word, and giue abfolute obedience to his commandements, then our faith is fuch as *Abrahams was.*

In the next place; Some may meruaile, why the Lord fhould commaund him fo hard a matter, and lay fo ftraite a commaundement vpon him, as to leaue his *Country and liuing*, which feemed vnreafonable; and his *kindred*, which was vnnaturall.

I an-

I answer: the reason is, not that God delighteth in *vnreasonable* or *vnnaturall* courses, or in laying heauy burdens vpon his children. But he did it for good and holy endes: as,

First, to prooue *Abraham*, and to see what was in him. As a friend is not tried in ordinary, but *in great matters*; so it is knowne, who is Gods friend in matters of *difficultie*. Hereby, therefore God made the faith and obedience of his seruant, to shine more gloriously.

Againe, to breake the corruption of his heart: for our wicked *natures* loue peace, and ease, and welfare, and hearts desire: but God will crosse those courses, and send vs troubles many wayes, that so he may pull downe the height of our corruptions, and humble vs to his owne hand.

The vse, is to teach vs to make true vse of our afflictions, and of those many hard crosses that must fall vpon vs in our course of seruing God; namely, to know that they are sent from God, not as a hard-hearted, or cruell *Iudge*; but as a wise and mercifull *Father*, who wisheth our good, and who will so blesse vnto vs the hardest and heauiest crosses, that befall vs in our liues (if we receiue them in patience and faith) that we shall say with *Dauid*, Psal. 119. 71. *It is good for vs that we haue beene in trouble, for thereby wee haue learned to know God, and our selues better.*

Thirdly, whereas *Abraham* at Gods commandement goeth out of his *Countrie* into another; we learne, that it is not vnlawfull for a Christian man, to *goe out* of his owne Country, and *trauaile* into another, & there to abide for some, or for a long time: Prouided, his causes be good & iust, as namely, these which follow;

First, if he haue a particular commandement of *God*, as here *Abraham* had.

Secondly, if he haue a lawfull calling of the Church or State, whereof he is a member: as if he be sent to a generall Councell: or, be sent as *Ambassadour*, either to stay for a time, or to stay there as Lieger.

Thirdly, if it be for the safetie of his life in a good cause. So *Moses* Exod 2. 14. 15. *fled into the land of Midian, and there stayed when Pharaoh sought his life*: And Christ himselfe fledde with his Father and Mother *into Egypt*; from the furie of *Herod*, Matth. 1. The like may be said for them, that to preserue *their libertie*, flie from the crueltie of their Creditors, who will not take honest and reasonable satisfaction; of a *surety* for another man; or of a child for the Fathers debts. But in no case for them, who *trauaile* in purpose to defeate their Creditors, or thereby to deliuer themselues from payment of their due debts, *beeing able to pay*. Of both these, we haue example in *Dauid*, & his followers. *Dauid* himselfe was faine to flie for his life from *Sauls* vniust crueltie, and therefore went and dwelt *amongst the Philistims*, 1. Sam. 27. 1. 2. And 1. Sam. 22. 2. there came to *Dauid such as were in trouble, and in debt*, and these

were with him in his trauaile, and persecutions. Now doubtlesse had they beene vngodly men (who had not cared how they came into debt, nor how they paid it,) *Dauid* would neuer haue beene *their Prince*; as that Text saith he was.

Fourthly, if it be for the maintenance of *pure religion*, and keeping a good *conscience*. This hath Christs warranty, Matth. 10. 23. *When they persecute you in one Citie, flie vnto another*. For this cause many of our fore-fathers in the former age, were faine to fly into *Germane*, *Switzerland: and to Geneua*. And for these causes diuers of other Nations doe repaire to this Nation, and are here entertained.

Fiftly, if it be for the getting, or encreasing of any good *learning*, and lawfull *knowledge*, especially diuine knowledge for matter of religion. Thus the Queene of *Saba* went out of the inmost parts of *Africa*, to *Ierusalem* in *Asia*, to see and heare *Salomon*: 2. Kings 10. and for that cause, she is highly commended by Christ himselfe, Math. 12. 42. Thus may yong men trauell for learning or the tongues, especially such as intend thereby to fit themselues for publike seruice, so it be with safetie of religion, and securitie of conscience.

Sixtly, if it be for the practise of a mans lawfull *calling*, as for trafficke: and thus *Merchants* may, and doe lawfully trauaile in all Nations, and haue their *Factors* there resident: prouided they loose not their soules, to gaine for their bodies: their trauailing is allowed by Christ in the Parable, where he saith, *The kingdome of heauen is like a Merchant man that seekes good pearles*, Matth. 13. 45.

Seauenthly, if it be to receiue and take possession of any goods or lands, lawfully descended or fallen vnto a man, in another Nation, as sometime it doth; This seemes to be allowed by Christ in the Parable, where he saith, *A certaine noble man went into a far Country, to receiue for himselfe a kingdome, and so to come againe*, Luke 19. 12.

In a word; if it be vpon any good and sufficient cause, allowable in good reason, & not contrary any part of Gods word. But as for such as leaue their Countries, and trauell into other;

Either, vpon *leuitie*, to see strange sights and fashions: Or, being *malefactors*, flie from their due punishment: Or, being in *debt*, goe away to deceiue their Creditors: Or, being *vaine-glorious*, to make themselues knowne: Or, being at *enmitie*, to fight *combats*, or to kill their enemies:

All these, and all such like, can haue no comfort in their *trauailes*: for they send themselues, God sent them not: they are out of Gods *protection*, because they goe without his warrant. And as many of them as goe away to escape the hand of the *Magistrate*; let them be assured they shall not escape the hand of God.

In the fourth place, here is a comfort for all such as are *banished* from their owne natiue Countries, for God and his Gospels sake. For,

Pfal.45.10, 11.

here *Abraham* the *Prince of Patriarkes*, was a banished man, and liued in a *strange Country*, the greater part of all his life. Let such men therefore take patiently what God laieth vpon them: for it is not their misery or mishap alone, but hath beene common to Gods children in all ages. Againe, Christ himselfe pronounceth them blessed, *who suffer persecution for righteousnesse sake*: for, though they bee exiles from their owne kingdome, or tossed vp and downe the *kingdomes of the earth*, yet *theirs is the kingdome of heauen*, Matth. 5. 10.

Lastly, though this commandement was *personally* directed to *Abraham*, and concernes not vs as it did him: yet it hath his force and vse euen to vs. For, though we are not to *goe out of our Countrie*, and leaue our liuings and habitations: yet we must doe that that is proportionable hereunto. That which is commanded to *Salomons* wife, is to all Christians; *Harken O daughter, and consider, incline thine eare, forget thine own kindred, and thy fathers house: so shall the King take pleasure in thy beauty.* This wife of *Salomon*, is the *soule* of euery Christian, the spouse of *Christ the true Salomon* who by nature is daughter to *heathen Pharaoh*, that is, to sinne, corruption, and wrath: but, beeing maried to Christ, must *forget her owne kindred and Fathers house*, that is, their owne nature and naturall affections, and carnall desires: and then shall Christ our King, and spirituall husband, *take pleasure in vs, and reioyce to doe vs good*. And this is the chiefe trauailing of all, and most acceptable to God, when a man *goeth out* of himselfe, and denieth his owne desires to obey God, and to serue *Christ Iesus*.

Thus we see the matter of his obedience; Now followeth the ende:

Which he should after receiue for inheritance.

The second particular in his obedience, is the *Ende*, why he went out of his owne Country; to inherit another, that is, the *land of Canaan*, called else-where the *land of Promise*, because God promised it vnto him, and to his seede. Now *Abraham* at Gods commandement, went out of his owne Country into this place, *to inherite it*, and to take possession of it.

But it may be obiected, He inherited it not; yea furthermore, *Stephen* saith, Act. 7. 4. *God brought him in, but gaue him no inheritance in it, no not the bredth of a foote.*

I answer, though *Abraham* did not inherite it *personally* himselfe, yet he may be said to inherite it two wayes:

1. *Sacramentally*, or Mystically:
2. In his *posterity*.

First, *Sacramentally* thus; The land of Canaan, is to be vnderstood, not onely as a Country of *Asia*, fruitefull and fertile, and plentifull of all good things, wherein the onely *visible Church* was confirmed till Christs comming. But further, as a Type of the *heauenly Canaan*, where the *triumphant Church* raignes in glory

with God. And thus *Abraham* did in his owne *person inherite it*: for he was translated from this world, after his death, into the glory of heauen. And in that respect, the glorie of heauen is rather called *the bosome of Abraham*, Luke 16. then of any other the Patriarkes, both for the excellencie of *his faith*, as also for that the promise of inheriting the land of *Canaan*, was first of all (*personally*) made to him; which because he enioyed not, he was recompenced with the fruition of the *true Canaan*.

From hence, we learne a notable doctrine: That God in performing of his promises, giueth not oftentimes the verie particular thing promised, but *something equiualent*, or proportionable to it, or else better. Thus in the fift commandement, obedient children are promised by God *long life*, as a reward for *honouring their Parents*. Now when hee takes them away in their best age, as hee did *Iosias*, 2. Kings 22.10.he giueth them *eternall life*, which is not onely proportionable, but farre exceeding the thing promised: So here, he promiseth *Abraham* the *land of Canaan*; but when it comes to the performance, he giues him a better, euen the true *Canaan*, the kingdome of heauen.

The vse hereof, is to teach vs wisedome for the true discerning of Gods mercifull performance of his promises: for he performeth them not alwayes one way vnto his children: sometime he giueth the particular thing promised, as vnto the children of *Israel*, their deliuerance out of Egypt: vnto *Hezekiah*, the restoring of his *health*, and such like. Sometime he giueth not it, but something which shall be as good or better vnto his children: as, when they are in some great *danger*, and craue *deliuerance*, or in some *necessitie*, and haue promise of *supplie*; God oftentimes deliuereth them not, but giueth them *patience*, and feeling of his fauour in such sort, as is many degrees more comfortable vnto them. And herein God heareth their prayers, and performeth his promise to them, to their full contentation.

Secondly, *Abraham inherited Canaan in his posteritie*. For though God promised it to himselfe, when he was 75. *yeares old*, Gen. 12.4. *and to him and to his seede*, Gen. 15. 7. yet neither he nor his immediate *seede* enioyed it, but his *posteritie* the Israelites, 430. yeares after the promise, as S. *Paul* prooueth, Galat.3.17. And so *Abraham* inherited it in his *posteritie*, which is a part of him; and they inherited it many hundreth yeares, euen vntill the comming of *Christ*.

As afore we learned, that God in the performance of his promises, giueth not alwaies the *thing promised*: so here let vs learne that he doth not alwaies performe them to the *same parties*, and yet most truly performeth them. If therefore God doth not to *our selues*, nor in our times accomplish his promises, or prophecies, we must not be impatient, but wait in patience. For as the Prophet saith, *The vision is yet*

for

for an appointed time, but at the laft it fhall fpeak
and not lie : though it tary, waite for it; it fhall
furely come and fhall not ftay, Habba. 2. 3. To
this ende *Dauid* alfo moft diuinely faith, Pfal.
97. 11. *Light is fowen for the righteous, and
ioy for the vpright in heart.* See light and ioy
belongs vnto them: but how? *It is fowen,* that
is, it is in hope and *expectation,* and not alwaies
in *fruition.* Therefore as the Husbandman cafts
his feede into the earth, and is content to ftay
almoft a ful yeere without it, or any profit of it,
and yet is patient all that while, becaufe hee is
fure *it will come,* and bring encreafe with it. So
muft we waite patiently on the Lord, & know
that whatfoeuer he hath promifed, we or ours
after vs, fhall be fure to enioy it. And though
we doe not, what great matter is it, *if our children doe?* For, We know, that oftentimes the
Father *foweth,* and dieth ere the harueft, and fo
the fonne *reapeth.* So for Gods great and gracious promifes, which are fowen vnto the Fathers ; if themfelues do not, their children are
fure to reape the côfortable harueft of performance. And thus we fee how *Abraham inherited the land of Canaan;* which is called the *land
of Promife,* becaufe it was fo long, and fo often promifed to fo many great *Patriarkes.*

In the fecond place, it is to be obferued,
when God promifed this vnto *Abraham;* euen
then when the land of *Canaan* was poffeffed
by many mightie Kings: So that it may be here
further doubted, how *Abraham* could take any
comfort in this promife, feeing it was at that
day held by almoft 40. Kings greater and leffe:
as we may fee in Iofhua, Chap. 10. 11. 12. and
further, *The people were many, and ftrong : the
Cities were well walled, and full of huge Giants,*
Num. 13. 28. 29. Yet for all this, he not onely *beleeues and obeyeth ;* but as God promifed,
fo he *went to it,* and *tooke poffeffion,* and died in
this faith, that God would performe his promife, and that his pofterity fhould inherit it all,
as afterward indeede they did, euen from *Mofes* to *Chrift.* If it be afked how this could be:
the anfwer is, that *Abraham* knewe that *God
was King of Kings,* and had the world, and
Kingdomes of the world *in his hand* and difpofition: and therefore affured himfelfe, that
he could bring to paffe what he had promifed,
and make good his word, notwithftanding all
fuch impediments to the contrary. And as hee
beleeued, it came to paffe; his pofteritie came
to it, entred *as conquerers,* vpon this gift of
God: and, by the power of God, fo amazed all
thefe Kings and their people, as fome fubmit-
ted, as the *Gibeonits;* and they that did not, were
all flaine, and their Countries conquered, as we
may reade at large in the booke of *Iofhua :* all
the Stories whereof are briefly comprehended
by *Dauid* in fewe words, where he faith, *Wee
haue heard with our eares, our Fathers haue told
vs, how thou O Lord droue out the heathen with
thy hand, & planted them in: how thou deftroyed the people, and made them grow,* Pfal. 44. 1. 2.

Out of which, we learne two inftructions.

Firft, that the *change of States,* and alteration
of Kingdoms or common-wealths, are in Gods
hand : and that hee can turne them one way or
other, as it pleafeth him. To this purpofe, faith
Dauid, in the fore-named Pfalme, *They inherited not the land by their owne fword, neither did
their owne arme faue them : but thy right hand,
and thy arme, and the light of thy countenance
becaufe thou didft fauour them.*

This muft teach vs to pray earneftly, in our
daicly prayers, for the good eftate of this Kingdome, wherein wee liue; and of that worthy
Prince and Queene, vnder whofe gouerment,
we haue beene fo long, and fo liberally bleffed.
For, the welfare and profperity, the certainty
and fecurity of it and her, is not in our policie,
might, munition, fhips: not in the ftrength of
our nauie, nor in the power of our armour, nor
in the chiualrie of our people, nor in the wifedome of our Counfell (though for all thefe we
are a people *honoured* of our friends, and *feared*
of our enemies): But in the mighty hand of our
God, who (as *Dauid* faith) *beareth rule ouer the
Kingdomes of the earth, and giueth them to
whomfoeuer he will,* Dan. 4. 22.

Seeing therefore the King of heauen is the
giuer and eftablifher, the *remoouer* and changer
of Kingdomes of the earth ; let vs affure our
felues, that the prayers of *Elifha,* are *the Horfes
and Chariots of Ifraell:* 2. Kinges, 13. 14.

And furely, if *Elifha* for his prayer was acknowledged by the King himfelfe, to be his Father ; then doubtleffe, the godly *Minifters,* and
fuch other in our Church, as *pray daily for the
peace of our Ierufalem,* are worthy to be accounted good *children* of our Church, and
worthy members of our State.

Secondly, here we learne what is the *ruine
of Kingdomes,* and ouerthrow of eftates: namely, *finne* and vngodlineffe. This is moft apparant in the prefent example. For, why did God
take this land from the *Cananites,* and giue it
to *Abraham* and his feede ? the Stories of the
olde Teftament anfwer, *nothing but finne.* In
Deuteronomie, *Mofes* chargeth the Ifraelites,
that they *doe not after the abhominations of the
heathen Cananites:* For, faith he, *becaufe of
their abhominable finnes God did caft them out
before you,* Deut. 18. 9. 12. And why did not
God inftantly giue it to *Abraham* (to *inherite*)
after the promife? euen becaufe *the wickedneffe
of thefe Amorites was not then full,* Gen. 15. 16.
that is, their finnes were not then ripe. For, we
muft know, that though God be the abfolute
and *foueraigne Lord* of all Kingdomes, and
may difpofe them as hee will: yet he rather exercifeth his *Iuftice* then his *power;* and neuer
ouerturneth any State, but vpon caufe of their
apparant finfulneffe. Nor can the Amorites or
Cananites pleade herein any hard meafure. For,
the *fame God,* dealt afterward in the *fame
Iuftice* with his owne people, giuing the Kingdome of Iudah to the *Chaldeans,* and Ifrael to

the

the *Assyrians:* and the cause is laide downe most memorably in the Storie; *When the Israelites sinned against the Lord their God, and walked after the fashions of the heathen, whome the Lord had cast out before them, and did secretly things that were wicked, & made Images, and serued idols: and though God warned them by his Prophets, yet would they not obey, but hardned their neckes, and so finally, left all the commandements of God; then the Lord was exceeding wroth with Israel, and cast them also out of his sight,* 2. Kings, 17. from the seauenth verse to the 19. Thus sinne is able to ouerturne Kingdomes, be they *Cananites, Israelites,* or whosoeuer.

Let this teach vs all to looke to our *liues,* and make conscience of all *sinne;* especially great & capitall, and *crying sinnes:* for the sinnes of a people are *wormes and Cankers,* eating out the life and strength of a common-wealth. And let our *State and gouernment* learne here to looke to the reformation of our people, especially *for great sinnes,* For, open *profanenesse,* or *vncleannesse,* or *oppressions,* or *iniustice,* or *extortions,* or *cruelties,* & exactions; all these, or any of these sinnes, raigning in a State, are able to ouerturne the best established Kingdome on the earth, and will at last (doe power and policie what they can) *make the land spewe out her inhabitants:* and in that meane time (let the wily wits of men, iudge as they list) it will proque true, that the sinfull and profane man is the *worst,* and the godly and conscionable man, the *best friend* to a State, and *best subiect* in a Kingdome.

Thus much for the second point in *Abrahams* obedience; namely, the ende of it.

The third and last point, is the manner of his obedience: which followeth in these words:

And hee went out, not knowing whither he went.

The manner of this his leauing his Country, in mans reason would seeme *strange;* nay, the world will condemne it for plaine *foolishnesse,* for a man to leaue a *certainty,* for an *vncertainty.* But it may here be doubted, how the *Apostle* can here say, that he knew not whether hee went; seeing these words are not in the Storie of the old Testament: doth not that practise allow *traditions* beside Scripture?

I answer first; We refuse no traditions, which are agreeable to the Scripture, and analogie of faith: but such as are agreeable to one of these, wee receiue them, though not as *Scripture.*

Secondly, if the Apostles in the new Testament doe adde any thing in any Storie, which is not in the olde (as S. *Paul* doth the names of the Sorcerers of Egypt, *Iannes and Iambres,* 2. Timo. 3. 8) that circumstance by them so added, is to be holden *as Scripture and no tradition;* because they hauing the same spirit of God, which the Writters of the olde Testament had, haue inserted it into the bodie of

Scripture: euen as the three sentences of the heathen Poets, alledged by Saint *Paul* (Acts 17. 28. 1. Corinthians, 15. 33. Titus, 1. 12.) haue now a *diuine truth* in them, which they had not before.

But yet will some say, the *Apostles* had these things from the olde Testament *by tradition;* seeing they were not written.

I answer: We may safely graunt it, and yet our cause loseth nothing, though it may be they had them *by inspiration,* and not by *tradition,* that beeing as likely, or much more then the other.

Thirdly, but for *this particular,* I answer, that the Apostle had the words, or at least the matter out of the Storie *in Genesis.* For thus go the words : *God said to Abraham, Goe out of thy Country, &c. into the land that I will shew thee:* He named none to him, but told him he would shew him *one.* So then *Abraham* went out at Gods appointment : and God knew, but *hee knew not whether he went:* hee knew well the land he left, but hee knew not the land hee should haue.

But it may be againe obiected, that this is not true: for it appeares, Gen. 12. 5. that *Abraham* with *Sarah* his wife, and all their substance, *departed to goe into the land of Canaan, and to the land of Canaan they came:* therefore he knew whither hee went; namely to that land.

I answer; It is true, *he went out,* with purpose and assurance, *to inherit a land promised* him by God, but not named to him. And whereas it is there said, *He went out to goe into the land of Canaan,* that is spoken in respect of the *performance* when he was come thither, not of the first *promise* made him at his departure : or, of the time when *Moses* wrote it, not of the time when God spake it to *Abraham.* And, that *he knew not* what land God did meane, vntill he came thither, is plaine in the 7. verse, where it is said, *That when Abraham had passed through all the countrey, and was come into Canaan, then God appeared to him, and saide, This land will I giue vnto thy seede:* But till then God neuer named it vnto him; and therefore we read afore, that *he beleeued and obeyed* vpon the generall promise: but now when God did *particularly* specifie and shew what land, he then shewed his thankefulnes to God, *and did there build an Altar vnto the God that had appeared vnto him.*

Thus it is cleare, that *Abraham went out, not knowing whither he went.* Which beeing so, it appeares that *Abraham* did that which the world would call, plaine *foolishnes.* To leaue knowne friends for vnknowne, *certen* liuing for *vncerten,* is a simple course in mans reason : at least (the world will say) he might first haue demanded of God, *what land* that was, which he should haue, before he left that which he had: but *Abraham* makes no such *questions,* mooues no such *doubts,* but beleeueth and obeieth, and goeth out of his certen dwelling (at Gods calling) *though he knew not where to lodge at night*.

This practife of faithfull *Abraham*, hath profitable vfe :

Firft, here we learne, that though Gods *commandements* feeme foolifh, and vnreafonable, yet we muft obey them. Chrift faith, *If a man will euer come in the kingdome of heauen, he muft be borne againe*, Ioh. 3. 3. S. Paul faith, *If any man among you feeme to be wife, let him be a foole that he may be wife*, 1. Cor. 3. 18. Chrift faith, *If any man will be my Difciple, he muft denie himfelfe and follow me*, Luk. 9. 23.

But how can thefe commandements be beleeued or done? how can reafon *beleeue* them? how can nature *doe* them? So difputed the woman of Samaria with Chrift, Ioh. 4. 11. when Chrift told her he would giue her *of the waters of life*; fhee replied, *Sir, thou haft nothing to draw with, and the well is deepe: whence then haft thou that water of life?* Thus we obiect and reafon againft God with carnall obiections, and waigh Gods commandements in the balance of reafon : thus God and his commandements are much abufed by vs. And this is the caufe we heare, and read Gods word, and profit not by it, becaufe we ponder it in our reafon, and allow nor follow it no further, then it agreeth with our naturall affections. As a man that will needes ftand vnder a *penthoufe*, hath no *water* falling on him, though it fhould raine neuer fo pretious water from heauen : fo, when the *water of life*, out of the word of God, fhould droppe vpon our foules, to comfort our confciences, and to wafh away our finnes; we haue our *deuices* out of wit, and *diftinctions* out of reafon, as penthoufes to keepe it from vs, that it flides away, and neuer hath any worke in vs. But contrariwife, we muft remember *Abraham the father of our faith*; and when we heare Gods word, we muft with him captiuate our reafon, and fubdue our affections to it : meafure them by Gods word, and not it by them; and what we cannot yeeld to in the obedience of reafon, we muft obey with *the obedience of faith* : and fo fhall Gods word haue a gracious and powerfull worke in vs.

Secondly, here we muft learne, that though we fee *no profit* come by obeying Gods commandements, yet we muft obey them. For what profit could *Abraham* fee in leauing a *certen liuing*, for an *vncertentie*? yet he obeyed and went, vpon the bare word of God, building vpon it, that God beeing his guide, he could not go aftray. So muft we follow God fincerely, and doe his commandements, though no profit feeme can come thereby. But fome will fay, Shall godly men be led like blindfold fooles? fhall they refufe all meanes of helpe, by wit and policie? this is the way to make them ridiculous, and *affes* for the wicked world to ride vpon.

I anfwer : let godly men vfe all their *wit*,

and looke with all their *eyes*, in their actions *with men of this world*. But in the obedience of Gods commandements, let them doe as *Abraham* did, *Follow Gods calling though it feeme to be to no ende*.

In obedience to God, we muft doe as *blind men* doe, who followe their *guides*, though it be through woods and rockes, hills, or dales, or dangerous places, regarding nothing, fearing nothing; onely following and trufting to *their guides*, who haue eyes for them, though they haue none for themfelues. So muft wee follow Gods calling, and yeeld abfolute obedience to his Commandements, fearing nothing but trufting to the faithfullneffe of his power, and affuredly beleeuing, that he beeing our *bleffed guide*, we fhall not be mif-led: thus to doe is true faith.

But alas, how contrary is the practife of the world! Men deale with God, as wee doe with *loofe Chapmen*, whom we will not truft without a good pawne. So we will no obey Gods *Commandements*, longer then his religion ferus our turne; nor will we truft and follow God without the pawnes of prophet and pleafure. Nay, wee doe worfe: moft men efteeme of God no better, nor vfe him any better then they doe *theeues* in their houfes. If a man come into our houfe, that is giuen to ftealing, wee truft him as long as he is in our fight: but if he be out of our fight, wee thinke euer he is ftealing: So, if men fee the meanes of Gods prouidence, they will take his word, and truft it; but elfe God muft excufe them, they may not truft him further then they fee him. And if the *Commaundements* of God found to their content, and tend to their profit, they will *obey them*: but, if not, they will caft them behinde their backe; at leaft, they will make a paufe at the mattter and take their owne time. And if Gods wayes feeme pleafant and profitable, they will *walke in them*: or elfe they will leaue them, and walke in their *owne*.

And hence is it, that men in deftreffes, runne to Wizards, and Wife-men: others deale fraudulently, and deceitfully: others worke on the *Sabath day*: and thus by indirect and vnlawful dealing, they labour to inrich themfelues, and to bring their purpofes to paffe. And why all this? but becaufe Gods commandements doe not found to their purpofe, nor tend to their profit, and therefore they will not obey them.

If thefe men had beene in Abrahams cafe, they would neuer haue gone out, *not knowing whither to goe*: but they would haue argued the matter with God, and haue thought it good wifdome to paufe well afore they leaue a *certentie* for an *vncertentie*. But contrariwife, *Abraham* thought it foolifhneffe to reafon with God, and therefore performed *abfolute obedience* : and for this caufe he and his faith are renowned to this day; namely, 3000. yeares after him, and fhall be till the worlds ende.

This

This was the obedience of faith: and this to doe, is to be true subiects to Gods kingdome. If the *King* call a man from his owne liuing, to come to himselfe and to the Court; who will not leaue what he hath of his owne, and *trust his word?* So, who will not leaue his owne wisdome, and relie on the *promise & word of God;* and obey his commandements, though there seeme at the first, no profit can come thereby. Thus shall we be sure, both to haue sufficient for this world, and shall also be true children of faithfull *Abraham.*

Hitherto of the first example of *Abrahams Faith.*

VERSE 9.

By faith, he abode in the land of promise, as in a strange countrey, as one that dwelt in tents with Isaak and Iacob, heires with him of the same promise.

Ere is the second example of *Abrahams faith*, and the fift in order; and is concerning *Abrahams* abiding, or dwelling in that land whereinto God had called him: and this he also did by *faith.* As he *went out* of his owne countrey, and came into *Canaan*, by the power and leading of his *faith*; so by the same *faith* he *abode* and dwelt *in the same land.*

The parts are two:
1. The *Action of Abrahams faith,* in the 9. verse.
2. The *Reason* of that his so doing, in the 10.

The *action* in the 9. verse. is spoken of two waies.
  1. It is *laid downe* to *be his abiding in the land of promise.*
  2. It is *amplified* by two circumstances:
    1. The *manner how* he dwelt there, in two points:
      1. As a stranger, or *in a strange countrey.*
      2. *As one that dwelt in tents,* and not in houses.
    2. The *persons with whome: with Isaac,* and *Iacob, Heires with him of the same promise.*
The first point in order, is his dwelling in

the land of Canaan (called here the land of Promise.)

By faith he abode in the land of Promise. Canaan is now called *the land of Promise*, because it was promised in the v. afore-going, as we then heard: so that the meaning is; he abode in that land, which was promised him, when he came out of his owne country. Which countrey *Abraham* knew not by name, when he left his owne, nor till he came thither: but then God told him, *This is the land I will giue thee and thy seede,* Gen. 12.7. In this Land thus promised, *Abraham* dwelt and remained the rest of his life, which was a hundreth yeares.

In this Action of *Abraham*, are three particular points.
  1. He *dwelt* in Canaan.
  2. That Canaan was the *land of promise.*
  3. He dwelt there *by faith.*

For the first: Concerning *Abrahams* dwelling in Canaan, diuers *questions* may be mooued;

First, how it is true, that he abode or dwelt there? seeing it is apparant in the Storie, he dwelt in Egypt, Gen. 12.10. *and in Gerar,* Gen. 20.1.

I answer: The meaning is not, that he staied there euery day of his life; but that he liued and died there, and made it the place of his residence and ordinarie habitation, whereunto he alwaies resorted againe, if any occasion drew him abroad.

And further, he went not into *Egypt*, but vpon such speciall cause, as could not be otherwise helped, as vpon a famine or such like, Gen. 12.10. *Then there came a famine in the land, therefore Abraham went downe into Egypt to soiourne there.* Where it appeares: first, that the cause was extraordinarie: secondly, that he went not to make any dwelling, but to soiourn there for a time, and then to repaire home againe.

Where we learne, that as a man is not to depart out of that land, where God hath appointed him to dwell, but vpon good and sufficient causes: so, when those causes cease, which drew him out, he is not to stay longer from home; but to repaire againe to the place of his ordinarie dwelling. God would haue a man dwell at home: and it is leuitie, and a token of an vnconstant minde, and a running head, for a man to desire to be alwaies abroad.

Birds flie abroad, but so as they may come to their neasts at night: so men should endeauour, as much as may be, to take few occasions of beeing from their dwellings: and when they needes must, to let it be for as short a time as may be. For, as it is a signe of a light woman, Prou. 7.11. *Her feete cannot abide in her house:* so is it of an vnstaied man, vpon euery occasion to be caried from home.

We must therefore follow holy *Abraham*, who is here commended for abiding, or dwelling in the countrey, which God had giuen him.

Againe, this practise of *Abrahams faith*, condemnes the *wandring beggers*, to be an vnfaithfull and vngracious generation. Our Land (by the abuse of our peace and plenty) is full of such. Aske them where they *dwell*: their answer is, They haue *small dwelling*; but, looke into the matter, and they haue the largest dwelling of all: for they dwell euery where, and all abroad; they count it bondage to be tied to one Town, or dwell in one Parish, and thinke it freedome and libertie to *dwell euery where*. These are Caterpillers of a Common-wealth, and the greatest robbers of the poore that are. Common Theeues steale from rich men: but these steale from the poore; they get that from men, which the true poore should haue. No good comes to Church nor Common-wealth by these men, but much hurt to both. For, a finger cut off from his place, is of no vse: so, a man liuing out of his calling, and out of his place, is of no vse in the body politique.

Happy will it be with our *Church and State*, when wee haue such lawes, and such execution of them, as that this disorder may be reformed, and euery man confined to his owne dwelling, and none suffred to liue in our Kingdome, who is not of some Parish: for let vs be assured, so many wandring beggers, so many blemishes in our gouernment.

Thirdly, *Abrahams dwelling in this Land* (beeing a fruite of his *faith*) teacheth vs it is no good token, but an ill signe for a man to be vncertaine in his dwelling. It is the fashion of many men, if they trauaile, they neuer lodge at one place twise: and for their dwelling, it is not certaine; but now in the *North*, now in the *South*: now in this Parish, now in that: now in this iurisdiction, now in another: Sometime in the Citie, sometime in the Countrie. Who bee these? But either such as be in debt, and purpose to deale ill with their Creditors; or that are malefactors, and hereby labour to auoide the censure of Authoritie: or else they bee Papists, which by this meanes labour to lurke vnseene, and to escape the law; as many of them doe, either by skipping out of one Parish, Diocesse, Countie, or Prouince into another, and so auoiding the authoritie of all: or else, by lurking in great Cities, and so lying as *Soiourners*, and not as *Parishioners*, vnseene or vnmarked in so great multitudes. Let our Authoritie take the more carefull notice of such men, the more craftily they labour to creep from vnder it: and let such men know, they discouer themselues the more by this practise, to be *vnfaithfull* either to GOD, or Men, or both; seeing that GOD here commends *Abraham* for dwelling or staying in that place, which GOD had appointed him. And so much for this question.

Againe, it may here be demaunded: How *Abraham* might lawfully *dwell in Canaan*, seeing it was then Idolatrous. It may seeme, that therefore it is not vnlawfull for men to dwell in Popish or Idolatrous Countries.

I answer: *Abraham* did not so vpon any priuate motion, nor for any worldly cause, but vpon speciall warrant and calling from God: otherwise his so doing, had not beene iustifiable: therefore that practise of his connot be a warrant for any to do the like, without the like cause and calling.

But how could *Abraham* be preserued from the contagion of Idolaters, liuing amongst them? I answer;

First, God that called him thither, did there preserue him. Againe, *Abraham* liued in the Country, but conuersed not with the people at all, but in some necessary and ciuill affaires: and by this meanes escaped the danger of infection.

Where we may learne, that if any man would liue in such places: without hurt to their conscience, let them first be sure that they haue a calling and warrant from God, to liue in those Countries. Secondly, let them conuerse with Idolaters warily and sparingly; and so shall they preserue themselues from the occasions of euil, as *Abraham* did, who abode in an Idolatrous Country; and so, though not without danger, yet without hurt to his religion. Thus we see *Abraham dwelt in the land of Canaan*.

Now secondly, this Land is called the *Land of Promise*: that is, the Land formerly promised him by God, when he called him out of his owne Country. And it is likely that the Apostle doth not here first of all call it so: but that it was knowne generally amongst the Patriarks by that name: and that *Abraham* himselfe did first of all so call it; who, when he looked vpon it, and considered the fruitfullnesse and excellencie of it, did euermore remember and call to minde, *this land is promised to me*, this is mine by promise. And herein he rested and satisfied himselfe, though he had not the possession of it.

Here we may see the excellency of true faith: which depends vpon the *promises* of God, though they be vnperformed. A Land *of promise* contents *Abraham*, he leaues *the possession* to his posteritie. It is hard to finde such faith in the world: It is land in possession which we looke for: a Land of promise cannot content vs: but let vs labour to practise faith, and to take comfort in the promises of God, and leaue the performance to Gods appointed time.

Thirdly, he dwelt in this land *by faith*. And no meruaile. For had it not beene by faith, hee would neuer haue dwelt there, where he had not so much as a roome for his Tent to stand in, but he must *borrow* it; nor to burie his dead, but he must *buy it*. This was against reason, yet *by faith he dwelt there*, as afore *by faith he left his owne*, which was also against reason. Where still the power of faith is magnified to be such, as it will carie a man ouer all impediments of obedience, and will giue him victory not against one,

one, but againſt all obiections; and power to performe not one, but many things contrary to carnall wiſedome.

We muſt here learne to examine, whether we haue a true and ſound *faith* or no. If wee haue, then we muſt not doe ſome one or fewe actions *in faith*, or *die in faith*, but we muſt liue by faith, the whole courſe of our liues. *We muſt walke by faith, and not by ſight,* ſaith the Apoſtle, 2. Corinth. 5. 7. So ſaith he of himſelfe, Galat. 2. 20. *I liue by the faith in the Sonne of God:* he ſaith not, *he hopes to die in that faith,* but *he liues by it.* And in the former place hee ſaith not, we muſt *ſet a ſtep* or two, but we muſt *walke by faith,* which argueth a continued action: and therefore it is that Saint *Peter* ſaith, Gods children *are kept by the power of God, through faith vnto ſaluation,* 1. Peter 1. 5. In which words two things are ſpoken of faith: the firſt is affirmed; namely, that *faith* preſerueth a man to ſaluation through all hindrances, either of inward temptations, or outward croſſes, which the deuill or the world can lay in his way. This *preſeruation* is one of the greateſt workes in the world, and therefore it is worthily aſcribed to God: the power of God preſerueth vs, but *through faith.* The ſecond is implyed; that therefore we muſt labour *to keepe that faith* euermore with vs, *which muſt keepe vs,* and to cheriſh and preſerue that that muſt *preſerue vs to ſaluation. Dauid* was an excellent practitioner hereof: no man was more tried and toſſed then he, *yet he euer drew neere vnto God,* Pſal. 73. 28. Indeede ſometime hee ſaid, *all men were liers, but that was in his feare,* Pſal. 116. 11. And againe, *I am caſt out of thy ſight, but that was in his haſte,* Pſal. 31. 22. that is, when the force of ſome paſſion, or the violence of ſome temptations did carie him headlong: but otherwiſe he euer *liued the life of faith.*

So muſt we, not thinke to liue in ſenſuality, and die in faith: but to liue by faith, in all our actions, from one day to another, meditating daily on Gods promiſes, and beleeuing them, and relying on them, and applying the generalls to our owne ſelues, and practiſing faith by making conſcience of ſinne, and inuring our ſelues to patience and long ſuffering. Thus doing, we ſhall be children of faithfull *Abraham,* who firſt *by faith* left his owne Country, and then *by faith* alſo dwelt ſtill in the Land of Canaan. And thus much for the *action of his* faith: *Hee abode in the Land of Promiſe.*

Now follow the circumſtances of the action, which are two: 1. The *manner* how: 2. The *Perſons* with whom.

The manner is laid downe in two points:

    1. As a ſtranger:

    2. As one that dwelt in tents.

The firſt point, for the manner, is laid downe in theſe words,

    As in a ſtrange Country.

The meaning is: he eſteemed it a *ſtrange* Country to him, & accounted himſelfe a *ſtran-*

ger in it. Againſt which it may be obiected, that he was familiarly acquainted with *Mamre, Aner, and Eſhcol,* three great and mightie men of that Country: that he and they were confederates together, Gen. 14. 13. therefore it ſeemes he liued not like a ſtranger in the Country.

Some anſwer, that theſe three were not *Cananits,* but neere a-kinne to *Abraham,* and had other names: but the Text is plaine in that place, that *Mamre* was an *Amorite,* and the other two were his brethren. Therefore the anſwer is, that in all likelyhood they three were *Proſelits;* and that by *Abrahams* godly perſwaſions they had renounced Idolatry, and were come to the knowledge of the true God, and that they ioyned with *Abraham* in the worſhip of the true God, and ſo were his conuerts: whereupon *Abraham* (as he might lawfully) conuerſed with them as his familar friends. And hereof there are two Inducements.

Firſt, it is ſaid, Gen. 14. 13. that *they were confederates with Abraham:* and it appeared ſo by their deedes; for they ioyned their powers, and aſſiſted him in the warre againſt the Kings, (Gen. 14. 24.)

Secondly, it is ſaid, Gen. 14. 13. *That Abraham dwelt on the Land of Mamre:* he was his Tenant or Fermour. Now, it is more then likely, *Abraham* would not haue ſo farre been beholden to them, but that they were true chriſtians, and of his owne religion.

Therefore this hinders not, but he might bee a ſtranger notwithſtanding, vnto the body of the people, and that it is true that *Abraham* ſaith of himſelfe to ſome of them, Gen. 23. 4. *I am a ſtranger and a Soiourner amongſt you.*

But it may be then demaunded, Why did *Abraham* liue amongſt them *as a ſtranger,* and in that Land as a Soiourner.

I anſwer: the reaſons were diuers: Firſt, hee had title giuen to that Land, but no poſſeſſion; he therefore contented himſelfe with that that God gaue him, and chalenged not any poſſeſſion all the dayes of his life, but bought or borrowed of *Mamre* the place where he liued and dwelt (Gen. 14. 13.) and of the Hittites a place of buriall, Gen. 23. 3. &c.

This may teach all men not to be too haſtie, in ſeeking for that, that it may be, is their right: let not men preſcribe their owne times, nor be their owne caruers, but leaue their affaires to Gods diſpoſing, and enter no further then they ſee God goeth afore them, *Abraham muſt be a ſtranger in his owne land;* and thou ſometime muſt be content for a time to be a *ſtranger* to that which is thine owne.

Secondly, they were all of them for the moſt part heathen *Idolaters,* amongſt whom *Abraham* would not conuerſe, but as ſparingly as might be. Now if *Abraham* would be *a ſtranger* in his owne Country, rather then liue familiarly with Idolaters; It ſheweth how litle faith, and leſſe conſcience they haue, who can be content to liue in the midſt of Idolaters,where they haue nothing to doe, and can conuerſe with them in all familiaritie,without any ſcruple of conſcience. *Abraham* made himſelfe a *ſtranger at home* to auoide Idolatry; but they wil make themſelues *at home in a ſtrange countrie*, to intangle themſelues in Idolatry : theſe men will hardly prooue the childrē of *Abrahā*.

Theſe reaſons *Abraham* himſelfe had in this his ſo doing.

There is a third, a more ſpirituall or myſticall reaſon; and that reaſon God had in making *Abraham* liue in Canaan *as a ſtranger*; Namely, to teach all Chriſtian men their dutie,to the worlds ende.

Abraham is the Father of the faithfull,Rom. 4. 11. And this is our honour to be the children of *Abraham*, we muſt therefore follow our Father *in his faith*, and in the practiſe of it: we muſt liue in this world as Pilgrimes and Strangers,euen in the midſt of all our peace and proſperitie, of all our libertie, riches,lands,and poſſeſſions ; yea, of all our worldly friends and acquaintance. If it ſeeme ſtrange how this can be: I anſwer, the practiſe of it conſiſts in ſixe actions.

Firſt, we muſt not bath our ſelues in the pleaſures of this world. *Pilgrims* take but little delight in their iournies , becauſe they thinke themſelues not at home. This is S. *Peters* argument: *Dearely beloued, as ſtrangers and pilgrims abſtaine from fleſhly luſts which fight againſt the ſoule*, 1. Pet. 2.11. Fot too much delight in fleſhly pleaſures, ſmothers the grace of God in vs,and lets looſe all ſinnes,and giues life vnto all corruptions.

Secondly, we muſt *vſe this world as though we vſed it not*; that is, euen the neceſſary comforts and delights thereof; they be the very words of the Apoſtle, 1. Cor.7. 31. For, ſo the *Pilgrime* , when he paſſeth through a ſtrange Countrie , hath not his minde troubled with looking or thinking on the goods and commodities of that Country where he is; but vſing as much thereof , as is neceſſary for him, all his thoughts are on his owne Country.So ſhould we,when we are in our beſt eſtates,in our greateſt iollity,in the midſt of our wealth and abundance of pleaſures, caſt our mindes from them, and haue our thoughts euen then conuerſing in heauen,where is the place of our abode.This is likewiſe the Apoſtles exhortation, Philip.3. 20.*Worldly men make their belly their God:* that is, drowne themſelues in carnall pleaſures , ſo farrey no they forget any other God, any other heauen. But we muſt not doe ſo: *our conuerſation muſt be in heauen* , from whence we looke for our Sauiour Ieſus Chriſt.

Thirdly, we muſt haue a ſerious care and endeauour to pleaſe god: for *all the earth is his*,& we are but ſoiourners in his ſight ; therefore as the Pilgrime is careful to pleaſe the Lord of tſe Country, by whoſe leaue he trauailes through it: ſo muſt we be to pleaſe the Lord; ſeeing as

God ſaith , Leuit. 25. 23. *The land is his, and we are but ſtrangers and ſoiourners with him.*

And hereunto adde a fourth, which is neere a-kinne vnto it : We muſt caſt all our care on God , ſeeing that he is the Lord of the earth, and we are but Pilgrimes and Soiourners. *Dauid* ſaith, Pſal. 24. 1. *The earth is the Lords, and all that therein is:* The ſame *Dauid* confeſſeth, Pſal. 39. 12. *He is a ſtranger before God, and a ſoiourner as all his Fathers were,* & thereupon deſireth God *to heare his prayer, hearken to his crie , and not to keepe ſilence at his teares:* as though he had ſaid , Inaſmuch as I ſoiourːe with thee,thou art to heare my complaint.Fo:, as a Soiourner carès , nor lookes for nothing, but depends on them for all things with whom he ſoiournes:ſo muſt we *caſt all our care on God; for he careth for vs* , he is our Landlord, we are his Farmours and Tenants , *we hold the earth from him*, by no leaſe of yeares,but at his will , and it is lent vs: let vs therefore but haue care to pleaſe this our Landlord, and caſe for nothing.

Fiftly, we muſt giue continuall thankes and praiſe to God for his good bleſſings we receiue in this world : for all are his, and we are but ſtrangers.Thus did all Gods Saints in old time; *Iaacob , He was leſſe then the leaſt of Gods mercies.*But eſpecially there is one memorable example of *Dauid*, and the Church in his dayes, 1. Chron. 29. 13,14, 15,16. When he had prepared abundantly for the building of the Temple,he proſtrated himſelfe before God,and in his owne name and the peoples ſaide thus; *Riches and honour come of thee, therefore our God we thanke thee,& praiſe thy glorious name. But who am I , and what is my people, that wee ſhould offer vnto thee ? for all is thine , and of thine owne haue we giuen thee: for wee are ſtrangers before thee, and ſoiourners, as all our Fathers were.* Thankefulneſſe beſeemes all men, eſpecially *ſtrangers*.Therefore,as Pilgrimes doe thankefully accept the fauours ſhewed them in a ſtrange Country:So muſt we,all the bleſſings God giues vs in this world , where we are but ſtrangers.

Sixtly and laſtly,we muſt haſten to the kingdome, as a Pilgrime doth to his iourneyes end, or to his owne Countrey: and till he can, is alwaies thinking of it , and ſighing after it: So muſt we (who are *not dwellers,but ſoiourners* in theſe houſes of clay) long after heauen, and (as S. *Paul* ſaith he did) *couet to remooue from hence, and to dwell with the Lord.*Strangers are not to take ſuch pleaſure in forraine Countries as to forget their owne. So Chriſtians muſt not be ſo in loue with this world, as to forget or neglect the world to come. If they doe , they are vnworthie of it , and ſhew themſelues not ſtrangers, as *Abraham* here was; but *men of this world , who haue their portion in this life.*

In performing theſe ſixe actions, men ſhew themſelues ſtrangers in this world. And thus muſt we doe , euen in the midſt of all worldly

Pſal.17.14.

profperitie,if we looke euer to enioy the glorie of a better: And thus doing, wee fhall be children of faithfull *Abraham*, who *dwelt in the land of Canaan, as in a ftrange Country.*

As one that dwelt in tents.

The fecond point for the manner, how *Abraham dwelt in Canaan,* is, that he built himfelfe no houfes, nor made Orchards or Gardens, *but dwelt in tents* or tabernacles; which were fuch houfes, as now are vfed in warre,and are yet called by the fame name, *Tents,* or Pauilions: whofe matter is not wood, nor ftone,but cloth, ftuffe,or skinnes:and are eafily reared, and foone taken downe: and when a man departeth,he may carie his houfe with him. That *Abraham* did thus, appeares in the Stories written of him. *He came to Bethell, and there pitched his tent,* Gen.12. 8: and Gen.13. 18.*he remooued his tent:*and 18.1. God appeared vnto him,*as he fate in his tent dore:*and 18. 9. being asked where *Sarah* was, he anfwered, *fhee is within the tent:* and thefe tents are called *his place,* Gen.18. 33. and *his houfe,*24.2.Out of all which places it is plaine, that *hee dwelt in tents,* and that not onely at his firft comming, when hee had not time to build him an houfe: but euen all the dayes of his life, after his comming into the land of Canaan.

But why did *Abraham* dwell in tents, and not in houfes? was it becaufe then there were no houfes? Not fo:For there were Cities built euen afore the flood, Gen. 4. 17. *Cain* bult a Citie: no maruell therefore if there were many after, as *Sodome, and all her fifters.*And though it appeares not they digged into the earth for naturall ftone, yet had they *Bricke,* which they made themfelues, Genefis, 11. 3. and furely, the world which built the huge tower of Babell, Gen. 11. would not fticke to build themfelues houfes. Nor can it be faid,that thofe Cities, Sodome, Gomorrah, and the reft, were nothing but a multitude of tents together. For, wee read Gen. 19. 3. that *Lot dwelling in Sodome, receiued 2. Angels into his houfe:* and in the 4. verfe, that the *Sodomits came and enuironed his houfe round about to take them,*thinking they had beene men: and when *Lot* refufed to deliuer them, that *they preffed fore vpon the houfe to haue broken vp the doore:* but all this might haue beene fpared,if it had bin nothing but a tent, which a childe may cut in peeces with a knife. It is manifeft then, that there were houfes in thofe daies. Why then did *Abraham* build none? was it becaufe he was poore and could not? Not fo: for contrariwife, Gen.12.5. *Hee carried with him from his owne country, all the fubftance hee poffeffed:* And what that was, is particularized, Gen. 13. 2. *He was very rich in cattell, in filuer, and in gold.* His riches were both great,and of the beft. So then hee could, but would not.But why *would* he not? Was it vpon a proud humour, or in a conceited fingularitie,becufe he would not be like other men, but haue a fingular way of his own?No: *Abra-*

A ham was none of thofe,who allow nothing,but that is done of themfelues;and who thinke nothing good,if it be ordinarie: for he was a holy man, and famous for his faith. So then none of thefe were the reafons of this his fo doing.

The reafons then why *Abraham*, and other holy Patriarches, vfed *to dwell in tents,* and not to build them houfes, were of two forts,*Ciuill,* and *Holy.*

The Ciuil or Politicke refpect that they had was this:

B They holding themfelues Gods feruants,did depend on his word; and therefore did fubmit themfelues to goe vp and downe the world, whither fo euer God did cal them.Beeing then to remooue, euery day (they knew not when nor whither) it was therefore both the fitteft and cheapeft,to *dwell in tents,*which were foone pitched vp, and foone taken downe. Neither neede it feeme ftrange that they could liue for cold, in thofe poore thin tents, all the yeare long: for the country and climate there was alwaies temperate enough for colde: and rather inclining to too much heate

The holy or religious refpect was this: They held themfelues but *ftrangers vpon earth,* and therefore would not build themfelues cities or houfes; as looking or caring to liue vpon earth: but *dwelled in tents,* as feeming defirous, to re-

C mooue from the earth to heauen:the fooner the better. And this did the Fathers of the olde Teftament:not that they thought it it vnlawfull to build cities, or dwel in houfes; but that they might teftifie their religion, and expectation of another world, in the midft of that profane age wherein they liued; wherein there were almoft none, that either regarded, remembred, or acknowledged a world to come.

And this was not the particular, or fingular deed of *Abraham* alone. All holy men in thofe dayes, liued in tents.Gen.9.21.It is cleere that Noah dwelt in tents, though then he was king of all the world. And fo did *Lot* alfo,as long as he liued with *Abraham:* Gen. 13. 5.*Lot had fheepe, and cattell,and tents.*And thus they did, becaufe (as the Apoftle faith) *they had here no*

D *enduring city, but they fought for one to come,* Heb. 13. 14. And they thought, they euer heard that voyce founding in their eares,(Mic. 2.10.) *Arife and depart, for this is not your reft.*

Contrariwife, the wicked of the world, becaufe they fet vp their reft in this world,and cared for no other: they began prefently to build them houfes,nay cities, (as *Cain* did euen in the beginning) Gen.4. 17.And the Sodomites had a citie euen walled(as is likely) *for Lot was fitting in the gate of Sodome, when the two Angels came to him,* Gen.19.1,2. And the Canaanites *had cities walled* exceeding high: (Num. 13.) But we finde not, that euer Gods children built them cities,vntill they came to haue a fetled Church of their owne. But contrariwife, it is worth obferuing, that God promi-

feth

seth his people, that *they shall come and dwell in cities which they built not* : namely, which were built by worldly men to their hand. And thus wee see the reasons why *Abraham* dwelt in tents. Now let vs see the vse of it.

First, here we learne *frugalitie*, out of the ciuill vse of their tents: that is, to vse the blessings and comforts of this life, and soberly and sparingly as may be : as to bestowe as little cost as may be of our selues, in such things *as perish in the vsing*: namely, meate, drinke, apparell, and houses. For what is spent herein, is spent onely on our selues : and beeing spent, is gone: therefore the lesse, the better: alwaies prouided, there be a discreet care had of our healths, and of the credit of the places we hold : and of our inabling to the duties of our calling. Which beeing sufficiently prouided for, it is a Christian frugality to spare, what further may be spared: And he hath the lesse to answer for, who spendeth the least in superfluities.

Againe, here we are taught *contentation* in the state which God hath appointed vs, and not to striue too fast to climb to wealth. These holy men can be content *to dwell in tents*, and tabernacles, though they might haue compassed much more : for they were great and mightie men. *Abraham* had 318.men, able to beare a sword, in his house daiely : and with them, and a little helpe more, hee ouerthrewe diuers kings, and rescued *Lot*, (Gen. 14. 14). He that durst encounter, and did ouercome such an hoste : How many inhabitants of the country, could he haue beat out of their houses? And how many tenants could he haue put out of their Liuing? And how much of that countrey could he haue inclosed to himselfe? Surely, euen as much, and as many as hee had pleased. Yet doeth he no such thing : but contrariwise considering himselfe to bee but a tenant vnder God, he is content to let euery man sit quietly by him, and himselfe *to dwell in tents*; rather then to incroach one foote further then God bad him, though he had beene able.

This checketh the pride, or couetousnesse, or ambition, or all, of such as *ioyne house to house*, *Land to Land*, Lordship to Lordship, Towne to Towne ; and care not how many mens houses they pull downe, to build one of their owne: nor how many men want land and liuing; so they haue their parkes, and pastures, gardens, and orchards, and all other delights they can deuise. These are so farre from *Abrahams* minde, who desired onely so much land, as his tent might stand on, and might feede his cattell; as they can inclose and make seuerall to themselues, that which in common should bee the liuing of many soules. But what can befall such men ? but that that *Esay* prophecieth to them, (Esay 5. 8.) *Woe bee vnto them that ioyne house to house, and land to land, till there be no place for the poore to dwell in.*

Thirdly, in that *Abraham* liued thus, as ready euer to depart into any other countrey, when God would call him: It sheweth that true *faith* doth neuer limit Gods hand, either in the greatenesse, or length of trialls, but submitteth it selfe wholly to his will, beeing resolued and content to suffer all trialls, how great soeuer, and how many soeuer God pleaseth to lay vpon a man. Reason would haue said, I haue left one country at Gods word : if I must leaue another, then I shall neuer know an ende, nor haue any thing certaine to trust to. But *faith* saith, As I haue left one country at gods calling, so vpon his word I will leaue twentie more: For God hath as good reason to bid me the second time as the first; and his loue cannot faile me: he may still try me, but can neuer leaue me. Thus spake *Abrahams* faith. And not he alone: For *Iob*, though he crie out of the violence of his temptation, *The arrowes of the Almightie are in me, and the venime thereof doth drinke vp my spirits, and the terrours of God doe fight against me* (Chap. 6.4.) Yet when faith comes to play his part, he then protesteth, that *though God kill him, yet he will trust in him, and he shall be his saluation.* (Chap. 13.15.) See *Abrahams* faith will lead him from country to country; and *Iobs* will carrie him through life and death. And noble *Dauid* is not behinde for his part, for he will lose his kingdome, if God will haue it so: 2. Sam. 15. 26. *If* (saith *Dauid*) *God say I haue no delight in thee*, loe here I am, let him *doe to me* (not what I in my reason could wish, but) *what seemeth good in his eyes.* Behold now in these holy men, the practise and obedience of true faith. It prescribes not God the measure how long, or how farre he shall afflict vs : but makes a man resigne vp himselfe wholly, his causes, his liuings, his countrie; his kingdome, his life and all, to be at Gods disposing. He that can doe thus, may haue ioy in himselfe, as beeing assuredly one of the children of faithfull *Abraham.*

Fourthly, in that *Abraham* in a strange country will not build him an house, but dwell in tents which daiely are remooueable ; Here may such men learne, as are trauailers, or factors, or soiourners in forraine countries, not to thrust themselues too hastily into societie and familiaritie with the people of those countries, where they soiourne. *Abraham* will not build him a house in a strange country, but will dwell in tents, that so he may the easier remooue: euen so, let no man fixe and fasten himselfe too hastily in a strange country, but liue so, as hee may easily remooue, when he seeth good cause.

Fiftly, *Abraham* who in his owne country (it is likely) had his house, in a strange country will haue none, but will *dwell in tents*. His practise much teach vs, euen so, not to build vs houses in this world, where we are strangers, but to set our tent here, and to looke for our house in heauen. Literally we are not bound to doe as *Abraham* did, but *mystically* wee must doe it:

the ſtate of our bodies here, is but a *tent* or tabernacle; the ſtate of our ſoules in heauen, is a *ſtrong* houſe. Wee muſt therefore ſay with the Apoſtle, (2. Cor. 5. 1, 2.) *We are willing that this earthly tabernacle were deſtroied, and deſire to be cloathed with our houſe which is from heauen.* Carnall and worldly men builde their houſe in this world; that is, haue all their care for their bodie: but if we follow our father *Abraham,* and eſteeme our life, and bodies, but as tabernacles preſently to be remooued, and build our houſes in heauen; then walke we here in the ſteps of his faith, and after this life, ſhall attaine his reward.

For the ending and knitting vp of this point, it may bee asked, How this can be any ſuch commendation to him, ſeeing that wicked men haue vſed to dwell in tents;

I anſwer, neuer any of them, but in two caſes: firſt in time of warre, where armies lying abroad in the fields, or in the ſiege of cities, muſt needes lie in tents; and ſo doe all men Chriſtian or Heathen to this day: or ſecondly, ſuch as kept ſheepe, did for their cattels ſake lie abroad in tents; as it is recorded of *Iabal,* one of *Cains* poſteritie (Gen. 4. 20.) that hee was the *father of all them that dwell in tents, and ſuch as haue cattell.* In which wordes, obſerue how their dwelling in tents, and hauing cattel are put together: And ſo the *Arabians,* great keepers of cattell, doe in *Arabia* (beeing a hot country) to this day. So that it is cleere, the wicked dwelt in tents, either for *neceſſitie* ſake in the warre, or els for *profit* ſake with their cattell; but that for no ſuch cauſe, but for their own ſakes: and becauſe they eſteemed themſelues *ſtrangers in the world,* it was neuer found that any vngodly man *dwelt in tents* all his life: but that it was alwaies a practiſe of holy and faithfull men, vntill they came to haue a ſettled Church and ſtate of their owne.

And thus much for the manner how *Abraham* dwelt in Canaan: 1. as a ſtranger: 2. dwelling in tents.

Now follow the Perſons with whom.

With Izack and Iacob heires with him of the ſame promiſe.

The ſecond Circumſtance is the Perſons with whom: they were *Izack and Iaacob:* his ſonne and his grandchild. But it may firſt of all be asked, to what clauſe is this referred, whether to *Abrahams* dwelling in Canaan, or to his beeing there a *ſtranger,* or to *his dwelling* there *in tents.* The anſwer is: to them all three: Hee *dwelt* there *with them,* hee was *a ſtranger with them,* he dwelt *in tents with them,* and they with him. Now the meaning is not, that they dwelt together with *Abraham* in the ſame tẽts, at the ſame time, (for *Iſaack* was not borne til *Abraham* was an hundred yeares old, & *Iaacob* was but yong when *Abraham* died): But that the ſame *promiſe,* made to *Abraham,* God *renewed* after to thẽ, firſt to *Iſaack,* & then

to *Iaacob:* which they alſo *beleeued* as *Abraham* did, and by the power of that faith were content to dwel in tents, as ſtrangers, as he had done before them.

But why doth he name none but *Iſaack* and *Iaacob?* did no other dwell in tents, and thinke themſelues ſtrangers, but they? yes, many other; but theſe two are named aboue any other, both for that they were next to *Abraham* in *time,* and in *blood,* and in *faith* alſo; for their faith was ſo excellent, as God is called *the God of theſe three men,* more ſpecially then of any other in the world: But in and vnder theſe two, are all other vnderſtood, who imbracing the ſame promiſe, did therefore as ſtrangers dwell in tents.

From hence we learne diuerſe excellent inſtructions.

Firſt, ſee here a notable worke of faith; I meane of true faith in the promiſes of eternall life: namely, that it conformeth the beleeuers one to another, both in the inward diſpoſition of heart, and outward conuerſation of life. God hath made this promiſe, That *he ſo loued the world, that he gaue his onely begotten ſonne, that whoſoeuer beleeueth in him ſhould not periſh, but haue life euerlaſting.* Now, as this promiſe is one, ſo is the faith that apprehends it; and this faith beeing one, conformeth all that haue it, and makes them like one to another in the obedience of Gods commandements. This is that that the Holy Ghoſt ſaith, Act. 4, 32. *The beleeuers were all of one heart, and one ſoule;* and that not one of them, but *the whole multitude of them that beleeued.* And *Eſay* propheſieth, that in the kingdome of Chriſt ſhall be ſuch vniformity & peace, as that though mẽ in their natures be as contrary one to another, as *ſheepe and wolues, lyons and kids, young children and ſerpents:* yet by grace and faith in Chriſt, they are changed, and all conformed one to another, ſo as they ſhall liue and conſent together in the vnitie of one obedience: Eſay. 11. 6. 7.

The Booke of the Pſalmes was penned by *Dauid, Aſaph, Moſes,* and others, and in ſeuerall ages and ſtates of the Church, and were appointed to be ſung then, for the preſent ſtate of the Church in thoſe dayes. It may therefore be demanded. Why then do we ſing them now in our Churches? The anſwer is: The Church in all ages conſiſts of a number of beleeuers, and the *faith* is alwaies one, and makes all that apprehend Gods promiſes, to be alike to one another in grace, in meditations, in diſpoſitions, in affections, in deſires, in ſpirituall wants, in the feeling and vſe of afflictions, in courſe and conuerſation of life, and in performance of duties to God and man: and therefore the ſame *Pſalmes, Praiers, and Meditations,* are now as fit for the Church in theſe dayes, and are ſaid and ſung with the ſame vſe and profit, as to the Church in thoſe dayes when they were made.

This doctrine hath profitable vſe.

First, if this be so, here is confuted the opinion and practise of many; who when they are taught, they ought to doe this or this, after the examples of holy men in times past: They answer, they were great and glorious men, they may not thinke to be like them; and their examples are to high: they may admire them, but not followe them. For example, when they are exhorted to *walke with God*, as *Henoch* did (Gen. 5. 24.) to refuse the world for Christ, as *Moses* did, (Exod. 2. 10.) to spare our enemie beeing in our power, as *Dauid* did, (1. Sam. 24. 5, 6, 7.) In Magistracie to be able to say, *Whose oxe or asse haue I taken, or whom haue I done wrong to?* as *Samuel* said, (1. Sam. 12. 3.) In the Ministerie, to followe the zeale, the patience, and the diligence of the holy Ministers of God in old time; They then answer: That they dare not looke at them, and that they may not thinke to be like them. But let these men knowe, that if they haue the same *faith*, they haue the same *conscience*; & that as *Izhak* and *Iacob*, though they had not the same measure of faith, that *Abraham* had, yet hauing the same faith, were therefore willing *to dwell in tents*, as hee had done: So if we haue the same *faith* that our fathers in times past had, then howsoeuer we cannot match them in holinesse, and vertues; yet we must seriously labour to bee like them, and must practise the same vertues, which they did: for if wee bee *heires with them of the same promise*, then must wee be practisers with them in the same obedience.

Secondly, this checketh a great and common profannesse, which now raigneth amongst vs. We all professe religion: yet come to the practise of religion, the hearing of the word, receiuing the holy Sacrament, or praier, or abstaining from fowle and common sinnes; let a man bee in any of these more forward then others, then some are so profane, as they sticke not to deride and reproach them. But, is this to be *heires of one and the same promise?* Let such men therefore know, that we in this age of the Church, are bound to conforme our selues to the holy liues of the Fathers of the old Church, or else we haue not the same *faith* that they had. Therefore our dutie is to striue, and by all meanes we can to endeauour who should come neerest to their faith, to their zeale, and to their obedience. And if any doe it more then we, we should rather honour, then reproach him.

In the next place, obserue here the power of a great mans example, how forcible it is; especially to them of the same kinred. *Abraham* a grand Patriarch, a man of honour, hee is content *to dwell in tents*, like a *stranger* in that land which was promised him to bee his owne. *Izhak* his sonne followeth him, and doth so also. *Iacob* his grand-childe comes after, and walkes in both their stepes. Let this teach all superiors (be they Parents, Ma-

gistrates, or Ministers) to looke to their wayes; for the higher they be, the more are they followed either in good or euil. We see in Courts, what Princes doe, they are imitated; and any fashion they take vp, or put in practise (be it neuer so strange) is followed of all men. And here we see, if *Abraham* will dwell in no house, but *in tents*, *Isaack* and *Iacob* will doe so after him.

Thirdly, obserue how these three holy men are called *heires of the promise:* and they are so called in regard of God. Who as he made the promise to *Abraham*, so he renewed it to them both seuerally, and withall, gaue them grace to apprehend it, and to shew the obedience of their faith as *Abraham* did.

But it is very notable, that they are not called *heires of the Land*, but of the *Promise*; for they inioyed not the land, but the promise, and their seede did afterwardes inioy the land it selfe: Wherein appeares the excellencie of their faith. For they who thus blessedly beleeued, and thus patiently and constantly obeyed God in all duties of holy obediēce, hauing but *bare promises*, how excellent and eminent would their faith and obedience haue beene, had they beene partakers of the *blessings themselues?* And here also must we learne our duties. For in greater matters than the land of Canaan, we enioy the things, whereas they had but the *promises:* as namely, the *Incarnation* of the Messias, and the *calling of the Gentiles*, these two great & grand mercies, were looked for by them, but enioyed by vs; they had the promises, but we the performance. Therfore if our obedience and patience, and other vertues, be behind theirs, our condemnation must needes be so much the deeper.

Much more is to be said of *Isaacks* and *Iacobs* faith: but they haue seuerall examples for themselues.

It followeth,

For he looked for a Citie hauing a foundation, whose maker and builder is God.

Thus we see the *fact* of *Abrahams faith:* now followeth the *reason* that mooued him to liue in the land of Canaan, as a stranger, and in tents. And the reason is, because *he looked for a City, &c.* that is, for euerlasting life in heauen. This is the substance of the reason; and then that life euerlasting is further described in diuers particulars: so that these two things are contained in this verse;

    1 Generally the state of the reason, shewing the height and eminency of *Abrahams faith:* he looked for *euerlasting life.*

    2. A particular description of that life eternall.

In the generall state of the reason, many worthy points are to be considered:

First, in the very contextion, and framing of the reason, obserue how *Abraham* therefore liueth as a *stranger*, patiently in that country

which

which was his owne, becauſe *he looked* for heauen after this life. Hence we learne, That hope
to winne heauen, worketh patience and contentation in all eſtates and conditions of life.
Thus reaſoneth the holy Ghoſt here; *Abraham*
was content to liue in no citie, but in tents, as a
ſtranger: for he looked for a better citie in heauen. So the Diſciples, grieued at Chriſts departure from them, he ſtrengtheneth them with
this conſolation, *In my Fathers houſe are glori-*
ous manſions, I goe to prepare a place for you:
Ioh. 14. 2.

The vſe of this doctrine is neceſſarie for theſe
our dayes; wherein are many that will ſay confidently they looke to be ſaued, and hope for
heauen: but let any man iniurie them, or croſſe
them in the leaſt meaſure, they breake out into
anger and impatience, yea often into ſwearing
and blaſpheming of Gods name. Or if God lay
his heauie hand on them or theirs, then inſtant-
ly they runne to wizards, and wiſe men, that is,
euen to the bottome of hell for helpe. Theſe,
and all ſuch, doe fowlely deceiue themſelues:
for if they truly hoped for that citie which is in
heauen, no ſmall croſſe in this world could
much trouble them: nor any ſo great, to driue
them into that diſquietnes, as by their oaths
they ſhall rend heauen and earth; and as it were,
confound God and all his creatures. Or, if they
truely perſwaded themſelues that God would
giue them *heauen* at their end; they would bee
afraide, and aſhamed, to runne to the deuill to
remooue Gods hand from them: for aſſuredly
that man cares not what God laieth on him in
this life, who is perſwaded, that after this life
God will giue him heauen.

Secondly, this doctrine giues vs a worthy
direction for comfort vnder the croſſe. For, if
Abraham bore all this patiently, becauſe hee
looked for heauen; then it muſt teach vs, that
when God laieth any croſſe on vs, if we would
haue the bitterneſſe thereof allayed, wee muſt
not looke on it with both our eyes, but with
one eie on the croſſe, and with the other on the
Citie prepared for vs in *heauen;* where is no
croſſe, no woe, no ſorrow, nor miſery; but
where *God himſelfe will wipe away all teares*
from our eies. There can bee no affliction ſo
bitter, but this meditation will mitigate it, and
yeeld comfort and contentment in the ſharpeſt
pangs thereof.

In the ſecond place, *Abraham waiting* for
heauen, when he ſoiourned on the earth, giues
vs an excellent pattern of chriſtian life. Whilest
we are on earth, wee muſt *waite for heauen,*
and looke, and long after it; there muſt our ioy
and our affections be. So teacheth the Apoſtle
(Coloſſ. 3. 1.) *If yee be riſen with Chriſt, ſeeke*
ye the things that are aboue. And (Phil. 3. 20.)
We muſt haue our conuerſatiõ in heauen, though
we liue on earth. How this may be, cannot be
better expreſſed, then by a compariſon:

A Merchant that is a free-man in *London,*
and there hath wife, children, and liuing; tra-

uaileth as a Merchant into Turkie, or Barbarie,
or Spaine; there he liues, there is his body, but
all his thoughts, and deſires of his heart, are at
home: and all the care there, is to maintaine his
good eſtate at home: and all the hazard of his
life and goods, are to preſerue and helpe his e-
ſtate there. So we in this world, are but *ſtran-*
gers; but we are *free-men in heauen:* therefore
our thoughts muſt be there; and all our cares
here ſhould be nothing, but how to procure vs
ſure and good eſtates in heauen. This if we doe
ſeriouſly intend, & carefully indeauour, then we
are good children of *Abraham* our father;
and thus doing, *wee haue our conuerſation in*
heauen, though we liue on the earth. And this
we ſhould doe the rather, becauſe generally the
world is full of ſuch men: who (as the ſame
place ſaith) doe *minde nothing but earthly*
things. Now it is a hard thing for a man to bee
vnlike the world, and to reſiſt multitudes, and
generall examples: but we muſt ſtill remember
we are *Abrahams* children, and children muſt
labour to be like their *father,* and not the common multitude: and it muſt more mooue a
good child, what his *father alone* doth, then
what is done by many other.

Thirdly, let vs obſerue, how God promiſing
Abraham onely the Land of Canaan, that is, a
temporall inheritance; he lookes further, for *a*
City in heauen. This he did out of his faith; for
he knowing that Canaan was but a type of heauen, therefore in conſideration of the earthly
Canaan, he aroſe to a conſideration of the heauenly: and in the promiſe of the earthly, apprehended the heauenly. This is the true and Chriſtian vſe of all Gods bleſſings, giuen in this life;
in them to behold better things laid vp in heauen, and ſhadowed in the other. Men vſe for
their vſe, ſpectacles in reading: but they take
no pleaſure in looking vpon them, but at other
things by and through them: So ſhould Chriſtians, through all temporall bleſſings looke *at*
ſpirituall and eternall, which are promiſed and
ſhadowed vnder the *temporal.* Thus doth Chriſt
himſelfe teach vs, in the very order of the *Lords*
prayer: directing vs to pray for *temporall* bleſſings firſt, in the fourth petition; and then for
eternall, in the fift and ſixt: as though that the
one were introductiõs & paſſages to the other.
And this made the Prophets ſo ordinarily couer ſpirituall bleſſings vnder temporall, and put
temporall deliuerances, for ſpirituall, and con-
fuſedly oftentimes one for another; becauſe that
the holy men of the old Church, did neuer reſt
in view of any tẽporall promiſe, or bleſſing, but
aſcended to contemplation of the higher things
in them. How pitifull then is the practiſe of
worldly men; who vſe Gods bleſſings ſo, as
they daily abuſe and peruert them: vſing meate
to gluttony, raiment to pride, learning to vain-
glorie, ſpeech to flatterie, wit to deceipt, authority to reuenge, callings to oppreſſió: whereas they are all giuen to be helps in Gods ſeruice, and furtherances in religion, and meanes

to helpe vs towards heauen. Thefe men looke at Gods gifts, with the eie of reafon, and no further; but if they looked at them, with the eie of faith, as *Abraham* did; it would teach them to make a heauenly and fpirituall vfe of them, as he did.

Laftly, in the generall ftate of the reafon, & of *Abrahãs* practife; obferue how he hauing promife of Canaan, *waited for heauẽ.* Now, no man waiteth for any thing, but that which he hath hope of; nor hopeth truely and properly, for any thing, but that which he hath affurance of: for *hope maketh not afhamed,* Rom. 5. 5. Not worldly hope, for that hath deceiued no more than euer trufted it: But *Hope in God* neuer deceiued man; nor went any away difappointed, that hoped in God. Therefore, here it is apparant, that hope of heauen goeth with affurance: and this affurance muft be particular to the beleeuer, as the beleife and faith is.

But the *Papifts* fay, This is true indeede of *Abraham,* he had not onely *hope,* but full *affurance;* but that came by extraordinarie reuelation: So that this is a rare example, and his particular reuelation, is no generall warrant to vs.

We anfwer from S. *Paul,* (Rom. 4. 11.) *that Abraham is the father of the faithfull;* and that his faith is a patterne for all Chriftians to follow: for elfe, why doth the Apoftle fo farre extoll, and fet forth that faith of his, aboue 1300. yeares after his death; fhall it be onely for his commendation, and not for our imitation alfo? Therefore euery man that will walke in the fteps of holy *Abraham,* may come with him to that meafure of *faith,* that he may waite for heauen, with affurance to enioy it.

Now let vs come to the particular defcription of that heauen, which *Abraham* thus waited for.

A City hauing a foundation, whofe maker & builder is God.

The defcription hath three parts.

    1. It is faid to be a *Citie.*
    2. That hath a *foundation.*
    3. That *God made and built it.*

For the firft:

Abraham by his faith waited for *heauen:* But for which? For there are three heauens, or differences of heauen in the Scripture.

The firft, that wherein we liue and breath, birds flie, and clouds mooue.

The fecond, that wherein the ftarres are.

The third is that, that is aboue them both, and is inuifible, the ftate of Gods glorie, where God reuealeth his Maieftie in fpeciall manner to men and angels. *This heauen Abraham waited for.* For as for the firft, he liued in it: And for the fecond, he knew it as wel as moft men; for it is credibly thought, he was a notable Aftronomer. So that it was the third heauen, *hee waited for:* which he knewe this world could not giue him: and therefore expected it in another.

Now, this heauen which was *Abrahams* hope, is called *a City.*

A City properly is a place for the habitation of men, compaffed with walls, and diftinguifhed by ftreets and houfes. Now, properly heauen (or the eftate of holy men in heauen) is not a *City;* but as elfewhere in the fcripture, it is called a *houfe,* a *tabernacle,* a *temple, an inheritance,* a *kingdome:* fo is it here called a *city;* namely, for the refemblance it hath thereunto, which confifteth fpecially in foure points.

    1. A *Citie* hath many houfes, greater, leffe, and for all forts. So in heauen alfo, there are *many manfions,* Iohn, 14. 2. Places of glorie for all men; none neede to feare that hee fhall not haue fulneffe of ioy, and perfect happineffe.

    2. A *Citie* is built, and at firft was ordained to this end; that many citizens might liue together in concord and amitie. So the kingdome of heauen, is a *heauenly citie,* where the Saints of God fhall liue in perfect peace and loue, with fulneffe of ioy euery one in himfelfe, and each one in another.

    3. The goodneffe or excellency of a *City* confifts in this; To haue good lawes, good Magiftrates to execute them, and good people performing fubiection and obedience. Therefore the kingdome of heauen is the moft perfect *Citie,* wherein Gods lawes are the onely lawes, and they fhall be written in mens hearts: where each one is a fufficient gouernour of himfelfe, and yet all fubiect to God; and their God vnto them all in all.

    4. A *City* is a place, where generally are all neceffaries and comforts for mans life: one part of the countrey hath this commoditie, another that; but in the citie are all, either brought into it, or of it felfe. So in heauen are all parts of perfection, and all complements of happineffe, to make the ftate of Gods children there infinitely bleffed.

Such a glorious place is the Citie that was *Abrahams* hope.

Now for the vfe hereof.

Firft, Is heauen fuch a *City?* Here is a notable comfort to the poore and plaine countryman, who liues in the fimplicity of the country life, tilling the ground, or keeping cattell; and it may be, neuer faue, or (at the leaft) neuer tafted of the pleafures and delights of *cities:* If he ferue God, and keepe a good confcience, here is his happineffe; he fhall be citizen in the high and heauenly Ierufalem, *that Citie which* was the hope of the holy men of God in all ages.

Secondly, this may teach *Citizens,* in the great, populous, and pompous cities of this world, to labour alfo to be *Citizens in heauen;* for that is a *citie* alfo, and the beft on earth are but fhadowes of it. And it may fhame them that are drowned in the pleafures & delicacies of earthly *cities,* and care not, nor looke after *the citie of the liuing God, the heauenly Ierufalem:*

lem: as it is called, Heb.12. 22. But alas, it seemes they care not for this shame; for where is securitie, wantonnesse, profanenesse, oppressions, so common, as in these great cities? And as in the Apostles times, the countrey towne *Berea,* was more zealous and religious, than the rich and stately citie of *Thessalonica,* Acts, 17. 11. So is it generally to this day, especially at such places in the country, where teaching and knowledge is. But let such *cities* know, that as they haue better means and more comforts, and their very nature should put them in mind and make them in loue with heauen; so they shall receiue greater damnation.

Lastly, *Cities* are places of freedome, and all such great places haue some notable priuiledges; therefore men desire to be free in such places: as is to be seene in *London, Rome, Venice,* &c. euen the greatest persons will be content to be free of them, and many seeke it, and pay deere for it; or at least, worke a long time for it.

But heauen is the *Citie of cities,* the perfection of beautie and true happinesse: therefore let euery one, that desires either honour or happinesse, labour and striue to be a *freeman of heauen,* and neuer rest till he know he be. And let those that liue in *cities,* when they are admitted freemen (as daily some are,) remember what a blessednesse it will be, if they can be admitted freemen of the glorious *Citie* which is aboue; and how little that shall auaile them, if they want this, which was the hope and ioy of *A-braham,* and all holy men.

To goe further: This Citie which *Abrahams faith waited for,* is described by two points:

    1. That *it hath a foundation.*
    2. That the *maker and builder was God.*

For the first: Heauenly Ierusalem hath a foundation, such a one, as no city in this world hath: and by this phrase, the holy Ghost insinuates vnto vs, what be the properties of heauen; which be two:

    1. The state of heauen is *vnchangeable.*
    2. *Euerlasting* and eternall.

First, the state of the Elect in heauen, and their glorie there, is not subiect to corruption, or the least alteration; as appeareth in that notable and loftie description of the heauenly Ierusalem, Apoc. 21. 14. and from the 10. v. to the 21. *It hath a great wall and high, twelue gates, twelue Angels for porters: and the wall had twelue foundations, of twelue sorts of most excellent pretious stones: and the wall it selfe was Iasper, and the citie pure gold, like crystall.* The state of it is shadowed by pretious stones, and gold; to signifie, as well the durablenesse, as the excellencie thereof. And in the 15. Psal. 1. it is called *the mountaine of Gods holines:* hills are hardly remooued, and therefore *Dauid* saith, that *Mount Zion can not be remooued, but remaineth for euer,* Psal. 125. 1. Now, if that be true of *Mount Zion,* in this world; which must needes be taken either *literally,* for

the state of the visible Church, which cannot be vtterly ouerthrowne: or *mystically,* for the state of Gods grace, which in this world can not totally & finally be lost: I say, if this Mount Zion standeth fast, and cannot be remooued; how much more true is it, of the state of glorie in heauen, and of the triumphant Church, and of heauenly Zion; that it is so vnchangeable, so durable, so vnremooueable, that it cannot be shaken, but standeth fast for euer. And in this respect, well may the Apostle say here, *It hath a foundation;* which the holy Ghost in the Reuelation saith, *to haue twelue foundations.*

Secondly, the state of the Elect in heauen, is not onely sure, but *euerlasting;* that is, without ende: Psal. 37. 18. *The Inheritance of holy men is perpetuall:* and therefore S. *Peter,* 1. 1. 4. saith, that the inheritance reserued in heauen for vs, is *immortall, and not fading away.* It fades not away; there is the *vnchangeablenes:* it is *immortall;* there is the *eternitie* of it. And this is meant, by *hauing a foundation:* for in this world, so much the longer doth any thing endure, as the *foundation* is stronger. Therefore, seeing the heauenly citie hath such a *foundation,* no maruell though it indure for euer.

Now put these two together, and they shew the perfect excellencie of that citie, which is both *vnchangeable and eternall.* Where we learne, the great difference betwixt the state of that world, and this present world, wherein we liue in the body. For what is there in this world so excellent, so pretious, so costly, so artificiall; but is subiect both to *alteration,* and in the end to *dissolution?* The longest *day* hath his night; and the longest *life* endeth in death, after many miseries, and tossings: the longest *Empires,* and mightiest *Monarchies,* had their period, after many mutations: the stateliest and strongest *cities,* ended in ruine, after many ciuill broyles, massacres, and other miseries. So that no glorie, no strength, no happinesse, nothing at all is there in this world, that is either *constant or perpetuall,* but subiect to vtter dissolution in the ende; and in the meane time, to pitifull alterations. So weake a *foundation* hath this world, and the best things in it. But contrariwise, the glorie of heauen hath such a foundation, as it is both *vnchangeable and eternall.*

The consideration of this difference, hath manifold and profitable vse. First, we may see how reasonable the counsell of the Apostle is, 1. Tim. 6. 17. *Charge them that are rich in this world, that they be not high minded, and put not their trust in vncerten riches, but in the liuing God.* For what a miserie and vanitie is it, to trust in that that is vncerten, and therefore will deceiue them? The Apostle tells them what to doe; namely, *Doe good, and be rich in good works, and be readie to distribute, laying vp in store for themselues a good foundation against the times to come, that they may obtaine eternall life:* that is, that they so spend their riches in holines and charitie, that they may in the ende attaine heauen, which is the *Citie that hath a foundation:* and who would not spend riches, which are so *vncertaine;* for heauen, which is so *certaine* a glorie?

Secondly, this must teach vs to followe the Counsell of Christ Iesus, Matth. 6. 19, 20. *Lay not vp for your selues treasures on earth, where moth and canker corrupt, and theeues steale: but in heauen, where is neither canker, moth, theefe, nor any other corruption.* Euery man naturally must haue his *treasure,* and that is it whereon he sets his heart; now that is vnworthy of a mans heart, which will be lost wee know not how soone. But let vs make *heaue our treasure,* the glory whereof is both eternall and vnchangeable.

Againe, seeing nothing here is certaine, wee must learne to seeke sound comfort, where it may be had. Seeke it in this world, and it will faile vs; but seeke it in the sincere worship of God, and that will minister such comfort in this life, and such glory in heauen, *as hath a foundation,* and will neuer faile vs.

Further, this must put vs in minde of the holy Kings aduise; which is, to *remember our Creator in the daies of our youth,* Eccles. 12. 1. Seeing this world is so vncertaine, and our life hath so weake a *foundation,* as we are not sure to liue to come to old age: euery man therefore, is to heare the conclusion of all; which is, *to feare God, and keepe his commandements:* and this, the sooner the better. For else, for a little foolish and vaine pleasure, transitory, and which *hath no foundation;* we shall venter the loosing of that glorious citie, *which hath a sure foundation.*

It followeth in the description;
*Whose maker and builder is
God.*

The second point in the description of this citie is, that *God was the maker, builder,* or author of it. These two words are both one, and therefore it is a needlesse labour of some that would distinguish betwixt them: for, the meaning is, *God made,* that is, prepared the glorie of heauen, and he *built it;* as though he should say, Heauenly Ierusalem is a glorious *citie:* and no maruell though it be so, for *God made it.* And if you will needs, that being *a citie,* it must be *built,* be it so; for God is *the builder of it.*

This doctrine is euident in the Scriptures, Psal. 136. 5. *God by his wisdome made the Heauens.* And here is another maine difference betwixt this world, and the glorie of heauen: The *Cities* of this world were built by man, but Heauen *by God himsefe.* The arte and skill of men built the cities of the earth, and sometime the couetousnesse, or other corruption of man, as is manifest in the beginning: for *Cain,* a couetous, cruell, and abitious man, built the first citie in the world: but holy and good men, haue not the honour to be *builders of this Citie;* No, they are *Citizens* of it, but God onely is the *author and builder of it.*

No man may doubt hereof, because this third heauen is invisible; for the *Angels* also are invisible, and yet Gods creatures. Besides, our Creed teacheth, that God is *Creator of all things visible and inuisible.*

If we doubt why God made it, seeing he made all things for man, and man in this world hath no sight nor vse of it. The answer is, God made it for two endes.

First, to be his owne glorious palace (not wherein he would confine his beeing, or his presence, but) wherein he would make his glory most apparant; and wherein his glorie should in a sort dwell. In which regards, it is called *his throne,* Esay 66. And in our Lords praier we say by Christs owne teaching, that God *our father is in heauen.* Therefore as Princes build themselues palaces, to shew their power and puissance, and to magnifie themselues, and to be fit habitations for their greatnesse; So God made the third heauen to be the *throne of his glorie.*

Secondly, he had also a respect herein to his creatures, for, he made that heauen, therein to reueale his maiestie and glorie to his reasonable creatures, *Angels and Men:* and (by shewing them his glorie) to glorifie them. *For in Gods presence is the fulnesse of ioy,* Psal. 16. *vltim.* And in this sense is it true, that *God made all things for man,* (*as man for himselfe:*) namely, all things, either for his soule, or body, or both; either for his vse in this life, or in the other. And so the third heauen was made for mans vse; not in this life, but in the life to come; for his *soule* vntill the last Iudgement; & after that, for both *soule and bodie.*

Hence we learne diuers instructions.

First, in that the third heauen, which neuer was seene with the eie of man, is here positiuely affirmed to be *made by God:* We learne, that therefore it is one of Gods creatures; and not eternall, as some hold, and goe about to prooue, thus: God is eternall; but he must be in some place: and heauen is the seate and place of God; therefore it is coeternall with God. But I answer, from Gods word; that though heauen be the seate and throne of Gods *glorie,* and where he manifesteth, and magnifieth his glorie; yet is it not the place of *his substance and beeing,* for that is infinite, and incomprehensible: and it is against the Christian faith, to imagine the Godhead to be comprehended or contained in any place. 1. King. 8. 27. *The heauens, yea the heauens of heauens cannot comprehend thee, O Lord; how much more vnable is this house that I haue built?*

Nor is it materiall, that we know not on what day it was created; or that it is not named amongst the works of the creation. For the same is true of the Angels *also:* and it pleased Gods wisedome, for speciall causes, to name no creatures particularly in the creation, but *visible;* whereas we know both from our Creede, and Gods word it selfe, that he is the creator of all things *both visible and inuisible*. Therefore though we know not what day the third heauen was made ; yet is it sufficient, that here is saide, *It was made and built by God himselfe*. Whereupon it necessarily followeth, it is a creature, and not coeternall with the Godhead.

Secondly, here appeares the weaknesse of one of the commonest arguments, vsed for the defence of the *Vbiquitie* and *Consubstantiation*. Christ (say they) is present bodily in the Eucharist, and they prooue it thus : Christ is in heauen, and he is God : but heauen is euery where; for God is euery where: and where God is, there heauen is: (as where the King is, there the Court is:) Therefore Christ may be in the Sacrament, and yet be in heauen notwithstanding.

I answer, the ground is false : *Heauen* is not euery where; for then it is in *Hell :* which to affirme, is absurditie, confusion, and impietie. Indeede *Gods presence* is euery where; and where his presence is, there is his *power :* as where the Kings presence is, there is also his power and authoritie ; and there may be any seate or court of Iustice : and so where he is, the court is. But if you take the Court, for some one of his chiefe houses, then the saying is not true. But contrariwise, as the Kings power is, wheresoeuer his presence is ; and yet he may haue one house more sumptuous, and magnificent then all the rest, which may be called his Court, by an excellencie aboue other : and that Court is not alwaies where the King is, but in some set and certen place, and not remooueable :

So Gods power and glorie is euery where ; and yet his most glorious Court, the *third heauen*, is not euery where, but in his limited and appointed place, where Gods glorie shineth more then in any other place.

Againe, if heauen properly taken, be euery where, then it is *God* himselfe: for that that is euery where, must needes be deified; and indeed some, to maintaine this opinion, haue said little lesse. But if the holy Ghost may moderate this disputation, he plainly tells vs here, *That God is the maker and builder of it*. Therefore assuredly it is not God, but one of Gods creatures.

Thirdly and lastly, let vs obserue the description of heauen, included in these two words, *maker* and *builder*. God *made it*, that is, it is one of his creatures ; he made it as well as the rest : and *he builded it*, that is, (as the word signifieth) made it with arte ; or he bestowed skill and wisdome vpon it. For, though we may not imagine any substantiall difference betwixt these two words, for matter ; yet in signification they differ : and so farre we are to obserue it.

Here then we learne, that the third *Heauen* is like a piece of worke, wherein an excellent workeman hath spent his arte, and shewed his skill ; that is, that the highest heauen is a most glorious place, and surpasseth all other crea-

tures of God in glorie and excellencie, so farre as therein shineth the glorie, skill, and wisdome of the Creator, more then in any other creature. In which regard, it is no maruell though the holy Ghost say in another place, That the *eye hath not seene, nor the eare heard, nor mans heart conceiued, what God hath there prepared for them that loue him*, 1. Cor. 2.9. And S. *Paul* himselfe, though he had the honour to be *taken vp into this third heauen*, and to *see and heare* the glorie which is there ; yet afterwards could not he expresse the glorie he had seene. And this was figured in the *Temple of Ierusalem*, which was the mirrour, and beautie of the world ; for the building whereof, God both chose the skilfullest men, & endued them also with extraordinarie gifts: namely, *Bezaleel and Aholiab*. Now, as thereby that *Temple* was the most excellent piece of worke that euer was in this world, made by man ; so the highest heauen (which was mystically prefigured in *Salomons* Temple) is the most excellent of all the works of God.

The vse of this doctrine is not to be omitted.

First, if that be so excellent and glorious a place, we must all labour to come thither ; for aboue all things, it seemes worthy to be sought for. People come out of all places of the countrey, to dwell in great townes, and rich *cities* ; and men labour to be freemen there, and to haue their children free in them : and euen the greatest men, will haue their houses either in, or neere them ; that so, though they will not alwaies dwell in them, yet they may soiourne in them at their pleasures now and then. And why all this? but because, first, they are places beautifull, and many waies pleasant to the eye. Secondly, full, and frequented with the best companie. Thirdly, replenished with abundance of all things needefull for mans life, for necessitie, comfort, and delight. Fourthly, they enioy many priuiledges and freedomes. And lastly, all this is most true of such cities, where the King keepes his Court.

If this be so, then how is heauen to be sought for? Behold here a goodly citie, a citie of God, (whereof, *London, Paris, Rome, Venice*, nay *Ierusalem*, are scarce shadowes) the true *Ierusalem*, the *ioy of the whole earth :* nay the ioy of the world, and the glorie of all Gods creatures, *made* immediately with the hand, and *built* with the skill and cunning of *God himselfe*. The Princes of the world, and euen of Rome it selfe, wondred at the beautie, and were amazed at the magnificence of Ierusalem and the Temple, and yet it was but a type and figure hereof. For that had indeede the glorie of the world vpon her : but the new Ierusalem hath the *glorie of God vpon her*, Rev. 21.4.

Shall we then seeke to dwell in the cities of this world, and not labour to come to heauen? Are they any way excellent, wherein heauen is not much more to be desired? Are they beau-

tifull,

tifull, and is not it the beauty of the world? Read the 21.chap of the Reue.and suppose that the beauty of it were but outward,and worldly and sensible to humane capacitie: yet is it farre more excellent,thē euer any was in this world. And is not there the company of the deitie, of Christs humanity, of the holy Angels, and all good men? And is not their aboundance of whatsoeuer belongs to perfect happinesse?And is not there freedome from the deuill,sinne,and death? And is it not the Court of God, the King of glorie?Then why doe we not sigh and grone, and long to be free-men of this glorious citie? And though we cannot come to it, as long as wee liue in this world; yet why doe we not striue to come as neere it as may bee?In this world, when a man cannot dwell in the heart of a *Citie*, yet he will rather dwell in the *suburbs*, then he will not be neere it; and beeing there, he knowes hee can soone steppe into the citie.So let vs in this life come as neere heauen as we may;let vs get into the *suburbs* and dwell there.

The *suburbs of heauen* is Gods true Church on earth, where his word is freely knowen and preached,and his holy Sacraments administred, and therein God truely serued. Let vs associate our selues to this Church, and liue according to the holy lawes thereof. This is the suburbs of heauen; so shall wee be readie to enter into the glorious citie it selfe, when the Lord calles vs.

And as this is for *our selues*; so if we loue *our children*, or care for their aduancement, let vs make them free-men of that citie, *whose maker and builder is God :* So shall we be sure to haue comfort and ioy *of them* here, and *with them* in heauen. But if we will haue them free-men in heauen,we must make thē *Gods apprentizes* on earth: they must serue out their time, else they get no freedome. This time, is all their life. Men are deceiued that let their children be the *deuills slaues* here, and thinke to haue them free in heauen : let vs then binde our chidren *prentizes to God*, that is, make them his seruants here: then assuredly, as in their repentance and regeneration here, they are borne free-men of heauen; so after this life they shall inioy the freedomes and priuiledges of that heauenly citie, which *was made and built by the wisdome of God.*

Lastly,here we see how true it is that *Dauid* teacheth, Psal. 15.4. *No vile person can come in heauen.* And no maruell: for if men thus and thus defamed, cannot be freemen in the *Cities* on earth, built by men; is it likely that sinners, and profane men, that care not for repentance, and regeneration, (for they be the vile men) shall be admitted into that citie, whose maker and builder is God? It is the holy citie, no vncleane thing can enter into it, Reuel. 21. It is Gods holy mountaine, how shall vngodlinesse ascend thither? Psal. 15. 1. It is the newe Ierusalem, how shall the old man, that is, sinnefull

corruption, get into it? We must therefore cast off the olde man, with his lusts, and be renewed in holynesse: we must become penitent sinners for our liues past, and *new men* for hereafter; or else let vs not looke to haue any part in heauen.

And good reason, for *God is the maker and builder of it :* But he is not the maker of sinne; but the deuill, and our selues brought it out: and thinke we the deuills worke shall come in heauen? or that God will build a house for the deuils slaues to dwel in?Let vs not be deceiued: But contrariwise, grace and holynesse is Gods worke:as our soules and bodies were the work of his hands, so our regeneration is much more the worke of his owne power and mercie.That man therefore, who can say, God as once he made me *a man*, so he hath againe made and built me a *new man*, and a new creature; that man is he, that shall be an inhabitant in that heauenly city, *whose maker and builder is the same God.*

In this holy way of faith and repentance,did the holy Fathers walke to this citie ; as *Dauid* saith, in the name of them all,*Thus I will waite for thee in holinesse.*

And thus doubtlesse did the holy Patriarke *Abraham*, who as he was the father of our faith, so was he also a patterne of repentance and holy life : and in that holynesse he waited *for this city that hath a foundation,whose maker and builder is God.*

Hitherto we haue heard the holy practise of *Abrahams faith*, in two examples.

There is much more spoken of the excellencie of his *faith:* but by the way,the holy Ghost interlaceth a worthy example, euē of a *womans faith* ; namely, *Sarah* his wife. The sixt Example, in the order of the whole, followeth in the words of the two next verses.

Sarahs faith.

Verse 11.

By faith, euen Sarah also receiued strength to conceiue seede, and was deliuered of a child, when shee was past age, because she iudged him faithfull which had promised.

Next to *Abraham*, who is called the *father* of our faith, or of faithfull men, followeth *Sarah*, who was also mystically the mother of *beleeuers:*

next to the husband followeth the wife: nay *Abrahams* faith is commended, both before her, and after her; and hers inclosed in the midst.

By the way, here obserue how God honours holy *mariage*, and obserues the *decorum*, and dignitie of it: He not onely allowes, or commends the faith of *Abel*, who it may be was vnmaried; but as we see, of *maried* men also. And it is worthy our obseruation, that of all these whom the holy Ghost here records for their faith and holinesse, they were all maried, except *Abel*; of whom, it is not certaine whether hee were, or no.

It appeares therefore, that God, as he *ordained* holy mariage: so he alwaies *honored* it, both with his *grace* on earth, and his *glorie* in heauen: as well, if not better, then any other state of life. They therefore doe spit in the face of God himselfe, who any way disgrace it, and they especially, who allow fornication, or adulterie, in any sort of men, rather then it, as some Papists doe. But here wee may obserue further, how God maintaines the *dignity and decorum* of it: hee placeth *Abraham* and *Sarah* together: and puts none betwixt them, to shew the inseparable vnitie, that is to be betwixt them: so farre, as that euen in storie, they are to bee set together: and how hainous their presumption is, that dare any way attempt to separate or part that vnitie.

He placeth *Abraham* first, to shew the dignitie and preheminence of the man, whome for her sinne, God hath set ouer her; not onely for her head, but for her guide and gouernour: and to teach the man, that he, and his example should be first, and should be a light vnto her; to shame them who come behinde their wiues in faith and holinesse. Hee placeth *Abraham* both afore and after her, and her in the midst; to teach her, that her glorie and honour, euery way, is in the vertue and worthinesse of her husband; her head vnder God: who is to goe before her, to giue her good example: and to come after, to ouersee her courses; and on all sides, to be a shelter and defence vnto her.

These things may not vnfitly bee noted in this contextion: Now let vs come to the words, wherein are these points;

    1. Who beleeued: *Euen Sarah.*
    2. What shee beleeued: *Gods promise to beare Isaac.*
    3. The impediments of that faith: which were two. 1. *Her age.*
                   2. *Her barrennesse.*
    4. The effects of this her faith: which were three,

        1. Thereby she *conceiued seed.*
        2. *Brought forth Isaac.*
        3. Had a *great issue and posteritie* by him.
    5. The ground of her faith: *shee iudged him faithfull which had promised.*

All these are laid down in this v. or the next.
The first point is, the person, of whome this

storie is: *Sarah, a woman*; euen shee beleeued. We haue heard some examples of notable men: but behold here, a woman chronicled for her faith, and holy obedience, as well as men.

Where we learne, that sauing faith, and consequently saluation it selfe, is not proper to one sexe, but to both; man and woman. The woman indeed was the first that brought in sinne; and beeing deceiued her selfe by the deuill, she deceiued man. In which sense the Apostle saith, 1. Tim. 2. 14. *The man was not deceiued, but the woman; and she was in the transgression.* And for that cause, grieuous calamities, and much bitternesse, was laid vpon that sexe, in bearing, and bringing vp children, and in subiection. In which regards they might thinke themselues forsaken of God, for their fault. For the preuenting whereof, the Apostle here, or rather the holy Ghost by him teacheth vs, that true faith and saluation by the Messias, belongeth to *Sarah*, as well as *Abraham*; to wemen, as well as to men. And Saint *Peter* also most plainely (1. Pet. 3. 7.) teacheth vs, that *they are heires together with their husbands, of the grace of life.*

The vse whereof, as it discouereth the monstrous and vnnaturall madnesse of some men, who haue called into question the possibility of their saluation; yea some, whether they haue soules, or no: so it giueth encouragement to women, to serue that God in zeale and sinceritie, which hath beene so mercifull vnto their sinne; and who, though he hath subiected them in bodie vnto their husbands, yet hath made their soules partakers with them, of the same hope of immortall life.

Yet withall we may obserue, howe few the holy Ghost here recordeth; namely, but one or two women, amongst many men. For so it hath beene in all ages, those that haue beene good, were excellent; but they were few in comparison of men: which, as it is the more commendation to them that are good, so it must stirre vp all women professing religion, to labour in the imitation of the faith of their grandmother *Sarah*; that so they may bee some of those fewe.

But let vs enter into further, and more particular consideration, who this *Sarah* was; especially seeing shee is the onely woman of the Iewes nation, whose faith is here remembred.

Shee was the wife of *Abraham*, the grand Patriarch of the Age betwixt the Flood, and the giuing of the Lawe. And of her we reade this storie, amongst other, Gen. 18. 13. God by his Angell appearing to her husband and her, made a promise, that within the yeare they should haue a sonne: both heard it, and both laughed to here it: *Abraham* in ioy and admiration, and therefore was not reprooued: shee in doubtfulnesse, and a conceipt of almost impossibilitie, and was for it sharply reprooued of the Angel. Yet behold this Sarah, that euen now laughed to heare such a promise, as beeing a fond conceipt, and meere impossible: yet afterward beleeueth, and in so good a measure, as her faith is here regiſtred to all poſterities.

In her example, we may learne a good leſſo. It was a bad thing in *Sarah* to *laugh* at Gods word, though it ſeemed neuer ſo high aboue her conceipt: But it was good and commendable, that ſhee correcteth her fault, and teſtifieth her amendment, by beleeuing. We all followe *Sarahs fault*; but fewe her *repentance*. Many in our Church are mockers of our religion, and of the Miniſters, and profeſſors thereof: and all religion that ſtandeth not with their humours, is no more regarded of them, then toyes, or deuiſes; and they are counted fooles, or hypocrites that thinke otherwiſe. But alas, theſe men know not how vile a ſinne they commit, while they laugh at Gods word. For, if her fault was ſuch, who laughed at that, that ſeemed to her almoſt impoſſible, and yet without any profaneneſſe; what ſhall become of them, that out of their carnalitie, and fleſhly profaneneſſe, doe make but a ſport at all Gods ordinances, promiſes, and commaundements; and at all religion, more then ſerueth their own turne? Let ſuch men bee warned, to ceaſe mocking, and lay aſide reuiling of others, and begin ſoberly and ſeriouſly to beleeue: elſe they will finde it ſharpe kicking againſt the pricke, and dangerous playing with edge-tooles.

Furthermore, *Sarah* that laughed in doubting, yet (withall) *beleeues.* This teacheth vs, that true *faith* is ioyned alwayes with doubting in all Gods children. If any obiect, that followeth not here: for, ſhee firſt doubted, and then beleeued; when ſhe doubted ſhe beleeued not, and when ſhee beleeued, ſhe doubted not;

I anſwer: It is not ſo, but the contrary, as I will prooue. For, *Sarah* was no Infidell, vtterly to denie and gaine-ſay Gods word, when ſhe heard it: but onely finding it in all reaſon, impoſſible, ſhe therefore preſently yeelded not to it, but laughed at it as a matter paſt ordinarie courſe, yet withall ſhe regarded who ſpake it; namely *God*, and therefore forthwith, iudged it poſſible with God, though impoſſible in reaſon, and ſo at laſt conſtantly *beleeued* it, yet ſtill her *reaſon* gaine-ſaying it: ſo that ſhee neuer doubted ſo, but that ſhee in ſome part beleeued it. And when ſhee beleeued it moſt ſtedfaſtly, yet ſhe ſomething doubted of it; reaſon ſaide it could not be, faith ſaide it might be. Therefore, as when reaſon ouer-ruling, yet ſhee had ſome ſparkes of *faith*: So, when her faith was predominant, there remained ſome reliques of doubting: for, as reaſon cannot ouerthrow true faith; ſo the beſt faith in this world, cannot fully vanquiſh reaſon.

This is the doctrine of Gods word, Mark. 9. 24. Ieſus bidding the father of the child poſſeſſed, *to beleeue*, and then his child ſhould bee diſpoſſeſſed: he anſwered, crying with teares,

Lord I beleeue, helpe my vnbeliefe. There is faith and vnbeliefe in one ſoule at one time, in one action, vpon one obiect: and what is vnbeliefe, but doubting or worſe?

And *Chriſt* often reprooueth his Diſciples, for their doubting, and calls them *O ye of little faith*; and ye all know that, that they then had true faith: yea, S. *Peter* himſelfe, moſt famous for his *faith*, is reprooued in the ſame words, *O thou of litle faith, wherefore didſt thou doubt?* He had a little *faith*, therefore ſome faith: a *little* faith, therefore much doubting: therefore it is apparant, a man may haue in his ſoule at once, both faith and doubting: yea, commonly we haue a *graine of muſtard-ſeede* or *a mite of faith*, and a mountaine of doubting.

The vſe of this doctrine; Firſt, diſcouereth the nakedneſſe of many profeſſing themſelues Chriſtians, who care not how they liue, yet ſay they beleeue in Chriſt, and looke to be ſaued by him. Aske how they know it: they anſwer, they know no other: Aske when they began: they ſay, they did euer ſo. Aske if they doubt; they anſwer, they would be aſhamed ſo to doe. But alas, here is nothing but ignorance and preſumption. Our *religion* can neuer be diſgraced by ſuch men; for they haue it not, they knowe it not: for, if they did, they would ſhame to anſwer ſo. Theſe men haue no *faith* at all: for, where it is, doubting doth alwaies ſhew it ſelfe. And he that knowes he *beleeues*, knowes alſo he *doubts*: and the more he *beleeues*, the more he knoweth & feeleth his doubting: for, where theſe two are, they are alwaies oppoſite, and ſhew their contrary natures: the one is the *ſpirit*, the other is *fleſh* and corruption. *And theſe*, ſaith the Apoſtle, *doe luſt one againſt another*, Galath. 5. 17. He therefore that thinketh he is wholy *ſpirit*, and hath no *fleſh* or corruption in him, is nothing but corruption: and he that imagineth, he hath perfect faith, and no doubting, hath no faith at all in him, but carnall preſumption.

Secondly, here is comfort to all ſuch as haue *faith* and grace, and yet are daily troubled with temptations: let not ſuch be diſmayed, though they finde in themſelues much doubting and diffidence. For *Sarah beleeued*, and yet ſhe doubted: yea, notwithſtanding all her doubting, ſhe *beleeued* ſo excellently, as her faith is here made a patterne, to all holy Matrons for euer. He therefore that is euen *buffeted by Sathan* with temptations of doubting, let not him bee diſmayed, as though he had no faith: but let him be aſſured, his doubting doth not bewray it ſelfe, but that faith makes the oppoſition; and therefore let him ſtriue with teares and prayers to God, & ſay, *Lord I beleeue, helpe thou my vnbeleefe.*

Thus we ſee the *perſon* who, *Sarah:* but what is the *action* which ſhe did? It is implied in theſe words,

Through faith Sarah, &c.

Her action is, ſhee beleeued. This vertue of

faith, and this action of *beleeuing*, is the matter of all this chapter. These holy men and women had other holy vertues: but their *faith* is that alone, which is here commended.

Now particuarly for *Sarahs faith*, here is one notable thing to be obserued; the very same word of God, which shee *beleeued*, and for beleeuing whereof shee is here regiſtred, at the same shee also laughed: but behold, her *faith* is recorded, her laughing is not; her faith is commended, her fault silenced. In which holy and mercifull practise of God, we learne;

First, that God accepteth *true faith*, though it be attended with many infirmities. As a King is content to giue a begger an almes, though he receiue it with a hand shaking with the palsey: So, God is well pleased with our faith, though diseased with infirmities, and beſtoweth grace on a beleeuing soule, though shaken with many temptations.

In a word, God accepteth soundnes of faith, though it be but small, and more lookes at (in his mercie) a mans little faith, then his many faults. *He will not breake the bruiſed reede, nor quench the ſmoking flaxe*, Eſay 42.3. When a man is broken in heart, and deiected in soule, in sight of his many sinnes, and little grace, God will not breake this *bruiſed reede*, but will comfort and ſtrengthen him. And when any life of grace appeares in a man (as *flaxe that ſmoketh*, but will not burne out) God will not *quench* it, but will rather kindle it, and giue life vnto it.

Let this teach vs to take in good part, the holy and honest endeuours of our brethren, though they cannot doe so well as they would, or should. Let vs not exact too much, and too haſtily vpon them, but expect in meekneſſe the working of Gods grace: and in the meane time, thinke well of *Sarahs* faith, though it bee with laughing.

Secondly, here we may learne, that God rather obſerues and regards good things in his children, then their faults and imperfections: he writes *vp Sarahs faith*, hee nameth not her laughing. This is from the goodneſſe of his nature, beeing *goodneſſe* it ſelfe, and therfore moſt eaſily apprehendeth, and takes notice of the leaſt goodneſſe, where-euer he findes it.

Thus ſhould wee deale one with another: what good thing we ſee in any man, we ſhould obſerue and commend it: his faults wee ſhould not ſee, but couer and omit them. But the courſe is contrary: the common table-talke of the world, is nothing but of mens faults, and to rip vp their imperfections: but if they haue neuer ſo many good properties, we can bury them all, or paſſe them ouer in ſilence. This argueth the malice and the naughtineſſe of our nature; which being euill, doth delight in nothing but euill; and being corrupt, feeds, as doth the filthy horſe-flie, on nothing but corruption. But let vs remember the practiſe of God, and learne to conceale faults, and vſe our tongues to talke

of the good things and vertues in our brethren: So ſhall we reſemble the Lord, who though *Sarah* laughed (not in a holy admiration, but in vnbeliefe) yet, foraſmuch as afterward *ſhee beleeued*, God hath matched her with the notableſt beleeuers, and holieſt men that haue bin in the world.

Thus much for the firſt point: the perſon, and her action, ſhe beleeued. Now the ſecond is, *what ſhee beleeued?* included and neceſſarily implied in the laſt words of the verſe: *ſhee iudged him faithfull which had promiſed.*

The thing ſhee beleeued, was the word or promiſe of God; Particularly his promiſe that ſhe ſhould beare *Iſaac* in her old age: of which promiſe, and the circumſtances of it, wee may reade, Gen. 18.13, &c.

Here the onely queſtion is, By what faith ſhe beleeued this?

And the anſwer is, by *true ſauing faith*: and it is prooued thus. *Abraham* beleeued this promiſe by *the faith that iuſtified him*, Rom.4. 10.11. But *Abraham* and *Sarah* beleeued it both *by one faith*: therefore *Sarah* beleeued that promiſe by the faith that alſo *iuſtified her.* Where we learne, that ſauing faith apprehendeth not onely the great promiſe of *redemption* by Chriſt, but all other inferiour promiſes that depend vpon it. For, here we ſee *Abraham* and *Sarah* take hold of the promiſe of a temporall bleſſing, by the ſame faith, whereby formerly they had laide holde on the promiſe of eternall ſaluation by the *Meſſias*: ſo that the obiect of true faith is,

　1. *Principall:* the promiſe of ſaluation by Chriſt.

　2. *Secondarie:* all inferiour promiſes annexed thereunto.

The maine promiſe is: *So God loued the world, that he gaue his onely begotten Sonne, to the end, that whoſoeuer beleeueth in him, ſhould not periſh, but haue eternall life*, Iohn 3.16. Now true faith, firſt of all, directly and plainely faſtneth it ſelfe on this: but after and with this, on all other promiſes that concerne ſoule or bodie. In the *Lords prayer*, wee are bid to pray for temporal bleſſings, health, peace, competencie of wealth, and all other, vnder the name of *daily bread*: and we are bound to beleeue, that God will giue them, if wee aske *in faith*. Neither is this faith conſtrained, but free and voluntarie, and on a good foundation. For, beeing perſwaded that God accepteth vs in Chriſt for ſaluation, we cannot but withall be perſwaded, that God will giue vs all things elſe needefull for vs.

This wee here note againe, becauſe we are wrongfully charged by the Papiſts, to hold, that faith apprehendeth the promiſe of ſaluation alone. But we paſſe it ouer, for that we haue already ſpoken ſomething of it.

Now followeth the third point: namely, the impediments of her faith, in theſe words,

When ſhe was paſt age.

The

The promife was to haue a child: *Shee be-leeued it.* Now againft child-bearing, there are two impediments: 1. *Barrennesse:* 2. *Age.*

If one be *aged,* or paft the ordinarie time, it is hard and vnlikely: but if one be *very aged,* and farre paft it, it is impoffible fhe fhould conceiue and beare a child: thus it ftands in reafon. Befides, though one be not *paft age,* yet if fhee be *barren* (as fome by fecret reafons in nature are) it is not to be expected, fhee fhould conceiue. Now, both thefe lay in *Sarahs* way; for, here it is faid, fhee was *paft age:* and another place (namely, Gen. 16. 1. 2). faith, *fhee was barren.*

But it may be obiected againft *Sarahs* age, that in the olde time they had children, till they were of great age. *Eua* had her fonne *Sheth* at 130. yeares olde (Gen. 5. 3.) For, *Adam* and *Eue* muft needes be both of one age: and after that, *Eue* bore *many fonnes and daughters.* Therefore, it may feeme, that *Sarah* was not paft age at 90. *yeares olde.* But we are to knowe, that they who began to beare at that age, liued eight or nine hundred yeares: but *Sarah* liued after the flood, when Ages were brought downe to 200. and for the moft part to 100. yeares. *Abraham* liued but 175. yeares, and *Sarah* but 127. She therefore who liued 127. yeares, and died an olde woman, muft needes bee paft age of childe-bearing, at 90. yeares olde.

And befides her age: fhee was alfo barren, by her naturall conftitution (as many are and haue beene) and brought *Abraham* no children. Yet vnto this woman comes a word from God, *Sarah fhall beare a fonne.* And beholde, this aged and barren woman, doth not obiect defperatly thefe her two hinderances (the one whereof in reafon is fufficient againft childe-bearing) but beyond all impediments, and aboue reafon beleeueth it fhall be fo, refting and relying onely and wholly on Gods word for it.

The vfe of which notable and faithfull pra-ctife (fo wonderfull in a woman) muft teach vs to reft on *Gods word* and promife, though wee haue no reafon fo to doe: for example,

When wee fee our friends, or childrens bodies caft into the earth to feede wormes, burnt by fire, or eaten by fifhes, reafon faith, they are gone, they can neuer be againe. We haue Gods word and aflured promife, *The dead fhall rife: with their bodies fhall they rife.* Wee muft therefore beleeue it; it we will be of the faith of *Sarah.* God faid to her; *Age and barrenneffe fhall haue a child.* fhe beleeued it. He faith to vs, Dutt & rottenneffe fhal liue again: nay he hath often faid it; and fhall not our faith acknowledg the voice of our God, and beleeue it as fhe did?

But let vs com to perfonall promifes, as hers was (for this is general) God hath proifed grace & pardon to euery penitent & beleeuing foule; yea no man is partaker of the fweetenes hereof, without the bitterneffe of many teinptations to

the cotrary, giuing him occafions of doubting, and often euen of difpairing of Gods fauour. What muft a man doe in this cafe? euen *beleeue,* though he feele no reafon why to beleeue; and *hope aboue hope.* Such was *Abrahams* and *Sarahs* faith. And for it, as they were regiftred in the Storie of Genefis: fo both here, and in the Romanes, Chap. 4. remembred againe, & commended for it. Now, fuppofe that thou, after thy comming to God by faith and repentance, fall into temptations of defertion, wherein to thy feeling, Gods heauie hand and wrath hath feized on thee, and the deuill layeth thy fins to thy charge, & tels thee thou art a damned wretch, for thou wert euer an hypocrite, and neuer hadft faith, & that therefore God is thy enemy; In this cafe, wherein in reafon or in feeling, there is not the leaft hope of faluation: what muft thou doe, defpaire? God forbid. For that is the downfall into hell. No, but *hope* when there is no *hope,* keepe faith when there is no feeling.

And to ftrengthen vs herein, remember the faith of *Iob* (tried and fifted, fo as few haue bin) who *though the arrows of the Almighty ftucke in him,* and the *venome thereof drunke vp his fpirits,* Iob. 6. 4. yet euen then he *beleeued:* and would not giue ouer, nor let goe his hold, and faide, *Though thou bring me to duft, yet will I not forfake thee: no, though thou kill me, yet will I truft in thee.* So, in the furie of temptations, when the venome of Gods wrath feemes to drinke vp our fpirits, then muft wee *beleeue:* and in the pangs of death, when God feemes ready to kill vs, then muft we *truft* in him. In fuch cafes is the life of faith to be fhewed: when *reafon and feeling* fay, God is a terrible Iudge, faith muft fay, he is a mercifull Father.

In our health, and welfare, and feeling of Gods fauour, this exhortation may feeme tedious: but if we belong to God, if it bee not paft already, the time is fure to come, when this doctrine will be needefull for the beft of vs all.

Thus we fee the excellencie of this womans faith: which is the more commended, by reafon of thefe two fo great hinderances. Now follow the effects of her faith, which are diuerfe: fome laide downe in this verfe, and fome in the next.

Receiued ftrength to conceiue feede,
And was deliuered of a childe.

In thefe words are two effects:

Firft, by power of her faith fhee was inabled to conceiue: which afore fhe did not, though there were the fame reafons in nature why fhee fhould.

Secondly, fhe was deliuered of a child in her old age, and that child was *Ifaac:* who is therefore called the promifed feede, and the child of the promife.

Out of the confideration of thefe two, wee may learne diuerfe good inftructions: for, feeing they are fo neere a-kin in their natures, we will fpeake of them both ioyntly together.

Firft, here we may fee that nothing is fo hard or difficult which God hath promifed, but faith can compaſſe it , and bring it to performance. Chriſt bad the *blind* ſee , the *lame* to goe: he ſpake, they beleeued, and they were healed.So, here God promiſeth a *barren old womã a child, ſhe beleeueth,* and lo, ſhee *conceiueth* and *brings forth a ſonne.*

The vſe of this doctrine is for two ſorts of people.

Firſt, many in our Church, beeing ignorant; when they are mooued to learne religion , anſwer: Alas they are ſimple, or not booke-learned, or they are dull, and heauie witted, or they be olde and weake , and therefore they can learne nothing; or if they doe, they cannot remember it. But here is nothing but vaine excuſes:For, they want not wit to learne religion, if they haue wit to buy and ſell , to knowe a faire day from a foule , good meate from ill, deere from cheape, Winter from Sommer. If they haue wit to practiſe the ciuill actions of the world, they haue wit enough to conceiue the grounds of religion, and to get ſo much knowledge as may ſuffice for a ground of that *faith,* which will ſaue their ſoules; So that they want nothing, but grace and diligence to vſe the meanes. To them therefore here is matter of good aduice. Let ſuch men learne but one promiſe of God out of the holy Scripture , as this; *Seeke firſt the Kingdome of God , and all things elſe ſhall be giuen vnto you,* Matth. 6.33. or this; *Caſt all your care on him, for he careth for you,* 1. Pet. 5. 7. or this ; *He that commeth vnto me, I caſt him not away,*Iohn 6.37.or but this: *Aske and ye ſhall haue, ſeeke and yee ſhall find,*Mat.7.7.Let them learne but one of theſe, and when they haue learned it, beleeue it , and let their ſoules daily feede on that faith; and they ſhall ſee what will followe : euen a wonderfull bleſsing vpon that poore beginning. This their faith, will ſo content and pleaſe their hearts, that it will vrge them forward to get more,and will make them both deſirous , and capable of more knowledge and grace;and will make them euen hunger and thirſt after knowledge and grace:(whereas, he that knoweth no promiſe, nor beleeues it , contents himſelfe in ignorance and errour).And this ſhall euery one finde , that will carefully vſe the meanes that God appoints,and will begin to learne but one leſſon at the firſt. For, as *olde barren Sarah,*beleeuing Gods promiſe , *conceiues and brings forth:* So, olde, ſimple, plaine, dull Countreymen,*beleeuing* but one promiſe of Gods word, ſhall conceiue and bring forth daily more and more bleſſed fruites of knowledge and grace.

Secondly, others who haue made better proceedings in religion , doe ſee their ſinnes, and doe much bewaile them , but they cannot ouercome their corruptions: yea , many there are, to whom their ſinnes, and inward corruptions are more grieuous, and burdenſome, then all bodily wants or miſeries in the world; yet ſee they not how to conquer their corruptions: but (alas)are oftentimes foiled by them, to their

great diſcomfort.

Let theſe men know, the want of faith is the cauſe hereof; for, that they doe not ſufficiently ruminate, & côſider the promiſes of God made in that behalfe , nor vſe the meanes God hath appointed: to the vſe whereof,he hath annexed his promiſes of helpe againſt ſinne. Let them therefore lay Gods word and promiſes vnto their conſciences in holy and frequent meditations. Let them carefully vſe the meanes God hath appointed, hearing and reading his *word,* receiuing the holy *Communion,*earneſt and frequent *Prayer,*crauing alſo the *praiers of others:* and let them ſharpen theſe holy exerciſes , by *faſting, watching,*holy *conferences* with others, *viſitations* of others afflicted like themſelues, oft reuealing their eſtate to their godly *Paſtors.* Let them continue thus doing , and reſt confidently on the word and promiſe of God, with the ſtedfaſt foote of faith , and they ſhall ſee, that *olde Sarah ſhall haue ſtrength to conceiue:* that is, that their poore ſoules ſhall receiue ſtrength to tread vpon Sathan,to conquer their corruptions, and to conceiue and bring forth many worthy fruites of holineſſe , to their ioy and comfort in their later experience; as *Iſaac* was to *Sarah,* in her elder age.

The next doctrine, we may here learne , is; That whereas *Sarah,* by her faith in Gods promiſe,conceiues and brings forth:therefore children are the immediate bleſsing of the Lord: for *Sarah* bare *Iſaac* , not by any ordinarie ſtrength or power of nature, but *through faith ſhee receiued ſtrength to conceiue,&c.*Neither is this ſo in her onely (wherein there was a miraculous worke of Gods power) but in all. Some are indeed barren by conſtitution , and theſe cannot conceiue,vnleſſe by Gods power as *Sarah* did. But ſome haue no children, who in all naturall reaſon might conceiue. For, as God gaue the Lawe, and thereby a gift and power *to encreaſe and multiply,* Gen. 1. 22. So, he reſerued the execution of it to himſelfe , and power to alter or diſpenſe, to adde,or diminiſh as it pleaſeth him. Therefore ſaith the Pſalmiſt, Pſal. 127. 3. *Lo, children are the inheritance of the Lord, and the fruite of the wombe is his reward:* And ſpeaking of them, Pſal. 128. 4. hee ſaith,*Loe,thus ſhall he be bleſſed that feareth the Lord.*

The vſe is , to teach *Parents,* therefore to bring them vp as Gods bleſsings,and not onely to giue them corporall neceſſities (for ſo they doe their beaſts) but to nurture them in holy Diſcipline, by ſowing the ſeedes of Religion in their hearts. If this they want, they haue nothing , though you leaue them Earledomes. And herein is the ſaying true, *Better vnborne then vntaught.*The Law and power to *encreaſe and multiplie,* is giuen to beaſts in their kinde, as well as to vs, Gen.1. 22. Therefore vnleſſe we doe more then prouide for their bodies, we differ little from thẽ:but, make thẽ know God, & ſo we make thẽ fellowes with the Angels. If

Parents did thus, it cannot bee expreſſed what bleſſings would come thereby to Church and Commonwealth.

Thirdly and laſtly, let vs here knowe and learne, that this holy Matron, *Sarah*, figureth vnto vs myſtically the ſpirituall Hieruſalem, the Church of God. *Allegories* are charily and ſparingly to be taught; els much vnſound doctrine may cumber mens conſciences: but this is found and ſure; for it is the Apoſtles, Gal. 4. 23, &c. *By Agar and Sarah, other things are meant*: for, *theſe two mothers are two Teſtaments: Agar, ſhe which gendreth vnto bondage. Sarah Hieruſalem, which is free, and from aboue, and is the mother of vs all.* Now, the reſemblance betwixt naturall *Sarah*, the wife of *Abraham*, and *myſticall Sarah* the ſpouſe of Chriſt the Church of God, ſtands in this; that as ſhe not by power in her ſelfe, but by Gods power, *and faith* in his promiſe *bare Iſaac*: So, the Church our mother, bringeth forth children to God, onely by the power of Gods word and ſpirit. And therefore as *Iſaac* is called the childe of Promiſe, and ſaid to *be borne by promiſe*, Gal. 4. 23. So, men regenerate and borne to the Church, are ſaid *not to be borne of blood, nor of the will of the fleſh, nor of the will of man, but of God*, Ioh. 1. 13. And S. Iames ſaith, 1. 18. *God, of his owne will, begat vs with the word of truth.* Thus the *word* of God and the *will*, that is, the ſpirit of God, theſe two together beget children to the Church.

The vſe is, to teach vs all to *honour* the Church as our mother; but to *worſhip* God alone, who is the father of our ſoule. The Church cannot make her ſelfe our mother, nor vs her children, when ſhe will: but it is God that muſt *ſpeake the word, and then we are made*, he muſt beget vs by the power of his ſpirit, and miniſterie of his word. And further, let vs learne here what account we are to make of Gods holy word, which is the immortall ſeede of our regeneration, whereby we are made Gods children, and heires of immortality.

Thus much of the two firſt effects of her faith:

The third is laid downe in the next verſe: which becauſe it is much ſtood vpon by the holy Ghoſt, we will put it off till then, beeing therefore worthy our deeper conſideration.

And now followeth in the end of this verſe, the fift and laſt point, which is, the *Ground of her faith:*

Becauſe ſhe iudged him faith hſhall which had promiſed.

The foundation, whereon ſhe built this her faith, that ſhe ſhould haue a ſonne, beeing *barren and paſt age*, was not the bare promiſe *of God*, ſo much, as the conceite or opinion ſhee had of him *that promiſed.* For, promiſes are not of value, ſo much by the things promiſed, though neuer ſo great or excellent (for they may promiſe much, who can performe nothing: or though they can, yet wil recal their word in

lightnes and inconſtancie) as by the worthines of the party promiſing. We ſay in this world, we had rather haue ſome mens word, then other mens bond: and rather haue a little promiſed of ſome, then much of others. Now ſuch was the Iudgement that *Sarah* helde of him that promiſed: namely, God: *Shee iudged him faithfull which had promiſed.*

Faithfull: that is, ſhe iudged him *able, and willing* to accompliſh what-euer he promiſed to her. So that the Grounds of our faith in God, and all his promiſes, muſt be a ſure apprehenſion and knowledge of theſe two things in God;

1. His *ability*, to make good what-euer paſſeth him in word.
2. His *carefulneſſe* to doe it, when hee hath ſaid it.

Some will promiſe any thing, though their abilities ſtretch not to performe: others are able enough, but haue no care of their word. But both theſe are in God; all-ſufficient ability, and moſt careful willingneſſe: So *Sarah* iudged of God, and therefore ſhee *beleeued* againſt reaſon: and ſo muſt we doe, if wee will beleeue Gods word aright. We may reade, and heare, and knowe Gods word, and haue the points therein ſwimming in our heads: but if we will conſtantly *beleeue*, with our hearts, his bleſſed promiſes, & in our conſciences feare his threatnings, we muſt be fully perſwaded of theſe two to be in him.

So are we taught by Chriſt (the wiſdome of God) in the Lords Prayer (afore wee pray for any thing) to be reſolued of Gods *power* and *will* to heare and helpe vs. Hee is our *Father*, therefore carefull and willing: *hee is in heauen*, and therefore able to heare vs, and to giue vs all things, Matth. 6. 9.

And the ſame commendation here giuen to *Sarah*, is alſo giuen to *Abraham*, Rom. 4. 21. *He doubted not, but beleeued aboue hope, &c. being fully aſſured, that he which had promiſed, was alſo able to doe it.*

The vſe hereof vnto vs is double:

Firſt, to aduiſe and guide vs for our promiſes; not to be too reckleſſe, as ſome are, what we promiſe: but to conſider aforehand, and if it be beyond our power, not to ſpeake the word, (for Chriſtian mens words muſt not be vain:) and if we haue promiſed any thing lawfull and in our power, to be carefull to performe it. Thus to doe, is to bee a *faithfull man*, and is a good ſigne of a holy man and Gods childe: prouided this be ſo,

Firſt of all towards *God*, that we make conſcience of performing the great vow wee made in our *baptiſme*, and all other ſerious and holy purpoſes of our heart made to God. For, otherwiſe, hee that breakes his vowe to God careleſly, by liuing profanely, he may in worldly policy keepe his word, but he cannot doe it in conſcience.

The Church of *Rome* is foully faulty in this

point, making no conscience of breaking promise and faith with vs , or any of our religion;
their nakednes herein is discouered in the face
of all Christendome: let them that are wise bee
warned of it. They make great ostentation of
their vowes, & of their care to performe them,
aboue any other religion: but it appeares hereby to be vile hypocrisie. For, if they were con-
scionably, and not politikely and formally carefull of their vowes of chastity, pouerty, and o-
thers , made to God , they could not but bee
likewise careful of their promises made to men:
for the one of these is the fountaine and roote
of the other. But the neglect of the one, sheweth the formality and hypocrisie of the other.

Let all that feare God , learne to make conscience of both these in their religion and seruice of God, and in all their dealings with men
in the world : that so the world may *iudge vs
faithfull men , when we haue promised.*

Secondly , let vs here learne how to helpe
and strengthen our weake *faith* in the great
promises of God. We haue a promise of *saluation , Whosoeuer beleeueth in Christ , shall not
perish, but haue life euerlasting.* Of our *resurrection,*Dan.12.2.*They that sleepe in the dust, shall
rise againe.* Of our *glorification,* Philip. 3. 21:
*The Lord Iesus shall change our vile bodies, and
make them like to his owne glorious bodie.* Of a
new world, 2. Pet. 3. 13. *We looke for new heauens, and a new earth, according to his promise.*

These be , as S. *Peter* calls them, *great and
pretious promises* , 2. Pet. 1. 4. And surely it
must be a great and precious *faith* , that can
constantly beleeue these. No better helps of our
faith can there be, then often and seriously to
consider of the *mercy* and *power* of him that
made them: if he be *willing*, and able, what can
let the performance of them? Let vs therefore
often say with holy *Paul , Faithfull is he which
hath promised, who will also do it,* 1.Thess. 5.24.
and with *Sarah* here , *Wee iudge him faithfull
which hath promised.*

Now followeth the last effect , in the next
verse.

v. 12. *And therefore sprang there of one, euen of one which was as dead, as many as the starres of the skie in multitude , and as the sands of the sea shore, which are innumerable.*

The third and last effect of *Sarahs* faith, is,
that by this sonne *Isaac*, whom she conceiued,
and brought forth *by faith*, she had a wonderfull great issue , and a *posterity almost without
number.* This effect consists not of it selfe, but
depends vpon the former. Her *faith* gaue her
strength to *conceiue Isaac*, though shee were

barren: and to *bring him forth* , though shee
were *olde and weake* ; and so her faith brought
him out, by whom shee was made *the mother
of many millions* of men.

The matter of this third effect, is the multitude of men, that came of *Abraham*, and *Sarah*
by *Isaac.*

This posterity or multitude , is discribed by
two arguments:

1. By the beginning or roote of it;
One that was as dead.

2. The quantity or greatnesse, laid down;

1. Generally to bee a *multitude* and *innumerable.*

2. Particularly, by two comparisons:

1. As many as *the starres in the skie.*

2. As *the sands by the sea shore.*

The first point , is the roote and beginning
of this multitude , in these words:

*And therefore sprang there of one, euen one
that was as dead.*

One; that is , one woman *Sarah:* or at the
most, *one couple, Abraham,* and *Sarah.* And
this *one* was no better the dead. Not dead properly and fully: for , none are so dead, whose
soules and bodies are not separate: but, *as dead,*
that is, as good as dead, or halfe dead; meaning,
that they were altogether vnfit for generation
of children, the strength of nature being decay-
ed in them; *Abraham* being an 100. & *Sarah*
90. yeares old. And if this be true of *Abraham,*
who was past age, how much more is it of *Sarah*, who was both past age, & was also barren
in her best age?

Here we are to note and learne many things:

First , *Multitudes came of one.* See here the
powerfull, and yet the ordinary works of God,
to reare vp goodly and huge buildings , vpon
small and weake foundations. So did he in the
beginning, and euer since. Indeede , hee made
at the first , thousands of *starres,* because they
must be no more then at the first they were; and
millions of *Angels,* intending they shall not
multiply; he could also haue made millions of
men in a moment: he would not, but onely one
couple, *Adam and Eue.* And of them came
the infinite race of mankinde. When sinne had
made an end of that world , hee founded not
the second that yet continueth , vpon a thousand couples ; but by three men & their wiues,
he multiplied the whole race of mankinde,
which since haue growen from three , to millions of millions. And so here of one olde man,
and a barren old woman , spring innumerable
multitudes.

This, God doth to magnifie his own power,
in the eies of the sonnes of men : and so he did
also in matters heauenly. The nuber of Christians since Christ , that haue growne to millions,
began in a poore number at the first. For, when
Christ himselfe was ascended , the number of
knowne beleeuers, was but 120. Acts 1. 15.

The consideration hereof should teach vs all
these duties;

First, not to meafure God by our lengthes, nor to tie him to our rules; but to efteem of his power and might, as wee fee it deferues: and to entertaine high and honourable thoughts of him and his Maieftie, who can reare vp fo great *works*, vpon fo *poore foundations*.

Secondly, not to defpaire of our felues or our eftates, though we thinke our felues neuer fo weake, fo poore, fo ficke, either in foule or bodie: but to remember him, that *of one made multitudes* to fpring out. Therefore when thou art brought neuer fo low, either in foule or bodie, by any miferies, either inward or outward; faint not, but *goe forward in the ftrength of the Lord thy God.* Particularly: If God haue afflicted thee with pouerty, that thou haue nothing to begin withall: or for thy foule; is thy knowledge in religion fmall, thy meanes poore, thy feeling of Gods fauour but weak? yet faint not, but lay faft hold on Gods power and promife, vfe carefully the holy meanes God hath ordained, remembring and relying on him, *who made millions growe out of one:* and affure thy felfe, as Iob faith, *Though thy beginnings be fmall, yet thy latter endes fhall greatly encreafe.*

Secondly, obferue here how old perfons are called *halfe dead,* or *as good as dead;* and that is true of them many waies.

Firft, their yeares and dayes, limited them, are as good as gone. For, fuppofe a man fhould be as fure to liue an 100. yeares; as the *funne* is to run all the day long his courfe, and at night to goe down: Yet as when the *funne* is paft the height, and drawing downeward, we fay it goeth faft downe, and the day hafteth away; So when a man is paft his middle age, when the funne of his life is paft the nonefteede, he declineth daily, and draweth faft away, and the night of his life approacheth, with haft and much horror, vnleffe he preuent it.

Secondly, their ftrength and vitall powers, by which their life is continued, and their fouls and bodies kept together, are fo much weakened, that they are almoft extinguifhed: whereby it comes to paffe, an old man may feele a manifeft defect in all powers of minde and body.

Thirdly, fickeneffes or difeafes growe vpon olde age: and as their ftrength faileth, fo the force of difeafes is redoubled on them: and looke what difeafes haue lurked in their bodies which either naturally were bred in them, or accidentally taken, they now fhewe themfelues more fenfibly, and the weaker a man is, the ftronger is his fickneffe. In thefe three refpects, an olde man or woman is *as good as dead.*

The vfe hereof is profitable;

Firft, they muft therefore be aduifed to *prepare themfelues for death.* Euery man is to prepare, I confeffe: then if euery man, efpecially they that be olde: The yong man may die, the olde man muft die; the yongeft cannot liue alwaies, the olde man cannot liue long; the aged mans graue is as it were made alreadie, and his

one foote is in it. And this is not mans conceit alone, but Gods owne iudgement, who as we fee here, calls an olde man *as good as dead :* and that not fo much in regard, that he is *fure* to die as that he is *neere* it : Therefore as euery man young or olde, is to make ready, becaufe his time is vnknowne, and no man is fure, that he fhall liue to be olde, & as the Pfalmift fingeth, *Euery man in his beft eftate is altogether vanity,* Pfal.39.6. So efpecially he to whom God hath beene fo gracious, as to let him fee old age, he fhould thinke of nothing but his ende, and prepare euery day *to dy in the lord.* His gray haires, his wrinkled skin, his withered face, his ill ftomack, his weake memory, his crooked body, and the manifeft and moft fenfible alteration & decay of his whole ftate of minde and body, fhould hourely all cry in his eares, *I am halfe dead, I will therefore prepare to die in the Lord.*

It is therefore a miferable fight to fee, that thofe who of all men fhould be moft willing to die, are for the moft part moft defirous to liue. And thofe who fhould be moft ready to die, are generally, moft ignorant, moft couetous, and their hearts moft of al wedded to the earth, and earthly things.

Secondly, olde perfons muft here learne S. Pauls leffon: 2.Cor.4.16. That *as the outward man perifheth, fo the inward man may be renued daily.* The outward man is the body; the inward man is the foule and the grace of God in it. They muft therefore labour, that as the ftrength of their bodies decay, fo the grace of God in their foules may quicken and reuiue. But alas, the common practife is contrary. For old men haue generally fo mifpent their youth, and in their olde age are partly fo backward, partly fo vnfit to learne religion, that when they come to their death-beds, they are then to be *Catechifed* in the very principles of religion: fo that when the body is halfe dead, religion hath no beeing in them; and when the body is a dying, religion and grace fcarce begin to liue in them: fuch men caft all vpon a defperate point. But let them that defire a ioyfull departure, thinke of thefe things aforehand : and as yeares draw on, and fo drawe life to his ende, and the body to the graue; fo let them weane their hearts from the world, and lift them vp to God, and fo fpend their laft dayes in getting knowledge, and in feruing God; that when their bodies are weakeft and fitteft for the earth, their foules may be the holieft and ripeft for heauen. To fuch men fhall it neuer be difcomfort to fee their bodies halfe dead, when for recompence thereof they finde their foules halfe in heauen. Thus we fee the *roote or foundation* of this pofteritie, how poore and weake it was. Now let vs come to the greateneffe of it.

Thereof fprang as many in number, &c.

This one olde couple, *Abraham & Sarah,* are made by gods power the father and mother of many nations: and he and fhee, of whom the world would haue pronounced, they should not haue left a name vpon the earth, haue now millions of children that sprang out of them. Here we may learne, That though God worke ordinarily, according to the courſe of Nature, which himſelfe hath eſtabliſhed; yet that he is not bound to it, nor will be: he bound it, therefore there is no reaſon it ſhould binde him. Here we may ſee the power and prerogatiue of Gods Maieſtie.

As in the beginning he made to be, thoſe things which were not: ſo ſtill he calleth *things that are not, as though they were*, Rom. 4. 17. and turneth and altreth the ſtate and nature of his creatures as pleaſeth him. He can take *life* from the liuing man, and leaue him *dead*; he can giue life to the dead man, and make him liue againe. So hath he dealt for the bodie, and for the ſoule he hath beene no leſſe wonderfull.

Saul, of a bloody perſecutor, he can make a zealous Preacher, Act. 9. euen a glorious inſtrument, and *a choſen veſſell to carie his name vnto the Gentiles*, euen he who thought to haue blotted out the name of Chriſt, and *all that called on that name* from vnder heauen, Act. 9. 14.

Rahab, a harlot, and a common woman, yet by Gods work ſo farre altred, that her faith is regiſtred in the 31. verſ. amongſt the moſt excellent beleeuers that haue bin in the world. Let this teach vs, when we ſee our owne ſinnes, how hideous and monſtrous they be, yet not to *deſpaire*. And when we ſee other men liue in extreame diſſolutenes, yet not *to iudge of them before the time*: but euen then, with hope and comfort, remember that God who *quickneth the dead, & calleth things that are not as though they were*.

And in that hope let vs perſwade our ſelues, that he may quicken our dead hearts, and reuiue vs by his grace. And therefore in that hope let vs raiſe vp our ſelues, to vſe all holy means, of Gods *Word*, *Sacraments*, and *Prayer*: which if we carefully and continually doe, we ſhall ſee wonders wrought in vs; that as they ſaide of *Paul, This man preacheth the faith which afore he deſtroyed, and therefore glorified God for him*, Galath: 1. 22. 23. So ſhall men ſay of vs, This man *hates* the prophannes that he *liued* in, and *loues* the religion that afore he mocked. Such miracles will the Lord worke in vs, if with faith and diligence we vſe the holy meanes; that ſo all that ſee vs, ſhall *Glorifie God for vs*.

Thus we ſee generally how great the iſſue and poſteritie of *Sarah* was.

But it is more particularly inlarged by two compariſons.

As many as the ſtarres in the skie, or the ſands by the ſea ſhore, which are innumerable.

His compariſons are two: One taken from the *heauens, as many as the ſtarres in the skie*: The other from the *earth, as the ſands in the*

sea. And theſe two are vſed by the holy Ghoſt, being things of incredible number, to expreſſe the multitude of the *Iſraelites*, that came all from *Sarah*.

Not but that other things alſo are of as great number; as the drops of water, duſt of the earth, and hairs of mens heads, &c. but theſe two are moſt common and prouerbiall phraſes, whereby to expreſſe a multitude. And againe, the *ſtarres of the skie* are rather named then any other, becauſe God in the beginning pleaſed to vſe it to *Abraham*, when he had neuer a child, Gen. 15. 8. God caried *Abraham* forth in the night, and bad him *count the ſtarrs if he could, and ſaid, ſo ſhall thy ſeede be*. And *Moſes* afterwards vſeth the ſame compariſon, Deut. 10. 22. *Our Fathers went downe into Egypt* 70. *perſons, and now the Lord hath made vs as the ſtarres of the skie in multitude*.

Now becauſe all men are not *Aſtronomers*, as *Abraham* and *Moſes* were, and that ignorant men might ſay, they can perceiue no ſuch matter in the *ſtarres*: Therefore he vſeth another compariſon, which euery Countryman may diſcern how innumerable they be; namely, the *ſands of the Sea ſhore*: And leaſt any ſhould ſay, I dwell in the mid-land Country, and neuer ſaw the ſea ſand, and am ignorant, and ſo cannot iudge of the *ſtarres*, therefore to put him out of doubt, the holy Ghoſt aſſures him, in the ende of the verſe, that they are both *innumerable*; that is, not in theſelues, or to God, but in regard of man, and mans skill vnable to be counted.

Concerning theſe two compariſons, let vs obſerue the *manner or the* phraſe of ſpeech in them vſed:

For the firſt, we are to know, that the ſpeech is not proper, but *figuratiue*. For properly, they were not as many as the *ſtarres*, or as the *ſands*: neither are the ſtarres or ſands *innumerable*: but it is a figure called by the Rhetoricians ὑπερβολὴ, which is an exceſſe of fineneſſe of ſpeech, or an exceſſiue elegancie. And as it is ordinarie in all Writers, and euen in common ſpeech: ſo it is not refuſed by the holy Ghoſt, but vſed both here, and in the two forenamed places: and the like alſo of the ſame nature (but in other phraſes) in other places, as S. Ioh. 21. 25. *I ſuppoſe* ſaith he, *if all the ſayings and doings of Chriſt were written, the world could not containe the bookes that would be written*. Meaning, they would be exceeding many, & more then would be needefull for ſaluation. And Deut. 9. 1. *Moſes* ſaith, *That the Cities of the Canaanites were great, and walled vp to heauen*. Meaning, that they were very high, and ſo high as was poſſible for Citie walles to be, and as was impoſſible to haue been ſcaled in all mens reaſons, had not God fought for them.

Theſe and ſuch like are common in the Scripture: and ſeeing we allowe that libertie to all Writers, and to our ſelues in common ſpeech, no reaſon to denie it to the Scripture, which was written for all mens vnderstanding, and therefore in such phrases as are vsuall and ordinarie with all men.

And the like libertie is here taken also in another figure, *as many as the sands by the shore of the sea:* the word properly signifieth and soundeth, *the lip of the Sea.* Now the sea hath no lippe, but it is a speech taken or borrowed from man or beast who haue lips, and the *sea shore* resembleth a *lippe.* For, looke what a *lippe* is to them, the *shores* are to the sea: as the two lippes doe inclose the mouth: so the two shores on both sides doe inclose the Sea, which lieth as in a mouth betwixt them. From hence we may learne profitable instructions.

First, that therefore *Rhetorike* is a warrantable, good, and lawfull Art; and it ariseth thus: That which the holy Ghost practiseth, must needes be not onely not euill, but good and warrantable. But the holy Ghost vseth and practiseth Rhetorike, here and in many other places else of the Scripture. Therefore it is a good and lawfull Art. The *proposition* is vndoubted, the *assumption* is cleare both by these places, & almost the whole bodie of the Scripture: many of S. *Pauls Epistles,* many of Christs owne Sermons, S. *Iohns* Gospel, many of the *Prophets,* especially *Isaiah,* haue as much and as elegant Rhetorike in them, as any writers in the world; and beside all other vertue and Diuine power in them, doe euen for figures and ornaments of Art, match any *Oratours,* that haue written in the *Greeke* or *Latine.* Nor would it be any hard task to vndertake to prooue, and illustrate euery approoued rule of *Rhetoricke,* out of some part of Scripture. Now if it be lawfull to practise the rules of Rhetoricke, then it is lawfull also to collect those rules together, to pen them, and to make an Art of them. They therefore that holding the contrary, do say, or teach, or write, it is vnlawfull, goe against the stream, and common practise of the Scripture, and rules of common reason.

Secondly, here it is apparant, that in preaching Gods word, it is lawfull, and warrantable for a *Minister* to vse Rhetoricke and eloquence. And the reason is good: for that which the holy Ghost vseth in *penning* of the Scripture, the same may Gods Ministers vse also in *preaching* the same. They therefore that denie that libertie to Ministers, are too rough and rugged, and pull out of the hand of the Ministers, one of his weapons, and out of the wings of the Scripture one of her feathers.

Yet we must know, that all, or any kinde of eloquence is not permitted to a Christian Minister; For, S. *Paul* saith, 1. Cor. 2013. *Wee speake the words of God, not in the words which mans wisedome teacheth, but which the holy Ghost teacheth, comparing spirituall things with spirituall things:* So that there is a holy, a sanctified, a *spirituall eloquence,* an eloquence fit for spirituall things, and that eloquence must be vsed. As the Israelits might marie the Midianite

women, whom they had taken in warre, but not till *they had purified them,* Num. 31. 18. 19. And more plainely and particularly, Deut. 21. 11, 12, 13. *Moses* explaneth what that purifying is: *And thou shalt bring her home into thine house, and shee shall shaue her head, and paire her nails, and put off the garment she was taken in, and then thou maist marie her:* So, humane eloquence must be *brought home* to diuinitie, and be pared, and shaued with spirituall wisedome, and then may lawfully and profitably be vsed.

For our more speciall direction herein; these cautions may be obserued.

First, the more *naturall* it is, and the lesse affected, the more *commendable* is it in the doer, and more *profitable* to the hearer.

Secondly, it must be graue, sober, and modest; remembering the height and holinesse of the place a man stands in, and of the worke he doth. Therefore it must not consist in telling strange tales, or vsing such gestures or words, manner, or matter, as may mooue *laughing,* and smiling in the Auditors. There may be wit in such doing; but it can hardly be the sanctified and spirituall eloquence, which S. *Paul* there speaks of.

Thirdly, it must be such as may be a helpe, and not a hinderance to the vnderstanding of Gods word: for, it is a damosell to Diuinitie, but not her Mistresse. Gods word therefore must not bowe and bende to her; much lesse be wrung and wrested to her, but she to Gods word.

It must in a word be such, as may most liuely, purely, plainely, and significantly expresse the meaning of Gods word. Therefore a man must endeauour that all his speech be in one language, at least in such as his hearers vnderstand: for else if he speak the body of his speech in one, and peece out the members in other, which the people vnderstand not; he may indeede *in his owne spirit speake mysteries, but to the hearer he speaketh parables.* And to his own vnderstanding, he may preach well, but *the hearer is not edified:* as the Apostle saith, 1. Cor. 14. 2. 17. Therefore let not eloquence, be a hinderance to the vnderstanding of the hearers, which God hath ordained to be a helpe and furtherance. And with these, or such like qualifications, eloquence may be vsed, with good warrant and much profit. And for cautions or qualifications herein, hardly can any man set downe better rules, then euery mans conscience will vnto himselfe.

Thirdly, inasmuch as the holy Ghost here and elsewhere vseth so much Rhetoricke, Diuines may learne where the fountaine of Christian eloquence is; namely, in the Scriptures of the olde and newe Testament. Which beeing compiled by the wisdome of God, we are to assure our selues they containe in them true wisdome of all sorts. *Precepts* of Rhetoricke, I confesse, are to be learned out of other books,

which

which purposely doe teach them; but the practise of those rules in examples, can be no
where better, than in *Moses*, the Prophets, and
the Euangelists. And this must needes followe
vpon that, that hath alreadie beene granted. For
if we yeeld, that *Rhetoricke* is good and lawful,
and practised in the scripture; then it must needs
follow, that it is there practised in the best
manner: for shall the *Diuinitie* there taught be
the soundest? the *Historie* there reported the
truest? the conclusions of *Philosophie*, *Astronomie*, *Geometrie*, *Arithmeticke*, *Cosmographie*,
and *Physicke*, there deliuered, the surest? the
Musicke there practised, the exactest? the *Logicke* there practised, the sharpest? the *Lawes*
there enacted, the iustest? and shall not the *Rhetoricke* there practised, be the purest? Surely, if
Moses had written a booke of his owne, as he
was a meere man, and as he was *Moses*, brought
vp in Egypt: or *Paul* writ a booke, as he was a
Pharisie, and Doctor of the Law; they would
haue beene full of all excellent learning: for
Paul was brought vp at the foote of *Gamaliel*,
Acts 22. 3. And *Moses* was exceedingly learned in all the learning of the Egyptians, and
mightie in word and deede, Acts 7. 22.

Shall they then be the Secretaries of the most
high God, the fountaine of wisedome, and
learning; and shall not their bookes be filled
with the most excellent learning in all kindes?
Doubtlesse, who euer searcheth it, shall finde it
to be so.

Seeing therefore Eloquence is lawfull, and
that Preachers may lawfully vse it; let them also knowe, where to haue it: let them studie
Gods Bookes; and there they shall finde not
onely Diuinitie, but knowledge and learning
of all sorts, and that most exquisite: and as excellent patternes and presidents of Eloquence,
as are to be found in any Authors in the world.
And let them, if they would preach with spirituall power and eloquence; looke how *Moses*,
the *Prophets*, our *Sauiour Christ*, and his
Apostles preached: for, to followe them is the
true way.

Thus we see the *manner* here vsed by the holy Ghost, in these two comparisons, to describe
the greatnesse of this her posteritie.

Now, the *matter* in them contained is, that
here is the performance of one of the greatest
promises made to *Abraham*. The promise is,
Gen. 22. 17. *I will surely blesse thee, and greatly multiply thy seede, as the starres in the heauen,
and as the sands by the sea shoare.* There is the
promise; and behold here the performance, in
the very same words, and that most true and
effectuall: For, at the time when the holy Ghost
wrote these words, the Israelites were multiplied to many millions; yea to a number past
number.

So that here we learne, *God is true* in all his
promises, be they neuer so great or wonderfull.
if he speake the word, if the promise passe him,
it is sure: Heauen and earth shall rather passe a-

way, then any one piece of his promise shall
faile.

The vse is to teach vs, first, *to beleeue God*
when he promiseth, what-euer it be; for, he is
worthie to be beleeued, who neuer failed to
performe what he promised. He promised these
Millions to *Abraham*, when he had but *one
childe*; nay when he had neuer a one: Gen. 15.
8. And *Abraham beleeued*. Such a faith was
excellent indeede, and deserues eternall commendation (as here it hath.) Let vs be *childrē of
this faithfull Abraham*, and the rather, seeing
we see the performance, which he sawe not.
We thinke it a disgrace, if we be not beleeued;
especially, if we doe vse te keepe our word: Let
vs then knowe thereby, what dishonour it is to
the Lord, not to beleeue him, which neuer
failed in the performance to any creature.

Secondly, we must here learne of God to be
true and faithfull in our words and promises.
God spake plainely, & deceiued not *Abraham*:
and after at the time performed it; So must we
deale plainly and simply in our words and bargaines, and thinke that to deceiue and ouer-
reach by craftie words, and double meanings,
and equiuocal phrases are not beseeming Christianity. And we must make conscience of a lie,
else we are like the deuill and not God. Also a
Christian man must take heede what, how, and
to whom he promiseth: but hauing promised,
he must performe, though it be losse or harme
to himselfe: if it be not wrong to God, or to
the Church, or State. Wrong to himselfe must
not hinder him from performance. Christian
mens words must not be vaine, they should be
as good as bonds, though I knowe it is lawfull,
and very conuenient in regard of mortalitie, to
take such kinde of assurances.

Lastly, *Abraham* had the promise his *seede
should be so*, Gen. 15. 8. and here we see it is
so, but he himselfe saw it not: so that *Abraham*
had the promise, and we the performance. So
Adam had the promise of the Messias, but wee
see it performed: The Patriarkes and Prophets,
the promise of the calling of the Gentiles, but
we see it performed.

See here the glorie of the Church vnder the
Newe Testament aboue the *Olde*. This must
teach vs to be so much better then they, as God
is better to vs, then he was to them: and to excell them in faith, and all other vertues of holynesse; or else their faith, and their holy obedience shall turne to our greater condemnation,
which haue had so farre greater cause, to beleeue and obey God, and so farre better meanes
then they. Which if it be so; then alas what
will become of them, who come behind them,
nay haue no care to followe them in their faith,
nor holynesse, nor any duties of holy obedience.

Thus much for the Example of this holy
womans faith, and of the commendation
thereof.

Now before he come to any more particular

examples of faith, the holy Ghoſt giues a general commēdation of the faith of all thoſe ioyntly which are ſpoken of already.

VERSE 13.

All theſe died in faith, and receiued not the promiſes, but ſawe them afarre off, and beleeued them : and receiued them thankefully, and confeſ- ſed that they were ſtrangers and pilgrimes on the earth.

Itherto the Holy Ghoſt hath particularly commended the faith of diuers holy beleeuers. Now from this verſe to the 17. he doth generally commend the faith of *Abraham, Sarah, Iſaac,* and *Iaacob* together; yet not ſo much their faith, as the durance and conſtancie of their faith. Particularly the points are two.

1. Is laid downe their conſtancie and continuance; *All theſe died in faith.*
2. That conſtancie is ſet forth by foure effects :
   1. *They receiued not the promiſes, but ſaw them afarre off.*
   2. *They beleeued them.*
   3. *Receiued them thankefully.*
   4. *Profeſſed themſelues ſtrangers and pilgrimes on the earth.*

The firſt point touching theſe beleeuers is; that as they begun, ſo they held on: as they liued, ſo they died in faith.

All theſe died in faith.

The truth of the matter, in the words, may be referred to all afore going, ſauing *Enoch* who *died not*; yet he continued alſo conſtant in his faith, and in that faith was taken vp: but as for *Abel* and *Noah, they died in faith.* Yet I take it, that principally and directly, the holy Ghoſt intended no more then theſe foure I named: and my reaſon is, becauſe the particular effects in this verſe, and the points where this their conſtancie is amplified in the three verſes following, doe all agree, eſpecially with theſe foure; and not ſo properly with *Abel* or *Noah:* ſo that I take, he meaneth by *all theſe,* all theſe men that liued in the ſecond world, ſince the flood. All theſe died *in faith*; that is, in aſſurance that the promiſes made vnto them,

should be performed in Gods good time.

Theſe promiſes were principally theſe two.
1. *Saluation* by the Meſſias.
2. The *poſſeſſion* of the Land of Canaan.

In this faith they died; that is, they held it (through all aſſaults and temptations to the contrary) euen to the laſt gaſpe, and died therein.

In this their practiſe, is commended vnto vs a moſt worthie leſſon of Chriſtianity: namely, that we muſt ſo liue that we may *die in faith.* Many ſay they liue in faith: and it is well if they doe ſo: but the maine point is, to *die in faith.* There is none ſo ill, but howſoeuer he liues, yet he would die well: If he would *die well,* he muſt *die in faith.* For miſerable is the death, that is without faith. And herein faith and hope differ from other graces of God; *Loue, ioy, zeale, holineſſe,* and all other graces are imperfect here, and are perfected in heauen : but *faith* and *hope* are perfected at our deaths; they are not in the other world, for there is nothing then to be *beleeued,* nor *hoped* for, ſeeing we then doe enioy all things: but as they are begun in our life, at our regeneration, ſo they be made perfect when we die; and they ſhine moſt gloriouſly in the laſt and greateſt combate of all, which is, at the houre of death. So that the death of a Chriſtian, which is the gate to glory, is to *die in faith.*

Beſides, as life leaues vs, ſo death findes vs; and as death leaues vs, ſo the laſt iudgement finds vs: and as it leaues vs, ſo we continue for euer and euer without recouerie or alteration.

Now to *die in faith,* is to die in an aſſured eſtate of glory and happineſſe; which is that, that euery man deſireth: therefore, as we all deſire it, ſo let vs *die in faith,* and we ſhall attaine vnto it.

Saint *Paul* tels vs, 1. Cor. 15. 55. *Death* is a terrible *ſerpent,* for he hath a poiſoned *ſting:* Now when we die, we are to encounter with this hideous and fearefull ſerpent. He is fearefull euery way, but eſpecially for his ſting; that *ſting is our ſinne:* and this ſting is not taken away, nor the force of it quenched, but by true faith, *which quencheth all the fierie darts of the deuill,* Eph. 6. 16. If therefore we would be able to encounter with this great enemie (in the conquering of whom ſtands our happineſſe; and by whom to be conquered, is our eternall miſerie) we muſt then ſo arme our ſelues with faith, that we may *die in faith*; for he that dieth in faith, that faith of his kills his ſinnes, and conquers death: but he that dieth without faith, death and ſinne ſeize on him, and his ſinnes liue for euer, and his miſerie by them.

Now, if we would die in faith, we muſt liue in faith; elſe it is not to be expected: For, ſo theſe holy Patriarchs *liued* long in this faith, wherein they died. For, their holy liues ſhewed plainly, that they liued in that faith, which the Apoſtle ftle faith) doth *purifie our hearts*, Acts 15.9. Now, if we would liue in true faith, the means to attaine it, fet downe by Gods word, are thefe.

First, we muft labour to get knowledge of the fundamentall points of religion; of God, of the Creation, the Fall, the immortalitie of the Soule, the two Couenants, of works by the Law, of Grace by the Mediator; and fuch other fubftantiall points, touching God, his Word, Sacraments, Law, Gofpel, Praier, good Works, &c. as the Scriptures, and the Creeds, and Ca-techifmes out of the Scripture doe yeeld vnto vs. Herein, the cafe of the common people of all nations, is miferable. In Poperie their Cler-gie is fo fatte and full, *they will not*; in our Chur-ches the Minifterie (a great part of it) fo poore, and ill prouided for, they *cannot* teach. Betwixt both, the people of the world doe *perifh for lack of knowledge*; for how can they but perifh, *that die not in faith?* How can they die fo, that liue not in faith? And how can they euer haue faith, that haue no knowledge, feeing know-ledge is the foundation of faith? Therefore, it needes the *helpe* of thofe that may, and the *prai-ers* of all, that our Church may haue *Teachers*, and our people *Catechifers*: for without lear-ning the Catechifme, it is impoffible to learne religion.

Secondly, when we haue got knowledge, and fo laid the foundation; then muft we learne the *promifes of God for faluation*, and we muft *hide them in our hearts*, as the Iewels of life and faluation. We muft beleeue them to be true and effectuall, to all that will take hold of them; and we our felues muft therefore take holde of them, and apply them to our foules.

Thirdly, after both thefe, we muft *conforme our felues* throughout (heart, and life) vnto the holy *laws* of God: we muft leaue all bad wayes, and vngodly courfes, though they be neuer fo deare vnto vs, or fo common in the world; and muft make confcience of all finne, and endea-uour to doe all duties to God and man.

The firft of thefe, is the *ground* of faith: the fecond is *faith* it felfe: the laft the *fruite* and ef-fect of it, and an affured teftimony of it to God, to his Church, and to a mans owne confcience. And to doe thefe three things, is to walke in the olde and holy way, confecrated by Chrifts blood, and troden in by all the holy Fathers: and Poperie, nor any other religion can appoint fo fafe, fo fure, nor fo direct a way. Thus liued *Abraham, Sarah, Ifaac*, and *Iaacob*, and after this courfe they *died in faith*, and now liue in glorie: and fo fhall we with them, if we will liue in faith, as they did; but elfe, we may long looke for heauen, before we come there. In-deede, God can make a man that liued not in faith, die in faith; but the matter is not what he can doe, but what is his ordinarie courfe; & that is this: *They that liue in faith, die in faith.* There-fore, let vs take the ordinarie courfe, and re-pent, and turne betimes, and liue the life of

faith; and leaue the late repentance to them that thinke it but a fport to venture a foule: that courfe may fpeede; but this courfe is fure to fpeed: he that liues in finne, *may hope* to die in faith; but he that liues in faith, *is fure* to die in faith, and to liue in glorie for euer.

Secondly, obferue how it is faid, *All thefe* died in faith: not fome, but al. *Abraham* the fa-ther, and the roote, and with him, the wife, the child, and the grand-child: behold a *true noble blood*, a holy kinred, a bleffed generation: wor-thy is *Abraham* of all the honour he hath, who was the roote of fuch a noble and bleffed brood. And worthie are *Ifaac* and *Iaacob* of fo good a father, who ftained not their blood, by forfaking their faith: but held it as they receued it, *and liued and died in it.* Let this teach vs, firft, if we be fathers, to fhine before our chil-dren, in a holy religion, true faith, and good life; and it is great hope that our wiues and children will follow vs in the fame.

Secondly, if we be fonnes, to looke which of our forefathers and aunceftors imbraced the moft holy religion; and to choofe, and liue, and die in their faith. Moft of our yong Papifts can fay no more for their religion, but this; my fa-ther and grand-father were of that religion. But they muft looke to all their fore-fathers: *Ifaac and Iaacob* would not be of their great grand-fathers (*Nahors* or *Terahs*) religion, but of their father *Abrahams*: and *Abraham* him-felfe, would not be of his father *Terahs*, or his grandfather *Nahors* religion; but he went vp a great deale higher, to his fore-fathers to the tenth generation, *Noah, and Shem*, and imbra-ced their religion. So that we fee, it is nothing to fay, I am of my fathers, or grandfathers reli-gion; vnleffe firft I prooue that theirs was of God: and then he is a Noble Chriftian man, which knowing that, will not forfake it, but will liue and die in it.

Thirdly, fee here *true honour and gentry* is to liue and die in the true faith, and holy religi-on of our aunceftors here is the fountaine of honour, to do as thefe did. *Abraham* perceiues he is wrong, and erred with his fathers; he therefore leaues his fathers and grandfathers religion, and goeth vp higher, and takes a bet-ter. *Ifaac* his fonne, makes himfelfe heire, not of his land alone; but of his fathers religion alfo: *Iaacob* the grand-child, follows both, and dieth in faith with them. Behold here *Iaacob*, a *true gentleman in blood*; his holineffe and re-ligion is in the third defcent: Let vs all learne to adorne our gentility and nobilitie with thefe enfignes of true honour.

And let all them, that fhame to ftaine their blood by treafons, or mifdemeanours; fhame alfo, to let their forefathers religion, holineffe, or vertues faile in them: but let them all fo liue in them, that with *Iaacob* they may *die in their fathers faith.*

Laftly, obferue how it is faid, they *died in faith:* they afore liued in it; but now their principall

cipall commendation is, *they died in it.*

Let vs learne here, to hold on in a good courfe when we haue entred into it; for conftancie and continuance is the true commendation : he that *dieth in faith*, is he that receiues the crowne. To this ende, let vs ftirre vp our felues with the Apoftles exhortation, Gal.6.9. *Let vs not be weary,of well doing, for in due time we fhall reape, if we faint not.*

And further, let this teach vs all to choofe that faith to liue in (with thefe holy Patriarchs) that we may boldly die in. It is a true obferuation, that *Poperie is a good religion to liue in, but ours to die in.*The Papifts vfurpe this faying, and turne it the contrary way; but they haue as much right to it, as the thiefe to the true mans purfe. The libertie, the pardons, difpenfations, fanctuaries, the pompe and outward glory of their Church; and their fafting and outward aufterities, beeing fowle and fained hypocrifies, and indeede, open licentioufneffe : thefe and many things more, may allure any naturall man in the world, to liue in their religion; but when they come to die, then they all know, and fome confeffe, it is fureft and fafeft to die in our religion. Let vs therefore cheerefully, and comfortably,liue in that religion,and faith, wherein wee may fo boldly die, that euen our aduerfaries confeffe it to be fafeft.

Now followe the foure *effects*, and fruits of their faith.

The firft is this: that

> *They receiued not the promifes, but faw them afarre off.*

By *Promifes*,we vnderftand, firft,the promifes of the Land of *Canaan*. Secondly, the fpirituall promifes of the kingdome of Chrift. Thefe they did *not receiue*;that is, fully;though in part they did: for, true *faith* doth alwaies receiue, apprehend,and apply vnto it felfe truely, though not fully,the thing promifed.God faid, he would giue them the Land of Canaan : but they did not fully enioy and poffeffe it: So likewife, the *Meffias* was promifed vnto them; but they neuer faw his comming in the flefh, and yet they beleeued Gods promife,and died in that faith.

Where we may fee, the inuincible force of their faith, that cleaued faft vnto the promife of God, euen vnto death; though they neuer enioyed the things promifed in this life: which plainely condemnes our age of vnbeleefe, for we haue more accomplifhed vnto vs, then euer they had. *Abraham* neuer *faw Chrift*, but *afarre off*; yet we haue him exhibited in the flefh: we fee and knowe he liued and died, rofe againe, and afcended,and now makes continuall interceffion for vs: and we haue the true facraments, which fhall laft for euer pledges of him, and of life euerlafting by him. And for temporall promifes, we haue farre more accomplifhed vnto vs then euer he had. But though we goe before *Abraham* in the frui-

tion of Gods promifes, yet we come farre behinde him in *beleefe*; for faith worketh by loue, and loue is feene in true obedience: but generally, this is too true, men make no confcience of *obedience*; which fheweth vndoubtedly, that there is little found *faith* among vs.And it may be feared, that thefe notable men, *Abraham, Ifaac, and Iaacob*, fhall ftand in iudgement againft vs;to our further condemnation;for they neuer receiued the accomplifhing of Gods *promifes*, and yet they beleeued: but we doe fee the fame *fulfilled* and exhibited vnto vs, and yet we will not beleeue.

> *But fawe them afarre off.*

Here is the propertie of their faith, and the power of it: the promifes were afarre off, and yet they faw them.The phrafe here vfed,is borrowed from Mariners: who beeing farre on the fea, cannot defcrie townes, and coafts afarre off, but onely by helpe of fome tower or high place, which their eie will fooner difcerne, though it be afarre off; And fo *Abraham,Sarah, Ifaac, and Iaacob*, beeing long before the day of Chrifts incarnation, could not other waies fee Chrift, but afarre off, by the eie of faith, in the promifes of the Meffias: for, this is the property of faith, to make a thing abfent, to be prefent,after a fort: *Faith being the ground of things hoped for, and the euidence of things which are not feene.*

Here we may learne a difference betweene the Church in the *olde* Teftament, and in the *newe*. We in the *newe Teftament*, haue greater meafure of knowledge, more liuely difcerning of the Meffias, and a clearer light of vnderftanding, in the myftery of our faluation by Chrift, then the Church had, vnder the *olde Teftament :* howfoeuer they excelled in faith, yet in the knowledge, and difcerning of Chrift, they were inferiour vnto vs. And therefore,the Lord made this promife to the time of the Gofpel, long before: that then *the earth fhall bee full of knowledge of the Lord, as the waters that couer the fea.*And S. *Paul* prooues this performed, when he affirmeth of the Church of the new Teftament, 2. Corinth. 3. 18. *But all we as in a mirrour behold the glory of the Lord,with open face.* And Chrift,Ioh. 6. 45. *They fhall be all taught of God.*

If this be true, that knowledge fhould fo abound in the time of the Gofpell; then all *ignorant* perfons of this latter age of the world muft knowe,that they haue much to anfwer for at the laft daie of iudgement: for, God in the newe teftament hath made his Church to abound in knowledge, fo that their ignorance (for which they thinke God will holde them excufed) fhall be a bill of inditement againft them at the laft day, to their further condemnation : becaufe the light of the Gofpel is fo clearely, and plentifully reuealed in thefe daies; that whereas the moft excellent Patriarchs of all, could then but fee Chrift afarre off, the moſt ſimple may nowe ſee him neere vnto them.

Againe, where is more knowledge, there ſhould be more obedience: therefore it concerneth all thoſe that profeſſe themſelues to be Chriſtians, and ſubmit themſelues to heare and learne the word of God taught vnto them; not to content themſelues with bare *knowledge*, though it be neuer ſo much: But withall, to bring forth the fruits of *obedience* in their liues and conuerſations. For, though *Abraham, I-ſaac, and Iaacob*, in regard of faith did goe far before vs: yet ſeeing we haue more knowledge then they had in the Meſſias, we muſt labour to become like vnto them in the *obedience* of our liues: their faith was ſtronger then ours: but our obedience ſhould be greater thē theirs, becauſe we haue more cauſe to beleeue then they.

2.Cor.3.18.

S. *Paul* ſaith, *We all behold as in a mirrour, the glory of the Lord with open face*: And the ende thereof is this, that we may be *transformed into the ſame image from glory to glory, as by the ſpirit of the Lord*. So that the more *knowledge* we haue, the more *ſanctification* we ought to haue, and the more hatred of ſinne, and more obedience to Gods commandements. But, the more is the pitie, the caſe goeth farre otherwiſe with the world: for euen many among vs that are no Students by profeſſion, haue great and commendable *knowledge in religion*. But where is the fruite hereof in holy obedience to the Lawes of God? God by calling hath made vs a pleaſant vine: but the ſower Grapes of ſinne, are our ordinarie fruite, they be *the Graps of gall* (as *Moſes* ſaith). For Atheiſme, blaſphemie, contempt of Gods word and worſhip, with open profaning of Gods Sabbath, doe euery where abound; to omit the hainous crimes againſt the ſecond table, as oppreſſion, adulterie, and blood touching blood: for all which, we may iuſtly feare, that the Lord will either remooue his Candleſticke from vs, and ſo of a Church and people of God, make vs no Church; or elſe ſweepe vs away by ſome fearefull iudgement, as with the beſome of deſtruction, becauſe we *withhold the truth in vnrighteouſneſſe*, Rom. 1. 18. For better it were not to haue knowen the way of righteouſneſſe, then to turne from the holy commandement giuen vnto vs : let vs therefore ioyne with our knowledge obedience, that ſo we may ſhewe forth our faith in doing the duties of pietie vnto God, and of brotherly loue & Chriſtianitie, vnto our brethren. Thus much of the firſt fruit of their faith.

Deut.32.33.

The ſecond fruite of their faith is noted in theſe words; *And beleeued them*. Where, by *beleeuing*, we muſt vnderſtand not ſo much the act of faith, for that was noted before, as the growth and encreaſe of their faith: for the word imports a confirmation of their hearts, and a reſolution in aſſurance of the promiſes made vnto them: which is not vnuſual in Scripture: for *Paul* prayeth for the *Churches* who

had true knowledge, faith, and loue, *that they might increaſe and abound therein more and more*, Ephe. 3. 16. 17. Philip. 1. 9. 11. Coloſ. 1. 9. 11.

Here then we may obſerue in the example of theſe Patriarchs, that it is the duty and property of euery true beleeuer, to goe forward and encreaſe in faith, till he come to a full perſwaſion and aſſurance in Gods promiſes. All the gifts of God (and therefore *faith*) are the *Lords talents*, and euery true beleeuer is the Lords ſeruant, called to occupie therewith. Now God, hauing put his *talent* into any mans hand, doth require the *encreaſe* thereof, as the Parable ſhewes, Luke 19. 13. And this *Paul* teacheth: for praying for the *Epheſians* that they may goe on, and be *ſtrengthened by the ſpirit in the inner man*, Eph. 3. 16. he ſignifieth, that he that doth truely beleeue in Chriſt, muſt goe on *from grace to grace*, till he bee a tall man in Chriſt: as a child groweth from yeare to yeare, till he come to be a ſtrong man. The nature of faith is like vnto *fire*, which will not goe out ſo long as wood, or other fewell is put vnto it, but will take hold thereof, and growe vnto a greater flame; and ſo will faith growe vp to a full perſwaſion in all thoſe that conſcionably applie themſelues to the Worde and Prayer.

But goes the caſe thus with vs in the matter of faith ? Nay verily, generally it is farre otherwiſe : for many among vs haue no regard of faith at all, but thinke they may liue as they luſt, their good meaning will ſerue the turne: others, and thoſe not a fewe, are ſo farre from *going forward in faith*, that they are euery day worſe and worſe, and ſtill *goe backeward* more and more. A third ſort we haue, that will heare the word, and receiue the Sacraments; but yet their growth in grace is very ſlender, they ſtand at a ſtay, and profit little.

Now, howſoeuer it may be thought but a ſmall fault, not *to profit in Religion*: yet vndoubtedly it is a fearefull Iudgement of God, when the hearers of the word in any congregation are daily taught, and doe not profit thereby; and therefore the holy Ghoſt noteth thoſe *women to be laden with ſinne, which are euer learning, and yet neuer are able to come to the knowledge of the truth*, 2. Tim. 3. 7. If a child lately borne, like not well, nor growe, when it hath good keeping: the common ſaying is, that it is a *Changeling*. So, if a man heare the word of God, and do not encreaſe in knowledge, faith, and obedience, we may moſt truly ſay of him, that he is a *ſpirituall Changeling*, and therefore to auoide this fearefull iudgement of God, we muſt labour for faith; and hauing gotten faith, *encreaſe therein*, and in other graces of God, *till we come to be ſtrong men in Chriſt*.

It is here ſaid, that thoſe Patriarchs encreaſed in faith : But it may be demaunded, how and by what meanes they did attaine hereto?

Anſ. In the booke of Geneſis, we may finde three wayes, whereby they were confirmed in the faith, and did grow vp in grace. The firſt meanes was from God himſelfe; for, when he had made his couenant with *Abraham*, mercifully renuing the ſame, during his life, as occaſion ſerued ſundry times, he ſtayed not there, ſuffering it to die with *Abraham*: but when *Abraham* was dead, God renued his couenant with *Iſaac* and *Rebecka*: and with *Iaacob* alſo after them. Now the tongue of man cannot vtter, what a wonderfull furtherance it was vnto their faith, to haue the Lord himſelfe to renue his gracious promiſes vnto them. The ſecond means of *encreaſing their faith*, was, their holy conuerſing one with an other: for the manner of the *Patriarchs*, was to teach and inſtruct their children, and to nurture them vp in the true worſhip and feare of God; by which meanes they did not onely implant Gods promiſes in the hearts of their children, but were themſelues confirmed in the ſame: for, he that teacheth another from a feeling heart, greately ſtrengtheneth his owne ſoule. Now God himſelf doth teſtifie this thing of *Abraham*, ſaying, *I know him, that he will commaund his ſonnes and his houſhold after him, that they keepe the way of the Lord, to doe righteouſneſſe and iudgement.* Now looke what *Abraham* herein did to *Iſaac*, that no doubt did *Iſaac* vnto *Iaacob*. The third meanes to encreaſe their faith was, from each one to himſelfe: for they gaue themſelues oftentimes in their owne perſons to muſe and meditate vpon the promiſes of God: ſo it is ſaid of *Iſaac*, that he *went out to pray or meditate in the field towards euening*: and we may perſwade our ſelues it was concerning this and other promiſes of God, and the accompliſhment thereof. And wee neede not to doubt, but that *Abraham* and *Iaacob* did the like.

These are the meanes, by which theſe godly Patriarchs were ſtrengthened in their faith. All which, muſt be marked of vs diligently, and put in practiſe: for, the cauſe why we heare the word often, and yet profit little by it, is chiefly this; becauſe the means by which men ſhould growe vp in faith, are ſo ſlenderly vſed among vs. For, the firſt meanes, which is on Gods behalfe to man; is through his great and vnſpeakable mercie, plentifully affoorded in many parts of the Land, in the holy Miniſterie of the goſpel: wherein Gods gracious promiſes of mercie, are opened and applied to mens hearts, and his iudgements againſt ſinne ſharpely denounced, to driue men to lay hold on Gods mercie in Chriſt. But, if we regard the ſecond meanes; which is, mutuall inſtruction, of father to child, of maſter to ſeruant, and of one neighbour to another; together with mutuall conference, about that we are taught; Or elſe if we regard the third meanes; which is, priuate meditation vpon Gods word and promiſes taught vnto vs; (which meditation, is to a Chriſtian ſoule,

Gen. 18. 19.

Gen. 24. 63.

like the chewing of the cudde vnto a beaſt; for as the chewing of the cudde turnes that which was eaten, into true feeding; ſo doth holy meditation, make Gods word, and promiſes, ſpirituall refreſhing, by digeſting them in the heart): If (I ſay) we take a view of theſe two latter, we ſhall finde them ſeldome vſed of very many, or not at all. Bleſſed be God, we neede not to doubt, but there be ſome, who vſe theſe meanes, with care and reuerence: but alas, theſe ſome, are very fewe. And becauſe this dutie is ſo ſlackely performed; hence it is, that though the couenant of mercie in Chriſt, be oft repeated, yet men reape little profit by it. So that we muſt learne to follow this notable practiſe of theſe godly Patriarchs, and looke what meanes they vſed for the increaſe of their faith; the ſame alſo muſt we vſe, and that diligently: ſo ſhall wee growe, and increaſe, and waxe ſtronge in faith, as they did.

The third fruite of their faith, is this,

*And receiued them
thankefully.*

Ασπασάμενοι, the word in the originall ſignifieth, *to ſalute*; and that not onely by ſpeach, but any way elſe: as by imbracing, &c. and therefore in this place, is not vnfitly tranſlated, *And receiued them thankefully*; that is, they tooke them kindely at Gods hands.

This is a notable fruite of faith, whereby they are commended; that *ſeeing the promiſes of God afarre off*, did yet take them moſt kindely at Gods hands. But here we muſt conſider, how they tooke them kindely: namely, by doing two things. 1. By an action of their heart. 2. By an action of their life. The action of their heart was this; that howſoeuer the promiſe was not accompliſhed in their dayes; yet they were wonderfully glad thereof: for our Sauiour Chriſt ſaid to the Iewes, *Your father Abraham reioyced to ſee my day, and he ſaw it, and was glad.* It did *Abrahams* heart good to ſee Chriſt afarre off: and ſo we may ſafly thinke of *Sarah*, *Iſaac*, *and Iaacob*, that their hearts were alſo rauiſhed with ioy, to heare the wonderfull promiſe of God, concerning the Meſſias; and to thinke of the moſt ioyfull performance, which they knew ſhould follow in due time.

Secondly, they tooke this promiſe kindely by the practiſe of their life; for when they came to any ſtrange place (as we may often read in the ſtory) there they built *vp altars*, and offered ſacrifice vnto God, and called on his name: All which they did, to teſtifie their inward ioy, and thankefull acceptance of Gods promiſes in Chriſt, and of the promiſed land, though neither were accompliſhed in their dayes.

Now, as touching our ſelues, the ſame maine promiſes of God, that were made to *Abraham*, *Iſaac, and Iaacob*, hath the Lord made and continued vnto vs: nay, wee haue the ſame alreadie *accompliſhed*; & we ſee the ſame veriſi

Ioh. 8. 56.

Gen. 12. 8. &
22. 9. & 33. 10.

ed more euidently and plainely, then any of the Patriarchs did. Which beeing true, our dutie is to take the same much more thankefully, and kindly, at Gods hands, then they did or could do; becaufe we haue more light and knowledge in the promifes of God, then euer the Patriarchs had.

But we haue iuft caufe to bewaile the dayes and times wherein we liue: for, whereas we fhould take the promifes of God moft ioyfully, and kindly; the cafe is farre otherwife. For generally, it may be faid of our nation and people, that in regard of the mercies and promifes of God, we are an *vnkinde people*. And that this is true (for the moft part) in all of vs, if we will but a little examine the matter, we fhall finde it too apparant, by many euidences: for firft, let any of vs be brought to a place, where we may behold fome vaine Enterlude, or Showe; a man would not thinke how wonderfully we are rauifhed therewithall, fo as we could finde in our hearts to fpend whole dayes in beholding them. But let vs be brought to heare the *Gofpel* of Chrift, his holy word preached and taught; as it was vnto *Abraham, Ifaac, and Iaacob* (wherein they much reioyced) and there we fit heauy and drowfie, fo as the word feemes loathfome vnto vs, and one houre is fo tedious, as we hardly hold it out without fleeping : and if it paffe the houre a little: O how impatiently our nature takes it! All which fhew plainly, that we haue no fuch ioy to heare of Chrift, and his mercifull promifes, as thefe godly Patriarchs had : fo that we are both hard hearted, and vnkind; and altogether infenfible of fo great fauours of our God towards vs.

Secondly, confider mens behauiour in Gods worfhippe : It is euident, that the greateft part of people, worfhip God but in formall fhewe, for fafhions fake. Thefe godly Patriarchs, *Abraham*, *&c.* built *altars* in euery place where they came, and offered *facrifice* vnto God, to fignifie their kindneffe, and willing heart, towards God for his promifes. But now men worfhip God formally, not in way of thankefulneffe; but either becaufe the *Law* compels them to it, or elfe becaufe it is a cuftome, and order which muft be kept. For proofe thereof take fome one of the common fort, and afke him why he commeth into the congregation? he will fay, he commeth to doe as other men doe; but what they doe, he knoweth not; nor what he himfelfe ought to doe, he cannot tell, nor careth much to know. Others alfo come to worfhip God: but afke them how they doe it, they will fay, by the faying ouer the tenne Commandements, the Lords praier, and the Beleefe. But, if the word be either *preached*, or *read*, they regard it not; thinking all Gods worfhippe ftands in the repeating of thofe three things. Which fheweth, that they worfhippe God but for fafhion fake, and with little more, then a plaine lip-labour.

Another fort there are, which come neere to God with their lipps, but their hearts are farre from him; for though their bodies be prefent in the congregation, yet their hearts are wandring about their worldly bufineffe, or the workes of finne: fo that we may truely fay, God is not worfhipped with faith, in the heart. And therefore we are an vnkinde people, and quite degenerate from the faith of our forefathers, thefe holy Patriarkes, who receiued Gods promifes fo kindly, and thankefully.

Thirdly, we haue the word of God daily preached and taught vnto vs: but how many be there that make confcience of obeying the fame in their liues and callings? Men doe come and heare, and fhould learne: but when they come home, they do flat contrary to that which is taught. Now there can be no greater vnthankefulneffe nor vnkindneffe towards God then this, that men fhould *heare* and not *obey*, *for difobedience is as the finne of witchcraft*: nay, [margin: 1.Sam.15.23.] the Lord himfelfe faith, that he that maketh no confcience of obedience in his life, is in his actions of Gods worfhip, no more acceptable vnto God, then a murtherer is *when hee killes a man.* [margin: Ifa.66.3.]

Wherefore, feeing obedience is fo rare to be found among vs, and difobedience aboundeth euery where, it is a plaine argument, that we take not the promifes of God kindely nor thankfully at his hands: for if we did, we would at leaft endeauour our felues, to doe what God commaunds in his Law, and defireth in his Gofpel, and fo be thankefull vnto God for his mercies, fhewing forth our thankefullneffe by our obedience. So that it ftandeth vs in hand, euery man to looke vnto himfelfe for his owne part, feeing God hath giuen vs his Gofpel the meanes of our faluation, that therefore we receiue and embrace the fame, leaft God doe either take the fame from vs, or vs from it: for, we may be fure that the one of thefe two will followe, if we doe daily heare and make no confcience to obey. And thus much of the third fruite of the Patriarchs faith.

The fourth fruite of their faith followeth: *And confeffed, that they were ftrangers and Pilgrimes on the earth.*

Herein we are to confider diuers points : 1. The Text faith, *They confeffed*; that is, they profeffed openly, what they were, and what their religion was; and that not onely amongft themfelues, but before the face of Gods enemies, and heathen men. Gen. 23.4. *Abraham* tolde the people of the Land of Canaan, that *he was a ftranger and a forainer among them.* And when *Iacob* came before *Pharaoh*, hee confeffed, that both *his dayes, and the dayes of his Fathers, were dayes of Pilgrimage*: Gen. 47.9. Now, affirming fo openly that they were ftrangers in thofe Countries, they intimated a plaine deniall and diflike of the religion and Idolatrie of thofe heathen Countries, and proclaimed themfelues to be of another religió: fo that this is true which here is said of them, that they made *confession* and profession of their estate and their faith, and that to the enemies of God.

Hence we learne, that we are not to be ashamed of that holy profession of *Christian religion* to which we are called. Our calling is to professe the Gospel and religion of Christ; now to many it is a reproach and ignominie: but we must learne this speciall lesson by the example of these men; that howsoeuer the world indge of *Christ* and his religion, yet we hauing entred into this holy profession, and beeing called hereunto, must neuer be ashamed of it; much lesse denie or forsake the same. In the primitiue Church it was a contemptible thing both among the *Iewes*, and Grecians to be a Christian: to the one, the Gospel was a stumbling blocke, to the other a laughing-stocke, 1.Cor. 1. 23. And yet *Paul* professed openly, *that he was not ashamed of that holy Gospel*: Rom. 1. 16 And so it ought to be with vs: we professe Christs religion, and therefore we must not be ashamed of it. Some there be that knowe but little, and yet haue a good minde to religion; but when they see some doe nothing else, but make a *mocke* and a iest of religion, they are thereby daunted and held back from the open profession, and embracing of it.

But if we looke to be saued by *faith*, as these men were, we must learne by their example, not to be ashamed of the profession of Christianity, whereto we are called: but must follow this notable example of *Abraham* and the Patriarchs, who were not ashamed, nor afraid to testifie their profession among the Heathen, whensoeuer any occasion was offred: for *whosoeuer is ashamed of Christ in this world, Christ will be ashamed of him at the last Iudgement; before his Father in the world to come*, Luke 9. 26.

To goe further: These Patriarchs professe two things: 1. That they were *strangers*. 2. That they were *Pilgrims*. A *stranger*, is one that hath his abode not in his owne, but in a strange Country, though he trauaile not.

And a *Pilgrime* is one that is a going thorough a forraine Country to his owne home. *Abraham, Isaac*, and *Iaacob* were *strangers*, because they dwelt as strangers in Tents, not in their owne Countries where they were borne; but in that strange Country, whither God had called them; and they were *Pilgrimes*, because they were alwaies readie to goe whithersoeuer God would call them: and in all places wheresoeuer they were, still they waited on God, and sought to him for the kingdome of heauen.

Now this was not proper to these Patriarchs, but is also common to all Christians, that looke to be saued by the same faith: for *Dauid*, long after them, confesseth vnto God, Psal. 39. 12. that he is a *Stranger and a Pilgrime, or soiourner with him, as all his Fathers were*. And euen

we also must follow their faith in the practise of this profession: dwelling here on the earth, we must testifie and professe our selues to be both *Strangers* and *Pilgrimes*.

But how (will some say) shall we be answerable to this profession? *Answ*. For the practise hereof, we must doe these three things: 1. We must *vse this world and the things thereof, as though we vsed them not*, 1. Cor. 7. 31. The temporall blessings we here enioy, we must so vse, as though they were not ours; but as strangers doe, onely for the present occasion: but we must not set our hearts thereon. And the rather to perswade vs hereunto, let vs consider the practise of these godly *Patriarchs*. They had the promise of the Land of *Canaan* distinctly and absolutely; so as no man in the world hath more right to any thing that he possesseth then they had to this land; yet when they came into it, they enioyed it and all things therein as *strangers*; and possessed nothing, but did euen buy ground to bury their dead in. And so must we vse the things that we haue in this world: for our houses, we must vse them as *Strangers* doe an Inne: and for our goods, we must vse them as *Pilgrimes* do other mens goods, where they stay for a night: we must so vse them alwayes, as beeing ready aud willing to leaue them the next morning or at any time when God shall call vs away.

Secondly, we must cast off all things in this world, that may any whit hinder vs in our iourney to the kingdome of heauen; like vnto good trauailers, who will carie nothing with them in the way, but that which may further them to their iournies end; and if any thing hinder them in the way, they will cast it from them, and rather loose it then be hindred from their home. But what is that which is burdensome vnto vs in this our iourney to heauen? This S. *Paul* sheweth, when he saith, 2. Tim. 3. 6. that certaine simple *women are laden with sinne*. Behold, sinne is that that ladeth vs: and the Author to the Hebrewes, calleth *sinne the thing that hangeth on so fast; and presseth vs downe:* (Heb. 12. 1.) Therefore if we will be good trauailers, and pilgrimes toward the kingdome of heauen, we must take heede of all sinne; for that will hold vs downe, that we cannot goe one step forward, but will drawe vs backeward vnto hell: for, the *way is straite that leadeth vnto life, and the gate narrow, and fewe there be that can enter into it*, Matth. 7. 13. He that would come hither, must come with an humble and pure heart: for the gate will not suffer any that is laden with sinne, to enter therein. The proud man, whose heart is puffed vp with pride: and the couetous man, whose heart is enlarged with a desire of gaine: the ambitious man, who is with child with worldly pomp and state: and the luxurious and voluptuous man, who fattes himselfe with earthly and carnall pleasures: all these are growne too bigge to enter into this straite gate. But the meeke in spirit, who lead an humble and innocent life, these shall tread in this path, though it be narrow, and enter in at this doore, though it be straite. And therefore, we must cast off euery sinne, by the practise of true repentance; and so make our selues fit pilgrimes for the way to heauen.

Thirdly, we must learne contentation of heart, in euery estate of life: which God shall send vpon vs: we must be contented as well in sicknesse, as in health; in pouerty, as in plenty; in trouble, as in peace; and in good report, and ill report; and in all estates of life & death. A pilgrime in his way taketh all things patiently, that befall him; and if he be iniured any way, he puts it vp quietly, without seeking reuenge or making complaint, til he come home; where he knowes he shall haue audience, and redresse. Euen so must we behaue our selues in this our pilgrimage to heauen; in hope of that redresse and rest we shall haue, we must beare all things patiently, that befall vs in this life, which is the way: and doing these three things, we shall become good *pilgrimes and strangers* in this world.

Here two questions offer themselues to be considered. First, if euery man both in profession and practise, must shewe himselfe to be a *pilgrime and stranger* in this world. Whether then, is it not a good state of life, for a man to contemne the world, and all things in it, and to betake himselfe to perpetuall beggerie, and voluntarie pouerty? *Answ.* The world in Scripture is taken diuers wayes: first, for the *corruptions* and *sinnes* in the world; and these must be contemned by all meanes possible: yea, that is the best religion, which teacheth best how to contemne these; and he the best man, who most forsakes them, in what calling soeuer he liues.

Secondly, for *temporall blessings*, as money, lands, wealth, sustenance, and such like outward things, as concerne the necessarie or conuenient maintenance of this naturall life. And in this sense, the world is not to be contemned, for in themselues, these earthly things are the good gifts of God, which no man can simply contemne, without iniurie to Gods disposing hand and prouidence, who hath ordained them for naturall life.

The Papists esteeme it an Angelicall state of perfection, approaching neere to the state of glorie, when a man forsaketh all, and betakes himselfe to voluntary pouertie; as begging Friers doe: But indeed it is a meere deuise of mans braine, and hath no warrant in Gods word, which decreeth thus; that he that will not labour (in some lawfull calling) shall not eate. *Obiect.* But here they will say, that our Sauiour Christ speaking to the yong rich man, bad him *goe and sell all that he had; and giue to the poore, and he should haue treasure in heauen.* Mar. 10. *Answ.* That commandement was not ordinarie, but speciall, belonging to that young man: It was a commaundement of triall, giuen to

him onely, as this was to *Abraham*, when God said, *Abraham kill thy sonne*, Gen. 22. 2. And the reason of that commaundement, was peculiar to him; namely, to shew him his corruption, and to discouer his hypocrisie. Againe, howsoeuer the yong man was commanded *to sell all*, yet he is not commanded *to giue all*; but onely thus, *Sell all, and giue to the poore.* 2.*Obiect.* Againe they obiect, that Christ himselfe was a beggar, and his Disciples also, and had nothing of their owne, but went vp and down the world, as beggars: and liued of that which others ministred vnto them. *Answ.* This is a meere forgerie, and cannot be prooued out of the word of God. The bagge which *Iudas* caried, doth prooue the contrary: for, he was (as it were) the steward in Christs family, who looked to their prouision, and to their contribution to the poore: as may be seene, Ioh. 13. 27. 28, 29. Yea Christs Disciples, though they left the *present vse* of their houses, and places: yet they gaue not ouer their title and possession in them: for, Christ went to *Peters* house, where he healed his wiues mother, Math. 8. 14. And after the time of Christs passió, *Peter* & the other *Disciples*, returned to their ships againe, and became fishers for a time. For Christ (Iohn 21.) after his resurrection, appeared to them while they were fishing.

2.*Quest.* Whether may a man lawfully seeke to be rich, seeing we must professe our selues to be *pilgrimes and strangers* in this life? *Ans.* Riches are taken two wayes: 1. for things *sufficient.* 2. for *aboundance.* For the first, by things sufficient, I meane things necessary and meete for a mans estate, to maintaine him and his family: and thus a man may seeke to be rich: for, so we are taught to pray in the fourth Petition, Giue vs this day our daily bread, that is, things meete and needefull for the day. From whence I reason thus: That which we may lawfully aske at Gods hands, we may lawfully seeke for: But we may lawfully aske of God all *things necessary* to this life; Therefore we may lawfully vse the meanes to attaine vnto them. And this *Agurs* prayer sheweth also, *Giue me not pouertie, nor riches, feede me with food conuenient for me.* Where we see, it is requisite a man should labour for things necessary to this life. Now, because mans corrupt nature is so gripple, that he would not be contented with the whole world though it were all his; therefore we must learne this rule of contentation for worldly things: namely, to follow the counsell of wise and godly men, who are neither couetous, nor riotous; but rest contented with that which is sufficient. As for the wearing of apparell, we haue no speciall rule, nor precept in Gods word: and therefore our direction, must be the example and fashion of the most graue and godly, in that calling whereof wee are; whose president must be our direction in all cases, whereof we haue no precept nor rule in Gods word.

But if riches be taken in the second sense, for

Prov. 30. 8.

aboundance, aboue that which is competent and ſufficient; then it is not lawfull for a man _to ſeeke_ to be rich: for proofe hereof, we haue the plaine teſtimony of the word of God ; _Paul_ ſaith, Tim. 6. 8, 9. _When we haue foode and raiment, we muſt therewith bee contented : for they that will be rich, fall into temptation , and ſnares,and into many fooliſh and noyſome luſts, which drowne men in perdition and deſtruction._ Where, the Apoſtle doth not ſimply condemne a rich eſtate , but rather the deſire to be rich, that is,a deſire to haue more then is neceſſarie for the maintaining of a mans eſtate. Yet this is the common ſinne of the world, men are ſo couetous that they will not be contented with that which is enough, but ſtil toile & moile for more;till they haue gotten ſo much vnder their hands, as would honeſtly and ſufficiently maintaine ten men of their eſtate and calling.But all ſuch are condemned, by the teſtimony of the holy Ghoſt,in the place afore named.

Queſt. What if God giue aboundance to a man,by lawfull meanes;what muſt ſuch a man doe? _Anſw._ When God ſendeth riches in aboundance to any man,he muſt thinke himſelfe to be appointed of God, as a ſteward ouer thē, for the good diſpoſing of them to the glorie of God,and the good of his Church ; alwaies remembring this rule of the Prophet _Dauid_,Pſal. 62. 10. _If riches increaſe, ſet not thy heart on them._ He ſaith not,If riches increaſe, refuſe thē; but,ſet not thy heart on them:and thus much of theſe Queſtions.

Now this practiſe of the _Patriarchs_ is as neceſſarie for vs in theſe dayes,as euer it was ; for the cauſe why we profit little after much hearing of Gods word,is this : we haue not behaued our ſelues like _Pilgrimes and ſtrangers_ in this world , but the _cares_ of the things _of this life haue choaked it vp_, Matth.13. 12. that it could take no ground, nor roote in our hearts: when we haue heard the word we remember it not, becauſe our hearts & the affections thereof,are ſet on the pleaſures and commodities of the world.We therefore muſt ſhake off this filthy ſinne, and learne to behaue our ſelues like _Pilgrimes and ſtrangers_, not intangling our ſelues with the things of this life , but _vſing them as though we vſed them not_,ſo as they bee no hinderance to the growth of Gods graces in vs.

For they that ſay ſuch things, declare plainly that they ſeeke a Country.

In the former verſe,was ſet downe the conſtancie of _Abraham, Sarah, Iſaac , and Iacob_, in the faith. Now in the 14. 15. and 16. verſes, the holy Ghoſt proceedeth to amplifie and inlarge the commendation of their perſeuerance in the _faith_ : for the ſcope of all theſe verſes, is to prooue, that all theſe particularly were _conſtant in the faith_ vnto the ende. The proofe is made by one ſubſtantiall reaſon; the ſumme whereof is this : _Abraham, Sarah, Iſaac, and Iacob, ſought for their Countrey,_

which was heauen,and therefore they were conſtant in the true faith.

But ſome may thinke that this reaſon is not ſubſtantiall, for men may ſeeke for heauen that neuer had true ſauing faith. As , _Balaam deſired that his ende might bee like the ende of the righteous_, Numb. 23.10. wherewith no doubt hee deſired the ſtate of the _righteous_ after this life.

I anſwer,that this deſire of _Balaams_ was not grounded vpon any conſtant perſwaſion , nor ſettled reſolution, but vpon ſome ſodaine motion. Secondly, though hee deſired _to die the death of the righteous_, yet he would not _liue the life of the righteous:_ he had no delight to walke in the way to come to that end which they walked in; without which, no man ordinarily can come to it.

Yet further ſome will ſay, _Many ſhall ſeeke_ (as our Sauiour Chriſt ſaith) _to enter in at the ſtraite gate of the kingdome of heauen, and ſhall not be able_ , Luke 13. 24. Therefore to ſeeke for heauen is no ſufficient argument of true _faith._

Anſwer. True indeede, many ſhall ſeeke to come to heauen, and ſhall not be able to enter; becauſe they ſeeke when the dore of mercy is ſhut,and when the day of _grace_ is paſt:for there is a time of grace wherein the Lord will be found. Now if men ſeeke him not in this time, though they ſeeke him neuer ſo long after, yet they ſhall not find him.But the ſeeking of theſe _Patriarchs_,was a ſound and conſtant ſeeking, and ſo a notable fruite of their true _faith_. For 1. they ſought a _heauenly Countrey_ : 2. they ſought it in due time; not for a brunt, but thorough the whole courſe of their liues: 3. they went the right way; denying themſelues and their eſtate in this life, as being ſtrangers vpon earth ; and they were willing to forſake all things in this world to attain heauen,eſteeming it as their true dwelling place,and their eternall reſt.

Now more _particularly_, the holy Ghoſt diuideth this reaſon into two parts, and handleth the ſame ſeuerally : 1. he prooueth that _they ſought a Country_, in this verſe;and 2. that _this Country_ which they ſought,_was heauen it ſelfe_, verſe 15. 16. For the firſt part; that _they ſought a Country_,is thus prooued,

    They which ſay they are Pilgrimes and ſtrangers, they ſhewe plainly that they ſeeke a Countrey :

    But _Abraham, Iſaac and Iacob_ ſaide of themſelues, that they were _Pilgrimes and Strangers_ :

    Therefore they ſhew plainly that they ſeeke a Countrey.

The firſt part of this reaſon is euident in it ſelfe : for he that ſaith he is a _Pilgrime and a ſtranger_ in any place , ſheweth plainely that he is forth of his owne Country , and therefore ſeeketh one. The ſecond part of the reaſon is aſſumed from their confeſſion,in the end of the former verse; *and confeſſed, that they were Pil-grimes and ſtrangers on the earth:*from whence, the concluſion is laide downe in this 14. verſe, that *therefore theſe Patriarchs ſought a Coun-trey.*

In this reaſon obſerue, firſt, that the Author of this Epiſtle had diligently read the Hiſtory of *Abraham, Sarah, Iſaac,* and *Iacob,* penned by *Moſes* in the booke of Geneſis: and in rea-ding, had obſerued that which they particular-ly confeſſed of themſelues in many places, of that booke; namely, that *they were Pilgrimes and ſtrangers:* yea, alſo he gathered from their confeſſion, this moſt heauenly meditation, that *therefore they were not in their owne Countrey, but ſought another.* Theſe three things then the Author of this Epiſtle vſed about the holy Scriptures: *Reading, meditation,* and *obſer-uation.*

Whence we learne, that all Gods *Miniſters,* and thoſe which prepare themſelues to the *worke of the Miniſterie,* are diligently to reade and ſtudy the holy *Scriptures,* and to meditate therein. No doubt, the Author of this Epiſtle was *an Apoſtle,* and had moſt notable giftes by vertue of his calling, and yet hee beſtowed paines in viewing the particular words of *A-braham, Iſaac,* and *Iacob,* recorded by *Moſes* in the booke of Geneſis. *Daniell* alſo was an extraordinarie Prophet: yet (as we may reade) Daniel 9. 2. he ſtudied with admirable dili-gence the prophecies of *Ieremie* and *Ezekiel.* And *Timothie,* though he were *a Diſciple* (Acts 16. 1) and well learned, yet *Paul* chargeth him *to giue attendance to reading; to exhortation, and to doctrine,* 1. Tim. 4. 13. And *Ezekiel* is commaunded to *eate the role, and to fill his belly with it,* Ezekiel 3. 3. And Saint *Iohn* likewiſe is commaunded *to eate vp the little booke,* Reu. 10. 9; 10. which thing he did, all which ſtrongly inforce the former duty, ſhewing that Gods ſeruant in the Miniſterie, muſt as it were, eate vp Gods booke; that in iudgement and vnderſtanding, he may digeſt as farre as is poſ-ſible the deepe things of God, and the hardeſt places of the Scripture: here muſt hee lay his foundation, and hither haue recourſe from all other writings whatſoeuer, in any matter of doubt.

This direction is moſt neceſſarie for the *Schooles of the Prophets,* and for all *Gods Mini-ſters:* and yet notwithſtanding, the contrary practiſe beareth ſway in the world. For, in the Popiſh *Vniuerſities,* moſt of their diuines apply themſelues to ſtudy the bookes of certaine *ſchoole-men,* and the Expoſitors or Commen-ters thereupon. Theſe are applied day & night, though they be both many and large, and full of needleſſe quiddities, and oftentimes they be alſo publikely expounded, whereas in the mean time the Bible lieth neglected, or little regar-ded: wherein we may ſee the notable worke of the *Deuill,* and his malice toward the Church of God; for the Schooles of the Prophets are

the *fountaines* of learning. Now, when as Sa-than by this meanes, doth ſteale away from them the ſtudy of the Bible, & in ſtead thereof foiſteth in corrupt humane writings; hereby he poiſons the fountaines, to the danger of infect-ing the whole Church. And as this is cõmon in the places of Poperie; ſo likewiſe ſome fault is this way committed among vs that be Prote-ſtants; for many in their priuate ſtudies take li-tle paines in the booke of God, but apply themſelues wholly to the writings of men; as Councels, Fathers, Schoole-men, and other Expoſitors: & in the handling of the Scripture, they glorie more to prooue a point of doctrine by multiplicitie of humane teſtimonies, then by the written word. But the truth is, thus to doe, is to preferre the handmaide before the Miſtris: and as for the opening and expounding of Scripture by other Writers, it is no ſuch point of deepe learning: a man of ordinarie ca-pacity and diligence, may eaſily deliuer what others haue done before him. But to open the Scripture ſoundly and purely, as it ought to be, is of another nature then theſe men take it: and hereto the ſound ſtudie of the Text it ſelfe, wil prooue the beſt helpe, as they will confeſſe who haue tried moſt of all. And though the beſt mens workes bee but baſe ſtuffe to the pure word of God, yet the writings of holy men muſt not be contemned; but muſt be read and regarded in their place, for our fruniſhing and and enabling to the ſtudy of the Scriptures, for the helping of our knowledge and iudge-ment in the word of God: they that hold or practiſe the contrary, knowe not what helpes they bee, and what light they yeeld to many darke places of Scripture: But ſtill aboue and beyond, before and after all, the word of God muſt be eaten vp of vs, and ſtudied with all di-ligence.

Secondly, in that the Author of this Epiſtle noteth their particular ſentence, and by conſe-quence gathereth this meditation out of it, *that they ſought a Country;* Hereby all men are taught to exerciſe themſelues in hearing and reading all the places of the Bible: euen the Hiſtories of men therein; and out of the wordes to gather godly meditations. So *Paul* ſaith to the Coloſſians, *Let the word of God dwel plen-tiouſly in you,* Coloſſ. 3. 16. The Prophet *Da-uid* alſo noteth it for the property of a good man, *to meditate in the Law of God day and night:* And the practiſe of the bleſſed virgine *Mary,* is regiſtred as an exãple for vs to follow; that ſhee *kept all the ſayings of Chriſt in her heart.* But pitty it is to ſee, how reading the word of God is laid aſide; for it is ſo little pra-ctiſed, that men now-adaies will not bee at charge to buy a Bible: for bookes of Statutes, men will not onely haue them in their houſes, but at their fingers ends; but Bible they haue none: and if they haue, it lieth on the deske, or table, and they read it not; and if ſometime they *reade,* yet they neuer *meditate* thereon, as wee

are

Pſal. 1. 2.

Luk. 2 51.

are taught in this place.

Further, whereas the holy Ghoſt reaſoneth thus vpon theſe examples; *Abraham, Iſaac, and Iacob, were ſtrangers and Pilgrimes,* therefore *they ſought a Country:* Herein he teacheth vs this ſpeciall point, to wit; that a doctrine, though it be not expreſſed in plaine words in the Bible; yet being gathered thence by right and iuſt conſequence, is no leſſe to be beleeued and receiued, then that which is plainely expreſſed: and therefore they are farre to blame which miſlike theſe tearmes in Diuinitie, *perſon, nature, ſacrament, conſubſtantiall, trinitie, &c.* becauſe they are not expreſſed in the word. But they may with good conſcience and much profit be retained; becauſe, though not literally, yet in ſenſe and meaning they are contained in the Scripture, and may by iuſt conſequence bee gathered thence. And, we denie not tranſubſtantiation, becauſe the word is not in the Scripture; but becauſe the matter is not there: nor can by neceſſary conſequence be deriued from it, but rather the contrary.

Againe, many refuſe theſe doctrines, the *proceeding of the holy Ghoſt from the ſonne;* and the *baptizing of children,* becauſe they are not expreſſed in the Scripture. But hence wee anſwer, that though they be not expreſly ſet downe in ſo many wordes, yet by iuſt conſequence they may be ſoundly gathered out of Scripture, and therefore are true doctrines, no leſſe to bee beleeued, then that which is plainly expreſſed. And thus much of the firſt part of the reaſon.

And if they had beene mindfull of that Countrey, whence they came, they had leiſure to haue returned.

But now they deſire a better, that is an heauenly: Wherefore God is not aſhamed of them to be called their God. For he hath prepared for them a Citie.

Here the holy Ghoſt prooueth the ſecond part of the former argument, by 2. reaſons: the firſt, is contained in the 15. verſe, and the beginning of the 16. It is taken from the diſtinction of Countries, and may bee framed thus;

They either ſought an earthly Country, or an heauenly Country:

But not an earthly: *Therefore they ſought an heauenly Country.* The firſt part of this reaſon is cleare of it ſelfe. The ſecond part is in the 15. verſe: from whence followeth the concluſion in the beginning of the 16. verſe.

To come to the firſt part, in theſe wordes: *And if they had beene mindefull of the Country, &c.* That is, if they had regarded, or thought vpon Meſopotamia, or Chaldea, from whence they came, and where they were borne; with any deſire to haue enioyed the profits, or pleaſure thereof; they had leiſure enough to haue returned backe thither, by reaſon of the length of their daies which they liued, in the land whither God called them.

A | Here obſerue two points: Firſt, that they are not *mindefull* of (or, as the word imports) they *remember not the countrey from whence they came:* but when God gaue them commaundement to depart thence, and not to returne to Meſopotamia againe; after this commadement giuen, they came forth, and did forget their owne countrey.

Whence we learne, that howſoeuer vſually, *Forgetfulneſſe* be a vice; yet ſome kinde of forgetfulneſſe, is a notable vertue: namely, to forget the things that diſpleaſe God, and which he would not haue vs to thinke vpon. Pſal. 45. 9. The *Church* is commanded *to forget her own people, and her fathers houſe:* that is, her owne will and deſires; ſhe muſt neuer thinke thereof, (nor of any other thing whereby God is diſpleaſed) vnleſſe it be with diſlike.

B | This condemneth the practiſe of many aged perſons, in theſe daies, who delight themſelues among the yonger ſort, to tell of the bad practiſes of their youth; in wantonneſſe, contentions, and breaking Gods commaundements: But, in ſo doing, they ſinne grieuouſly; for, a man muſt not remember his ſinnes, but with diſlike, and deteſtation; beeing grieued with them, and angry with himſelfe for them; or elſe to teach others how to auoide them.

And as this kinde of *Forgetfulneſſe,* is a good vertue; ſo there is alſo a vertuous and good Remembrance: namely, to bee mindefull of that which may pleaſe God: as of Gods *Iudgements,* to be humbled thereby: and of his *Mercies,* to bee thankefull vnto Almightie God for them: and of his *Commandements,* to become obedient to his will. Theſe things therefore, wee ought to imprint by diligence in our memories.

C | Secondly, here obſerue, God calleth them out of their owne countrie, and biddeth them liue in the land of Canaan, as ſtrangers and pilgrimes; and ſo they doe, abiding there, without any purpoſe to returne; nay, they are not mindefull of their former home.

Hence we are taught, to be conſtant in that calling whereunto God hath called vs. It is a fearefull ſinne, for a man to goe backe from that calling, in which God hath placed him. When the Iſraelites abode not patiently and conſtantly with God in the wilderneſſe, but deſired to ſhake off the calling of God, and to returne to Egypt, there to ſit by the fleſh-pots againe; they had Gods hand vpon them grieuouſly: as we may read at large, Pſalm. 78. *Lots* wife, for looking backe, when ſhe was commanded to the contrary; was fearefully, and ſtrangely puniſhed, beeing turned into a pillar of ſalt, Gen. 19. 26. And our Sauiour Chriſt ſaith, Luk. 9. 62. *No man that putteth his hand to the Lords plough, and looketh backe againe, is apt to the kingdome of God.* As though he had ſaid, He that ſtarteth from the plough, is not fit for the field: no more is he that ſhifteth from his calling, fit for Gods ſeruice.

To

To apply this to our selues: God hath called vs to professe Christian religion, whence we are called *Protestants*; We therefore must professe the same constantly and hold it fast, without wauering or doubting (euen without beeing mindefull of that spirituall Egypt of darkenesse and superstition, whence wee are deliuered) much more, without turning to any other; this beeing the *true religion*, which is grounded on Gods word.

Againe, in this our calling of Christianitie, wee haue vowed vnto God for our selues, to renounce the flesh, the world, and the deuill. Now, this beeing our calling; as we haue promised, and vndertaken it: so we must obey it in our liues, fighting manfully euery day, against the world, the flesh, and the deuill. For, if we professe religion in word, and doe not obey it in deed; we make our selues vnfit for the kingdome of heauen. But alas, men are like to the *Swine* that returneth to the puddle, though he be washed neuer so cleane: and to the *Dogge*, that returneth to his vomite: for, most men do but serue the flesh, and the world, and the lusts thereof; therein is their ioy, and their hearts ease: take away these things from them, and take away their liues: so farre are they from seeking the kingdome of heauen, as these Patriarchs did.

Thus much for the first part of the reason.

Now followeth the second part, which is this; *But they sought not a place in earth*: and therefore the conclusion followeth, *That they desire a countrey, which is heauen*: in these words,

But now they desire a better.

But some will say, the Patriarchs were dead many hundred yeares, before this was written; How then can they bee now said, *to desire a countrey? Answ.* The Author of this Epistle, here obserueth, and followeth the manner of them that write Histories; who speake of things past long agoe, as though they were now present.

Now, it is said, *they desire a better countrey.* These Patriarchs had laid before them two countries, the Land of Canaan, and the kingdome of Heauen; and of these two, they might choose whether they would, to be their portion, and inheritance, vpon which they would bestow their hearts: Now, they esteemed heauen (though it was to come) better then Canan, though present; and therefore made choice of heauen, and longed for it.

Where we learne, that as we must be thankfull to God, for all his blessings; so among them all, we should choose the best. This *Dauid* doth: for beeing put to choose, whether he had rather liue in safe-guard, and in solace, with the wicked and vngodly; then in base estate, and in great danger, neere to Gods sanctuarie: He saith, Psal. 84. 10. *Hee had rather bee a doore-keeper in the house of his God, then to dwell in the Tabernacles of whickednesse.* And

Salomon is highly commended by the holy Ghost, 1. King. 3. 10. 11. for choosing a *wise and vnderstanding heart, before riches and honour. Moses* also (as we shall see afterward) had his choyce, whether he would liue gloriously, & at ease, in *Pharohs* court; or with the Church of God in aduersitie: now *Moses* hauing the gift of discerning, *refused to be called the sonne of Pharaohs daughter, and chose rather to suffer aduersitie with the people of God, then to enioy the pleasures of sinne for a season.* Which holy examples, doe all teach vs; that when God setteth before vs diuers sorts of his blessings, we in spirituall wisedome, must make choyce of the best. On the contrary, *Esau* had this choyce set before him; his brothers *red broth*, and his *birth-right*: but he chose the worse: and therefore, in the new Testament, the holy Ghost noteth him with this marke, to be *profane Esau* for his labour. And the Gaderens also are branded with a note of infamie to all ages, for choosing their *hogs* before *Christ*, and his saluation. And the like choyce is set before vs euery day: for God of his mercy, in the preaching of the word, for his part, doth set forth vnto vs *Christ Iesus* crucified: and in him, remission of sinnes, and saluation. Now, on the other side, commeth the deuill, and setteth before vs, all sorts of vaine pleasures, and delights; shewing to euery man those sinnes, to which he is giuen; and with them, all the profits or pleasures that vsually accompany such sinnes. Now, most men hauing this choyce set before them, doe leaue the true and substantiall blessings of God, and come to Sathans painted Pageants, and there make choyce of sinne, with those base companions that do attend her. This is too apparant to be denied: for, howsoeuer the word of God be preached vnto vs, and we doe heare the same, yet we preferre the vanities & pleasures of the sinnefull world, before *Christ crucified*: making no account of him, nor of our own saluation by him, in comparison of the present profits and pleasures of sinne. But we must pray to God to giue vs spirituall *wisedome*, and the gift of discerning, that now when God sets before vs things so farre differing, wee may haue grace to discerne betweene them: and withall, to preferre and make choise of the best, and to refuse the worst. But as for them that are so mad in their choise, that they now preferre sin before the blessings of God in *Christ*, they shal see the day, when they would wish themselues to be Dogges, Toades, or Serpents, rather then men and women: and yet (though they would be glad of that exchange of state) they shall neuer compasse it, but shall remaine woefull men and women for euermore, because that once they made so profane a choise: when the path of life was set before them, they chose the way of death rather then of life; and therefore when they would desire death, they shall not haue it, but shal liue a life more bitter for euer then any death in the greatest pangs.

Thus

Thus we see in generall their choise was of the better, Particularly the Text addeth,

That is, an heauenly.

In which words is laid downe the last and chiefe point in this reason, to wit, that the Patriarchs desired a better Country then the Land of Canaan, and that was an *heauenly Countrey,* euen heauen it selfe: the proofe whereof is principally intended in this place.

Now whereas the Patriarchs, beeing our fore-fathers in faith, and patternes whome wee must followe, *did desire heauen:* by their example euery one of vs is taught the same duty, to aime at another and a better *Country,* then that in which we liue, euen at the kingdome of heauen: and not to thinke that this world is the Country wee are borne for. This better Country we must all seeke for, whatsoeuer we be, high and lowe, young and olde, learned and vnlearned, if we will followe these godly Patriarchs. And this wee must doe not at death onely, seeking this world all our life long, for that is to despise heauen: but euen in the time of our youth, and strength of our daies, must we set our hearts on heauen: endeauouring so to vse this world, and the things thereof, that when we *die,* we may com to heauen, that blessed country, which we desired, and sought for in our liues.

And to perswade vs hereunto, consider the reasons following. First, worldly wisedome teacheth this: If a man dwell on his owne land, and in his owne house, he is carelesse: But if in another mans house, whereof he hath no lease, but contrariwise, is certaine to be put out, he knoweth not when: this man in time will prouide himselfe of another, that so he may remoue into it, and not be destitute: and if it be within his power, he will prouide a better, that so hee may not remooue for the worse. Beholde, while we liue in this world, our bodies are tents and tabernacles wherein our soules doe dwell, for a time: and besides, this time is vncertaine; for there is no man that can say certainely, he shall liue to the next houre. Therefore, we must euery one of vs, prouide for himselfe a dwelling place in heauen, where we may abide for euer, in all blessednesse.

Again, consider the state of all sorts of men in the world: for sinne, Atheisme, and profanenesse abound euery where, the blaspheming of Gods holy name, and the breaking of his Sabbath: besides daily sinnes against the second table. Now, all these are continually *for ven* geance, & for Gods iudgements to be inflicted vpon vs, and we know not how God will deale with vs for our sinnes: whether hee will take from vs our goods, and good name, our health, friends, or life it selfe: and therefore it standeth vs in hand to prouide for our selues a resting place, wherein we may abide for euer, after this fraile life full of misery is ended.

Thirdly, if we shall not doe this, marke what followeth: this, and no other, is our estate; By nature, we are the children of wrath, and of the deuill: and by our manifolde sinnes, we haue made our case farre worse: Now, what is due vnto vs, for this corruption, and for these transgressions? Surely, not heauen, but another place; euen the contrary, the place of eternall woe and destruction, the bottomlesse pit of hell. Now, if this be our due by nature, then let not sinne, nor Sathan deceiue vs; perswading vs, that we may come to heauen, and still continue in the state of our corrupt nature: but let vs labour by all meanes, to eschew this place, which is due vnto vs by nature; that thorough the gift of faith in Christ, wee may come to the heauenly citie, which these godly Patriarchs so seriously sought for. But if we remaine in our sinnes, and so die, wee are sure to goe to the place of destruction, and there to remaine in woe and torments, with the deuill, and his angels for euermore: so that it stands vs in hand, to vse all good meanes to come to heauen, or else our case will be the most miserable of all creatures; for, perdition & destruction will be our portion world without ende.

This must awake and stirre vp our dead and drowsie hearts, that are so besotted with sinne, that though we heare, yet we neither learn, nor practise. In worldly things, wee can take care and paines: but if we will doe any thing for our owne euerlasting good, let vs labour by all meanes to come to heauen; for if we misse of that citie, it had beene good for vs, we had neuer beene borne: or that wee had beene the vilest creatures in the world, rather then men. For, when the vnreasonable creatures die, there is an ende of all their miserie; but, if we die, and be not prepared for that place, our death will bee vnto vs the beginning of all woe and miserie.

Wherefore God is not ashamed of them to bee called their God, for he hath prepared for them a citie.

In these words is laid downe a second reason whereby is prooued, that these Patriarchs *died in faith, seeking their country in heauen.* The reason is drawen from the testimony of God himselfe, recorded by *Moses* in the booke of Exodus, where God saith, He is *the God of their Fathers, the God of Abraham, Isaac, and Iacob,* Exodus 3.61.

The exposition. Wherefore] that is, that this might appeare and be euident, that these Patriarchs died in the faith, and sought this Country of heauen, God was content to vouchsafe and grant vnto them this fauour, to be called their God.

Was not ashamed] To be, or not to be ashamed of one, properly belongs to men; and it cannot be affirmed properly of God, that *he is ashamed* or *blusheth* (as the word signifieth,) but the meaning is, that God vouchsafed vnto them this fauour, and shewed them this honour and dignity. *Quest.* What was this honour and dignity which he shewed vnto them? *Answer.* To

be

be called their God. By which is meant thus much, that God accepted them in his mercie, to be such, with whom he would make his couenant of saluation, and not with them alone, but with their seede after them. Secondly, that he chose them, to make the couenant in their names for all the rest. Thirdly, he vouchsafed them a speciall and extraordinarie fauour, euen that himself would beare their names, and they should beare his; making his glorious name renowned to the worlds end, by this title, *The God of Abraham, Isaac, and Iacob.* Hereupon the reason is framed thus; God would not bee called in speciall manner the God of vnfaithfull men, but rather would bestowe such a speciall fauour vpon Beleeuers: but that fauour did God vouchsafe to these three Patriarchs; therefore doubtlesse they liued and died in that holy faith.

In that it is said, *God was not ashamed to bee called their God;* Here first we learne, that God doth not vouchsafe his mercie equally to all men, but some men haue more prerogatiue in his fauours & mercies then others. *Kings* make choise among all their subiects, of some men, whome they will preferre to be of their counsel or guard, and to whome they will giue speciall countenance, and dispence their fauours more liberally then to all; Euen so God among all *Abrahams* kindred maketh choise of these three persons, *Abraham, Isaac, and Iacob,* to bestowe on them such speciall honour, as hee vouchsafed not to any of their fore-fathers afore them, nor posterity after them. No meruaile therefore though he bestowe not his speciall mercie vpon all, seeing he dispenceth not his inferiour fauours vnto all alike. And yet for all this, he is no *accepter of persons:* for, he onely is properly said, to bee an accepter of persons, that preferreth one before another, in regard of some quality in the person: but God vouchsafed this honour vnto these three, only of meere mercy and good will, and not for any thing hee respected in them.

This confuteth the conceite and errour of many men broched abrode in this age, that God doth equally loue al men as they are men, and hath chosen al men to saluation, as they are men, and hath reiected none: for (say they) it standeth with equity and good reason, that the Creator should loue all his creatures equally, and this opinion they would build vpon the generall promise made to *Abraham:* because that *in him* God said *all the nations of the earth should bee blessed,* Gen. 22. 18. But wee must vnderstand, that (All) is not alwaies taken generally, but sometime indefinitely for many: and so *Paul* speaking of this couenant of grace in Christ, saith; The Lord made *Abraham a father of many natiõs,* Rom. 4. 17. where repeating the couenant recorded by *Moses,* he putteth *many* for *all.* Againe, graunt that *Abraham* were the *father of all nations,* and that in him *All the kindreds of the earth were*

A | blessed: Yet it followeth not, that therefore God should loue *all men* equally and alike, for hee may loue the *faithfull* of all nations, and yet not loue *all men in all nations:* for, in his bountifull mercie in Christ, he preferreth some before others. And this answer seemes the better, because we may haue some reason to thinke, that God will saue of euery nation some, but no ground to imagine he will saue all of any nation: much lesse all of euery nation.

2. Here wee may see, *that God honoureth those his seruants that honour him,* as he saith to *Ely* the priest, 1. Sam. 2. 30. Which is a point to be marked diligently; for, this God is the glorious king of heauen and earth: yet he abaseth himselfe, and is content to be named by his Creature, aduancing them by abasing himselfe to be called their God, *the God of Abraham, Isaac, and Iacob.* Where we may apparantly see, rather then God wil not haue them honoured that honor him, he will abase himselfe, that they thereby may be honoured.

B |

Hence we may learne many things. First, that all that professe religion truly, must inure themselues to *goe through good report and ill report,* and in all estates to be content, for Gods honours sake: as *Paul* saith; *I haue learned in whatsoeuer state I am, therewith to be content: I can be abased, and I can abound; euery where, in all things I am instructed, both to be full, and to bee hungry; to abound, and to haue want.* Thus spake that holy man of God: and so must wee all endeauour to say, and accordingly to practise. And the reason is good, because if a man honor God, howsoeuer he be contemned, or not regarded in the world, yet God will honour him, and esteeme highly of him: that will prooue the way to all true honour, as it hath done, euen in this world to all that tried it.

C | Phil. 4. 11.

Secondly, hence we learne which is the true way to get sound honour amongst men; namely, to honour God. Good estimation in the world is not to bee contemned, for the Lord commaundeth all inferiours to honour their superiours, whereby he also bindeth euery man to preserue his owne dignity. Now God honoureth them that honour him; therefore the surest way to get true honour among men is this. Let a man first lay his foundation well, and begin with God, and set all the affections of his heart and thoughts on this, To honour God. *Quest.* How may a man honour God? *Ans.* By forsaking the rebellious wayes of sinne and vngodlinesse, and walking in the way of righteousnesse through the course of his life. This doth God take to be an honour vnto his high Maiestie. And when a man doth this vnfainedly, then God will honour him, euen among men, so farre forth as shall be for his good; for God hath all men hearts in his hand, and will make them to honour those that honour him: so S. *Paul* saith, *If any man therefore purge himselfe from these, he shall be a vessell vnto honour:* not onely in glorie eternall after death,

D |

2. Tim. 2. 21.

but

but alſo in grace & fauour with Gods Church. This confuteth the opinion, and condemneth the practiſe of many, who would faine haue good report in the world, and be ſpoken well of by all men:but what courſe(I pray you)take they to come by this good name?They doe not begin with God, and lay their foundation by honouring him; but they ſtriue to pleaſe men, whether it be by doing well or ill, they care not; their onely care is to pleaſe all: for, that is their rule and reſolution, all muſt be pleaſed, and becauſe moſt men are il,they rather chooſe oftentimes to doe ill, then they will not pleaſe the greater ſort. But he that beginneth to get honour by pleaſing men, beginneth at a wrong ende; for, by the teſtimony of the holy Ghoſt in this place the way to get ſound approbation before men, is firſt to begin with God, and to honour him.

Thirdly, if God will honour them that ho-nour him, then by the contrary,conſider what a miſerable caſe many a man is in:*For,thoſe that diſhonour God,God will diſhonour them againe;* as we may ſee at large,and very plainely, in the example of *Elie*, and his two ſonnes: for, *them that honour me*(ſaith the Lord vnto him) *I will honour, & they that deſpiſe me,ſhall be deſpiſed,* 1.Sam.2.30. And in Zachary we may read,that *the man that by blaſphemie, theft, or periurie, diſhonoureth God, the flying curſe of the Lord ſhall enter into his houſe, and remaine in the midſt thereof, and conſume it with the timber thereof, and the ſtones thereof;* Zach.5.4. And becauſe *Elie* did *more honour his children then God,* 1.Sam.2.31. therefore the Lord threat-neth the deſtruction both of him & his family: and according as the Lord had threatned,ſo it came paſſe.For when the Iſraelites fought with the Philiſtims (Chap.4.11.) his two ſonnes were ſlaine,and he at the hearing of the newes, *fell downe and brake his necke.*

Now, if this be ſo, what ſhall we ſay of our owne nation and people, amongſt whom it is as common to diſhonour God, as euer it was amongſt the Papiſts or Pagans;partly,by light vſing of his holy titles, and taking his name in vaine: and partly, by ſwearing, and open bla-ſphemie: and ſometime, euen by abhominable periurie. Nay, it is many mens rule, that they may ſweare, diſſemble, lie, and forſweare for aduantage. Theſe ſinnes are ſome of them rife in all ſorts of people,and hardly ſhall you talke with a man, that doth not by vaine othes di-ſhonour God: yea, it is ſo common, that chil-dren, ſo ſoone as they can crawle, or liſpe out a word; the firſt thing they can ſpeake, is to curſe, or ſweare, and take Gods name in vaine, whereby God is diſhonoured euery way: ſo as it is a wonder,that the earth doth not open and ſwallowe vp many men quicke, for their ſwea-ring & blaſphemy. And whereas Gods Iudge-ments are often grieuouſly inflicted vpon vs, in many places of the Land; we may perſwade our ſelues, that among other ſinnes it is for

our blaſphemy, and taking Gods name in vaine. And if it be not ſpeedily redreſſed, it is to be feared, leaſt God will raine downe his iudgements vpon vs, and in his wrath ſweepe vs all away; and take away the father with the child, the good with the bad, becauſe there is no reformation of ſo vile, and yet ſo needeleſſe a ſinne.

To be called their God.

Obſerue here further, that *Abraham,Iſaac, and Iaacob*, could all of them ſay, *God is my God.* Now that which theſe worthy Patriarchs could ſay of themſelues, we muſt euery one of vs in our owne perſons labour for;for, their ex-ample is and muſt be a rule for vs to followe. We therefore muſt labour for this aſſurance, by Gods grace to ſay, as theſe holy Patriarchs did ſay, *The true Iehoua is my God:*and of this I am reſolued, & vndoubtedly aſſured in mine own conſcience.

*Queſt.*How ſhall we be able to ſay vnfained-ly, God is my God? *Anſ.* By becomming his ſeruants and people in deede and truth; for, to him who is one of Gods people,God is alwaies his God. But how ſhall we become Gods true ſeruants? *Anſw.* By ſetting our hearts vpon the true God, and giuing them wholly vnto him, and to his ſeruice; and reſtraining our ſelues from all occaſions of ſinne, becauſe ſinne diſpleaſeth him. *Queſt.*But how ſhall a man ſet his heart wholly on God?*Anſw.* This he doth, when he loueth him aboue all, and feareth him aboue all, and aboue all things is zealous for Gods glory; when he hath full confidence in Gods word and promiſes, and is more grieued for diſpleaſing God, then for all things in the world beſides. Or more plainely thus: then a man doth ſet his heart on God, when his heart is ſo affected, that when God commaunds, he is alwaies ready to obey:So the Lord ſaith,Hoſ. 2.23. *I will ſay to them that were not my people, Thou art my people; and they ſhall ſay, Thou art my God.* And in the Pſalmes, the Lord ſaith, Pſal.27.8. *Seeke yee my face:* Then the holy mans heart, as an Eccho giueth anſwer, *I ſeeke thy face, O God.* And ſuch a one is the heart of him, that is indeede the ſeruant and child of God, and one of Gods people.

For he hath prepared for them a city.

Theſe words are a reaſon of the former, prouing that God was not aſhamed to be cal-led their God, becauſe he prepared a city for them. And indeede, this ſhewes euidently that God was greatly delighted with them, rather then aſhamed of them; for had he beene aſha-med of them, he would haue ſhut them out of his preſence. Herein therefore he declared his loue and fauour, that by preparing this citie,he procured that they ſhould liue in his ſight for euermore.

Hence we learne, that he which hath *God for his God,* hath all things with him; accor-ding to the common prouerbe, *Haue God,and haue all.* And on the contrary, *Lacke God,and lacke all.* And therefore *Dauid* ſaith, Pſal. 145. 15. *Bleſſed are the people whoſe God is the Lord.* Other things which here might be added, haue beene handled before.

Abrahams Faith.

VERSE 17.

By faith Abraham offered vp Iſaac, when he was tempted; and he that had receiued the promiſes, offered his onely begotten ſonne.

18. To whom it was ſaid, in Iſaac ſhall thy ſeede be called.

19. For, he conſidered that God was able to raiſe him vp, euen from the dead: from whence he receiued him alſo, after a ſort.

IN the former verſes, we heard the faith of *Abraham, Iſaac, and Iaacob* commended iointly together. Now the holy Ghoſt returneth to the commendation of their faith ſeuerally. And firſt, he beginnes with *Abrahams* faith; whereof, he had formerly propounded two works, or actions: 1. His going out of his owne Country. 2. His abode in a ſtrange Land. Now, here followeth the third, which is the moſt notable worke of all, wherein his faith ſhines moſt gloriouſly; and his example herein is vnmatchable. The particular points herein, are theſe: 1. The worke of his faith is plainely laid downe, *in his offering vp of Iſaac.* 2. The ſame worke of faith is notably commended, by three ſpeciall arguments; to wit, 1. by three great impediments that might haue hindered this worke of faith: as we ſhall ſee in their place, v. 17. 18. 2. by his victory ouer theſe impediments, v. 19. 3. by the iſſue of this temptation, and his work of faith therein, in the ende of the 19. ver.

For the firſt. The fact of *Abrahams* faith here commended, is this: *That he offered vp Iſaac his ſonne.* It may firſt of all be demaunded, How *Abraham* could offer vp his ſonne *by faith,* conſidering it is againſt the Law of nature, and the law of God, for a man to kill his owne ſonne: which *Abraham* muſt doe, if he did offer him vp in ſacrifice vnto God. For anſwer hereunto, we neede goe no further then the Story, Gen. 22. where we may ſee, he had

a ground for his faith: for though the generall comandement be, *Thou ſhalt not kill,* yet he had a ſpeciall commandement, *Abraham, kill thy ſonne:* and by vertue of that, he did it: and did it in and by faith. But if that be ſo, then thereupon riſeth another and a greater doubt: namely, How can theſe two commandements ſtand together, one beeing contrary to the other? *Anſ.* Here a ſpeciall point is to be obſerued: namely, that whenſoeuer two commandements are ſo ioyned, that a man cannot practiſe both, but doing the one, the other is broken; then one of them muſt giue place to the other: For, howſoeuer all Gods commandements binde the conſcience: yet ſome binde it more, ſome leſſe, becauſe ſome are greater, and ſome leſſer then others. Whence this rule may be ſet downe; that when two Commandements of God croſſe one another, then a man muſt preferre the greater. As for example this is Gods Commandement, *Honour God,* commanded in the firſt Table. Againe, the 5. Commandement ſaith, *Honour Parents and Magiſtrats.* Now, if parents or magiſtrates command any thing, the doing whereof would diſhonour God, beeing contrary to the firſt table; then the 5. Commandement giueth place vnto the firſt: and a man muſt rather diſobey magiſtrates and parents, then diſhonour God: for, the maine duties of the firſt table, take place before the maine duties of the ſecond. And therefore Chriſt ſaith, *If any man come to me, and hate not his father and mother, wife and children, brethren and ſiſters, yea, and his owne life alſo, he cannot be my diſciple;* meaning, that if father or mother, wife or children would drawe vs from God, we muſt hate them rather then diſobey God. Againe, a commandement *ceremoniall,* and a commandement *of loue and mercie* concurre together, and it ſo falleth out, that they ſhould be both keept, and cannot: in this caſe therefore the ceremoniall Law of the firſt table, muſt giue place to the Law of Charity and Loue in the ſecond table: becauſe the ceremonies are the inferiour duties of the firſt, but charitie and mercie the principall duties of the ſecond table: For example, the Lord enioyneth vs in the fourth commandement to reſt on the Sabbath day. Now it falls out, that our neighbours houſe is on fire vpon the Sabbath day: whether then may I labour with my neighbour that day to ſaue his houſe? *Anſ.* I may; for the ſtrict obſeruation of reſt on the Sabbath day, is a ceremonie: but the quenching of fire in my neighbours houſe, is a worke of mercie, and a maine duty of the ſecond table, and therefore muſt take place before a ceremoniall duty of the firſt table.

Thirdly, God hath giuen vs tenne commandements, concerning all ordinary duties both of pietie and of mercie: yet if God giue vs a particular and ſpeciall commandement contrary to any of the tenne; that muſt ſtand, and the ordinary commandements muſt giue place

and

and yeelde vnto it : as for example ; the second commandement forbiddeth any man *to make any grauen Image*; yet *Moses* by a speciall commandement, made a brasen serpent in the wildernesse to be a figure of Christ. So the sixt commandement, *Thou shalt not kill*, is an ordinary commandement, and bindeth the conscience of euery man to obey the same ; yet God comes with a speciall commandement to *Abraham*, and saith, *Abraham, kill thy sonne :* and therefore the ordinary commandement of the second table, giueth place for the time. And so all the commandements, *thou shalt doe thus and thus*, vnlesse God command otherwise: for God is an absolute Lord, and so aboue his owne Lawes, he is not bound vnto them, but may dispence with them, and with vs for the keeping of them, at his will and pleasure. And thus was *Abraham* warranted to sacrifice his Sonne; namely, by vertue of a speciall, and personall commaundement to himselfe alone.

But if *Abraham* had not had this particular commandement, the sacrificing of *Isaac* had beene vnlawfull and abhominable; for, the killing of a man is a hainous sinne : much more is the killing of a mans owne sonne without a speciall commandement ; for that is against nature : and therefore the Lord by *Ieremie* doth seuerely condemne the Iewes *for burning their sonnes and daughters in sacrifice*, Ier. 7. 31. without any warrant from him ; though it may be they would pretend their imitation of *Abraham* in the sacrificing of *Isaac:* yea, and to shew his detestation of that fact, he changeth the name of the place, calling it the *valley of slaughter*, ver. 32. and in the new Testament it is vsed to signifie *hell*, Matth. 5. 29. 30. And because this sinne is so odious, it is rather to be thought, that *Iephte* did not kill his daughter in sacrifice to the Lord (as some thinke he did) especially beeing a man commended for his faith by the holy Ghost : but thereof wee shall speake when we come to his example, ver. 32.

Thus wee see *Abraham* had ground for this fact to doe it by faith, euen Gods speciall commaund. But here it will be said, that *Abraham* did not offer vp his sonne indeede: for though he had bound him, and laide him on the Altar, yet when he lifted vp the knife to haue killed him, the Angel staid his hand, and suffered him not, Gen. 22. 11. 12. How then can it be true which is here said, that he offered him vp? for the writer of the story must make true reports; but it seemes the writer hereof is deceiued in the very principall point, affirming *Isaac* was offered, when in truth he was not. *Answ.* God is the Author and inditer of this Story, and in Gods sight and estimation he was offered, though not in the worlds : and therefore it is so said, in regard of Gods acceptance; because *Abrahams* purpose was to haue done it; and if he had not beene staide, he had done it.

Where we note a point of speciall comfort,

to wit, that God in his children and seruants, doth accept the will for the deed: so *Paul* saith, 2. Cor. 8. 12. *If there be a willing minde, it is accepted according to that a man hath, and not according to that he hath not:* speaking of their releeuing of the poore he telleth them, that God regardeth not so much a mans worke, as the heart wherewith he doth the worke. And therefore the *poore widowe* in the Gospel, Luke 21. 3. is saide by our Sauiour Christ, to haue cast more into the treasury (though it were but *two mites*) then many rich men that cast in great abundance : more in heart, not in substance.

This serueth to stay the heart of many a man that is found bruised in conscience; for, seeing his weake obedience, and the greatnesse of his sinnes past, he begins to call his election into question : now what must a man doe in this case? *Answ.* Surely he must goe on forward in obedience, and endeauour himselfe to continue therein : and then though he faile many times through infirmity, yet for his endeauour, God will accept of him, & be pleased with the same.

This doctrine is very comfortable to a distressed conscience; but yet it must not make any man bold to sinne: for many abuse this Doctrine, and say, that though they liue in sinne yet God will accept them, for they loue God in their heart. But they deceiue themselues: for, this mercifull dealing of God in accepting the will for the deede, is onely towards those that endeauour themselues sincerely to leaue their sinnes, to beleeue in God, and to walke in obedience; but such as flatter themselues, lying in their sinnes, *God will not be mercifull vnto them*, Deut. 29. 19. 20.

Here further it may well be demaunded; How *Abraham* could take *Isaac* and bind him, and lay him on the altar to haue offered him: for, though the common opinion be, that hee was but 13. yeares olde, yet the more receiued opinion of the best Writers is, that *Isaac* was 25. or 27. yeares olde. How then could *Abraham* beeing an olde man of more then 120. yeares, be able to binde *Isaac* beeing a yong and lusty man, and lay him on the altar to kill him? For though *Abraham* had a commandement to kill *Isaac*, yet we finde not that God commaunded *Isaac* to suffer himselfe to be killed; now Nature mooues euery one to seeke to saue his owne life, and to resist such as would kill vs. How then was *Isaac* brought to yeeld thus farre to his Father?

For answer hereunto, we are to knowe, that *Abraham* was no ordinary man, but a Prophet, and that an excellent and extraordinary Prophet: So God himselfe testifieth of him to *Abimelech*; *He is a Prophet, and he shall pray for thee :* yea he was esteemed and reuerenced as a Prophet, and an honourable man, euen of the Heathen. The Hittites tell him : *Thou art a Prince of God amongst vs*, Gen. 23. 6.

Now beeing a man of so high place, and so great regard euen in the world; doubtlesse he was of much more authorititie in his owne house. It is therefore very likely that hee tells *Isaac* his sonne, that he had a speciall commandement from God, to kill him in sacrifice. Now *Isaac* beeing a holy man, & well brought vp, hearing this, is contented to be sacrificed, and obeyes his Father herein.

This I speake not as certaine, but as most probable; and it is the iudgement of the best learned, who haue good experience in the Scripture.

This circumstance well obserued, serues greatly for the commendation of them both: of *Abraham* the Father, that had so religiously brought vp his onely Sonne, that was most deere vnto him, that he would not resist the will of God reuealed vnto him, though it cost him his life. Oh that Parents would follow *Abraham*, in so doing to their children; then would it goe well with the Church of God. Againe, *Isaacs* behauiour is here admirable, that hee would not resist his weake and aged Father, but suffered him to binde him, and to lay him on the Altar; yeilding himselfe vnto death, when his Father told him, My sonne, God will haue it so.

This example must be a patterne of obedience, not onely for children towards their parents; but for vs all towards Gods ministers, when they shall tell vs, what God would haue vs doe: we must submit our selues, and yeelde though it turne to our bodily paine and griefe; for *Isaac* yeelds, though it were to the losse of his life. But alas, who will followe *Isaac*? For, let the minister speake against our carnall pleasure, and vnlawfull gaine; let him crosse our humour, and affections, then we refuse to heare, and will not obey. Nay, if the minister of God, as the Lords priest come with the sacrificing knife of Gods word, to the throat of our sinne, to kill the same in vs, that so we may be pure and acceptable sacrifices vnto God; doe we not resist him, and say in our hearts, We will none of this doctrine? Or, if he like a Prophet of God, come and offer to binde our consciences with the cordes of obedience, and to lay our affections on the altar of the Law; then we resist, and are either too yong, or too olde; too rich, or too learned; or too great to be taught and bound to obedience. But let vs know, that if we will be true *Isaacs*, euen the sonnes of faith and obedience, and the true heires of *Abrahams* faith (as we would beare the world in hand) then as he did submit himselfe to bee bound of his father; so must we yeeld our selues to the ministers of God, to be bound by his word: and suffer the same word to be in vs, the two edged sword of the spirit, to cut down sinne and corruption in vs, and to make vs new creatures; that so both in body and soule, wee may become pure and acceptable sacrifices vnto our God. Thus much of the fact it selfe, wherein *Abrahams* faith is set forth.

Now follow the Arguments, or reasons,

whereby the same worke of faith is commended vnto vs. The first Argument is taken from the great impediments which might hinder his faith; and they are in number three: First, that he was brought to this worke, not by ordinary command, but by an extraordinary course in temptation: *Beeing tempted.* Secondly, that he was to offer his owne child: yea, *his onely begotten sonne.* Thirdly, that he *who had receiued the promises,* must offer him and kill him, *in whom the promise was made.*

For the first impediment. In the ordinary translation, it is read thus, *When he was tried:* But that is not so fit, beeing rather an exposition of the meaning, then a translation of the word. For the very word signifieth, *to be tempted:* and the meaning is, when he was *tried.* I would therefore rather read it thus: *when he was tempted;* or, *being tempted,* as the word signifies.

In the handling hereof, first wee will intreat of the nature of this temptation, and then come to the circumstances belonging to the same.

Temptation (as it is here vsed, may be thus described) *It is an action of God, whereby hee prooueth, and makes experience of the loyaltie and obedience of his seruants.* First, (I say) *it is an action of God:* This is plaine by the testimony of *Moses* in Gen. 22. 1. where (if we read the history) we shall finde, that *God did prooue Abraham.* *Obiect.* But against this it may be obiected, that Saint *Iames* faith, Iam. 1. 13. *God tempteth no man:* and therefore no temptation is the action of God? *Answ.* That place in *Iames* is thus to be vnderstood: *God tempteth no man:* that is, God doth not stirre vp, or mooue any mans heart to sinne. Yet further it will be said, That temptation is an action of Satan: for so in the Gospel we may read (Matt. 4. 3.) that he is called the *tempter? Ans.* Some temptations are the actions of God, and some the actions of Satan: God tempteth, and Satan tempteth: but there is great difference in their temptations: first, in the manner: for, Satan tempteth a man to sinne against the will of God, and to doe some euill; God tempteth a man to doe something, which shall be onely against his owne affections, or his reason. Secondly, God tempteth for the good of his seruants: but Satan tempteth for the destruction both of their bodies and soules.

Againe I say, *Whereby he maketh triall, &c.* Here some will say, God knowes euery mans heart, and what is in them, and what they will doe, long before; and therefore hee needeth not to make triall of any man? *Ans.* God makes triall of his seruants, not because he is ignorant of that which is in their heart; for he vnderstandeth *their thoughts long before:* but because he will haue their obedience made knowne; partly to themselues, and partly to the world: so that he makes triall of his seruants, not for himselfe, but for our sakes.

Now further, God tempteth men three

wayes; firſt by his Iudgements, and Calamities in this world: ſo the Lord ſaith to the Iſraelites, Deut. 8. 2. *Thou ſhalt remember all the way which the Lord thy God ledde thee this fourtie yeares in the wilderneſſe, for to humble thee, for to prooue & to know what was in thy heart.* That iourney might haue been gone in *fourty dayes*, but God did lead them in it *fourty yeares*, to prooue and trie by this vnwontted calamity, whether they would obey him or not. So likewiſe God ſuffered *falſe Prophets*, and *Dreamers of dreames*, to come among the people; for this ende , *To prooue them, and to knowe whether they loued the Lord their God, with all their heart, and with all their ſoule*, Deut. 13. 3. Now this firſt kinde of temptations, by *outward Iudgements*, is moſt grieuous; when the Lord laieth his owne hand vpon his ſeruants ſo heauily, as they ſhall thinke themſelues to be quite forſaken. In this temptation was *Dauid* as we may reade at large: Pſal. the 6: and Pſal. 38: and Iob beeing afflicted not only outwardly in body , but inwardly in minde , crieth out, that *the arrowes of the Almighty were in him*, Iob. 6. 4. and through the whole chapter he bewaileth his grieuous eſtate by reaſon of this temptation.

Secondly, *God tempteth* his ſeruants by withdrawing his graces from them, and by forſaking them in part; and this temptation is as grieuous as the former: herewith was good King *Hezekias tempted:* for as we may read, God left him to a ſinne of vaine glory, and the ende was *to try him, and to prooue all that was in his heart*, 2. Chron. 32. 31.

Thirdly , God tempteth his ſeruants by giuing vnto them ſome ſtrange and extraordinarie commandement : As in the Goſpel, when the *young man* came to our Sauiour Chriſt, and asked him, *what good thing he might doe to haue eternall life?* Matt. 19. 16. Chriſt biddeth him, *goe and ſell all that he had, and giue to the poore.* This commandement had this vſe, to be a commandement of triall *vnto the yong man*, whereby God would prooue what was in his heart, that the ſame might be manifeſt both to himſelfe and vnto others. And vnder this kind, we muſt comprehend this temptation of *Abraham :* for when God ſaid, *Abraham, offer vp thy ſonne in ſacrifice*; it was not a commandement requiring actuall obedience, (for God meant not that *Abraham* ſhould kil his ſonne) but only of triall, to ſee what he would do. And theſe are Gods temptations, whereby he proouth his ſeruants.

Yet farther the temptations of God whereby he tempteth his children, haue two endes: 1. they ſerue to diſcloſe and make euident the graces of God, that be hidden in the hearts of his ſeruants : ſo S. *Iames* ſaith, *My brethren count it exceeding great ioy when yee fall into diuerſe tentations:* Iam. 1. 2. The reaſon followeth : *Knowing that the triall of your faith bringeth forth patience*, v. 3.

Where wee ſee this ende of temptation ſet downe , To manifeſt the gift of patience wrought in the heart. And S. *Peter* ſaith to the Church of God , *That they were in heauineſſe through manifold tentations , that the triall of their faith beeing much more precious then gold that periſheth (though it be tried with fire) might be found vnto their praiſe, and honour, and glory, at the appearing of the Lord Ieſus*, 1. Pet. 1. 6. 7. Where temptations haue this vſe, to make manifeſt the ſoundneſſe of mens faith in God, as the fire doth prooue the gold to be good and pretious. So in this place , The temptation of *Abraham* ſerueth for this ende, to make manifeſt his notable faith and obedience vnto God, with a reuerend feare of his Maieſtie, as the Lord himſelfe teſtifieth, ſaying, *Now I knowe that thou feareſt God, ſeeing for my ſake thou haſt not ſpared thy onely ſonne*, Gen. 22. 12. Meaning this: Now I haue made thy faith, and loue, and feare of me ſo manifeſt, that all the world may ſee it and ſpeake of it.

Secondly, Gods temptations ſerue to manifeſt hidden ſinnes and corruptions, partly to a mans owne ſelfe, and partly to the world. And for this ende God tempted Hezekias. For, beeing recouered of his ſickeneſſe , after that the King of *Aſhur* his great enemy was vanquiſhed, eſpecially when the Embaſſadours of the King of *Babell* came *to enquire of the wonders which were done in the Land*; God left him that he might ſee his ſinnes, and the corruptions of his nature , as pride, and vaine-glory, wherewith he was puffed vp at the comming of the Embaſſadours to him. And thus hee who little thought, that pride and vaine-glory could haue taken ſuch hold on him , perceiuing how his heart was lift vp in him , was doubtleſſe much humbled at the ſight of this his ſo great corruption; for when the Prophet came vnto him, he ſubmitted himſelfe to the word of reproofe, Iſay 39. 18.

Firſt, whereas *Abraham* the ſeruant of God was tempted, that is, was prooued and tried by God himſelfe ; Here we are taught, that if we perſwade our ſelues to be the ſeruants of God, as *Abraham* was, then we muſt looke to haue temptations, at Gods owne hand; for his example is a patterne for vs: and therefore in him we muſt ſee that which we muſt looke to haue; for it could not be needefull for *Abraham* , but it may be alſo needefull vnto vs. In regard whereof, Saint *Peter* counteth it as a thing neceſſary, that men ſhould *fall into ſundry temptations, that the triall of their faith might be vnto their praiſe.* So, that in this life we muſt looke for triall: and the more glorious our faith is, and the more like to our Father *Abrahams*, the more trialls ſhall we vndergoe.

Againe, ſeeing we muſt be tried , therefore euery one of vs muſt labour for ſoundneſſe of grace in our hearts; as of faith, repetance, hope, and of the loue of God (though they be but little in meaſure) for, we muſt come to triall, and

2.Chr.32.31.

1.Pet.1.16.

and it muſt appeare, whether we be hotte or colde. Now, if we haue not ſoundneſſe of grace in vs, in the time of triall, then looke, as the dreſſe conſumeth in the fire, when as gold commeth out more cleare; ſo ſhall hypocriſie, formality, and all temporizing profeſſion, come to nothing, in the midſt of tentation; when ſound grace, and a good conſcience, ſhall paſſe thorough, and ſhine more pure and perfect after then before.

Thirdly, conſidering we are to looke for *trials and temptations* from God; therefore we muſt be carefull to remember, and practiſe that counſell of Chriſt to his Diſciples, before his paſſion: *Watch and pray leaſt ye enter into temptation,* Matth. 26. 41. And becauſe they were careleſſe in practiſing this dutie, therefore they fell into temptation; eſpecially *Peter* fell moſt grieuouſly, by denying his maſter. We muſt perſwade our ſelues, that the ſame commandement is giuen to vs; for God will prooue vs by temptations, to make manifeſt the corruptions that be in our hearts: we therefore conſidering our owne eſtate, muſt pray for Gods aſſiſting and ſtrengthening grace, that when temptations ſhall come, we may be found ſound and ſtedfaſt in the triall.

Thus much of the nature of *Abrahams* temptation; now followe the *circumſtances* to be conſidered therein: And firſt, of *the time* when *Abraham* was tempted. Hereof we may reade, Gen. 22. 1. *After theſe things,* ſaith Moſes, *God did prooue Abraham.* The words will admit a double reference. But this I take to be moſt proper and fit for that place, to wit; that after God had made moſt excellent promiſes vnto *Abraham,* and giuen him moſt wonderfull bleſſings and priuiledges, *then he tempted him.*

Hence, we learne this notable leſſon: That thoſe people in Gods Church, which receiue from God more graces then others, muſt looke for more temptations. This we ſhall ſee to be true in *Chriſt Ieſus* the head of the Church: for when he was *Baptized,* and *had receiued the holy Ghoſt,* Matth. 3. in the forme of a Doue, and had this voyce of God the Father pronounced vpon him, that *he was his wel-beloued ſonne in whom he was well pleaſed*; then preſently followeth this, that *he was led into the wilderneſſe to be tempted of the deuill:* Matth. 4. 1. beeing full of the holy Ghoſt, as Luke ſaith: So likewiſe when God had teſtified of *Iob,* that he was *an vpright and iuſt man, one that feared God, and eſchewed euill,* Iob. 1. 8. then Satan tooke occaſion thereby to tempt him: as in all the whole courſe of that booke we may plainely ſee, wherein are ſet downe moſt wonderfull temptations and trials whereby he was prooued. So *Iaacob* muſt *wreſtle with the Angel,* Gen. 32. 24. 28. and by the power of God ouercome God himſelfe. This was a notable prerogatiue, To preuaile with the Lord; but yet hee muſt *preuaile with his foyle* (v. 31.) and

Luk. 4. 1.

at the ſame time, and euer after draw one of his legges after him, euen to his dying day. Saint *Paul* was *rapt vp into the third heauen, into Paradiſe, and heard words which cannot be ſpoken; yea, which are impoſſible for man to vtter: yet leaſt he ſhould be exalted out of meaſure, through aboundance of reuelations, there was giuen vnto him a pricke in the fleſh, the meſſenger of Satan to buffet him:* 2. Cor. 12. 7. God will honour him with reuelations, but yet Satan ſhall haue leaue to buffet and beate him as it were blacke and blewe. In all which we may ſee, to whom God vouchſafeth a greater meaſure of grace, to them he appointeth ſingular trialls and temptations aboue other men. And the reaſon is: Firſt, becauſe Gods graces doe better appeare in temptations then out of them: as golde is beſt tried in the fire, and thereby prooued moſt pure and perfect: Secondly, temptations ſerue to abaſe the ſeruant of God, and to bring him downe in his owne conceite, that he be not proude of thoſe things that are in him, or puffed vp with conceite that there is more in him, then indeede there is. This we ſawe in *Pauls* example; *He was buffeted of Satan, leaſt he ſhould be exalted with aboundance of Reuelations.* We may ſee a type hereof in worldly affaires: The beſt ſhip that floateth on the Sea, when it carieth in it moſt precious Iewels, is ballaced with grauell or ſand, to make it ſinke into the water, and ſo ſayle more ſurely, leaſt floating too high, it ſhould be vnſtable: euen ſo dealeth the Lord with his ſeruants, when he hath giuen them a good meaſure of his graces, then doth he alſo lay temptations vpon them, to humble them, leaſt they ſhould be puffed vp in themſelues.

The ſecond circumſtance to be conſidered in this temptation, is the *greatneſſe* thereof. It was the greateſt that euer was, for ought we reade of, That *God ſhould command him to kill his owne ſonne.* For, if God had tolde *Abraham,* that *his ſonne Iſaac* muſt haue died, it would haue beene very grieuous and ſorrowful newes vnto him: and yet more grieuous if he had told him, that he ſhould haue died a bloody death. But yet this was moſt grieuous of all, that *Abraham* himſelfe with his *owne hand,* ſhould ſacrifice his owne ſonne; nay his *onely* ſonne; and that which is more, he muſt kill his onely childe, in whom the *promiſe* was made, that in *him ſhould his ſeede be called:* this muſt needes be a great wound vnto his heart; and yet to augement his griefe, he muſt not doe it preſently, nor where he would, but goe three daies iournie in the wilderneſſe. During which time Satan vndoubtedly wrought mightily vpon his naturall affections, to diſwade him from obedience: which could not chooſe but be far more grieuous vnto his ſoule.

Out of the grieuouſneſſe of this temptation, wee may learne this leſſon: that God in tempting a man, doth ſometime proceede thus farre, Not onely to croſſe his ſinnes and corruptions,

tions, but euen to bring him to nothing, in regard of humane reason and naturall affections. For, this commaundement (*Abraham kill thy sonne*) might haue made *Abraham* (if he had consulted with flesh and blood) euen distracted in himselfe, and without reason, not knowing which way to turne himselfe. And accordingly, let all Gods children, especially such as haue the greatest graces, looke for such temptations as shall lay their humane reason flat vpon the ground, and bring them to this point, euen vtterly to denie themselues.

The third Circumstance in this Temptation, is this; What *Abraham* did when hee was tempted? the Text telleth vs, that *by faith hee offered vp Isaac, beeing tempted.*

Abraham beeing thus tempted, whether he would obey Gods Commaundement, or not; obeyes God in offering vp his sonne, and yet layes holde vpon Gods promise made in him. For, we must know, that *Abraham* had a promise of blessing, in *Isaac*: and beeing now commanded to kill *Isaac*, hee did not now cast off his hope, and desperately thinke it could not be performed, if this commaundement were obeyed; but by the great power of faith, he both obeyes the commandement, and yet still beleeues the promise: For, so saith the text, *By faith he offered vp Isaac.* Therefore, in the very action of killing *Isaac*, hee beleeued the promise, that *Isaac* should liue. And this was the excellency of *Abrahams* faith. For, if God should with his owne voyce bidde a man kill his sonne, it may be some would be found, that would doe it; but to doe it, and still to beleeue a contrary promise made before, betokeneth the vertue of an admirable faith.

In this circumstance we may learne a good instruction; to wit, in all temptations that befall vs, still to hold fast the promises of God. Though in the deuills purpose, they tend to the loosening of our holde; and in all common reason, we haue good cause to let them goe: yet for all that, wee must neuer let goe, but still hold the promise fast, and rather let goe all reason in the world, then Gods promise. And this is not onely true faith, but euen the excellencie of faith. For example, Gods promise is (Ioh. 3. 16.) *God so loued the world, that hee gaue his onely begotten sonne into the world, that whosoeuer beleeued in him, should not perish, but haue euerlasting life.* Now, when wee are in the extremitie of all temptations, we must still holde fast this promise, and venture our soules vpon the truth of it. This was *Abrahams practise*; for in this temptation, Gods meaning was to trie *Abraham*, and to see what he would doe: Now *Abraham*, he holdes fast the promise, and yet obeyes God; though all the reason in the earth, cannot tell how that promise, and that commandement could stand together. But this was *Abrahams* faith, though I know not, nor reason knoweth not; yet God knoweth: and therefore, seeing I haue his commaundement, I will

obey it; and seeing I haue his word and promise, I will beleeue that also, and neuer forsake it. And euen thus must we striue to doe in all temptations whatsoeuer; yea, euen in those that come from Satan, which are full of malice and all violence. In our heart and conscience we must still hold and beleeue the promise of God: and this is euer the surest and safest way to get the victorie ouer Satan, To hold, that Gods promise shall be performed, though wee know not how, but rather see the contrary. And though in humane reasoning, it bee a note of ignorance, and want of skill, to sticke alwaies to the conclusion and question; yet in spirituall temptations, and trialls, this is sound diuinitie, Alwaies to holde Gods promise, and to sticke fast to that conclusion: and not to follow Satan in his Arguments, neither suffer him by any meanes to driue vs from it.

Further, in that this fact of offering vp *Isaac*, was onely *Abrahams* triall; we may obserue, that it did not make him iust before God, but onely serued to prooue his faith, and to *declare* him to bee *Iust*. And therefore, whereas Saint *Iames* saith, Iam. 2. 21. *That Abraham was iustified through workes, when hee offered his sonne Isaac vpon the altar.* His meaning is, that *Abraham did manifest himselfe to be iust before God,* by offering vp his sonne; and not, that by this fact *Abraham* of a sinner was made iust; or, of a righteous man, was made more iust: For indeede, good workes doe not make a man iust, but onely doe prooue and declare him to bee iust.

Thirdly, God gaue *Abraham* this commandement; *Abraham kill thy sonne* ; but yet hee concealed from him, what was his purpose and intent herein; for God meant not that *Abraham* should kill his sonne indeede, but onely to *trie* what he would doe; whether he would still *beleeue* and obey him, or not. Where wee see, that God, who is truth it selfe, reueales to *Abraham* his will; but not his whole will: whence ariseth this question;

Whether it be lawfull for a man, according to this example of God, when he tels a thing to another, to conceale his meaning, in whole, or in part? For answer hereunto, we must knowe, there are two extremities, both which must bee auoided in this case. 1. That a man must alwaies expresse all that is in his minde. 2. That in some cases a man may speake one thing, and thinke another; speaking contrary to his meaning: But this latter is no way lawfull, and the other is not alwayes necessarie. Wee therefore must holde a meane betweene both; to wit, that in some cases a man may conceale his whole meaning, saying nothing, though he bee examined: namely, when the concealing thereof, doth directly stand with the glory of God, and the good of his brother.

Thus godly Martyrs haue done: for, beeing examined before tyrants, where & with whom, they worshipped God; they haue chosen rather to die, then to difclofe their brethren: and this concealing of their mindes was lawfull, becaufe it touched immediately the glorie of God, and the good of his Church.

Secondly, a man may conceale part of his minde: but that muft be alfo with thefe two caueats; Firft, that it ferue for Gods glorie: Secondly, that it bee for the good of Gods Church.

Thus did *Ionas* conceale the condition of mercie from the Niniuites, when hee preached deftruction vnto them, faying; Within fortie daies and Niniuie fhall be deftroyed: though it is euident by the euent, that it was Gods will they fhould be fpared, if they did repent. But that Condition God would haue concealed, becaufe, it would not haue beene for the good of the Niniuites to haue knowen it; fith the concealing of it caufed them more fpeedily, and earneftly to repent.

But out of thefe cafes, a man (beeing called to fpeake) muft declare the whole truth, or elfe hee finnes greatly againft Gods commandement, forfaking the property of the godly, Pfal. 15.2.

And thus much of the firft impediment of *Abrahams* faith.

The fecond impediment to *Abrahams* faith, is contained in thefe words,

Offered his onely begotten fonne.

We know that the loue of Parents defcends to euery childe naturally, but efpecially to the onely begotten; vpon whome (beeing but one) all that is beftowed, which, when there are many, is diuided among them. And therefore in all reafon, this might greatly hinder *Abrahams* obedience, That God fhould commaund him to offer his fonne, yea, his only begotten fonne: But yet by faith he ouercommeth this temptation, breaks through this impediment, and offers vp his *onely fonne.*

Where we note, that true *faith* will make a man ouercome his owne nature. Loue is the ftrongeft affection in the heart, efpecially from the father to the childe, euen his onely childe: And a man would thinke it impoffible to ouercome this loue in the parent, vnleffe it were by death; there beeing no caufe to the contrary in the childe. But yet beholde, *Abraham* by faith fubdued this fpeciall loue which he bare to his onely childe: God himfelfe teftified of *Abraham*, that his loue to *Ifaac* was great, Gen. 22.2. and yet by faith he ouercometh this his loue.

This point is carefully to be marked, as declaring the great power of true fauing faith; for, if faith can ouercome created and fanctified nature, then vndoubtedly the power thereof, will inable man to ouercome the corruptions of his nature, and the temptations of the world, for it is an harder thing to ouercome our nature which wee haue by creation, then to fubdue the corruption thereof, which coms in by tranf-

greffion. And hence fuch excellent things are fpoken of faith: it is called *the victorie that ouercommeth the world.* 1. Iohn 5.4. And *God* is faid *by faith to purifie the heart: faith ftrengtheneth the heart:* Acts 15.9. And *through faith we are kept by the power of God vnto faluation.* 1. Pet. 1.5.

Is this the power of faith to ouercome nature, and the corruptions thereof? then howfoeuer religion be reeeiued, and faith profeffed generally among vs, yet vndoubtedly there is little true faith in the world: for, euen among the profeffours thereof, how many bee there that fubdue the finnes of their liues, and fuppreffe the workes of their wicked nature? furely very few. Now where corruption beareth fway, and finne raigneth, there found faith cannot be, for, if faith were found in men, it would *purifie their hearts:* and cleanfe the corruptions therof: and bring forth obedience in life.

Secondly, this power of true faith in mans heart muft teach vs, not to content our felues with a general faith and knowledge in religion, but to goe further, and to get a found faith that may *purifie the heart*, at leaft in fome true meafure; for, fauing faith wil cleanfe a man in euery part of foule & bodie, and ftrengthen his foule in temptations.

Queft. Here it may be asked, how it can bee truely faide, that *Ifaac* was *Abrahams* onely begotten fonne, feeing *Ifmaell* was alfo his fonne, and was borne before *Ifaac*, as is euident, Gen. 16? I anfwer two wayes: firft, that *Ifmaell* by Gods appointment was put out of *Abrahams* houfe, (for it was the expreffe commaundement of God, *to put forth the bond-woman and her fonne*, Gen. 21. 10.) and fo was made no childe of *Abraham.* Secondly, *Ifmaell* was his childe indeede, yet not by *Sarah*, but by *Agar* a bondwoman; and fo was (as I may fay) bafe borne, whereupon hee is reputed for no fonne: but *Ifaac* is his onely begotten lawfully; which may be an *Item* to beware of the bed defiled, feeing fuch off-fpring is fo debafed with the Lord.

Now followeth the third impediment of *Abrahams* faith; which is alfo a notable circumftance whereby the fame faith is commended: and it is taken from the perfon of *Abraham:* in thefe wordes, *who had receiued the promifes.*

The meaning of the words. Who.] This muft be referred to the perfon of *Abraham* of whom the holy Ghoft here fpeaketh. *Receiued the promifes.*] That is, by faith; for, when God made his promifes vnto *Abraham*, hee did not onely heare them; but (which is the principall point of all) he beleeued them, and applied the fame effectually vnto his owne foule; fo much doth the word [*receiued*] import. Now it is faide that he receiued (not one promife) but the *promifes* plurally; for thefe caufes; firft, becaufe God hauing made one maine promife vnto him touching Chrift, did repeate and renue the same diuers times. Secondly, becaufe God had made diuers particular promifes vnto him; as firft, *that he would be his God, and the God of his feede:* Gen. 17.7. Secondly, *that he would giue him a child in his olde age:* Gen. 17.19. Thirdly, *that vnto him and his feed, he would giue the Land of Canaan for euer:* Gen. 13.15. Fourthly, *that in Ifaac he would bleffe all the Nations of the earth.* Gen. 21.12.

And becaufe the receiuing of Gods promifes in generall could feem no great impediment to *Abrahams* worke of faith; therefore the holy Ghoft annexeth his receiuing of a particular promife in *Ifaac* in the 18. verfe, *To whom it was faid, in Ifaac fhall thy feede be called.* Which might feem impoffible to ftand with the doing of this worke in facrificing his fonne; and therefore the confideration of it in *Abraham*, muft needes be a great impediment to him in this worke: for, he goes about to kill *Ifaac* (in obedience to Gods commaund) in whofe life hee beleeued to receiue the bleffings promifed of God.

Here then, obferue a moft wonderfull impediment to *Abrahams* faith: which aboue all might haue hindred him from obeying God; for, how could he choofe but reafon thus with himfelfe? God hath made vnto me many gracious promifes, and that which is more, he hath faide, *That in my fonne Ifaac the fame muft bee accomplifhed:* and, *in him all the nations of the earth muft bee bleffed:* Now then, if I fhall kill and facrifice my fonne, how fhall thefe promifes be accomplifhed? And reafon in this cafe would fay, I fee no way, but that the promife is gone, and all hope loft. But what doth *Abraham* in this cafe? for all this, hee doth *facrifice his fonne,* and that *by faith;* ftill beleeuing and holding affuredly, that though *Ifaac* were facrificed and flaine, yet in him fhould all the nations of the earth be bleffed.

Here then we note this fpeciall point, wherin the faith of *Abraham* doth notably appeare; THat when *Abrahams* cafe, in refpect of inioying the promife of God, might feem defperate, and void of all hope and comfort, then he beleeueth: for, when *Ifaac* was dead, in all reafon hee could haue no hope of the accomplifhing of Gods promifes vnto him, becaufe they were made to him in *Ifaac: Ifaac* was the man in whom *all the nations of the earth fhould be bleffed*; and yet when all hope is paft in mans reafon, then good *Abraham* fet his heart to beleeue.

This practife of *Abraham* muft be a pattern for vs to obferue and followe, al our liues long, in the matter of our faluation: if it fall out that we fhall doubt of our faluation, and feele many things in vs that would carie vs to defpaire; when we are in this cafe, and feele no comfort, then let vs call to minde *Abrahams* practife, who beleeues Gods promife, when the foundation thereof is taken away: euen fo let vs doe at the fame inftant, when the promife of God

feemes to be fruftrate, and we haue no hope of the accomplifhment thereof, then we muft caft our foules vpon it. For wee muft not onely beleeue, when we feele comfort in our confcience concerning Gods mercies; but euen then when God feemes to ftand againft vs, and when wee feele in our foules the very gall of hell, then (I fay) we muft beleeue.

In *Paules* daungerous voyage towards Rome, when he was in the fhippe with the Mariners and Centurion, there arofe a great tempeft, *and neither funne nor ftarres appeared for many dayes:* fo that, as the Text faith, *All hope that they fhould be faued was taken away,* Acts 27.20. Now, what faith *Paul* in this extremitie of danger? *Now I exhort you to bee of good courage: for there fhall bee no loffe of any mans life, faue of the Shippe onely,* (Verfe 22.) and fo perfwaded them to take bread. Euen fo, when our cafe falles out to be this; that either by reafon of finne and of the temptation of Satan: or elfe by reafon of fome outward calamities and troubles, we feele our foule (as it were) ouerwhelmed with forrow, and euen entring into deftruction, and can neither fee (as it were) *light of funne or ftarres;* then wee muft fet before vs Gods promifes, and labour to beleeue the fame. So *Dauid* beeing in great affliction, and grieuous temptation, faith thus of himfelfe, Pfal. 77.2,7,8,9,10. *In the day of my trouble I fought the Lord, my fore ranne and ceafed not in the night, my foule refufed comfort.* Yet at the very fame inftant he prayed, *When his fpirit was full of anguifh;* and though hee feemed (as it were) to defpaire (when he faid, *Will the Lord abfent himfelfe for euer? and will he fhew no more fauour? Is his mercie cleane gone? Doth his promife faile for euermore? And hath God forgotten to be mercifull? &c.)* Yet he checkes himfelfe, and faith, *This is my death, and my weakeneffe.* Euen fo, euery true member of Gods Church, in the extremitie of all temptations, and in the time of defperation, is bound to beleeue the promifes of God; and indeede, that is the fitteft time for *faith* to fhewe it felfe in: for *faith* (as we haue before heard) *is the ground of things hoped for, and the fubfifting of things which are not feene.*

Now further it it faid, *Abraham receiued Gods promifes;* that is, he applied them to his owne foule and confcience, and beleeued them, and made them his owne by faith. This is a notable point, and worthy the marking: God made his promifes to *Abraham:* now *Abraham* he doth not onely heare, and learne the promifes; but applies them to himfelfe, and by faith makes them his owne. And thus ought we to doe with all the gratious promifes made in Chrift. But the manner of our daies is farre otherwife; for, when the mercifull promifes of God, are laid downe vnto vs in the minifterie of the word, we are content to heare, and (it may be) to learne, and knowe the fame: But where is the man to be found, that will apply

them

them to his owne conscience, & by faith make them his owne? Men commonly are like vnto way-faring men, or trauellers on the sea, that passe by many goodly faire buildings, rich townes, and Islands; which, when they behold, they admire, and wonder at: and so goe their way, without making purchase of any of them. And thus deale the most men with Gods mercifull promises. In the ministerie of the word, God laies open vnto them his rich mercies, and bountifull promises in Christ; and men approoue thereof, and like them well: whereupon, many doe willingly apply themselues to know the same; but for all this, they will not *receiue them by faith*, & so apply them to their owne soules.

But we must take a better course: and when we heare of the promises of God made vnto vs in Christ: we must not content our selues with a bare knowledge of them, but labour to beleeue them, and apply them vnto our selues, to our soules, and consciences: & so by faith make them our owne. As it is said of *Abraham*, and in him, of all the faithfull; *The blessing of Abraham cam on the Gentiles, thorough Iesus Christ, that wee might receiue the promise of the spirit, through faith*: Gal. 3. 14.

Further obserue, the holy Ghost setteth down that particular promise which God made to *Abraham*, in his sonne *Isaac*: *To whom it was said, in Isaac shall thy seede be called*, Gen. 21. 12. Rom. 9. 7. In which places it is saide, that *in Isaac should his seede bee called*. The meaning whereof is plaine, and thus much in effect: *Ismael shall not be thy sonne and heire, but Isaac is the childe which shal be thy heire; he it is, in whome I will accomplish the promises of life and saluation made to thee*.

From the words thus explained, first wee must obserue *Pauls* collection gathered from Gods dealing with those two persons (Rom. 9. 7:) namely, that God before all worlds hath chosen some men to saluation in his eternall counsell, to manifest the glorie of his grace; and hath refused and reiected others, leauing them vnto themselues, to shew forth his Iustice vpon them.

This doctrine is gathered out of this place, after this manner: Such as is Gods practise and dealing towards men, in time; such was his eternall counsell and decree (for as God before all time determined to deale with men, so in time he dealeth with them.) Now Gods practise and dealing with *Isaac* and *Ismael* is this; *Ismaell* is vouchsafed to bee made partaker of temporall blessings; but yet he is cut off from the spirituall couenant of grace, and *Isaac* is the man that must receiue the Couenant, and by vertue thereof be made partaker of life euerlasting. And so accordingly it is with others; God hath decreed to chuse some men to saluation, and these are admitted into the Couenant: others he hath decreed to reiect, and they are cut off from the Couenant, and from life euer-

lasting. These two persons, *Isaac* and *Ismaell*, are Types of these two sorts of people whome God doth elect, and reiect: *Isaac* representeth those that are chosen to saluation, who become the true members of Gods Church; and *Ismael* is a type of those that are reiected. Now in regard of this different dealing of God with mankinde, chusing some, and refusing others, wee must all put in practise Saint *Peters* lesson with feare and trembling, beeing very carefull, and *giuing all diligence to make our election sure*, 2. Peter 1. 10. for, all be not elected to saluation, but some are reiected; all bee not *Isaacs*, but some are *Ismaelites*. If all were elected and chosen to saluation, then no man needed to care for it; but seeing some are reiected, and neuer vouchsafed to come within the couenant indeed, therefore it standeth vs greatly in hand to take the good counsell of the Apostle, and *to giue all diligence to make our election sure*.

Secondly, whereas it is said, *Not in Ismaell, but in Isaac shall thy seede be called*: Wee may note the state of Gods Church in this world, in regard of the different sorts of men that liue therein. For *Abrahams* family was Gods Church in those daies, and therein were both *Isaac* and *Ismaell*; though both his children, yet farre differing in estate before God. *Ismaell* indeede was borne in the Church, and there brought vp, taught, and circumcised; but yet he was without the Couenant in Gods sight: Now *Isaac* was not onely borne, and brought vp in the Church, and circumcised, but also receiued into the Couenant; and herein differed farre from *Ismael*: for, he is the sonne of *Abraham*, in whome God will continue the Couenant of grace vnto life euerlasting, to his posteritie. And so it is with Gods Church at this day: in it there be two sorts of men; one, which are baptized and brought vp in the Church, heare the word, and receiue the Sacraments; but yet are not saued, because they haue not the promise of the couenant effectually rooted in their hearts. The other sort are they, which beeing baptized in the Church, heare the word effectually, and receiue the Lords supper worthily, to their saluation; because God doth establish his Couenant in their hearts. This difference is plaine in Scripture, in the parables of the draw-net, (Matth. 13.) of the Sower, and of the tares: as also by Christs behauiour at the last iudgement, (Matth. 25. 32.) seuering the sheepe from the goates, both which, liue together in the Church. And by Saint *Paul*, who speaking of those which are borne and brought vp in the Church, saith; that some are *children of the flesh*, & some *children of the promise*, Rom. 9. 8.

This beeing so, that euery one which liues *in the Church*, is not *of the Church*; that is, is not a true member of the Church, and the true childe of *Abraham*: it must make vs all carefull, to vse all holy meanes, whereby wee may bee fully assured that the Couenant of grace be-

longs

longs vnto vs; for, it is not enough for vs to dwell in the Church, to heare the word, and to receiue the sacraments (for so did *Ismael*, and yet neuer was saued) vnlesse therewithall wee haue the couenant of grace belonging vnto vs, and the assurance thereof sealed in our consciences, by Gods holy spirit.

Againe, consider who spake these words; *But in Isaac shall thy seed be called:* Wee shall finde in Gen. 21. 12. it was God himselfe. *Let it not* (saith God vnto *Abraham*) *be grieuous in thy sight for the childe, and for the bond-woman: in all that Sarah shall say vnto thee, heare her voice;* which was, to *cast out the bond-woman and her sonne Ismael.* For (saith God) *in Isaac shall thy seed be called.*

Here obserue a notable practise of *Abraham*, as a good direction how wee ought to iudge of all those that liue in the Church, submitting themselues outwardly to the ministerie and regiment thereof. *Abraham* here hath two sonnes, *Isaac*, and *Ismael*; hee circumciseth them both, and instructs them both (for *hee taught all his houshold to knowe God, and to feare, and obey him*, Gen. 18. 19.) he iudgeth them both to be in one state, in regard of Gods couenant; though they were not: but that difference is made by God. *Abraham* doth not on his owne head, and by his owne will, put *Ismael* out of the Church, which was in his family; but God bids him put him out, and then he put him out, and not before: till such time he kept him in, and held him to be within the couenant, as well as *Isaac* was. Euen so must we deale towards those that liue in the church: secret iudgement must be left to God; and (till God manifest the contrary) in the iudgement of charity, we must holde them all elect. This is the practise of Saint *Paul* in all his Epistles: writing to the Corinths (1. Cor. 1.2.) he calls them *all sanctified:* and to the Galatians (Gal. 1.2.) he calles them *all elect:* speaking so in the iudgement of charitie, although he knew that among them there were many profane and wicked men : and though hee reprooue many great errors and hainous sinnes among them.

And thus much of the first argument whereby *Abrahams* faith is commended vnto vs; namely, the great impediments which might hinder the same.

Now followeth the second Argument or reason, whereby his faith is commended ; to wit, *Abrahams* victory ouer these impediments, or the meanes whereby hee ouercame them, and induced himselfe to obey God, in these words:

Verse 19.

For he considered, or reasoned, that God was able to raise him vp, euen from the dead.

HEre is the true cause that made *Abraham* to offer his sonne, and yet beleeue the promise, *that in him his seede should be cal-*

led. We may perswade our selues, that *Abraham* had rather haue died himselfe (if it might haue stood with the will of God) then to haue sacrificed his sonne. How then doth he induce himselfe to offer him vp? *Answ.* By this wich is here set downe : *he reasoned that God was able to raise him vp, euen from the dead.*

Here are diuers points to be considered of vs : First obserue, the text saith not, that *Abraham* murmured, or *reasoned against God:* but *reasoned with himselfe, that God was able to raise vp his sonne againe :* and thereby induced himselfe to sacrifice his sonne vnto God.

Hence we learne, that when God laies vpon vs any hard commandement, we must not plead the case with god, or murmure against him: but with all quietnesse and meekenesse obey. This is a notable grace of God commended vnto vs by God himselfe: *In rest and quietnesse* (saith God, Isay 30. 15.) *shall bee your strength : in quietnesse and confidence shall ye be saued.* Many thinke it impossible, to endure or doe some things, which God imposeth on his children : But our spirituall strength stands in these two, in *silence*, or *rest*, and in *quietnesse*; by these we shall be enabled. When *Nadab* and *Abihu*, the sonnes of *Aaron*, offered strange fire before the Lord, which hee had not commaunded, *There went out a fire from the Lord, and deuoured them ; so they died before the Lord.* Now when *Aaron* their father asked *Moses* a cause hereof, *Moses* saide, *It was that which the Lord spake, he would be glorified in all that came neere him*; which when *Aaron* heard, the Text saith, *He held his peace, and said not a word:* so *Dauid* behaued himselfe in the case of distresse. *I helde my peace and saide nothing, because thou Lord diddest it.* And this is a speciall point for vs to learne and practise; we must not grudge or repine at Gods hard commaundements, nor pleade the case with him, but in all quietnesse and silence obey God in all that he saith vnto vs.

Againe, whereas it is said, that *Abraham reasoned, that God was able, &c.* Here we learn, that it is a necessarie thing for a man that beleeues, to haue good knowledge in Gods word: that when a temptation comes against his faith, by knowledge & reasoning out of Gods word, he may be able to put backe the same ; for, all our reasoning in matters of faith, must bee grounded on the word: so doth *Abraham* in this place, against this strong temptation, reason out of Gods word to stay himselfe : so that knowledge in the word of God, is necessarie to him that beleeues. And therefore that Doctrine of the Church of Rome is erronious, and here condemned, which saith; that if a man become deuout, and beleeue as the Church beleeueth (though he know not what the Church beleeueth) yet this faith will saue him: but this is a meere deuice of their owne, and hath no ground in the word of God: for (as we see here) knowledge in the word is necessary for him that

hath

Lev. 10. 1, 2.

hath true sauing faith.

But what is *Abrahams* argument, whereby he mooues himselfe to obey God? Surely this; *He reasoned that God was able to raise vp Isaac from the dead.* One part of his reason he takes for graunted, which here he conceales: for this promise was made vnto him, *In Isaac shall thy seede be called.* Now this he takes for graunted, *that God will neuer change his promise.* From whence he reasoneth thus: *God is able to raise vp Isaac my sonne from the dead to life againe;* and therfore I wil sacrifice my sonne according to his commaundement: for, this I know certainly, that *in Isaac shall my seede be called,* seeing God hath promised that, as well as he commandeth this other.

In this example, we see a meanes set downe vnto vs to induce vs to obey God in all hard and difficult cases imposed by God: which is a point to be considered carefully of euery one of vs. For, say that any of vs shall be so touched in conscience for our sinnes, that we euen despaire of our owne saluation: what must we doe in this case? we must take *Abrahams* course, and dispute with our selues for our selues, and we must drawe our arguments from the *promise* of God, and from the *power* of God; wee must ioyne the promise and power of God together. As for example: thus we must say; *God hath made this promise,* this I haue heard, and I doe beleeue it, *that God so loued the world, that* *he gaue his onely begotten sonne, that whosoeuer beleeued in him should not perish, but haue euerlasting life.* This is Gods promise, and it shall neuer be changed. Now therefore howsoeuer my case be heauie and desolate, yet God is able to comfort me, & to bring my soule out of hell, and from this case of desperation; therefore though he kill me, I will trust in him, and I will vse all holy meanes whereby I may ouercome this hard and grieuous temptation. So, if it shall please God to call vs to suffer any thing for the name of Christ, and his holy profession; flesh & blood we know, is weak, and Nature wil make this obiection, *that life is sweete:* what course therefore shall we take? we must doe as *Abraham* here doth; vnto the certainty of Gods promise we must adioine his *power,* & reason thus; *God hath made this promise,* that he wil be with them that suffer any thing for his owne name sake, and I know that he is able to deliuer me: and though he will not, yet he can make me able to beare it; therefore I will patiently suffer, and abide whatsoeuer his holy hand shall lay vpon me. Thirdly, is a man so troubled with some sinne, that he cannot get out nor ouercome it? Then also let him set before him this fact of *Abraham;* and vnfainedly endeuour to doe hereafter. For that which is past, let him labour to beleeue this promise of God, *At what time soeuer a sinner doth repent him of his sinne, he will put all his wickednesse out of his remembrance.* And for the time to come (beeing first resolued, that God can inable him to leaue his

Ioh.3.16.

sinnes) let him striue by good meanes to leaue his sinne, auoiding the occasions of it, and praying against it; and this will be as a cable-rope to draw him out of the pit of sinne: This course we must take, and this doe, in euery hard case that shall befall vs.

And thus much of the meanes whereby *Abraham* induced himselfe to obey God.

The third and last reason whereby *Abrahams* faith is commended vnto vs, is the issue & euent thereof, in these words,

> *From whence he receiued him also after* *a sort.*

From whence; that is from death: *After a sort,* or (as it may be read) *in some shewe.* This is said, because *Isaac* in the thought & purpose of *Abraham,* was but a dead man: for, *Abraham* was fully resolued with himselfe vpon Gods commaund, to haue sacrificed him; yea, hee had gone so farre, as to put the sacrificing knife vnto his sonnes throate, and had slaine him indeed, had not the Angell of God staied his hand: and therefore when the Angell said, *Lay not thy hand vpon the childe, neither doe any thing to him,* euen then did *Abraham* in some shew receiue *Isaac* from death.

Here we learne diuers points: 1. That whosoeuer shall rest on Gods prouidence, & good pleasure, euen in cases of extremitie, when hee shall be out of all hope with himselfe; shall at the last haue a good issue. This wee see to bee true by *Abrahams* example in this place. As we said before, he himselfe (no doubt) had rather haue died ten thousand times, then to haue *Isaac* slaine, in whom the promise was made: but yet, beleeuing Gods promise, that that should neuer change, he rests himsefe on Gods good pleasure and prouidence, and goes on in obedience; and so in the end receiued a blessed issue. This is very cleerely set downe vnto vs in the History recorded by *Moses.* For, when *Abraham* had gone three daies iourney in the wildernesse, and had built an Altar, then *Isaac* said vnto *Abraham,* Gen. 22. 7. *Father, here is the fire and the wood, but where is the lambe for the burnt offering?* Then *Abraham* said, *My sonne, God will prouide him a lambe for a burnt offering,* Vers. 8. And thus yeelding himselfe to Gods good pleasure and prouidence, he receiued his sonne againe; as a dead child restored to life. So, when wee are in cases of extremitie, when all goes against vs, and when we can see no hope of any good issue or end, and all good meanes seeme to faile vs; if we can then cast our selues on Gods prouidence, and rowle our selues vpon God, we shall haue comfort in the ende, and a good issue out of all. We doe all of vs in word acknowledge Gods prouidence: but when we come to the pinch, that wee fall into cases of extremitie; the we vse vnlawful means, and doe not with *Abraham* cast our selues vpon God, but seeke helpe of the deuill, and wicked men. But all such persons must looke for a cursed issue. They threfore, that feare the Lord,

beeing

being put to any plunge, or extremity, must cast themselues vpon God wholly, and wait for his good time & pleasure: and then wil the issue be both ioyous and comfortable vnto their soules.

Here some circumstances of this fact are to be considered, out of the larger storie. The first is this: What did God vnto *Abraham* at this time, when he was about to kill his sonne? *An.* God now gaue him a commandement, to *stay his hand, and not to slay his sonne:* By vertue whereof, *Abraham* staies his hand. God before commãded him *to goe three daies iourney in the wildernesse, and there to sacrifice his sonne:* Hereupon *Abraham* goes; but now beeing come to the place, hauing bound his sonne, and being ready to cut his throat; god bids him *stay his hand:* and then also *Abrahã* obeieth God, & doth not kill his sonne. Here we see, *Abraham* is at Gods command; and (as we say) at his becke: He doth not follow his owne will and pleasure, but when God calles, he is wonderfull pliable to doe Gods command, whatsoeuer it be, one way or other.

This practise of *Abraham*, must be a looking glasse for vs, wherein to see, what manner of persons wee ought to bee. Looke what God commands vs to doe, that we must doe; and what he forbids vs, that we must not doe. But this is a rare thing to be found in these daies: our practise generally is contrary; for in our liues we followe our owne humors and affections, neuer regarding what God doth either will or nill. But if we will be *Abrahams* children, we must follow *Abrahams* practise in this place; For, *the sonnes of Abraham will doe the works of Abraham*, Ioh. 8. 39. Good seruants will come and goe, doe and vndoe, at their Lords pleasure; and forget themselues, to obey their masters: And so must it be with vs, if we call God our good Lord and master.

The second circumstance to bee considered, is the *time* when *Abraham* receiued his sonne from death; to wit, at the very same time when his knife was at his sonnes throate, and he himselfe ready to offer him vp for a sacrifice vnto the Lord: at that same instant God spake vnto him by his Angel from heauen, and said, *Abraham stay thy hand*, Gen. 22. 10. This circumstance is worth the marking: for, God lets him alone three whole daies in great perplextie; and *Abraham* goes forward, according to Gods cõmand, euen to lay his knife to his sõns throat.

Here then we see what is the Lords dealing with his seruants; He lets them alone for a long season in temptation and pitifull distresse: and at the length, when it comes euen to the extremitie, and when the knife is (as it were) at the throat; then he shewes himselfe, and brings comfort vnto them.

The Spouse (in the Canticles) which is the Church of God, or a true Christian soule, whether you will (for it is true both in the generall, and particular) Cant. 3. 2. 3. *She seekes Christ euery where, in the streetes and open places, but*

she finds him not; *then shee goes to the watchmen* (which are Gods ministers)*and there inquires after him whom her soule loued,* and they cannot tell her where she might finde him; so that now all hope of finding him might seeme to be past: but when she was *a little frõ thẽ, then she found him*, & Christ comes to her when she was most in feare not to haue found him at all.

The people of Israel, were many yeares in bondage in Egypt: and when the time came that *Moses* was sent of God to fetch them thence, & to be their guide and deliuerer, when he had brought them out, and carried them to the red sea, then came *Pharaoh* with a huge armie after them to destroy them, Exod. 14.25. Before, they had beene in great affliction and bondage: but now they were quite past all hope of recouery; for they had before them the red sea, and on each side of them great hills and mountaines, and behinde them the huge hoast of *Pharaoh*; and therefore they cried out vnto *Moses*; who then by Gods commandement did diuide the red sea, and made it drie land, and deliuered them through the midst of the redde sea: but as for their enemies, *Pharaoh* and all his hoast, the Lord drowned thẽ in the midst therof.

So for our selues, when God shall excercise any of vs in cases of extremitie, we must looke to be so dealt withall at Gods hand; He will let vs alone for a time, and neuer helpe vs, till the pinch: & therefore, we must waite for his good pleasure with patience; for, this he will doe to try vs to the full, and to make manifest the graces of God wrought in vs.

The third circumstance to be considered, is this: *In what manner did Abraham receiue his sonne from the dead.* This we may read of, Gen. 22.13. He must take a *Ramme that was caught behind him in a bush, and offer him in stead of Isaac:* so *Isaac* is saued, and the Ramme is sacrificed and slaine.

Now whereas *Abraham* offered *Isaac* in sacrifice to God, and yet *Isaac* liueth, and the Ram is slaine in his steade: Hence some gather this vse, and we may profitably consider of the same; to wit, that the sacrifices which we offer vnto God, now vnder the Gospel, must be liuing sacrifices: for, *Isaac* he was offered in sacrifice to God, and yet he liued and died not, but the Ramme is slaine for him. So must we offer our selues in sacrifice vnto God, not dead in sinne, but liuing vnto God in righteousnesse & true holinesse. And thus shall we offer vp our selues liuing sacrifices vnto God, when as we cõsecrate our selues vnto Gods seruice, & obey him in our liues & callings. And looke, as vnder the Law the burnt offerings were burnt all to smoake & ashes; so must we in our liues, wholly and altogether, giue our selues vnto God, & renouncing our selues, be nothing to the world, but wholly dedicated to God. Neither must we come vnto him in our sinnes: for sinne makes our sacrifice dead, lame, halt, and blinde, which God doth abhor; but we must bring our selues

Matth.8.9.

Luk 6.46.

liuing ſacrifices vnto God (as *Paul* ſaith, Rom. 12.1.) *I beſeech you brethren, by the mercies of God, that you giue vp your bodies a liuing ſacrifice, holy and acceptable vnto God, which is your reaſonable ſeruing of God.*

Hence alſo ſome gather, that this ſacrificing of *Iſaac* was a ſigne and type of Chriſts ſacrifice vpon the croſſe. For, as *Iſaac* was ſacrificed and liued, ſo did Chriſt; though he died, yet roſe againe, and now liueth for euer: but becauſe it hath no ground in this place, though it be true which is ſaid of both, therefore I will not ſtand to vrge the ſame.

And thus much of this third reaſon, whereby *Abrahams* faith is commended, with the circumſtances thereof: and conſequently, of all the examples of holy *Abrahams* faith.

Iſaacs Faith.

VERSE 20.

By faith Iſaac bleſſed Iaacob & Eſau concerning things to come.

IN the three former verſes, the holy Ghoſt hath particularly commended the faith of *Abraham:* Now in this verſe, he proceedes to ſet downe vnto vs the faith of Iſaac particularly alſo. Wherein we are to marke theſe foure points : Firſt, a bleſſing wherewith Iſaac bleſſed Iaacob and Eſau: Secondly the *cauſe* of this bleſſing, that is, his *faith:* Thirdly, the parties bleſſed, which are, Iacob and Eſau: Fourthly the *nature* and *matter* of this bleſſing in the ende of the verſe; *Concerning things to come.* Of theſe in order.

Firſt, for the bleſſing. That we may knowe the nature and quality of it, we muſt ſearch out the kinds of bleſſings how many they be.

In Gods word we finde three kinds of bleſſings; 1. whereby *God bleſſeth man.* Now, God bleſſeth man, by giuing vnto him gifts and benefits either temporall or ſpirituall: and ſo he bleſſed all his creatures in the beginning, but eſpecially man.

The 2. kinde of bleſſing, is that, whereby *man bleſſeth God:* and this, man doth by *praiſing God,* and *giuing thankes vnto him, who is the Author of all bleſſings.* So Paul ſaith, *Bleſſed be God euen the Father of our Lord Ieſus Chriſt, which hath bleſſed vs with all ſpirituall bleſſings in heauenly things in Chriſt:* Eph. 1.3. beginning his epiſtle, with this kind of bleſſing, that is, by *praiſing God.* And ſo *Zacharie* after the birth of his ſonne, and the receiuing of his ſight, he ſings vnto god this ſong of praiſe, *Bleſſed be the Lord God of Iſrael,* Luk. 1.68. that is, praiſe and thankſgiuing be vnto the Lord, &c.

The third kind of bleſſing, is that, wherby one man doth bleſſe another : & vnder this kind we muſt vnderſtand Iſaacs bleſſing in this place.

Now further, this kinde of bleſſing, where-

by one man bleſſeth another, is either *priuate* or *publike.* A *priuate bleſſing* is that, whereby one priuate man whatſoeuer he be in his place, praies to God for a bleſing vpon another. And this is common to all men: for euery man may bleſſe another, that is, pray to God for a bleſſing vpon another; but eſpecially it belongeth to Parents thus to bleſſe their children by praying to God for a bleſſing vpō them. And therefore the Cōmandement goes thus, *Honour thy father and thy mother, that they may prolong thy dayes in the Land which the Lord thy God giueth thee,* Exod, 20.12. Now Parents prolong their childrens dayes by bleſing them, that is, by teaching and inſtructing them in religion, and by praying vnto God for a bleſſing vpon them, that he would bleſſe them. Secōdly, there is a publike kinde of bleſſing, which is done by the miniſter of God, in the name of God. And after this ſort *Melchiſedech bleſſed Abraham, as he returned from the ſlaughter of the Kings,* Heb. 7.1. *and without all contradiction,* (ſaith the Author of this Epiſtle) *the leſſe is bleſſed of the greater* (v.7.) Further, theſe publike kind of bleſſings are of two ſorts; either *ordinary* or *extraordinary.* An *ordinary* kinde of publike bleſſing is that, which is pronounced, and vttered out of Gods word by an ordinary miniſter, vpō the people. Example of this we haue in the ordinarie Prieſts in the olde Teſtament; whoſe duty was in the ſeruice of God to bleſſe the people, before their departing. And the forme of bleſing which they ſhould vſe, is preſcribed vnto them by *Moſes,* after this manner from the Lord: *Thus ſhal ye bleſſe the children of Iſraell, and ſay vnto them: The Lord bleſſe thee, and keepe thee, the Lord make his face to ſhine vpon thee, and be mercifull vnto thee: The Lord lift vp his countenance vpon thee, & giue thee peace.* Where we ſee the manner of the Prieſt was to bleſſe the people, not in his owne name, but in the name of God, ſtreching out his hand ouer the heads of the people.

This kinde of bleſſing was then ordinarie; and yet ſome way figuratiue; ſignifying vnto them the bleſſings which Chriſt Ieſus the Mediator, God and man, ſhould not onely pronounce, but euen giue vnto the Church in the newe Teſtament: which our Sauiour accordingly performed to his diſciples at his Aſcenſion. For the Story ſaith; When he was riſen againe, he led them to Bethania (where he aſcended) *and lift vp his hands and bleſſed them.* And *S. Paul* declareth this bleſſing of Chriſt more at large, ſaying; Epheſ. 4.8. 11.12. *Chriſt aſcended on high, and led captiuity captiue, and gaue gifts vnto men: ſome to be Apoſtles, ſome Prophets, & ſome Euangeliſts, and ſome Paſtors and teachers; for the gathering together of the Saints, for the worke of the miniſtery, and for the edification of the bodie of Chriſt.* Where we ſee, that our Sauiour Chriſt did not onely pronounce a bleſſing vpon his Church, but was alſo the author thereof from God his father. And as the

Num.6.23.

Priests in the olde testament had an ordinary kinde of blessing the people: so the ministers of God in the new Testament, they haue the same in substance; for the ministers may blesse their people two waies: First, by praying vnto God for them: Secondly, by pronouncing a blessing vpon them, according to Gods holy word. A forme of this blessing we haue from the Apostle Saint *Paul*, who blessed the Corinthians after this sort; *The grace of our Lord Iesus Christ, and the loue of God, and the communion* (or fellowship) *of the holy Ghost be with you all.*

2.Cor.13.13.

Secondly, an extraordinarie kinde of blessing is, whē an extraordinary Prophet, or seruant of God, doth set downe and pronounce a blessing vnto any, and foretelleth their estate from God. Thus did *Noah* blesse his two sonnes, *Shem* and *Iaphet*, (Gen.9.25.26.27.) and pronounced a curse vpon wicked Canaan. This he did, not as an ordinary father, but as an extraordinary Prophet; not only praying for a blessing vpō his two sonnes, but also foretelling them what should be their condition or estate afterward. So in this place, whereas *Isaac blesseth Iaakob and Esau*, it is no priuate blessing, but a publike; and yet indeede, not an ordinarie publike blessing, but extraordinarie, by telling vnto *Iaacob* and *Esau* before hand, what should be their particular estates and conditions, and what blessings they should haue from God, both in this life, and in the life to come. For we must not here conceiue of *Isaac*, as an ordinary father, but as a holy Patriarch and Prophet of the Lord, and an extraordinary man; foreseeing, and foretelling by the spirit of prophecie, the particular estate of his two sonnes; and also what particular blessings they and their posteritie should receiue from God.

The meaning then of these words, *Isaac blessed Iaacob and Esau*, is this, that *Isaac* beeing a Prophet, an extraordinary man, and a famous Patriarch, did by the spirit of Prophecie foresee, and set downe, and tell before hand, what should be the particular estate of his two sonnes, *Iaacob* and *Esau*: and as hee did foretell it, so likewise he praied vnto God that the same might come to passe; as it did afterward. And thus much for the meaning.

Now, though this were an extraordinary kinde of blessing, which *Isaac* vsed; yet from hence, we may all of vs learne an ordinary duty: for, looke as *Isaac* blessed his two sonnes, so we by his example must learne to abstaine from all wicked speeches: as cursing and banning, and exercise our tongues in *blessing*, not making them the instruments of sinne, to curse, and reuile as many doe: for *vengeance is mine* (*saith the Lord*). He must curse, that hath absolute power and authoritie to inflict the same; when he will. But we are not absolute Lords ouer any man, nor any creature; and therefore we must remember S. *Peters* lesson, 1.Pet.3.9. *We must not render euill for euill, nor rebuke for rebuke, But contrariwise blesse*: & he rendreth a reason,

Knowing that we are thereunto called, to be heires of blessing. Farre be it from vs therfore, to open our mouthes to curse either men or any of Gods creatures: & indeed, vile & abominable is the practise of many, who exercise their tōgues in cursing and banning, not onely men, but also other creatures of God. But let such as feare God, both learne and practise the contrarie.

The second point to be considered, is the cause of this blessing; to wit, *Isaacs* faith: *By faith* Isaac blessed *Iaacob and Esau.*

Here first we are to consider, how *Isaacs* faith blessed *Iaacob* and *Esau?* surely thus: He did most notably gather together all the promises of God made to him, and to his two children, which were specially three. First, *I will be thy God, and the God of thy seede*. 2. God had promised, that *he and his seede should possesse the Land of Canaan*: 3. That his two children should be two mightie Nations, and that *the elder should serue the yonger.*

Now *Isaac* doth not consider these blessings a-part one from another, but hath them all in memory; and on them all (receiuing them by a liuely faith) he builds his blessings: for, by faith in these promises, he did certainly fore-see what should be the future estate of his two sonnes, and accordingly doth he pronoūce particular blessings vpon them both.

But it may be thought, that *Isaac* did not blesse his sonnes *by faith*; for if we reade the Historie in Genesis, we shall see, that he blessed them by errour, and was deceiued therein: for, he was purposed to haue blessed *Esau*, onely with the speciall blessing, when as he gaue the same to *Iaacob* vnwittingly; how then could he doe this by faith? For the answering of this, we must consider two things: First, it is true indeede, that *Isaac* was blinded ouermuch with a fond affection, toward *Esau*, and loued him otherwise then he ought, and therefore was purposed to haue blessed *Esau* with the speciall blessing. This was a fault in *Isaac*: but yet it takes not away *Isacs* faith, nor makes it to be no faith: But it shews that *Isaacs* faith was weake, and ioyned with some infirmitie in forgetting Gods particular promises. Secondly, howsoeuer at the first *Isaac* erred in his purpose for the blessing of his chidren, yet afterward he corrects himselfe for it. For as we may read in the Historie, after he had indeede blessed *Iaacob*, supposing it had beene *Esau*, when *Esau* came for his blessing with his venison, the Text saith, *That Isaac was strioken with a meruailous great feare*, and said, *I haue blessed him, and therefore he shall be blessed*; correcting his fault in his former purpose: yea, and though *Esau* sought it with teares, yet he could not mooue *Isaac* to repent himselfe of blessing *Iaacob*, Heb.12.17. wherefore it is vndoubtedly true, that he gaue these blessings vnto his children by faith.

Now from this that *Isaac blessed his children by faith*, we learne many instructions. The first concerneth Parents; that, howsoeuer they cannot as *Isaac* did, like Prophets and Patriarchs pronounce blessings vpon their children, and foretell what shall be their particular esttae afterward: yet if Parents would as farre as they may, follow the practise of *Isaac*, they should bring great cõfort & cõsolation vnto their own soules, both in this life and in the life to come.

Isaac set before his eies all the promises that God had made both concerning him and his sonnes, and by faith in these promises is mooued to blesse his children: so if Parents would haue true comfort in their children, they must search through the whole booke of God, and see what promises God hath made vnto the godly and to their seede; and withall, they must by faith apply vnto their owne soules, all those gracious promises, endeauouring also to make their children to knowe the same, and to walke worthie thereof: & then as their obedience shal increase, so will their ioy increase, not onely in God, but mutually one in another. This wil stay their hearts in al assaults, yea euē in death it self.

Secondly, whereas *Isaac* blessed his children by faith: here we may take iust occasion to speake of such wicked persons as are commonly called blessers; who are too much esteemed of, by many at this day, and their wicked practises counted blessings, and good meanes of helpe: when as indeede they are most vile and wretched creatures. This may be thought a hard censure, because they are taken for cunning men and women, and for good people following *Isaacs* example in blessing mens children and cattell: they are thought to doe no harme at all, but much good by helping strange mischances that befall men in their bodies, children, or goods. Thus would some excuse and defend these wizzards and blessers, who are the wretched limbs of the deuill: but let vs know, that if they will blesse aright, it must be by faith. Now, what faith haue they? hath God made any promise to them, that by their meanes he will helpe those that come to seeke helpe at them for their children and cattell? nay verily, there is no such matter: God neuer made promise to any such; nay, hee hath flatly forbidden, not onely such practises as they vse, but also for men *to seek* to any such persons: and therefore they cannot blesse mens children and cattell by faith. But they say they doe these things by faith: yet it is by faith in the deuill, and in his promises. For this is certaine, that as God hath his Lawes and Sacraments for those that enter couenant with him: so on the contrary, the deuill hath words, spells, and charms, as his Lawes and rites, wherein he excerciseth his slaues: and by a Satanicall faith in the deuils word and promise, doe these Wizzards and wise-women blesse mens goods and children. This is true by the common confession of many of them, to omit all other proofe. And therefore we must hold thē for the limbs of the deuill, and his wicked iustruments to drawe men from God; and so in no case goe to them for

Lev.19.31.

helpe: for in so doing, we *forsake the liuing Lord* and his helpe, and seeke for helpe at the deuill; then which what can be more odious? But say we receiue some outward helpe by their meanes: yet marke the issue; the Lord hath said, Leuit. 20.6. *If any turne after such as worke with spirits, and after southsayers to goe a whoring after them, then will I set my face against that person, and will cut him off from among his people.* Therefore vnlesse we feare not the curse of God, we must be warned hereby, not to seeke for helpe at their hands. For they are gracelesse people; who haue no feare of God before their eyes: but they set themselues against God and his word. And indeede these common blessers which seeme to doe no hurt, but to blesse mens children & cattell, are more dangerous then notorious Witches, who can onely hurt mens bodies and goods, when God permits; whereas these blessers ensnare the soule, & draw whole Townes and Countries to the approbatiõ & partaking of their wickednes.

The third point to be considered is, the parties blessed, that is, *Iacob and Esau.* Here marke first the order which the holy Ghost vseth: hee setteth *Iacob* in the first place, and yet *Esau* was the elder brother: what is the reason of this? *Ans.* We must know, that the Scripture vseth a three-fold order in the naming of persons.

1. The order of *Nature:* as when the first borne is put first. And thus *Dauids* sonnes are numbred according to their age; first, *Ammon*, then *Daniel*, the third *Absolon*, &c.

*1.Chron.3.
1,2,3.*

2. The order of *dignity*, when as those are put in the first place, not which are the eldest, but which are best and most in Gods fauour. This order the holy Ghost vseth in naming *Noahs* sonns, Gen.5.31. saying, *Noah* begat *Shem, Ham, and Iaphet*; when as *Iaphet* was the eldest, & by order of nature, should haue bin put first: yet with *Shem* god continuedthe couenãt.

3. The order of *History*, when as one that is first or chiefe in dignitie, is placed last, because his History begins in the last place. So our Sauiour Christ is mentioned last in the Genealogie made by S. Matthew, because his History began in the last place, though in dignity he were first and principall. To apply this to our purpose: The order which the holy Ghost here vseth, is not the order of *history*, nor of *Nature*, but of *dignity*; because *Iacob* was chiefe in the fauour of God, therefore the holy Ghost putteth him in the first place.

Here then we see in this order of dignitie, that the first blessing (of life euerlasting) belongs to *Iacob:Esau* must haue his blessing, but in the second place.

Here obserue these two things: First, *Iacob* is receiued into Gods couenant, and *Esau* put by. Iacob getts the principall blessing, and *Esau* looseth it: but what? are these things so for Iacobs desert, or for the default of Esau? Nay verily: the good pleasure of God is the chiefe cause heereof: for touching the blessing;

if we read the Hiſtorie, we ſhall ſee, that *Eſau* at his Fathers commandement, went and hunted, and tooke paines, and got his Father veniſon, and told him nothing but truth. But *Iacob* neuer went to hunt, but gets a Kid dreſſed, and comes to his Father with it, and while he talkes with his Father doth foully gloaſe and lie: ſo that in all reaſon it might ſeeme, that *Eſau* deſerued the better bleſſing: yet God will haue it otherwiſe, and the principall bleſſing belongs to *Iacob.* Wherein we may note, that Gods ſpeciall loue to a man, whereby he receiues him into his couenant, is not grounded on mans behauiour, but on his owne good will and pleaſure.

Secondly, in that *Iaacob* here had the principall bleſſing: we learne that the counſell of God doth ouerrule the will of man. For, Father Iſaac had purpoſed to haue bleſſed *Eſau* with the chiefeſt bleſſing: but yet Gods counſell was contrary, and the ſame ouerrules Iſaacs will. For, though *Iſaac* had cauſe to ſuſpect that it was not *Eſau*, both becauſe he came ſo ſoone, as alſo for that the voice was apparant not to be *Eſaus*, but *Iacobs* voice: yet Gods counſell ouer-ruled his will: and when he came to handle his ſonnes hands, he could not diſcerne betweene a Kiddes skinne, and the skinne of a man: whats the cauſe hereof? Surely it was Gods will and counſell, that *Iaacob* ſhould haue the chiefeſt bleſſing: and therefore hee o-uer-rules *Iſaacs* will, and blindes his ſenſes, and makes him to bleſſe *Iacob* with the chiefeſt bleſſing.

The conſideration hereof is profitable vnto vs: for it is a receiued opinion with many at this day, that God did purpoſe to ſaue all men. Now when queſtion is made, Why then are not all men ſaued? They anſwer, becauſe men will not, though God will. But this opinion is erroneous: for, it makes mans will to ouer-rule Gods counſell: as if they ſhould ſay, God willeth it not, becauſe men will it not: or elſe (which is worſe) God willeth it, but it commeth not to paſſe, becauſe man will not doe it. But Gods will and counſell is the higheſt and chiefeſt cauſe of all: and looke whatſoeuer hee willeth that bringeth he to paſſe: and becauſe all men are not ſaued, therefore we may ſafely thinke, and ſay, that God did neuer decree to ſaue all men.

Now further, more particularly of *Iaacobs* bleſſing: firſt, it may be asked, How could *Iacob* be bleſſed, ſeeing he came diſſemblingly and lying to his father.

Anſw. We muſt knowe, that howſoeuer *Iaacob* ſought the bleſſing by fraude, yet hee might be bleſſed: for he failed not, neither did amiſſe in ſeeking for the bleſſing, but onely in the manner of ſeeking it: it was his duty to ſeeke it, though not after that manner which he did: he ſhould rather haue ſtaied that leiſure and time, wherein God had cauſed *Iſaac* to bleſſe him, without his ſinne in ſeeking it.

Secondly, conſider the manner how *Iacob* receiues his fathers bleſſing; namely, in his elder brother *Eſaus* garment.

Here we may ſee a notable reſemblance of Gods manner of bleſſing vs: When we looke for a bleſſing at Gods hand, we muſt not come in our owne garments, in the rotten ragges of our owne righteouſneſſe; but we muſt put on Chriſts garment, the long whit robe of his righteouſneſſe. And ſo comming vnto God, as *Iſaac* ſaid of the ſauour of *Eſaus* garments, which *Iacob* had put on, (Gen. 27. 27. 28.) *Behold, the ſmell of my ſonne is as the ſmell of a field; God giue thee therefore of the dewe of heauen, and the fatneſſe of the earth, and plenty of wheate and wine:* So will God ſay vnto vs, that the *righteouſneſſe of Chriſt*, which we haue put on by faith, *is a ſweet ſmelling ſauour in his noſthrils*, Eph. 5. 2. Now ſeeing all the bleſſings we enioy, come to vs in Chriſt, and our acceptance with God, is in his righteouſneſſe; wee therefore muſt labour to put on Chriſt euery day, by becomming new creatures: we muſt ſeeke to reſemble him in knowledge, righteouſneſſe, and holineſſe: ſo ſhall our aſſurance of Gods bleſſings increaſe vpon vs more and more.

Laſtly, marke that howſoeuer *Iaacob* was bleſſed otherwiſe then *Iſaac* had purpoſed; yet, after the bleſſing is pronounced, it muſt needs ſtand: for, ſo when *Eſau* came, *Iſaac* ſaid vnto him, *I haue bleſſed Iaacob; therefore he ſhall be bleſſed:* Eph. 27. 33. Euen ſo, the Miniſters of Gods word, in the aſſembly of the Church, who haue power to pronounce Gods bleſſing vpon the people; howſoeuer they be but weake men, and may be deceiued, beeing ſubiect to error, as other men are: yet when they pronounce Gods bleſſing vpon their congregation in the miniſterie of the word; if they doe it in ſinceritie of heart, and vprightneſſe of conſcience, that bleſſing ſhall ſtand. And ſo on the contrary, looke whom they curſe, for iuſt cauſe out of Gods word; their curſe ſhall ſtand.

Further, as *Iſaac* bleſſed, but knewe not whom; ſo the Miniſters of God in the diſpenſation of the word, they muſt bleſſe Gods people, though they knowe not who they are particularly, that doe receiue it.

Thus much of *Iſaacs* bleſſing *Iacob.* Now I come to his bleſſing of *Eſau*: for he alſo was bleſſed, as the Text ſaith; yet in the ſecond place though he were the elder brother. *Queſt.* How could *Eſau* be bleſſed at all, ſeeing *Iſaac* had but one bleſſing? *Anſw. Eſau* was onely bleſſed with temporall bleſſings, and not with ſpirituall. *Obiect.* But ſome will ſay, *Eſau* was a bad man, and wicked; now it is ſaide, that to the *impure all things are impure:* how then could the beſtowing of temporall things be bleſſings to him? *Anſ.* Temporall things beſtowed on the wicked are bleſſings, and no bleſſings: they are bleſſings in regard of God that giues them; but they are no blessings, in regard of men that receiue them and vse them amisse.

Quest. How came it to passe, that *Esau* beeing the elder brother, looseth his birth-right, and blessing both; how came it to be *Iaacobs?*

Ans. The cause was his profanenesse, as we may see and read in the next chapter; where it is said, (Heb. 12.16.) that *he solde his birth-right for a portion of meate:* euen for a messe of redde broth; and beeing so profane, as to contemne so high an honour, he must be content to haue his blessing in the second place. And hence we may obserue a good instruction.

There is many a young man in these our dayes, baptized as *Esau* was circumcised, and liuing in the Church, as he did in *Isaacs* house; who, during the prime of his age, is giuen to nothing but to his pleasure; that is as good to him as *Iaacobs* redde broth was to *Esau:* take this pleasure from him, and take away his life: herein is all his ioy, & he delighteth in nothing so much, as to spend his time in hunting, hawking, dicing, gaming, wantonnesse, and drinking. Now know for certaine, this is a right *Esau;* and yet many such haue we among vs, who thinke of themselues, that they are the iolly fellowes, and they onely carrie the braue mind: but as for *Iaacob,* & such as make conscience of their waies and words; those alas are silly fellowes. Now, what is to be said or thought of these? Surely this, if they doe not (and that in time) looke to their estates, and to themselues, it will cost them their liues; euen the life of their soules. *Esau* lost his birth-right by his profanenesse: and so will these men doe if they continue in this estate; they will blot their names out of the booke of life, and roote themselues quite out of the kingdome of heauen. Therefore let all yong men whatsoeuer they be, high or lowe, take heede how they liue in sinne, and goe on in their wickednesse; for if they take *Esaus* course, and continue in profanenesse, doubtlesse they will haue *Esaus* ende. How wonderfully doth Satan bewitch them, that while they goe on in sinne, they should thinke so highly of themselues, and so basely of those that make conscience of their waies? Wherefore in the feare of God let such betime redresse their waies and courses; least when Gods curse is vpon them, they crie too late for mercie. And thus much of the parties blessed.

The fourth point to be considered, is the nature or matter of this blessing, in the ende of the verse;

Concerning things to come.

The meaning of these words is this: That olde *Isaac* their father did pronounce blessings vpon his sonnes, not onely for the time present, but for the time to come; in blessings temporall and spirituall, (as we may read Gen. 27. 28. 39.) where he giueth to them both *the fatnesse of the Land, and plentie of wheat and wine:*

and especially, to *Iaacob,* that *he should be Lord ouer his brethren.* But some will say, it may seeme to prooue otherwise; for while *Iaacob* liued, he was alwaies humble and subiect to *Esau:* and when he came to his owne country from among the Aramites, as he met with *Esau,* he sent presents to him: and when he sawe him, *he went before, and bowed himselfe to the ground 7. times, vntill he came neere to his brother. Answ.* That prophecie of *Iaacob* and *Esau,* that *the elder should serue the yonger,* must not be restrained to the persons of *Iaacob* and *Esau,* but referred to their posterity; especially in the dayes of *Dauid* and *Salomon:* for then were the Edomites who came of *Esau,* in subiection to the Israelites, the posterite of olde *Israel.* Whereupon, *Dauid* speaking as a King, saith, Psal.60.8. *Moab shall be my wash-pot, ouer Edom will I cast my shooe:* meaning thereby, that he would bring the posteritie of *Esau* into a base and low estate of subiection vnto him; according as we may see verified, 2.Sam. 8.14.

But some will say, that *Isaac* when he blessed *Esau* pronoūced that he should haue *a fertile soile, and the fatnesse of the earth should be his dwelling place* (Gen. 27. 39.) whereas in Malachie the Lord saith (Mal. 1. 3.) *he hated Esau.* And a token thereof was this; *that he had made his mountaines waste, and his heritage a wildernesse for dragons:* meaning, that he should dwell in a barren Land. How can these two agree? *Answ.* First, we may say thus: That the land of Edom was a fertile land; but yet in respect of the Land of Canaan, but a barren and waste Land. Secondly, *Isaac* speaks here of *Idumea,* as it was in his time; not as it was afterward: for it might be fertile in Isaacs time, and yet after become barren: for God will curse a Land by turning *fruitefullnesse into barrennesse, for the wickednesse of them that dwell therein,* Psal. 107. 34.

And thus much for the example of *Isaacs* faith. Now followe the examples of the faith of *Iacob.*

Iacobs Faith.

VERSE 21.

By faith Iacob when hee was dying, blessed both the sons of Ioseph, and worshipped on the ende of his staffe.

IN these words the holy Ghost layes down the notable and worthie example of *Iacobs* faith: which is here commended by two actions; First, his blessing of the two sonnes of *Ioseph:* Secondly, his *adoring or worshipping of God.* In the first action consider these points:

1. The

1. The *bleſſing* it ſelfe: 2.The *circumſtances* belonging to the ſame; As 1. *the time* when Iaacob bleſſed them, that is, *when he was dying:* ſecondly, by what meanes did he bleſſe them, namely, *by faith*, thirdly, the *parties bleſſed: Ephraim and Manaſſes*. Of theſe in order.

Firſt, for the *bleſſing*: Of this kind of bleſſing, wee entreated in the former verſe, in the example of *Iſaacs* faith; and therefore need not now repeate the ſame. Onely this we muſt remember, that this bleſſing of *Iacob* is not the common or ordinarie bleſſing of a father, but the extraordinarie bleſſing of an holy Patriarch and Prophet of God. The bleſſing it ſelfe ſtands in three things: *Iacob* makes the ſonns of *Ioſeph* his own ſonnes, adoping them and taking them into his family. And this is the meaning of thoſe words in Geneſis, where *Iacob* ſaith as he is bleſſing them, *Let my name bee named vpon them, and the name of my Fathers, Abraham & Iſaac;* Gen. 48. 16. that is, they ſhal be receiued into my family, and be my children, called after my name.

2. He giues them two portions in the Land of Canaan: for *Iacob* was made an inſtrument of God, by way of propheċie to diſtinguiſh and diuide the Land of Canaan among his children.

3. He doth as a Prophet, by the ſpirit of prophecie, foretell the condition and eſtate of *Ephraim* and *Manaſſes* in their poſterity; to wit, that they ſhould be great Nations, and of them ſhould come two great people: in theſe three things doth *Iacobs* bleſſing conſiſt.

Out of this bleſſing of *Iacob*, we learne two things: Firſt, that God alloweth this liberty to a maſter of a family, to adopt and chuſe for the vpholding of his houſe a child or children, in the want of iſſue from his owne bodie. For here old *Iacob* for the continuance of his poſterity, and the enlarging of the Church of God, adopteth his ſonnes ſonnes into his owne family, to be his owne ſonnes: And this he doth *by faith*. And therefore a Lord and Maſter in his family may doe the like: but yet with this caueat; he muſt euer take heede that in this adopting he doe not vniuſtly hinder his owne iſſue or kindred.

Againe, whereas *Iacob* bleſſeth theſe two ſonnes of *Ioſeph*, by fore-telling the particular eſtate of their poſterity, for their portion in the Land of *Canaan*; here we learne, that in many things God doth vouchſafe to reueale his will and counſell in a ſpeciall manner vnto them that be his children: As, in this place he reueaeleth vnto *Iacob* the particular eſtate of the two ſonnes of *Ioſeph*. In like manner, when God was to deſtroy the Sodomites; *Shall I hide* (ſaith the Lord) *from Abraham that thing which I doe, ſeeing that Abraham ſhall bee indeede a mighty Nation? for I know him that he will commaund his ſonnes and his houſhold after him, that they keepe the way of the Lord.* And the Prophet *Amos* ſaith; (c. 3. 7.) *Surely the Lord*

Gen. 18. 17,
18, 19.

will doe nothing, but he reuealeth his ſecrets to his ſeruants the Prophets. So ſaith our Sauiour Chriſt to his Diſciples, *Ye are my friends*: and hee giueth a reaſon, *becauſe* (ſaith he) *I haue reuealed vnto you all that I haue heard of my Father*, Ioh. 15. 15. So that thoſe which are (in Chriſt) the friends of God, they ſhall in a particular and ſpeciall manner knowe thoſe things which God wil not reueale vnto others. And looke as this is here verified to *Iacob* in a ſpeciall manner, ſo it is true generally in all Gods ſeruants and children; he reuealeth ſome particular things vnto them, more then he doth vnto others. For, beſides that generall knowledge which they haue in his word, he reueales particularly vnto them the knowledge of their owne *election, of their iuſtification, ſanctification, and glorification to come*: though not by way of prophecie, yet by the working of his ſpirit in the miniſterie and meditation of his word. And thus much of the bleſſing. Now followe the Circumſtances.

The 1. Circumſtance to bee conſidered, is the *time* when *Iacob* bleſſed the two ſonnes of *Ioſeph*; noted in theſe words, *when he was dying:* that is, beeing ready to die, not in the act of dying.

In this circumſtance we may learn two eſpeciall duties: one for maſters of families; the other for the Miniſters of Gods word; for, here *Iacob* beares the perſon not onely of a Father, but of a Prophet. Firſt, Maſters of families are here taught to ſet in order their houſes and families whereof they haue charge, before they die: for, *Iacob* hauing a great charge, and many children, cals for the ſonnes of *Ioſeph, Ephraim*, and *Manaſſes*, before his death, and makes thē his owne, to perfect his family.

Queſt. How (will ſome aſke) muſt a man ſet his houſe in order when he dies. *Anſwer.* By doing two things after *Iacobs* example: for, firſt, he diſpoſeth of his temporall things, and diſtributeth his temporall inheritance in the Land of Canaan. Secondly, hee giues them charge of ſome duties concerning himſelfe and ſome others, eſpecially concerning religion and Gods worſhip, and then he dies: and it is ſaid, *When he had made an end of giuing charge vnto his ſonnes, he plucked vp his feete into his bead, and gaue vp the ghoſt*, Gen. 49. 33. So likewiſe Maſters of families, they muſt ſet their houſes in order by the like two duties: 1. By a due diſpoſing of their temporall goods and poſſeſſions: and 2. by giuing exhortation and charge vnto their children and family, concerning the worſhip of God, and the practiſe of true Religion. This (as we may alſo reade, 1. Kings 2.) was the practiſe of good King *Dauid:* when he was about to die, and as hee ſaith, *to goe the way of all fleſh*, he calls for *Salomon* his ſonne, and makes him King in his ſtead, and giues him a moſt notable charge concerning Gods worſhip, Verſe 3. reade the place, it is worth the marking. So the Prophet *Iſaiah*, when he comes to *Hezekiah* from the Lord, he aimes at thefe two : and bids him *fet his houfe in order, for hee muft die and not liue: Ifay 38.* 1. and fo ought euery Mafter of a family, after their example, both learne & practife thefe two duties.

Secondly, Gods Minifters muft hence learne their dutie : for, *Iacob* was a notable Minifter and Prophet in Gods Church, which was then in his family. *Iacob hee bleffeth the fonnes of Iofeph,* that hee might receiue them into his family, and into the couenant; that fo he might continue and preferue the Church of God after his death: for, looke as *Ifaac* his father did call him into the couenant, and bleffed him; fo dealeth he with the two fonnes of *Iofeph*. And accordingly euery Minifter of God, in his place, ought to haue fpeciall care to conuay and deriue true religion, and the Gofpel of Chrift from hand to hand, fo much as they can while they liue; that fo after their death it may bee publifhed and maintained. In the new Teftament we haue a worthy commaundement for this purpofe; S. *Paul* hauing inftructed and taught *Timothy* in the wayes of godlines and religion, chargeth him, *that what things he had heard and learned of him, the fame he fhould deliuer to faithfull men, which fhould bee able to teach other alfo* : that fo Gods Gofpel and religion going on from hand to hand, and from perfon to perfon, might increafe from time to time. S. *Peters* practife herein, was notable, 2. Pet. 1. 15. *I will endeauour therefore alwaies, that ye may be able to haue remembrance of the things of God after my departure* : hauing profeffed before, that *while he liued he would ftirre them vp by putting them in remembrance, v.* 1 3. And in like fort, all Gods faithfull minifters muft doe their whole endeauour before they die, that the Gofpel may bee preached when they are gone.

2. *Circumftance.* By what meanes did Iacob bleffe the two fonnes of *Iofeph*? *Anf.* By faith in the promifes of God; fo the text faith, *By faith Iacob bleffed the two fonnes of Iofeph.* And if we confider the matter well, wee fhall fee it was a notable faith: for, he was now a poore pilgrime in Egypt, and yet by faith giues them portions in the land of Canaan.

Queft. Why (will fome fay) did hee not keepe himfelfe in the Land of Canaan ?

Anfw. Iacob indeede dwelt there for a time, but yet as a foiourner, hauing no more liberties then he bought for himfelfe; no not fo much as water for his camels, or a place to bury the dead: and befides, he was driuen out of this his owne Land by famine, and was faine to flie into Egypt for food and fuftenance ; and there to liue as a poore pilgrime and ftranger, forth of his owne country: And yet for all this extremitie (as though he had bin fome mighty potentate of the world, or fome Emperour) he makes his Will, and bequeathes vnto his children the Land of Canaan, allotting to euery one his part

and portion; which muft needes be a worke of a notable faith, wonderfully apprehending and applying the promife of God.

In his example we are taught a notable dutie in the matter of our faluation: When as any vs (by reafon of the rigorous temptation of finne and Satan, and by their affaults) fhall feeme to our felues to be (as it were) thruft out of our inheritace in the heauenly Canaan, what muft we doe? We muft not defpaire ; but euen then fet before our eies, and call to remembrance the promifes of God made vnto vs in Chrift, concerning life euerlafting: and thereon we muft reft and ftay our felues. Then let temptations affault vs, and driue vs whether they can: ftill wee muft hold faft the promife with both hands of faith ; and aboue hope, *by faith* appoint and defigne vnto our felues, a part and portion in the kingdome of heauen. And fo doing, we fhall be true Ifraelites, & true followers of this faithfull Patriarch; who by faith (beyond all likelihood) allots the Land of Canaan to his pofterity.

3. *Circumftance.* The *parties* whom he bleffed; namely, *the two fonnes of Iofeph, Manaffes and Ephraim.* Hereof wee may reade at large, Gen. 48. 8, 9, &c. where among many things, obferue this one: *Iofeph* brings his two fonnes, *Manaffes* and *Ephraim,* vnto *Iacob* his father, that he might bleffe them, as he lay on his bed. Now, *Iofephs* minde was, that *Manaffes* (the elder) fhould haue the chiefeft bleffing ; and therefore, he fet *Manaffes* at *Iacobs* right hand, and *Ephraim* (the yonger) at his left : But *Iacob* beeing to bleffe them, laies his hands acroffe, putting his right hand on *Ephraims* head, and the left on the head of *Manaffes;* whereby, he gaue the birth-right (which was a principall prerogatiue) vnto *Ephraim,* contrary to *Iofephs* defire. Vnto *Manaffes* he gaue a bleffing alfo, but farre inferiour to *Ephraims.* Now, here we may not thinke, that *Iacob* did this vpon any fond affection (as parents oftentimes do, becaufe they loue one childe better then another) but he did it after a fpeciall manner ; by the direction and inftinct of Gods fpirit, which fo appointed it: For, when *Iaacob* bleffed them, he knew not (of his owne knowledge, by the benefit of his fenfes,) which was *Ephraim,* and which *Manaffes.* Againe, looke as *Iacob* gaue the bleffing at this time, the principall vnto *Ephraim,* and the leffer to *Manaffes* ; fo afterward they came to paffe: For (as we may read) the tribe of *Ephraim* was farre more populous, and more glorious then the tribe of *Manaffes.* And therefore, in the bookes of the Prophets (Hof. 4. 16. and 5. 9. and 6. 4. &c.) wee fhall finde, that the name of *Ephraim* is giuen to all the ten tribes; and they are called by that name, becaufe it was the moft noble tribe of all, and the moft valiant, and, (as it were) the fhelter of all the reft. Yea further, of this tribe came (1. Chron. 7. 27.) *Iehofua,* that noble captaine; & (1. King. 11. 26.) *Ieroboam,* and many other

mighty

mighty Kings of Ifrael.

Where we may learne, that God is the difpofer of honours and dignities in this world; he giueth thefe to whome he will, to fome more, and to fome leffe, as pleafeth him: yea fometime he raifeth vp men of bafe and lowe degree, to great dignitie; as *Dauid* faith, Pfal. 113.7. *He raifeth the needy out of the duft, and lifteth the poore out of the dongue.* Now whence comes this? Is their learning, their great ftrength, their beautie, or wonderfull skill, and knowledge, the caufe of their preferment? or the wealth of their parents, or any thing in them? No furely: If we fpeake of the firft caufe, we fee in this example, that the preferment of *Ephraim* aboue *Manaffes*, was for no caufe in *Ephraim*; for, what was in *Ephraim*, that was not in *Manaffes*, when *Iacob* bleffed them? Surely, nothing: for, he was but a childe as the other was, and a yonger childe alfo; but he was preferred by reafon of Gods good will towards him. And fo it is with all thofe that are aduanced to preferment in this world. Wherefore, feeing honour and dignity commeth not from themfelues, or any thing in them; therefore they muft not afcribe it to their owne wit, learning, ftrength, or friends; but wholly to the gift of God, as the firft caufe: and fo muft labour to vfe it to the honour of him that onely giues it, of his good pleafure; elfe they facrifice to their owne net: Hab. 1.16.

Queft. Why doth the holy Ghoft in this place put *Iofephs* name downe, who was not bleffed, & conceale the names of the two children that were bleffed? *Anfwer.* If we reade the Hiftory in Genefis, we fhall fee the reafon hereof. For, when *Iofeph* heard that his Father *Iacob* was fick; though he was a mighty Prince and a noble Potentate among the Egyptians, and his Father but a poore Pilgrime: yet hee comes to his ficke Father before his death, and brings his two fonnes with him, to haue his Father to bleffe them before he died; and therefore the holy Ghoft here nameth *Iofeph*, to fhew vnto vs what refpect hee had of his Fathers bleffing: he made more account thereof, and did more efteeme it, that fo hee might haue his fonnes within the couenant, then of all the Kingdomes in the world: and therefore hee brings them both to his Father to be bleffed, a little before his death.

Now looke what minde and affection *Iofeph* beares, the fame fhould be in euery one of vs. Whatfoeuer our eftate be, whether honourable, or bafe and meane; wee muft with *Iofeph* efteeme more of Gods couenant, and to bee members of Gods Church, then of all the honour in the world befides; and we muft efteem our place, and preferments that we haue, or our children may haue, to be nothing in comparifon of the bleffing of God, and his fauour. Yea, we muft chufe with *Iofeph* rather to leaue our honours and dignities for a time, or (if it were) for euer; then to loofe the bleffing of Gods

grace: and bleffed fhall thofe Fathers bee with *Iofeph*, who had rather haue their children bleffed of God, then aduanced in the world. The fecond action of *Iacobs* faith, is in thefe words; *And worfhipped on the end of his ftaffe:* and it is a notable worke for the commendation of his faith. But before we come vnto it, there are certaine queftions which may profitably be confidered: As firft, for the tranflation; how the words fhould be read. The Papifts reade them thus: And adored the toppe of his Rod; that is (fay they) the top of *Iofephs* Scepter who came to vifit him. From whence they would gather and ground their abominable Idolatrie, in the Adoration of creatures, and namely of noly things, as Crucifix, Reliques, Images, as alfo of God at & before fuch holy things. But we muft know, that their tranflation is falfe and erronious, and cannot be iuftified, howfoeuer they may bring fome mens witneffe and teftimonie for the fame. For in reading it thus, *and adored the top of his Rod;* they leaue out a fubftantiall word of the text, to wit, this word *vpon;* wherby they corrupt the Text, & depraue the meaning of the holy Ghoft.

Againe, their obferuation and collection hence, is moft abhominable: for, to worfhippe an Image or other holy thing, or God himfelfe in or at the fame, is flatly forbidden in the fecond Commaundement, *Thou fhalt not make to thy felfe any grauen Image, &c. Thou fhalt not bow downe to them.*

But our Tranflation in this place is true and right, according to the words of the Text, and the meaning of the holy Ghoft, *that he worfhipped vpon the ende of his ftaffe.*

Yet further, there may be a queftion mooued about the words, for, if we reade the Hiftorie in Genefis, it is there faid, that *Iacob* worfhipped *towards the ende or top of his bed*, Gen. 47.31.

Now, there is great difference betweene thefe two, *To worfhippe on the toppe of his ftaffe: and on the toppe of his bed.*

How therfore can they ftand together? *Anf.* They may ftand well together, and bee both true: for when *Iacob* was about to giue vp the Ghoft, and was ready to die, hee raifed vp himfelfe vpon his pillowe towards the beds head, and thereon refted his body. Now becaufe his body was weake and feeble, he ftaide himfelfe alfo vpon his ftaffe: and thus comparing the places together, wee fee there is no repugnancie in them. Againe, this wee muft know, that the fame fentence of Scripture may be diuerfly read in diuers places of Scripture, without any impeachment to the truth, certaintie, or perfection of Scripture: for, when the holy Ghoft fpeaketh the fame thing often, yet in different tearmes (as in this place) the diuerfity of words doth enlarge or open the fenfe and meaning, but no way corrupt or depraue the fame. And thus much for the words.

Now to come to the fact it felfe: in *Iacobs*

worſhip, three circumſtances are to be conſidered: 1. The occaſion: 2. The time: 3. The manner of it.

The occaſion of *Iacobs* worſhip here ſpoken of (as we may reade , Gen. 47.) was this: when the time drew neere that *Iacob* muſt die, he called for his ſonne *Ioſeph*, and charged him deeply, That *he ſhould not burie him in Egypt when he was dead, but that he ſhould carie him thence, and burie him in the buriall of his Fathers*; *Ioſeph* conſents vnto his Fathers requeſt: and yet *Iacob* for certaintie makes him to *ſweare* that he ſhall doe ſo, and *Ioſeph* ſware vnto him. Now vpon this iſſue that *Iacob* had with *Ioſeph* , the Text ſaith, *That Iſrael worſhipped towards the beds head*: that is, he praiſed God, and gaue thankes vnto him for this benefit that he ſhould be buried with his Fathers, *Abraham* , and *Iſaac*. And yet this benefit did not ſo much concerne himſelfe as his children: for, the carying of his bones thither , was to be a token and pledge, and a certaine aſſurance vnto them , that the Land of Canaan ſhould be theirs, and that God would bring them thither againe.

In this circumſtance , obſerue a notable dutie belonging vnto Fathers & Maſters of families: they muſt in their life time haue care of their poſteritie, & vſe all meanes to helpe them, and benefite them in the faith; not onely while they are aliue, but alſo after they are dead, after the example of this holy Patriarch : and when they haue obtained this benefite for them, they muſt be glad in their hearts and reioyce , and thereupon take occaſion to praiſe the Lord, as *Iacob* did in this place.

2. Circumſtance. The *manner how he worſhipped:* Which is ſet downe in theſe words; *on the end of his ſtaffe*. This circumſtance is worth the marking: for, good *Iacob*, by reaſon of the weakeneſſe of his bodie and olde age , was not able to come forth of his bed , and kneele downe or proſtrate himſelfe ; but raiſeth himſelfe vp vpon his pillowe towards his beds head: and by reaſon of feebleneſſe beeing not yet able to ſit vpright, he doth leane and beare himſelfe vpon his ſtaffe.

Here we learne , that wee muſt not onely worſhip God with our ſoules and hearts , but with our bodies alſo : for God hath created both, and therefore will be worſhipped in both, 1. Cor. 6. 20. Olde *Iacob* might haue excuſed himſelfe, that by reaſon of the weakeneſſe of his bodie , hee was not able to adore God with any bodily reuerence : but yet we ſee hee leanes vpon his ſtaffe; and ſo, making ſupply to his bodily weakeneſſe, adoreth God with his bodie.

Queſt. In what kind of geſture then muſt we worſhip God; with our bodies?

Anſwer. The word of God doth not preſcribe any, by way of limitation. For ſometimes our Sauiour Chriſt prayed *kneeling* , Luk. 21. 41: ſometimes *groueling*; Matth. 26. 59: ſometimes *ſtanding*; Ioh. 11. 41. as alſo did the Apo-

ſtles. And the Scripture approoueth the Publican, who ſtoode a-farre off and prayed , Luke 18. 13. *Elias* alſo , 1. King. 18. 42. is ſaid to pray *with his head betweene his legges*; ſo that we haue no certaine forme preſcribed vs: onely this , we muſt vſe that geſture which may beſt ſet forth and declare our humble heart , & holy affection vnto God.

Here then is confuted an opinion of thoſe, which thinke that a man may worſhip God with his heart, and yet worſhip images with his bodie ; that hee may be preſent at idolatrous worſhip, yet keep his heart vnto God. But *Iacobs* behauiour , in this place, doth both confute and condemne them: for, hee thought his body as due to God, as his ſoule; and therefore worſhipped God with both.

3. *Circumſtance: The time* when hee worſhipped God thus; namely, *when he was dying*, euen then he worſhipped God. In this circumſtance we may note diuers things.

Firſt , here behold the bad practiſe of the world ; for , many men when they are dying, now-adaies, are ſo farre from following *Iacobs* example in worſhipping and praiſing God; that then they are faine to cal for men to teach them how they ſhould worſhip God: hauing ſpent the former part of their life careleſly, in regard of their ſoules ; following worldly profits and pleaſures, neuer thinking of their duty to God, till they die. But what a fearefull courſe is this, that men ſhould thus brutiſhly goe on from day to day, not knowing how to worſhip God? Well, all ſuch as loue their owne ſoules, and would be like to godly *Iacob*; or (as our Sauiour Chriſt ſaid to *Nathaniel*) would be *true Iſraelites*, Ioh. 1. 47. the naturall ſonnes of olde *Iſrael* indeed; they muſt haue care ſo to liue in this world, that they may *worſhip God* when they die: and therefore they muſt not deferre, but learne betime the knowledge and feare of God; that when death comes , they may bee able to ſhewe forth, and practiſe the ſame. It is a lamentable thing, to conſider how the deuill bewitcheth mens hearts, ſo as they liue in the world, as though they ſhould neuer goe out of it ; neuer caring for religion till the day of death come vpon the͂ : and then it is too late to learne. But this is to followe *Eſau*, and not *Iacob*; who is therefore condemned by the holy Ghoſt.

2. Againe , in this that *Iacob* worſhipped God at his death, we learne this ; *That as men liue, ſo they die, for the moſt part* : *Iacob* was brought vp in Gods worſhip, and therein liued all his life long; and looke as he liued ſo he died : for , when hee died, *he worſhipped God, reſting his bodie on the end of his ſtaffe*. This ſame truth is verefied now, and ſhall bee for euer; let a man worſhip God through the courſe of his life, and when hee dieth he ſhall be able to worſhip and praiſe God. On the other ſide (take notice of it) he that liues in couetouſnes, in profaneneſſe, in fornication , and wanton-

nesse, for the most part so dies : Come to a co-uetous man at his death, and talke with him, and you shall finde nothing in him ordinarily, but rauing, and talking about his bargaines, his billes, and indentures, and other worldly things. And so we may say of other lewd liuers: looke what minde they had while they were liuing, and that shall you finde most in their mouthes while they are dying: which shewes plainely, that as men liue, so they die.

But some will say, that oftentimes the godly man raues and speakes lewdly, and (it may be) profanely, before his death; *Answ.* It is true indeede : the best man is not freed from any kind of bodily sicknesse, but is subiect to them, as well as the wicked; as, to burning feuers, and such like : by the violence and rage of which diseases, they are often driuen to raue, to speake fondly, and sometimes lewdly; yea (it may be) profanely. But what is that to the purpose? for though a godly man (for the time of his fit) cannot expresse the grace of his heart, but ra-ther the corruption of his nature; yet when hee hath recouered himselfe, hee is sory for the same, and is then ready and willing to praise God with all his heart. So that if we would die well, as *Iacob* did, praising God, then let vs lead our liues as he did; namely, by faith, and the direction of his word and promises. Then come death when it will, and how it will, we may indeede be sore assaulted by sicknesse and temptatió; but yet we shal neuer bee ouercom: for, God is faithfull that hath promised an issue to his children in temptation, 1. Cor. 10. v. 13.

Lastly, whereas *Iacob worshipped God at his death*; Here we learne, that *sound zeale will ne-uer decay*. Many men haue zeale indeede, but it comes onely from the strength and sound-nesse of their bodily constitution: and looke, as strength decaies, so doth that kinde of zeale. But sound zeale will not decay and weaken with the bodie: but(as *Dauid* saith of the righ-teous, Psal. 92. 13, 15.) will *flourish like a palme tree, and growe like a Cedar in Libanon, it shall still bring forth fruite in a mans age, and flourish*. This wee see was true in Iacob; for, though hee were olde, and feeble with sick-nesse, yet he sheweth forth sound zeale in his heart, at the houre of his death. Euen so will it be with vs, that professe religion : if zeale bee found in our hearts, it will shewe it selfe : and the older wee are, the more fruites of grace wee shall bring forth : and then shewe forth more true zeale, then in yonger yeares. For, though bodily strength decay, yet sound zeale will neuer decay : but when strength faileth, then will zeale flourish (if it bee found) like to the palme tree, which wil bud & sprout, though the roots of it be cut of. Where-fore, if we would shew forth zeale in our age, we must get soundnes of it in our youth : for that will put forth it selfe in the time of death. And thus much of *Iacobs* example.

Iosephs Faith.

VERSE 22.

By faith, Ioseph when hee died made mention of the de-parting of the children of Is-rael, and gaue comandement of his bones.

Ee haue heard in the former verses the seue-ral examples of the faith of the three Patriachs, *Abraham*, *Isaac*, and *Iacob*. Now in this verse the holy Ghost setteth downe the example of Iosephs faith. The words in this verse are plaine and easie, and neede no exposition : They are a plaine and briefe summe of the ende of the 50. Chapter of Genesis. Let vs therefore come to the points of doctrine, and instructions which are to bee learned and gathered forth of the words.

First, note in generall, the great resemblance of this example with the former : of Ioseph a godly sonne, with Iacob a godly father : for, both of them shew forth their faith when they die. For, it is said of both, *By faith when he died*: So that in ground & circumstance of time, they both agree.

Herein we may obserue: first, that the good exáples of *Superiours* (whether they be ciuill or Ecclesiasticall) are of great force to bring other men on, and to make them forward in the du-ties of religion : their zeale (as *Paul* saith to the Corinthians in the case of almes) prouoketh many. Iacob the father, a worthy Prophet and Patriarch, and giuing an holy and blessed ex-ample vnto Ioseph and his children, doth shew forth at his death most notable behauiour: wherein, he worthily expresseth the truth of his faith. Now, his example works with Ioseph, and he in his death behaues himselfe in the same manner that his godly father did before him: and therefore *superiours* must looke to all their sayings and doings carefully, that they may be worthy examples to their *inferiours*, to drawe them on in religion, and in the feare of God.

Secondly, hence inferiours also must learne to follow the godly, holy, & religious examples of their gouernours and superiours (whether they be ciuill or Ecclesiasticall): as we may see in this place, Ioseph doth imitate the godly ex-ample of his father Iacob. Hereof Saint *Paul* giueth straite charge vnto the Philippians, say-ing: *Brethren be followers of me, and looke on them which walke ſo , as yee haue vs for an ex-ample*, Phil. 3. 17. And in the next Chapter, exhorting them to honeſt conuerſation , hee biddes them *doe thoſe things which they had heard, receiued, and ſeene in him*. But are theſe duties practiſed among vs ? bee the elder ſort teachers of good things to the yonger? and doe the yonger follow their elders in well-doing? nay verily: but ſuch are our times, too many a-mong vs, both thoſe that giue, and thoſe which follow good examples , are as *ſignes and won-ders* ; as the Prophet ſpeaketh; they are made a reproach, and a by-word among men , and are foully diſgraced by odious tearmes, *Iſay* 8. 18. But this indeede is a practiſe of *Iſmael* , that mocked *Iſaac*, Gen. 21. ver.9. And we againe, muſt vndoubtedly know , that vnleſſe it be re-formed , that hand of God which hath beene ſtretched out againſt vs in manie feareful iudge-ments, will not be pulled backe , but ſtretched out ſtill, till it bring vs to deſtruction: for, God will not ſuffer his ordinances to be contemned, and his holy ones to be abuſed: he looketh for better fruites at our hands , and therefore wee muſt learne of theſe godly Patriarches, both to giue and to followe good examples.

In the example of *Ioſeph*, more particularly we are to obſerue two points: 1. *Ioſephs* faith: 2. The actions of his faith whereby it is com-mended.

For the firſt : it is ſaide, that *by faith Ioſeph when he died , &c*. *Ioſeph*, for ought wee finde in Scripture, had not ſuch meanes to come by faith, as his Aunceſtors had before him. For the three Patriarches, *Abraham, Iſaac*, and *Iacob*, had otherwhiles the appearance of God vnto them , otherwhile his holy Angels brought them meſſages from God, and ſometime they had his wil reuealed vnto them by dreames and viſions ; all which were notable healpes and meanes both to beginne and to encreaſe *faith* in them: but *Ioſeph* wanted all theſe meanes, or at leaſt many of them. For , reade his whole Hiſtorie , and you ſhall not finde, that either Angell appeared ynto him, or elſe that God by dreames and viſions ſpake vnto him : and no meruaile. For he liued out of the viſible Church where Gods preſence was, in ſuperſtitious and Idolatrous Egypt : and yet for all this, hee is here matched in the matter of faith , with the three worthie Patriarchs.

It is then a good queſtiõ; how *Ioſeph* ſhould come by this faith?

Anſw. We muſt knowe this, that though he had not the like extraordinary meanes with the Patriarches; yet he wanted not all meanes: for, in his yonger dayes , hee was trayned vp in his Father *Iacobs* family, and by him was inſtructed in the wayes of God, and in the practiſe of re-ligion; and in his latter dayes alſo , hee had the benefit of his Fathers company and inſtructi-ons in Egypt. Now *Iacob* was not an ordinarie Father , but a notable Patriarch and an holy Prophet ; in whoſe family God had placed his

viſible Church in thoſe dayes, wherein *Iacob* was the Lords Prophet and Miniſter. Now *Ioſeph*, both in his young age, and alſo after his Father came to Egypt, did heare and learne of him the wayes of God ; and by that meanes came to this excellent faith, for which hee is ſo commended here, & matched with his Fathers the holy Patriarchs.

Hence we learne, that the preaching of Gods word by his Miniſters (though extraordinarie meanes, as reuelations, and viſions, be wanting) is ſufficient to bring a man to faith; yea, to ſuch a faith as the three Patriarchs had. Indeede in the miniſterie of the word, hee which ſpeaketh vnto vs, is but a man as others are ; but yet the word which he deliuereth is not his owne, but the mighty word of God: and looke what is truly pronounced by him vnto vs out of Gods word, the ſame is as certainly ſealed vnto vs by his ſpirit, as if God himſelfe from heauen ſhould extraordinarily reueale the ſame. And howſoeuer in former times men had viſions & dreames, and Angels from God himſelfe to re-ueale his will vnto them: yet this Miniſterie of Gods word in the new Teſtament, is as ſuffici-ent a meanes of the beginning & encreaſing of true faith, as that was then.

This plainly confuteth all thoſe that neglect or contemne the Miniſterie and preaching of the word , and looke for extraordinarie reuela-tions, and for viſions and dreames , for the be-getting and encreaſe of faith and grace in their hearts. But our Sauiour Chriſt doth notably checke all ſuch in the Parable of the rich man, by the words of *Abraham* to *Diues*; ſaying, of *Diues* brethren, that *they had Moſes and the Prophets; if they will not heare them, neither will they beleeue though one ſhould come from the dead againe*, (verſe 31): in ſinuating , that if a man will not beleeue by the preaching of the word, there is nothing in the world will make him to beleeue; neither reuelations, nor viſions, no not the words of them that riſe againe from the dead.

Secondly, the conſideration of the ſufficien-cie of Gods ordinance in the holy Miniſterie, to beget and to encreaſe true faith, muſt ſtirre vs vp to all care and diligence, not onely to heare the word of God preached vnto vs, but to pro-fit by it both in knowledge and obedience: and thus much for the firſt point.

The ſecond point to be handled, is the com-mendation of *Ioſephs* faith by two actions thereof: to wit, 1. His *mention of the departure of the children of Iſraell out of Egypt :* 2. His *commaundement concerning his bones*. Of both which we will ſpeake briefely, becauſe the ſpe-ciall points herein were handled in the former verſe.

For the firſt: *Ioſeph when he died made menti-on of the departing of the children of Iſrael*, that is, *out of Egypt into Canaan*.

Here we may obſerue a moſt notable worke of *faith* : it makes a man to keepe in memory

the

the mercifull promifes which God hath made vnto him. This is it which comends *Iosephs* faith for a liuely faith, That being about to die, hee remembreth this mercifull promife of God, made to his fore-fathers touching their pofterity; to wit, that *after they had continued as feruants in a ftrange Land 400. yeares, they fhould then haue a good iffue and a happy deliuerance, and bee brought into the Land of Canaan.* Gen. 15. 13. This is a notable worke of faith, as may appeare by two notable effects hereof in the life of a Chriftian: For firft, by this remembrance of Gods mercifull promifes, the feruant of God at all times, and in all diftreffes and extremities doth finde comfort vnto his foule. This brings to his memory the wonderfull goodneffe and mercie of God, by which he is comforted. When *Dauid* was in a moft defperate cafe, fo as hee cried out by reafon of affliction and temptation, *Will the Lord abfent himfelfe for euer, and will he fhew no more fauour? Is his mercie cleane gone? doth his mercie faile for euermore?* Pfal. 77. with fuch like moft fearefull fpeaches; How did he then comfort himfelfe in this diftreffe? *Anfw.* Surely *by remembring the workes of the Lord, and his wonders of olde, and by meditating on all his workes* and gracious acts which hee had done for him. So likewife in another place in great anguifh of fpirit, he faith to his foule, *Why art thou caft downe my foule,* and *why art thou difquieted within me?* Pfalm. 43. 5. Yet in the next words he thus ftayes himfelfe; *Waite on God, for I will yet giue thankes vnto him: hee is my prefent helpe, and my God.* How came *Dauid* to fay fo, in this diftreffe? *Anfwer.* By meanes of faith, which doth reuiue and refrefh the dead heart of man, by bringing to his remembrance the mercifull promifes of God.

Saint *Paul* preffed with corruption: cried out: *O wretched man that I am, who fhall deliuer me from the body of this death?* Rom. 7. 24. Yet in the next words he faith, *I thanke my God through Iefus Chrift our Lord: Then I my felfe in my minde ferue the law of God, &c.* How com the latter words to followe on the former? *Anf.* In the firft words indeede, he is caft down with the vew and fight of his naturall corruption, which drew him headlong into finne: but yet the latter words are a remembrance of the mercifull deliuerance from finne which God had wrought in him by *Chrift*: and therefore he breaketh out to this faying, *I thanke my God through Iefus Chrift, &c.*

Secondly, the remembrance of Gods promifes ferueth to be a meanes to keepe a man from finne: for mans nature is as readie and prone to finne, as fire is to burne when fewell is put to it. But when by faith he calls to minde Gods mercifull promifes, efpecially thofe which are made vnto him in Chrift: then hee reafoneth and ftriueth againft temptation, and layes the word as a fhield vnto his foule, to keepe out the fierie darts of Satan; yea, hee

applies the fame word to his owne foule, as a corrofiue vnto corruption: whereupon it is faid, that faith purifieth the heart, Act. 15. 9. How? namely, befide the applying of Chrifts blood, it brings to memory Gods mercifull promifes in Chrift: which ftay a man from committing fuch things as would pollute and defile the hart. And therfore is *faith* faid to be *our victory ouer the world:* 1. Ioh. 5. 4. becaufe by applying to our foules gods promifes in Chrift, we doe not onely contemne the world, in regard of Chrift; but alfo ftand againft the affaults thereof: fo that it is a moft notable and excellent worke of faith.

Laftly, obferue the circumftance of time, when *Iofeph* made remembrance of their departing. The text faith, *When hee was dying.* Hereof we haue fpoken in the former verfe: yet this one thing may here againe be well remembred; *Iofeph* cals to minde the promifes of God at his death, which concerne the temporall deliuerance of his people: and we by his example, when we are dying, muft learne to call to remembrance the gracious promifes, which God hath made vnto vs in Chrift, touching our eternall deliuerance from the fpirituall bondage of the deuill. Oh! great will bee the fruit hereof, not onely for inward comfort to our owne foules, and ioy to fuch as loue vs; but alfo wee fhall hereby giue a worthy euidence to the world, that we haue beene found in the faith: wherein, wee fhall leaue a good prefident to thofe that follow vs.

The fecond fact of *Iofephs* faith is this; *He gaue commaundement concerning his bones.* The meaning thereof is this: that *Iofeph* lying on his death bead, gaue a folemne charge to his brethren, to haue fpeciall care how and where they buried him; that his bones might not be loft, but fo preferued while they ftaied in Egypt, that at their departure they might be caried into the land of Canaan, and there buried in the fepulchre of his fathers. The caufes why *Iofeph* gaue this commandement were thefe: 1 Hereby to teftifie vnto his brethren and pofterity, that howfoeuer he liued a long time in the pompe and glory of Egypt, yet his heart was neuer fet thereon; but hee had greater delight, and more efteemed to be counted a true member of the Church of God, then to bee a noble prince in the Land of Egypt. For, if he had loued and liked the pompe of Egypt, he would haue had his fepulchre among them; but giuing commaundement to the contrary, it fheweth plainely, that his heart was neuer fet on that glory and pompe in which he liued.

By whofe example wee are taught, that in vfing the world, and the things thereof, wee muft not fet our hearts on them; but as the Apoftle faith, 1. Cor. 7. 31. *Vfe them as though we vfed them not:* ftill hauing our affections fet on heauen, which is our fpirituall Canaan.

2. Hereby *Iofeph* would teftifie vnto his brethren, what he efteemed his chiefe happineffe;

namely, that in faith and hope hee was ioyned vnto his fathers, and auncestors, that beleeued in God, and that he was of their religion, and looked for a resurection & another life, as they did. And this he would haue knowen, not only to his brethren and posteritie, but to the Egyptians also, among whom he liued.

3. *Ioseph* hereby intended principally, to confirme the faith of his brethren and posterity in Gods promise, for enioying and possessing the Land of Canaan after his death: and this was a notable way to strengthten their faith. For, when they shlould see or remember his corps, it was vnto them as a liuely sermon, to shew them plainely, that howsoeuer they liued for a while in bondage in Egypt: yet the day should shortly come, wherein they should bee set at libertie, and brought (as free-men) into the land of Canaan: And vndoubtedly, *Ioseph* would therefore haue his bones kept among them, that they might be a pledge vnto them of their deliuerance.

Yea note further, the story saith, (Gen. 50. 15.) that *Ioseph* did not onely charge his brethren generally; but binds them by an oath to cary his bones: hereby shewing, that it was a matter of great weight which he did inioyne them; euen a signe and pledge of the truth of Gods promise in their deliuerance. Whence we learne, that it is a matter of great moment, for euery Christian, both carefully and reuerently to vse the *sacraments*, which God hath giuen as pledges of his couenant of grace, made with vs in Christ. For, shall *Ioseph* cause his brethren and posteritie to sweare concerning his bones, that so they might more reuerently regard that pledge and signe of their outward deliuerance? And shall not we with all reuerence and good conscience, both esteeme and vse those holy pledges of our eternall deliuerance by Christ Iesus?

The Papists, from this place, would iustifie their practise, in reseruing and honouring the Reliques of Saints. Now by Reliques, they mean the parts of the bodies of saints departed; as the head of *Iohn Baptist*, the armes or bones of this or that Saint, the milke of the virgin *Mary*, and also the parts of the crosse whereon Christ suffered, with such like. *Answ.* First, let vs know, that their Reliques are nothing else but forged deuices of their owne, and no true Reliques of Saints; as by one instance may appeare. For, the parts and parcels of wood, kept in Europe, which they say are parts of the crosse whereon Christ died, are so many, that if they were all gathered together, they would load a ship: which shewes plainely, that herein they vse notorious forgerie, for it was no greater then a man may beare. And the like is their behauiour in the rest. Secondly, the keeping of *Iosephs* bones, was for a good end & purpose; namely, to testifie his owne faith, and to confirme theirs, in beleeuing Gods promise for their deliuerance out of the bondage of Egypt: but their Reliques serue rather to extinguish faith in Christ, then to confirme it; for, they nourish men in fond deuices, and foule superstitions, and not in the truth of Gods promises. Thirdly, wee doe not reade in all the Bible, that *Iosephs* bones were euer worshipped; and therefore from this place they haue no ground whereon to build their superstitious *worshipping of Reliques*. And thus much of the example of *Iosephs* faith.

Moses Parents Faith.

VERSE 23.

By faith, Moses when he was borne, was hid three moneths of his parents, because they saw he was a proper child: neither feared they the kings commandement.

N this verse the holy Ghost proceedeth further, and setteth downe vnto vs a notable and worthy example of the faith of *Moses parents*. If we would see the history at large, we must reade the 2. Chapter of Exodus; of which, these words are an abridgement, or briefe Epitome. Now, here the faith of *Moses* parents is commended vnto vs by two notable actions: 1. The hiding of *Moses* their child when he was borne; 2. Their courage and boldnesse in that action; in *not fearing the Kings commandement*. Of their hiding of him, wee will first intreat generally, and then come to the circumstance thereof. In generall, Their hiding of the childe was this: They kept him close, and vnknowen to the Egyptians for three moneths space; because the King had giuen commandement and charge to all his people, that they should *drowne euery man childe borne among the Hebrewes.* Exod. 1. 22. In this action of their faith, we may obserue some speciall points.

First, *Moses* was to be a worthy Prophet, & Captaine, or guide vnto the people of Israel: and therefore howsoeuer other men-children were drowned vpon the cruell commaund of *Pharaoh*, yet the Lord prouides for him so soone as hee is borne, that he shall be hid, & so preserued frō the tirannie and rage of *Pharaoh*.

Whence we learne, that God in the middest of all persecution, doth euermore preserue the seede of his Church. There bee two estates of Gods Church in the world: the first is quiet and peaceable, when the Gospel is publikely

likely profeſſed, taught, and receiued without hoſtile oppoſition, as by Gods great mercie it is in our Church at this day. The ſecond is an hidden eſtate, when as it cannot ſhew it ſelfe viſible, but the open profeſſion of the Goſpel is ſuppreſſed by the rage of the enemie the de-uill, and by wicked and cruell men that be his inſtruments. Thus God ſuffereth his Church ſometimes to be ſhadowed, and in theſe times many of his deere children to be ſlaine and put to death for the ſinnes of his Church, yet ſo, as that alwaies hee preſerues the ſeede of his Church. When *Iſay* had ſhewed the Iewes the fearefull deſolation of their Land; that the Ci-ties ſhould be waſted without inhabitant, and their houſes without man; yet then hee ſaith, *There ſhall bee a tenth in it, and the holy ſeede ſhall bee the ſubſtance* or *vnderprop thereof*, verſe 13. God doth not deale with his Church, as he doth with the enemies thereof: hee but loppes off the branches in his Church, when as hee ſtockes vp the roote of the enemies, *Iſay*, chapter 27. verſes 7, 8. When he viſited So-dome and Gomorrah, he deſtroyed them vtter-ly out of the earth: but the Lord doth euer keepe faſt the ſeede of his Church, that when the ſtorme of perſecution is blowen ouer, his Church may ſpring and flouriſh after-ward.

Here ſome may ſay, Seeing God purpoſed to make Moſes ſuch a worthy mã ouer his people, why did he not by ſome wonderfull, powerfull, and mighty manner preſerue him againſt the rage of *Pharaoh? Anſw.* God indeede was a-ble to haue ſent a legion of Angels for his pre-ſeruation, or to haue done it after ſome ſtrange viſible manner; but yet he would not: for wee muſt knowe and remember, that it is Gods pleaſure to ſhew his power in weake meanes. He can preſerue euery ſeruant of his from all kinde of iniurie: but he will not alwaies doe ſo. When Chriſt himſelfe our Sauiour, was in his infancie perſecuted by *Herod*, God his Father was then able to haue preſerued him in Iudea, and to haue ouerthrowen his perſecutor by many legions of angels; yet he would not, but onely vſeth the poore helpe of *Ioſeph* & *Marie*, with the ordinarie weake meanes of flight; and all this he did, that he might be glorified in the weakeneſſe of his ſeruants; for, when all meanes faile, then doth hee magnifie his power and prouidence in preſeruing thoſe that truſt in him. And thus much of this Action in generall.

The circumſtances to bee conſidered in the hiding of Moſes, are foure: 1. The time when he was hid: the Text ſaith, *When he was borne.* Moſes (as we ſaide) muſt be afterward a nota-ble ſeruant, and a worthy inſtrument of God, whereby hee would worke the deliuerance of his people, out of the bondage of Egypt: and yet we ſee, he is faine to be hid ſo ſoone as he is borne.

Hence we learne; that thoſe that be the ſer-uants of God, & are in ſpecial fauour with him,

muſt look for trouble and affliction in this life, from the cradle to the graue, from the day of their birth, to the houre of their death. Moſes is in danger of his life by *Pharaoh*, ſo ſoone as hee is borne. And ſo was our Sauiour Chriſt by *He-rod*, when he was but a babe: whereupon his Parents fled with him into Egypt for his ſafety. And anſwerable to their infancie was the reſt of their life: full of danger, full of trouble: And as it was with them, ſo is it with others: 2.Tim. 3. 12. *He that will liue godly muſt ſuffer perſe-cution:* and he that *will be Chriſts Diſciple, muſt take vp his Croſſe euery day and followe him,* Luk. 6. 23.

This is a point which all of vs muſt marke; wee muſt not looke to haue eaſe and ioy in earth: It is enough for vs to enioy that after this life. If Chriſt himſelfe carie his croſſe out of the gate, we then with his diſciples *muſt take vp our croſſe and followe him euery day.*

The 2. circumſtance to be conſidered, is this: How long was Moſes hid? namely, *three moneths. Queſt.* Why was hee hid no longer? *Anſ.* Becauſe they could not; for it is likely, there was ſearch for him, and therefore *they made a baſket of reed, and dawbed it with ſlime and pitch, and laide the childe therein, and put it among the bulſhrues by the riuers brinke.*

Thus did the Parents aduenture the childes life, for the ſauing of their owne: wherein we may ſee a great want & weaknes in their faith; for they kept their child a while by faith: but af-terward committed him to the dangers of the waters, of whilde beaſts, and fowles of the aire. So that it is plaine their faith was weake, and mingled with feare and with ſome doubting. For in keeping the childe three moneths, they ſhewe forth liuely faith; but when as they expoſe him to danger for their owne ſafety, herein they bewray ſome want of loue, and weakeneſſe of faith: and yet we ſee they are here commended for their faith. Which ſhew-eth plainely, that if a man haue true and ſound faith, though it be but weak, yet God in mercy will take knowledge of it, and commend it, paſſing by the weakeneſſe of it; yea and vnto that faith will giue the promiſes of life euer-laſting made in Chriſt.

The third circumſtance to be conſidered, is this; Who it was that kept Moſes three mo-neths. In Exodus it is ſaid that *his mother kept him*; but here it is ſaid, *his parents kept him:* where the holy Ghoſt includes his father alſo. How can both theſe be true? anſw. We muſt know, that the Mother was the chiefe doer, in this worke, and the father, though he was not a doer, yet he gaue his conſent. Now we muſt remember, that conſent is a kinde of doing, whether it be in good things, or in euill: for, when *Saul* did but *keepe the perſecutors clothes that ſtoned Stephen,* (Act. 7. 58.) whereby hee ſignified his conſent; thereupon hee confeſ-ſeth himſelfe to be *guiltie of his death,* Act. 22. 20.

Laſtly, obſerue the Cauſe, or rather the Occaſion that mooued the Parents to ſaue their childe. It was a notable *comlineſſe* and *beautie*, which did appeare in the body of the childe, when hee was borne. This mooued them to reaſon thus with themſelues: Surely God hath giuen ſuch beautie and comlineſſe vnto this childe, that it is very likely hee will vſe him hereafter, to bee ſome notable inſtrument of ſome great worke: we therefore will keepe him aliue. This point muſt be marked of vs: for, beſide their naturall affection, this alſo was a motiue to make the parents ſaue their childe.

Hence wee may learne, that thoſe whome God will imploy aboue others in ſome ſpeciall ſeruice for his owne glory, are vſually endowed with ſome ſpeciall gift aboue others; yea many times with outward grace and comlineſſe in the body. For, this beauty in *Moſes* body, mooued his parents to ſeeke to ſaue his life; they perſwade themſelues that God had not imprinted that in him for nought. *Saul* (we know) was made King ouer Iſrael: and it is noted, that the Lord had giuen him a goodly ſtature: for he was *higher then any of the people from the ſhoulders vpward.* So *Dauid* had a *good countenance,* and *a comely viſage:* for the Lord purpoſed to make him king ouer Iſrael. Now as he did excell his brethren in beauty & comelineſſe, ſo he was to be far aboue them in this ſpeciall ſeruice of God, in gouerning his people.

Hence we learne, firſt, that comelineſſe and beautie is a gift of God: Secondly, that thoſe which excell others in theſe gifts of nature, muſt looke alſo that anſwerably they excell them in holineſſe, and zeale in the ſeruice of God, and doing good vnto men, as Moſes and *Dauid* did. But alas, wretched is the practiſe of theſe times: for commonly thoſe which haue comelineſſe and beauty aboue others, doe vſe it as a bait and occaſion vnto all ſinne, and naughtineſſe; as to whoredome and laſciuiouſneſſe, that thereby they may more fully ſatisfie their owne wretched and Satanicall luſts: but this muſt carefully be looked vnto, of all ſuch as haue the gifts of nature in more excellent manner then others. For if they vſe them, or rather abuſe them to be meanes of ſinne, and to ſet forth the pride and vanitie of their hearts, they haue much to anſwer for vnto God, at the dreadfull day of Iudgement. Hath God giuen thee beauty and comelineſſe? and doeſt thou vſe it as a baite to enſnare others for the ſatisfying of thy luſt? then looke vnto it thou euill ſeruant, for thou doeſt not hide, but conſume thy Maſters talent, imploying it to his diſhonour; therefore it ſhall be taken from thee: and in ſtead thereof, thou ſhalt haue vglineſſe and deformity, and ſo in ſoule and body be tumbled into hell with vncleane ſpirits. And thus much of the firſt action of their faith, with the circumſtances thereof.

The ſecond action, whereby the faith of

1.Sam.10.23.
1.Sam.16.12.

Moſes Parents is commended vnto vs, is this; *They did not feare the Kings commaundement.* Theſe words muſt not bee vnderſtood abſolutely and ſimply, but with limitation. For many places of Scripture are ſpoken ſimply, which muſt bee vnderſtoode with reſpect: as when it is ſaid, Matth. 11.18. *Iohn came neither eating nor drinking,* that is not, *eating nothing at all,* but *eating little:* and *Chriſt* ſaith, Matth. 10.34. *He came not to bring peace, but the ſword:* that is (as *Luke* expounds it, Luk. 12.51.) *rather debate,* then *peace.* And ſo in this place, Moſes parents feared not the Kings commandement; that is, they did not feare it ouermuch, or wholly, or onely, or ſo much as others did in the like caſe.

Here then firſt wee may learne, how farre forth we muſt obey ſuperiours and magiſtrates; wee muſt obey them, not ſimply, but *in the Lord:* Epheſ.6.1. that is, in all their lawfull commands: but when they commaund things euil and vnlawfull, then we muſt ſtay our ſelues, leſt obeying them we rebell againſt God. For this, we haue ſufficient warrant in this place, as alſo in the Apoſtles; who beeing commanded (Act.4.18,19.) that *in no wiſe they ſhould ſpeake or teach in the name of Ieſus:* anſwered, *Whether it be right in the ſight of God, to obey you rather then God, iudge ye.* And the *midwiues* of Egypt are commended of the holy Ghoſt, Exod. 1.17. for ſauing the young children aliue, againſt the Kings commandement. And the three men of the Iewes, *Shadrach, Meſhach* and *Abednego,* are renowmed with all poſterity, for diſobeying the commaundement of *Nebuchadneſſar* (Dan. 3.16,17.) of worſhipping the golden Image. By which examples, wee may ſee plainely, that our obedience to men muſt be in the Lord onely. Neither is our refuſing to doe their vnlawfull commaunds, any diſobedience indeede: becauſe the fift commandement in this caſe ceaſeth to binde, and giues place to the commandements of the firſt table, which are greater; as we ſhewed before, v. 17.

Secondly, ſee here this godly boldneſſe, in not ouermuch fearing the Kings commaundement, is made a worke of faith: whence wee learne, that true faith in the promiſes of God, doth ſerue to moderate a mans affectiós. There is no man, but if he be left to himſelfe, he will goe too farre in the ſway of his affections: experience ſheweth that many through anger, & ioy, haue loſt their liues; ſome for feare haue forſaken religion, and ſorrow hath coſt many a man his life: yea, any affection if it be not moderated and ſtayed, will bereaue a man of his ſenſes, and make him a beaſt, and no man.

But behold the vſe and power of true faith: It ſerueth to mitigate a mans affection; ſo as if a man be angry, it ſhall be with moderation: and ſo we may ſay of feare, ioy, hatred, or any other affection; faith will aſſwage and ſtay the rage thereof. For vndoubtedly, Moſes parents

rents might haue beene ouerwhelmed with feare of Pharaohs tyrannie and cruelty, but that God gaue them faith, which did moderate this feare. There is none of vs, but if wee looke well into our ſelues, wee ſhall ſee that we are exceſſiue in many affections, ſometime in feare, ſometime in anger, ſometime in ſorrow, and ſuch like. Now, would we know how to bridle theſe ſtrong paſſions? Then get true faith: it is the meanes whereby a man may moderate and ſtay the rage of his affections, ſo as they ſhall not breake out into extremitie. Is a man angry? why, if he haue faith, he will bridle his anger. Is he ſorrowfull? yet it is in meaſure: and ſo for the reſt, faith will rule them all, and yet extinguiſheth none. Which ſhould greatly prouoke vs to labour for true faith, ſeeing it is of ſuch vſe and power in the ſtay of our affections.

v. 24. By faith, Moſes when he was come to age, refuſed to bee called the ſonne of Pharaohs daughter.

25. And choſe rather to ſuffer aduerſitie with the people of God, then to enioy the pleaſures of ſinne for a ſeaſon.

26. Eſteeming the rebuke of Chriſt greater riches then the treaſures of Egypt: For he had reſpect vnto the recompence of reward.

HEre the holy Ghoſt comes to the commendation of Moſes faith, and in theſe three verſes propounds a moſt notable example hereof.

By Moſes faith, in this place, we muſt vnderſtand ſauing faith; which is nothing elſe, but a gift of God, whereby Moſes receiued the promiſe of god touching ſaluation by the Meſſias, and of the promiſed Land, made to Abraham and to his ſeede afrer him, and applied the ſame vnto himſelfe particularly.

Now in the firſt entrance of this example, the holy Ghoſt ſetteth downe a wonderfull thing of Moſes; namely, that Moſes had faith, and by it did this great worke. This (I ſay) is ſtrange, becauſe hee was brought

vp by Pharaohs daughter in the Court of Pharaoh, where was no knowledge of the true God, and indeede nothing but idolatry, wantonneſſe, and profaneneſſe. And yet here it is teſtified of him, by the ſpirit of God which cannot lie, that he had faith; which is a wonderfull thing. And the like is recorded of others in the word of God: As in Ahabs Court (who was a King that had ſold himſelfe to worke wickedneſſe) yet the ſpirit of God teſtifieth, that euen there was good Obadiah, a man that feared God greatly. And Herod was a moſt deadly enemie to Chriſt: and yet Ioanna the wife of Chuza Herods friend, miniſtred of her goods vnto Chriſt. And Paul ſaith, The Saints which are of Caſars houſhold ſalute you: Where, by Cæſars-houſe, is meant the Court of Nero, who was a moſt bloody man, and a wicked perſecuter; and yet in his houſe were the profeſſors of Chriſts Goſpel. By theſe examples we learne, that Chriſt hath his children and ſeruants in the middle among his enemies: for, theſe three Courts, of Pharaoh, Herod, and Nero, may be called a kinde of hell; and yet there were ſome of Gods ſeruants in them all. Which ſheweth vs clearely the truth of Gods word, which ſaith of Chriſt, that hee raigneth in the middle among his enemies. Howſoeuer they rage, and ſeeke to blot out his name, and roote out his kingdome, yet mauger their throats, he will rule in the middle of their kingdomes, and there haue thoſe which truly ſerue him and feare his name, Reuel. 2. 13. God had his Church in Pergamus where Satans throne was.

Againe, this faith of Moſes ſerues to checke many a man in this age, that is brought vp in the Church of God, and vnder godly Parents and gouernours, and yet is a hater and mocker of the religion of Chriſt. Surely Moſes in the day of iudgement ſhall ſtand vp againſt all ſuch, and condemne them. For he had faith, though he were brought vp in a moſt profane place: and they are voide of faith, nay, enemies vnto it; though they liue in the boſome of the Church.

But let vs come to the ſtrange fact which Moſes did, for which his faith is ſo commended. The Text ſaith of him firſt of all, That when hee was come to age, he refuſed to bee called the ſonne of Pharaohs daughter. How Moſes became her ſonne, wee may reade at large, Exod. 2. where it is ſaid, that ſhee hauing found Moſes in the baſket, preſerued him aliue, and brought him vp as her owne childe, purpoſing to make him her owne ſonne and heire. But this honour of hers hee would not accept; this he refuſed by faith, and this is that notable and famous act, for which his faith is here commended vnto vs.

But ſome will ſay, This fact of Moſes may ſeeme rather worthy of blame then praiſe, as beeing a practiſe of great rudeneſſe and ingratitude: for ſhee preſerued his life from death,& brought him vp as her own child, and vouchſafed him this ſpeciall fauour to make him her heire;and therefore *Moſes* ſhould not thus haue contemned her fauour. *Anſwer.* Indeede it had beene *Moſes* part to haue ſhewed himſelfe thankfull, in accepting this fauour at her hands, and alſo in enioying the ſame, if he might haue done it with the feare of God, and keeping a good conſcience. But, that he could not doe : for, if he had dwelled ſtill with her, and beene her ſonne and heire, he ſhould haue beene vndutifull vnto God. Now this is a rule to bee remembred and practiſed alwaies ; that in dúties of like nature, the Commaundements of the ſecond table doe binde vs no further then our obedience thereto may ſtand with obedience vnto the Commaundements of the firſt table:and when theſe two cannot ſtand together, then we are freed from obedience vnto the ſecond table; as, from performing honour and thankfulneſſe vnto men, when wee cannot therewithall perforne obedience and ſeruice vnto God. And this was *Moſes* caſe : becauſe he could not both ſerue God, and continue his thankfulneſſe, to *Pharaohs* daughter (for in ſtaying with her, hee ſhould haue made ſhipwracke of true religion)therefore hee forſaketh her fauour and honour;and for this cauſe is here commended vnto vs. The like did our Sauiour Chriſt, for when *the people would haue made him King , he refuſed it , and fled from among them,* Ioh. 6. 15. becauſe it would not ſtand with that calling , for which he was ſanctified and ſent into the world : therefore *Moſes* fact was commendable,& doth greatly ſet forth vnto vs his holy faith.

In this fact of *Moſes* thus generally conſidered, obſerue a notable fruite of true faith : It makes a man eſteem more of the ſtate of adoption to be the childe of God, then to bee the childe or heire of any earthly Prince. This is plaine in *Moſes* in this place. And the like wee may ſee in *Dauid:* for though he were a King, yet he ſet all his royalty & maieſtie at naught, in regard of Gods bleſſing of adoption ; and therefore ſaith , *The Lord(not the Kingdome of* Iſrael*) is my portion.* And againe , when hee was kept from the Lords tabernacle , and the company of Gods Saints, through perſecution; he ſaith , *The Sparrowes and Swallowes were more happy then he,* Pſal. 84. becauſe they had neſts where they might keepe their young, and ſit, and ſing; but he could not come neere the Lords Altar.And yet more fully to expreſſe the earneſtneſſe of his affection this way; hee ſaith, he had rather be a man of a baſe office, euen *a dore-keeper in the houſe of God,* then a man of renowne in *the tents of wickedneſſe.* But howſoeuer, theſe men were of one minde herein; yet come to our age, and ſeeke in Towne, Country,and people,and we ſhall ſee this fruite of faith is rare to bee found : for generally (though I will not ſay all) the moſt of thoſe that are borne of good parentage, as the

Pſal. 16.

ſonnes of Knights or Squires, and eſpecially of Nobles,are ſo bewitched with the pride of their earthly Parentage, that they haue ſcarce a thought after adoption in Chriſt.Gods heauenly graces will take no place in their hearts , but they vtterly contemne all other eſtates of life in regard of their owne. And this is the common ſinne of the whole world : for at earthly preferments men will ſtand amazed; but ſeldome ſhall you finde a man that is rauiſhed with ioy in this , that hee is the childe of God,as *Moſes* was. But his practiſe muſt bee a preſident for vs to followe: we muſt learne to haue more ioy in beeing the ſonnes of God, then to be heires of any worldly Kingdomes; and to take more delight in the grace of adoption through Ieſus Chriſt , then in the ſonſhip of any earthly Prince.

It is a great prerogatiue to be heire to a King or Emperour: but yet to be the childe of God, goes farre beyond it : euen aboue compariſon. For, the ſonne of the greateſt Potentate may be the childe of wrath: but the childe of God by grace, hath Chriſt Ieſus to bee his eldeſt *brother*,with whom he is *fellow heire* in heauen; he hath the holy Ghoſt alſo for his *comforter,* and the Kingdome of heauen for his euerlaſting *inheritance.* And therefore wee muſt learne of *Moſes,* from the bottome of our hearts,to prefer this one thing, To be the childe of God, before all earthly things, either pleaſures, riches, or any other prerogatiues whatſoeuer.

Now more particularly in this fact of *Moſes* note two circumſtances: 1. The *manner* how: 2. The *time* when, he refuſed to bee called the ſonne of *Pharaohs* daughter.

For the firſt ; his refuſall was not in word, but in deede: for,if we reade the whole Hiſtory of *Moſes* , we ſhall not finde , that either hee ſpake to *Pharaob*,or to his daughter, or to any other to this effect, that he would not bee her heire, nor called her ſonne ; but we finde that he did it indeede: for, when he came to age, he left the Court oftentimes,and went to viſite his brethren, to comfort them, to defende them, and to take part with them. And hence wee muſt learne, not ſo much to giue our ſelues to knowe, and to talke of matters of religion,as to doe and practiſe the ſame both before God and men. This did *Moſes.* It is the common fault of our age , that wee can be content to heare the doctrine of religion taught vnto vs ; yea, many will learne it, and often ſpeake thereof: but but fewe there be that make conſcience to doe the things they heare and ſpeake of. But let vs learne of *Moſes* to put thoſe things in practiſe which wee learne and profeſſe , and in ſilence doe them : for, the fewer words the better, vnleſſe our deedes bee anſwerable. If any of vs were to walke vpon the top of ſome high mountaine, wee would leaue off talking, and looke vnto our ſteps for feare of falling. Behold, when wee enter the profeſſion of Chri

Phil.3.14.

ſtianitie , we are ſet vpon an high mountaine: for the *way of life is on high*; and Chriſtianity is the *high calling of God.* We therefore muſt be *wiſe* as *Salomon* ſaith, Pro. 15.24. and looke well to our conuerſation, hauing a ſtraite watch ouer all our waies, through the whole courſe of our life, euen to the ende of our daies: and not ſtand ſo much on ſpeaking & talking, as on doing: *for the doer of the work ſhall be bleſſed in his deed,* Iam.1.25. This is the thing we muſt looke vnto , as the onely ornament of our profeſſion, declaring that we haue the power of godlineſſe: but if deedes be wanting, our religion is vaine, we are like the *Figtree* which Chriſt curſed, *hauing leaues and no fruite.*

Matth.21.19.

The 2. circumſtance to be conſidered, is, the time whē he refuſed this honour: namely, *when he came to be a man of yeares and diſcretion.* A man in common reaſon would iudge thus of *Moſes* fact: *Moſes* hath rare fortune offered him , he might haue bin ſonne and heire to a Princeſſe : ſurely this is a raſh fact of his, and voide of conſideration, to refuſe it; vndoubtedly he farre ouerſhot himſelfe herein, either thorough raſhneſſe or ignorance. But to preuent ſuch carnall ſurmiſes, the ſpirit of God ſets downe this circumſtance of time; ſaying , that he did not refuſe it in his youth: but *when hee was come to age, that is, to perfect yeares of diſcretion,* and by reaſon thereof, muſt needs haue conſideration and iudgement to know what he did; then did he refuſe this honour, to be *Pharaohs* daughters ſonne and heire. In the ſeuenth of the Acts, we ſhall ſee that he was *fourty years ólde* when he did this. And therefore this is true which is here ſaid, that *when he was come to age* and ſtaiednes : then he refuſed this honour: for, fourtie yeares is a time, not onely of ripeneſſe for ſtrength : but of ſtaiedneſſe in iudgement and diſcretion.

Out of this circumſtance we learne two points. 1. That it is a common fault of yong yeares , to be ſubiect to inconſideration and raſhneſſe: for, *Moſes* did not refuſe the honour of *Pharaohs* daughter, when he was young, leſt it ſhould ſeeme to be a point of raſhneſſe: but *when he was come to age* (as the text ſaith): inſinuating , that if he had done it when he was young, it might haue beene eſteemed but a raſh part, and done in ſome haſtie paſſion of youth. Euery age of man hath his faults: and this is the fault of youth, to be heady and raſh in their affaires, for want of cōſideration and experience. And therefore all young perſons muſt haue care of theſe ſinnes of youth, and watch the more againſt them, becauſe they are ſo incident to their yeares. Now the way to auoyde them, is to followe Chriſts example , Luk.2.52. to labour *to growe, as in yeares, ſo in wiſedome and grace:* and to obey the counſell of *Paul* to *Timothy,* 2.Tim.2.22. to *fly the luſts of youth: following after iuſtice, faith, charity, and peace, with all that call vpon the name of the Lord with a pure heart.*

Secondly, this circumſtance of time, noting *Moſes* deliberate ſtaiedneſſe in this fact, doth plainely aduertiſe vs, what is, or ſhould be, the vertue of old age, and the ornament of yeares: namely , *ſtaiedneſſe* and *diſcretion:* whereby I meane , not onely that naturall temper of affection, which olde age bringeth with it: but ſuch religious diſcretion , whereby men of yeares doe all things in faith, ſo as their works may be acceptable and pleaſing vnto God. For, when a man is growen in yeares , and hath had experience and obſeruation in the Church of God, he muſt not onely haue a generall knowledge and wiſedome, but a particular wiſedome, whereby he may do in faith, whatſoeuer he takes in hand, and therein pleaſe God. But alas, this may be ſpoken of old men in theſe daies, that in regard of this wiſedome , they are very babes: a thing greatly diſgracefull to their condition. For, *Paul* biddes the Corinthians , 1.Cor.14.20. that *they ſhould not be childrē in vnderſtanding, but of ripe age:* yea, and he forbiddes the Epheſians, Eph.4.14. to *be children ſtill, wauering and carried about with euery winde of doctrine.* Whereby we may ſee, that aged perſons doe quite degenerate from that they ought to be, when they are babes in knowledge, voide of ſpirituall wiſedome. Indeede, we muſt graunt, that our aged perſons are worldly wiſe; and he muſt haue a cunning head, and (as we ſay) riſe early, that herein goes beyond them: But bring them to the book of God, and to giue a reaſon of their actions , that they are done in faith; herein, they are meere babes, and ignorant: neither cā they tel what it is to do a thing in faith, ſo as it may be acceptable to God. Herein, many that are yong in yeares, doe quite outſtrippe them. What would we thinke or ſay of a child, that being ſet to a good ſchoole, ſhould ſtill be in the loweſt forme, though he had long continued at it? Surely we would iudge him either exceeding negligent, or deſtitute of ordinary capacitie.

Behold, the Church of God is the ſchoole of Chriſt: and if a man haue liued long therein, (as twenty, or fourty yeares) and yet be no wiſer in religion, then a young child; is it not a ſhame vnto him? and ſhall we not condemne him of great negligence? Wherefore, let all aged perſons here learne their dutie; which is, to growe to ripeneſſe in ſpirituall wiſedome, that ſo their *age may be to them a crowne of glory, beeing found in the way of righteouſneſſe,* Prou.16.31.

VERSE 25.

And choſe rather to ſuffer aduerſitie with the people of God , then to enioy the pleaſures of ſinne for a ſeaſon.

THe meaning of theſe words is this: *Moſes* caſt with himſelfe, that if he ſhould yeild to become heire to *Pharaohs* daughter, he muſt liue with her, and pleaſe her in all things, and ſo alto-

altogether leaue Gods Church, and people, and Gods holy religion; which thing to doe, he abhorred in his heart: and withall, he muſt leaue and loſe the eternall bleſſedneſſe of Gods chil-dren, for the honours, and ſinnefull pleaſures of the Court, which were but momentany. Theſe things conſidered, he chooſeth rather to be in affliction and miſerie with the people of God, then vpon theſe conditions, to liue in *Pharaohs* Court, and to become his daughters ſonne and heire.

And becauſe this may ſeem a ſtrange choiſe, the holy Ghoſt doth afterward render a reaſon hereof, which is this; Becauſe *Moſes* liked ra-ther to inioy the prerogatiues of Gods Church (though it were in miſerie) then to enioy any honour in a wicked Court, ſuch as indeed *Pha-raohs* was.

In this verſe therefore, we are to note a ſe-cond fruit of *Moſes* faith; to wit, that he prefer-red the fellowſhip and communion of Gods Saints, before all other ſocieties in the world. The ſame alſo was *Dauids* practiſe, Pſal. 16. 3. *All my delight* (ſaith he) *is in the Saints that dwell on the earth.*

This fruite of *Moſes* faith, doth diſcouer vn-to vs a grieuous fault, which raigneth in this age; to wit, the neglect and contempt of the communion and ſocietie of Saints. There is a ſo-cietie and fellowſhip that is loued and magnifi-ed among vs: but what manner of ſocietie is that? ſurely of ſuch as giue themſelues to drin-king, ieſting, ſcoffing, riot, mirth, gaming. This is the common and generall good fellowſhip: through which, God is greatly diſhonoured. For moſt men ſet their delight therein, and are neuer merrie but in ſuch company, wherein in-deede they delight themſelues in their ſenſuali-tie. True it is, men pleade that this good fel-lowſhip is a vertue. But then was *Moſes* farre ouer-ſeene: for in *Pharaohs* Court he might haue had all kinde of ſuch good fellowſhip and company; yet he likes it not, but rather choo-ſeth affliction and miſerie with the people of God, then to enioy ſuch fellowſhip in *Pha-raohs* Court. And as for the goodneſſe of it, it is neither ſo eſteemed, nor called by any, but by them that call good euill, and euill good. Wee ſee, *Moſes* a man of wiſedome and learning, Acts 7.23. no child, but a man of xl. yeares old, hates and abhorres this good fellowſhip, as the worſt eſtate in the world: rather chooſing the ſocietie of a miſerable and perſecuted Church, then the beſt of that fellowſhip which a Kings Court could yeild. Let vs therefore learne more wiſdome out of his practiſe. Some ſay, this good fellowſhip is harmeleſſe; and ſuch men who thus merrily paſſe their times, doe no ſuch hurt as many others doe. But I anſwer, men are borne to doe good. Againe, to miſſpend time, wealth, & wit, are not theſe euil and harmefull, both in themſelues, and in the example? And which is worſt of all, it is no fellowſhip with God, nor any part of the communion of Saints,

but rather a fellowſhip with Satan: therefore, let all that will, like true Chriſtians, haue true comfort in that article of their Creed, *the com-munion of Saints,* eſteeme the fellowſhip of good and holy men aboue all other. For, by this communion with Gods Saints, a man reapes great profit, when as the other brings to a man the ruine both of his bodie and ſoule. By the ſociety of the godly, we are firſt made partakers of their gifts and holy graces; and ſecondly, of their prayers, and the bleſſings of God vpon them: which things, if there were no other, might mooue vs to embrace this bleſſed ſociety before all other. And yet further; by beeing of this ſociety, a man auoids many of Gods iudge-ments: If there had beene tenne righteous men in *Sodome,* they had all beene ſpared from de-ſtruction. Wherein we may ſee that they that cleaue to ſuch as feare the Lord indeede, neuer receiue harme, but rather much good; for, *for the elects ſake* it is, that the world yet ſtandeth: and if they were gathered, heauen and earth would goe together; but for the calling of the Elect, the hand of God is yet ſtaied. Why then ſhould not *Moſes* example be our rule, Aboue all worldly pleaſure to reioyce in the ſocietie of Gods Saints.

Thus much in generall: Now, in the particu-lar words, are many notable points of doctrine, which we will touch in their order. *And choſe rather, &c.*] Marke here a rare & ſtrange choiſe as euer we ſhall reade of. There are two things propounded to *Moſes:* The firſt is, honour and preferment in *Pharaohs* Court; to be ſonne & heire to *Pharaohs* daughter: wherewith he might haue enioyed all earthly pleaſures and delights. The ſecond is, the miſerable afflicted condition of Gods Church and people.

And of theſe two, *Moſes* muſt needs chooſe the one: well what chooſeth he? Surely he refu-ſeth the prerogatiues and dignity, that he might haue had in *Pharohs* Court, and makes choiſe of the miſerie and affliction of Gods people in aduerſitie; that ſo he may enioy the priuiledges of Gods Church. A wonderfull choiſe: for which, his faith is here commended, and he re-nowned to all poſteritie. The ſame choiſe hath God ſet before all men in all ages. In former times God ſet before *Eſau* two things; A meſſe of redde broth, and his birth-right: but profane *Eſau* chooſeth the worſer, he forgoes his birth-right, ſo he may haue the broth. But far worſe did the Gaderens; there was ſet before them Chriſt Ieſus the Lord of life, and their hogges and cattell: Now they preferre their hogges be-fore Chriſt; A moſt miſerable and ſenſeleſſe choice. And is it not as ill with vs? There is ſet before vs on the one ſide heauen, and on the o-ther ſide hell; but men for the moſt part chooſe *hell* and forſake heauen. Ciuill worldly men whoſe delight is all in riches, they prefer earth before heauen, the ſeruice of ſinne, which is the greateſt ſlauerie, before the ſeruice of God, which is perfect freedome, and glorious liber-

Gen.18.32.

ty of the Saints in light : and thus doe all men without Gods speciall grace. Whereupon *Paul* prayes in his Epistles for the Churches, that God would giue vnto them *the spirit of wise-dome, that they may be able to iudge betweene things that differ.* And this wisedome we must labour for, that when these different things are set before vs, we may make a wise choice: other-wise, we shew our selues to be like bruite beasts without vnderstanding, & do quite ouerturne our own saluation. In the Ministery of the word we haue *life and death, good and euill,* set before vs, as Moses said to the people, Deut. 30.15.19. Let vs therefore endeauour our selues to chuse life by embracing and obeying the word of God: and so shall we followe both his precept and practise.

To suffer aduersitie with the people of God. Here we may obserue what is the ordinary state and condition of Gods Church and people in this world: namely, to be in affliction and vnder the crosse. Hence *Paul* saith, *That we must come to heauen through manifold afflictions,* Act. 14.22. The Lord knoweth what is best for his seruants and children : and therefore he hath set downe this for a ground, that *all that will liue godly in Christ Iesus, must suffer persecution,* 2. Tim. 3. 12.

Thus the Lord dealeth with his children for speciall causes : for first, all crosses, as losse of goods, friends, libertie, or good name, they are means to stirre vp and awake Gods people out of the slumbring fit of sinne ; for the godly are many times ouertaken this way. The wise vir-gins sleepe, as well as the foolish: Now, afflicti-ons rouze them out of the sleepe of securitie. See this in *Iosephs* brethren, who went on a long time without any remorse for selling their brother : But when they were staied in Egypt, then they are rouzed vp, and can say, Gen. 42. 21. *This trouble is come vpon vs, for selling our brother.*

Secondly, afflictions serue to humble Gods children, Leuit. 26. 41. So the Church of God speaketh, *I will beare the wrath of the Lord, be-cause I haue sinned against him,* Micha.7.9.

Thirdly, they serue to weane the people of God, and to driue them from the loue of this world : for, if men might alwaies liue in ease, they would make their heauen vpon earth; which may not be. And herein God dealeth with his children like a Nurse; when she will weane her child, she layes some bitter thing vp-on the pappes head, to make the child to loath the pappe; so the Lord, to drawe our hearts from the world, and to cause vs to loue and seeke after heauen & heauenly things, he makes vs to taste of the bitternesse of affliction in this world. Fourthly, afflictions serue to make Gods children to goe out of themselues to seeke sin-cerely vnto God, and to relie onely vpon him: which in prosperitie they will not do. This, *Paul* confesseth of himselfe and others; *We* (saith he) *receiued the sentence of death in our selues, be-*

cause *we should not trust in our selues, but in god:* 2. Cor. 1. 9. So good King *Iehosaphat,* when he was compassed of his enemies, *He cried to the Lord, and said; Lord we knowe not what to doe, but our eyes are towards thee:* 2. Chron. 20. 12. Yea, the rebellious Iewes are hereby driuen to seeke the Lord, whom in prospertie they forsooke; as wee may see at large, Psal. 107. 6. 12.13.19.

Lastly, afflictions serue to make manifest the graces of God in his children. *The Lord* (saith Iob) *knoweth my way and trieth me,* Iob 23.10. Deut. 8. 2. *Remember all the way* (saith Moses to the Israelites) *which the Lord thy God ledde thee this fourty yeares, for to prooue thee and to knowe what was in thine heart.* Hence *Iames* calleth *temptations, the triall of faith,* Iam.1.2, 3. And *Paul* makes patience, *the fruite of tri-bulation,* Rom. 5. 3. For looke as the showers in the spring time cause the buds to appeare: so doe afflictions make manifest Gods graces in his children. Patience, hope, and other vertues, lie close in the heart in the day of peace: but when tribulation comes, then they breake forth and shew themselues.

Hence we learne, that it is not alwaies a to-ken of Gods wrath, To suffer affliction. If any man or people be laden with crosses, it is no ar-gument, that therefore they are not the children of God: for, as *Peter* saith, *Iudgements begin at Gods house,* 1. Pet. 4. 17. and any crosse vpon a people, family, or particular persons, if it bring forth the fruite of grace in them, is a true signe, they belong to God. Yea, when men wander from God by an euill way, these afflictions are meanes to call them home to God. Psal. 119. 67. *Before I was afflicted, I went astray.* And they that forsake their sinne & returne to God in the time of affliction, are certainely Gods people: for, the wicked man fretteth and mur-mureth against God when a crosse commeth, and he cannot abide it. But the godly man is humbled thereby, and it makes him more obe-dient in all duties vnto God.

This we should consider: for by an outward profession, we beare the world in hand, that we are Gods children, and therefore we come to heare Gods word, and to learne how to be-haue our selues as beseemeth his children. But if we would be knowne to be Gods children indeede, then when any of Gods iudgements doe befall vs ; we must make this vse of them; namely, labour thereby to be humbled for our sinnes, and to forsake our sinne, and to make conscience of all bad wayes for euer afterward; and then we shew our selues to be Gods chil-dren indeede : but if vnder the crosse, or after the crosse, we be as dissolute as euer we were, and still followe our olde sinnes, then we can-not be iudged to be Gods people and chil-dren, but rather a wicked & stubborne genera-tion, which the more they are corrected, the worse they are; like a stithy, the more it is bea-ten, the harder it is. Let vs therefore by the

Philip 1.20.

vfe of Gods iudgements, fhewe our felues to be Gods children : fo fhall we fay, with *Dauid* with much ioy and comfort, *It is good for vs that we haue beene in trouble,* Pfal.119.71.

Thus we fee Mofes choife: now come we to the thing he refufed; *To enioy the pleafures of finne for a feafon.* By pleafures of finne, we muft vnderftand the *riches and dignitie that* Mofes *might haue had in Pharaohs Court and Kingdome* Which are called *the pleafures of finne*, not becaufe they were fo in themfelues; for, fo they were the good gifts of God: but becaufe Mofes could not enioy them in *Pharaohs* Court, without liuing in finne; for, he muft haue refufed the focietie of Gods Church and people, and fo haue beene a ftranger from the couenant which God made with *Abraham, Ifaac*, and *Iaacob*, and with his feede after them, if he would haue beene fonne to *Pharaohs* daughter.

Here then the holy Ghoft fetteth down two notable reafons, which induced Mofes to refufe thefe honours and dignities : Firft, becaufe *they were the pleafures of finne*; And fecondly, becaufe he fhould enioy them but *for a feafon.*

The firft reafon affordeth vnto vs many notable points worthie our confideration. 1. Here we learne, that riches, honour, and dignity feuered from true religion, are nothing but the pleafures and profits of finne. This was Mofes iudgement, as the holy Ghoft here teftifieth: and it is the plaine truth of God, as *Salomon* after lamentable experience difputeth, and prooueth at large: concluding of riches, honour, pleafures, and all earthly things feparated from the feare of God, that they are nothing elfe but *meere vanity and vexation of fpirit.* And *Paul* faith, *To the impure all things are impure*; his meate, drinke, and apparell, which in themfelues are otherwife the good gifts of God.

The confideration hereof is of great vfe: for, firft it lets vs fee what is the ftate of thefe men which lay afide religion and good confcience, and betake themfelues wholly to the world, to get riches and preferment: moft men are of this difpofition, and fuch indeed are onely counted wife. For, let there be fpeech tending to a mans commendation, vfually this is the firft matter of his praife, that he is a fubftantiall wealthy man; and one that lookes well to himfelfe: as though riches, or honour were a mans chiefe happineffe. But, howfoeuer the world iudgeth of thefe men; yet hereby we may fee and know, that their cafe is miferable. For, without religion and the feare of God, their riches and honours are but the pleafures and profits of finne: & therfore the more they heape vp riches after this fort, not regarding Chrift, nor his Gofpel; the more they heape vp to themfelues the treafures of finne, and confequently the greater condemnation : for worldly treafures feuered from religiõ, are but the Mammon of iniquity, which caufeth damnation. Hence Chrift faid

vnto his Difciples (vpon occafion of the young rich man) that it was *as eafie for a great Camell to goe through the eye of a needle, as for a rich man to enter into the kingdome of heauen*; that is, fuch a rich man as fets his heart to get riches and honour, not regarding the religion of Chrift. Whence alfo in another place he pronounceth this fearefull fentence againft them: *Woe be to you that are rich, for you haue receiued your confolation*: Luk. 6. 24. They therefore that lay afide religion, and giue themfelues wholly to feeke gaine and honour, are before God moft wretched and miferable: and the longer they continue in this courfe, the more miferable they are; for the more finne they heape vp, and fo the deeper fhall be their condemnation. Wherefore if any of vs haue beene thus minded hertofore, let vs now leaue this courfe, as moft dangerous to our foules: for what will it profit a man to gaine the whole world, if he lofe his foule?

2. Hence we muft all learne, efpecially they that haue any meafure of wealth more or leffe, to ioyne with the vfe of our riches the feare of God, and the practife of true religion: for, feuer thefe afunder, and riches are nothing elfe but finnefull pleafures. It is a good confcience which rectifieth the owner in the right vfe of his honour and treafures: but without that, he pollutes the bleffings of god which he enioyes, and they beeing polluted fhall turne to his greater woe. A man would haue thought that King *Belfhazzer* had been an happy man, when he kept his royall feaft, and dranke wine in golden bowls before a thoufand Princes that were vnder him, and before his Concubines: but the ende of all that his iollity may fhewe vs the nature of fuch profperitie. For fo foone as he faw *the fingers of a mans hand, writing vpon the wall*, he became quite confounded in himfelfe: *his countenance was changed, and his thoughts troubled him*; fo that *the ioynts of his loines were loofed, and his knees fmote one againft the other:* What comfort had he now from all his riches and pleafures? So *Diues*, while he liued, might feeme for his wealth and riches to be happy : yet all this did him little good; for, *he had but his pleafure for his life time,* Luk. 16 25. and after this life, his foule went downe to hell. A worldly man would iudge the rich man in the Gofpel, a moft happy man, that faide to his foule, by reafon of his great aboundance of outward wealth, Luke 12.19. *Soule, foule, thou haft much goods laide vp for many yeares, liue at eafe, eate, drinke, and take thy fill:* yet becaufe herewith he wanted religion, a good confcience, and the feare of God, this fentence was denounced againft him; *Oh foole this night will they fetch away thy foule: then, whofe fhall thefe things be?* Wherefore, vnleffe we will wilfully caft away our owne foules, let vs fanctifie our intereft in all earthly bleffings, by a fincere endeauour in all things, to fhew forth the feare of God, with the keeping of faith and a good con-

ſcience: & let vs begin with this, as Chriſt ſaith, *Firſt ſeeke Gods Kingdome and his righteouſ-neſſe,* Mat. 6. 33. Let vs hereby ſeeke to haue our hearts acceptable vnto God; and then all things ſhall be cleane vnto vs.

Thirdly, are riches and honour, beeing ſeue-red from true religion, but the pleaſures of ſinne? then vndoubtedly all recreations, all ſports, and paſtimes, ſeuered from religion and a good conſcience, are much more the pleaſures of ſinne. This *Salomon* knewe well: for, ſpea-king of ſuch mirth, he calles *laughter madneſſe; and to ioy (he ſaith) what is it that thou doeſt?* Eccle. 2.2. Oh then how manifold be the ſinnes of al ſorts of men? for who almoſt doth not neg-lect religious duties for matters of ſport and pleaſure? Wherefore if we deſire ioy indeede in any worldly things, let vs firſt lay the foundati-on in our owne hearts, by getting and keeping true faith and a good conſcience.

Secondly, whereas *Moſes* refuſeth dignitie and honour onely for this, Becauſe they would be vnto him *the pleaſures of ſinne*; here we are taught in what manner and order we ought to enioy worldly riches and honour. *Moſes* pra-ctiſe here, muſt be our direction; we muſt en-ioy them and vſe them with thankfulneſſe to God, ſo farre forth as they will further vs in the courſe of religion and true godlineſſe. But if the caſe ſtand thus; That we cannot enioy them both together, then we muſt followe *Moſes* ex-ample; chooſe religion and a good conſcience, and let honour and preferment goe. This is *Moſes* practiſe: and we may reſolue our ſelues, that if he might haue enioyed them together, he would haue refuſed neither; but becauſe he could not haue them both, therefore he prefer-reth the religion of Chriſt with a good conſci-ence, before the honour and wealth of E-gypt.

Thirdly, note this, *Moſes* doth not onely re-fuſe the riches and pleaſures of Egypt, when they would become vnto him the pleaſures of ſinne; but rather then he will enioy them, he is content to ſuffer great miſerie and aduerſitie with Gods people. Where, behold a ſingular vertue in *Moſes*: He iudgeth it to be the grea-teſt miſerie, *to liue in ſinne;* and therefore he chooſeth rather to ſuffer any aduerſitie and re-proach in this world, then liue and lie in ſinne: becauſe thereby, he ſhould diſpleaſe God, his moſt louing father in Chriſt. A moſt notable vertue in this ſeruant of God: & the like minde beare all thoſe, that haue the ſame graces of ſa-uing faith, and true repentance that Moſes had. S. *Paul* eſteemed the Temptations vnto ſinne, which Satan ſuggeſted into his minde, to be as *beatings and buffettings,* & as *pricks and thorns in his fleſh,* 2. Cor. 12.7. And *Dauid* ſaith, Pſal. 119. 136. *His eyes guſh out riuers of waters, becauſe men brake Gods commandements.* Was *Dauid* thus grieued for other mens ſinnes? Oh! then what a griefe did he ſuffer, when he him-ſelfe brake Gods commandements, and there-

by diſpleaſed God?

Now, looke how theſe ſeruants of God were affected, ſo muſt euery one of vs, that profeſſe the faith and religion of Chriſt, labour to be affected towards ſinne; we muſt iudge it the greateſt miſerie and torment in the world, to doe any thing that ſhal diſpleaſe God. But alas, come to our daies, and the caſe is farre other-wiſe; for, to moſt men, it is meate and drinke vnto them to commit ſinne: ſo farre are they from counting it a miſerie. Yea if a man be or-dinarily addicted to ſome ſpeciall ſinne, you then may as ſoone take away his life, as bereaue him of his ſinne: he will aduenture the loſſe of heauen for euer, for the pleaſure of ſinne for a time. But all ſuch, are farre vnlike theſe holy ſeruants of God; for they counted it the grea-teſt croſſe, and miſerie that could be, to doe a-ny thing that diſpleaſed God, and did checke and break the peace of a good conſcience. And if we looke to enioy like peace and comfort with them; we muſt ſtriue againſt our owne corrupt diſpoſition, and labour to finde ſinne to be our greateſt ſorrow. Worldly miſeries may affect vs: but, in reſpect of ſorrowe for ſinne, all worldly griefe ſhould be light vnto vs. Indeed, we are otherwiſe minded naturally: but herein, we muſt ſhewe the power and truth of grace, that to diſpleaſe God by any ſinne, is our grea-teſt griefe.

The ſecond reaſon, that mooued Moſes to refuſe the honours and pleaſures of *Pharaohs* Court, was, becauſe he ſhould haue enioyed them but *for a time*: for, the time of his naturall life, was the longeſt that poſſibly he could haue enioyed the. And the ſame reaſon muſt mooue euery one of vs, to vſe this world, and all things herein (euen all temporall benefits) as though we vſed them not: being alwaies willing and ready to leaue them whenſoeuer God ſhal call. This ſame reaſon doth *Paul* render when he perſwades the Corinthians to the ſame dutie, 1. Cor. 7. 31. *Vſe this world (ſaith he) as though you vſed it not; for the faſhion of this world go-eth away.* As if he ſhould ſay, All things in the world laſt but for a time; and if a man would neuer ſo faine, he could but enioy them to the ende of his life: & therefore, vſe them as though you vſed them not. But pitty it is to ſee, how farre men are from the practiſe of this duty; for, they ſet their whole heart vpon the world: and to get riches is their delight, and their god. This ought not ſo to be. God hath not laid downe theſe precepts and examples in vaine: vndoubtedly, if they drawe vs not to the like practiſe, they ſhall riſe vp in iudgement a-gainſt vs, at the laſt day. And thus much of *Moſes* choyce, and refuſall.

Verse 26.

Eſteeming the rebuke of Chriſt greater riches, then the treaſures of Egypt; for he had reſpect to the recompence of reward.

MOses (as we haue heard) *refused* the ho-nour and wealth of Egypt, and *chose* to liue in affliction with Gods people. Now, be-cause this might seeme to be a strange choyce, and a naturall man would soone condemne him of folly for his labour: therefore here the holy Ghost laies downe a reason that mooued Moses thus to doe : to wit, Moses chose rather to suf-fer affliction with Gods people , then to enioy the pleasures and honours of Egypt:because he was perswaded,that *reproach for Christ his sake, was greater riches, then all the wealth in Egypt.* So that he refused not absolutely riches, ho-nour, and other comforts : but chose the best riches and honour , and left the worser, vpon a sound iudgement betweene things that did differ.

Hereby we may obserue in generall, how needefull a thing it is for euery Christian, to haue sound knowledge and vnderstanding in the word of God. For,he that would walke vp-rightly , and approoued of God, must be able to iudge betweene things that differ: not onely betweene good and euill, but betweene good and good, which is the better: and so of euils, which is the worser.Which, no man can do, but he that hath a sound and right iudgement in the word of God: for therein is attained the spirit of discerning.Many there be,that by the course of their liues choose hell , and refuse heauen: which , vndoubtedly, comes from their igno-rance in the word. But ignorance will excuse none. He that will come to heauen, must be a-ble to discerne good from euill : & according-ly, to chuse the good, and to refuse that which is euill; which, without diuine, and supernatu-rall knowledge, no man can doe.And therefore all ignorant persons, and all such as are blinded through the deceitfulnesse of sinne, must shake off their securitie, and get sound knowledge in Scripture , with a good conscience; that when things which doe differ are set before them, they may with *Moses* choose the better.

But let vs come to *Moses* iudgement more particularly. *He esteemed the rebuke of Christ, &c.*that is , he was firmely resolued, that re-proach and contempt for Christ his sake , was greater riches vnto him , then the treasures of a whole kingdome. But some will say, This is a very strange iudgement: can it possibly be true and good? *Ans.* Yes vndoubtedly , it is most sound iudgement,and worthy eternall re-membrance of euery one of vs;that to suffer *re-proach for Christ his sake,is greater riches,then al worldly wealth.*The truth herof is prooued by many reasons out of Gods word. 1. God hath made *a promise of blessednesse* to those which suffer for Christs sake. *Blessed are you (saith Christ) when men reuile you,and speake all man-ner of euil sayings against you for my names sake, &c.*And S. *Peter* saith, *If ye be railed vpon for my names sake, blessed are ye.* And least any should doubt how this can be, Christ shewes wherein this blessednes consists, saying; *He that*

*forsaketh houses, or brethren,or sisters,or father, or mother, or wife, or children , or lands, for my names sake ; shall receiue an hundred fold more, and shal inherit eternall life.*A most worthy pro-mise, assuring vs that no man looseth by suffe-ring for Christs sake; for , he shall be rewarded an hundred fold ouer. In stead of earthly friends, and worldly comforts , he shall haue the loue and fauour of God shed abroad in his heart; which will be an ouer-flowing fountaine of comfort for soule and bodie for euer, far more worth then the wealth and treasures of all the kingdomes in the world. A small springing fountaine (we know)is better to an house,then a hundred Cisterns full ; because of continuall supply from the springing fountaine, when the Cisterns will be spent. Behold the loue of God in Christ, with other spirituall graces, shall be in all that suffer for the name of Christ,as liuing streames flowing vnto life eternall;when as the cisterns of all worldly pleasures and treasures, shall be spent and dried vp. 2. By suffering af-fliction for Christs sake, we are made confor-mable vnto him in his humilitie ; that so we may be made like vnto him after this life in glorie . So *Paul* saith, *Our light affliction cau-seth vnto vs an eternall weight of glory,*2. Cor. 4. 17. And againe, it is a true saying; *If we be dead with Christ, we shall also liue with him : If we suffer we shall also raigne with him,* 2.Tim.2. 11. 12. This assurance can no worldly riches giue: and therefore we may boldly say, that the suffering of reproach for Christ his sake,is grea-ter riches then the treasures of a whole king-dome. 3.To suffer for Christ his sake,is a token of Gods speciall loue : & therefore S.*Paul* bids the Philippians, *Not to feare their aduersaries: which is a token of saluation vnto them,and that of God ; because it is giuen to you* (saith he) *for Christ, that you should not onely beleeue, but suf-fer for his sake.* Wherefore if suffering for Christ haue a promise of blessednesse;if it make vs conformable vnto Christ, and be a signe of Gods speciall loue ; then it is to be esteemed aboue the riches and honours of the whole world.

Are afflictions for Christ to be esteemed a-boue the treasures of a kingdome?then we must all learne to reioyce in the troubles and wrongs which we suffer for Christs sake. So did the A-postles, Act. 5. 41. *They departed from the Councel,reioycing that they were counted worthy to suffer affliction for his name.* And S. *Paul* brags thereof greatly,saying; *I beare in my bo-die the marks of the Lord Iesus ,* Gal. 6. 17. And looke , as these seruants of God reioyced in their sufferings for Christ: so likewise must we labour for the same heart and affections in the like case; for, who would not reioyce to be made partaker and possessor of the treasures of a kingdome ? Well, the rebuke of Christ is greater riches then the treasures of a king-dome.

This lesson is of great vse: for howsoeuer

many among vs come to heare Gods word, yet there be many also, that scoffe and mocke at religion, and at the Gospel of Christ, and the professors thereof; whereby, the most are hindred in profession, and many daunted, and quite driuen backe. But we must here learne, not to be discouraged by these mockes. Indeede we must take heede, we giue them no iust occasion to mocke vs; and then if we be scoffed at, we shall neuer be hurt by it: nay (though that be farre from their intent) yet in mocking vs, they doe vs great honour. For the word of God that cannot lie, is this; that to suffer affliction for Chrisls sake, is greater honour and riches, then the treasures of a kingdome. And if Moses iudgement be good, which God himselfe doth here commend; then we are happy & blessed, in enduring these mocks and scoffes for Christ.

Secondly, we must here learne instruction for the time to come: We haue a long time, through the great goodnes of God, enioyed peace and wealth, with the Gospel of Christ; but vndoubtedly, these daies of peace will haue an ende, they cannot last alwaies, Gods people must passe through the fierie furnace of affliction. Well, when this is come vpon vs, how shall we be able to beare it? Surely, we must now learne to be of this opinion that Moses was of; we must iudge it to be the greatest honour and riches that can be, to suffer affliction for Chrisls sake: and this will be the ground of all constancie, courage, and Christian boldnes in the day of triall. For he that is of this minde, will neuer feare affliction, nor reproach for Chrisls sake: nay, he will be so farre from fearing it, that he will reioyce and triumph therein.

Further, whereas it is said, *Esteeming the rebuke of Christ*; here marke, the rebuke of Gods Church & people is called *the rebuke of Christ*. The people of God in Egypt were laden with reproaches and rebukes: and behold, Christ accounts it his rebuke, and the holy Ghost so cals it. Where learne this, *That Christ esteemeth the reproach and affliction of his Church, as his owne affliction*. When Saul went to persecute the brethren at Damascus, Act. 9. 2. 4. Christ Iesus calls to him from heauen, saying; *Saul, Saul, why persecutest thou me? Saul* went to persecute the Christians, and yet our Sauiour Christ taketh it vnto himselfe. And after his conuersion he saith, 2 Cor. 4. 10. *Euery way we beare about in our bodies, the dying of the Lord Iesus*. And againe, *Let no man put me to businesse: for I beare in my bodie the markes of the Lord Iesus*, Gal. 6. 17. This is a point of speciall vse.

First, hence we learne, that Christ hath a speciall care of his Church and children, in that he iudgeth their afflictions to be his owne afflictions; and therefore he can no more forget, or leaue off to helpe them in distresse, then denie himselfe.

Secondly, here is a speciall comfort for Gods children that be in affliction: their afflictions are not their owne alone, but Chrisls also; he is their partner, and fellow sufferer. This may seeme strange, but it is most true: Christ puts (as it were) his shoulders vnder our afflictions, and takes them to himselfe, as though they were his owne; then which, what can be more comfortable? For, though thou thy selfe cannot beare it, yet trust vndoubtedly, that Christ who beares with thee, will giue thee strength to vndergoe it vnto victorie.

Thirdly, if the afflictions of a Christian, be the afflictions of Christ; then it is a fearefull sinne for any man to mocke or reproach his brother, in regard of his profession and religion: for, *mocking is persecution*, Gal. 4. 29. with Gen. 21. 9. And that reproach which is cast vpon a Christian, is cast vpon Christ; and Christ takes it as done vnto himselfe: the persecutor wounds Christ Iesus through the sides of a poore Christian; which is a fearefull thing. For in so doing, he sets himselfe against the Lord Iesus, he kickes against the prickes; and if he so continue, he must needes looke for some fearefull ende: *for who hath euer beene fierce against the Lord, and hath prospered?* Iob 9. 4. Wherefore, if any of vs be guiltie of any sinne in this kind, let vs repent: for vnlesse we turne, our condemnation will be remedilesse.

Againe, the afflictions of the Israelites, are here said to be their sufferings for Christ: where note, that though Christ his comming were then a farre off, yet the Israelites then knew of Christ: for else they could not suffer for him.

This confuteth those which hold, that euery man may be saued by his owne religion, whatsoeuer it be, if he liue ciuilly and vprightly therein. Their reason is taken from the Iewes, who (they say) had onely the knowledge of outward ceremonies, and so were saued. But that opinion is here disprooued: for the Iewes knew Christ, and professed him, or else they would neuer suffer for him: and therefore they were saued by him, and not by their obedience to outward ceremonies. And thus much of the reason, which mooued *Moses* to make such a choise as he did.

Now in the ende of the verse is added a reason, why *Moses* was of this strange iudgement, to thinke the *reproach of Christ greater riches then the treasures of Egypt*: namely, *because he had respect to the recompence of reward*. That is, he often set his eye to behold, and his heart to consider, how God had made a promise of life euerlasting after this life, vnto all those that obeyed him, and trusted in him after this life: for the enioying whereof, he preferred that estate wherein he might liue in the feare of God, though it were a state of reproach, before all other whatsoeuer. Where we see, what it is will bring a man to esteeme affliction, with the feare of God, better then the treasures and pleasures of an earthly kingdome: namely, as we set the bodily eye to behold the affliction; so wee must lift vp the eye of the minde by faith, to behold the recompence of reward; that is, the state of glorie in heauen prepared for Gods children. Thus did the Christian Hebrewes in the primitiue Church, Heb. 10. 37. *They suffered with ioy the spoyling of their goods.* (A very hard thing, but yet most true, for it is the word of God.) And the reason is rendred, *They knewe in themselues how that they had in heauen a better and more enduring substance.* And our Sauiour Christ *endured the Crosse, and despised the shame, for the ioy that was set before him,* Heb. 12. 1. that is, in consideration of that ioy in glory, whereto hee should be aduanced himselfe, and bring all his members. This we must make vse of: for if we will liue godly in Christ Iesus, we must suffer affliction. This flesh and blood will not yeeld vnto: and therefore, to perswade vs to suffer with ioy, we must with *Moses haue respect to the recompence of reward.* We must say thus to our soules, The day will come wherein we shall haue euerlasting life in the Kingdom of heauen, if we now serue and feare him: Shall we not then for his sake be content to suffer a short affliction; seeing the greatest of them are not worthie of the glory that shall be reuealed? Rom. 8. 18.

Quest. But why doth the holy Ghost call euerlasting life, a reward? *Ans.* It is not so called because *Moses* did procure it, and deserue it at Gods hand by the dignitie of his works in suffering: for sure no man can merit any thing at Gods hands. The case is plaine: For, Christ as he is man (consider his manhood a-part from his Godhead) could not merit any thing at Gods hands: for, he that would merit of God by any worke, must doe three things: 1. He must doe the worke of himselfe, and by himselfe; for if he doe it by an other, the other meriteth, and must haue the reward and praise of the worke. Secondly, he must doe it of meere good will, and not of dutie: for that which is of duty, cannot merit because a man is bound to doe it. 3. The worke done to merit, must be of that price and dignity, that it may be proportionable to life euerlasting, which is the reward. Now, though Christ as he is man, be aboue all men and all Angels in grace and dignitie: yet consider his manhood a-part from his Godhead, and he could not doe a worke with these three properties. For first, the works done of the manhood were not done of it selfe, but from that fullnesse of the spirit wherewith he was endued. Secondly, Christ as man is a creature: and so considered, his works are of duty to the Creator, and so cannot merit. Thirdly, Christs works as man simply considered are finite; and so could not merit infinite glory.

Quest. How then did Christ merit at Gods hands? *Ans.* Partly by meanes of Gods promises made in the Law, which was this; *Doe this and thou shalt liue:* but properly and chiefely, because he was not a meere man onely, but (withall) true and very God: for, because his obedience both in his life and death (though

performed in his manhoode) was the obedience of him that was God and man, euen from the infinite excellencie of the person whose it is, it becomes meritorious. In his manhood, he obayed the Law, and suffered for our sinnes: but the dignitie thereof came from the Godhead: for, he that did these works for vs, was both God and man.

Now, if Christ considered as man onely cannot merit: then much lesse can any other man merit at Gods hands. And therefore *Moses,* though he were a worthie man, yet because he was but a man, and a sinnefull man also, he could not by any work deserue life euerlasting at Gods hands.

But *life euerlasting* is called a reward in the Scripture, because it is the free gift of God, promised by God to his children in Christ; for this ende, to allure and drawe them on in obedience. And it must not seeme strange, that we say a *reward* is a *free gift:* for so it may be, as we shall see by comparing two places of Scripture together; to wit, Matth. 5. 44. with Luk. 6. 32. For, whereas Matthew saith, *If you loue them that loue you, what reward haue you:* Saint *Luke* repeating the same thing, saith, *What thanke haue you,* or (as the word signifies) *what fauour, or free gift haue you?* Secondly, there may be another cause rendred, why life euerlasting is called a reward; to wit, not in regard of the worke done: but in regard of the worker considered in Christ: for Christs merit makes life euerlasting to be a reward. Now, euery true beleeuer that endeauours to doe the will of God, is in Christ: and so Christs righteousnesse with the merit thereof, is his, so far forth as serues to make his person acceptable to God. Whereupon, he hath a promise of reward made vnto him vpon his obedience; yet not for his worke, but for the worke of Christs obedience in whom he is: And so must these words here be vnderstood.

1. The consideration of this reward of life eternall giuen, through Christ, to those that suffer for his sake, may make vs ioyfull and patient in all our afflictions for righteousnes sake. A naturall man will endure much for a good recompence in the ende. Now Christ saith, *Great is your reward.* And therefore let vs reioice in suffring for Christ; *holding fast our confidence, which hath so great recompence of reward.* Matth. 5. 12. Heb. 10. 35.

Secondly, is life euerlasting a *recompence,* that is, a *giuing of a reward?* Then here is condemned the desperate practise of many a one, who spend their whole life in a greedy pursuite after the profites and pleasures of the world: as it were running themselues out of breath in the way to hell, without all regard of their soules, till death come; thinking, that if at the last gaspe they can crie God mercie, and commend their soules to God, all is well. But all such persons for the most part deceiue their owne soules, not considering that life euerlasting is giuen as a reward. Now, we

know

knowe that no reward is giuen to any man, till the worke be done which he is set about; he must come worke in the Vineyard some part of the day that would haue his pennie at night: as for those that neither stirre hand nor foote to doe the worke, what reward can they looke for? And yet this is the state of carnall liuers, they addict theselues wholly to earthly things. But if we looke for any reward at the day of death, we must labour in the works of godlinesse all the dayes of our life; for, therefore were we redeemed, Luk. 1. 74. 75.

In the whole booke of God, we finde but one man that liued wickedly, and repented at his ende: that is, the thiefe vpon the Crosse. Which shewes that it is a most rare thing for a man to haue the reward of life euerlasting after this life, that labours not in the works of godlinesse in this life.

Thirdly, the consideration of this reward, must stirre vp all Gods children vnto all diligence in the duties of godlinesse, and that with cheerefulnesse, through the whole course of their liues. When we shall die, we will looke earnestly for this reward; and therefore while we liue, we must diligently doe the works that God commaundeth: and then when death comes, we may assure our selues that God will giue vs this reward; not because we did deserue it by our works, but because he hath promised it in Christ, vpon our endeauour in obedience and true repentance. And thus much for the reason of Moses choice.

VERSE 27.

By faith he forsooke Egypt, and feared not the fiercenesse of the King. For, he was couragious, as he that saw him that is inuisible.

IN this verse, the spirit of God proceedeth to another example of Moses faith: and hereto also in the verse following, he addeth a third. Now he is thus large in the commendation of his faith, for this ende; to perswade the *Hebrewes*, to whom this Epistle is sent, that they were not to looke for any Iustification by the works of the Law: and his reason is; because if any man could be iustified by the works of the Law, it must be Moses, who gaue the Law to the people from the Lord, and did excell in obedience to both Tables, and therefore is a renowned Prophet vnto all posteritie in *speciall fauour with God*, Num. 12. 7, 8. But Moses could not be iustified by the works of the Law; for here the holy Ghost prooues, that Moses was iustified and saued by faith. The thing that commends Moses and makes him stand before God, is not his works but his faith: and therefore the conclusion is; that as Moses was not iustified by his works but by faith, no more must they stand vpon their works to be iustified thereby, but labour for such faith as Moses had. Now, this faith of Moses is a true sauing faith, founded on these two promises of God: 1. On this great and maine promise made to *Abraham*, *I will be thy God and the God of thy seede*: 2. On another particular promise rising from the generall, made vnto him when he was called to fetch the Israelites out of bondage; which was this; *I will be with thee and guide thee*. And in this place Moses is said to haue faith, not onely because he *beleeued that God would be his God*, as he was the God of all *Abrahams* seede; but because *he beleeued particularly that God would be his God, and defend and be with him in the deliuerance of the Israelites out of Egypt.*

Exod. 3. 12.

To come particularly to this fact, *By faith, Moses forsooke Egypt*. *Moses* departed from Egypt twise: First, when he had slaine the Egyptian, and fledde from Pharaoh vnto Midian, and there kept *Iethroes* sheepe. Secondly, fourty yeares after when he ledde the people of Israel out of Egypt into the land of Canaan: and here some make it a question, whether of these departures is meant in this place. *Answ.* It is most like, that this place is to be vnderstood of his second departure, rather then of the first: And the reason is taken out of Exodus, Chap. 14. 15. where we finde that the first time, *he fledde for feare*: for, so soone as he heard that his slaughter of the Egyptian was knowen to *Pharaoh*, he fled in such feare, as that he durst not returne againe, of fourtie yeares. Now these words are not to be vnderstood of such a flight: for here it is said, *He departed, not fearing the Kings wrath or fiercenesse.*

Here some will say, This is no commendation: for, malefactors and rebels doe flie their Country? *Ans.* They flie indeed, yet not in faith, but in feare. *Moses* fled in faith: and hereby his faith is commended, that he *fled not fearing the King*. But malefactors flie for feare of punishment. *Moses* departed with courage and boldnesse, and therefore fled not as a malefactor: for he feared not the King, as appeareth plainely in the Historie; for, though *Pharaoh* had said vnto him, Exod. 10. 28. *Get thee gone, see thou see my face no more: for when thou commest in my sight, thou shalt die*; yet *Moses* went once more: namely, the tenth time, and told him of the tenth plague, and said, That *Pharaohs* seruants should come downe vnto him, and fall downe, and pray him to goe hand out with the people and their cattell. And when the Israelites murmured against him at the red sea, when *Pharaoh* was at their heeles, and they had no way to flie, *Moses* encourageth the people, saying, *Feare not, stand still, and behold the saluation of the Lord which he will shew you this day: for the Egyptians whome ye haue seene this day, shall ye neuer see againe*, Exod. 14. 13. Whereby, it notably appeares, that Moses departed in faith without feare of Pharaoh.

But ſome will ſay; For a man to come into another mans Kingdome, and to carie away his Subiects without the Kings conſent, is a fact of rebellion and ſedition : and therefore worthie no commendation, but rather ſhame and puniſhment : And this did Moſes, he comes from Midian, and caries away the Iewes which had beene a long time *Pharaohs* ſubiects ; and for whoſe ſeruice he might plead poſſeſſion, and a long preſcription : therefore it ſeemes to be no fact of faith. *Anſ.* Indeede if Moſes had done this on his owne head, he might worthily haue beene thus cenſured. But when he came to E-gypt, he had a calling immediatly from God to doe as he did ; and for confirmation hereof, he had Gods promiſe of aſſiſtance in working ſtrange miracles : and when he caried the peo-ple out of Egypt, he did it by commandement from a King that was higher then *Pharaoh.* Neither yet did Moſes carie them away as a priuate man : for he was a publike perſon, an high Magiſtrate, and no ſtranger, but one of themſelues : yea, he was a *King,* as may appeare in Gods word: for, Deut. 33.5. he is plainly cal-led *a King* : and Gen. 36.31. it is ſaide, *There were ſo many Kings in Edom, before there raig-ned any King ouer the children of Iſrael.* Now, the laſt of thoſe Kings raigned at that time when Moſes went with the Iſraelites out of E-gypt : ſo that Moſes was their King, and had the authoritie & gouernment of a King ouer them from the Lord : and therefore it was no fact of rebellion in him, but a worke that did greatly commend his faith, beeing grounded vpon Gods commandement and promiſe.

Thus we ſee how we muſt conceiue of *Mo-ſes* fact. Now we come to ſome particular points to be conſidered therein.

How came it to paſſe, that Moſes now had this courage, to depart from *Pharaoh* not fea-ring his commandement; whereas 40. yeares before, beeing called *to ſhew himſelfe vnto his brethren, as one whome they were to reſpect as their deliuerer,* Act. 7.23.25. he fled immediat-ly out of Egypt vpon the notice of one fact of defence in behalfe of the Iſraelites ? why did he not ſhew as much courage when he ſlew the Egyptian, as at his ſecond departure ? *Anſw.* The cauſe of his courage at this latter time was this; God now renued his commiſſion, and con-firmed his former calling. For when he was firſt called, he did his dutie and reuenged their wrongs : but yet beeing in danger, and his cal-ling beeing as yet but a ſecret inſtinct, he was fearefull, and fled. But now when God called him the ſecond time, and confirmed the ſame calling both by promiſe and commandement, and power to worke miracles, then fearefull Moſes becomes couragious and bold.

Here then obſerue, that there is a difference of Gods graces; there is a firſt grace, and a ſe-cond grace. The firſt, is that which God giues to any man for any calling : the ſecond is that, which God addes to the firſt, for the confir-ming thereof. And the firſt, is not effectuall without the ſecond ; As here we ſee, Moſes firſt calling was not effectuall with him, till the ſecond came. And ſo Gods firſt grace is not ef-fectuall till the ſecond come; by which the for-mer is confirmed, ſtrengthened, and encreaſed. And the ſecond is confirmed by the third : and ſo we muſt goe on from grace to grace, if we will be bold and couragious in any dutie, ei-ther of our generall or particular calling. This muſt be well conſidered ; for, that any man ſtands in grace, or encreaſeth therein, either re-ſpecting his particular calling, or his Chriſtian conuerſation, it comes from this, that God addes a ſecond grace vnto the firſt. And there-fore whoſoeuer is enabled for any dutie, hath great cauſe to praiſe God : for, whether we continue in grace, or encreaſe therein, it comes from the goodneſſe of God, who addeth grace to grace: which if he ſhould not doe, we ſhould fall away, and not be able to goe forward in the feare of God, and the duties of our calling ; for the firſt grace would not ſuffice to ſtrengthen vs againſt temptation. And therefore howſoe-uer God hath ſtrengthened vs for the time paſt, yet ſtill we muſt pray to God to deliuer vs from euill : which plainely imports, that our ſtanding is from his daily ſupplie of new grace.

2. *Point.* When went Moſes out of Egypt ? The time is directly ſet downe, Exod. 12.41. *Euen the ſelfe ſame day when the promiſe of God was expired : for when the foure hundred and thirtie yeares were expired, then went all the hoaſt of the Lord out of Egypt,* neither before, nor after, but the very ſame day. Indeede Moſes was choſen to be their captaine 40. yeares be-fore, and ſent vnto them by God: and S. *Steuen* ſaith, *He thought they would haue vnderſtood ſo much.* But then they would not take him for their guide. Yet now 40. yeares after, when Gods determinate time of 430. yeares was ex-pired, he comes againe vnto them, to cary them out of Egypt; & then they acknowledge him, & follow him out, according to Gods comiſſion.

Hence we learne, firſt, that no creature can alter the rule of Gods prouidence. Fourtie yeares before, Moſes would haue deliuered the people ; but he muſt ſtay till the time of the Lords promiſe was accompliſhed, and then he caries them away. Secondly, this muſt teach vs, not onely to beleeue, that God both can and will keepe his promiſes ; but alſo by faith to waite for the time, wherein he will accompliſh the ſame vnto vs. Moſes is faine to waite 40. yeares for the fulfilling of Gods promiſe. When *Daniel* vnderſtood how long the Iſraelites muſt be in captiuitie, he would not pray for the ſhortning of that time : but when he knew that the time of their returne drew neere, then he praied vnto the Lord moſt earneſtly, waiting for the accompliſhment of Gods promiſe in their deliuerance. And *Dauid* thus waited on God for deliuerance in all his troubles. And their examples muſt we follow, for the frui-tion

Dan.9.

Pſal.42.11.

tion of all Gods bleſſings.

3. *Point.* In what *manner* doth *Moſes* depart? The text ſaith, He went out, *not fearing the Kings commandement* : ſo that his departure was with *courage.* Whence we learne ſundry inſtructions. Firſt, here is a notable preſident for the framing of our lines, which muſt be a rule vnto vs. We muſt walke diligently in our callings, as *Moſes* did; and though croſſes meete vs, ſo that *Pharaoh* fall out with vs; if Kings become our enemies:yet we muſt not lay aſide the duties of our callings;but after *Moſes* example, goe on therein with courage. Moſes *without fearing the Kings wrath, went and ledde all the people away.* And ſo muſt euery one of vs do: although dangers come, we muſt not feare, but ſtand faſt in our profeſſion, and goe on in the duties of our callings : Ecclef. 10. 4. *If the ſpirit of him that ruleth riſe vp againſt thee, leaue not thy place.*

Secondly, hence we may learne, that Magiſtrates which are to gouerne the people, ought to be men of courage, in performing the duties of their calling. When too heauy a burthen lay on Moſes,in iudging all the congregation himſelfe; *Iethro* his father in law biddes him *prouide among all the people men of courage, fearing God, to be Rulers,* Exod.18. 13. 21. Now their courage muſt not be a proud hautineſſe, or an indiſcreete crueltie;but a godly boldnes,which may inable them to the duties of their calling, without feare of man. To this ende, the Lord put *of his ſpirit* vpon the *ſeuenty,* which were to rule with Moſes, Num.11. 17.Now, the ſpirit of God, is not a ſpirit of feate,but of *power, and of loue, and of a ſound minde,* 2. Tim. 1. 7. Which ſhewes, that in a Magiſtrate muſt be courage to call,and (if neede be) to compell others to the duties of their calling, how great ſoeuer they be. And it is a matter of great waight and moment in Gods Church: for, the Miniſter may teach and ſpeake as much as he will, or can; yet vnleſſe with the ſword of the ſpirit, there be ioyned the temporall ſword of the Magiſtrate ; to reforme mens liues, and to keepe them from open ſinne againſt the law of God, and to vrge them to the duties which the miniſter teacheth: ſurely, their teaching and preaching will be to ſmall effect.

Laſtly, Moſes went with courage out of Egypt. This departure of his, was a ſigne of our ſpirituall departing out of the Kingdome of darkeneſſe: for, ſo *Paul* applieth it, 1. Cor. 10. And therefore after Moſes example, we muſt with courage come euery day more and more out of the kingdome of darknes, marching forward with couragious faith & heauenly boldneſſe towards our bleſſed Canaan, the glorie of heauen : we muſt not leaue this to the laſt breath, and then thinke to haue heauen gates ready open for vs:but we muſt enter into Gods Kingdome, in this life. Looke as Moſes by his faith did depart boldly out of Egypt, ſo muſt wee in heart by faith depart out of the King-

dome of ſinne. This we ſhall doe, when we vſe meanes to eſtabliſh the Kingdome of Chriſt Ieſus in our hearts, and doe forſake the works of ſinne and darkeneſſe. For, looke where there is no departing from ſinne,there is no faith:and therefore let vs ſhew our ſelues to haue true faith, by departing more and more boldly and ioyfully out of the Kingdom of ſinne and Satan; that ſo it may appeare, we loue the light,and hate darkeneſſe. And in this iourney, let vs not feare any contrary commandement, nor the furious wrath of ſpirituall *Pharaoh* the deuill, nor all the gates of hell: for Chriſt Ieſus is our guide.

Becauſe a man might thinke at the firſt, that it was a raſh and deſperate part in Moſes, thus boldly to take away the Iſraelites, not regarding *Pharaohs* commandement; therefore in the latter part of the verſe, the holy Ghoſt ſetteth down a reaſon, that mooued Moſes to doe ſo, in theſe words:*For he endured,or was couragious,* that is, he tooke heart to himſelfe. Why ſo? *Becauſe he ſaw God that is inuiſible.*That is, he caſt the eie of faith vpon God, who had promiſed the euidence of his power and preſence, in their deliuerance. So that it was the worke of Moſes faith, laying hold on the promiſe of Gods preſence, and protection from the rage of *Pharaoh,* that made him thus confident and bold.

Hence we learne, that the true valour and manhood that was in Moſes, and is in all Gods children, like vnto him, is a gift of grace. Among many gifts of the ſpirit, powred vpon our Sauiour Chriſt,*the ſpirit of ſtrength, or courage, is one,* Iſay 11. 2. And *Iethroes* counſell to Moſes is notable this way; he biddes him prouide for gouernours,*men of courage, fearing God,* Exod. 18. 21. Inſinuating, that true courage is alwaies ioyned with the feare of God, and is a fruite of grace. But ſome will ſay, that many heathen men, who neuer knewe the true God, nor what the gifts of the ſpirit meant,had that courage. *Anſ.*Tiue it is,they had courage indeede: but it was nothing but a carnall boldneſſe (not worthy the name of courage; beeing onely a ſhaddow of true fortitude) ariſing from ambition,pride,and other fleſhly humors; whereas Moſes his courage ſprang from the grace of faith,in the mercifull promiſes of God made vnto him concerning his deliuerance and ſafetie. And indeede, howſoeuer wicked men haue a notable ſhewe of diuers vertues, yet in the triall they prooue but ſhaddowes; for, true valour, and other vertues, doe alwaies accompany regeneration.

As he that ſawe him that is inuiſible.

Here is the cauſe that made Moſes thus couragious: and this will make any man bold,if he can be perſwaded in his conſcience of Gods ſpeciall preſence with him, and prouidence and protection ouer him.

Here then obſerue a ſingular fruite of faith: it makes God who is indeede inuiſible, to be after a ſort viſible vnto vs. *Moſes* by faith ſawe him that was inuiſible; for, by faith he was perſwaded of Gods prouidence, and ſpeciall protection in the deliuery of his people, though *Pharaoh* ſhould rage neuer ſo much. So *Enoch* is ſaid to haue *walked with God*, becauſe he ſaw him by the eie of faith, in all his affaires. And when *Ioſeph* was allured to ſinne with his Miſtres, what ſtaied him? ſurely, the feare of God, whom he ſaw by faith. *How can I doe this great wickedneſſe* (ſaith *Ioſeph*) *and ſo ſinne againſt God?* As if he ſhould ſay, I am alwaies where God is preſent; how then ſhould I doe ſo wickedly, and God ſee it? And the ſame is the ſtate of all true beleeuers; their faith makes the inuiſible God, to be after a ſort viſible vnto them: ſo as a faithfull man may ſay, God is preſent with me, and protecteth me. Whereby we may ſee, what little faith is in the world: for fewe can truly ſay, they ſee God: which, faith inables a man to doe. Yea, moſt men care ſo little to ſee God, that he is farre from their very thoughts. Many haue made meanes to ſee the deuill: but where is he that labours for ſuch a meaſure of faith, that he may ſee the inuiſible God? If wicked men runne to Coniurers, to ſee the deuill, whom they ſhall once ſee to their ſorrowe; let vs labour for faith in the word and ſacraments, and this faith will make vs ſo to indure in all tribulation, as though we ſawe God.

Furthermore, ſeeing *Moſes* by faith endured, as he that ſaw God: we learne, that the ſeeing of God by faith, takes away feare and giues ſpirituall boldneſſe. This is a point of ſpeciall vſe: for naturally men are fearefull: ſome cannot endure the darke, nor ſolitary places, for feare of the deuill: yea, the ſhaking of a leafe, or the crawling of a worme doth terrifie others. Now, howſoeuer ſome mens conſtitution may helpe forward this feare, yet many times it comes from an accuſing conſcience, as a fruit of ſinne. And the way to remooue it, is here to be learned: namely, to doe as *Moſes* did: that is, labour to be reſolued of Gods preſence with vs, and prouidence ouer vs: and this will arme vs againſt all ſatanicall and fooliſh feare. For, if God be on our ſide, who can be againſt vs, to doe vs harme? Againe, the Souldier, by his place and calling ought to be a man of courage: for elſe the ſtate of his life, and the thought of his enemies will much affright him. Now how may he become couragious? They vſe to ſound the drumme and trumpet for this ende: and it muſt be graunted they are good incitements and prouocations vnto battell: but, when it comes to the point of danger, theſe cannot giue heart. Others vſe againſt the battell to fill themſelues with wine, and to make themſelues valiant by ſtrong drinke. This indeede may make them ſenſeleſſe and ſo deſperate. But the true way is, to become Chriſtian ſoldiers, knowing, and fearing God: & with their bodily armour, to bring alſo the ſhield of faith: whereby their hearts

may be aſſured, that God hath called them to that fight: and that he is preſent with them, to couer their heads in the day of battell. This will make them to take heart and courage to themſelues, and to become truly valorous: though by nature they be weake and timorous.

Thirdly, who knows whether God wil bring vs to this triall: either to lay downe our liues, or forſake his truth: for, he may iuſtly take frō vs theſe golden daies of peace, for our ingratitude. Now, if ſuch times come vpon vs, what ſhall we doe? Shall we denie the faith of Chriſt? God forbid. But how ſhall we ſtand out in ſuch a triall? Surely, we muſt followe *Moſes*, and *labour to ſee him that is inuiſible, by faith*. This will make vs couragious, and without feare in Gods cauſe: remembring this alſo, that among thoſe which are reckoned to goe downe to hell, the *fearefull man* is one, (Reul. 21. 8.) who dares not ſtand to the truth of God, but for feare of men denies it. Let vs therefore now begin to ſettle our hearts in the aſſurance of Gods prouidence and protection: that ſo, when triall comes, we may be bold in the caſe of God.

Him that is inuiſible.] That is God, who is a moſt ſimple eſſence, voide of all compoſition, or corporall ſubſtance: for, *God is a ſpirit*, (Ioh. 4. 24.) and therefore inuiſible, and not ſubiect to mans ſenſes. But ſome will ſay, God is ſaid to haue head, heart, hands, and feete: with other parts of mans body: and therefore he is viſible? *Anſw.* The holy Ghoſt ſo ſpeaketh in Scripture of God, by way of reſemblance of him vnto man: that we might the better thereby conceiue of his works: for, therefore are the parts of mans bodie aſcribed vnto God in Scripture, that we might knowe he doth ſuch works by his diuine power, as man doth by the parts of his body. Man ſheweth his ſtrength and valour in his arme: and by reſemblance vnto man, God is ſaid to haue an *Arme, to note out his power and valiant acts*. And ſo God is ſaid to haue eies, becauſe we ſhould conceiue that by his infinite wiſdome he ſeeth al things more cleerely, than man doth any thing at noone day, with his bodily eies. And ſo of the reſt.

But *Moſes* is ſaid, *to talke with God face to face*: and, *to ſee his backe-parts*, Exod. 33. 11. 23. *Anſw.* This imports not, that he ſawe the ſubſtance of God; but onely, that God did after a familiar manner, reueale himſelfe vnto him, and in ſome reſemblance ſhew him his glorie, ſo farre forth as *Moſes* was able to behold it: for the text is plaine, *My face cannot be ſeene. There ſhall no man ſee me and liue*, verſe 20.

Here we learne, that when we pray to God, we muſt not conceiue of him by any forme or image in our mindes; for ſo we make an idol of God. *Queſt.* What then muſt we doe? for, how (will ſome ſay) can I pray to him, and not thinke of him? *Anſ.* When we thinke of God, or pray vnto him, we muſt conceiue of him

Gen. 5. 22.

Gen. 39. 9.

in our mindes, as he hath reuealed himselfe in Scripture; that is, by his workes, and by his properties: wee must thinke in our mindes of an *eternall essence*, most *holy, wise, &c. who made all things, and gouernes them by his mighty power.*For, euery image to resemble God by, either to the minde, or to the eye, is a plaine lie; making him visible, who is inuisible: as saith the Prophet, Hab. 2.18. *The image, what profiteth it, for it is a teacher of lies?* Which flatly ouerthroweth the opinion and practise of the Romish Church, who resemble the true God, euen God the Father, and the holy Trinitie, in images: what else doe they herein, but make a lie of God?

But the Papists say, they deuise no image to resemble God in, but onely such whereby hee hath shewed himselfe; as the Scripture testifies: as the *Father*, like an *old man*; the Sonne, as hee was incarnate; and the holy Ghost, *like a doue*, Matth. 3.16. *Answ.* We must not conceiue of those formes, of *an olde man*, or of *a doue*, to haue beene euer any image of the Father, or of the holy Ghost; but onely signes and pledges for a time, whereby those persons did then manifest their presence. Nowe, there beeing an expresse commaundement against all representation of God by images, not excepting those very shapes, whereby it pleased God for a time to signifie his presence; it must needs be idolatrous presumption to make any image of God, or of the Trinitie. And indeede, God being inuisible (as the text saith) it is impossible to make any true image or resemblance of him.

Verse 28.

By faith, hee ordained the Passeouer, and the effusion of blood: least he that destroyed the first borne, should touch them.

IN the former verses, the author of this Epistle hath shewed vnto vs, the notable faith of *Moses*, by two worthy acts: 1. His *refusing to be called the sonne of Pharaohs daughter.* 2. His *departing out of Egypt.* Now, here in this verse, he commends his faith vnto vs by a third action; which is, the ordination, or celebrating of the Passeouer. This verse is the summe of the 12. Chap.of Exodus, the effect whereof is this: After that God had sent nine seuerall plagues vpon the land of Egypt, which were occasions to harden *Pharaohs* heart; at last he sends *Moses* to certifie *Pharaoh*, that vnlesse he would let the people goe, hee would send a tenth plague, which should bee more grieuous to them, then all the former; euen *the slaughter of al the first borne in Egypt, both of man and beast.* Yet *Pharaohs* heart was not softened, neither did he let the people goe. Therefore *Moses* de-

parted from him, & (according to Gods commandement) assembles the Elders of Israel together, and causeth them to kill euery man a lambe of a yeare olde, and to eate it, roste with fire; and to take the blood, and sprinkle it vpon the doore cheekes, and vpon the posts of their houses: for a signe vnto them, that the Angel of the Lord, (seeing the blood sprinkled vpon their doores) should passe ouer them, and touch none of their first borne, neither man nor beast. This is the summe and meaning of that history. Now let vs come to the consideration of this fact more particularly; and first, to the meaning of the wordes of this verse, because there is some difficultie in them.

Through faith he ordained the Passeouer.

The *Passe-ouer* here named, may bee thus described; *It is one of the Sacraments of the old Testament, seruing for a signe to the people of Israel, both of their temporall deliuerance from the bondage of Egypt, and from the slaughter of the first borne; and also of their spirituall deliuerance from euerlasting death, by the sacrifice of Christ Iesus the immaculate Lambe of God.*

Touching this description: first, I call it *one of the Sacraments of the old Testament:*because they had beside this, *Circumcision*, another ordinarie Sacrament. Next I say, It serued for a signe to the people of Israel, to shew that it was properly a sacrament vnto them. For, it is of the nature of a sacrament, to signifie and seale vp some blessing of God to his people: now that the Passe-ouer did so, is plaine, where the Lord calls it a signe or token of deliuerance vnto them. But some will say, this Passe-ouer was a *sacrifice:* for so it is called, *This is the sacrifice of the Lords Passe-ouer.* And, *Thou shalt not offer the blood of my sacrifice with leauened bread, &c. Ans.* It is called a sacrifice, because it was killed, also the blood thereof was sprinkled, and some parts of it, as the *fat*, with the two kidneies were burnt in sacrifice to the Lord. For, when *Iosias* kept that famous Passe-ouer with all the people, the Priests that slew the Passe-ouer, and sprinkled the blood thereof, did *first take away that which was to be consumed with fire, and then gaue to the people according to the deuisions of their families, as Moses appointed.* Now, in regard of these properties of a sacrifice which were in the Passe-ouer, it is truly called a sacrifice. And yet more properly it was a Sacrament, because it was a visible signe of speciall blessings from the Lord.

But what did this Sacrament of the Passe-ouer signifie; *Ans.* It did signifie a double deliuerance; one *temporal*, as well from the destroying Angell, as also from the bondage of Egypt: The other *spirituall:* from the curse of the Law, and from the wrath of God. The first is plaine, where the Lord saith, *The blood beeing sprinkled vpon the doore posts, shall be a token for you that I will passe ouer you.* And verse 17. *Yee*

Exod.12.27.

Exod.23.18.

Levit.3.4.

2.Chr.35.12.

Exod.12.13

ſhall keepe the feaſt of vnleauened bread: for that ſame day will I bring your Armies out of the Land of Egypt. And touching the ſecond, that it was a ſigne of a more heauenly deliuerance from the bondage of ſinne and Satan, *Paul* telleth vs plainely, when as hee ſaith, *Chriſt our Paſſe-ouer is ſacrificed for vs:* giuing vs to vnderſtand, that the Paſchall Lambe in the olde Teſtament, was vndoubtedly a true ſigne of the true Paſchall Lambe Chriſt Ieſus: to which purpoſe *Iohn Baptiſt* ſaith; *Behold the Lamb of God that taketh away the ſinnes of the world:* Ioh. 1. 29. Where he calleth *Chriſt the Lambe of God,* making there an oppoſition betweene him and the Paſchall Lambe of *Moſes,* which may be called the Paſchall lambe of men; for herein alſo they differ. The Paſchall Lambe was ſeparated by men, though by Gods appointment; but Chriſt the true Lambe of God, was ſet a part before all worlds by God the Father. And thus we ſee briefly what this *Paſſe-ouer* is. It followeth.

Ordained the Paſſe-ouer. The word tranſlated, *ordained,* ſignifieth, *He made,* or *did celebrate:* for the better vnderſtanding whereof, we muſt haue recourſe to the Euangeliſts. Matthew ſetteth downe Chriſts ſpeach to his Diſciples about the Paſſe-ouer, which he kept with them a little before his paſſion, thus: *My time is come, I will make my Paſſe-ouer at thine houſe.* Now, S. *Luke* repeating the ſame Story, mentioneth, firſt the *killing,* and then the *eating* of it: by which two words hee explaneth what Chriſt meant by making (which here is tranſlated *ordaining*) the Paſſe-ouer; to wit, firſt, the killing and preparing of the Paſchall Lambe, and then the eating of it as the Lords Sacrament. But this is a ſtrange kind of ſpeach (will ſome ſay) how can the Paſſe-ouer be killed or eaten? ſeeing properly the Paſſe-ouer is nothing elſe, but the act of the Angell paſſing ouer the houſes of the Iſraelites, when hee ſmote the firſt borne in euery houſe of the Egyptians. *Anſ.* The phraſe is improper: yet it muſt not ſeeme ſtrange, becauſe it is vſuall in Scripture, entreating of the Sacraments, ſometime to giue the name of the ſigne to the thing ſignified: as 1. Cor. 5. 7. Chriſt is called our Paſſeouer; & on the otherſide, to giue the name of the thing ſignified to the ſigne: as in this place, *he ordained the Paſſe-ouer;* that is, the Paſchal Lamb, which was a ſigne of the Angels paſſing ouer their houſes. So, *This is my bodie,* that is, a ſigne of my bodie. *The rock was Chriſt.* The reaſon of theſe figuratiue ſpeeches, whereby one thing is put for another, is the Sacramentall vnion of the ſigne with the thing ſignified: which yet is not *naturall* according to place, either by change of the ſigne into the thing ſignified, or by including the thing ſignified in the ſigne, or faſtning it vpon it; but *reſpectiue* and analogicall, by reaſon of that agreement & proportion, which is betweene the ſigne and the thing ſignified: which ſtands in this, that looke when

the *outward ſigne* is preſented to the outward ſenſes, at the very ſame time the *thing ſignified* is thereby, as by certaine viſible words, preſented to the minde. And indeed looke what coniunction is betweene words, & the things ſpoken of, in the minde of the vnderſtanding hearer; the ſame is betweene ſacramentall ſignes, and the things ſignified, in the minde of a diſcerning receiuer. But when words of ſenſe are ſpoken to the eare, the vnderſtanding minde doth therewith apprehend the thing ſpoken of. And euē ſo the mind of the diſcerning receiuer doth inwardly apprehend the thing ſignified, & apply it to his ſoule, when the ſacramentall ſign is preſented to the outward ſenſe. And this coniunction ariſeth not from the nature either of the ſigne, or the thing ſignified; but from the inſtitution of the Lord. The meaning then of the holy Ghoſt here is this, That *Moſes* by faith did ordaine and appoint the killing and eating of the Paſchall Lambe, which was the ſigne of the paſſing ouer of the Lords Angell, when the firſt borne in Egypt were ſlaine.

It followeth: *And effuſion of blood;* that is, the ſprinkling of the blood of the Paſchall Lambe; which was a notable rite and ceremony vſed in this firſt Paſſe-ouer, after this manner: The blood of euery Lambe was put into a baſon, and ſprinkled with a bunch of Hyſope vpon the doore poſts of euery mans houſe among the Iewes. Now this rite did not continue alwaies, but was peculiar and proper to this firſt Paſſe-ouer kept in Egypt at the inſtitution theereof beeing then practiced (but not after) in regard of that ſpeciall deliuerance then at hand, whereof, it was an aſſurance: for it ſignified vnto them, that the Angell of the Lord, comming to deſtroy the firſt borne of Egypt, and ſeeing that blood ſo ſprinkled, ſhould paſſe ouer their houſes, and touch none of their firſt borne, of man nor beaſt. This ende of the ſprinkling of this blood, is here likewiſe ſet downe in theſe words; *Leaſt he that deſtroyed the firſt borne ſhould touch them.* He: that is, the Angell of the Lord, who was ſent to deſtroy the firſt borne throughout all Egypt both of man and beaſt, ſaue onely of thoſe who had their doore poſts ſprinkled with blood. And thus much for the meaning of the words.

Firſt, obſerue what the holy Ghoſt ſaith of this fact of *Moſes,* in ordaining the Paſſe-ouer: namely, that *he did it by faith.* Hence we learne, that the Sacraments of the new Teſtament muſt be celebrated in faith: for, herein we are to ſeeke to be acceptable to God as *Moſes* was. The Lords ſupper in the new Teſtament ſucceedeth the Paſſe-ouer in the olde: for, that was a ſigne to the Iewes, that Ieſus Chriſt the immaculate Lambe of God, ſhould afterward be ſacrificed for their ſinnes; and this is to vs a ſigne of Chriſt already ſacrificed. Now looke as that was ordained and receiued vnder the Law, ſo muſt this be adminiſtred and receiued vnder the Goſpel. But in the olde Teſtament *Moſes*

cele-

celebrates the *Paſſe-ouer through faith*, and enioines the Iſraelites ſo to doe ; therefore accordingly muſt wee by faith celebrate and receiue the Lords ſupper vnder the Goſpel. *Cains* ſacrifice was fruitleſſe to him , and odious to God, becauſe he offered not *in faith* ; and no leſſe were all other faithleſſe ſacrifices: euen ſo euery Sacrament & ſpirituall ſacrifice receiued or offered in time of the Goſpel, is vnprofitable to man, and vnacceptable vnto God , if it be not receiued in faith. In euery Sacrament we receiue ſome thing from God, as in euery ſacrifice wee giue ſome thing to God . In the Lords ſupper , as the miniſter giues the bread and wine into the hand of the receiuer , ſo the Lord God giues his ſonne vnto their hearts. Now if faith bee wanting, Chriſt crucified is not receiued: for, faith is the hand of the ſoule, without which, there is no receiuing of Chriſt, and his benefits; but contrariwiſe, a heauie and fearefull ſinne, heaping vp Gods wrath againſt vs. Hereby we learne , how ſundry ſorts of people ſinne moſt grieuouſly againſt God: for, many come to receiue the Lords ſupper , who are altogether ignorant in the nature and vſe thereof, not knowing what the ſacrament meaneth; & yet becauſe it is a cuſtom in the church, they will receiue (at leaſt) once a yeare, though they know nothing therein as they ought. Now ſuch perſons muſt know, they ought to come *in faith*; which they cannot do, becauſe they want knowledge: and therfore in receiuing it ſo, they commit a grieuous ſinne, and ſo indanger their owne ſoules, becauſe they receiue it vnworthily. And this is not the fault of young ones onely ; but of many , whoſe yeares might ſhame them for their ignorance, if they were not paſt all feeling of ſpirituall wants. A ſecond ſort there are, who receiue the Lords ſupper , and ſay they will doe ſo , becauſe they haue *faith.* But theſe are like the former: for their faith is nothing but *honeſt dealing among men* ; thinking, that if they bring that to the Lords Supper, though they haue no more, yet all is well. The greateſt ſort are of this minde, taking *fidelitie* for *true faith:* and it is a plaine point of popery, ſo commõn, as almoſt in euery place, men doe embrace it. But theſe deceiue themſelues: for another kinde of faith is required of thoſe that receiue the Lords ſupper worthily; namely, ſuch a *faith*, whereby we doe not onely beleeue the remiſſion of ſinnes in Chriſts blood; but alſo are aſſured, that the bread and wine receiued worthily , are ſignes and ſcales of the ſame bleſſing exhibited vnto vs by Chriſt. Hee that comes onely in a good meaning, deceiues himſelfe , and receiues to his condemnation. And yet alas , many euen of the ancient ſort, haue no other faith, but their good meaning.

A third ſort there are, who yet goe further; and knowing the vanitie of this opinion , that a mans fidelitie in his dealing with men, ſhould be his faith, to commend him vnto God ; they hold and know, that true faith , is to beleeue

their owne ſaluation in the blood of Chriſt: and theſe are to bee commended in reſpect of the former. But herein they faile; that comming to receiue, they bring not with them a liuely faith: for, it is not onely required in a communicant, that he profeſſe the faith of Chriſt aright: but a worthy receiuer muſt looke to his owne heart, that his faith therein, be a liuing faith, ſuch as worketh by loue, and ſhewes it ſelfe by obedience. Now herein, many that haue good knowledge doe grieuouſly offend, That howſoeuer they make a ſhew of faith, in an orderly and religious carriage of themſelues on the Communion day; yet when that time is a little paſt, they returne to their former ſinnes againe, neuer els hauing any care (nay , not ſo much as making any ſhew) of laying away their ſinnes, ſaue onely at the receiuing of the Lords ſupper. And thus doe too many of thoſe, who make a faire profeſſion. Theſe men bring faith in profeſſion, but yet their faith is dead ; for, if it were a liuely faith, it would purifie their hearts , and cauſe a change in them from euill to good, and from good to better , euery daie more and more. But bleſſed be God, by whoſe mercie it comes to paſſe , that there are ſome in his Church, who come with ſuch a faith, and thereby communicate acceptably to God , and fruitfully to themſelues. Yet we muſt confeſſe, they are but fewe in compariſon. But as for all the other three ſorts of people, they ſinne grieuouſly , becauſe they bring not the hand of a liuely faith, to receiue thoſe things which their God offereth vnto them. Wee therefore in this example are admoniſhed, to celebrate and receiue the Lords ſupper in ſuch ſort, as *Moſes* did: namely, in faith: and that not in an idle, or dead, but in a liuely faith: which may, both before and after the receiuing of this ſacrament, bring forth good fruits , to the reforming of our liues, in continuall obedience, of Gods glorie , and our owne comfort and ſaluation in Chriſt.

2. Obſerue further : *Moſes ordained and made the Paſſe-ouer.* We may not thinke, that *Moſes* killed all the Lambes that were to bee ſlaine at this Paſſeouer: but in his owne family he killed his own lambe, and inioyned the people from God, to doe the like in theirs. The like phraſe is often vſed in the Scripture , Ioſua 5. 3. *Ioſua* is ſaid *to circumciſe the ſonnes of Iſrael:* which was almoſt a thing impoſſible for one man to doe: But the meaning thereof is this; that *Ioſua* inioyned and procured, that all the people ſhould bee circumciſed , and ſawe it done. And ſo wee muſt vnderſtand this place.

Now in this, that *Moſes* did in this manner celebrate this Paſſeouer, wee are taught this leſſon; that *Gouernours* and *Superiours* in their place , muſt procure, that thoſe which be vnder their gouernment, doe keepe the commandements of God; and eſpecially thoſe , which concerne Gods worſhip. It is the commandement of the Lord by *Moſes*, that *the King ſhould haue the law written; that he may learne to feare his God, and keepe all the words of this lawe written, to doe them*. Now, how ſhall the King doe all the words of the lawe? ſeeing there be many commandements, that doe not concerne him, nor his place: but his ſubiects, and other particular men, of other callings. Surely thus: He muſt doe thoſe in his own perſon, that concerne him in his place; and then ſee that his ſubiects and ſeruants doe likewiſe ſuch duties, both towards God and man, as concern them in their places. This is a ſpeciall point concerning all Magiſtrates and Superiours whatſoeuer; and therefore *Paul* ſaith, Rom. 13. 4. *The Magiſtrate beareth not the ſword for nought, but for the wealth of Gods people:* that is, for their good; not in body onely, but principally, for the good of their *ſoules*. And therefore euery gouernour, either of towne or kingdome, and euery maſter of a family, within the compaſſe of his calling, is to ſee that thoſe which are vnder him keepe Gods commandements: eſpecially thoſe which concerne Gods worſhip. When a magiſtrate ſhall doe this, then the praiſe and honour of the whole is giuen to him; as here the killing of the Paſſe-ouer is aſcribed to *Moſes*, becauſe he ſaw that the people did it. So on the contrary, if the Magiſtrate be negligent in his dutie, hee becomes the greateſt ſinner of all; for then the ſinnes that are committed through his default, are aſcribed to him. *Nehemiah* reproouing the *Rulers, tels them that they brake the Lords Sabbaoths*, Nehem. 13. 15. when as not onely they, but the people alſo brake them: yet there he chargeth the ſinne of the people vpon them, becauſe it came through their negligence. As, if any ſinne be committed in a family, through the defect of the gouernour of the family; it is not onely the ſinne of the particular partie, but the gouernours ſinne. And ſo, when any man ſinnes in breaking the ſabbaoth, it is not onely the ſinne of that particular man, but of the gouernours to whom hee is ſubiect. And therefore gouernors muſt ſee that Gods commandemēts be kept of thoſe that be vnder their gouernment. But here ſome may obiect (as indeede ſome abuſe the place to this ende) that it ſeemes no man may be barred from the Lords Supper; for the like reaſon is in the Lords Supper, that was in the Paſſeouer: but *Moſes* kept the Paſſeouer himſelfe, and commanded all the people of Iſrael ſo to doe; therefore no man is to be put from Gods table. *Anſ.* It is true indeede, that in Egypt at the celebration of the firſt paſſeouer, *Moſes* kept it himſelfe, and commanded euery Maſter of a family among the Iſraelites to doe the ſame; and the reaſon hereof was, becauſe at the firſt inſtitution, the Paſſeouer was both a ſigne and a means of a temporall deliuerance, beſides the ſpirituall: and therefore there was great reaſon then, why all the Iſraelites ſhould eate the Paſſeouer,

and none be put back; becauſe all of them were to eſcape the temporal puniſhment, which God was to inflict vpon the Egyptians. But afterward the Lord made a lawe, that if any were but *legally vncleane*, hee might not eate the Paſſe-ouer, but muſt ſtay till the next moneth, and then come, and onely the cleane muſt eate thereof: ſo that the Lord himſelfe did inhibit ſome from that Sacrament: whereby it is plain, that the celebration of the Paſſeouer is ſo farre from giuing warrant to this confuſion, & careleſſe admitting of all to the communion, that rather it prooueth that there muſt bee a diſtinction made, and a ſeparation of the vnworthy from the Lords Table. Thoſe which are fitly prepared are to be receiued; but notorious offenders, who are morally and ſpiritually vncleane, are to bee put backe, till by repentance they haue teſtified their worthineſſe.

3. Let vs conſider the ſignification of the *Paſſe-ouer.* For the *Paſchall Lambe* was a ſigne of Chriſt the true Lambe of God, ſhadowing out diuers things worthy our obſeruation: as firſt the Lambe, for the Paſſe-ouer was to be a Lamb of a yeare olde, without ſpot or blemiſh: which ſignified vnto vs, that *Chriſt* was *that immaculate Lambe of God* and without ſpot, as *Peter* calleth him, 1. Peter 1. 19. Secondly, the *Paſchall Lambe* when hee was killed and eaten, had no bone of it broken, ſo was it commanded, Exod. 12. 46. and Numb. 6. 12. ſignifying, that Chriſt when hee was crucified, ſhould not haue a bone of him broken, as S. *Iohn* applieth the former Texts, Iohn 19. 36. Thirdly, the *Paſchall Lamb* muſt be eaten with ſower hearbs, Exod. 12. 8. ſignifying that no man can feele any ſweetnes in the blood of Chriſt, till he haue his heart full of bitterneſſe for his ſinnes; and, with *Hanna*, be ſore *vexed and troubled in minde, ſo as he can poure out his ſoule before the Lord*, 1. Sam. 1. 15. The want of this is the cauſe why ſo many do heare Gods word, and receiue the Sacraments, and yet reape no benefit by them. Fourthly, before the *Paſchall Lambe* was eaten, all leauen muſt bee remooued out of their houſes. This had a notable ſignification: which we neede not to gheſſe at, ſeeing the holy Ghoſt hath ſet it downe; namely, that wee muſt remooue all *old leauen of corrupt doctrine* (Matth. 16. 12.) out of our hearts; and the *leauen of ſinne and wickedneſſe*, out of our liues, if we profeſſe communion with Chriſt. This is a point worth our marking; for, vnleſſe we doe ſo, we ſhall haue no benefit by the ſacrifice of Chriſt: for if wee wil liue in this old leauen, we muſt neuer looke to receiue Chriſt into our hearts. Laſtly, euery perſon receiued the Paſſeouer *in haſt, with ſhoos on their feete, with ſtaues in their hands, and their clothes girt vp*, Exod. 12. 11. yet this we muſt vnderſtand onely of the firſt paſſeouer in Egypt; for Chriſt did eate it *ſitting.* Now this ceremonie vſed in the firſt paſſe-ouer, ſignified thus much, that if we looke to haue benefit by

1. Cor. 5. 7.

Luk. 22. 14.

Chriſt,

Christ, we must be of this minde to be alwaies ready to leaue this world, and bee prepared to goe when and whither God shall call vs: Wee must not haue our hearts glewed to earthly things, but alwaies ready to receiue Gods commaund, and to goe at his call. These be the significations of the Passeouer: which we must remember to make good vse of in the course of our liues. And thus much of the first branch of this act of *Moses* faith, in *ordaining the Passe-ouer*.

The second branch of this worke is this; *And the effusion of blood:* that is, the sprinkling of the blood of the Lambe vpon the posts of their houses, and vpon the doore cheeks; which was a token to the Israelites, that the destroying Angell should not strike the first borne of the *Israelites* either man or beast. In mans reason, this may seeme to be a weake and simple meanes; yet God ordaines it to preserue all the first borne among the Israelites. And thus the Lord vseth to deale, that his people, through the weakenesse of the meanes, might be brought to acknowledge God to bee their protectour and defender. When the *Israelites* were stung with the serpents, a man would haue thought it had bin the best way for their curing, to haue giuen them cunning Surgeons; but the Lord ordaines onely a dead serpent of brasse, which they must looke vp vnto, and be cured. A weake meanes it was, and yet the Lord vseth it; because he would haue them to giue all the glorie vnto him, and not to ascribe the same either to themselues or to the meanes.

Further, this *sprinkling of the blood* vpon the doore cheeks and the posts of their houses, had a notable signification: namely, *of the sprinkling of the blood of Christ* vpon the doors of our hearts, to which *Peter* alludeth, 1. Peter 1. 2. *Through the obedience and sprinkling of the blood of Iesus Christ.* And *Dauid*, when he saith, *Sprinkle me with Hysope, and I shall be cleane:* *Dauid* knew wel that the blood of beasts could not take away sinne, and therefore no doubt by his sauing faith, he had an eye to the blood of the Messias vnder legall tearmes. Whence, we are taught this lesson: that as the *Israelites* with their bodily hands did sprinkle the blood of the *Paschall Lamb* vpon their doore cheeks, and the posts of their houses: so by the hand of faith, euery one of vs must sprinkle *the blood of Christ* vpon our owne hearts: which wee shall then doe, when we doe not onely in generall beleeue that Christ is a Sauiour and Redeemer, but particularly that he is a Redeemer vnto vs; and that the merits of his death, and the benefit of his blood are ours.

Obiect. But some will say, If this be so, then all is well, for I doe beleeue this. *Ans.* Herein very many deceiue themselues, thinking that they haue faith, when indeede they haue none. For, looke vnto their wayes, and see into their hearts by their liues; and it will easily appeare,

that they haue nothing in them but ignorance, security, and presumption in sinne. Now such men are deceiuers of their owne soules; for after this *sprinkling* followeth sanctification, and rising from dead workes to newenesse of life: so that they that liue in sinne, and yet say they haue faith, deceiue themselues. For, if a mans heart bee sprinkled with the blood of Christ through faith, it will change his life and conscience, and make him a new creature; for, Christs blood is a cleansing & purifying blood, insomuch as where it is truly sprinkled, it certainly cleanseth: Heb. 9. 14. And thus much of this ceremonie of *sprinkling*.

Now followeth the ende of both these actions, in these words: *Least he that destroyed the first borne should touch them.* Let vs examine the words in order: First, by *the destroyer*, is meant the Angell of God (as we may see in the Storie, Exod. 12. 19.) who at midnight smote all the first borne of Egypt both of man and beast. Where by the way wee may take a view of the wonderfull power and strength of Gods Angels, and also of their admirable swiftnesse and readinesse in doing the will of God, that in one night euen at midnight, one of them could passe through the Land of Egypt, and kill all the first borne of man and beast, in euery place of the Egyptians. The like wee may see in the destruction of *Senacheribs* host, by one Angell in one night.

The first borne: that is, both of men and beasts. So it is in the Storie, Exod. 12. 29. But beeing so, it may not vnfitly bee demanded, How this *Passe-ouer* could bee a Sacrament, when as euen the *beasts* of the Israelites had benefit by it; for they were spared by reason of this *sprinkling of the blood of the Paschal Lamb?* *Ans.* That hindreth not why it should not be a Sacrament. For wee must consider this *Passe-ouer* two waies: First, as a meanes of temporall deliuerance; and so the beasts had benefit by it. Secondly, as a signe and seale of our spirituall deliuerance from hell by the sacrifice of the Lambe of God Iesus Christ, which is the thing signified; and so it is a Sacrament for mans saluation: and thus the beasts had no benefit by it. The water that flowed from the rock in the wildernesse, was a Sacrament, and the beasts dranke of the water, but yet they did not partake of the Lords Sacrament: for we must consider that water two wayes; first, as a meanes to quench thirst, and consequently as an outward benefit to preserue the life of the creature, and so the beasts had a benefit by it: but consider it as a signe and seale of the water of life, and so their beastes had no benefit by it, but onely the beleeuing people.

It followeth; *Should touch them.* Here is the very vse & end of both the former actions; *That the Angel might not hurt them,* but passe by the Israelites houses. Here consider a notable point, concerning Christ, the true Passe-

ouer:

ouer:namely,that they which haue their hearts ſprinkled with his blood, ſhall be preſerued from euerlaſting damnation; and not onely ſo, but hereby they ſhall haue deliuerance, from all temporall iudgements in this life, ſo farre forth as they are curſes,and hurtfull vnto them. So we may reade, before the deſtruction came to the citie of the Iewes, the *angel* of God went through the citie *with a writers inkhorne, to ſet a marke vpon thoſe that did mourne and crie for their ſinnes*. And *Dauid* ſaith, *the righteous man ſtandeth vpon a rocke, ſo as the floods of many waters ſhall not come neere him.* This is a point of great vſe:and the conſideration hereof, ſhould mooue all perſons that haue beene careleſſe in religion, now to become carefull and deſirous to haue their hearts waſhed in *the blood of Chriſt:* and thoſe alſo which haue any care, muſt haue double care hereof; for they haue freedome and ſecuritie,both in temporall, and eternall iudgements.

Obiect. But many of Gods deare children are taken away in common iudgements. *Anſ.* True: but yet they are neuer hurt thereby; but the iudgement and affliction is ſanctified vnto them, becauſe they haue their hearts *ſprinkled with the blood of Chriſt*.And as for thoſe whom God knoweth it good for,they are deliuered in generall iudgements, and preſerued for his glorie, and vſe of the Church.

But how did the *Angel* deſtroy the firſt borne in Egypt, both of man and beaſts? *Anſ.* By taking from them their temporall liues, by deſtroying or killing their bodies. That is the ſenſe and plaine meaning of the holy Ghoſt:and to this ſignification anſwereth the word in the originall. Now ſome doe abuſe this place, and ſuch like, for the ouerthrowing of the ancient cenſure of the Church in *excomunication:* for (ſay they) the practiſe of S. *Paul,* 1. Cor. 5. is the principall ground of excommunication; where *Paul* biddes that the inceſtuous man *be giuen to Satan for the deſtruction of the fleſh.* Now they that denie excommunication,would haue that place to be interpreted by this, becauſe the ſame word is there vſed:and therefore (ſay they) *Pauls* words muſt be vnderſtood, of deſtroying the inceſtuous mans bodie, and taking away his temporal life.This interpretation doth quite ouerthrowe excommunication: for, if nothing elſe be there vnderſtood, but onely the tormenting of the bodie,then excomunication is not thence prooued.But the truth is,that the cenſure which the Apoſtle vrgeth there, cannot be vnderſtood of the puniſhment of the bodie: which I prooue thus. In that place S. *Paul* oppoſeth the *fleſh and the ſpirit.* Now vſually, when he maketh this oppoſition, *Fleſh* ſignifieth the *Corruption* of the whole man: and the *Spirit* ſignifieth the *grace* of God in the man:ſo that his plaine meaning is this, *Let him be deliuered to Satan for the deſtruction of the fleſh*; that is, for the deſtruction of his naturall corruption, and of the bodie of ſinne.

Ezck.9.4.
Pſal.32.7.

Further, where it is ſaid, *the firſt borne;* we muſt vnderſtand it of the firſt borne among the Egyptians, both of man and beaſt.And whereas he ſaith, *ſhould touch them;* he meaneth the Iſraelites, who were not touched in this deſtruction.

Hence we learne two points further. 1. The firſt borne of Egypt are deſtroyed, both of man and beaſts. This is markeable: for the Egyptians in former times deſtroyed the Iſraelites children, and eſpecially their firſt borne; for they ſlewe all the males, leaſt they ſhould increaſe in their land: and now it comes to paſſe, that their children, euen the principall of them, their firſt borne are ſlaine for the Iſraelites ſake; and when they are preſerued. Where we may obſerue a moſt righteous, and yet an vſuall kinde of iudgement with God. He doth often puniſh the wicked in their kind,with their own ſinnes: This is true euen in the beſt,ſo far forth as they are ſinnefull. The ſame iniurie which *Dauid* did to *Vriah,* was done vnto him by his owne ſonne,euen by his ſonne *Abſalon,*2.Sam. 10. 10, 11. and 16. 22.And this our Sauiour Chriſt teacheth vs, ſaying, (Matt. 7. 1.) *Iudge not, that ye be not iudged.* We finde this true likewiſe by experience: they that giue themſelues to backe-biting, rayling, and ſlandering, by the iuſt iudgement of God, haue for the moſt part the ſame done vnto themſelues by others; ſo that men are often puniſhed in their owne ſinnes. For, God hath his ſtorehouſe full of iudgements, and he can puniſh men what way he will.But he oft obſerueth this order,to puniſh men by their owne ſinnes, and to catch the wicked in their owne deuiſes.

This muſt be a motiue to make vs to looke vnto our ſelues, and to haue care againſt all ſinnes of the ſecond table; for looke wherein thou takeſt thy pleaſure to Gods diſhonour, therein ſhalt thou feele and ſee Gods iudgements vpon thee, to thy correction and confuſion. Pſal. 109. 17. *As he loued curſing,ſo ſhall it come vnto him; and as he loued not bleſſing, ſo ſhall it be farre from him.* This, *Adonibezek* felt and confeſſed, when his thumbes were cut off, Iudg.1. 6, 7. *As I haue done,ſo God hath rewarded me.*

Laſtly, in that *the deſtroyer killeth the firſt borne of Egypt,* marke a ſtrange kinde of Gods iudgements. King *Pharaoh* & his people ſinne, becauſe they will not let the Iſraelites goe; but the puniſhment of their ſinne, is laide vpon their children and cattell. The like we read of, 2. Sam. 12. 14. when *Dauid* had committed thoſe grieuous ſinnes of adulterie and murther, a part of his puniſhment was the death *of his child*.When he numbred the people,the plague light on them, 2. Sam. 24. Now we muſt not too curiouſly prie into the reaſon of Gods indgements: for he is not bound to giue account of his actions, and yet in reaſon we may ſee the equitie thereof. For, we muſt conſider of kingdomes and ſocieties, and of twones and

fami-

families, as of bodies : euery focietie is a bodie, and the particular perfons therein, are members of that bodie. Now looke, as it is in the naturall bodie; fo it is in the bodie ciuill or politike. Oftentimes in the naturall bodie, when the ftomach is ficke, the head aketh ; the braine is wounded, and the heart aketh; the foote is hurt, and the head aketh; and the offence of the tongue may be punifhed with ftripes vpon the backe: Euen fo it is in ciuill focieties, the Prince finneth, and the people are punifhed; or, the people finne, and the Prince is punifhed. This is no iniuftice with God: for fith Prince and people make but one bodie, and fo Parents and children, God may iuftly lay vpon any member, the temporall punifhment of finne committed by another. And thus much of this example ; and of the faith of *Mofes* alone.

The Ifraelites Faith.

Verse 29.

By faith, they paffed through the redde fea, as by drie land : which, when the Egyptians had affaied to doe, they were drowned.

Itherto we haue heard the faith of *Mofes* alone, highly commended, in two examples. Now followeth a commendation of his faith with others : fo that here is a new example of faith ; to wit, of the *Ifraelites* together with *Mofes.* For, Mofes is here to be confidered not onely as one of them, but as a principall agent in this worke of faith. And here their faith is commended vnto vs by a wonderfull ftrange action, which they did, through the power and goodneffe of God : namely, by their *paffing through the red fea:* not by paffing ouer it : for, that might haue beene by Art ; but *through* it : which is aboue nature and Art, and meerely miraculous. This fact of theirs is largely fet downe, Exod. 14. And, that it might appeare to be euery way wonderfull as it is indeede, the Author of this Epiftle commends it by two circumftances; which notably fet forth vnto vs the ftrangeneffe hereof. Firft, by their *manner* how

they paffed through ; namely, *as by drie land.* Secondly, by the time when; namely then, when *the Egyptians following them, were drowned.* Here firft we will fpeake of the fact it felfe, and then of the circumftances.

The fact is fet downe in the firft words ; *By faith they paffed through the redde fea.* The words are plaine of themfelues ; and offer vnto vs fundrie points worthie our obferuation. And firft, it may be asked, who they were that here paffed through by faith ? The anfwer is, *the Ifraelites.* But fome will fay, we read in the Hiftorie, that when the people came to the redde fea, they were wonderfully afraid, and murmured againft Mofes, faying, That *it had beene better for them to haue liued in the bondage of Egypt, then to come into the Defart and there die.* Now, how can they murmure impatiently and fearefully, and yet *paffe through by faith ? Anfw.* At the firft indeede they murmured, when they faw the danger they were in, hauing the huge armie of *Pharaoh* following them, and the redde fea before them, and hills and mountaines on each fide. But howfoeuer they murmured at the firft, yet when Mofes fpake words of comfort vnto them in the name of the Lord, bidding them *not to be afraid, &c.* and when he held vp his rod, and entred into the red fea before them, then they followed him *by faith :* and hereupon the holy Ghoft giues vnto them the title of true beleeuers.

Here we may learne, that true faith in Gods children, is mingled with vnbeleefe. The Ifraelites faith was true faith, but yet it was very imperfect and weake : for, if it had beene perfect and found faith, they would neuer haue murmured, nor haue beene impatient and fearefull. But looke as it is in nature, fo it is in grace. In nature we cannot paffe from one contrarie to another, but by the mixture of the contraries : as, in light and darkneffe, the one doth not follow the other immediately ; but firft, there is a mixture of them both in the dawning of the day, and clofing of the night : and fo it is in other contraries, euen in thofe which concerne the foule: vnbeleefe is a finne ; faith is a vertue and grace contrarie to it. Now vnbeleefe cannot be expelled by faith, before there be a mixture of them both, and fo when faith preuaileth, vnbeleefe decaieth ; neither can faith be euer perfect, becaufe it is euer mingled more or leffe with vnbeleefe.

This plainely ouerthrowes the opinion of the Church of Rome, who fay, that after a man is regenerate, and beleeues, there is nothing in him that God can hate. For they imagine that he is fo foundly fanctified, that there is nothing in him which may properly be called a finne : but here we fee their doctrine is falfe, feeing faith and vnbeleefe are alwaies mingled together.

Secondly, as it falls out with faith, fo it is with the reft of Gods graces : looke as faith is not perfect, but mixed with vnbeleefe ; fo are all other graces of God whatſoeuer. The feare of God is not perfect in a man, nor the loue of God: for, the feare of God is mingled with the feare of men: and the feare of God for his mer-cie, is mingled with the feare of God for his iudgements. And hereby many are deceiued; for when they feare God for his puniſhments, they thinke themſelues to bee moſt miſerable & voyde of grace: but they deceiue themſelues. For there is no man vpon the earth that feareth God onely for his mercies, and doth not feare God alſo for his puniſhments in part; for Gods graces in this life are euer mingled with their contraries. And therefore to imagine that a man may feare God for his mercies onely, and not for iudgements alſo, is to conceiue of ſuch a man as none is, nor can be in this life ; for the beſt feare that is in any man liuing, is a mixt feare.

Further, when *Moſes* had ſpoken words of comfort vnto them, the vnbeleeuing and feare-full Iſraelites, doe ſtir vp their hearts to be-leeue. So we accordingly muſt labour and ſtriue againſt that in-bred vnbeleefe which is in vs : for euery man hath innumerable ſinnes in him that reſiſt faith; and if they be not checked and ſuppreſſed, they will maſter his faith : but hee that would haue faith to continue and laſt, muſt ſtriue againſt naturall vnbeleefe, as the Iſrae-lites doe in this place ; and as the man in the Goſpel, *Mark. 9. 24.* when hee ſaid to Chriſt, *Lord, I beleeue, helpe my vnbeleefe,* knowing that his vnbeleefe did ſuppreſſe his faith. And ſo did the Diſciples of our Sauiour Chriſt, when they prayed, *Lord increaſe our faith,* Luk. 17. 5. And *Dauid,* beeing oppreſſed with deadneſſe of heart, ſtirres vp his faith, ſaying, *Why art thou caſt downe, my ſoule? &c. waite on God,* Pſal. 42. v. 11. For, he that hath faith, is troubled with vnbeleefe; & the more it trou-bles him, the leſſe he beleeueth, vnleſſe he ſtriue againſt it manfully.

2. *Queſt.* But how many of the Iſraelites be-leeued, and went ouer by faith? *Anſ.* Not all: for *Paul* ſaith, *With many of them God was not well pleaſed; for they were ouerthrowen in the wil-derneſſe:* 1. Cor. 10. 5. Which ſhewes, that all that paſſed ouer had not true faith; for, ſome be-leeued: and by the force of their faith, all went ouer ſafely.

Hence we note this (which hath beene of-ten taught vs) that an vngodly man receiueth many temporall benefits, by the ſocietie of Gods people which beleeue: as here the vnbe-leeuing Iſraelits had this benefit, to go *through the redde ſea* ſafely, by reaſon of thoſe that be-leeued. And in the former example, the brute beaſts were freed from killing by the Angell, becauſe they belonged to the hoſt of the Lords people. Now, ſhall a brute beaſt haue benefit, by beeing with Gods people, and ſhall not a man much more? Yes vndoubtedly: for, ſo we may reade, that for *Pauls* ſake, all the Mariners and Souldiers that were in the Shippe, were

ſaued from drowning, Act. 27. 24. This point muſt perſwade euery one of vs, to make choyce of the godly for our ſocietie, and com-pany, with whome wee liue and conuerſe; for, by them wee reape many benefits, and freedome alſo from many heauie iudge-ments.

The third point is this: *When did the Iſrae-lites beleeue ?* This circumſtance is worth the marking : They beleeued *when they paſſed through the redde ſea* ; for, they beleeued not onely in generall, that God was their God, as hee had promiſed to their fathers, but they beleeued, that God would bee with them, and giue them life in the middle of the redde ſea. A notable point. They beleeued (as it were) in the middle of their graues (for ſo might the redde ſea be well called) that God would giue them life euerlaſting, and preſerue them ſafely through the ſea, and from their enemies.

In their example we are taught the ſame du-tie, to doe as they here did. The childe of God in this life hath innumerable cauſes of deſpera-tion : and ſometimes his owne conſcience will take part with Satan, in charging the ſoule to bee in ſtate of damnation. In this heauie caſe, what muſt bee done? Surely, at this time, when a man is a caſt-away in himſelfe, he muſt euen then beleeue; beeing in hell (as it were) hee muſt beleeue that God will bring him to hea-uen. It is nothing for a man to beleeue in pro-ſperitie, and peace; but in time of deſperation to beleeue, that is a moſt worthy faith: and in-deede, then is the right time for a man to ſhew his faith, when there is in himſelfe no cauſe of beleeuing. *Obiect.* But when a man is in this caſe, he cannot beleeue. *Anſ.* Indeede to be-leeue then, is a wonderfull hard thing, and a miracle of miracles. But yet this is the propertie of true faith, ſo to doe; and if there be but one dramm of true faith in the heart that deſpaires, howſoeuer it may for a time lie hidde, as dead; yet at the length it will make him to hope, and waite for mercie and life at the hands of Al-mightie God. And therefore, if it ſhall pleaſe God at any time to lay a torment vpon our conſciences, ſo as we ſhall ſtriue with the wrath of God, thinking that he hath caſt vs away; yet for all that, then we muſt beleeue Gods promi-ſes, and ſet before vs his mercies, and therewith refreſh vs. And if this faith were not, the childe of God many times were in a moſt miſe-rable caſe; the Lord therefore hath moſt mer-cifully prouided to helpe him, by the grace of faith. When a man is paſt all hope of life, he muſt then beleeue and hope for life, as the Iſ-raelites did in the red ſea, for preſeruation. And vndoubtedly, this is a comfortable ſigne of grace, if a man in the horrour of con-ſcience, can ſhewe forth the leaſt ſparke of true faith.

Fourthly, note the effect & iſſue of this faith. *They paſſed through the red ſea.* We ſay vſual-ly, that water and fire be vnmercifull creatures;

and

and therefore the naturall man feares them both : but the *Israelites faith* makes them not to feare the water ; but it makes them bold, e-uen to passe *through the sea.* The like we may see for fire, in the three children, Dan.3.16.23. who were not afraid of the hot burning ouen, but were as bold in it , as out of it. Rauenous and wild beasts are terrible vnto men ; but faith makes a man not to feare them : and therefore *Daniel* feares not the Lyons , though he were throwne into their denne to be deuoured, Dan. 6.22. Great is the fruit and force of faith : it takes from a man the feare of those creatures, which by nature are most terrible. And here we see a cause, why the holy Martyrs of God died most cheerefully. A man would thinke it strange, that one should goe into the fire, reioy-cing, as many of them did : but the reason is, Because they had faith in their hearts, which taketh away the feare of the most fearefull creatures.

But if it be so (may some say) that the Israe-lites *by faith went through the redde sea,* not fearing the water ; why may not we that be-leeue, now doe the same ? for we haue the same faith that they had. *Ans.* We haue indeede the same faith, and yet we cannot passe through waters as they did. For their faith rested on two promises : first, on this made to *Abraham, I will be thy God, and the God of thy seede :* secondly, on a particular promise made to *Moses.* For, when he commanded him to goe through the red sea, withall he made a promise, to keepe and preserue them : and this they beleeued , and so went through. Now , howsoeuer we haue iu-stifying faith, hauing the same generall promise; yet we haue not the like particular promise, That if we passe through the red sea , God will be with vs and saue vs. And therefore, if any man shall aduenture to doe so , let him looke for nothing but death ; for it is not an action of *faith,* but of *presumption.* And therefore *Peter* sunke, when he would needs walke vnto Christ vpon the sea , hauing no such hold vpon Gods speciall promise, as here they had : and the E-gyptians following presumptuously were drowned. Wherefore, let vs here be warned, not to attempt to doe extraordinarie workes, without Gods speciall warrant : for a particular faith, requires a particular promise, besides the generall promise of God in Christ.

Further , let vs here obserue a wonderfull worke of Gods mercie and power. When these seruants of God were brought into extremitie of daunger, so as they were in a desperate case for their temporall life; yet then the Lord findes a way of deliuerance. And indeede , if a man consider aright of it, he must needes acknow-ledge that these Israelites were in a pitifull case; for, they had the red sea before them, & moun-taines on each side , and themselues hindred from flight, by their bagge and baggage, and with their children, and the huge hoast of *Pha-raoh* behinde them ; so as to mans reason, there

was nothing but present death to be looked for : yet the Lord in mercie to saue them , makes a way where there was no way, and o-pens them a gappe to life, when naturall rea-son could lay before them nothing but violent death. Which shewes the wonderfull mercie of God, to his owne people and seruants. And the like thing we may read of in *Dauid,* when he aboad in the wildernesse of *Maon :* for there *Saul followed him, and he and his men compassed Dauid and his men round about,* 1.Sam.23.26, 27. Now, what hope of deliuerance was there for *Dauid? Ans.* Surely this onely: *Dauid* was the seruant of God, and the Lord preserued him, that he might rule his people after *Sauls* death ; and therefore he escapeth, though won-derfully : for *a messenger comes to Saul, and bids him hast, for the Philistims inuaded the land : and so Saul returned from pursuing Dauid, and went against the Philistims.*

Hence we learne this generall rule, that in the extremitie of all danger, God hath meanes to preserue and saue his owne children and people. Which must teach vs, to commend our case to God, and to rest on him in all dangers ; for when our case is desperate in our sight, then are we fittest for Gods helpe. Let vs therefore in such cases, learne to practise our faith ; and then especially to cast our selues vp-on God. This, *Iehosaphat* did most notably : for, beeing assaulted with the huge armies of the Moabites, Ammonites, &c. he prayed vnto the Lord most feruently, saying, 2.Chron.20.12. *Lord , there is no strength in vs, we know not what to doe : but our eyes are towards thee :* and thus doing, was preserued : for, God will in no extremitie whatsoeuer forsake them that trust in him.

The redde sea.] In many places of the Old Testament, it is called *the sea of rushes,* Psal. 106.7.9.Or, *the sea of sedges,* Ier.49.21. It is a corner of the Arabian sea , that parteth Egypt and Arabia. Those which haue seene it in tra-uell, say, it hath no other colour then all other seas haue ; Why then is it called *the redde sea ? Ans.* To omit many supposed causes hereof, there be two especially, for which it is so cal-led. 1. Because of the red sand ; for both the bottome of the sea, and the shoare , are full of redder sand, then ordinarily is else-where. 2. Some thinke it is called the red sea, by reason of the sedges and bul-rushes, which growe much at the sea side, and be of a redde colour ; which, by reflection, may make the same colour appeare on the water. But this neede not to trouble any man : for the holy Ghost vseth the same name, which commonly the men of that countrey gaue it. And thus much of their fact, that *they by faith passed through the redde sea.* Now we come to the two circumstances, whereby it is commended.

The first circumstance is, the *manner* of their going through the red sea : *they went through as on drie land.* This must not be conceiued to

*surely because
Edom ete
... ...
sea signifies
Red*

be, by helpe of bridge or shippe, nor by meanes which men vse, as swimming, sailing, or wading; but their passage was miraculous: for, the waters stood like walles on both sides of them. And the channel of the sea was as a *pauement or drie land*; Exod. 14. 22. which notably setteth forth the strangenesse of this fact, shewing that it was a wonderfull work of God. And this also confuteth certaine enemies of the Scripture: who haue cauilled at all the miracles which are recorded therein: accounting of *Moses* but as a *Magician* and Sorcerer, and of the miracles which hee did, as of illusions: and for this miracle they make no account of it; for (say they) *Moses* beeing a great scholler, and a wise man, knew the time of the rise and fall of the waters, and knewe the fords and shallowe places: therefore he tooke his time, and found a place so shallow, that when the tide was past, the sands were bare and dry (as the marshes in England are) and then he led the hoast of Israel through. But *Pharaoh* and his hoast following them, were drowned, because they went thorough at the flowing of the sea. *Ans.* Whereas they say that this their passage was no miracle, here we see it is ouerthrowen by this circumstance of the manner of their passing ouer : for, the bottom of the sea was as a pauement, and as ground on which no waters fall. Now, in most places of the sea, where the waters ebb & flowe, the ground is neuer fully *dry*, but watery and full of moist places.

Againe, the waters passed not away as at an ebbe, but *stood as walles on each side of the hoast of Israel, both on the right hand and on the left:* both which shewe plainely, there was no vantage taken by the ebbing and flowing of the water (as vngodly Atheists doe cauill, deriding Gods workes to their owne destruction) but a mighty and miraculous worke of God, first making the waters stand like two walles, and then making the earth vnder it firme and dry, contrary to nature in them both.

The 2. circumstance is, concerning the *time* when they passed through; euen then when the *Eyptians assaying to doe the same, were drowned.* Marke the words; for the thing is strange. The *Egyptians* come armed afer the *Israelites,* with a huge great Armie. Now, the *Israelites* they take into the sea; and the *Egyptians* seeing them, stand not still vpon the banke, but aduenture after them, not by ship, but the same way that the Israelites tooke before them: but yet without any warrant or commaundement from God : so great was their malice against them ; and yet a man would haue thought they durst neuer haue aduentured into the sea after them, especially as they did.

Here, by this fact of *Pharaoh* and his men, we learne, that when God forsakes a man, and leaues him to himselfe, he doth nothing else but run headlong to his owne destruction. *God* (as *Moses* saith) *raised vp Pharaoh to shew his power vpon him:* and now it pleaseth God to leaue

him to himselfe, and he pursueth the Israelites to his owne destruction. And this is the course and state of all those that are forsaken of God. The consideration whereof must teach vs a speciall clause to be vsed of vs in our prayers : wee must euer remember to pray for this, That God would neuer wholly forsake vs, nor cast vs off. This condition is more fearefull then the estate and condition of any creature in the world besides: for when God forsakes a man; all that he doth, is hastning himselfe to his own destruction. *Dauid* knew this well, and therefore hee prayes, *Oh knit my heart vnto thee, that I may feare thy name,* Psal. 86. 11. And againe, hee praieth that the Lord would not *forsake him ouer-long,* 119. 8. as if he should say, if it bee thy pleasure to try me by leauing me to my selfe, yet, *O Lord, let it be but for a while, forsake me not ouer-long.* This is the scope of the sixt petition, *Leade vs not into temptation:* where wee are taught to pray, that God would not forsake vs, or leaue vs to our selues ; or to the power of Satan; but that he would be with vs, and shewe his power in our weakenesse continually. And this may enforce vs vnto this petition: for, the consideration, That men forsaken of God, doe nothing but worke their own destruction, is many times a cause of great trouble of minde. For, some desiring to see such as hang or drowne themselues, by beholding of them get this conceite in their heads, that God will likewise forsake them as he hath done these whom they behold, and so shal they make away themselues ; whence followeth great trouble, and anguish of soule for a long time. Now, how must a man or woman in this case helpe themselues? *Ans.* The best way is, by prayer to craue at Gods hands, that hee would euer be with them, and neuer wholly forsake them. And further, this must bee remembred withall, that God will neuer forsake any of his seruants before they first forsake him: and therefore they that can say truly and vnfainedly, that they desire to serue God, & to be his seruants, and seeke his blessing by prayer, they may stand fast on this ground, that God will neuer forsake them, till they first forsake him. And therefore *Azariah* the Prophet saith notably to King *Asa,* 2. Chron. 15. 2. *The Lord will be with you while you be with him; and if ye seeke him, he will be found of you: but if ye forsake him, hee will forsake you.* And *Iames* saith, *Draw neere to God, and he will draw neere to you,* Iames 4. 8. It was neuer heard that God did euer forsake any that did seeke him. And if the causes were knowen why men make away themselues, it would prooue (generally) to be thus ; because they first by some fearefull sinnes haue forsaken God, and then he in his Iustice forsakes them. And therefore they that are troubled with this temptation, must pray earnestly that they may sticke fast vnto God by faith and holinesse : and so will hee neuer forsake them.

Exod. 14. 22.

Secondly, in this circumstance, that the *E-*
gyptians following the Israelites, were drowned,
we haue a notable patterne of the state and
condition of all persecuters of Gods Church.
In *Pharaoh* and his hoast we may see their end,
which is vsually destruction: that is their reward
for persecuting Gods Church. *Cain* slaies *A-*
bel that notable seruant of God: but his reward
was this, he was *cast forth of Gods Church,*
Gen.4.11.13. and striken in Gods iust iudgement with finall desperation. *Saul* persecuted
Dauid: but his ende was to kill himselfe *with*
his owne sword, 1.Sam. 30.4. And *Iesabel* shee
persecutes the Prophets and children of God:
but her ende was this, *the dogges did eate her*
flesh. The whole stocke of the *Herods* were
great enemies to Christ: but their name was
soone rooted out; and *Herod,* called *Agrippa,*
that slew *Iames,* and persecuted *Peter,* was eaten vp of wormes. Many great Emperours in
the primitiue Church were persecuters: but
they died desperately. And *Iulian,* for one, once
a Christian, died blaspheming Christ: and, ca-
sting his blood vp towards heauen, cried, *Thou*
hast ouercome, O Galilean, thou hast ouercome.
And to come neere these times; what reward
from God the persecuters of the Church haue
had, we may read in the booke of Acts and Monuments, which was penned for that purpose.
And to come to these our daies, the whole
band of those that call themselues leaguers, in
France, Italie, Spaine, &c. like the *Tabernacles*
of Edom and the Ismaelites, Moab, and the A-
garims,&c. Psal. 83.5,6. they vow the destruction and persecution of Gods Church: but yet
Gods Church stands; and he so contriues the
matter, that they draw swords against themselues, and slay and poison one another. Herein
doth God graciously make good his promise
to his Church, that *the weapons made against*
her shall not prosper. And Zachar. 12.3. there is a
prophecie of the Church in the new Testament: the Lord saith, *He will make Ierusalem*
(that is, his Church) *an heauie stone: for all peo-*
ple that lift it vp shall be torne, though all the
people of the earth be gathered against it: where
the Prophet setteth downe notably, what shall
be the condition of those that persecute Gods
Church: the more they persecute her, the more
they shal haue Gods hand against them to confound them. Dan. 2.34. there is mention made
of *a stone hewen out of a rocke without hands,*
which smote the image vpon the feete, which
were of yron and clay, and brake them to pieces.
By that stone, is meant the kingdome of Christ,
which shall dash in pieces the kingdomes of
the earth, which set themselues against Christ,
and his kingdome. For Christ must raigne till
he haue put all his enemies vnder his feete: so
that destruction is the ende of the enemies of
Gods Church. For, *the hand of the Lord shall be*
knowne among his seruants, and his indignation
against his enemies, Isa.66.14. And thus much
of the second circumstance.

Now, in this whole fact of the Israelites passing through the redde sea, towards the land of
Canaan, there is a notable thing signified;
namely, *Baptisme.* So *Paul* saith, *The Israelites*
were baptized vnto Moses in the sea, 1.Cor.
10.2. Yet we must remember, it was not ordinarie *Baptisme,* but extraordinarie; neuer administred before, and neuer shall be so againe, for
ought we know. The minister of this Baptisme,
was Moses; an extraordinarie minister, as the
Baptisme was extraordinarie. The outward
signe was the *red sea;* or rather the water of the
red sea. The departing of the children of Israel
out of Egypt through the red sea, signifieth the
departing of the children of God out of the
kingdome of darknes, from the power of sinne
and Satan. And the drowning of *Pharaoh,*
with all his host in the red sea, signified the subduing of the power of all spirituall enemies,
with the pardon and death of sinne; which
stands partly in the abolishing of sinne, and
partly in newnesse of life. And to this alludeth
the Prophet *Micah,* saying, *He will subdue our*
iniquities, and cast all their sinnes into the bot-
tome of the sea, Mic. 7.19. As if he should say;
Looke as God subdued *Pharaoh,* and all his
host, in the bottome of the sea; so will he cast,
and put away the sinnes of his people.

From this we learne two points: 1. That
the *Baptisme of infants* hath warrant in Gods
word, howsoeuer some men be of a contrarie
opinion: for, here we see all the Israelites were
baptized in the sea; and among them no doubt
were many children. If it be said, this baptisme
was extraordinarie, and is no ground for ours:
Answ. True: it was extraordinarie for the
manner; but yet herein, the matter and substance, and the thing signified is ordinarie, and
the ende all one with ours: and therefore the
baptizing of infants in the red sea, is some warrant for the baptisme of infants in the Church
now a daies.

Secondly, here we may learne another instruction. As the *Israelites* went through the
redde sea (as through a graue) to the promised
land of Canaan; so we must know, that the
way to the spirituall Canaan, euen the kingdome of heauen, is by dying vnto sinne. This is
a speciall point to be considered of euery one
of vs: we professe our selues to be Christians,
we heare Gods word, and receiue the Sacraments, which are the outward badges of Christians, and we perswade our selues of life euerlasting after death: well, if we would haue that
to be the ende of our iourney, then we must
take the Lords plaine way in this life; which is,
to die vnto all our sinnes. So it is saide, *They*
which are Christs, haue crucified the flesh with
the affections and lusts thereof: where, this dutie
is inioyned to euery Christian; he must crucifie
the lusts and affections of the flesh, and not liue
in sinne. For, a man cannot walke in sinne, and
so runne the broad way to hell, and yet wait for
the kingdom of heauen; these two wil not stand

together : and therefore , if wee would walke worthy the calling of Chriſtianitie , wee muſt haue care that all our ſinnes, whether they bee of heart or life, little or great, new or olde, may be mortified and aboliſhed. Many will for a time become ciuill,and ſeeme to be religious, eſpecially when they are to receiue the Lords ſupper; but when that time of the Sacrament is paſt, then they returne to their olde cuſtome in ſinning againe : whereby it appeares , that their change was but in ſhew, to blind the eies of men. Aud doe we not each Sabbaoth pro-feſſe our ſelues good Chriſtians, and ſeeme to glory in it , by keeping this day with ſuch ſo-lemnitie ? But alas! as ſoone as that day is paſt, many(and ſome euen this day) runne into all ryot. This is not Chriſtianity; this is not the way to heauen: but if euer we thinke to come to Canaan, we muſt kill and bury our ſinnes,we muſt die vnto them ; or elſe wee ſhall neuer come to the ende of Chriſtianity: namely, e-ternal life.And thus much of this circumſtance, and also of the example it ſelfe.

Ioſuahs Faith.

Verſe 30.

By faith, the walles of Ie-richo fel downe , after they were compaſſed about ſeuen daies.

FRom the beginning of this chapter , to this 30. verſe, we haue heard two ſorts of examples of faith: the firſt, of belee-uers from the beginning of the world to the flood. The ſecond, of ſuch as were from the time of the flood, to the giuing of the Law in Mount Sina: and of both theſe, we haue hi-therto intreated. Now here , and ſo forward, to the end of this chapter, is ſet downe a third order of examples of faith; namely, of ſuch as liued from the time of the giuing of the Lawe, to the time of the raigne of the Maccabees.

This 30. verſe containes the firſt example of this ranke ; namely, the example of *Ioſuahs* faith , and of thoſe that went with him into Canaan. And their faith is commended vnto vs by a notable fact of theirs ; *the cauſing to fall the walls of Iericho :* the Hiſtorie whereof wee may reade at large, Ioſuah 6. The ſumme of it is this; Whereas the *Iſraelites* came vnto *Ca-naan*, and could not enter into the Land, by reaſon of the ſtrength of Iericho, by which they muſt needes paſſe, nor could win it by reaſon of the huge walles of *Iericho*; the Lord promiſeth to deliuer *Iericho* into their hands: onely the people muſt doe this; they muſt *com-*

paſſe-about the walls ſeauen daies, and carie the *Arke* of the Lord with them , ſounding with Rammes hornes, and ſhowte, and ſo the walls ſhould fall downe. Now , the Lord hauing made this promiſe vnto them ; the Iſraelites, and ſpecially *Ioſuah*, obey his commaunde-ment,and beleeue his promiſe: and thus doing, *by faith the walls of Iericho fell downe, after they were compaſſed-about ſeauen dayes*. Indeed the power of God was the principall cauſe of this ruine of the walls ; but yet becauſe vpon their beleeuing , God ſhewed this power, therefore is the downefall of them aſcribed to their faith.

Here are many notable points to be learned. 1. Whereas the text ſaith , *By faith the walls of Iericho fell downe*;we may obſerue the wonder-full power of true faith. *Ioſuah* and the Iſrae-lites beleeued Gods promiſes, that hee would ouerturne the *walls of Iericho:* and as they be-leeued , ſo it came to paſſe. So our Sauiour Chriſt ſaith,Matth. 17. 20. *if a man had but as much faith as a graine of muſtard-ſeed, hee ſhall ſay vnto the mountaine, remooue hence , and it ſhall remooue, and nothing ſhall be vnpoſſible vn-to him:* ſignifying , that by the power of true faith, ſuch things as are impoſſible to mans reaſon, ſhall be brought to paſſe, if God haue promiſed them : as wee ſee in this place, the mighty walls of Iericho fall downe by faith, which to mans reaſon is impoſſible. So , the Lord promiſeth to *Abraham, That he ſhould be the Father of many Nations:*yea, *that all the Nations of the earth ſhould bee bleſſed in him.* This was ſtrange; but *Abraham* beleeued it: and as hee beleeued, ſo it came to paſſe: for, many Nations deſcended from him : and after the time of Chriſts aſcenſion, when all the Na-tions of the world were called to the light of the Goſpel, they were bleſſed in Chriſt, the promiſed Seede of *Abraham :* and therefore is he called *the Father of the faithfull* in all Nati-ons. And to come vnto our ſelues : To miſera-ble men it may ſeeme a ſtrange thing , that the power of the deuill and the ſtrength of the fleſh, ſhould be ouercome in vs: yet let a man beleeue this promiſe of God ; *God ſo loued the world , that he gaue his onely begotten ſonne, that who ſo beleeued in him,ſhould not periſh,but haue euerlaſting life*, Ioh. 3. 16. I ſay, let him beleeue this effectually , and hee ſhall finde by faith the Kingdome of ſinne and Satan, in his heart and conſcience , weakned euery day more and more. And therefore S.*Iohn* ſaith not without cauſe, *This is the victorie that ouer-commeth the world, euen our faith ,* 1. Iohn 5. 4.

2. Here obſerue, that among the cauſes of the change and ouerthrowe of Townes, Cities, and kingdomes, this is one ; namely, *faith in Gods promiſes.* Many men haue written of the change of Kingdomes,and doe giue diuers rea-ſons thereof:But moſt of them omit the princi-pall, and that is *faith*; by vertue whereof many

Gen.17.2. and 18.18.

times Kingdomes and Townes are brought to ruine and ouerthrowe. God promised to *Abraham* and to his feede, that he would giue them the land of *Canaan* for their inheritance: now, they beleeued this promife, and here we fee it comes to paffe as they beleeued; *Iericho by faith is ouerturned* and the reft of their Cities, and the people of Canaan difpoffeffed. So that we fee, faith in Gods promifes, is a meanes to Gods people, to ouerturne cities and kingdomes, that are enemies to Chrift and to his Gofpel. God hath made a promife vnto his Church, that the *whore of Babylon*, Reuel. 18. 2. that is, the Kingdome of Antichrift fhall flourifh for a while, but after it fhall be deftroyed; yea, fuch a ruine fhall come vnto it, that the *Kings of the earth, and all great men and Merchants fhall bewaile the deftruction thereof.* Now, this promife beeing receiued by faith, and beleeued of Gods Church, fhall vndoubtedly come to paffe. It is in fome part verified already (for we fee, fome Kingdomes and people haue renounced the curfed Doctrine and tyrannie of Rome; and many Chriftian Princes haue already fhaken off the Popes yoke) yea, and this promife fhall come to paffe daily more and more. Let all the Kings of that fort doe what they can, and let the people fet themfelues neuer fo much againft Gods Church, yet *Babylon fhall downe:* for God hath promifed fo to his Church, and his Church beleeueth the fame; and therefore by their faith it fhall be brought to paffe, in defpite of the deuill.

Thirdly, here we learne, that when any City, Towne, or Kingdome, is to make warre either in defence of themfelues, or in lawfull affault vpon their enemies; a fpeciall meanes for good fucceffe herein, is true faith. Chriftian policie is a commendable thing in this cafe: but if policie be feuered from faith, it is nothing. Faith in Gods promifes of protection and affiftance, doth farre furpaffe all worldly wifedome. And therefore, good King *Iehofaphat*, when he was to fight againft the huge Armies of the Moabites, and Ammonites, giues this counfell to his people, 2. Chron. 20. 20. *Put your truft in the Lord your God, and ye fhall be affured: Beleeue his Prophets, and ye fhall profper,* giuing a moft notable inftruction, and fhewing that the beft helpe for our defence, is faith in God, whereby we reft vpon his word and promife, that he will helpe vs: yet this taketh not away the vfe of meanes, but it giues the bleffing and efficacie vnto them. *Faith* we knowe, is called *a fhield,* among the fpirituall armour of God, whereby a man awards the blowes of Satan: and though that be the principall vertue of it, yet is it alfo a notable fhield to defend men, euen againft their outward vifible enemies, and a moft ftrong engine againft them, to worke their ouerthrowe. Hence *Dauid* faith, *He will not be afraid for ten thoufand of the people, that fhould befet him round about.* They therefore that would defend themfelues againft their e-

nemies (yea, and ouercome them in lawfull affault) muft embrace and obey true religion; and with Chriftian policie, ioyne faith in Gods promifes: for, by faith we make God our Captain, and through him we fhall doe valiantly, and beate downe our enemies on euery fide.

Laftly, here we may learne, what a vaine thing it is to truft in outward worldly meanes. *The wals of Iericho* were both ftrong and high, and hard it had been to haue ouerthrown them by ordinarie meanes: but yet we fee, it prooued but a vaine thing to truft vnto them, as the men of *Iericho* did: for they found but little reliefe and defence in them: for, the Lord layes them flat to the ground; and fo the people of Ifrael went ftraight forward and tooke the Citie. So likewife it is a vaine thing to truft to mans ftrength, or in the ftregth of an horfe, or in the number of men, or in riches, or in gifts of wifedom and learning, or in any other outward meanes whatfoeuer: the reafon is, becaufe God can ouerturne them with the leaft breath of his mouth.

This muft admonifh vs, that howfoeuer we vfe odinarie meanes of our preferuation and helpe, yet euer we muft caft our whole care on God, and put all our confidence in him for helpe and fafetie: for, without him all other outward meanes are nothing but vaine helps; *For, vaine is the helpe of man.* And thus much for the fact it felfe.

Further, this fact is fet out vnto vs by two circumftances; to wit, by the *meanes* which they vfed, and by the *time* which they obferued for this exploit. For the firft: when they come to Iericho, this ftrong Citie, which they muft needes fubdue (or elfe they could not this way enter and poffeffe the Land) they doe not goe about to ouerturne the Citie by vndermining, battering, or fcaling the walls; but, according to Gods appointment, they goe one by one in order round about the Citie walls day by day for one weeke fpace: and on the feauenth day, they compaffe it feauen times; during all which time they kept great filence, faue onely that feauen Priefts founded vpon feauen trumpets of Rammes-hornes before the Arke, till *Iofuah* bade them fhout. Now, in common reafon, a man would iudge this rather to be fome childifh fport, then a meanes to fling downe thefe great walls. Nay, confider it well, and it may feeme a courfe tending rather to ouerthrowe themfelues, then the walles of Iericho: for, they marched not in battell ray, as though they would pitch a field againft the people of Iericho, or lay fiege to their Citie; but they went in length one before another, fo as they might compaffe the Citie about. Now, if the men of Iericho fhould haue come forth, and made affault vpon them, in all likelihood the Ifraelites had beene ouerthrowne; fo weake and feeble were the meanes. And yet the Lord for waighty caufes, prefcribes this courfe vnto them: to wit, Firft, hereby to trie the faith of his people, whether they will beleeue his promiſes or no, when they are enioyned to vſe weake, & feeble meanes, and in mans reaſon fooliſh.

Secondly, to make manifeſt in the weakeneſſe and inſufficiencie of the meanes, his own all-ſufficient power and wiſedome, for the furtherance of his glory: for, *through weakeneſſe is Gods power made perfect*, 2. Cor. 12. 9. Hence, our Sauiour Chriſt, when hee was to cure the man that was borne blinde, *tempers clay of ſpittle, and layes it to his eyes*, Ioh. 9. 6. A meanes in common reaſon, rather fit to make a man blinde, then to recouer his ſight: and yet Chriſt vſeth it for the furtherance of Gods glory, in the manifeſtation of his Diuine power, whereby the people might knowe hee was able in himſelfe, to doe whatſoeuer he would.

Now, looke what courſe the Lord here takes for the battering of *the walles of Iericho*, the like hee vſeth in ouerthrowing the kingdome of the deuill, *the ſpirituall Iericho*; eſpecially in the new teſtament. For, after Chriſts aſcenſion, when hee intended to deſtroy the Kingdome of darkeneſſe, vnder which all the nations ſate, hee ſets apart a fewe fiſher-men, ſimple perſons, wanting worldly wit and policy; neither did he put a ſword of fleſh into their hands, but the word of God into their mouthes: and thus ſent them to diſpoſſeſſe the deuill out of all the world, and to batter down the kingdome of darkeneſſe by their preaching. And now in theſe latter daies, wherein the Antichriſtian kingdome of the Pope had ſpread it ſelfe through all places almoſt, God vſed the ſame weake meanes to ouerthrow it. For, hee ſet apart a ſilly Monke, and indues him with gifts to preach the truth: by which meanes, the kingdome of Antichriſt receiued a greater wounde, then if tenne Princes had ſet themſelues againſt it. And ſtrange it is to ſee, how God ouerturneth all the ſtratagems deuiſed againſt his Church, and how he vanquiſheth the power of ſinne, by the weake meanes of the Goſpel preached, and by the praiers of the Church; then which, to the world nothing ſeemes more feeble or fooliſh.

The conſideration hereof, is of ſpeciall vſe: for, it may be we ſhall ſee Kings and people of great power and number, to make reuolt from the Goſpel of Chriſt, and to fall to Antichriſt, embracing popery: hereat indeede, we muſt be grieued, but yet withall, here is good cauſe of comfort vnto vs; for we muſt know, that Satans kingdome muſt bee battered downe, not ſo much by the power of Kings, as by the breath of Gods mouth: not ſo much by the ſword of fleſh, as by the *ſword of the ſpirit*. So it is ſaid, that *the man of ſinne*, euen *Antichriſt muſt bee aboliſhed*: not by the power of Princes; yea, let all the princes and potentates in the world doe their beſt for him, yet his kingdom muſt downe in Gods good time; *for God wil conſume him with the breath of his mouth, and aboliſh him by*

the *brightneſſe of his comming*, 2. Theſ. 2. 8. that is, by the preaching of the word, in the mouthes of his Miniſters, who are me voyd of all worldly power and policie.

Yet further, obſerue the meanes. *They walke about the walles of Iericho ſeauen daies together*. If men ſhould attempt the like enterpriſe at this day, in all likelihood it would coſt them their liues; for, now there are deuiſed ſuch inſtruments of warre, I meane great ordinance, and field pieces, that will kill afar off: and vndoubtedly, if there had bin ſuch inſtruments of war in this city, the Iſraelites could not ſo ſafely haue compaſſed the walles ſo many daies together. Whereby it appeares more then probable, that in thoſe daies there were no gunnes knowen; no not amongſt the heathen, which at this day are ſo rife amongſt Chriſtians. Whence may be gathered, that theſe later daies are perillous times; for now mens heads are ſet to deuiſe more hurtfull meanes againſt the life of man, then euer the ſauage heathen knew. For, beſide the inuention of gunnes, which put downe all euidence of proweſſe and valour, ſeene in Ancient warres; our age exceedes in contriuing ſuch ſtrange kindes of poyſons, as were neuer knowen in former times. For, men haue now deuiſed poyſon of that ſort, that will kill a man, not preſently; but a weeke, or a moneth, or a quarter of a yeare after; as appears by the confeſſion of thoſe, that haue giuen themſelues to ſtudie and practiſe ſuch hurtfull deuiſes. And it is worth the marking, that the principall inuentors and practiſers of ſuch hurtfull inuentiôs, haue bin of the Romiſh religion.

The ſecond circumſtance to be obſerued, is the *Time* of this exploit. It was not on any of the ſixe daies, but on the ſeauenth; and that after they had that day compaſſed the citie about ſeuen times: then when the Prieſts blew the trumpets, and all the people ſhowted as *Ioſuah* bade them, the walles of Iericho fell downe; for this was the time which God had appointed for this exploit. The reaſon why God appointed ſeauen daies, and ſeuen times compaſſing on the ſeuenth day, is not reuealed vnto vs in the word of God: & therefore we may not curiouſly prie into it, nor yet (as ſome do) hence gather, that ſeuen is a perfect number. But from the conſideration of the very time wherein the walles fell down, we may learne this; that if wee would haue God to accompliſh his promiſes vnto vs, we muſt waite for that time & ſeaſon which hee hath appointed: we muſt not thinke that God wil accompliſh the when we appoint. But we muſt beleeue gods promiſe, & alſo wait his good leiſure, and then will it come to paſſe. The Iſraelites compaſſed about Iericho one day, and the walles neuer ſtirre; yea, they doe ſo ſixe daies together, and ſixe times more on the ſeuenth day, and yet they ſtand faſt: The reaſon is, Becauſe Gods appointed time was not yet come. But on the ſeuenth daie, when they had compaſſed them about the ſeauenth

time,

time, all the people gaue vp the fhowt, and then they fell downe; becaufe that was the particular fet time, wherein God would accomplifh his promife.

Further, whereas they *compaffe about the walles feuen daies together*; it muſt needes be, that they went about them on the Sabbath day, for that was one of the feuen. Now here a doubt arifeth: for, this was a feruile worke vpon the Sabbath, contrarie to Gods commandement; which inioyneth fo ſtrict a reſt vpon the Sabbath day, that they might not kindle a fire thereon: how then could they lawfully compaffe the citie on the Sabbath day? *Anfw.* All Gods commandements in the morall law, muſt be vnderſtood with this exception; *Thou ſhalt doe thus and thus, vnleſſe I the Lord command thee otherwiſe*: for, God is an abſolute Lord, and fo aboue the Law; and therefore may lawfully command that which the Lawe forbiddeth. In the fecond commandement he faith, *Thou ſhalt not make to thy felfe any grauen image, &c.* and yet *Moſes* by Gods ſpeciall appointment fet vp *a braſen ſerpent*, which was a figure of Chriſt. Vpon ſuch a ſpeciall command, *Abraham* lawfully offers to kill *Iſaac*; the Iſraelites at their departure fpoyle and rob the Egyptians; and *Ioſuah* with the people, here compaſſe the walls of Iericho on the Sabbath day.

Rahabs Faith.

VERSE 31.

By faith, Rahab the harlot periſhed not, with them which obeyed not, when ſhee had receiued the Spies peaceably.

IN this verſe the holy Ghoſt proceedes further, in declaring the power of faith; and, for this ende, commends vnto vs the faith of *Rahab*. The words contain the ſumme and abridgment of the fecond and fixt chapters of *Ioſua*: the meaning of them is plaine.

The points herein to be confidered, are three: 1. The perſon beleeuing; to wit, *Rahab*. 2. The reward of her faith giuen by *Ioſuah*: Shee *periſhed not, but was preſerued in the deſtruction of Iericho*. 3. The teſtimonie of her faith, fo called by S. *Iames*, 2. 25. and fet downe in the end of this verſe, *When ſhe had receiued the ſpies*

peaceably.

For the *perſon*: *Rahab* was a woman of Canaan, dwelling in Iericho; as we may read, Ioſuah 2. there ſhe liued and had her abode: ſhe was no *Iſraelite*, but a forrainer in regard of her birth, and a Stranger from Gods Church. How then comes it to paſſe, that ſhe is commended for her faith, and here put into the Catalogue of theſe renowned beleeuers? Why are not the reſt of the Cananites preferred to this honour as well as ſhe? *Anſw.* We muſt knowe this, that from the beginning of the world to the time of Chriſts aſcenſion, the Church of God was ſmall; ſometime ſhut vp in ſome fewe families, as, from the flood, to the giuing of the Law; and after limited to a ſmall Kingdome and people in the Land of Canaan, where the Lords people dwelt. During which time, all other Nations and people of the world befides this little company, were no people of God, but ſtrangers from the couenant of promife, and (as *Paul* faith) *Without God in the world*. And howſoeuer Gods Church was thus ſhut vp, as it were in a corner; yet now and then it pleaſed God to reach out his mercifull hand to ſome of the heathen, calling them into his Church, and receiuing them into his couenant: and they are called in the newe teſtament, *Proſelytes*. In *Abrahams* familie, his *bond-men and ſeruants were circumciſed*, and made members of the Church of God. And in *Moſes* dayes *Iethro Moſes* father in Law, a Prieſt of Midian, obtained this at Gods hands, to be ioyned vnto Gods Church: and fo was *Ruth* the Moabite, Ruth 1. 16. and *Naaman* the Aſſyrian, 2. Kings 5. 17. and as ſome thinke *Nabuchadonozer*, Dan. 4. 3. but that is not fo certaine. And fo was the *Eunuch of Ethiopia, Candaces the Queene of Ethiopias chiefe gouernour*, Act. 8. 27. Now, as God in mercie dealt with theſe, fo did he in like mercie call *Rahab* the harlot aboue all the people of Iericho: for, they truſted to their ſtrong walls, and therefore died: but *Rahab* beleeued, that the God of Iſrael was the true God, and fo had mercie ſhewed vnto her. Now, after the time of Chriſts aſcenſion, God dealt more bountifully with the world: for he fent the light of his Goſpel into all Nations: and (as the Scripture faith) *their ſound went thorough all the earth, and their words to the ends of the world*, Rom. 10. 18.

The confideration of this limited eſtate of the Church of God for fo long a time, ſerues to difcouer vnto vs the errour of thoſe, that maintaine and hold *vniuerſall calling* of all and euery man to the eſtate of grace and faluation: but if that were fo, then in former ages the Gentiles would haue beleeued; whereas we fee, that before the aſcenſion of Chriſt, the Church of God was but a ſmall remnant, among the people of the Iewes onely: and not one of tenne thouſand beleeued among the Gentiles. Now, if all men had beene effectually called, then all would haue receiued the promife of the Goſpel: but

many

Eph. 2. 12.

Gen. 17. 27.

Exod. 18. 11, 12.

many Nations in former ages neuer heard of Chrift: and therefore there was neuer in all ages a generall effectuall calling of all men.

Obiect. Paul faith, *God reconciled the world vnto himfelfe by Chrift*, 2. Cor. 5. 19. and if that be fo, then he called all men effectually. *Anf.* We muft vnderftand the Apoftle according to his meaning: for, Roman. 11. 15. he expounds himfelfe, and fhewes what he meanes by the *world*; faying, That *the falling away of the Iewes, is the reconciling of the world:* which cannot be vnderftood of men in all the ages; but in the laft age of the world after Chrfts afcenfion, wherein God offered to all the world life euerlafting by Chrift.

Further, *Rahab* is here noted by a notorious vice, fhe is called a *harlot*; whereby, fhe was infamous among the men of Iericho. Certaine of the *Iewes* which are enemies to the new Teftament, fay, That the Author of this Epiftle, and S. *Iames* doe great wrong vnto *Rahab* for calling her an *harlot* ; for (fay they) in *Iofuah* fhee is called but a *Tauerner* or *Hoftefle.*

Anfw. We muft know that the word which is vfed in *Iofuah*, fignifieth two things; a *Tauerner* and an *harlot.* Now, take the word properly, as it is generally vfed in the olde Teftament, and then moft commoly it is put for an harlot. And therefore in the newe Teftament, *Rahab* hath no wrong don her by this title. For it is the thing that *Iofuah* intended, to fhewe what a one fhe had been: and therefore in fpeaking of her to the fpies, he bids them go into *That harlots houfe*, Iof. 6. 22. vfing fuch an Article as implyes, that fhe had beene infamous and notorious in that kinde. And yet we muft not thinke that fhe playd the harlot, after fhe had receiued grace to beleeue, but long before; for, *faith purifieth the heart*; neither will it fuffer any finne to raigne therein. She is called a *harlot*, therefore, in regard of her life paft; for which, fhe was infamous among the men of Iericho, before her calling to the faith.

Queft. How could fhe beleeue, beeing a harlot in former times? for it is faid, That *neither fornicators, nor adulterers, fhall inherite the Kingdome of heauen*, 1. Cor. 6. 9. *Anf.* That is true according to the Law: but the Gofpel giues this exception, *vnlefle they repent*. And fo are all legal threatnings to be vnderftood in the word of God.

In this circumftance of the perfon, and in the qualitie of her finne, we may note the endlefle mercie of God towards finners ; for he hath vouchfafed to call moft notorious and grieuous finners to the ftate of faluation: as *Ifay* faith, *The Lord is very ready to forgiue*, Ifay 55. 7. yea, *with the Lord is plentifull redemption*, Pfal. 130. 7. This appeares, by vouchfafing mercie to *Rahab* a notable harlot : and as he dealeth with *Rahab* here, fo hath he fhewed like mercie to other notorious finners. King *Manaffes* had fold himfelfe to *Idolatry* and *witchcraft*, and had fhed innocent blood exceeding much, &

caufed *Iudah to finne*, 2. Kin. 21. 6. 16. for which he was led captiue : yet *when he hubled himfelfe and prayed*, *God was intreated of him*, 2. Chr. 33. 13. And *Paul* faith of himfelfe; *When he was a blafphemer and a perfecuter, and an oppreffor, he was receiued to mercie, though he were the head of all finners ; that Chrift might firft fhew on him all long fuffering, vnto the example of them , which fhall in time to come beleeue in him vnto euerlafting life*, 1. Tim. 1. 13. 16.

The confideration of this exceeding mercie of God towards finners, is of great vfe. Firft, it armeth a poore foule againft defpaire: whereinto the deuill would drawe it vpon the viewe of the multitude and greatnefle of his finnes: for, many reafon thus: My finnes are fo haynous, fo many , and fo vile , that I dare not come to God, neither can I be perfwaded of the pardon of them. But behold here the endelefle mercie of God, in forgiuing finnes to them that repent, though they be like crimfon and fcarlet, and neuer fo many. This muft comfort the wounded foule, and encourage all touched hearts, to repent, and to fue to the Lord for mercie and pardon.

Secondly , it muft mooue euery one of vs now to begin to repent, if we haue not repented heretofore: and if we haue begun, to doe it more earneftly; for God is moft mercifull , *and with him is plentifull redemption*. Yet we muft beware that we take not occafion hereby to liue in finne, becaufe God is mercifull: for this is *to turne the grace of God into wantonnes*; which S. *Iude* makes a brand of the vngodly, and a figne of the reprobate, who (as the Apoftle there faith) *are appointed to condemnation*: yea, this is a *defpifing of the bountifulnefle of God, which fhould lead them to repentance*; and hereby *they heape vp vnto themfelues wrath againft the day of wrath*, Rom. 2. 4, 5. Let vs therefore remember this counfell of *Paul* , *Shall we finne that grace may abound? God forbid.* We muft all, but efpecially young men take heede of this courfe : for, if we blefle our felues in our heart, and fay we fhall haue peace, though we liue in finne, God will not be mercifull vnto vs, but his wrath fhall fmoake againft vs.

Further note, that howfoeuer fhe was a finner , and a moft infamous *harlot*: yet when fhe repents, God doth honour and grace her with the title of a *beleeuer*; & that among thofe moft renowned beleeuers that euer liued before *Chrift*: euen to be one of that *cloud of witneffes*, in whom faith is commended to the Church for euer. Hence alfo it is, that S. *Matthew* reckons her in the *Genealogie of Chrift* , to be one of his predeceffours: when as *Amafia*, *Achas*, and fuch like , (who for ought we knowe) did neuer repent, are not once named. Herein we may fee Gods wonderfull mercie in honouring finners, if they doe repent. The confideration whereof muft mooue vs, not only to learne the doctrine of Repentance , and to haue it in our mouthes, but to labour that it may be fettled in our

hearts;

Iude 4.

Dent. 29. 19, 20.

Heb. 12. 1.

Matth. 1. 5.

hearts : that we may shewe forth the power thereof in our liues. All of vs desire honour and reputation among men. Well: if we would be honoured indeede, we must repent, and then God himselfe will honour vs; neither haue our sinnes made vs so infamous, as by our repentance God shall make vs honourable.

Further, concerning the partie: How could *Rahab* come by faith? seeing she liued out of the Church, where the word was neuer preached vnto her.

Ans. If we reade the Story, we shall finde that she came *to beleeue, by a report* of Gods meruailous acts: for, when the Lord deliuered the *Israelites* out of *Egypt* through the red sea, and drowned *Pharaoh* therin with al his hoast; as they went further, he deliuered the Kings of the Nations into their hands: as *Og* the King of *Baashan*, with the Kings of the *Amorites* and *Amalekites.*

Now, the report hereof came to the people of *Iericho*; whereupon they were stricken with a wonderfull great feare. And howsoeuer the men of *Iericho* made no other vse of it, but to arme and prepare themselues to resist and beate backe the Israelites : yet this report wrought further with *Rahab*; and therefore she came to the Spies, whom she had receiued, and hid vpon the roofe of her house, and their confessed the God of Israel to be the true God, in heauen aboue, and in the earth beneath.

Here we may note, that when ordinary meanes faile, for the beginning and encrease of faith; as the word preached, and the Sacraments : then God can worke faith extraordinarily, euen by reports, and rumors. For, thus *Rahab*, and many of the heathen came to beleeue. We say of the Church of Rome, that it is no true Church, and that their religion cannot saue a man : Hereupon many that fauour that way, reply and say: Will you therefore condemne all your forefathers, that liued and died in time of Popery? We answer, no; we dare not giue such censure vpon them : but rather iudge charitably of them : yea, we haue great hope that many of them were saued. For though they wanted preaching and reading, yet God might worke faith in them extraordinarily, and blesse euen good reports and speeches vnto them, with the reading of other godly bookes, besides Gods word, which some of them had. We need not then giue so hard a censure of them : because God is not tied to ordinarie meanes, but can saue extraordinarily, when meanes faile.

Further, concerning *Rahabs* faith, it may be demanded whether it was weake or strong? because, before she had done this fact of faith, her whole abode was among the heathen. *Answ.* We must knowe, that there is in the child of God a certaine seede, or beginning, or preparation to a true and liuely faith ; which our Sauiour Christ in the Scriptures, doth honour with the title of a true and liuely faith: as when a man knowes no more but this, that *Christ Ie-*

sus is the true Messias; hauing withall, a care and conscience to profit and increase in the true knowledge of the Gospel, and to ioyne practise therewith, in his life and calling. Examples hereof, we haue many in Gods word : A certaine *Ruler* came to Christ, and besought him *to goe downe and heale his sonne*, Ioh. 4. 49,50. &c. Iesus but said vnto him, *Goe thy way, thy sonne liueth; and the Ruler beleeued the word that Iesus spake vnto him, and his sonne liued*. Now, inquiring of the hower, and finding it to be the same time when Iesus said, *Thy sonne liueth*; the text saith, *He beleeued and all his houshold*. Now what was this mans faith? Surely, he onely acknowledged, that *Christ was the true Messias*: and withall, resigned himselfe and his family to be instructed further therein. And though they knew nothing particularly, of the meanes whereby Christ should be a Sauiour; yet for this willingnesse in embracing Christ, and readinesse to be taught, the holy Ghost saith, *they did beleeue*. So in the same Chapter, ver. 29. the *woman of Samaria* (beeing conuicted in her conscience, of the things that Christ told her) runnes to the towne, and saith; *Come see a man that hath told me all things that euer I did: Is not he the Christ?* Then the text saith, *Many of the Samaritans beleeued, because of the saying of the woman.* Now what *faith* had these *Samaritans?* Surely, they did onely acknowledge him to be the true Messias, and were willing to be further instructed in his doctrine; which they testified, by going to heare him in their owne persons. So likewise, Christ giues a notable testimony to the confession of the *Apostles faith* (Matt. 16.17, 18.) in the person of *Peter*, saying; *Thou art Peter, and vpon this rocke* (that is, vpon this your *faith*, which thou confessest) *will I build my Church*; and yet the *Apostles* were ignorant of some maine points of the Gospel. For a little after, when Christ tels them of his going to Ierusalem, and of his passion, for the redemption of them, & all the elect, *Peter* perswades him to the contrary, saying ; *Master, spare thy selfe, these things shall not be vnto thee*. Whereby it appeares, that *Peter* did not know *how* Christ should be a Sauiour ; neither did the Apostles particularly know Christ his *resurrection*, till he was risen againe : yea, at the very time of his *ascension*, they knewe not the nature of Christs Kingdome; and therefore they asked him, *Lord, wilt thou now restore the Kingdome to Israel?* (Acts 1.6.) dreaming still of a temporall Kingdome: for which Christ rebukes them. And notwithstanding all these wants, Christ saith, they had true faith; yea, such faith as *the gates of hell should neuer preuaile against*. This then is a most comfortable truth, That if a man (in the want of meanes of further knowledge) doe holde Christ Iesus to be the true Messias, and yeelde himselfe willing to learne the doctrine of the Gospel, and (withall) ioyne obedience to his knowledge, the Lord is willing for a time, to accept of this as of true faith.

Now,

Now, to apply this to *Rahabs* faith: Her faith was but a weake faith, or rather the seede and beginning of a liuely faith afterward. For, as we may reade, all that she knew was this, that the God of Israel was the onely true God, and that hee would certainly deliuer the Land of Canaan into the Israelites hands. This was a notable perswasion wrought by a report; and accordingly she ioynes her selfe to Gods people, & resignes her selfe to obey the God of Israel: but whether she knewe the particular doctrine of saluation by Christ, it is not here set downe; and it is very like, that as yet she was altogether ignorant of it. For, here are all things set down, that tend to her commendation. So that her faith was very weake, and onely the seede of a liuely faith: and yet here the holy Ghost doth commend her for her faith, among the most renowned beleeuers that euer were.

Hence we may learne many good instructions. First, That God makes much account of a little grace: if hee see in a man but the seeds of grace, he doth highly esteeme thereof. When the young man came to Christ, and asked him *what he should doe to be saued*; Christ tells him, *hee must keepe the commaundements*: the young man answers, that *hee had kept them from his youth*; at which answer it is said, *Christ looked vpon him, and loued him.* This he did for the shewe of Grace, which appeared in his answer: much more then will he like of that, which is true grace indeede. So, likewise Christ reasoning with the Scribe, concerning the first and great commandement, and perceiuing that hee had answered discreetly, hee said vnto him; *Thou art not farre from the Kingdome of God*, Mark. 12. 34. shewing hereby how deeply hee tenders the sparks and seedes of true grace: nay, hee makes much of a very shew of grace: which if it be so, then if God haue giuen to any of vs but one sparke of true grace, how ought we to tender it, and cherish it, and to reioyce therein, with all thankfulnesse to God for it? yea, wee must seek to encrease the same: for according to our grace is our acceptance & respect with God in Christ.

Secondly, whereas *Rahabs weake faith* is thus commended, here is comfort for all those that are willing to learne Gods word, and to obey the same. Many are willing to learne: but they are so wonderfull troubled with dulnesse and want of memory, that they cannot learne; and hereupon they growe to doubt much of their estate towards God. But these men must comfort themselues: for though they haue but little knowledge, yet if they haue care to encrease in knowledge, and make conscience of obedience to so much as they know, God will account of them as of true beleeuers: and in truth such are to be commended aboue those which haue much knowledge, and so seeme to haue much faith, and yet shewe forth no obedience answerable to their knowledge; for, they haue a shew of godlines, but want the

power of it.

Thirdly, this confuteth our ignorant boasters, who say they haue as much knowledge as any man needes to haue: for, they knowe, that a man must *loue God aboue all*; and, that *Christ Iesus is the Sauiour of the world*: and this (say they) is enough; and hereupon they take vp their rest for matters of religion, and seeke to go no further. But these men know nothing at all: for, if they would adde to this which they know, though it be but little, a care to encrease in knowledge, and with their knowledge ioyne obedience, then it were something. But whiles they haue no care neither to get more knowledge, nor to shewe forth obedience to that they knowe, they doe hereby shew plainly, that there is no drop of sauing knowledge, nor true faith in their hearts.

Fourthly, seeing God commends the seedes of true faith, for true faith indeede; This must encourage all men to vse all good meanes to come by true faith and repentance. For though as yet thou hast but little knowledge, and therfore but little faith and repentance: yet if thou ioyne hereto an endeauour to get more knowledge, and haue also care to practise that which thou knowest; then will the Lord encrease thy knowledge and thy small faith, till thou haue sufficient, and in the meane time accept of thee as a true beleeuer. And thus much for the measure of *Rahabs* faith.

The second point to bee considered is, the *reward* which *Rahab* receiued at the hands of *Ioshua*, and the *Israelites*, for her faith; *Shee perished not with them that obeyed not*: that is, she with her family was preserued aliue, when as *Iosuah* destroyed all that liued in *Iericho*, young and olde, man, woman, and childe.

But some will say; The *Israelites* were the people of God, a religious people: now, it may seeme to be a cruel part to destroy all; for, what had the young Infants done? *Ans.* In mans reason it may seeme so indeede: yet it could not bee a cruell part, because they did no more then that which God commaunded them. For, it was Gods ordinance, that the *Cannanites should bee rooted out, and that the Israelites should shewe no compassion on them*, Deut. 7. 3. Besides, euen in reason the *Israelites* had some cause to deale thus: for, God gaue this charge to the *Israelites*, that when they came to any Citie or people, First, *they must offer peace; and if they answered peaceably, then they must bee saued, and become their tributaries & seruants*: Deut. 20. 10. but if they would not make peace, *then they must put them to the edge of the sword* (v. 17) man, woman, and child, beeing inhabitants of Canaan, or neere adioyning. And thus no doubt *Ioshua* dealt when he came to *Iericho*; first, he offered peace if they would become their tributaries: but they trusted to their strong walles, and would not yeeld to become their seruants; for which cause he put them all to the edge of the sword: and there-

fore

fore it was no cruelty, becaufe it was Gods commandement; for Gods will is the rule of iuftice.

But was not this partiall dealing, to fpare *Rahab* with her family, who were inhabitants of *Iericho*, as well as the reft? *Anfw.* There were two caufes why fhe fhould efcape: Firft, becaufe fhe yeelded her felfe to the people of *Ifraell*, and ioyned her felfe vnto them, and was content to become one of their religion; and therefore the commandement of putting all to death, did not take hold of her. Secondly, *Rahab* obtained this of the fpies, and bound them to it by an oath, that when they came to deftroy *Iericho*, they fhould fpare her and her family: and therefore alfo did fhee efcape.

In this preferuation of *Rahab*, we may learne fundry points: firft, whereas fhe is faued aliue, becaufe of the oath of the fpies, we fee what fpeciall care euery one ought to haue for the doing of thofe lawfull things whatfoeuer they are, whereto he binds himfelfe by an oath.
Iofh.6.22. *Iofhua* knowing this bond of the fpies to *Rahab* (as we may reade) giues fpeciall charge for her preferuation. Hence *Dauid* faith, If a man binde himfelfe with an *oath*, he muft keepe it, *though it be to his owne hinderance*, Pfal. 15. 4. Euery fingle promife bindes a mans confcience, if it be lawfull: But when an oath is adioyned, then there is a double bond. And therefore the
Heb.6.17,18. Author to the Hebrewes faith, that *God*, *To make knowen the ftablenefe of his counfell promifed, bound himfelfe with an oath: that by two immutable things* (to wit, Gods promife, and oath) *we might haue ftrong confolation:* fo that an oath binds a man double to the performing of his promife. And that this confcience is to be made of a lawfull oath, appeareth thus: If a man make a lawfull oath, and yet be induced to doe it by fraud; he muft performe it, and not faile: as appeareth by *Iofuahs* fact to the *Gibeonites*, Iof. 9. 19. For, when they came to the *Iewes* craftily, as though they had beene men of a far country, and had brought them to fweare that they would not hurt them: though the hoaft of Ifrael murmured at it, when they came to their cities; and though they might haue reafoned thus, that they got it of them by fraud, and therefore they would not keepe it: yet, this is the anfwer of *Iofuah* & the Princes vnto the people, That *they had fworne vnto them, by the Lord God of Ifrael, and therefore they might not touch them*. And when king *Saul*, in zeale to Ifrael, had broken this oath of *Iofuah, and the Princes*, by deftroying the *Gibeonites*, 2. Sam. 21. there came a plague vpon the Land, for three yeares fpace; and was not ftaied, till feauen of *Sauls* fonnes were hanged, for *Sauls* fact. So that the breach of an oath is a moft dangerous thing: and therefore, he that hath bound himfelfe thereby, muft haue great care to keepe it.

Yet here fome cafes may be propounded,

worthie our confideration. For firft, what if a man haue taken an oath to doe an vnlawfull thing, muft he then keepe his oath? *Anf.* If his confcience tell him, out of Gods word that the thing is not lawfull, then he muft not keepe it: for an oath may not be the bond of iniquitie: the keeping of it is a doubling of the fin. *Dauid* in his anger, had fworne *to flay Nabal, and all the men of his family*, for denying reliefe vnto his feruants, 1. Sam. 25. 22. This was a rafh oath, and therefore afterward, when he was preuented by *Abigails* good counfell, he bleffeth God for it, and breaks his oath which he had made, ver. 32.

Queft. 2. What if a man take an oath, and yet afterward in confcience doubts of the lawfulneffe of that which he hath fworne to doe: what muft be done in this cafe? *Anf.* So long as he doubteth, he muft defer the performance of it. For, he that doth a thing doubtingly, condemnes himfelfe in the thing he doth, *becaufe he doth it not of faith: and whatfoeuer is not of faith, is finne*, Rom. 14. 23.

Queft. 3. What if a man be vrged by feare to take an oath, muft he afterward keepe it? As for example; a man is taken of theeues; nowe, wanting money, they charge him on paine of death, to fetch them money, and they binde him hereto by an oath: what muft be done in this cafe, confidering there muft fuch great care be had in keeping of an oth? *Anf.* So long as the thing which he is bound by oath to doe, refpecteth his priuate damage onely, he muft keepe his oath; yet fo as he declare his cafe to the Magiftrate, becaufe their courfe is againft the common good: now the Magiftrate hearing of it, is according to equitie, to prouide for his defence, and for the fafetie of his goods.

A fecond point to be confidered, in *Rahabs* preferuation, is this; *Rahab* efcaped a common danger (but not without all meanes) onely ftaying her felfe on the bare promife of the fpies: but, as fhe beleeued in the true God, fo fhe vfed meanes, whereby fhe might be fure of her preferuation, and that is this; *She bindes the*
Iofh.2.18.21. *Spies by an oath*, to faue her life, and to fpare her houfhold: alfo *fhee keepes within*, and *ties the cord of red threed in her windowe*, according to the mutuall couenant. Thus fhe vfeth meanes for her temporall fafetie: and fo haue other of Gods children done in like cafe. When King *Hezekiah* (2. Kings 20. 6.) was ficke, he was certified by the Prophet from God, that he *fhould liue fifteene yeares longer*, yet he neglected not the means whereby he fhould be healed, and liue: for, he applied dry figges to his byle; and vfed foode, and raiment for his bodily life, during the whole fpace of thofe fifteene yeares. So the Apoftle Saint *Paul*, in his voyage by Sea to *Rome*, was affured by a vifion, that *none of them that were with him fhould perifh, but all come fafe to land*; and yet, notwithftanding, *when the Mariners would haue gone out, he tells the Centurion*, that

*vnleſſe thoſe ſtaied in the ſhip (*that ſo they might vſe ordinarie meanes*) they could not bee ſafe.* Now, as it fareth *temporally* for the ſauing of the body; ſo is it in the *ſpirituall* caſe, for the ſaluation of the ſoule: men muſt vſe meanes to come by grace, and ſo to ſaluation. But, many in this regard be great enemies to their owne ſoules; they ſay, God is mercifull, and Chriſt is a Sauiour, and I hope hee will ſaue me; yet they will not vſe the meanes to come to ſaluation. But if we would be ſaued, then with our inward faith, we muſt ioyne the obſeruation of the outward ordinarie meanes whereby God vſeth to ſaue mens ſoules; as namely, the hearing of Gods word, calling vpon God by prayer, and the receiuing of the ſacraments; that thereby our ſinnefull lyues may be amended, and our faith ſtrengthened. This muſt be remembred of vs: for, they that contemne or neglect the meanes, deſpiſe the grace and mercie of God offered therein: and therefore *Paul* ſaith of the Iewes, when they put the Goſpel from them, *that they did iudge themſelues vnworthy eternall life,* Act. 13.46. It followeth;

With them that diſobeyed: That is, with the people of *Iericho. Queſt.* How did they diſobey? *Anſ.* Thus: When *Ioſuah* and the people came vnto them, and offered them peace, if ſo bee they would become their tributaries and ſeruants, the inhabitants of *Iericho* would not yield vnto them, but ſet themſelues againſt the people of *Iſrael,* and ſo againſt God, in that they would not vndertake that eſtate which God offered vnto them: and therefore they are here eſteemed diſobedient.

Hence we learne, that if it ſhall pleaſe God at any time to put vs out of theſe temporary benefits which we enioy in goods and poſſeſſions; we muſt be contented with Gods will and prouidence, and ſeeke to obey God therein. The inhabitants of *Iericho* pay deerely for their diſobedience in this caſe: God ſets the *Iſraelites* as Lords ouer them: and becauſe they will not yeild to become their ſeruants, they die for it. *Dauids* practiſe was commendable in this caſe: for, when hee was put out of his owne Kingdome, by his owne ſonne, hee murmured not, but ſaid thus; *If I ſhall finde fauour in the eies of the Lord, he will bring me againe: but if hee ſay thus, I haue no delight in thee; beholde, here I am, let him do to me as ſeemeth good in his eies,* 2. Sam. 15.25, 26. In other countries, we ſee Cities and Townes ſpoyled and ſacked: what muſt the people doe? *Anſ.* They muſt ſubmit themſelues to the Lords pleaſure; knowing that he permitteth it, who may doe what he will. And ſo, if it ſhall pleaſe God to bring vs into the like caſe; as to ſuffer our enemies to haue dominion ouer vs, and to diſpoſſeſſe vs of our places: we muſt ſubmit our ſelues to Gods good pleaſure, when we ſee no helpe by lawfull meanes: wee muſt not murmure or rebell; for, that is but to diſobey, as the people of *Iericho* did: and ſo ſhall we bee

deſtroyed, as they were. And thus much for the ſecond point.

The third thing to be conſidered in this example, is the *teſtimony of her faith, in receiuing the ſpies peaceably.* This was a notable worke of faith, as Saint *Iames* noteth, Iam. 2.25. and the more commendable, becauſe ſhe receiued them into her houſe, and entertained them: yea, ſhee preſerued them in danger of her owne life; for, ſhee did it contrary to the pleaſure of the State vnder which ſhe liued. But againſt this may be obiected, firſt, that ſhee lyed in this fact; for, when the King of *Ierichos* meſſengers came to ſearch for the Spies, whom ſhe had hid in the top of her houſe, ſhee ſaid to the meſſengers, *they were gone another way.* Now, how can it bee a good worke, which was don with lying; eſpecially to our Superiour, who hath power to aske vs, and to whome we are double bound to ſpeake the truth? *Anſw.* Wee muſt know that the worke was good which ſhe did; and a worke of mercie, to preſerue Gods people, although ſhe failed in the manner of doing it: ſhee receiued them by faith, though ſhee ſhewed diſtruſt, in lying for their ſafetie. It was a notable worke of *Rebecca,* Gen. 27. to cauſe her ſonne *Iacob* to get his fathers bleſſing; for ſo God had determined, and yet ſhee failed in the manner.

Queſt. But how could this worke be good, being faultie in the manner of doing it? *Anſ.* It might: for *Rebecca's* perſon ſtood righteous before God in Chriſt. Now, the worker beeing acceptable vnto God, the worke muſt needes be good alſo: and though the worker failed in the circumſtances; yet the euill of the worke, was couered in the obedience of Chriſt; and ſo the goodnes of it was approoued, and the fault thereof couered.

The vſe of this doctrine is two-fold: firſt, it ſhewes that the works of Gods children, are partly good and partly bad; euen the beſt works they doe are imperfect. Secondly, this ſhewes the true meaning of Saint *Iames,* when he ſaith, that *Rahab was iuſtified by her works:* hereby he meanes, that by her works ſhe declared her ſelfe to be iuſt. For, that ſhe was not iuſtified by her works appeareth plaine; becauſe the worke which ſhe did, was faultie in the manner, and not perfectly good: and therefore could not be anſwerable to the perfect iuſtice of God.

But ſome will further ſay, that this concealing of the Spies, and lying to the Kings meſſengers, was a worke of treachery againſt her own country; and therefore was a notorious fault, and ſo no worke of faith? *Anſ.* Treacherie indeede, is as great vilany, as one man can practiſe againſt another; and therefore ought to be abhorred and deteſted of al men: but yet we muſt knowe, that *Rahab* in this place is no Traytor. For, ſhe had a plaine Certificat in her conſcience, that the Land of Canaan, and the city *Iericho* were giuen by the Lord to the people of Iſraell, and that they were the right

Lords

Lords thereof, and should enioy them : so that she hid the Spies, not in *treachery, but in faith.*

Thus we see her fact. The duties which wee learne hence, are these: First, it is said that this harlot *Rahab,* being by calling an Hosteffe and a Victualler, receiued the spies peaceably. Hence, Inn-keepers are taught their duty. First, if they will shew themselues faithfull, they must haue speciall regard & respect vnto such guests of theirs, as be the seruants of God, and feare him. This was the worke of *Rahabs* faith towards the spies of Gods people. *Dauid* makes this the property of euery godly man, *That in his eyes a vile person is contemned, but he honoureth the that feare the Lord,* Psal. 15. 4. And therefore if Inn-keepers will shew themselues godly, they must so do. And to encourage each one hereto, our Sauiour Christ makes this notable promise (Matth. 10.41.) *He that receiueth a Prophet, in the name of a Prophet, shall receiue a Prophets reward: and hee that receiueth a iust man, in the name of a iust man, shall receiue a iust mans reward.* And, *if any shall giue, to one of these little ones to drinke, a cuppe of colde water onely, in the name of a Disciple: Verily I say vnto you, he shall not lose his reward.*

Also *Strangers* are here taught, that in seeking places for their abode, they must make choyce to bee with those that feare the Lord: so God directs these spies to doe. And when Christ sent his Disciples to preach, hee bade them (Matth. 10. 11.) when they entred into a Citie, *To enquire who is worthy in that Citie, & there to abide till they departed.* But alas, these duties are little performed; especially the first. For, *In-keepers,* & such as entertaine Strangers, doe make most of those that giue themselues to riot & good fellowship: they are best welcome, that spend most in gaming, drinking, & lasciui-ousnes. These might learne otherwise of *Rahab,* who did better, though she had been an harlot.

Thirdly, *Inn-keepers* must here learne, that when a man comes into their house (if he be no malefactor) they must giue him protection. Thus, *Rahab* doth here to the spies of the Israelites, euen with the danger of her owne life. The like also we may reade of *Lot:* for, when two Angels in the likeneffe of men came into his house, and the men of Sodome would haue had them out; *Lot besought them to let them alone,* Gen. 19. 8. And his reason is, *because they came vnder the shadow of his roofe.*

Againe, hence we may learne another generall dutie; to wit, that a Christian man in the time of persecution and danger, is not to disauer his fellow brethren, or to detect them; but must rather indanger his owne life, by concealing them for their preseruation. This was practiced by good *Obadiah:* when *Iesabel* killed the Lords Prophets, he hid them by fifties in a Caue; which if it had beene knowen, would haue cost him his life. And so did the Apostles and brethren in the Primitiue Church; when the Iewes would haue slaine *Paul* in *Damascus,*

the brethren tooke him by night, and let him down through the wal in a basket to saue his life, Act. 9. 25. And since those times, in the Historie of the Church vnder the Gospel, we may finde, that when the Christians were vrged by persecuters to reueale their brethren, they rather chose to lay downe their owne liues, then to betray their brethren into their enemies hands. And this is true loue indeede, such as the holy Ghost commendeth, *When a man will giue his life for his brother,* 1. Ioh. 3. 16.

Gal. 4. 22.

Lastly, whereas *Rahab* receiued the spies peaceably, we note that it is a speciall fruite of faith, to bee peaceable and kinde. The holy Ghost, repeating the fruites of the spirit, names *Peace and meekeneffe among them.* Now, this *peace* is, when a man is kinde and peaceable to all, but especially to those that be of the *houshold of faith.* And vndoubtedly it is a fruite of faith, which the Prophet *Isay* fore-told should be vnder the Gospel, Isay 11. 6. that then *the Wolfe should dwell with the Lamb, and the Leopard lie with the Kid:* signifying, that howsoeuer men by nature were as sauage as Wolues, yet beeing conuerted to the Kingdome of Christ, they should become gentle as *Lambes,* beeing kinde and peaceable one to another. This peaceableneffe is especially to be shewed in the place and calling where a man liues: for, there did *Rahab* shew forth hers, whe the spies came vnto her. And, where this is truly in outward action, there is *faith* in the heart: it is a good token that a man is at peace with God, when he liues peaceably with men. Which being so; we must learne, not to giue place to our heady affectios, but must rather bridle the rage of malice and anger, and endeauour to liue peaceably with all, especially with those that bee members of Gods Church. And thus much of this example.

The Iudges Faith.
VERSE 32.

And what shall I say more? For, the time would be to short for me to tel of Gedeon, of Barac, & of Samson, & of Iephte: Also of Dauid, and Samuel, and of the Prophets. Which through faith subdued Kingdoms, wrought righteousneffe, &c.

Hitherto, the Author of this Epistle hath set downe vnto vs examples of faith, more at large. But from this verse to the ende of this Chapter, he heapes vp briefly together many examples of faith, one vpon another. The reason whereof is; First, because the number of true beleeuers which are mentioned in Scripture, is very great, and therefore he could not here stand to set them downe in order one by one. Secondly, by handling all the examples at large, which the Author propoundeth in this short Epistle, he should haue seemed to haue restrained the name and title of faith to a very few: for, all that are here named and commended for their faith, are but few, in comparison of all that truly beleeued in the old Testament. And therefore he heapes vp the rest together, to intimate that the number of beleeuers, was more then he could record. And this he doth, by a Rhetoricall preterition or passing ouer, called in Schooles, _Paralepsis_; whereby matters are briefly dispatched and passed ouer, with the very naming onely.

What shall I say more?] That is, as if he had said; I haue propounded diuers worthie examples of faith: and, besides these, there are also many more; but the time of writing an Epistle, will not suffer me to handle them all at large.

First, in this particular quicke dispatch of beleeuers, by our Apostle, we may obserue a difference betweene the infinite vnderstanding of God, and the created vnderstanding that is in mans minde. Man indeede vnderstands the things that are reuealed to him of God; but yet in a manner and order, farre different from that which is in God: for man cannot conceiue in his minde all the things he knowes, at once, by one act of his vnderstanding; but must haue distinct time to conceiue of them, one by one distinctly. For looke as he vtters them distinctly, one by one (as we see in this place,) so likewise doth he apprehend them in conceit, and vnderstanding. But with God it is not so; for God at once, by one act of vnderstanding, without distinction of time, doth conceiue of all things at once, both past, present, and to come; and so could vtter and expresse them, if any creature were able in conceit so to comprehend them.

Secondly, whereas the holy Ghost saith, _The time would be too short, &c._ he giues vs to vnderstand, that the _number of beleeuers_ is very great; and that a long time would not serue to repeat them, or to write of them. This directeth vs vnto a good answer to a question, which much troubleth our common people; to wit, How great is the number of them that shall be saued; whether it is greater then the number of them that shall be damned? _Ans._ We must consider the number of the Elect two waies: first, in comparison of them that shall be condemned: secondly, in themselues. If we compare the elect with the reprobate, the number of the Elect is but a small number: for in most ages, the Church of God hath beene but a handfull, to the rest of the world. And in the

Church this likewise is true, _Many are called, but few chosen_, in respect of them that are called. But yet consider the _Elect_, as they are in themselues, and they are a huge great number; yea, innumerable, as Saint _Iohn_ saith, speaking of the Elect among the Gentiles, beside the chosen Iewes: for all that doe truly beleeue shall be saued. Now, beleeuers are innumerable: This the Author of this Epistle would insinuate vnto vs by his phrase of speech, _What shall I say more? &c._

In handling these examples, we must obserue the order here vsed by the holy Ghost: for in this 32. verse he sets downe the names of the persons that beleeue, all ioyntly together, rehearsing them one by one: and in the 33, 34, 35. verses, he laies downe briefly the fruits of all their faith; in number, tenne most notable actions, seruing all and euery one of them, most worthily to commend their faith. In handling of them, we will follow the order obserued by the holy Ghost: and first speake of the persons; then of their actions.

The foure first are these: _Gedeon_, _Barac_, _Samson_, and _Iephte_: these foure were _Iudges_ in Israel: the fift is _Dauid_, who was both a _Prophet_ and a _King_: the sixt is _Samuel_, both a _Iudge_ and a _Prophet_: lastly, the _Prophets_ generally; by whome we must vnderstand especially these three, _Elias_, _Eliseus_, and _Daniel_.

In speaking of these persons here commended vnto vs; first, we will intreate of them generally, and then in particular. In generall, let vs first obserue _the order_ which the holy Ghost here vseth in naming them. _Gedeon_, for time, was after _Barac_; and yet here he is first named: so _Samson_ was after _Iephte_, and yet here he is put before him. This, the holy Ghost would neuer doe, without some speciall cause. We therefore must know, that the Scripture vseth a two-fold order in reckoning vp of persons: to wit, the _order of time_: when as he that liued first, is first named: and the _order of dignitie_; when the most worthie and excellent is named first, though he were later in time. Now, the Scripture accounteth best of them that did excell in faith, and in the fruits thereof: so in this place whereas _Gedeon_ is set before _Barac_, and _Samson_ before _Iephte_; the holy Ghost obserues not the order of time, but the order of dignitie, according to the excellencie of their faith; naming them in the first place, that were most famous for this grace of faith, and did excede the other in the fruits thereof.

Here we learne this speciall point: That the more men excell in faith, and other graces of God, the more God will honour them: for, looke who most honour God, shal be most honoured of him: but the more a man excells in grace, the more he honours God. And for this cause is _Gedeon_ preferred before _Barac_, and _Samson_ before _Iephte_; because they were more plentifull in the fruits of faith. This must mooue vs, not onely to feeke to haue faith, but to labour euery day more and more for the increafe of faith, and of obedience: for, the more a man abounds in grace before God, the more will God honour him, both here and in heauen. And thus much for the order wherein they are propounded.

Secondly, let vs confider what manner of perfons thefe were, *Gedeon, Barac* and the reft: They were extraordinary men, in their time, raifed vp by God, for the fpeciall good of his Church, and the common wealth of the Iewes, that they might helpe and defend them in diftreffe. And therefore, as their calling was extraordinarie; fo God indued them with extraordinarie gifts of *wifedome, ftrength, zeale, and authoritie*; for which, they are here renowned in this Catalogue of moft worthie beleeuers.

In their example we may obferue this point: That whom God doth raife vp extraordinarily, for fome fpeciall good in his Church, them he endues with extraordinarie gifts to difcharge that calling: and withall, he giues them the fpirit of grace, with a true and liuely faith. This (befides the inftance we haue in hand) appeares plainly in Chrifts Apoftles; they were called by Chrift to preach the Gofpell to all the world, and to plant his Church vniuerfally; and thereupon (howfoeuer they were fimple mē before) were furnifhed with extraordinary gifts of wifedome, zeale, and knowledge, and with this excellent grace of fauing faith, which did fanctifie their other gifts: for, howfoeuer *Iudas* was numbred among them, hauing been a Difciple; yet he neuer came to the excecution of the Apoftlefhip, but went aftray from that miniftration, Acts 1.25. And in thefe latter dayes, when God reftored his Gofpel to light out of the darke myft of Popery, he raifed vp extraordinarie men, whom he endued with wifedome, zeale, & iudgement; which giftes alfo he fealed vp in them by a liuely faith, which they teftified by their piety and godlineffe in life and converfation. And this courfe he obferueth vfually, in all thofe whom he raifeth vp extraordinarily for the good of his Church.

This we muft obferue, to acquaint vs with a fpeciall difference, betweene thofe whom God raifed vp extraordinarily for fpeciall good, and all arch-heretiques and traytors that fet vp themfelues, vnfent of God. For, many fuch wretches haue excelled in wifedome, in worldly policy, in zeale and authoritie: whereupon they haue pretended and perfwaded many, that they were called of God. But hereby efpecially they are to be difcouered, that they are voide of this rare gift of true fauing faith: for looke at their liues, and ordinarily for impietie they haue beene and are arch-deuils. So that, though they wanted not authoritie, or outward zeale, and wifedome: yet they wanted faith, which fhould *purifie their hearts*; or elfe they would neuer haue liued in fuch notorious finnes, as they were difcouered to doe. And

this is the trial which our Sauiour Chrift directs vs vnto; faying, *Ye fhall knowe them by their fruites*. Math.7.16. Let them therefore pretend what knowledge, what zeale, or authoritie foeuer they will; if the fruites of faith appeare not in their liues by obedience, they are not called of God, for the fpeciall good of his Church.

Thus much of thefe men in generall: now we come to entreate of them feuerally, as they are propounded in the Text.

THe firft perfon here commended vnto vs, is *Gedeon*: the Hiftory of whofe acts, is laid downe at large, Iudges 6. In his example note one point efpecially, to acquaint vs with the manner which God vfeth in begetting and encreafing true faith in the hearts of his children. If we read the Storie, we fhall fee, that the Lord, in the likeneffe of an Angel, called *Gedeon*, once, twice, yea thrice to be a Iudge to his peoole. But *Gedeon* greatly doubts of his calling; and therefore defires a figne of the *Lord*; which God gaue him: For, *the facrifice which he offered, was burned vp with fire from heauen*: yet ftill he doubted, and was in a greater feare then before, euen of death it felfe: but beeing confirmed by the Angel, and fet a woik, he brake downe the Altar of *Baall*, and built one to the true God, and thereon offered facrifice as God commanded, though with fome feare. And, when the *Midianites* and *Amalekites* came armed againft Ifrael, he is ftirred vp by the fpirit of God for their defence: but yet ftill he doubted of his calling, and therefore againe asked a figne at Gods hands, and had it; and after that asked another, which God alfo graunted. Now, hauing all thefe one in the necke of another, at length he knowes his calling, and fo goes in faith, and defends Ifrael: fo that he got the affurance of his calling, by fundry particular fignes and confirmations of his faith. And though he doubted greatly at the firft: yet, after hee beleeues, not onely that he fhould be a Iudge and Deliuerer of Gods people out of the hands of their enemies; but this principally, that God was his God, and would giue vnto him euerlafting life.

Here then we haue a notable precedent of the manner of Gods working true and found faith in the hearts of his children. They receiue not this grace at once, but, by degrees, God workes it in them by little and little. When a man is firft called of God, he hath much doubting & feare; but then God fends fundry helps to weaken this ftate and doubting: and as they decreafe, fo is faith increafed. No man beleeues foundly at the firft, but weakely; euen as he growes in yeares, fo he muft grow in faith: and the encreafe of our faith is by continuance in the meanes, and by the experience of Gods loue and fauour. And indeede the more faith encreafeth, the more we vfe the means to grow therein, and the more wee delight in the meanes; and at length, after long experience of

Gods

Iudg.6.12.
14.16.

Gods mercie, we shall haue wrought in our hearts this gift of true and liuely faith, which shall be able to preuaile against all feare and doubting. And thus much for the person of *Gedeon*.

The second person commended vnto vs, is *Barac*; of whom we may read, Iud. 4. His Storie is large and plaine enough: and therefore we will not stand vpon it.

The third person is *Samson*; of whom we may also reade Iudg. 13. 14. &c. Now touching *Samson*, this question may well be asked, how he can be iustly commended for his faith, seeing it may seeme he killed himselfe? *Ans.* *Samson* did not kill himselfe: for he was called extraordinarily to be a Iudge ouer *Israel* for their defence and deliuery out of the hands of the *Philistimes*. Now, when the Princes of the Philistimes were gathered together, beeing his enemies, and the enemies of God and his people, he cast the house downe vpon their heads to kill them therein, because (beeing blinde) he could not pursue them in battaile. And therefore hauing them by Gods prouidence in his hands, he destroyed them, as his calling was: albeit, he lost his life in the same action.

Againe, *Samson* in pulling down the house purposed not directly and wilfully to kill himselfe, but to aduenture his owne life, by taking iust reuenge vpon his enemies, and the enemies of God: and therefore as Gods seruant, he praied first vnto God: and so did no more then the Souldier in the field ought to doe: who, bearing a louing minde towards his Country, is content to aduenture his owne life for the destruction of his enemies, in the defence of his Country: and is resolued, that if he die in that defence, he dieth in his lawfull place and calling, and dieth Gods seruant, yea, Gods Champion. This did *Samson*, and therefore may iustly be commended for his faith: neither is this fact of his any disgrace, but rather a notable commendation of his faith, and an euidence of great zeale for Gods glorie, and of singular loue to his people.

The fourth person commended here, is *Iephte*, of whom we may reade, Iudg.11. *Iephte was the base sonne of Gilead, borne of an harlot*. To be base borne, is noted in Scripture as a matter of reproach: and therefore the Lord forbad *a bastard to enter into the congregation of the Lord, to beare any office, vnto the tenth generation*. Deut.23. 2. So ignominious is this kinde of birth, by the iudgement of Gods spirit, vnto that party on whom it falls. For, this sinne of fornication doth not onely hurt the persons committing it, but euen staines the children base born vnto the tenth generation. Yet howsoeuer *Iephte* was base borne, and so suffered for it great reproach: here we see, he is commended vnto vs for his faith, among the most worthie beleeuers that euer were. Indeede, besides *Iephte*, we shal not find the like example in Scrip-

ture. Yet in *Iephte* we may see, that howsoeuer it be a reproachfull thing, to be borne of fornication: yet that doth not hinder, but the party so borne, may come to true faith, and so to the fauour of God, and to life euerlasting. Such persons as are base borne, vpon view of that reproach, which the Scripture fasteneth vpon them, might take occasion to thinke miserably of themselues; euen that God hath reiected them: but, this example serues to shew, that it hindereth not, but that they may come into the fauour of God, and by faith get honour of God, to counteruaile that discredit, which they haue by their base birth.

Further, whereas we commonly say, that such as are base borne are wicked persons; here we see the contrary in *Iephte*: and therefore, we must not for this cause condemne any for wicked or vngodly. Indeede, the Lord hath branded this estate with reproach, that men should shunne the sinne of fornication the more.

Againe: whereas *Iephte* is here commended for his faith; we may probably gather, that their opinion is not true, who hold that *Iephte* sacrificed and killed his owne daughter. For, beeing commended here for his faith, certaine it is, he had knowledge in Gods will & word: and therefore, we must not thinke, but that he knewe, God would neuer accept of such a vowe; by the performance whereof, he should commit wilfull and most vnnaturall murder. This his faith shewes, that it was not his intent to kill the first person that met him out of his house; for, by the light of nature he might knowe, that God would neuer accept thereof: and therefore it is not like he so made his vow; for, this faith, and such a vow cannot stand together.

But some wil say, the text is plaine (Iudg.11. 31.) that *He vowed to offer for a burnt offering, the thing that came out of the doores of his house to meete him when he came home*. *Ans.* It is so indeede, in some traslations: *It shall be the Lords, (And) I will offer it, &c.* But the words, in the originall, may as well be translated thus: *It shall be the Lords, (or) I will offer it, &c.* And this latter translation is more sutable to the circumstances of the place; for, this was *Iephtes* meaning, that whatsoeuer met him first, he would *dedicate* it to God: and, if it were a thing that might be sacrificed, then his purpose was to offer it vnto the Lord in sacrifice.

Quest. But if he did not kill her, why did hee then so lament for her? *Ans.* Because, by his vowe, he was to dedicate her to God; and so shee was to liue a Nazarite all her life long: which must needs be a very bitter thing to him, who had no childe but her; it beeing so great a reproach, & in some sort, a curse in those daies, to want issue. I speake not here, how well or ill *Iephte* did in making her a Nazarite: But, this may no way bee admitted, That beleeuing and godly *Iephte* should aduisedly kill his owne daughter. Vndoubtedly, hee could not thinke,

that

that God would be pleaſed, with ſuch an abhominable ſacrifice. Thus much for theſe perſons:
the reſt, I paſſe ouer, becauſe this ſtory is plaine
and large in Scripture.

The Faith of the Iudges
and Dauid.

VERSE 33, 34, 35.

Which through faith ſub-
dued Kingdomes, wrought
righteouſneſſe, obtained the
promiſes, ſtopped the mouthes
of Lions,

Quenched the violence of
fire, eſcaped the edge of the
ſword, of weake were made
ſtrong, waxed valiant in bat-
tell, turned to flight the Ar-
mies of the Aliants.

The women receiued their
dead raiſed to life.

N theſe words, the Apoſtle
propounds vnto vs ten ſe-
uerall fruits of faith: the
nine firſt whereof, are the
particular actions of the
parties ſpoken of in the former verſe; and they are here
related for the commendation of their faith.
The firſt is, *Subduing of Kingdomes*; which
ſerues chiefly for the commendation of the
faith of the foure Iudges there named, and of
Dauid. For, as we may reade in the bookes of
Iudges, and of *Samuel,* all theſe *ſubdued King-*
domes; as, the *Canaanites*, Iudg. 4. the *Midi-*
anites, Iudg. 6. the *Philiſtims,* Iudg. 15. and
16. 2. Sam. 8. 1. the *Ammonites,* Iudg. 11.
Moabites, and *Aramites,* 2. Sam 8. 2. 6. Now,
how did they ouercome and ſubdue them? The
text ſaith, *by faith*; which, we muſt not thus
vnderſtand, as though onely by the very act
of faith they ſubdued kingdomes: But the meaning of the holy Ghoſt is, that they beleeued
the promiſes which God made vnto them, of
deliuering theſe kingdomes into their hands; and
according to their faith, God accompliſhed his

promiſes vnto them: and ſo they ſubdued Kingdomes by faith.

In this worke of faith, we may learne two
things: firſt, that it is lawfull for Chriſtians in
the newe Teſtament to make warre; for, that
which may be done in faith, is lawfull for Gods
ſeruants: but, warre may be made in faith; for,
theſe ſeruants of God, ſubdue kingdomes in
warre, and that by faith: and therefore it is
lawfull for Chriſtians, vpon iuſt cauſe to make
warre. The *Anabaptiſts* of Germany ſay, It
is not lawfull for a Chriſtian vnder the Goſpel
to carry a weapon, or to make warre. But, this
one place of Scripture (if there were no moe) is
alone ſufficient to prooue the lawfulneſſe of
warre vnder the Goſpel, if it be vſed according
to Gods will and word. When the *Souldiers*
came to *Iohn Baptiſt,* and asked him, *What they*
ſhould doe? he bids them not leaue off their calling; but this: *Doe violence to no man, neither*
accuſe any falſly, and be content with your wa-
ges, Luk. 3. 14. And our Sauiour Chriſt repor-
teth of a *Centurion* (which was captaine of a
Band) when he came to haue his ſonne healed;
that *hee had not found ſuch faith in Iſrael.* And
hee was not a Centurion, onely afore he beleeued; but euen afterward, when Chriſt commended his faith: yet did he not diſlike his calling. The like may bee ſaid of *Cornelius,* Act.
10. All which, ſhewe plainely, that vpon
iuſt cauſes, Chriſtians may lawefully make
warre.

Ob. 1. But to defend their opinion, they
obiect ſome places of Scripture; as Matth. 5.
39. *Reſiſt not euill ſaith Chriſt:* therefore (ſay
they) a man may not weare a weapon, nor vſe a
ſword; leaſt thoſe make him to reſiſt, and ſo to
breake this commandement of Chriſt. *Anſ.*
That place muſt bee vnderſtood of priuate reuenge: and ſo it maketh nothing againſt lawfull warre. For, what though a priuate man may
not reuenge himſelfe, nor make warre; yet that
hindereth not, but that a Magiſtrate who bears
the ſword, may lawefully vſe it. Againe, it is
friuolous to imagine, that reſiſting is onely by
a weapon; for, the chiefe reſiſtance that God
reſpecteth, is in the heart and affection. And a
priuate man may reſiſt; that is, breake this commandement, by vnlawfull reſiſtance, though he
carry no weapon: &, the publike perſon breake
it not, though he make warre.

Obiect. 2. Secondly, they obiect the prophecy of *Iſay,* who ſpeaking of the kingdome
of Chriſt, vnder the Goſpell, ſaith; *That then*
they ſhall turne their ſwords into ſcithes, and
their ſpeares into mattocks: therefore (ſay they)
there muſt be no warre vnder the Goſpel. *Anſ.*
That Prophecy ſignifies, that in Chriſts kingdome, there muſt bee great loue, and peace,
and wonderfull concord among all the true
ſeruants of God. But, here they take aduantage, and ſay; If this be ſo, what then needeth any warre? *Anſ.* We muſt know, that as
there be two kindes of Kingdomes, a ſpirituall
king-

Matth. 8. 3.

kingdome, and a politicke; so, there be two
kindes of peace, spirituall, and politicke. *Spiri-*
tuall peace, is inward, in the Church: and politicke peace, is outward, in the common wealth.
Spirituall peace, is begunne, and preserued by
spirituall meanes of grace in the ministery of
the Church; but warre is an ordinarie meanes
for the establishing and preseruing of politicke
peace.

Secondly, hence we learne, that Gods people may make warre, not onely by way of defence; but also, in assault vpon their enemies,
and that according to Gods word. For here it
is said, that *Gedeon, Samson, Dauid,* and the rest,
by *faith subdued Kingdoms*, making warre a-
gainst them by way of assault, and not in defence onely. Indeede, speciall care ought to be
had, that offensiue warre, in assaulting an enemie, bee made vpon iust and good grounds:
one speciall ground or cause is here implied
in this worke of faith; to wit, the recouery of
iust right in matters of importance: for, the
Kingdoms of Canaan were giuen to the Israelites by God himselfe, and for the recouery of
them, they made warre by way of assault. So,
when *Lot* was taken captiue by *Keder-laomer,*
and the Kings of the Nations; *Abraham, Lots*
kinsman, gathers his seruants together, and
pursues the Kings, and ouertaking them, destroyed them for the recouerie of *Lot* and his
goods. Other respects there be, for which offensiue warre in assault may bee made: but because they are not here mentioned, I will not
propound them.

The second fruite of their faith is this; they
wrought righteousnesse: that is, some of these
men in their places wherein God had set them,
gaue to euery man his owne. This *working of*
righteousnesse consists in two things; First, in
giuing rewards to such as deserued them. Secondly, in inflicting due punishment according
to mens deserts. In both these, the men before
named did all excell; but especially two of
them, *Dauid and Samuel.* For *Dauid,* it is a
wonder to see how *righteous* he was: for when
he was anointed King in *Sauls* stead, and *Saul*
reiected, how did he behaue himselfe towards
Saul? Did he seeke *Sauls* blood? No: But when
Saul hunted him, *as the hunter doth the Par-*
tridge; Dauid euen then gaue himselfe to *studie*
and practise righteousnesse: yea, when *Saul* was
fallen into his hands both in the *Caue* & *asleepe*
in the campe, 1.Sam. 24. 5, 6. &c. and 26.7,8.
hee would not touch him, nor suffer others to
doe him hurt, *because hee was the Lords an-*
nointed: yea, so righteous was *Dauid* towards
Saul, that *his heart smote him for cutting-off*
but the lappe of his coate. Therefore *Dauid* is
here commended especially, for this effect of
faith, *the working of righteousnesse.*

To applie this vnto our times: If this bee a
fruite of faith thus to *worke righteousnesse,* then
what may be said of the Church of Rome, and
of the Popish sort among vs? They pretend the

auncient faith, and none must bee so good beleeuers and Catholikes as they: but how doe
they shewe this their faith? Is it by the *practise*
of righteousnesse? Doe they giue to euery one
his due? Nay verily: but they set themselues to
worke the ruine of Kingdomes, that ioyne not
with them in religion. This, witnesse their manifold and deuillish plots against our state from
time to time. This did not *Dauid,* no not a-
gainst *Saul,* though he were reiected of God,
and also most vniustly sought his death. But
they haue many times sought the death of the
Lords anointed ouer vs: whereby they declare
their state to all the world, that they haue no
sparke of true faith, at all: for, true faith will
make a man practise righteousnesse and innocencie. And therefore we may iudge of them,
and all their adherents that be of this minde to
allow such practises, that they haue none other
but the faith of deuills: which is, to beleeue the
word of God to be true. This the deuils doe
with trembling. And as their *faith* is deuillish,
so are the *fruites* thereof: namely, treachery and
falshood, such as the deuil most approoues. But
wee must learne, that true faith is especially
commended by these fruites, The studie and
practise of innocencie, and the maintaining of
peace in Christian estates: for, true faith, and
treachery, and contention, will no more stand
together, then light and darknesse.

Secondly, *Samuel* also *wrought righteous-*
nesse; as appeareth by his protestation before all
Israel, when hée gaue vp his office of gouernment ouer them vnto *Saul,* 1.Sam. 12. 3: *Be-*
hold (saith he) *here am I: beare record of mee*
before the Lord, and before his anointed: whose
Oxe haue I taken? or whose Asse haue I taken?
or whome haue I done wrong to? or whom haue I
hurt? or of whose hand haue I receiued any
bribe, to blinde mine eyes therewith? and I will
restore it.

Now, as these two, *Samuel* and *Dauid* were
famous, for this fruit of faith in working righteousnesse: So likewise were the Iudges and
Prophets, before named, in their places carefull of this vertue: & did practise the same, partly in rewarding the good, and partly in punish-
ing the wicked.

But some will say; To worke righteousnesse,
cannot be a fruite of faith: for, the very Heathen, which neuer heard of Christ, by the light
of nature haue done Iustice, and are highly
commended by Heathen Writers, for the same.
Now, that which the Heathen can doe by the
light of nature, is not thus to be extolled as a
fruite of faith? *Ans.* True it is, the Heathen
haue done many works of iustice: but we must
wisely consider, that euery iust worke is not a
fruite of faith, vnlesse it be done by *a righteous*
person in obedience to God, and *for his glory.* But,
in all these, the Heathen failed in their workes.
For, though the things they did were good in
themselues: yet seeing the Heathen were corrupt trees, remaining in the sinnefull state of

Gen.14.

corrupt nature,their works muſt needes be corrupt fruite; as comming from them. For, an e-
uill tree cannot bring forth good fruite. The
heart is the fountaine of euery action: now,
their hearts were corrupt, beeing deſtitute of
faith which purifieth the heart: and therefore
their works muſt needes be ſinnefull. Againe,
they did not their works in obedience:for, they
were guided onely by the light of nature, and
knew not God aright, nor his cõmandements.
And laſtly,they propounded not the glorie of
God,as the end of their works,but the praiſe of
men, their owne profit, or ſome ſuch ende. But
theſe worthie perſons do not onely ſuch things
as were iuſt in themſelues: but they do them in
faith,in obedience, and for Gods glorie, and ſo
pleaſe God.

Now, ſeeing theſe renowned Princes and
Iudges,haue their faith commended vnto vs by
their practiſing of righteouſneſſe; we muſt
learne to followe them within the compaſſe of
our calling, doing Iuſtice and righteouſneſſe
in ſuch things as concerne vs. There be many
reaſons ſet down in Gods word,to perſwade vs
hereunto. As firſt, for this ende hath God cauſed the Goſpel to be publiſhed.Tit. 2.12. *The
ſauing grace of God hath appeared:* but to what
ende? *To teach vs, that we ſhould denie vngod-
lineſſe, and liue ſoberly and righteouſly:* that is,
that we might *doe Iuſtice.* Vnleſſe therefore we
worke righteouſneſſe, we make the Goſpel a
vaine word vnto vs. Secondly, we deſire to be
counted iuſt before God and men;and it would
grieue vs, if we ſhould be otherwiſe thought
of: but if we would be iuſt indeede both before
God and man, then we muſt worke righteouſneſſe: for(as S. *Iohn* ſaith) *He that doth righ-*
1.Ioh.3.7.
teouſneſſe is righteous: Thirdly, there is no man
ſet ouer a family, but he either doth, or ought
to endeauour to bring a bleſſing vpon his family. But this he cannot doe, vnleſſe he *worke
righteouſneſſe,* and doe Iuſtice: for, *Salomon*
Prov.20.7.
ſaith: *He that walketh in his integritie, is iuſt,
and bleſſed ſhall his children be after him.* Laſtly, we doe all of vs deſire to eſcape hell: well,
then we muſt remember to *practiſe righteouſneſſe;* for,the Apoſtle ſaith,*no vnrighteous man,*
1.Cor.6.9.
that is none practiſing vnrighteouſneſſe, *ſhall
enter into the kingdome of heauen.*So that within the compaſſe of our calling, we muſt all endeauour to doe Iuſtice.

Here ſome will aſke:How ſhall I do Iuſtice,
and worke righteouſneſſe? *Anſw.* For doing of
it, wee muſt remember to practiſe theſe rules
that followe: 1. That which is both the word
Matth.7.12.
of God, and the rule of Nature; *We muſt doe to
all men,as we would they ſhould doe vnto vs: this
is the Law and the Prophets*(ſaith our Sauiour
Chriſt.) Now, the ſquare for all our actions,
muſt bee the word of God: and Gods word
giues this direction: Do thou to thy neighbour
as thou in thy reaſon and conſcience thinkeſt
he ſhould do to thee, if thou wert in his caſe,&
he in thine.

A

The 2. rule,is that which *Paul* teacheth vs,
ſaying, *Giue vnto euery man that which is their
dutie: tribute to whom tribute belongeth,&c.*
Rom.13.7.
That which Gods word, and our conſcience,
and the wholeſome lawes of the realme binde
vs vnto, that we muſt giue vnto euery man.

The 3. rule is this: *Euery man within the
compaſſe of his calling, muſt not onely intend and
labour for his owne good; but for the common
good, in that Church & common wealth wherein he liueth.* The blinde would out of their carnall mindes, haue learned this for a rule, *Euery
man for himſelfe, and God for vs all:* and this
is many a mans practiſe, he wil labour diligently in his calling: but, all is for himſelfe. But, he
B
that propoundeth onely this end in his calling,
to benefit himſelfe alone, dealeth vniuſtly,both
towards the Church and common wealth, in
which he liueth; who ought to haue a part of
his care with himſelfe.

The 4. rule is taught vs alſo by S. *Paul: Defraud or oppreſſe no man in any matter.*This rule
concerneth our manner of dealing in common
affaires: In all our traffick and bargaines, as
we would benefit our ſelues; ſo we muſt ſeeke
to benefit thoſe with whom we deale.This rule
is very neceſſarie to be learned: for, this is the
common practiſe of men in their traffique, To
vſe all meanes whereby they may defraud o-
thers; ſo that they get vnto themſelues, they
care not how it come. But in the feare of God,
C
let vs remember, that the practiſe of iuſtice (to
which we are all bound) ſtandeth in this; that
we defraud or oppreſſe no man in any thing.
And thus much of this ſecond fruite of their
faith.

The third fruite and effect of theſe mens
faith, is this: *They obtained the promiſes.*]By
promiſes, we muſt not vnderſtand the maine
promiſe,concerning the *Meſſias* comming; for,
that they obtained not as yet: for,(as it appears
v. 39)*they receiued not that promiſe;* for, Chriſt
was not incarnate in their time. But,by*Promiſes* are here meant certaine ſpeciall and particular promiſes, made vnto them alone, and not
common to all: ſo that the meaning of theſe
words is this; *They obtained the benefit and accompliſhment of thoſe* particular promiſes that
D
God made vnto them.This effect is ſpecially to
be vnderſtood of *Caleb,* and *Dauid:* for, *Caleb*
entred into the Land of Canaan, and there enioyed his poſſeſſion, according to Gods promiſe made vnto him, Ioſ. 14. So, *Dauid* had
a particular promiſe made vnto him, that he
ſhould be king ouer Iſrael; this he long waited
for, and reſting herein,he was not onely anointed King, but in due time actually made King
ouer all Iſrael.

Whereas theſe worthie men, by *faith obtained theſe promiſes:*Hereby we may be directed,
to ſee the true cauſe, why after ſo long preaching of the word, and often receiuing of the
ſacraments, men reape ſo little profit; eſpecially, conſidering that God hath made a promiſe

of

of grace and saluation, by meanes of his word & sacraments. Hence therefore we must learne, that the word of God preached, and the sacraments receiued, are vnprofitable, not because God altereth his willh, auing promised his blessing in these meanes; for herein the will of God is vnchangeable; but the cause is, the great measure of vnbeleefe, in those which heare and receiue. They therefore profit not, because they receiue them without faith. For, howsoeuer men say they haue faith; yet the works of their liues, and their estate in sinne, after long hearing, shewe plainely, they haue none at all. Take a vessell that is close stopped, and cast it into a riuer, or into the sea; yet it receiues no water, because it hath no place of entrance: Euen so, bring a man that wants faith, to the word and sacraments, wherein, God hath promised the fulnesse, of his grace: yet he receiues none, because his heart is closed vp through vnbeleefe. This is it which makes the heart like a stopped vessell, which hath no entrance for Gods grace. We therefore, in the feare of God, must labour to haue, our hearts purged of this vnbeleefe and lip-faith, and to be endued with true sauing faith; whereby we may profitably heare the word, and receiue the sacraments, and so enioy Gods most excellent promises in Christ. Men may lie, and be deceiued; but God is truth it selfe, and cannot lie: and therefore, as he shah made his promise of life to beleeuers, and to no other: so wil he assuredly accomplish the same to them, and to no other. Wherefore if we loue our soules, and desire life, let vs get into our hearts the grace of faith. And thus much of the third effect of their faith.

The fourth and fift effects, which I will handle together, are these: *Stopped the mouthes of Lyons: Quenched the violence of the fire.*] For the fourth. Whereas some of these persons are said to haue stopped the mouthes of Lyons, it is to be vnderstood of *Daniel*; as appeareth in the 6. Chap. of that booke. For, *Daniel* (thorough the malice of others that incensed the Kings wrath against him) was cast into the den of hunger-bit Lyons. But, *Daniel* euen then beleeued in the Lord, and put all his trust in God, and for this cause, *the Lord by his angel stopped the mouthes of the Lyons,* & (as it were) sealed vp their pawes, that they could not hurt him.

The fift effect, in *quenching the violence of the fire,* must be vnderstood of *Shadrach, Meshac, and Abednego,* the companions of *Daniel:* which three (as we may reade, Dan. 3.) refused to worship the golden image, which *Nabuchadnezar* had set vp. For which cause, they were cast into an hot burning Ouen; but they put their trust in God, and claue fast vnto him in obedience, euen to the hazard of their liues. Whereupon, the Lord by his omnipotent power, did most miraculously preserue them, by staying the rage of the fire contrary to the nature thereof, that it had no power ouer their

bodies; nay, it did not burne the haire of their heads, nor cause their garments to smell. And therefore they are said, to *haue quenched the violence of it,* because it had no power ouer them, though it burned most fiercely; but was to them, as though it had beene quite put out and quenched.

Now, ioyne these two effects together, and they affoord vs good instructions. First, here we learne how to behaue our selues in time of danger, and at the point of death. Euen as these foure men did, so must we from the bottome of our hearts forsake our selues, and put all our trust in Christ. This did *Daniel,* when he was in the *Lyons den:* and this did the 3. *Children,* in the hot fiery furnace. And this hath beene alwaies the auncient practise of Gods children in all ages; At the very point of death, and in the extremitie of all danger, they rested themselues wholly vpon the mercifull promises of the true God. The time will come vpon vs all, wherein we shall be called to the practise of this duty: for, we must all passe the doore of death, and once lie in the pangs thereof. Now, what shall we doe when we lie halfe dead, gasping and panting for breath, able to speake to no man, not to heare any speaking vnto vs, when all comfort of the world failes vs? Surely, we must then, at that very instant, labour to leaue our selues and this world, and yeeld vp our selues by faith into the hands of God, and cleaue fast vnto Christs Passion, from the bottome of our hearts, and he will surely deliuer vs from the danger; stopping the mouth of Satan that roaring Lion, and quenching the fire of hell, that it shall not touch vs.

But some will say, if this be all we must doe, then all is well; for, this I can soone doe when time serues, and therefore I will take no care till then? *Ans.* Beware of spirituall guile; for, it will be found a most hard matter, for a man to relie and cast himselfe wholly vpon Christ, in the houre and pang of death. For, then aboue all times, is the deuill busie against vs: then will the conscience stirre, if euer; and the body beeng tormented, the soule must needes be wonderfull heauie. This we may see by the state of our Sauiour Christ, in his agony and passion; and therefore we must not reckon so lightly of this dutie.

Quest. But, if it be so hard a thing, how could *Daniel* and the three children doe it? *Ans.* They were prepared for it: for, they rested vpon God in the time of peace: and so were enabled to relie vpon him in time of perill. Euen so, if we would beleeue in God when we die, and then shewe forth our faith, we must while we liue put our trust in him, and shewe it by obedience: for rare it is to finde a man that liues in vnbeleefe, to shewe forth faith at his ende. And therefore while we haue health, strength, and peace, we must labour to beleeue, and then shall we find the comfort of it in time of perill, and of death.

Secondly, from thefe two effects of faith, wee obferue further, that Gods diuine prouidence doth firmely rule and gouerne the whole world. Ordinarily God gouernes the world by fecondarie caufes, fetting one creature ouer another, and ordaining one to doe this thing, and another that, and accordingly they worke: but we muft not thinke that God is bound to any of thefe meanes, but is moft free to vfe thē, or not to vfe them. Ordinarily hee executeth this or that punifhment by this or that creature, and fo by meanes conuayes his bleffings: but yet he can worke without them, as here we fee. For, he preferues his creatures againft the ordinarie meanes; as, *Daniel* from the Lions, whofe nature is to deuoure: and againft the nature of fire, hee faued *the three children* in the fire. So that God worketh by meanes, but yet freely; becaufe he can worke at his pleafure either without or againft meanes: and his powerfull hand, fauing againft meanes, fhewes his ruling and difpofing prouidence ouer all things.

Thirdly, by thefe effects of their faith we learne, that Gods goodneffe and mercy towards beleeuers, is farre greater, and more vnfpeakeable then euer hee promifed, or they could expect. This point is carefully to bee confidered of vs all; for, it is of fingular and extraordinarie vfe, efpecially in time of perill and trouble: and yet wee fee it is the plaine truth of God; and therefore *Paul* giues thanks and praife vnto God, *who is able to doe for vs* Eph. 3. 20. *exceeding aboundantly aboue all that we aske or thinke*. *Daniel* put his truft in the Lord, when he was in the Lions den: and what doth he obtaine for his labour? the Lord neuer promifed to ftop the Lions mouthes, neither did *Daniell* euer prefume vpon that deliuerance; and yet the Lord faued him. And fo the three children, though they made no account of their liues, becaufe God had not promifed to keepe them from burning, yet they come out in fafety. For, God in mercie fo quenched the heat of the fire vnto them, that though it burnt to death thofe that caft them in; yet did it not fo much as burne their garments, or the hair of their heads, to caufe the fame to fmell. And the like is his goodneffe towards all his feruants. *Dauid* Pfal. 21. 3. faith, *The Lord preuented him with liberall bleffings*, that is, when *Dauid* neuer asked fuch bleffings at Gods hand, euen then did the Lord beftowe his liberall bleffings vpon him: as namely this, when *Dauid* was *following his Fathers fheepe*, and walking in his calling, hee neuer dreamed of any Kingdom: yet thence the Lord tooke him to be King ouer his people Ifrael. So the Ifraelites hauing beene 70. yeares in captiuity, neuer thought of returne; and yet then were they deliuered: and their deliuerance was fo ftrange and miraculous, that they *were like them that dreame*, Pfal. 126. 1. When Act. 12. 4. *Peter* was caft into prifon by *Herod*, and committed to foure quaternions of Souldiers to be kept, the Angel of the Lord came and awoke him as he flept, and ledde him out of prifon, paft the watches, and through the iron gate, and then left him. Now, this deliuerance was fo ftrange vnto him, *that he knewe not whether it was true, but thought he had feene a vifion*. From hence it is that God hath made this gracious promife vnto his Church, *to anfwer before they call, and to heare while they fpeake*, Ifay 65. 24. So endleffe is his mercie, and his goodneffe fo vnfpeakeable towards his feruants, that if they cleaue vnto him vnfainedly, they fhall finde his bounty farre furpaffing all that they could aske or thinke.

The confideration hereof ferues to ftirre vp euery one of vs in our places, to cleaue vnfainedly vnto the true God, with all our hearts by faith, in due reuerence and obedience. If a feruant were to choofe his Mafter, and among an hundred fhould heare of one, that befides his wages, would giue vnto his feruants, gifts which they would not thinke of; this feruant would forfake al the reft to come vnto this one. Behold, the Lord our god is this bountiful mafter: who doth not onely keepe couenant with his feruants, in a full accomplifhment of his promifes; but is exceeding gracious, preuenting them with liberall bleffings, aboue all that they can wifh for themfelues: wherefore let vs forfake all our bad Mafters, the world, the flefh, and the deuill, in the feruice of finne; and refigne our felues with full purpofe of heart, to ferue this our good God, to the ende of our dayes. There is no man liuing, that can haue fuch true ioy in heart, as Gods feruants haue; for, God fhewes more kindneffe vnto them, then they can aske or thinke of. And take this for truth alfo: there be none that thus giue thēfelues to ferue God faithfully with all their hearts, but before they die they fhall finde this to be true, that God is a moft mercifull God, and his goodnes endleffe towards them aboue their deferts.

Secondly, this endleffe mercie of God, muft mooue vs all to repent vs of our finnes, and to truft in him for the pardō of thē, be they neuer fo many or haynous: for, they cā neuer reach to the multitude of his mercies. Though they be in number like the fand of the fea, they muft not difmay vs from comming vnto him: but confidering that his goodneffe is endleffe, and his mercie is ouer all his workes, we muft come vnto him for the pardon of our finnes. For, God is mercifull to performe his promife; yea, & beyond his promife, to doe for vs more then we can thinke of. Many indeede abufe this mercie of God, by prefuming thereon to goe on in finne: but fuch deceiue themfelues: *For, God will not be mercifull vnto them*, Deut. 29. 20. It is the penitent perfon that fhall finde mercie.

The fixt effect of their faith, is in thefe words: *Efcaped the edge of the fword*. The words in the originall, are thus: *Efcaped the mouth of the fword*: which is the Hebrewe phrafe in the olde

Tefta-

Testament, and here followed by the Pen-man of this Epistle:& before, where he calleth the word of God *a two mouthed sword*,Heb. 4. 12: hereby meaning (as it is translated) *a two edged sword*. This effect must be vnderstood of two worthy Prophets, *Elias* and *Elizeus*: for *Elias*, wee may reade, that when he had slaine *Baals* Priests (1. Kings 19. 1.) *Iezabel* the Queene threatned to kill him : which he hea-ring, fled into the wildernesse , and thence was led to Mount *Horeb*,& there escaped by means of his faith. And for *Elizeus*,we may reade,that when he disclosed the King of *Syriah* his coun-sell to the King of *Israel* (2. Kings 6.) hee was compassed about in *Dathan*, the city where he lay, with a huge hoast of *Assyrians*; but, pray-ing to the Lord, the Lord smote the hoast with blindnesse , and so the Prophet led them in safetie to *Samaria*.So then, the meaning of this effect, is,that when these seruants of God were in distresse , and danger of death , they denied themselues, and their owne helpe, and by faith relied vpon God vnfainedly,from the bottom of their hearts ; and so found deliuerance with God, from the perill of death.

First, here we learne, that God prouides for the safetie and deliuerance of his seruants , in the extremitie of perill and danger, when both might and multitude are against them. This point we haue touched in diuers examples be-fore,and therefore doe here onely name it.

Secondly, in that these men in the extremity of danger beleeued , and so *escaped the edge of the sword*; we learne,that when we are in grea-test danger,so as we see no way to escape;euen then we must put our trust in the true God,and he will saue vs. This wee must doe , not onely for the safety of our bodie; but more especially, for the saluation of our soule. Put the case a man were in despaire of his saluation, and that he sees *legions of deuils* compassing him about to take him away : what must this man doe in this case? *Ans.* Looke what *Elias* and *Elizeus* did, the same thing must he doe ; he must not lie dead in desperation, yielding thereto: but, at the very same time , when such terrors op-presse him, he must by faith list vp his heart to God,and put his trust and confidence in him, thorough Christ. And, if he can this doe, hee may assure himselfe, that he shall certainely es-cape these fearefull terrors of conscience , and the torments of hell, as *Elias* and *Elizeus* did the edge of the sword: for, let a man put his whole trust in God,& whatsoeuer his troubles bee, God will deliuer him. *Great are the trou-bles of the righteous : but the Lord deliuers him out of them all*, Psal. 34. 19. Indeede,we must not limit God, for time , or manner of deliue-rance; but, waite on God by faith , accounting his grace sufficient, till deliuerance come. And thus much of the sixt effect.

The seauenth effect of their faith is this: *Of weake were made strong*. Or thus: *Of weake were restored to health*. This must bee vnder-

stood of *Hezekias.*, a worthy king of Iuda, who (as wee may reade, 2.Kings 20.) beeing sore sicke , euen vnto death, was restored to health, and obtained of God the lengthning of his daies,for the space of fifteene yeares.Which wonderfull recouery,he obtained by meanes of his faith, which he shewed in time of his sick-nesse, by a prayer he made vnto God; the sub-stance whereof,stood in these two things:First, beeing very sicke, hee praied for the pardon of his sinnes. This appeareth by his thanksgiuing, vpon his recouery, Isay 38. 17. where he con-fesseth, that *God had cast all his sinnes behinde his backe*,Now,looke for what he gaue thanks; that (no doubt) he had before begged of God in praier, Secondly, he made request vnto God for prolonging of his daies , for some reasons which did concerne himselfe: and this hee also prayed for in faith. Now, the reasons moouing him to pray for longer life, were these: First,he had then no issue to succeed him in his King-dome; and therefore hee praied for life, to be-get a childe , which might sit vpon his throne after him. And the ground of this praier was this : God had made a particular promise vnto *Dauid* and *Salomon*, 1. Kings 8. 25. *that they should not want issue after them, to sit vpon the Throne of Israel*,so that *their children took heed to their way,to walk before the lord,as Dauid did.* Now, King *Hezekiah*, knowing this promise, had regard hereunto: and, building himselfe hereon , his conscience bearing him witnesse, that hee had walked before the Lord vpright-ly, he praies for issue to succeed him : and, for that cause, hee desires strength of bodie, and length of daies. This appeareth notably by his praier, 2. King. 20.3. *Lord* (saith he) *I beseech thee now remember how I haue walked before thee in truth , and with a perfect heart.* The summe of his prayer is this: All the kings suc-ceeding *Dauid* and *Salomon*, which walke in Gods commandements, shall haue issue to sit on their thrones after them.Now, from hence he praies thus : *Oh Lord, I haue walked before thee, in truth and sincerity of heart :* and here-upon the conclusion followes,*grant me issue to sit vpon my throne after me*; and therefore , life and health to accomplish the same.

Secondly, hee praied that he might liue to glorifie God, in that weighty calling, wherein God had placed him ouer his people. This ap-peareth likewise, by his thanksgiuing vnto the Lord, vpon his recouerie: where he saith , Isay 38. 20. *The Lord was ready to saue me : there-fore wee will sing my song all the daies of our life in the house of the Lord.* Thus by his worthy prayer, hee shewed forth his faith notably : by vertue whereof, beeing sicke vnto death , hee obtained of the Lord, the prolonging of his daies,for the space of fifteene yeares.And,so we see, to whom this seauenth effect of faith is to be referred.

Here we are taught a speciall dutie , for the recouery of our health, in the time of sickenes:

to wit, before we vfe the ordinarie meanes of Phyficke, we muft (according to this example) firft put our faith in practife, by humbling our felues for our finnes paft, confeffing them truly vnto God, and praying for pardon, from a refolute purpofe of heart, to lead a new life; and also, by intreating health of God, and his good bleffing vpon the meanes which we fhall vfe for our recouerie. Thus haue other of Gods feruants done, befide *Hezekias.* When *Dauid* was grieuously ficke, the principall thing he did, was this practife of faith; in humbling his foule before God for his finnes, and intreating earneftly the pardon of them, as we may fee, Pfalm. 6. and 38. This is the principall thing, which in thofe Pfalmes is propounded of *Dauid.* And fo the Apoftle counfells, Iam. 5. 14, 15. *Is any man ficke among you? let him call for the Elders of the Church:* and what muft they doe? furely, firft pray for him; and then (as the cuftome was in thofe daies) *anoint him with oyle, in the name of the Lord.* And the praier of faith fhall faue the ficke, and the Lord fhall raife him vp againe: and if he haue committed any finne, it fhall be forgiuen him.* And here we muft be admonifhed, to beware of the bad practifes of the world, in this cafe: the moft men in their fickneffe, firft feeke to the Phyfitians; and if that faile them, they fend for the Minifter. This was King *Afa* his practife, for which he is branded to all pofteritie, that *beeing difeafed in his feete, he fought vnto Phyfitians, and not vnto the Lord,* 2. Chron. 16. 12. though otherwife, he had good things in him, 1. King. 15. 14. And many doe farre worfe, who feeke to Witches and Inchanters, when they, or theirs are in diftreffe: but this is to forfake God, and to feeke helpe of the Deuill, like to *Ahaziah,* who fent to *Baalzebub the God of Ekron, to know of his recouerie, when he was ficke vpon a fall,* 2. King. 1. 2. This fhould be farre from all Gods children: for, as *Ahaziahs* fickneffe became deadly, through his fending to *Baalzebub;* fo vndoubtedly, many difeafes become incurable, by the bad and prepofterous dealing of the Patient, who either vfeth vnlawfull meanes, or lawfull meanes diforderly, or trufteth therein. We therefore, in this cafe, muft remember our dutie in the practife of faith, as *Hezekiah* did.

The eight fruit of faith, is this; *Waxed valiant in battell.* This effect may well be vnderftood of all the *Iudges* before named, and of all the good Kings in Iuda and Ifrael. But yet there be two efpecially, to whom we may more peculiarly referre it: to wit, *Samfon,* and *Dauid.* For *Samfon,* he by meanes of faith, came to be fo mightie (Iudg. 15. 15.) that *with the iaw bone of an affe he flew a thoufand Philiftims.* And for *Dauid,* he likewife was fo incouraged by faith, that with the fame fling, wherewith he kept his fathers fheepe (which was but a flender weapon for warre) he encountred with *Goliah* that huge Philiftim, and hit him with a ftone in the forehead, and flew him. Both thefe facts, were the fruits of their faith, which made them bold to encounter with thefe mightie enemies.

In this effect of their faith, firft, we may obferue, that true fortitude and manhood, right valour and courage, comes from true faith. It muft be graunted, that many heathen men had great ftrength and courage; but indeede, it was but a fhadowe of true valour; for right valour comes from a beleeuing heart. And, therefore it is faid, that thefe Iudges & Princes of Ifrael, *waxed ftrong in battell by faith.*

Secondly, Doth true faith make men valiant in battell? Then fhould the preaching of the word, be fet vp, and maintained, as well in the Campe, and Garifon, and among Souldiers on the Seas, as in Cities and Townes of peace. For, the preaching of the word is the meanes of this faith which giues valour in battell, to them that fight in a good caufe.

Hence it was, that the Lord enioyned by *Mofes,* that when the people of Ifrael went out to battell, *the Priefts fhould come forth, and incourage the people, that their hearts might not faint, nor feare, nor dread their enemies; becaufe of the powerfull prefence of God fighting for them.* The Papifts obiect this (by way of reproach) againft *Zwinglius,* who was one of the reftorers of the Gofpel: That he died in the fielde among Souldiers: But, this indeede is no reproach, but rather a matter of great commendation vnto him: in that, for the increafe of faith and knowledge, in them that were weake Chriftians about him, he was content to hazard his owne life. And thus much of the eight effect.

The ninth effect of faith, for which thefe worthy men are commended, is this; *They turned to flight the Armies of the Alients.* This may be vnderftood of the moft of the *Iudges,* and of the good *Kings* of Iuda and Ifrael. But I will make choyfe, efpecially of two, *Gedion,* and *Iehofaphat:* for, *Gedeon,* one of the Iudges, *with three hundred Souldiers* (Iudg. 6. 7.) altogether vnweaponed, onely *with light pitchers in their hands,* put to flight a mighty huge Armie of the *Midianites.* And *Iehofaphat* a godly King, beeing affaulted with a mighty and great Armie of Moabites, Ammonites, and men of mount Seir, knewe that by force of armes hee could not withftand them; and therefore by faith makes a worthy prayer vnto the Lord, and the Lord heard him, and fet his enemies one againft another, and fo did he put them to flight: which he could neuer haue done by any ftrength of his owne.

Here we may learne, how Kingdomes and people may become able to put to flight their enemies. The beft way is, to put in practife their faith in God; by humbling themfelues truly for their finnes paft, with vnfained confeffion of them vnto God, praying withall earneftly for the pardon of them; and for Gods aide, affiftance, and protection againft their

Deut. 10. 2, 3.

enemies. The power of this meanes is euident in Scripture : and therefore when *Eliah* was taken vp, *Elisha* cried, *My Father, my Father, the Chariot of Israel, and the horsemen thereof*, 2. King. 2. 12. giuing him this notable commendation, that he was as good to Israel, by meanes of his faith, as all their chariots and horsemen. *Quest.* How could that possibly be true? *Ans.* If we read the Storie, we shall finde it to be most true, that by his prayers which he made in faith, he did as much or more then all the strength of the land could doe. And so it shall be with all Christian Kings and people : if they can shew forth their faith, by praier vnto God, they shall doe wonderfull much hereby, in subduing of their enemies.

To applie this to our selues : We haue had many and dangerous assaults from Popish enemies, both domesticall and forraine, who haue of long time, and no doubt still doe purpose our ouerthrow. Now, how shall we be able to withstand their might, and to escape their malice? True it is, Christian policie, and warrelike prouision must be vsed : yet our stay and rest must not be thereon ; but we must stirre vp our faith, both Magistrates and Subiects, Prince and people : and first of all humble our selues for our sinnes, and shew forth our repentance by new obedience in time to come ; and then pray for a blessing vpon the outward meanes which shall be vsed. This is the right practise of faith, in the case of daunger by our enemies ; which we shall finde (if we exercise it vnfainedly) to be a surer meanes of safetie and victorie against our enemies, then all worldly munition and policie. For hereby we shall haue the Lord for our protection, and his blessing vpon the outward meanes, giuing strength and good successe thereunto ; when as, omitting this dutie, the Lord will not be with vs, and then we shall finde that vaine is the strength or wit of man. Let vs not therefore betray our selues wilfully into our enemies hand ; but by this practise of faith, enable our selues against all our enemies whatsoeuer : otherwise we may iustly feare to be deliuered into their hands, for a pray vnto their teeth. And therefore, if we loue our owne safetie, and the wel-fare of our Land, let vs practise this dutie : *For, the praier of faith auaileth much with God, if it be feruent* ; and therefore the Lord saith to *Moses*, when he fell downe before him, to turne backe the wrath that was broken in vpon the people, *Let me alone :* as though Moses had held, or bound the Lords hand by his praier, that he could not smite his people. And thus much for the ninth fruit of faith.

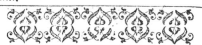

The faith of the widow and the Shunamite.

VERSE 35.

The women receiued their dead raised vp to life.

His is the tenth and last fruit of their faith, which must be vnderstood of these two women especially ; the *widow of Zarephath*, and the *Shunamite*. The *widow of Zarephath*, giuing entertainment to *Eliah* in the great famine, had this blessing vouchsafed vnto her for her faith, that her dead sonne was restored to life by the Prophet : And the *Shunamite* that prouided lodging for the Prophet *Elisha*, had her onely sonne restored to life from death by the Prophet through faith. Now here we must obserue, that these two women did not onely beleeue in the true God ; but more particularly, that God would vse these his seruants, as meanes to restore to life their two children that were dead : as appeares by this, that both of them made meanes to the Prophet, for the reuiuing of their children ; which they did, by faith.

But some will say, This last effect of faith, may seeme to crosse the Scripture else-where ; which saith, that *Christ is the first fruits of them that sleepe*. How then could these that were before Christs incarnation, be restored from death to life? *Answ.* Saint *Pauls* meaning is this ; that Christ is the first of all those that rose from death to life, to die no more, but to liue for euer. So, indeede, Christ is the first fruits of them that sleepe : for, he rose to liue for euer. As for these two, and some other, mentioned both in the old Testament and the new, that were raised from death to life, they rose not from the sleepe of death, to liue for euer, but to die againe.

In this tenth fruit of faith, all Parents may learne their dutie towards their children, in the case of sicknesse, or such like. They must follow the example of these two godly women, and labour especially to shew forth their faith in such duties as God requireth in such a case : to wit, they must humble themselues for their owne sinnes, and for the sinnes of their children and family ; praying earnestly to God for the pardon of them (for God may visit the iniquitie of the Parents vpon the children in bodily iudgements) and entreating the Lord to restore them to health and libertie : and withall, they must vse the ordinarie lawfull meanes of recouerie in physicke and such like, praying to God for a blessing thereupon.

This is their dutie ; but (alas!) the manner and practise of many Parents, is farre otherwise : for, whereas they should first seeke vnto the Lord, and come to his Prophet, they either runne first to the ordinarie meanes of physicke ; or, beeing worse disposed, seeke helpe of wizards and blessers by their charmes and sorceries forsaking God and running to the Deuill. Indeede, the vse of lawfull meanes is not to be discommended simply: but this preposterous course is blame-worthie, and depriues many of Gods blessing in the meanes, That they seeke helpe of Physicke, before they haue sought to the Lord, in this holy practise of faith.

Quest. But how can the parents faith benefit the childe? *Ans.* It cannot procure vnto it eternall life: for euery one must be saued by his owne faith in Christ. And, yet the childe receiues many a good blessing at Gods hand, by meanes of the Parents faith; as namely, the benefit of the couenant of grace in the seales thereof; besides the fruition of many temporall blessings, as life it selfe in this place.

The consideration hereof, must mooue all parents, aboue all things to labour for true faith: for, by the practise hereof, they shall be able to bring the greatest blessing vpon themselues, and their children, and vpon the lawfull meanes which they shall vse for their good. Say the Lord shall lay his hand vpon children and seruants in a family, what must parents and masters doe? Surely, the best way for helpe, is the practise of faith, in true humiliation for sinne, and prayer to God for mercie, and for a blessing vpon the meanes which they shall vse. In all societies this is true, that by the faith of the gouernours, many curses are remooued, and many blessings procured. God sends his iudgements among vs daily, and we know not when other moe shall befall vs: but, for the remoueall and preuenting of them, we must giue our selues to true humiliation and praier; and so shall we finde the Lords mercie towards vs, as these two women did.

And thus much of this tenth fruite of faith, and of them all seuerally.

Now, from them all ioyntly together, obserue this speciall point; *That faith is such a grace of God, as doth bring downe from heauen vpon euery beleeuer, all Gods blessings that are needefull for him:* Who is hee that desires not to be made partaker of Gods blessings needefull for him, both in soule and body? Well: the onely way and meanes hereto, is to get a true and a liuely faith, and to put the same in practise, in all such duties as God shall require at our hands. The worthie men before named, obtained all the former most wonderfull blessings, by meanes of their faith: *By it they escaped the edge of the sword, they quenched the violence of the fire, waxed mighty in battell, &c.* as we haue heard.

Now if faith be such a notable grace of God, then aboue all things in this world, let vs labour for it. We must not content our selues with lip-faith, and so presume vpon Gods mercies; but we must labour for a true and a liuely faith in Christ, which may purifie our hearts, and bring forth fruite in our liues. Here are strong motiues to perswade vs hereunto: for, what doe we desire? riches, honour, or fauour,

and grace in the world? would we haue health, and strength? nay, the fauour of God, which is all in all? then, looke to get true faith: for, in the practise thereof, thou shalt obtaine of God, all needefull blessing, both temporall and spirituall. Many toyle themselues exceedingly, by worldly meanes to get temporall blessings, as health, wealth, honour, &c. and yet neuer attaine thereto, because they seeke them not by faith. I confesse, naturall men get many good things: but to them they are no blessings: because they want faith both in getting, and keeping of them: for they lay all religion aside, and toyle themselues wholly in worldly means. This course the childe of God must beware of. Say, that a Prince bids one of seruants goe to his Treasurie, and there inrich himselfe with Iewels, with gold, and siluer, and with whatsoeuer he lacketh: what will this man doe? Surely, first he will call for the keyes, whereby he may vnlocke the doores and chests; for else he can get nothing. Behold, in the Ministerie of his word, God shewes vs his full treasury, wherein we may enrich our selues, with all his blessings: Now, we must not with the foole, runne without the key, but labour first, for true faith; which is that key, whereby Gods heauenly treasures are opened vnto vs: and, we must be sure that we haue a sound key; that is, a true and sound faith, which may strongly turn about the lockes of Gods treasury. For, this is most certaine, he that doth vnfainedly beleeue, shall neuer want any thing, either in body or soule, that is good for him to haue. Euery one will say, he beleeues; but the truth is, that true faith is rare: for mens hearts are not purified, nor their liues changed; but they remaine as sinnefull as euer they were, which causeth Gods indgements to be rife among vs. Wherefore, as we desire our owne good, both in soule and bodie; so let vs labour for true faith, and shewe forth the power of it in our liues. And thus much of these Iudges and Prophets, and of the fruits of their faith.

Beleeuers vnder the Maccabees.

Verse 35.

Others also were racked, and would not be deliuered, that they might receiue a better resurrection.

IN these words, the Author of this Epistle proceedes to the fourth order of Examples of faith, contained in this Chapter: wherein (as in the former lastly handled) he proceedes briefly, heaping vp in few words, many worthie examples of faith, concealing the names of the parties, and onely setting downe those things, for which their faith is commended vnto vs. And this fourth and last order of examples, comprehendeth such beleeuers as liued vnder the regiment of the Maccabees, and afterward to the comming of Christ. For, of beleeuers in former times, it cannot be vnderstood, because there is a manifest distinction put betweene these beleeuers, and the former Iudges, Kings, and Prophets; in these words, *others also*: whereby it is plaine, that here he propounds examples of beleeuers different from those which he mentioned before. And it is also plaine, that these beleeuers liued before the comming of Christ. For, howsoeuer the Christians in the primitiue Church, were racked, scourged, and tormented after this sort; yet of them this place cannot be vnderstood, because they enioyed *the promise of the Messias*: but, these here mentioned, enioyed *not that promise in their daies*, but waited for it by faith, and therein died, v.39. And indeede, in the time of the Maccabees, the Church of the Iewes was wonderfully persecuted by *Antiochus*, about two hundred yeares before Christ; as we may see, 2.Maccab.4.and 6.chapters.

Quest. Where had the Author of this Epistle this large narration of these strange persecutions, seeing they are not registred in the bookes of the old Testament?

Ans. We may iudge, that he gathered it out of the Stories and Records of men: which (howsoeuer they be not now extant) yet in his daies in the primitiue Church were extant, knowne, and approoued. Neither must this seeme strange vnto vs: for, the spirit of God, in the olde Testament speaking of men, hath oftentimes reference and relation therein to humane writings; as this phrase (*The rest of the acts of such and such, are they not written in the bookes of the Chronicles of the Kings of Iudah and Israel*) so often vsed in the bookes of Kings and Chronicles, doth euidently declare.

Now, those *bookes of Chronicles*, were not parcells of holy Scripture, but ciuill or Ecclesiasticall Stories, like to our bookes of Martyrs and Chronicles. 2.Tim.3.8. S. *Paul* saith, *Iannes and Iambres resisted Moses*. Now, in the booke of *Exodus*, we shall not finde the Sorcerers that withstood *Moses*, once named. And S. *Iude* maketh mention of a *prophecie of Enoch*, v.14. which in all the old Testament is not recorded: and it is like, that Moses was the first penne-man of holy Scripture. Whence then had these Apostles these things? *Answ.* No doubt, the holy Ghost might reueale such things vnto them, though they had beene vn-

knowne in those times: but it is more probable, that the Apostles had them out of some Iewish writers, or records then extant, and approoued among the Iewes. So *Paul*, preaching to the Athenians, alleadgeth the saying of *Aratus* an Athenian Poet: *For, we are his generation*. And to the Corinthians, he propoundeth a sentence of *Menander*; *Euill words corrupt good manners*, 1.Cor.15. And to *Titus*, he alleadgeth *Epimenides*, a Cretian poet; *The Cretians are alwaies liers, euill beasts, slow bellies*, Tit.1.12.

Now whereas the spirit of God taketh these sentences out of the writings of men; we may learne, that to read the writings of men is not vnlawfull, but a thing of good vse to the seruants of God. But whereas some would hence prooue, that their authoritie may be alleadged ordinarily at euery mans pleasure in the publike ministerie, it hath no ground in these places. For, first, the Apostles were so guided by the holy Ghost in their publike Ministerie, that they could not erre: but no Ministers at this day haue such a priuiledge. Secondly, the Apostles, alleadging or recording the sayings of men, in their Sermons or writings, did thereby sanctifie them, and make them to become a part of holy Scripture. This, no ordinarie Minister can doe: but let him alleadge a humane testimonie tenne thousand times, yet still it remaines humane, and is not Gods word. Thirdly, they that would warrant their practise, in alleadging humane testimonies in their sermons, by the Apostles, ought to follow the Apostles in their manner of allegations. Now, the Apostles were so sparing herein, that in many bookes we shall not finde one: for, there are onely three, in all the new Testament. Againe, the Apostles did it without ostentation: for, the names of the Authors are concealed, whence they tooke their testimonies.

And lastly, the Apostles did it vpon weightie cause and iust occasion; to wit, when they were perswaded in conscience, that those testimonies would conuince the consciences of their hearers in those things for which they alleadged them. Now, how farre many differ from the Apostles in their allegations, let the world iudge.

Yet before we come to speake of these examples of faith in particular, there are sundrie generall points to be handled. In the three former verses, the spirit of God hath set downe the prosperous successe of beleeuers, through faith: But here he comes to acquaint vs with a different estate of other beleeuers, vnder grieuous persecutions and torments, euen vnto most cruell and bitter kinds of death.

From this which the Apostle here obserueth, we may take a view of the state of Gods Church and people here in this world. For, God vouchsafeth peace, and prosperous successe to some, as a iust reward of faith and obedience: but others must want the comfort of

outward peace and welfare, and vndergoe
most grieuous trials and persecutions. Looke,
as there is a continuall interchange betweene
day and night, and the one doth constantly
followe the other, so as it is one while day, and
another while night: so is it with the Church
of God, and with true beleeuers in this world;
sometime they haue peace and prosperitie; and
this continueth not alway: but another while
they are in trouble, miserie, and persecution.

To make this point more plaine, because it
is of some importance; we may behold the
truth of it, in the Church of God from the beginning. *Adams* familie was Gods Church, and
therein was first notable peace: but when God
accepted *Abels* sacrifice, and refused *Caines*,
then persecution began, and *Cain* slew his brother *Abell*. *Abraham* is called the Father of the
faithfull, and his familie in those dayes, was the
true Church of God; wherein, we may notably
see this changeable estate: for, God calls him
out of *Charran*, to dwell in the land of Canaan,
Exod. 12. 1. 10. But, within a while, the familie was so great in the Land, that he was faine
to goe downe into Egypt, to soiourne there.
And, there the Lord blessed him exceedingly,
and enriched him so greatly, that he became
a mighty Prince, able to encounter with the
Kings of those nations in battell, after his returne to Canaan, Exod. 14.

The Israelites, Gods chosen people, were
400. yeare in bondage in Egypt; but, at the appointed time God gaue them a glorious deliuerance: and, yet they were tried in the wildernesse 40. yeares; after which time, they were
planted safely in the fruitefull Land of Canaan,
a Land that flowed with milke and hony. And
there also, the Church of God was in this case;
sometime in prosperitie, and otherwhiles in aduersitie; for, when it was ruled by Iudges (as in
that booke appeares) for ten, twenty, thirty,
or fourty yeares together, the Israelites for their
sinnes, were in subiection and bondage to the
nations round about them; as the *Moabites*, the
Philistims, the *Ammonites*, &c. Yet then, when
they cried to God, he sent them some mighty
Iudge to deliuer them, for so long time againe.
This was the interchangeable estate of the
Church, all the time of the *Iudges*. And afterward, when it was gouerned by Kings, it was
in the same case: for, one while God gaue them
good Kings, who would aduance religion, and
maintaine and cherish the Priests and Prophets
of God; and for their time the Church prospered. But otherwhiles, for their sinnes, God
would send them wicked Princes; which persecuted the Prophets, and the godly in the Land.
This is plaine in the bookes of the Kings and
Chronicles. After the raigne of good king *Iosias*, came the captiuity into Babylon, and 70.
yeares expired, the Lord by K. *Cyrus* returned
them againe. After their returne, they were one
while in peace, and another while in distresse:
as we may see in the bookes of *Ezra* and *Ne-*

hemias: but, aboue all other, that persecution
of *Antiochus Epiphanes*, was most notorious,
which was foretold by *Daniel* in his Prophecie,
Dan. 11. 36. and is recorded in the books of the
Maccabees.

To come to the time of the Gospel: The
Primitiue Church, after the ascension of Christ,
in the first 360. yeares, suffered ten most bloody and grieuous persecutions: betwixt each of
which, she had some times of peace, and (as it
were) respite to breath in. And, after the tenth
persecution ended, the Lord raised vp the good
Emperour *Constantine*; who brought peace, and
welfare vnto the Church. But, soone after him,
the heresie of *Arrius*, raised vp by the deuill,
brought as grieuous persecutiōs on the church,
as euer the Pagans did; beeing a most blasphe-
mous heresie, denying the eternall deity of
Christ, and of the holy Ghost: and, it preuailed
in the Church for 80. yeares. Not long after the
suppression of that heresie, began the idolatry
and tyrannie of *Antichrist* to preuaile in the
Church, for many hundred yeares. And nowe,
about some fourescore yeares agone, the Lord
in mercie raised vp worthie instruments, by
whose meanes he deliuered his Church from
that idolatry and blindenesse: yet so, as still the
Church hath felt the bloody hand of *Antichrist*
in grieuous persecutions. All which, shewes
this to be most true: that the outward state of
Gods Church, is interchangeable, hauing one
while peace, and another while grieuous persecution.

To apply this to our selues: God hath planted his Church among vs in this land, and for
many years together, hath blessed vs with prosperitie and peace; which, in great mercie he
hath giuen vs as a reward of the faith of his
seruants which are among vs: and, during this
time, we haue had great freedome and liberty
in Gods holy ministery, for the word, praier,
and sacraments. But, we must know, that the
state of Gods Church, for peace and trouble is
interchangeable, as day and night, for light and
darkenesse. Wherefore we must be aduertised,
to looke vnto our selues: for our estate in peace
must not last alwaies, these golden dayes will
haue an ende, and troubles and afflictions will
vndoubtedly come. Indeed, God onely knoweth, what kinde of afflictions shall befall, and
the particular time thereof: but that they shall
come in the time appointed of God, wee
may resolue our selues by the reasons following.

First, the tenour of the Law, is this; that
the curse doth followe the transgression: so that
when any man, or family, or people, liue in the
breach of Gods commandements, they must
looke for Gods iudgements to be powred vpon them. Now, we may too truely assume,
that this our nation and people abound with
grieuous sinne in all estates: For, in the ciuill e-
state (to omit the manifold practises of oppressi-
on) Where is iustice without bribery? or bargai-

ning,

ning,without fraud and deceit ? And in the miniſterie (beſide many abuſes) where is that care
which ought to be for the building of Gods
Church ? And for the bodie of our people(beſide groſſe ignorance, and ſuperſtition) what
fearefull blaſphemie, whoredome, ſwearing,
and Sabbath-breaking, doth euery where a-
bound ? beſide fearefull Atheiſme, which is a
mother of abhominations : whether we reſpect
naturall Atheiſme, whereby many denie God
by their works ; or., learned Atheiſme in ſome,
who diſpute againſt the truth of God, reuealed
in his word. All theſe, and many other ſinnes a-
mong vs, crie loud for Gods iudgements vpon
vs ; euen for that fearefull iudgement, the re-
mooueall of Gods kingdome in the Goſpel of
peace.

Secondly, conſider what manner of perſons
of place, and note, both in Church and Commonwealth, God takes from vs by death, euen
in their beſt time : are they not ſuch as excelled
among vs,for great wiſdome and learning, and
for true pietie and good conſcience? now,how-
ſoeuer this may ſeeme but a ſmall thing in the
eyes of many ; yet vndoubtedly,it is a forerunner of Gods iudgements : for *the righteous periſh,and no man conſidereth it in heart;and mercifull men are taken away,and no man vnder-
ſtandeth that the righteous is taken away from
the euill to come,*Iſa.57.1.

Thirdly, God hath ſent his fearefull iudgements among vs,and about vs,warre and ſword
in our neighbour nations; which alſo hath been
oft ſhaken at vs : alſo, famine and peſtilence
throughout our owne Land, by intercourſe
and long continuance, Leuit.26. Now this is
the truth of god,that,*when God ſends his iudgements vpon a people ; if they doe not repent, one
iudgement is but the forerunner of another more
grieuous and terrible then the former.* But,little
or no repentance appeares among vs ; nay rather, we fall away more and more, and ſo ſtand
ſtill in danger of more fearefull iudgements.

Laſtly, it is vſuall with God, thus to deale
with his owne ſeruants : as he doth ſometime
reward their faith and obedience with peace ;
ſo,otherwhiles he will trie their faith by affliction. Thus he dealt with his ſeruant *Iob*, though
there were none for pietie like him in his time,
through all the world. Now, God hath his ſeruants among vs:for the triall of whoſe faith,we
may perſwade our ſelues,ſome tribulation ſhall
come vpon vs ; *For, all that will liue godly in
Chriſt Ieſus ſhall ſuffer tribulation,*2.Tim.3.12.

This beeing ſo, that our peace ſhall be turned into trouble (as by the former reaſons,
which directly faſten themſelues vpon our
Church and ſtate,may euidently appeare)let vs
then here learne our dutie.

Firſt,we muſt caſt with our ſelues,what may
be the worſt that can befall vs, when triall and
perſecution ſhall come. This is the counſell of
our Sauiour Chriſt to thoſe that would follow
him conſtantly as good Diſciples : they muſt,as

good builders, conſider of the coſt, before they
lay the foundation; and,like *good warriers*,con-
ſider of their ſtrength, before they goe out into
the field, leaſt they leaue off ; and turne backe,
like fooles and cowards, Luk.14.28. &c. We
by Gods mercie doe now profeſſe the true religion of Chriſt, with hope to be ſaued thereby : therefore, we muſt caſt with our ſelues,
what our religion may coſt vs, and ſee before-
hand, what is the worſt thing that may befall
vs,for our profeſſion of Chriſt and his Goſpel.
If we haue not done this at the beginning of
our profeſſion,we muſt now doe it : for, better
late,then neuer : leaſt going on ſecurely, without this account making,we ſhamefully forſake
Chriſt when triall comes.

In former times, the conſtant profeſſion of
Chriſt, hath coſt men loſſe of friends, loſſe of
goods,and libertie ; yea,the loſſe of their hearts
blood:and the ſame caſe may befall vs. Wherefore,we muſt caſt with our ſelues, and ſee whether we be willing to ſuffer the loſſe of goods,
and friends ; yea, the loſſe of our liues, for the
defence of Chriſts true religion.

Againe, as this eſtate of the Church muſt
mooue vs to make this account, for reſolution
in ſufferings ; ſo it muſt teach vs to labour for
thoſe ſauing graces of Gods ſpirit, which may
inable vs to ſtand faſt in all temptations, troubles, and perſecutions. We muſt not content
our ſelues with blazing lamps, as the fiue fooliſh virgins did ; but get the oyle of grace into
the veſſels of our hearts. Knowledge in the
word, is a commendable thing ; but not ſufficient to make vs ſtand in the day of triall. We
therefore muſt labour for true ſauing graces; e-
ſpecially for this,to haue our hearts rooted and
grounded in the loue of God, through faith :
whereby we are aſſured, that God is our father
in Chriſt, and Ieſus Chriſt our Redeemer, and
the holy Ghoſt our comforter and ſanctifier.
This aſſurance of faith will ſtabliſh our hearts
in all eſtates: come life, come death, we neede
not feare ; for,nothing ſhall be able to ſeparate
vs from this loue of God in Chriſt Ieſus.

And thus much of the coherence of this
verſe with the former. Now to the words.

Others alſo were racked, &c. Here the holy
Ghoſt beginnes to propound the fruits of faith,
for which this laſt ranke of beleeuers are commended vnto vs. And they are not ſuch famous
exploits as the former, but *nine ſeuerall kinds
of ſufferings* ; vnto all which, we muſt remember to applie this clauſe *by faith*, from the 33.
verſe:as thus, *Through faith, they endured racking,mocking,* and ſo for all the reſt.

Out of theſe effects in generall, we may
learne two things: Firſt,a ſingular fruit of faith,
for which it is here ſo highly commended in
this laſt ranke of examples: to wit,that by it the
child of God is inabled to beare whatſoeuer
the Lord ſhall lay vpon him. The torments
wherewith mans bodie may be afflicted, are
many and terrible ; and yet, be they neuer

so many, nor so terrible, true sauing faith will make the child of God to beare them all for the honour of Christ.

The effects of faith before set downe, were many and singular: but vndoubtedly, this strength of patience, which it giueth vnder the greatest torments for Christs sake, is one of the principall.

This, Paul doth notably testifie in this profession, (Rom. 8. 38,39.) *I am perswaded, that neither death,nor life, nor Angels, nor principalities, nor powers ; nor things present; nor things to come ; nor height, nor depth , nor any other creature , shall be able to separate vs from the loue of God, which is in Christ Iesus our Lord.* Oh singular power of faith! which so firmely vnites the beleeuer vnto Christ, that no torments in the world , no not all the power of Satan , and his angels , can separate them asunder.

Quest. How doth faith worke this indissoluble power in cleauing vnto Christ? *Ans.* After this manner : It is the propertie of faith, to perswade the conscience, of Gods loue and fauour in Christ : and vpon this perswasion, the heart beginnes to loue God againe. Now, by this *loue* doth faith worke, and make a man able to beare all torments that can be inflicted for religions sake : for, *Loue suffereth all things,* 1. Cor. 13. 7. euen that loue wherewith one man loueth another:how much more then shal this loue wherewith we loue God in Christ, make vs to suffer any thing for his names sake? Hence it is,that *loue is said to be strong as death: and the coales thereof are fierie coales,and a vehement flame : yea , much water cannot quench loue, neither can the floods drowne it :* that is, grieuous persecutions and torments cannot extinguish the same. Nay, such is the power of loue to God when it is feruent, that it makes a man so zealous of Gods glorie, that if there were no other way to glorifie God, then by sufferings ; the childe of God would rather yeeld himselfe to endure the torments of the damned , then suffer God to lose his glorie. This we may see in *Paul,*Rom. 9. 3. *I would wish my selfe*(faith he)*to be separate from Christ for my brethren that are my kinsmen, according to the flesh:* that is , the Israelites ; meaning for the aduancement of Gods glory in their calling and saluation. Such zeale we may see in *Moses:* for, thinking that God should lose his glory, if the Israelites were destroyed, he *prayes the Lord to pardon their sinne : But if thou wilt not,* then (saith he)*raze me out of the booke which thou hast written.*

This beeing the fruite of faith, To make a man able and willing to suffer any thing for Christs sake;we must hereby be mooued to labour for true faith : for, tribulation may come; nay, some affliction will come on euery childe of God, more or lesse. Now, without faith we shall neuer be able to glorifie God vnder the crosse. *The iust must liue by faith in* this estate

Heb. 10. 38.as , here they endure racking, burning,hewing asunder,&c. and all by faith.

Secondly, out of all these sufferings here endured by faith , note the minde and disposition of godly men towards Gods Church and people ; they are most bitterly and bloodily bent against them: for, here they put in execution vpon Gods children, whatsoeuer cruelty the deuill could suggest into their hearts. And this hath been their disposition and behauiour, not onely before Christs incarnation , but also euer since : as may appeare by the manifolde strange tortures , deuised against Christians in the Primitiue Church; and both then and since inflicted vpon them. Beholde it in the Church of Rome , especially in their late Inquisition: whereby, beside the cruell racking of the conscience by vniust inquiries, they put the Protestants to most cruell torments.

The consideration of this cruell disposition in the wicked, against the godly, is of speciall vse. First , it prooues vnto vs, that the religion which by Gods mercie we professe, contained in the bookes of the olde and new Testament, is no politique deuice of man, but the sacred ordinance of the euerliuing God.For, if it were the inuention of man, it would so fit their humour, and accord with their nature, that generally it would be loued and embraced, and not one of an hundred would mislike it.But, we see it is generally detested; *This sect is euery where spoken against,* Act. 28. 22: naturall men reiect it , and persecute it , and the professours of it vnto the death. This they doe,because true religion is contrary to their nature , as light is to darknesse ; and condemnes those wayes and courses which they best like of. This reason shall iustifie true religion, to bee Gods owne ordinance,euen to the conscience of the worldly Atheist:his deuillish malice against it,proues Gods diuine truth to be in it.

Secondly , doe the wicked hate the godly, because of their religion and profession? then on the contrary, we must learne to loue religion, because it is religion; and the professours of it , for their professions sake. This is Christs instruction, *to loue a disciple because he is a disciple,* Matth. 10. Indeede wee must loue all men;but especially those that embrace the Gospel of Christ,and be of the housholde of faith: for, all such are brethren, hauing one Father, which is God ; and brethren ought to loue one another.But alas this lesson is not learned: for, the world generally is giuen to mocking, and scoffing, and the matter of their mocking is religion , and the professors thereof. This ought not to bee so: for, howsoeuer men may faile both in knowledge and practise , yet the professers of religion should not so be despised. This abuse is growen to such a hight,that many refraine the diligent hearing of the word preached , least they should bee mocked. But let these mockers know, that herein they shake hands with the deuill, and with the persecuters of Gods Church: for, *mocking is a kinde of perfecution*. Young Chriftians fhould not be fo dealt with ; but rather encouraged, for the aduancement of the Kingdome of Chrift. Thus dealt our Sauiour Chrift with thofe that gaue any teftimonie of the fparkes of grace: when the *young man* faid , *Hee had from his youth kept Gods commaundements* , the Text faith, *Iefus beheld him, and loued him*, Mark. 10. 21. and, hearing a *Scribe* anfwer difcreetly, he faid vnto him; *Thou art not farre from the Kingdome of God*, Mark. 12. 34. Now, we muft be followers of Chrift, and walke in loue, iudging and fpeaking the beft of all profeffours, accounting none for hypocrites , till God make their hypocrifie knowne. It is a note of a Chriftian to loue a man, becaufe he loues religion: on the contrary, to hate a man, becaufe hee is a Chriftian , is a note of a perfecuter, and an enemie to Chrift. And thus much in generall.

Now wee come in particular to the feuerall kindes of fuffering, which thefe beleeuers endured by faith: the firft whereof, is *racking*; in thefe words : *others alfo were racked*: or, as fome tranflate it; *And others were beaten with clubbes*. For, the worde in the originall will beare either tranflation: and, both of them fitly agree to this kinde of fuffering. For, in thefe times, the enemies of Gods Church, vfed to fet the bodies of them that were to be tormented, vpon rackes, and engines; whereon , they ftretched out euery ioynt , and then did beat the whole body thus racked, with clubs, till the party were ftarke dead. An example of this kinde of fuffering, we haue in *Eleazer a Iewe*, 1. Mac. 6. who vnder *Antiochus* was firft racked, and then beaten on euery part of his body, vnto the death; becaufe he refufed to eat fwines flefh.

But fome will fay, This cannot be any commendation of faith, to be racked and beaten to death: for, malefactors and traytors are fo vfed. *Anf.* To preuent this obiection, the holy Ghoft addeth thefe words ; *and would not bee deliuered*: or, *would not accept deliuerance* : to fhewe , that this fuffering was a notable commendation of true faith. The meaning of the words in this; That whereas fome Iewes in the olde Teftament, were condemned to death for their religion, by perfecutors: and yet, had life and libertie offered vnto them, if they would recant, and forfake their religion; This proffer of life they refufed, *and would not be deliuered*, vpon fuch a condition.

In this example of faith, wee are taught to hold faft true religion , and to preferre the enioying of it, before all the pleafures and commodities in the world ; yea, before life it felfe. This point, *Paul* vrgeth in fundry exhortations; faying, *Let him that thinketh he ftandeth, take heede leaft he fall*: 1. Cor. 10. 12. forbidding vs to preferue our outward peace, by communicating with idolaters. And againe, *Stand faft in the faith*: 1. Cor. 16. 13. Yea, this

is one maine point that *Paul* vrgeth to *Timothy*, in both his Epiftles; *to keepe faith , and a good confcience*. And our Sauiour Chrift in one of his parables , Matth. 13. 44. compares the Kingdome of heauen , *to a treafure hid in the field : which, when a man findeth, hee hideth it, and goes home and fels all hee hath, to buy the field*. Whereby hee would teach vs , that euery ones duty , who would enioy the Kingdome of heauen, is this: In regard of it, to forgoe and forfake all things elfe, efteeming them to bee droffe and dongue , as *Paul* did, Philip. 3. 8. What though a man had all the riches and pleafures of the world , and all things elfe for this life, that his heart could wifh ? yet , if he want religion, and a good confcience, all he hath is nothing: for , fo he wants the loue and fauour of God, and fhall lofe his foule; for the ranfome whereof, all the world can doe nothing. Wherefore, we muft hereby be admonifhed, to haue more care to get and maintaine true religion, and a good confcience, then any thing in the world befides.

Now, becaufe nature will iudge it a part of rafhneffe, to refufe life, when it is offered: therefore, to preuent this conceit, againft thefe beleeuers, the holy Ghoft fets downe a notable reafon of this their fact: to wit , They refufed deliuerance, *that they might receiue a better refurrection*. Many interpreters vnderftand thefe words, of the refurrection at the day of iudgement fimply ; as though the holy Ghoft had faid, Thefe Martyrs therefore refufed to be deliuered from death; becaufe, they locked to receiue, at the day of iudgement, a greater meafure of glory: euen for this, that, in obedience to God, for the maintenance of true religion, they were content to lay downe their liues. This (no doubt) is the truth of God , that the more we humble our felues, in fuffering for the name of Chrift in this life; the greater fhall our glorie be, at the generall refurrection ; *for our light affliction, which is but for a moment , caufeth vnto vs, a farre more excellent, and eternall waight of glory*, 2. Cor. 4. 17. And yet (as I take it) that is not the meaning of thefe words; but , their *refurrection* at the laft day , is here tearmed *better*, then the temporall deliuerance offered vnto them. For, beeing in torments on the racke, they were but dead men; and, when life was offered vnto them, it was (as it were) a kinde of refurrection, and in regard of the enemies of the Church , a good refurrection: but, for that, they would not lofe the comfort of refurrection to life, at the laft day.

Here then , are two refurrections compared together. The firft, is a deliuerance from temporall death ; the fecond, is arifing to life euerlafting at the day of iudgement. Now, of thefe two, the latter is the better ; and that in the iudgement of Gods feruants, and Martyrs. So then, the true meaning of thefe words, is this : Thefe feruants of God, refufed deliuerance from temporall tortures and punifhments;

ments; becaufe their care and defire was, that their bodies might rife againe to life euerlafting, at the day of iudgement: which rifing againe to life at that day, they iudged farre better, then to rife to a temporall life, for a while in this world.

This reafon, well obferued, may teach vs thefe two fpeciall duties: Firft, to be carefull aboue all things, for affurance in our confciences (as thefe feruants of God had) that our bodies fhall rife againe to life euerlafting at the laft day. True it is, we make this confeffion with our mouthes, among the articles of our faith; but we muft labour to be fettled and refolued effectually in our hearts, that thefe our bodies (be they neuer fo miferably tormented here) fhall one day rife to life and glory, by Iefus Chrift. All the true Martyrs of Chrift, knewe and were refolued of this: and this it was, that made them fo confident in their fufferings. And if we can attaine vnto it, we fhall finde great vfe hereof, both in life and death. For our liues, this will mooue vs to embrace true religion from our hearts, and in all things to endeauour to keepe a good confcience. This *Paul* teftifieth, Act. 24. 15. 16. for, hauing made profeffion of his hope in the refurrection, both of iuft and vniuft, he faith, *And herein I endeauour my felfe to haue alwaies a cleare confcience, both towards God, and towards men.* And for death, this perfwafion alfo is of great vfe: for, it will notably ftay the heart, againft the naturall feare of death. It is a wonder to fee, how terrible the thoughts of death are to many a one. Now, this feare arifeth hence, that they are not in heart refolued of their refurrection, to life and glorie at the laft day: for, if they were, they would endeauour themfelues with patience and with comfort, to vndergo the pangs thereof, though neuer fo terrible.

Secondly, hence we muft learne fo to lead this temporall life, that when we are dead, our bodies may rife againe to life eternall. Thefe Martyrs are a notable prefident herein vnto vs: for, they are fo refolute to hold that courfe of life, which hath the hope of glorie, that they will rather lofe temporall life, then leaue that courfe. And indeede this dutie is fo neceffarie, that vnleffe we order well this temporall life, we can neuer haue hope to rife to glory. *Queft.* How fhould we leade this temporall life, that we may rife to glorie, after death? *Anf.* This S. *Iohn* teacheth vs, Reuel. 20. 6. *Bleffed and holy is he that hath his part in the firft refurrection: for on fuch the fecond death hath no power.* We muft therefore labour earneftly to haue our part herein. This firft refurrection is fpirituall, wrought in the foule by the holy Ghoft; caufing him that is by nature dead in finne, to rife to neweneffe of life: whereof whofoeuer is true partaker, fhall vndoubtedly rife to glorie. For, they *that are quickened in Chrift* from the death of finne, *are made to fit together in heauenly places in Chrift Iefus,* Eph. 2. 5. 6. Natu-

rall death may feuer foule and bodie for a time: but it can neuer hinder the fruition of eternall life. Wherefore, as we defire this life which is eternall when we are dead: fo let vs frame our naturall liues to die vnto finne while we are aliue.

Verfe 36. *And others haue beene tried by mockings, and fcourgings: yea, moreouer by bonds and prifonment.* The fecond kinde of fuffering, wherewith the feruants of God were then tried, is mocking. Touching the which we may obferue diuers points: Firft whence it came. No doubt it came from vngodly perfons, that were enemies to Gods Church, and true religion; for here it is made a part of the triall of Gods Church, by the enemies thereof.

Here, then beholde the ftate of mockers and fcoffers at the feruants of God: they are here accounted wicked wretches, and enemies to God, and to his truth. So Saint *Iude,* fpeaking of certaine *falfe Prophets,* which were crept into the Church, calls them *vngodly men,* Iude 4. which he prooues afterward, by there blacke mouthes in *euill fpeaking,* ver. 8. 10. And *Ifmaell* is accounted a *perfecuter,* by the holy Ghoft, for *mocking Ifaac,* Gal. 4. 29. And *Dauid* reckoning vp the degrees of finners, makes the chaire of the fcornefull, the third and higheft, Pfal. 1. 1. All thefe places fhew the haynoufnes of this finne: and therefore if any of vs, young or olde, high or low, haue beene ouertaken with it heretofore, let vs now repent and leaue it; for, it is odious in Gods fight. Thou that art a fcoffer, mayft flatter thy felfe, and thinke all is well, let the matter prooue how it can, words are but winde. But knowe, thy cafe is fearefull; for, as yet thou wanteft the feare of God, and art an enemy to Chrift and his religion: and one day thou fhalt be iudged, not only for thy wicked deeds, but *for all thy cruell fpeakings,* Iude, verfe 15.

Secondly, whereas thefe feruants of God *were tried by mockings,* it fhewes that Gods Church in this world, is fubiect to this affliction. It is not a thing newely begun in this age of ours, but hath beene alwaies in Gods Church from the beginning. Gen. 21. 9. *Ifmaell mocked Ifaac;* and *Ifay* brings in Chrift complaining thus: Ifay 8. 18. *Behold, I and my children whom the Lord hath giuen me, are as fignes and wonders in Ifraell.* And *Ieremie* faith, *I am in derifion daily: euery one mocketh me,* Ier. 20. 7. Yea, our Sauiour Chrift vpon the Croffe, when he was working the bleffed worke of mans redemption, was euen then *mocked* by the fpitefull Iewes, Mat. 27. 41. And *Paul* was *mocked* of the Athenians, for preaching Chrift and the refurrection. Act. 17. 18.

Now, if this haue beene the eftate of Chrift our head, and of his moft worthie Prophets, and Apoftles, to be mocked and fcorned; then muft no child of God at this day thinke to efcape: for, if they haue done this to the greene tree, what will they doe to the dry? Wherefore,

if

if we belong to Chrift, wee muft prepare for it, and arme our felues with patience to vndergoe this triall. *The Difciple is not aboue his mafter, nor the feruant aboue his Lord. If they haue called the Mafter of the houfe Beelzebub, how much more them of the houfe?* Matth. 10. 24, 25.

Thirdly, whereas thefe feruants of God were tried by mockings, and did endure the fame, by faith; here we learne how to behaue our felues, when wee are fubiect to mocking and derifion, efpecially for religions fake. Wee muft not returne mock for mock, and taunt for taunt: but with meekeneffe of heart learne to beare the fame. When Chrift was vpon the croffe, the Iewes moft fhamefully mocked him: yet euen then did Chrift pray for them. And the fame was *Dauids* behauiour, as wee may reade notably, Pfal. 38. 12, 13, 14. *When his enemies fpake euill of him,* what did he? Did hee raile on them againe? No; *Hee was as a deafe man, and heard not; and as a dumbe man which openeth not his mouth; euen as a man that heareth not; and in whofe mouth are no reproofes.* This was a rare thing in *Dauid,* that hee could thus bridle his affectiõs in the cafe of reproach: but, read the 15. v. and wee fhall fee the caufe; *Hee trufted in the Lord his God:* alfo, he confidered the hand of God in their reproches, as 2. Sam. 16. 10. and thefe things made him filent. This example we muft looke vpon, and learn hereby with patience to poffeffe our fouls vnder reproach.

The third kinde of fuffering, is *Scourging.* They were not onely *mocked* for religion, but alfo *whipped* and *fcourged.* The fourth, is *Bonds and imprifonment.* The fift is ftoning, verfe 37. *They were ftoned.* The fixt, is this, *They were hewen afunder.* Thefe were all worthy fruits of faith, beeing endured for religions fake: but the particular points that might here be obferued, haue beene handled before; and therefore I paffe them ouer.

The feauenth kinde of fuffering, is this: they were *tempted.* Thefe words, by the change of a letter in the originall may be read thus, *They were burned.* And fome doe fo tranflate it; thinking, that they that writ or copied out this Epiftle at the firft, did put one letter for another. Their reafon is, becaufe examples of grieuous punifhments are mentioned both before and after this: and therefore they thinke this fhould be *burning,* which is a fore and grieuous death. But we may fafely and truely reade the words thus, *They were tempted:* conceiuing hereby that they were enticed and allured by faire promifes of life, to forfake their religion. So the fame word is vfed by Saint *Iames,* faying; *Euery man is tempted, when hee is drawne away by his owne concupifcence, and is enticed,* Iames 1. 14. If any aske, why this triall in *tempting,* fhould bee placed among fuch cruell torments? I anfwere, becaufe it as great a triall as any can be. For, it is as

dangerous a temptation to ouerthrow religion and a good confcience, as any punifhment in the world. This appeares plainely in Chrifts temptations by the Deuill: for, in thofe three, Satan bewraies his malice and craft againft Chrift and his Church moft notably. Now Satan, not preuailing with the two firft, makes his third and laft affault from the glory and dignity of the world: for, fhewing vnto Chrift *all the Kingdomes of the world, and the glory of them,* hee faith, *All thefe will I giue thee, if thou wilt fall downe and worfhip mee,* Matth. 4. 9. Indeede, Chrifts holy heart would not yeeld vnto it: but, that it was a grieuous temptation, appeares by Chrifts anfwers. For, in the former temptations, hee onely difputed with Sathan out of Scripture: but when this temptation comes, Chrift bids him (as it were in paffion) *auoide Satan*; fignifying thereby not onely his abhorring of that finne, but alfo the danger of that affault by the world. And indeede, thefe temptations on the right hand (as we may call them) will moft dangeroufly creepe into the heart, and caufe fhipwracke of faith and a good confcience. All *Dauids* troubles and perfecutions could not bring him to fo grieuous finnes, as did a little eafe and reft. A huge great Armie cannot fo foone giue entrance to an enemie into a Citie, as riches and faire promifes: neither can bodily torments fo foone preuaile againft a good confcience, as will worldly pleafures and faire promifes. In regarde whereof, we muft take heede that we be not deceiued by the world: for, the view of the glory and pompe thereof, will fooner fteale from a man both religion and a good confcience, then any perfecution poffibly can doe. And indeede, who doe fo oft change their religion when trialls come, as they that haue the world at will?

The eight example of fuffering is this, *They were flaine with the fword.* There can be nothing faide of this, which hath not beene fpoken in the former examples: and therefore I omit it.

The ninth and laft example of fuffering is this; *They wandred vp and downe in fheepe skins, and Goais skinnes, beeing deftitute, afflicted, and tormented:* That is, beeing either banifhed, or conftrained by flight to faue their liues, they wandred vp and downe in bafe attire, and were deftitute of ordinary foode and comfort; and fo in great affliction and torment.

Here we fee thefe feruants of God, were driuen from their owne Country, friends, and families, by perfecution. Whence we obferue, that in time of perfecution, a Chriftian man may lawfully flie for his fafety, if he be not hindred by the bond of priuate or publike calling. For, thefe feruants of God, here commended for their faith, did flie when they were perfecuted; and that by faith: therefore the action is lawfull, as I might prooue at large, but that I haue fpoken of it heretofore. When our Sauiour Chrift knew that the Pharifies heard of

the

the multitude of Disciples which he made, Ioh. 4.1.3. *hee left Iudea, where they had greatest iurisdiction, and came into Galile*, for his safety. The Prophets in the old testament did flie: as, *Elias* from *Iezabel*, 1. King. 19. 3. And, so did the *Apostles* in the new; and that by Christs direction, Matth. 10. 23.

Obiect. 1. But some will say, Persecution is the hand of God, and therefore no man may flie from it; for so he should seeme to flie from God himselfe. *Answ.* We must consider persecution two wayes: first, as it is the hand of God: secondly, as it is the worke of the wicked enemies of Gods Church. For, them God vseth sometimes as instruments, in laying his hand vpon his Church, either for chastisement, or for triall. Now, a Christian beeing persecuted for the truth, and hauing libertie to flie, cannot be said to flie from Gods hand; vnlesse he went away contrary to Gods commaunde, as *Ionas* did, beeing sent to Niniue: and beside, he knowes that is impossible. But, his intent is to flie from the wrath of his enemies, to saue his life, for the further good of Gods Church. Againe, the reason is not good, To say persecution is the hand of God, therefore a man may not flie from it. For, so might a man conclude, that none ought to flie from sicknesse, or from warre: both which, a man may doe with a safe conscience, not beeing hindred by some speciall calling.

Obiect. 2. But euery one is bound to testifie his faith and religion, before his enemies; and therefore may not flie in persecution. *Answ.* True indeede: a Christian man must so testifie his faith, if he bee called thereto of God: but if God giue him libertie, and opportunitie to flie, then he will not haue him, at that time, to iustifie his religion by that meanes.

Obiect. 3. But, if it be lawfull to flie, how then comes it to passe, that some of Gods children, when they might haue fled, would not; but, haue stood to iustifie their profession vnto death. *Ans.* We must iudge reuerently of them, and thinke they did it by some speciall instinct and motion of Gods spirit; as appeareth by their patience and constancy in their greatest torments. Examples hereof, we haue in our English Acts and Monuments, in men worthy of notable commendations for their constancie, and zeale for the truth of the Gospel.

Quest. If flight in persecution, may bee an action of faith; Whether may not the minister of Gods word flie in time of persecution?

Answ. There bee some cases, wherein the Minister may lawfully flie: 1 When that particular Church and congregation, ouer which he is placed, is dispersed by the Enemies: so as he hath no hope to gather and call them backe againe: then (no doubt) hee may flie, till his congregation be gathered againe. 2. If the persecutors doe specially aime at the Ministers life, then with the consent of his flocke, he may goe apart for his owne safetie, for a time.

So it was with *Paul*: when the Ephesians were in an vproare about their *Diana, Paul* in zeale would haue entred in among them; but the Disciples suffered him not, Act. 19. 30. This they did for *Pauls* safetie, and the good of the Church; for they knewe, those Idolaters would haue beene most fierce against *Paul*. And so ought euery particular Church, to haue speciall care of the life of their Minister. Other causes there be, in which he may flie: but I will not stand to recite all; because there be so many circumstances, which may alter the case, as well respecting his enemies, as himselfe, and his people: making that vnlawfull at one time, and to some persons, which to others, or at another time, may be lawfull.

Secondly, whereas it is said, *These seruants of God wandered vp and downe*: we doe learne, that a man may lawfully goe from place to place, and trauell from country to country; if so be, he goes in faith, as these men did. Againe, their going was to keepe faith and a good conscience: and, for the same ende, may a man lawfully trauel from place to place. But when men goe not in faith; nor yet, for this ende, the better to keepe a good conscience: there vndoubtedly their trauell is not lawfull.

By this then, we haue iust cause to reprooue the bad course of many wanderers among vs: as first, of our common beggars, whose whole life is nothing else, but a wandering from place to place; though not in faith, nor for conscience sake: but they finde a sweetenesse in their idle kinde of life; and therefore they wander, because they would not worke. Now, this their course (hauing no other ground, but loue of idlenesse, and contempt of paines in a lawfull calling,) cannot be but greatly displeasing vnto God; who enioynes, that euery man should *walke in some lawfull calling, and eate his owne bread.* This they doe not; and therefore the curse of God pursueth them: for, generally they are giuen vp to most horrible sinnes of iniustice, and vncleannes: they walke inordinately; for, they range not themselues into any families, but liue liker bruite beasts, then men: they are not members of any particular congregation, but excommunicate themselues from all Churches; and so liue as though there were no God, no Christ, nor true religion. And, herein we may see Gods hand more heauie vpon them, that they take all their delight in that course of wandring, which in it owne nature is a curse, and a punishment.

Secondly, we may here also iustly reprooue the course of some others among vs, who will needes be trauellers; not for religion sake (for that were commendable, if they had such need) nor yet, by vertue of their calling (which were lawfull) but, onely for this ende, to see fashions, and strange countries: and, they refraine not from such places as Rome, Spaine, &c. wherein that cruell Inquisition will hardly suffer any to passe, with safetie of a good conscience. But,

shall

shall wee thinke that this their trauell is commendable? No surely: for, the ende of lawfull trauell, is the preseruation of faith and a good conscience ; or, the bond of some lawfull calling. Now, these men trauelling vpon no such grounds, but onely vpon pleasure ; how shall wee thinke they will stand to the truth, when they thrust themselues into such needlesse danger, and triall? The crazed consciences of many at their returne, shew sufficiently, the badnesse of that course.

Further, note the state of these beleeuers, for their attire; it was of *sheep skins*, and *goates skins*. The like may bee obserued, in other famous Prophets, and seruants of God: *Elijah* wore a garment of heire, and thereby was knowen, 2. King. 1. 8. And so did *Iohn Baptist*, Matth. 3. 4. Yea, the false Prophets went so arraied, that they might the rather be respected of the people, Zach. 13. 4. And, our Sauiour Christ saith, *The false Prophets shal come in sheepes clothing*, like the true Prophets; when as indeede, *they are rauening Woolues*. Now, the true Prophets of God, went thus basely attired : that not onely by word and doctrine, but also in life and conuersation, they might preach repentance vnto the people. And indeede, euery Minister of the Gospel, ought to be a light vnto his people, both in life and doctrine: and, he that preacheth well, and doth not liue according to his doctrine, buildes with the one hand, and pulls downe with the other. Now, whereas these seruants of God, went vp and downe in such base attire, as sheepe-skinnes, and goat skinnes : it was for pouertie's sake, beeing depriued of friends, goods, house, and lands; and so, destitute of prouision for better attire.

In their example, we may note that Gods seruants and children may be brought to extreame pouerty, and necessitie; so as they shall want ordinarie foode, and raiment, and bee faine to couer themselues with beasts skinnes. This was the poore state and condition of godly *Lazarus*. Yea, Christ Iesus, for our sakes, did vndergoe a meane estate; for, *he had not a place whereon to lay his head*: and at his death, hee had not so much ground of his owne, as might serue for a buriall place; but, was laid in *Iosephs* toombe: which is a great comfort to any child of God in like distresse. For, why should any bee dismayed with that estate, which Christ Iesus and his deerest seruants haue vndergone for his example.

Here some may aske, how this can stand with that saying of *Dauid*, *I haue beene young and am olde : yet I neuer saw the righteous forsaken, nor his seede begging bread*, Psalm. 37. 25.

Ans. *Dauids* saying may be taken two waies: first, as his owne obseruation in his time. For, he saith not, *The righteous is neuer forsaken* ; but, that *he neuer saw it*: and indeede it is a rare thing, to see the righteous forsaken.

Secondly, (which I take to be *Dauids* meaning) the righteous man is neuer forsaken, and his seede too. For, if God lay temporall chastisement on any of his seruants, suffering them to want, yet he forsaketh not his seede after him; but renueth his mercie towards them, if they walke in obedience before him: he may make triall of godly Parents by want, but their godly children shall surely be blessed : so that this hindereth not, but that the godly may be in want.

Further, whereas they are said to goe vp and downe in *Sheepes skinnes and Goates skinnes*, we must vnderstand, that they did it by faith. From whence we learne, that when all temporall blessings faile, then the child of God must by faith lay hold vpon Gods gracious promises of life eternall, and stay himselfe thereon.

This point must be remembred carefully: for say we should want all kind of temporall benefits, must we thereupon despaire, and thinke that God hath forsaken vs? God forbid: nay, when all meanes faile, and the whole world is against vs, yet then we must lay hold vpon the promise of life eternall in Christ, and thereupon rest our soules. Thus did these beleeuers in this place. And this faith did *Iob* notably testifie, when god had taken from him children, goods, health, yea, and all that he had, yet then he said, Iob 13. 15. *Though he kill me, yet will I trust in him.* And so must we endeauour to doe if that case befall vs: for, when all worldly helps and comforts faile vs, this promise of life in Christ, will be a sweete and safe refuge for our soule.

Beeing *destitute, afflicted, and tormented.*] Here the Apostle amplifieth their miserie in their wandring estate, by three degrees of crosses, which did accompany the same. First, they were *destitute* of all temporal blessings: secondly, they were *afflicted* both in body and minde: Thirdly, *tormented*, that is, euill entreated. These are added for a speciall cause ; to shewe that these seruants of God were laden with afflictions: They were *banished* and driuen to extreme pouertie; they were *depriued* of all their goods, and of all societie of men: they were *afflicted* in body and in minde, and euill entreated of all men; no man would doe them good, but all men did them wrong; whereby, we see that euen waues of miserie ouerwhelmed them on euery side.

Hence we learne that Gods seruants may be ouerwhelmed with manifolde calamities at the same instant, beeing pressed downe with crosses in goods, in body, minde, friends, and euery way. This was *Iobs* case, a most worthie seruant of God; he was afflicted in bodie, in friends, goods, and children, and (which was greatest of all) he wrestled in conscience with the wrath of God; Iob 13. 16. *Thou writest bitter things against me, and makest me to possesse the iniquities of my youth.* And the like hath beene the e-

state

ſtate of many of Gods children : Pſal. 88. 3. 7. *My ſoule is filled with euils: thou haſt vexed me with all thy waues, &c.*

Queſt. How can this ſtand with the truth of Gods word, wherein are promiſes of all manner of bleſſings both temporall and ſpiritual, to thoſe that feare him : Deut. 28. 1, 2. &c. *If thou obey the voyce of the Lord thy God, all theſe bleſſings ſhall come vpon thee, and ouertake thee: bleſſings in the Citie, and in the field: in the fruite of thy bodie, and of thy ground and cattell.* Pſal. 34. 10. *They that ſeeke the Lord, ſhall lacke nothing that is good.* For, *Godlineſſe hath the promiſes of this life, and of the life to come,* 1. Tim. 4. 8. And therefore *Dauid* compareth the godly man *to the tree that is planted by the water ſide, which bringeth forth much fruite; and is greene and well liking,* Pſal. 1. 3. How then comes this to paſſe, that Gods owne ſeruants ſhould be thus oppreſſed, & laden not with one calamitie or two, but with ſundry and grieuous afflictions at the ſame time? *Anſ.* True it is, the Scripture is full of gracious promiſes of temporall bleſſings vnto Gods children : but they are conditionall, and muſt be vnderſtood with an exception, to this effect; *Gods children ſhall haue ſuch and ſuch bleſſings, vnleſſe it pleaſe God by afflictions to make triall of his graces in them, or to chaſtiſe them for ſome ſinne :* ſo that the exception of the croſſe, for the triall of grace, or chaſtiſement for ſinne, muſt bee applied to all promiſes of temporall bleſſings. And hence it comes to paſſe, that the moſt worthy and renowned ſeruants of God for their faith, are ſaid to be afflicted and in miſerie. For, his promiſes of temporall bleſſings, are not abſolute, but conditionall. *Al things are theirs (as Paul ſaith)* 1. Cor. 3. 21. and they ſhall haue honour, wealth, fauour, &c. vnleſſe it pleaſe God to prooue their faith, or to chaſtiſe their ſinnes by croſſes and afflictions.

Qu. How can Gods ſeruants be able to beare ſo many croſſes and grieuous at once, ſeeing it is hard for a man to beare one croſſe patiently? The anſwer is here laid downe, to wit, *by faith;* for many and grieuous were the miſeries that lay on theſe ſeruants of God: and yet by beleeuing the promiſe of life in the Meſſias, they were enabled to beare them all. This is a ſoueraine remedy againſt immoderate griefe in the greateſt diſtreſſe : and vndoubtedly the floods of affliction ſhall neuer ouerwhelme him, that hath his heart aſſured by faith of the mercie of God towards him by Ieſus Chriſt. This made *Dauid* ſay, *He would not feare euill, though hee ſhould walke through the valley of the ſhadow of death,* Pſal. 23. 4. and *Paul* ſpeaking of *tribulation, anguiſh, famine, perſecution, yea, and death it ſelfe,* ſaith, *In all theſe we are more then cōquerers through him that hath loued vs,* Rom. 8. 37. And frō this faith it was, that he was able to endure all eſtates ; *to be hungry, to want, &c.* Phil. 4. 12. 13.

If this be true, that Gods children may bee

afflicted with manifold calamities at once; then the opinion of naturall and vngodly men is falſe, who iudge him and thinke him to be wicked and vngodly, whom God ladeth with manifold calamities. This was the iudgement of *Iobs three friends,* and the ground of all their diſputation againſt him; that, becauſe God had laid ſo many croſſes vpon him, therefore he was but an hypocrite. And, this is the raſh iudgement of naturall men in our dayes, eſpecially vpon thoſe that make profeſſion of religion : when Gods hand of triall or correction lies vpon them, they preſently cenſure them for hypocrites : but this is a wretched opinion; for Gods deareſt children may be preſſed downe with manifolde calamities.

Secondly, ſeeing faith in Chriſt will ſupport the ſoule vnder manifolde croſſes, be they neuer ſo grieuous; we muſt labour in the feare of God, to haue our hearts rooted and grounded in this faith: and when afflictions come we muſt ſtriue to ſhew forth the fruite and power of it, by bearing them patiently.

And thus much of the ſeuerall branches of affliction, in this laſt example of beleeuers.

Verse 38.

Whom the world was not worthie of, they wandered in the wildernes, and mountaines, and dennes, and Caues of the earth.

IN theſe words, the holy Ghoſt doth anſwer to a ſecret obiection or ſurmiſe, which a natural man might conceiue againſt the beleeuers ſpoken of before. For, it beeing ſaid, *That they wandred vp and downe:* ſome man might thinke thus: no meruaile though they wandred vp and downe; for it may be, they were not worthy to liue in the world. This, the holy Ghoſt doth flatly denie, and auoucheth the cleane contrary of them; to wit, *that they wandred vp and down by faith;* and the Lord cauſed them ſo to do, *becauſe the world was not worthy of them,* they were too good to liue in the world.

In this anſwer to this ſurmiſe, wee may obſerue what is the opinion of naturall men, concerning the children of God; to wit, that they are not worthy to liue in the world, but the earth wheron they tread, is too good for them. This hath beene, is, and will bee the worlds eſtimation of Gods children. Matth. 24. 9. *Yee*

shall bee hated of all nations for my names sake.
Ioh. 16. 2. *They shall excommunicate you; yea,
the time shall come, that whosoeuer killeth you,
shall thinke he doth God good seruice.* Act. 22. 22.
Away (say the Iewes, of *Paul*) *with such a
fellowe from the earth: it is not meete that hee
should liue.* And hence he saith of himselfe, and
the other Apostles, 1. Cor. 4. 13. *They were made
the filth of the world, and the off-scouring of all
things.*

In the time of the persecuting Emperous
in the Primitiue Church, when any common
calamitie befell the people or State: as famine,
dearth, pestilence, or such like, they straight-
way imputed it to the Christians: saying, That
*they and their wicked religion were the cause
thereof.* And though we haue religion maintained among vs, yet the poore seruants of God
finde the like welcome in the world: for, thus
the wicked censure them euery where, That
they are dissembling hypocrites, and none so
bad and vile persons as they are. Now, if any
man aske, how comes it to passe, that the world
should slander them so, and thinke so vilely of
them. *Ans.* First, because *they be taken out of the
world, in regard of state and condition in grace,*
Ioh. 15. 19. *therefore the world hateth them,*
Ioh. 15. 19. Secondly, *the world knowes them
not,* 1. Ioh. 3. 1. and therefore speakes euill of
them, Iude 10. Thirdly, the wicked measure
others by themselues; and therefore despise the
godly, that ioyne not with them, 1. Pet. 4. 3.
Lastly, there is a secret enmitie betweene the
seede of the wicked, and the seede of the
Church: (1. Ioh. 3. 12.) the wicked are of
that *euill one,* the *deuill*; and therefore, must
needes hate the godly, who are borne of God.
So that, when we shall see or heare, that vngodly persons shall in any such sort abuse the
children of God; we must not maruell, nor bee
troubled at it, for it is no newe thing, it hath
beene from the beginning: but wee must pray
that God would open their eies, that they
may turne from their sinnes to repentance;
and then (no doubt) they will change their
conceite: and alter their behauiour towards
them: as *Paul* did, Gal. 1. 13. 15. Acts, 9. 1.
26.

To come to the words more particularly;
the Holy Ghost saith, *The world was not worthy
of them:* that is, the company of vngodly liuers,
without Christ, and voyde of grace, were not
worthy the societie of these holy ones; and for
this cause, did the Lord take them from among
them.

Here note a singular fruit of true faith: it
brings a man to that estate, and giues him that
excellencie, that hee is more worth, then the
whole world. I meane by the whole world, the
estate of all those that liue in the world, out of
Christ. If then a man, would haue true and
stable dignity, let him labour for true faith: for
faith hath this priuiledge, to aduance a beleeuer to true honour and excellencie. And there-

fore our Sauiour saith, *As many as receiued him
by faith, to them he gaue power, or prerogatiue,
to bee the sonnes of God.* Wee take it for a great
prerogatiue, to bee the childe of an earthly
prince; and so it is: but, to be the sonne of God
(who is King of Kings) is a preheminence and
dignitie aboue all dignities; and, no tongue
can expresse the excellency thereof. For, what
more can a man desire, then to bee heire of
glory in life euerlasting? and, yet true faith
bringeth this to a beleeuer. It is an excellent
dignitie, to be matched with Angells; and no
prince in the world, by all humane wit or
power can attaine vnto it: but yet, the childe
of God can, beeing ioyned to God by faith in
Christ; whereby (in some sort) he is aboue the
Angels themselues: for, our nature in Christ, is
aduanced aboue the nature of Angels.

Honours and dignities, in Politicke or ciuill
estates, are the good gifts of God, and his own
ordinances, whereby men are in higher places,
and in account one aboue another: but yet, all
the dignity, honour, and pompe of the world,
seuered from that dignitie which faith bringeth to the beleeuer, is nothing worth. Indeede,
if worldly preheminence be ioyned with faith,
it is a great and excellent prerogatiue; for, faith
makes it acceptable vnto God: but, seuer faith
from worldly dignities, and what are they, but
vanitie of vanities? which will turne to the greater condemnation of him that enioyeth them.
If a man haue fauour in the Court, and yet
want the Kings fauour, it is nothing: and, such
are all temporall dignities, without Gods fauour; for, at his indignation they vanish away.
Now, his fauour without faith, can no man
haue; for, *hee that commeth vnto God must beleeue,* vers. 6.

Here, all these that are in place aboue o-
thers, either by birth, or speciall calling, must
learne aboue all things to labour for the dignity of faith. When we haue such things wherein
wee delight, wee desire continuance of them.
Beholde, the dignitie of faith is euerlasting:
and besides, it sanctifies all ciuill dignities, and
makes the owners of them glorious, and acceptable, both before God and man; when as o-
therwise, without faith, they are nothing: and,
they that haue them, can doe nothing but abuse
them.

Againe, the holy Ghost saith, *The world was
not worthy of these men,* for another cause; and
that is this: Euery Christian man by his faith,
brings many blessings among those parties, and
to that place where he liued: now, the world
deserues no such blessings, and therefore is
vnworthie of the persons by whome they
come.

Quest. How doe Christians bring blessings
to places where they liue? *Ans.* First, by their
presence: for, as God said to *Abraham* the Father of the faithfull, *Thou shalt be a blessing,*
Gen. 12. 3. so is it with all beleeuers. *Laban*
confesseth *that he perceiued that the Lord had*

blessed

blessed him for Iacobs sake, Gen. 30. 27. And *Potiphar* sawe that *Ioseph* was a blessing in his house: *For, the Lord made all that he did to prosper*, Gen. 39. 2. 3. While *Lot* was in Sodome, the *Angell could not destroy it*. Gen. 19. 22. And *if there had beene tenne beleeuers in Sodome, the Lord would haue spared all for tennes sake*, Gen. 18. 32. Now, bringing good things, and keeping backe Gods iudgements by their presence, they are thereby blessings. Secondly, they are blessings *by their prayers. Abraham* prayed for *Abimelech*, Gen. 20. 17. 18. and, *God healed him and his family of barrennesse.* At *Moses* prayer, Gods iudgements were taken from Egypt, Exod. 7. 12. 13. 30. and his wrath appeased toward his people, Exod. 32. 11. 14. And some thinke that *Stephens* prayer at his death for his persecuters, was one meanes for mercy vnto *Saul*, that then consented to his death. Act. 7. 60. and 8. 1. Thirdly, they bring blessings vpon a place, by their *example: for,* when men shall see godly persons, walking before them in the feare of God, and making conscience of all manner of sinne, it is a speciall meanes to cause others to turne from their wicked wayes, to newnesse of life. And therefore *Peter* exhorts the Christians *to haue their conuersation honest among the Gentiles; that they which speake euill of them as of euill dores, might by their good workes which they should see, glorifie God in the day of their visitation.* 1. Pet. 2. 12. And he bids *godly wiues* so walke, that *their husbands may bee wonne without the word, by beholding their pure conuersation which is with feare.* 1. Pet 3. 1. 2. And *Paul* bids the Philippians, *to walke blamelesse in the middle of a wicked and crooked nation, as lights in the middle of the world*, Phil. 2. 15. that those which were to be conuerted, by their good conuersation might bee wonne to the truth. God sent a flood vpon the world for the grieuousnesse of mans sinnes: Now, why doth he not still send more floods? are not men now as wicked as they were then? Yes vndoubtedly; man for his part deserues it now: as well as they did then: and therefore our Sauiour Christ faith, as it was in the dayes of *Noah*, so shall it be in the dayes of the sonne of man; so that euery day wee deserue a new flood: but yet the Lord stayes the execution of his iudgements for a time, that his elect may bee gathered and conuerted. And so soone as that is done, heauen and earth shall goe together: and God will not stay one moment, for all the world besides. So that euery nation and people in the world haue benefit by Gods children; because for their sakes doth the Lord stay his wrath, and deferre his iudgements, euen the great iudgement of fire, wherewith the world shall bee consumed at the last day. These things the world should take notice of, as well to mooue them to repentance of their sinnes, whereby they are made vnworthy the presence of a godly man, as also to perswade them to better behauiour, and

cariage towards the godly by whom they are so many wayes blessed.

The holy Ghost addeth, that *they wandred in wildernesses, and mountaines, and dennes, and Caues of the earth*. These were desolate places, and not inhabited: and yet for the wickednesse of the world, God will haue these beleeuers here to wander. We must not thinke, that they betooke themselues voluntarily to this solitary life; but onely vpon necessity beeing constrained by persecution to flie into the wildernesse, for the sauing of their liues, and the keeping a good conscience.

This serues to descry vnto vs the blinde errour of many ages afore vs, wherein it hath beene thought, and is by Papists at this day, to bee a state of perfection, to liue a Monke or Hermite out of all societies, in some desert place, and there to spend the whole life in contemplation onely, and that voluntarily: and they magnifie this estate so much, that hereby they thinke to merit eternall life at the hands of God. But these beleeuers did neither voluntarily, nor with opinion of merit, betake themselues to this solitarie life, but on necessity. And, indeede this kinde of life hath no warrant in Gods word: for, euery Christian is a member of two Kingdomes; of Christs Kingdome of grace, and of that particular state where he dwelleth: and by reason hereof hath a twofolde calling; a temporall, and a spirituall calling. In both of which, he must walke diligently, so long as he can, doing the duties both of a childe of God, and of a member of that common-wealth where hee liueth. Now, when a man goes voluntarily to leade a solitary life, he forsakes his temporall calling altogether, and performes the other but negligently: for, hee withdrawes himselfe from many duties of piety, whereby the people might be furthered to God-ward: which none can doe with a good conscience.

Further, obserue the places where they are constrained to wander, to wit, in *Wildernesses, Caues, and Dennes*; places where wilde beasts haue abode and recourse: & yet here they liue, when as men will not suffer them to liue among them. Where note, that many times more mercie may be found among wilde and sauage beasts, then with some men; so mercilesse are the wicked when God forsakes them, and leaues them to themselues. The *Lions* entreat *Daniel* better, then *Darius* Courtiers and seruants doe; Dan. 6. And *Lazarus* findes more kindenesse with the doggs at *Diues* gates, then with him, and all his family besides, Luk. 16. 21. The consideration whereof must teach vs to nippe sinne in the head at the beginning, and not to suffer it to growe: for, if it get a head and raigne in vs, it will make vs worse then bruite or sauage beasts, and cruell as the Deuill himselfe; as we may see in the worlds vsage of these beleeuers.

Thus we see the state of true beleeuers, vn-

der

der many and grieuous miseries, which wee must well obserue, to arme our selues against the times of aduersities, which God may sende vpon vs. We must not iudge it a cursed estate to be vnder the Crosse: for, here we see, the faith of his seruants is commended for suffering *nine* seuerall kinds of miseries. If we shall thinke that these were but a fewe; we must know, that in them the holy Ghost setteth downe the state of his Church vnto the ende; for, these things were written for ensamples vnto vs. And therefore if calamities come, and such miseries befall vs, as doe driue vs toward distrust, as though God had forsaken vs, we must remember that God did not forsake these his children in their calamities, and therefore also will not forsake vs. And thus much for this last example.

VERSE 39.

And these all through faith obtained good report, and receiued not the promise.

He holy Ghost hauing set downe at large a worthy and notable Catalogue of examples of faith in sundry beleeuers, that liued from the beginning of the world, to the time of the Maccabees, doth now for a further commendation of their faith rehearse the same things that before he had said in the 2. and 13. verses of this chapter. In saying, that by *faith they all receiued good report*; his meaning is, that they did beleeue in the true Messias, and looked for saluation in him alone, whereupon they were approoued of God himselfe; who gaue testimony hereof, partly by his word, and partly by his spirit in their consciences, and partly by his Church: by all which they were commended, and assured to be Gods seruants. And yet notwithstanding this good report, *they receiued not the promise*; that is, the promise of Christs incarnation in their dayes. They receiued Christ truely by faith, and so saw his day; but his actuall incarnation in the flesh, they liued not to see.

Whereas it is said, That *by faith they obtained testimony*; Here first obserue, that there is nothing in man, that makes him acceptable to God, but faith onely. God regards no mans person: he accepts not of a man, because he is a King, or because he is wise, or rich, or strong, &c. But, if a man beleeue, then the Lord is readie to giue testimony of him, that he likes well of him. In regard whereof, we must all labour diligently, aboue all other things, to get true faith in Christ, that so we may haue approbati-

on at Gods hands; without which, there is no saluation to be hoped for.

Secondly, here also learne the right way to get testimony, approbation, and credit with men; a thing, whereof many are exceeding glad; and which, the childe of God must not contemne. Now, the way is this: He must first labour to get approbation at Gods hands; which indeede he cannot doe any other way, saue onely, by a true and liuely faith, as we haue heard before. Now, the Lord God approouing of him, he hath the hearts of all men in his hands, inclining them whether he will: and if it stand with his glorie, he will cause them to like, and to speake well of him, that doth beleeue.

Many, indeede, get great applause in the world, which little regard true faith; but in the ende, this their glory and applause, will be their shame: for, *They that honour me, will I honour,* saith the Lord: *but he that despiseth me shall be despised,* 1. Sam. 2. 30.

Lastly, whereas the holy Ghost saith, That all these worthy men *obtained testimony of God, and yet receiued not the promise*: We are hereby taught, that we which now liue in the Church, are much more bound in conscience to beleeue, then they that liued in the olde Testament. For, we haue receiued the promise of Christs incarnation: They receiued it not, and yet beleeued. Wherefore, in the feare of God let vs labour for true faith. But some will say, What should we heare so much of faith? we doe all beleeue. *Answ.* Indeede, we say so with our mouthes: but it is a rare thing to find true and sound faith in the heart; for, grosse and palpable ignorance abounds euery where, and yet men will needes be good beleeuers, which is a thing impossible: for, how should faith be without knowledge? And, as men are ignorant, so they haue no care to learne, nor to get knowledge, that so they might come by true faith. Their hearts are wholly taken vp with the world, for matters of profit and delight; that they can spare no time, to seeke for this pretious gift of faith. Againe, many haue knowledge, with whom true faith is rare: for, faith purifies the heart, it is ioyned with a good conscience, and shewes it selfe by obedience, thorough loue. Now, (to leaue the heart to God) where almost is the man that walkes answerable to his knowledge? May we not truely say of many, that as the word commeth in at the one eare, it goeth out at the other? And, among those which learne, and beare away something, there is little care to practise it in life.

But, we must knowe, that if we would be approoued of God, we must beleeue. Now, so long as we remaine ignorant; or else hauing knowledge doe not ioyne practise therewith, in obedience from a good conscience: vndoubtedly we haue no sparke of true faith in vs. We may make a shew of faith, and so beare the world in hand wee beleeue: but certainely, this will prooue a very dead faith; and in the ende,

and

and finishing of all, appeare to be nothing, but bare lip-faith, and meere presumption. Now, to conclude this point, we must know, that vnlesse we get true faith, as these beleeuers had, (which we must shewe by good fruits, as they did)euen they shall rise vp in iudgement against vs to condemne vs, at the last day. For they beleeued; though they had not the ground of faith so laid before them as we haue. Wherefore, let them that want knowledge, labour for it; &, they which haue it, let them ioyne obedience with their knowledge, that the faith of their hearts, may be seene by the fruits of their liues: for, true faith cannot be hid, but will breake out in good works.

VERSE 40.

God prouiding a better thing for vs, that they without vs should not be made perfect.

BEcause some man might much meruell, that such men as receiued testimony of God for their faith, should not yet receiue the promise; therefore here the holy Ghost renders a reason thereof: the good pleasure of God, appointing that Christ should be incarnate at such a time, as was most conuenient for the perfect consumation of the whole Church, consisting of Gentiles, as wel as Iewes. For, though these auncient beleeuers, were in time long before; yet God prouided Chrifts incarnation so fitly for vs, that they without vs should not haue perfect consummation in glorie.

The Exposition. God prouiding a better thing *for vs.* The word in the originall, translated *prouiding,* signifieth properly *foreseeing;* wherein is likewise included, Gods decree and ordination. Now, this we must knowe: that it is a peculiar prerogatiue, belonging to the true God alone, to be able to forsee things to come: and that many 1000. yeares before: no creature of himselfe can do it. And, yet it is true, that this propertie to *foresee,* is ascribed vnto God, not properly; but in regard of our capacitie: for if we speake of God properly, God cannot be said *to foresee* any thing; because all things be present to him, whether past, or to come.

This prescience, or foreknowledge in God, puts a difference betweene the true God, and all creatures: for, the true God foresees all things that are to come; so can no creature doe. Indeede, some creatures foresee and foretell some things: yet herein, they come short of the diuine propertie: for, God foresees all things by himselfe, without signes, and outward means. But creatures onely foresee some things not of themselues: but, by meanes of signes, and outward causes, or by reuelation from God; otherwise can no creature foresee things to come.

Now, as we said before, this *fore-sight* in God includes his decree and ordination: for, therefore did these things so come to passe, because God ordained them. Whereby we see, that Gods prescience or foreknowledge is not idle, but operatiue, and ioyned with his will: for, Matth. 10. 29. 30. *an haire cannot fall from our head: nor a sparrowe light vpon the ground, without his will.* As all things in time come to passe; so God, before all worlds *willed,* that is, decreed and appointed them. And, vnder this large extent of Gods will or decree, we must include the sinnefull actions of men; for, God doth not barely foresee them, but decree the beeing of them, and so will them after a sort; though not to be done by himselfe, yet by others. When *Iudas* betrayed Christ, and *Pilate* with the wicked *Iewes* condemned and reuiled him, they sinned grieuously; and yet herein, *they did nothing, but that which Gods hand and counsell had determined before to be done.*

This point well considered, confutes their opinion, who indeede inlarge Gods prescience or foreknowledge ouer all things good and euill; but yet exclude sinne from without the compasse of his decree, and ordination. But here we see Gods foresight includes his decree; and nothing comes to passe simply without his will: howsoeuer many things be done against his reuealed will; yet without his absolute will, can nothing come to passe. *He worketh all things according to the counsell of his owne will:* doing himselfe those things that be good, and willingly permitting euill to be done by others, for good ends.

But, what did God here prouide and foresee for vs? *Answ. A better thing:* that is, God in his eternall counsell prouided a better estate for his Church in the newe testament; then he did for beleeueres in the olde.

Hence we learne, that as God hath his generall prouidence, wherby he gouerneth all things; so also, he hath his speciall and particular prouidence, whereby in all things, he prouides and brings to passe, that which is best for his church. For, in the olde testament, God prouided that for his Church, which was meete for it: But considering that the Church in the newe Testa-(in some respects) was to haue a better estate, then the Church in the old testament had there fore, he prouides for it a better state. And look, as in his eternall wisedome he foreseeth what is best for all estates and times; so in his prouidence doth hee accomplish and effect the same.

For vs.] That is, for the Church in the new testament: where note, that Gods Church, and the

the ſtate thereof in the new Teſtament, is better then it was in the old, before the comming of Chriſt. The holy Ghoſt here ſpeakes this plainly; and therefore, we neede no further proofe thereof.

Queſt. How ſhould it bee better with the Church now, then it was then? *Anſ.* True it is, that God gaue the couenant of grace in the beginning, to our firſt parents in Paradiſe: the ſumme whereof was this; *The ſeede of the woman ſhall breake the Serpents head.* And this couenant did God renue and reuiue vnto his Church, from time to time, in all ages, vnto this day. Both circumciſion and the Paſſeouer, were ſeales of this couenant, as well as our Sacraments bee: ſo that in ſubſtance they differ not; the free gift of grace in Chriſt belonged to them as well as vnto vs. The beleeuing Iewes in their Sacraments, did eate the ſame ſpirituall meate, and drinke the ſame ſpirituall drinke with vs (as the Apoſtle witneſſeth, 1. Cor. 10. 3): and beleeuers then, obtained the ſame eternall life that we doe now by faith. And yet if wee regard the manner of adminiſtring the couenant of grace in Gods Church, vnto the people of God; Herein doth the Church of the new Teſtament farre ſurpaſſe the Church of God in the olde: and, indeede herein conſiſts the preheminence of the Church vnder the Goſpell; which ſtands in fiue things eſpecially.

Firſt, in the olde Teſtament, ſpirituall and heauenly were propounded vnto the Church, vnder temporall and earthly bleſſings. This is plaine by Gods dealing with the Patriarchs, *Abraham, Iſaac, and Iacob;* for, the Lord promiſed vnto them the temporall bleſſings of the Land of *Canaan;* vnder which hee ſignified the gift of life euerlaſting, in the Kingdome of heauen. But, in the new Teſtament, life euerlaſting is plainly promiſed to the beleeuer, without any ſuch type or figure.

Secondly, in the olde Teſtament Chriſt was ſhewed and ſignified vnto them in ceremonies, rites and types; which were in number many, and in ſignification ſome of them darke and obſcure: but now theſe types and ceremonies are aboliſhed, the ſhadowe is gone, and the ſubſtance come: and in ſteade of dark ſignes and figures, we haue two moſt plaine and ſenſible Sacraments. More plainely, the couenant of grace in the olde Teſtament, was ſealed by the blood of Lambs, as ſignes of the blood of Chriſt: but now to his Church in the new Teſtament, Chriſt himſelfe hath ſealed his Teſtament by his owne blood.

Thirdly, in the olde Teſtament all the knowledge they had was in the Law: and their vnderſtanding in the Goſpel was obſcure and very ſlender: but, in the new Teſtament, not onely the Law is made manifeſt, but alſo the ſupernaturall knowledge of the Goſpel.

Fourthly, the Law was onely committed and publiſhed to one nation and people: but the

Goſpel is ſpred and preached to all the world.

And *laſtly,* the Church in the old Teſtament beleeued, in Chriſt to come: but, now the Church beleeues in Chriſt, which is already come and exhibited: in all which reſpects, the Church in the new Teſtament doth exceed the Church of the olde.

Now, where the Text ſaith, *God prouided a better thing for vs,* we muſt not vnderſtand it of all theſe prerogatiues, but onely of the fift and laſt, touching the actuall exhibiting of Chriſt in the fleſh: as Chriſt alſo imports, Luk. 10. 23, 24. *Bleſſed are the eyes which ſee that ye ſee; for, I tell you, many Prophets and Kings haue deſired to ſee thoſe things yee ſee, and haue not ſeene them:* Which things we muſt vnderſtand of the incarnation of Chriſt. And that this is ſuch a prerogatiue to the new teſtament, appeareth by olde *Simeon,* who when hee had ſeene Chriſt in the Temple, as it was promiſed to him, ſang vnto God this ſong (Luk. 2. 29) *Lord, now letteſt thou thy ſeruāt depart in peace, according to thy word; for, mine eyes haue ſeene thy ſaluation:* as if he ſhould ſay, I haue now Lord liued long enough; let me now depart in peace, ſeeing now I haue ſeene thy Chriſt my Sauiour(where we ſee he makes it a matter of full contentment vnto his ſoule) which the beleeuers vnder the Law ſaw not.

Hence we muſt learne our dutie: for, if our ſtate bee now better then the ſtate of the olde Teſtament was, and if wee enioy priuiledges denied to Gods ancient ſeruants before and vnder the Law; then vndoubtedly we ought to ſtriue to goe before them in grace and obedience; for, euery mans accounts ſhall be according to his receits. He that receiues fiue talents, muſt mak account to returne moe, then he that receiues two: where God is more abouudant in his mercy, there he looks for anſwerable thankfulnes & obedience. We go beyond the ancient Church in fiue things: and therefore we muſt ſtirre vp our hearts to be anſwerable in grace & obedience going beyond thē. But if for all this, wee come ſhort of them in theſe things, then ſurely our caſe is fearefull, and our puniſhment ſhall be the greater: for, they that had leſſe prerogatiue, ſhal be witneſſes againſt vs, if they goe beyond vs in obedience.

That they without vs might not be made perfect: that is, might not be fully glorified. Here is the reaſon why Chriſt was not exhibited in their dayes. Indeede all true beleeuers before Chriſt, were iuſtified, and ſanctified, and in ſoule receiued to glory before vs; yet perfected in ſoule and body both, they muſt not bee before vs: but wee muſt all bee perfected together. Now, his will herein he bringeth thus to paſſe; All muſt bee perfected in Chriſt: But hee will not haue Chriſt to come and ſuffer, til the fulnes of time came, *in theſe laſt daies,* Heb. 1. 2. (as the Apoſtle ſpeaketh) that the beleeuers liuing in theſe dayes, might haue time of beeing in the Church to be called, iuſtified,

and

and fanctified; that fo they might be glorified with them that liued before. For, put the cafe that Chrift had fuffered in the dayes of *Abraham*, or *Dauid*, or thereabout; then the ende of the world muft needes haue come the fooner: for, fo it was foretolde, that Chrift fhould come in the latter ages of the world. 1. Pet. 1.20. Now, if the world had beene fooner cut off, then had there not beene time of birth and calling, for all the elect that now liue and fhall liue: therefore for their fakes was Chrifts comming deferred, till the fulneffe of time. And this I take to be the meaning of the words.

Now, in that the holy Ghoft here faith, *The members of Chrift in the newe Teftament muft be perfected, with all the ancient beleeuers in the olde*; we muft hereby be admonifhed, to conforme our felues vnto thefe auncient Fathers in the participation of grace and practife of obedience in this life. For how can we looke to be glorified with them after this life, if here we be not like them in grace. Chrift tells his followers, that *many fhould come from the Eaft and from the Weft, to fit with Abraham, Ifaac, and Iacob, in the kingdome of heauen*, Matth. 8.11. 12. (becaufe they were followers of thefe Patriarchs in the faith) *when as the children of the Kingdome*, that is, many Iewes by birth, borne in the Church, *fhould be caft into vtter darkeneffe*. Now, if Chrift denie to glorifie the children and pofteritie of thefe auncient beleeuers, becaufe they did not follow them in grace and in obedience: how can we which are by nature finners of the Gentiles, looke to be glorified with them, vnleffe in grace and obedience we conforme our felues vnto them? Thus much for thefe examples of faith: now fomething muft be added out of the next chapter; becaufe there the holy Ghoft makes vfe of all thefe worthie examples.

A COMMENTARIE
VPON PART OF THE
12. Chapter to the Hebrewes.

VERSE 1.

Wherefore, let vs alfo, feeing we are compaffed with fo great a cloud of witneffes, caft away euery thing that preffeth downe, and that finne that hangeth fo faft on : let vs runne with patience the race that is fet before vs.

IN thefe words, the holy Ghoft propoundeth a worthy exhortatió to the Chriftians of the newe Teftament; that they fhould labour to be conftant in the profeffion of the faith: that is, in holding, embracing, and beleeuing true Chriftian religion. And his reafon is framed thus; *The Saints of God in the olde Teftament, were conftant in the faith: and therefore, you muft likewife be conftant in the faith that liue in the newe Teftament.* The firft part of the reafon is laid downe in all the examples of the former chapter. The conclufion or fequell is contained in this firft verfe. Wherein, we may obferue two points: an exhortation vnto conftancy in true religion; and the way or meanes to attaine thereunto. The exhortation is inferred vpon the former examples; which are all here applied as prefidents and directions vnto vs, for conftancy and and perfeuerance in the faith: in thefe words; *wherefore, feeing we are compaffed about with fuch a cloud of witneffes*: that is, Seeing *Abel, Enoch, Noe, Abraham*, and all the reft of the holy Fathers, who are a cloud of witneffes vnto vs (that is, lights, and leaders before vs) were conftant in true religion (whether we refpect their faith in Gods promifes, or obedience to his commandements) therefore, we alfo muft be conftant in the faith. The way or meanes hereunto, ftands in three duties, in the words following; *Let vs caft away, &c.*

For the *exhortation*: Firft in generall, the very inferring of it from the former examples, teacheth vs this fpeciall duty; That euery one in Gods Church muft apply vnto himfelfe thofe inftru-

instructions, that are laid downe, either generally in doctrine, or particularly in example. And therefore the holy Ghost here saith not, Let the *Galatians*, or the *Corinthians* (which were renowned Churches) be constant in the faith; but, *Let vs*, that is, *you Hebrewes*, with my selfe be constant in the faith, following the example of your auncient Fathers. It is saide of the auncient Iewes, that *many of them heard Gods word; but it was not profitable vnto them, because it was not mingled with faith in them.* What is it to mingle the word with faith? It is, not onely to receiue it by faith, beleeuing it to be true; but also, by the same hand of faith, to apply it to a mans owne soule, to his heart, and life. And vndoubtedly, Gods word thus applied to a mans particular person, hath in it great power and fruite; whether we regard information of iudgement, or reformation of life. But, it is a hard thing to doe, and rare to finde a man that doth sincerely apply vnto himselfe, either generall doctrines, or particular examples. We are all prone to shift it from our selues, and lay it vpon others, saying; *This is a good Item, or a good lesson, for such a one, and such a one, if he were here; or, if he would marke it.* In the meane while, what benefit reape we to our owne soules? for, the word not applied to our selues, doth vs no good : it is like Physicke not taken, or food not eaten. And, hence it comes to passe, that though we heare much; yet we profit little by the ministery of Gods word. We must therefore learne to followe *Maries* example, *who pondered Chrifts words, and laid them vp in her owne heart.* When an exhortation is giuen, we must not post it off, and lay it vpon other mens shoulders; but apply it to our selues, and lay it to our owne hearts, saying, This instruction is for me. Hereby (no doubt) we should feele greater blessings vpon the preaching of the word, then yet we doe. And, to mooue vs hereunto, let vs consider, that Satan our vtter enemie (who seekes nothing but our destruction) is most busie to hinder this application of the word, either by the minister, or by a mans own conscience. As for example: when the minister (by occasion out of Gods word) shall confute, either errour in iudgement, or misdemeanour in life ; then, men that heare, and are guilty thereof, should say, *This is mine errour, or my fault ; now am I confuted, or reprooued.* And God (no doubt) if men would thus doe, would make it effectuall vnto them at the length. But, instead of this applying to our selues (either through our owne corruption, or Satans suggestion, or both) we shift it from our selues, and say, Now he reprooues such a one, and such a one; and speakes against such and such: and indeede, Satan (by his good will) would neuer haue a man to apply the word rightly to himselfe. Therefore, seeing Satan is so busie, and this is his deceit to make a man shift off an exhortation or reproofe from himselfe, and to lay it on others: we must be as carefull to apply

Heb. 4. 2.

it to our selues, and to lay it to our owne consciences: and then (no doubt) we shall finde it to be a word of power, able to reforme both the misdemeanour of our liues, and the errours of our mindes.

Now, to, the reason more particularly. *We must be constant in the faith*, because we are compassed about with so great a cloud of witnesses. Here the auncient Fathers of the olde Testament, which in the former chapter were commended vnto vs for their faith, are compared to a *cloude*, and then to a cloude *compassing vs*. Lastly, to a cloud of *witnesses*.

They are compared to a cloude (as I take it) by allusion to the cloude which directed and led the Israelites in the wildernesse : for, when they came from Egypt, and were 40. yeares in the Desert of Arabia; all that while, they were *directed by a pillar of cloude by day*, Exod. 13. 21. Now, looke as that cloud guided the Israelites from the bondage of Egypt, to the Land of Canaan: so doth this company of famous beleeuers, direct all the true members of Gods Church in the new Testament, the right way from the Kingdome of darkenesse, to the spirituall Canaan the kingdome of heauen. And this is the true cause why these worthie beleeuers are compared to a cloude.

Marke further, they are called *a cloud*: but what *a cloud*? namely, *compassing vs.* A compassing cloud they are called, by reason of the great company of beleeuers : so as which way soeuer a man turnes him, he shall see beleeuers on euery side: and they are said *to compasse vs*, because they giue vs direction in the course of Christianitie, as the cloud did the Israelites in the wildernesse.

Now, whereas the whole company of beleeuers is called *a cloud compassing vs* : here is answered a common obiection of temporizers, which argue thus against religion: There are so many kindes of religion now a-dayes, that no man can tell which to be of: and therefore it is good to be of no religion, till we bee certified, which is the true religion. This carnall reason is here answered; for, howsoeuer in some things, there be variety of opinions in Gods Church, yet for the substance of religion all agree in one. For, the company of beleeuers in this world, resembles a cloud that goes before vs, shewing vs the right way which we are to walke in, to the Kingdome of heauen. Secondly, in that these auncient beleeuers are called *a cloud compassing vs*, we are taught, that as the Israelites did follow the cloud in the wildernesse from the Land of Egypt to Canaan; so must we follow the examples of these ancient beleeuing Fathers and Prophets, to the kingdome of heauen. It is a strange thing to see how the Israelites followed that cloud. They neuer went, till it went before them: & when it stood still, they stood stil also, though it were 2. yeares together: & when it begā to moue, they moued with it. So in the same manner must we set be-

fore

Rom 15.4.

fore our eyes, for a patterne of life, the worthy examples of beleeuers in the old Testament: *for whatsoeuer was written, was written for our learning.* We must therefore be followers of them in faith, obedience, and other graces of God; and so shall wee be directed to life euerlasting, in the spirituall Canaan the kingdome of heauen. And yet we must not followe them absolutely. For, all of them had their infirmities, and some of them had their grieuous faults, whereby they were tainted, & there commendation somewhat blemished: but, wee must followe them in the practise of faith and other graces of God. The cloud that guided the Israelites, had two parts; a light part, and a darke.

Exod. 14.20.

The *Egyptians* who were enemies to Gods people, had not the light part before them, but the darke part: and so following that, they rushed into the red sea, and were drowned; when as the Israelites following the light part went through, in safety: Euen so these beleeuers had in them two things: their *sinnes*, which be their darke part, which if we follow, we cast our soules into great danger and destruction: and faith with other graces of God, which are their light part, which we must followe as our light: which if we doe carefully, it will bring vs safe to the Kingdome of heauen. So *Paul* bids the Corinthians, *bee followers of him*; yet not absolutely in euery thing, but *as he followes Christ:* and so must we follow the Fathers, as they went on in faith in Christ.

Further, they are *a cloud of witnesses:* that is, a huge multitude of witnesses. And they are so called: First, because by their owne blood they confirmed the faith which they professed: Secondly, because they did all confirme the doctrine of true religion, whereof they were *witnesses*, partly by speaches, and partly by actions in life and conuersation. And so is euery member of Christ a witnesse: as the Lord often calls the beleeuing Israelites, *his witnesses.* Quest.

Isa. 43.9, 10. 12.

How came this to passe, that these beleeuers should be Gods *witnesses*? *Ans.* Surely, because they testified the truth, and excellencie of Gods holy religion, both in word and action, in life and conuersation.

Now, seeing these in the old Testament were Christs witnesses; First, hereby all ignorant persons must be stirred vp to be carefull to get faith, and to learne true religion. If any thing will mooue a man to become religious, this will: for, out of all the world, God will chuse faithfull men to be his witnesses, to testifie his religion vnto others. If a man were perswaded that some worthie mightie Prince would vouchsafe to call him to beare witnesse of the truth on his side, he would be wonderfull glad thereof, and take it for a great honour to him. How much more then ought we to labour for knowledge, faith, and obedience in true religion, that we may become witnesses vnto the Lord our God? if it be a dignitie to be witnesse to an earthly Prince; oh then what a

great prerogatiue is this, for a silly sinfull man, to become a witnesse to the truth of the euerliuing God, who is King of Kings, and whose word needes no confirmation? This must make vs all to labour for knowledge, and for faith, and for the power of religion: but, if we will remaine still in our ignorance, and neuer labour for knowledge, then shall these seruants of God that beleeued in the old Testament, stand vp and witnesse against vs at the day of iudgement: for, they had not such means as we haue, and yet they became most faithfull witnesses.

Secondly, this must teach vs to be carefull, that as in word we professe Christ, so in deede we may confesse him, expressing the power of his grace in vs. For, by this true confession of Christ, we are made his witnesses: but when we confesse Christ in word onely, and yet in life and practise denie him, then we are vnfaithfull witnesses: for, we say and vnsay. In an earthly court, if a man should one while say one thing, and another while another thing, he would not be accepted for a witnesse, but rather be excepted against, as altogether vnworthie; and so would prooue a discredit to his friends cause, and a shame to himselfe: so it is with vs in Christs cause; if we professe in word, and denie in deede, we discredit Christ and his profession, and shame our selues for euer. And therefore we must be carefull not onely in word & iudgment, but in life and conuersation, to make a true and constant confession of Christ and of his truth. And thus much for the exhortation.

Now followeth the second point to be obserued in this verse; namely, the *manner* how Gods Church and people may put in practise this worthie exhortation of the holy Ghost, To be constant in the faith. And this consists in three duties: 1. They must *cast away that which presseth downe*: 2. They must cast away that *sinne that hangeth so fast on*: or, *sinne which so readily doth compasse vs about*: 3. They must *runne the race that is set before them, with patience.* Whosoeuer in Gods Church either Iew or Gentile, can performe these three things, shall be able no doubt to follow the counsell of the holy Ghost, and continue constant in the faith vnto the ende. Of these three in order.

The first thing then to be done, is this, *We must cast away that which presseth downe:* or thus, *Cast away the waight, or burthen* (for so much the word in the originall signifieth) euen that burthen which so presseth down the poore Christian, that he cannot goe on forward in the course of godlinesse and Christianitie. By *burthen* or *weight*, here we must vnderstand fiue things: First, the loue of temporall life: secondly, Care for earthly things: thirdly, Riches and temporall wealth: fourthly, Worldly honour and preferments: fiftly, Worldly delights and pleasures. All these are things which lie heauie on mans soule, as weightie burthens which presse it downe, especially then when the

soule

soule should lift vp it selfe to seeke heauenly things. So in the parable of the Sower, *riches, pleasures,* and *cares* for the things of this life, are called *thornes, which choake the word of God in a mans heart* , and make it vnfruitfull. And, *surfetting* and *drunkennes,* are said to be things which *oppresse the heart, and make it heauy.* And, easie it were, to shewe by many testimonies, that all these fiue things doe presse downe the heart; especially then, when it should bee lifted vp in the seeking of heauenly things.

Now in this, that these fiue things are waighty burdens, we may learne; first, what is the cause, that in these our daies, euery where the Gospel of Christ, beeing published, preached, and expounded, takes so little place in mens hearts; whether wee regard knowledge and vnderstanding, or affection and obedience. For, Gods word, is a word of power, mightie in operation : how comes it to passe then that the ground is barren, where it is cast? why makes it not men learned and religious? *Ans.* Surely, in euery place where the word of God is preached, especially among vs, these fiue things possesse the hearts of men, and exercise all the thoughts of the minde, and affections of the heart. From whence it commeth to passe, that after long preaching, there is little fruite, or profit; either for knowledge, or obedience: for, where the heart is pressed downe with the waight of these earthly things; there the word of God can take no place, nor bring forth fruit. And, this is generally true among vs; though we heare Gods word from yeare to yeare, and thereby might increase in knowledge, and obedience, if we would; yet in many, there is little shew of either: and, the cause is in these worldly cares, which take place in our hearts. For, this is a most certaine truth, that so long as our hearts are addicted to the greedy seeking after these earthly things, honours, pleasures, &c. so long will the ground of our hearts bee barren. The good seed of Gods word may be sowen therein; but little fruite shall come therof, saue briers and weeds, which will increase our damnation.

Againe, whereas the loue of temporall life, and care of earthly things, &c. are *sore burdens pressing downe* a mans heart from heauen to earth, and making it heauy, and sad, and dead in regard of all spirituall exercises and contemplations : hereby we are taught, oftentimes to giue our selues to eleuate and lift vp our minds and hearts to God, partly by meditation in his word, partly by inuocation on his name, and partly by thankesgiuing. And to doe these things the better, we must remember to set apart some speciall time euery day, for this speciall worke: so as we may say with *Dauid,* Psal. 25. 1. *Lord, I lift vp my heart vnto thee. Dauid* was well acquainted with this exercise, and so was *Daniel*: for both of them vsed this, as we may reade, Psal. 55. 17. *Euening and morning (saith Dauid) and at noone will I pray, and*

make a noyse. And *Daniel* vsed to pray vnto God three *times a day* : wherein, he would heartily and vnfainedly call vpon God, with thanksgiuing. And, great reason we should doe so; for, we liue in this world, wherein are innumerable weighty things, which presse downe our hearts from looking vp to heauen: & therefore, we must often practise our selues in holy meditation and prayer vnto God; that so we may lift vp our soules vnto God, from the things of this world. To vse a fit comparison: We know that those who keepe clocks, if they would haue the clock stil going, must once or twice a day wind vp the plummets which cause the wheeles to goe about; because they are still drawing downward : Euen so, seeing our hearts haue plummets of lead, which are worldly cares and desires, to presse them down, from seeking vp to heauen; we must doe with our hearts, as the clock-keeper doth with his plummets, winde them vp vnto God euery day: and, for this ende, must set apart some particular time to doe the same, in holy duties. Why doth God command the seauenth day to bee sanctified, and set apart, from all bodily exercises, and worldly cares? vndoubtedly, it is for this ende; to cause men to eleuate their hearts from all worldly things, to seeke the things aboue : else, if the minde should bee alwaies pressed downe with worldly cares, it could neuer attaine to heauens ioyes. Hee that hath not conscience on the Lords day, to lift vp his heart to heauē, by praier, & hearing Gods word, with meditation thereon; cannot possibly haue any soundnes in religion, nor his heart firmely setled on heauenly things.

Thirdly, whereas the holy Ghost saith, That the Hebrewes must cast away *the weight that presseth downe*; Here wee are taught, in what manner, and how farre forth we must vse the things of this life; as *riches, honours,* and lawfull *pleasures* ; yea and all *temporall blessings* whatsoeuer: namely, so farre forth, as they will further vs in the course of religion, and in the exercises of godlinesse, and vertue; and no further. But (finding by experience, that these temporall things be a burden vnto vs, pressing vs downe, and making vs vnfit for spirituall exercises) we must leaue them, and abstaine from them. This is that moderation, which we must vse in temporall things: for, the maine end that euery man must propound to himselfe in all things, is this; *That God may be glorified.* Now, that a man may glorifie God, it is necessarie that he should walke in the waies of godlinesse, and of true religion. Therefore, looke as riches and worldly commodities may further vs in Christian religion, and godlinesse; so farre forth must we vse them, & therein giue glory to God: but, when they hinder vs therein, then we must leaue them, & cast them off. The Mariner that is vpon the sea in a great tempest, seeing his ship too sore ladē, wil cast out any of his cōmodities; first, that that is the heauiest, and at last (if neede

Dan.6.10.

be) the most pretious iewels that be in his ship, before he will see it lost : Euen so must we doe in the sea of this world, when we see riches, honours, and lawfull pleasures, to make vs vnfit and vntoward for the exercises of pietie, and religion; then away with them, we must cast them off, how deare soeuer they be vnto vs. And thus much for the first duty.

The second duty that we must performe, for constancie in religion, is this; we must *cast away the sinne that hangeth so fast on* : or as the words will better beare, *We must cast away the sinne; that is so fit, or so ready to compasse vs about euery way.* By *sinne* here, we must not vnderstand *actuall sinne,* the practising of vngodlinesse in life and conuersation ; but, *originall sinne,* which is the corruption of nature, in which men are conceiued and borne. Now this originall sinne, is said to *be ready to compasse vs about;* because (as *Paul* saith of himselfe) *when a man would doe good, it causeth euill to be present with him; so as that good thing which he would doe, that he doth not: but the euill that he would not do, that doth he.* And it is said, *to compasse vs about;* because, whatsoeuer in heart a man doth desire, or affect, or purpose to doe, this originall sinne doth corrupt and defile the same vnto him: and, whatsoeuer in action a man would bring to passe, it doth likewise pollute it. By reason whereof, it comes to passe, that we may truely say, that all the thoughts, affections, wills, and purposes, yea and euery action of Gods children, are all mixed and stained with the corruption of this sinne. So that this hinders Gods deare seruants and children, that they cannot goe on in the course of godlinesse and christianitie, as they would; but, either they fal in their iourney many times: or, if they stand, yet they doe often stagger, and goe very faintly and haltingly forward.

From this that the holy Ghost saith, *Originall sinne compasseth the beleeuer about,* we are to obserue and learne sundry points. First, this serueth notably to confute some errours maintained and vpheld by the Church of Rome: for they say, that after a man is regenerate by Gods spirit, there is nothing in him that God can iustly hate ; and they doe curse all that holde the contrary. Now, to ratifie this their doctrine, that originall sinne, after regeneration, is not sinne properly; They say, that after regeneration, it is no more sinne, then Tinder is fire; which in it selfe is no fire, but very apt and fit vpon the least occasion, to be set on fire. But this opinion is here ouerthrowne, by this that the holy Ghost saith; That the beleeuing Hebrewes, that is, Gods Church *must cast away this sinne.* Where it is plaine, that after regeneration, whereby a man receiueth the spirit of sanctification, and adoption, he hath sinne in him ; for this sinne is most apt and ready to hinder him in the course of Christianity and godlinesse. Now, if sinne were not properly sinne, it must lose it owne nature and qualitie; and if it had

lost it proper qualitie, it would not be so ready to hinder a man in the course of godlinesse; both in thought, words, and deeds. So that here it is manifest and plaine, that in a regenerate man, there is sinne properly: And, howsoeuer he be free from the guilt and punishment of sinne; yet the corruption remaineth still in him, though greatly weakned through Sanctification.

Againe, here obserue, that the opinion of many men concerning their sanctification, is erroneous : for, some there be, who haue thought that a man might be perfectly sanctified in this life, and haue originall sinne quite abolished. But this is most false: for this Church of the Hebrewes had as worthie men in it for godlinesse and sanctification, as any are in these daies ; yea, and the author of this Epistle was (no doubt) a man that had receiued a great measure of sanctifying grace : yet including himselfe among them, he exhorts the Hebrewes thus; *Let vs cast off the burden, and sinne, that is so ready to compasse vs about.* What? had the Apostle, and these Christians sinne in them? Yes; or else the holy Ghost would neuer bid them cast it off: for, it were a vaine thing, to bid them cast off that which they had not. Therefore, they were not perfectly sanctified ; as indeede no man euer was, or shall be, in this life, Christ onely excepted. We must not maruell at this, that no man is perfect in this life : nay, we must rather maruell at this, that God hath giuen to any of vs, any droppe of sound grace, beeing such miserable wretched sinners as we are.

The Lord himselfe hath giuen many reasons, why men should not be perfect in this life. As first : If a man were perfectly sanctified in this life, then were he perfectly iust and righteous in himselfe before God, and so should be saued; yet not by free grace and mercy alone in Christ; and thus should Christ not be a whole and alone Sauiour; but onely a meanes to conuay into a man that sauing grace whereby a man should be saued. But Christ is our whole and onely righteousnesse, whereby we are iustified and saued ; and this may our corruption teach vs, which still remaines in vs, not quite mortified till the houre of death. Secondly, whatsoeuer grace we receiue of God, it comes by meanes of faith, which God worketh in vs: And looke how it stands with vs in regard of faith, so is it with vs for all other graces. But, faith in the best beleeuer is imperfect in this life, and mixed with much doubting; and therefore all other gifts and graces which come by faith, as righteousnesse, repentance, and sanctification, are also imperfect in this life.

From this, that sanctification in this life is imperfect, we learne (for the ouerthrowing of another errour of the Church of Rome) that no *man can stand at Gods tribunall seat, iustified by inherent iustice or righteousnes.* For that which we call Sanctificatio, the Papists call the *Iustificatio of a sinner;* making two parts of iustification: the first, whereby a finner of an euill man is made good; by the pardon of finnes, and the infufion of inward righteoufneffe, ftanding in hope and charity efpecially: And the fecond, whereby of a good man, one is made better, and more iuft: and this they fay, may proceede from the merit of a mans own workes of grace; and hereby they holde a man ftands righteous before God. But look how it ftands with grace in vs in this life, fo likewife fhall it ftand with the fame graces at the laft day; if they be imperfect now, and fo not able to iuftifie vs before God, they fhall alfo be found imperfect then to that purpofe and effect: But now they are imperfect, as hath beene fhewed, and therefore cannot then ftand for our righteoufneffe; vnleffe we will imagine that God will then accept of an imperfect Iuftice. Wherefore, their Doctrine is erroneous, and a doctrine of all terrour and defperation: for, who dare aduenture the faluation of his foule vpon his owne righteoufneffe? We denie not, but that God accepteth of our fanctification; yet not as the matter of our iuftification vnto life: that onely is the obedience and righteoufneffe of Iefus Chrift, accepted of God for vs, and made ours by faith; for, that alone is aunfwerable to the rigour of the Law.

Thirdly, this alfo fheweth the errour of thofe, who hold that concupifcence or original finne, is not a quality, but an *effence or fubftance liuing and fubfifting by it felfe*. For, here we fee a plaine difference betweene a mans bodie and foule, and *originall finne that compaffeth them;* elfe the holy Ghoft would not bid vs to caft off this finne: for, that which is of the fubftance of man, cannot by man bee caft off. And to make this more plaine, we muft know, that in man defcending from *Adam*, there be three things: 1. The fubftance of his foule and body: 2. The powers and faculties in them both. 3. The corruption or bad difpofition in thofe powers and faculties, whereby a man is vncomformable to the will of his Creator, and prone to that which is euill. And this third thing is it, which is here fpoken of, different from mans fubftance and faculties; and fo is not a fubftance in man, or mans nature corrupted, but an ill difpofition therein. Fourthly, hence alfo we learne, what a regenerate man doth moft feele in himfelfe; namely, *originall finne, the corruption of his nature:* for, that hangs on faft, and hinders him in the practife of all good duties. This *Paul* knew well; and therefore confeffeth, that *hee faw another Lawe in his members, rebelling againft the Law of his mind, and leading him captiue vnto the law of finne, which was in his members,* Rom. 7. 23. This caufeth him *to leaue vndone the good which he would haue done; and to doe the euill, which he would not doe,* v. 19. And *Dauid* felt the the fame thing when hee faide; *I will runne the way of thy commaundements, when thou fhalt enlarge my heart.* Why doth *Dauid* fpake of the *enlarging of his heart?*

Surely, hee felt in himfelfe this originall finne, which did ftreicten his good affections, fo as he could not put them forth fo much as hee would toward the Law of God. And when hee faith, Pfal. 51. 12. *Stablifh me oh Lord by thy free fpirit;* he would giue vs to vnderftand, that by originall corruption hee was reftrained of his Chriftian libertie, and hindred in all good affections, holy actions, and heauenly meditations: which caufeth him to pray for libertie and freedome by the fpirit. So that it is plaine, the feruant of God feeles this corruption, clogging and hindring him from all good duties.

This ferues to admonifh all fecure perfons, which neuer felt finne to be a clogge or burden vnto them, of their fearefull and dangerous eftate. For, to euery childe of God, originall corruption is a grieuous burthen. Now, conferre with a naturall man, and aske him what imperfections and wants hee feeles in himfelfe: his anfwer is; hee neuer was hindred by any corruption in all his life, he neuer felt doubting or want of loue, either to God or to his brethren: he feeles no pride of heart, no hypocrifie, nor vaine glory, &c. If wee take thefe men vpon their words, they are Angels among men: but indeede they are blinde and ignorant, and wonderfully deceiued by Satan: for, all Gods feruants in this life doe continually bewaile the corruption of their nature, crying out againft originall finne, that it *hinders them in doing the good things which they would doe; and caufeth them to doe that euill which they would not*. Thefe men therefore, that are neuer troubled with corruption, but (to their owne thinking) haue grace at will, are in a fearefull cafe, their mindes are ftill blinded, and their hearts hardned; they are dead in finne, abiding in darkneffe vnto this houre. And if they goe thus on to death, they fhall finde that finne will vnvizor himfelfe, and then they fhall knowe what finne meanes, and finde the terrour, and feele the burthen of it when it is too late; like the foolifh virgins that knew what the want of oyle meant, when the doores were fhut.

Secondly, this fhewes vnto vs, what is the ftate and condition of the childe of God in this life; Hee is not here a Saint feeling no corruption, perfectly fanctified and freed from all finne: but fuch a one as feeles the burthen of corruption, hindring him in his Chriftian courfe; vnder which he fighes and groanes, labouring by all good meanes to be difburthened, and to caft it off. It is indeede a matter of great comfort for a man to feele Gods graces in himfelfe; as *faith*, loue, repentance, fanctification, and fuch like; but no child of God can alwaies or alone feele the comfort of grace; moft commonly he fhall bee troubled with finne, if he be Gods childe. Now, if feeling it, he diflike himfelfe, and ftriue to be eafed of it, this is a fure argument of his happy eftate.

Fiftly, this commaundement to *caft away*

sinne that presseth downe, teacheth euery childe of God to labour earnestly for the gouernment and direction of Gods spirit: for we haue within vs originall corruption, that like an armed man besets vs about, and hindreth vs in euerie good thing wee take in hand. We must therefore pray vnto God daily, that hee would guide vs by his good spirit: for, by reason of the corruption of our nature, and the deceitfulnesse of sinne, we shall vtterly faile, vnlesse Gods spirit gouernes vs, both in the thoughts of our hearts, in the words of our mouthes, and the actions of our liues. This *Dauid* knew well, and therefore prayeth to the Lord *for his good spirit, to leade him into the Land of Righteousnesse.* Psal. 143. 10.

Lastly, seeing wee haue this corruption of nature in vs, wee must *keepe our hearts with all diligence*, and set watch and ward about them. So *Salomon* saith: *Counterguard thy heart my sonne*, Prou. 4. 23. Why doth *Salomon* giue this commaundement? Surely, for speciall cause: for, euery man while he liues on earth, is compassed about with his own corrupt nature; which like a home-borne traytor seekes to deliuer the heart into the possession of Satan, and so to defraude God of his right. Againe, the heart is mans Treasure, from whence comes all actions good and badde: now, if it bee well kept and guarded, the Lord will dwell in thy heart, and thence will proceede the issues of life: but, if it be left open, for corruption to enter and take place; then is it made an habitation for the deuill.

If a citie were besieged about by bloody enemies, the inhabitants thereof would set watch and ward in euery place, to keepe out the enemie: so, we hauing originall sinne, as a fierce enemie compassing vs about, for to worke our destruction some way or other, must labour to haue our hearts guarded with a watch of grace; that our corruption may not let in Satan there to dwell, or to haue any abode.

But (will some say) how shal we get a watch that may thus keepe our hearts?

Answ. Wee must labour that the word of God may dwell plentifully in our hearts; and there, as the scepter of Christ, to be held vp by the grace of faith, ruling our wills and affections, & bringing into subiection euery thought to the obediece of Christ. In such a heart Christ dwells, who is stronger then Satan: and, here can neither corruption set open the doore to Satan, nor Satan enter; but all things are in safety. Also the actions, that proceede hence, shalbe the issues of life, being holy and pleasing vnto God.

And thus much of the second point.

The third duty to be performed for our continuance in the faith, is this: *We must runne with patience the race that is set before vs.* In these words the holy Ghost borroweth a comparison from the games of men that did runne a race: and thus we may conceiue it; The race that the holy Ghost propounds vs to runne, is the race of *Christian religion :* the parties that must runne in this race, are all *Christians*, men or women, high or low; not one excepted: the *price* and crowne for which we runne, is *euerlasting glory :* the iudge of the runners is the *Lord himselfe*, who hath appointed this race vnto euery Christian in this life; who also, will giue the reward to euery one that runneth well.

In this comparison, we may obserue many good instructions. First, in that *Christian religion* is compared to a *race* ; We are taught, that euery one that professeth religion must goe forward therein, growing in knowledge, faith, pietie, and in euery grace of God. He that runnes a bodily race, must neither stand still, nor goe backward (for then he shal neuer get the price) but still goe forward to the race ende: So must euery Christian goe forward in grace, following hard towards the marke, for the price of the high calling of God. If we care not for eternall life, then we may take our ease, and let grace alone; but if we tender our owne saluation, we must goe on in the graces of religion, as a runner doth goe forward in his race. This beeing well obserued, would rouze vp our drowsie Christians, that make no progresse in religion.

Secondly, this resemblance of Christianity to a race, teacheth vs all to striue to goe one before another in knowledge, faith, and holy obedience: thus runners doe, that runne a bodily race. Also in the world, the manner of men is, to labour and striue to goe one before another in riches, preferment, in fine apparell, and in all bodily delights: now, shall men striue to be first in these transitory things, and shall wee neglect our duty about these spirituall graces? wherein, the more wee excell, the more acceptable wee are to God, and shall bee more glorious in the world to come.

Thirdly, seeing Christianitie is a race, we must remember to be constant therein, till we come to the ende of our faith; euen the saluation of our soules. It hath beene the manner of our people, to turne in religion with the State and Time; and yet, to this day many thousands come to our assemblies, that would turne to Poperie, if that abhomination should be set vp againe : for (say they) It was a merrie world, when that religion was vp. But, this is not the propertie of good runners; If we would haue the crowne of life, we must hold true religion constantly vnto the death.

Lastly, like good runners we must minde our way, and haue our hearts set vpon the end of our race; which is, euerlasting life. Each ordinarie traueller, is very inquisitiue of his way, and all his care is to goe the neerest way he can to his iourneys ende. Behold, we are trauellers, and our iourney is to heauen; we must therefore endeauour to goe the straightest way we can, to come to life euerlasting: neither must we make delaies in this way, but vse all helpes to further vs herein; for the matter is of great importance whereabout we goe.

Here some will say, We like this well; but, true religion hath alwaies many enemies, and few hearty friends: besides, if a man runne this way, he must runne alone, and suffer many crosses and reproaches. *Ans.* This is most true: and therefore the holy Ghost addeth; That we must runne this race *with patience:* We must not be discouraged because of these crosses and afflictions; but labour with patience to beare that part of affliction, what-euer it be, that shall light vpon vs in our iourney. This is Christs counsell to his Disciples, Luke 21. 19. *Possesse your soules in patience:* as if he should say, If you would saue your soules, you must labour to beare all crosses that fall on you, with patience. In the parable, Luk. 8. 15. *They that receiue the seede in good ground, are they, which with an honest and good heart heare the word, and keepe it, and bring forth fruit.* But how? *with patience.* Euery one that heares Gods word, and makes conscience thereof, shall haue enemies to scoffe and mocke, and to afflict him; which the deuill sets a worke, to hinder the growth of the word in his heart: but, must he therefore cease to bring forth fruit? no, he must bring forth fruit with *patience.* And so must we do in the race of true religion: for crosses, afflictions, and mockings will come; but these stormes must not turne vs backe: nay, the more they beate vpon vs, the more must we arme our selues with patience, by which we shall be able to beare them all. And thus much for this third duty; as also of the exhortation vnto Constancie in the faith; after the example of all these godly Fathers.

FINIS.

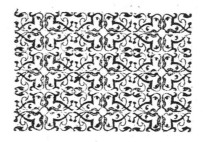